D0944331

USED

English Prose

of the XVII CENTURY

English Prose

of the XVII CENTURY

SELECTED AND EDITED BY

ROBERTA FLORENCE BRINKLEY

Professor of English
Duke University

W · W · NORTON & COMPANY, INC.

New York

Copyright, 1951, by

W. W. NORTON & COMPANY, INC.

FIRST EDITION

PRINTED IN THE UNITED STATES OF AMERICA
FOR THE PUBLISHERS BY THE VAIL-BALLOU PRESS

Preface

It is with some diffidence that the editor has undertaken a companion volume to *English Poetry of the Seventeenth Century*, for it is even more difficult to make a satisfactory selection from prose than it is to make a collection of poems. It is the purpose of this volume to provide a body of significant material which will give some knowledge of the contrasting prose styles which developed and the great diversity of types which arose in the period. The general principle of selection is the same as that for the volume of poetry: the familiar passages which one would not willingly do without have been included, and some that are less generally known have been added in order to introduce them. There is, for example, a section of James Howell's *Instructions for Foreign Travel*, which will afford comparison with what Bacon, Milton, and others have to say about travel. Fuller's *The Phoenix* is included to show another phase of his many interests, and William Allen's *Killing No Murder* is given in its entirety as a seventeenth-century example of prose satire done in the manner of Swift. The life of the Duchess of Newcastle provides an example of a complete short autobiography, which not only portrays many interesting people but also gives a picture of the social life and customs of the day, and the selection from Thomas Ellwood's *Life of Himself* recounts Ellwood's connection with Milton. In addition to its own value, Locke's *Some Thoughts Concerning Education* offers a comparison with Milton's little tract and with other writings on the subject. Particular attention has been given to the development of certain types, such as the essay and various kinds of biographical and autobiographical writing.

This book is prepared for readers inexperienced in the eccentricities of seventeenth-century spelling and punctuation, and therefore the text has been sufficiently modernized for there to be no barrier of mechanics between the reader and the content.

I wish to record my indebtedness to various friends who have given me suggestions concerning material, and especially to Professor R. C. Cawley, of Princeton, who read the manuscript as originally submitted and requested additional selections, a number of which were incorporated. I also wish to express my thanks to the staff of the British Museum, of the Huntington Library, and of the Library of Duke University. That I had the privilege of working on this anthology at the Huntington Library, I owe to the Carnegie Foundation for the Advancement of Teaching, from which I received a grant for use in the summer of 1948.

Because of the opportunity to use the British Museum and the Huntington Library, it has been possible for the editor in most cases to go back to the first editions for the text, but in several instances a later edition was chosen because the author himself had made interesting additions to his material or because the first edition was not available.

I wish to make acknowledgment to the following publishers who have granted permission to use works controlled by them:

The Nonesuch Press, Ltd., for the sermon "Death's Duel," by John Donne, from *X Sermons*, edited by Geoffrey Keynes, published in *XXVI Sermons*, by John Donne, copyright, The Nonesuch Press, 1923.

G. Bell and Sons, Ltd., for selections from the *Diary* of Samuel Pepys, edited with additions by Henry B. Wheatley.

Percy Dobell and Son for selections from *Centuries of Meditations*, by Thomas Traherne.

ROBERTA FLORENCE BRINKLEY

Contents

English Prose

of the XVII CENTURY

The Seventeenth Century in England

THE MODERN world evolved in the seventeenth century. The ideas which are basic in our thought were developed and systematized from an embryonic and chaotic state by the zeal and almost superhuman efforts of the giant intellects that dominate the period. These ideas did not come forth without conflict: the monarchy was overthrown and then restored; the church suffered an upheaval; and religious faith felt the impact of the materialistic view resulting largely from the new science. The very turn of the century is marked not only by an attempt to crush out the new science but also by the beginning of experimental methods. It was in 1600 that Bruno, who accepted and expanded the Copernican idea of the universe, suffered martyrdom and that William Gilbert published the first great scientific work to be published in England, *On the Magnet, on magnetic bodies, and on the earth as a great magnet, a new physiography, demonstrated by many arguments and experiments.* In differentiating between arguments and experiments, Gilbert led the way toward the true scientific method.

The century is marked by a tireless search for truth, regardless of the consequences. Bacon set this keynote when he said, "The inquiry, knowledge, and belief of truth is the sovereign good of human nature." He reasoned against the practice of the schoolmen, who "have withdrawn themselves from the contemplation of nature and experience and sported with their own reason and the fictions of fancy"; he criticized the method of Aristotle, who "did not consult experience in order to make right propositions and axioms, but when he had settled his system to his will, he twisted experience round and made her bend to his system"; and he substituted for these means the scientific method of the wide observation of facts. At the beginning of the century he advanced the idea that man was merely on the threshold of truth and must assume the obligation of adding to the store of the world's knowledge.

The need of more practical means for the discovery of truth was answered by the development of mechanical instruments to insure precision. The first of these was the telescope. It gave evidence to the physical sense which reason alone could not have fathomed, and it revolutionized man's conception of his relation to the universe and to God by furnishing physical evidence of the Copernican theory. The Ptolemaic system had made the earth and man the focal point of the universe and of God's attention. The extent of space was comprised within ten concentric spheres, limited, patterned, and accountable. The Copernican system, however, changed the fixed center from the earth to the sun and greatly extended the conception of space, though leaving it still bound by the outer sphere of fixed stars. Bruno, in interpreting the Copernican theory, gave evidence that there were no bounds to space and that man is on the smallest of countless universes, whirling in illimitable space about the sun. The sudden projection into infinity staggered man's imagination and necessitated a thoroughgoing readjustment of his ideas. In the first place, the heliocentric theory of the universe was held to be contrary to the Scriptures: it changed the location of heaven and hell and violated the literal interpretation of various passages, which were eagerly cited as evidence against the new theory. In the second place, it revealed that the stars, which according to the old belief governed man's fate by their influence, were other worlds, remote and not concerned about man's affairs. Comets, long held to be miraculous portents of death and disaster, were discovered to have a place in this universe; and their supernatural powers vanished when it was found that their return could be accurately predicted. The old science of astrology had to pass. Speculations arose as to whether other creatures dwelt upon these newly discovered worlds and vied with man for the attention of a God suddenly lost in an infinity of space, and whether voyages could be made to the moon. Comedy, satire, and serious study reflect the different attitudes of thought concerning the possibility of such a voyage and the nature of the inhabitants of the moon. The telescope became increasingly popular, and even literature is full of references to it: in Daniel's masque *The Vision of the Twelve Goddesses*, for example, a sibyl used a telescope to describe the goddesses, who descend from a mountain; and in *Paradise Lost* Milton's recollection of the appearance of the moon's surface as he had seen it through Galileo's telescope in Fiesole was used in figuratively portraying Satan's shield. In Restoration England a private individual might have a telescope on top of his house, as did Pepys, for the entertainment of his friends or join the crowds which gathered to look through the great telescope in St. James's Park. The Royal Society spent much time in improving the instrument and recording observations made under various conditions.

A second mechanical instrument which changed man's thoughts about himself and his world was the microscope. This revealed to him the marvelous perfection of his body in even its most minute organisms, and the structural infinity and complexity of tissue. He learned many things about the structure of the human organs and for the first time became acquainted with the basic facts of modern physiology. The discovery of the capillaries added the final proof to Harvey's theory of the circulation of the blood; the corpuscular composition of the blood was ascertained; and vast realms of living creatures of which man had never dreamed became visible. The microscope led also to the study of plant anatomy and to a classification of plants based upon structure instead of upon a description of external appearance. Furthermore, sex was recognized in plants and the primary facts in plant reproduction were understood. Nature seemed excessive, terrifying in its fecundity. Milton expresses this idea in *Comus* when he speaks of the seas with their "spawn innumerable," the teeming earth, and the air crowded with birds. Man felt overwhelmed by the stupendous sweep of the new cosmos, so crowded with worlds and packed with creatures; and a spirit of melancholy became prevalent. Some would not accept the evidence of the senses; others refused to look through the telescope and the microscope, holding that faith must be preserved even if it meant the denial of actuality. With great humor Galileo wrote to Kepler of a professor of philosophy at Pisa who tried "with logical arguments, as if with magical incantations, to charm the new planets out of the sky." [1]

Donne said that the "new philosophy calls all in doubt," but the disturbing evidence to the physical senses afforded by these two instruments was less significant than the profound shock to faith occasioned by the development of mathematics and the application of the laws of mathematics to astronomy and physics. The importance of the gift of the seventeenth century in mathematical notation can hardly be overemphasized, for modern algebraic symbols were first originated. Other very significant developments were: the decimal system, analytical geometry, logarithms, and calculus. Tycho Brahe and Copernicus had been obliged to make their computations through laborious arithmetical processes. If no quick and accurate method of computation had been devised, the century could never have made the steps of progress which it achieved, for the new mathematics made it possible to work out the laws of nature through formulæ. The application of mathematical laws to the phenomena of motion led men to see that nature operated by laws which could be depended upon as invariable and to question whether God were necessary to the mechanism of the universe. Descartes argued that there was no place for an active Providence who could interfere in the working of these laws. The development of mathematics also led to greater confidence in reasoning and fuller reliance on the rational. The determination of the unknown from the known, the

---

[1] Quoted by O. Lodge in *Pioneers of Science* (1893), p. 106.

steps in analytical generalization, the trustworthiness of the law of cause and effect—all these were found valuable not only in science but also in the more abstract realm of philosophy.

In the mental confusion which resulted from the conflict between science and religion, some found a safe retreat in mysticism, where the individual could depend upon the personal experience of religious ecstasy instead of upon the evidence of his senses. Donne in *The Second Anniversary* questions the soul:

> When wilt thou shake off this pedantry
> Of being taught by sense and fantasy? [2]

Browne thinks that faith is strengthened by being challenged, and holds that there are not enough doubts for an active faith to overcome. Direct communion with God will give all one needs to know, and this contact can be secured through contemplation or found revealed in nature and the happy innocence of childhood. Donne, Herbert, and Crashaw are the poets of mystic contemplation; Vaughan and Traherne, of nature and childhood. Milton, on the other hand, holds that the new science is based on theories and that theories are relatively unimportant. Others follow Hobbes in the denial of faith and the acceptance of a purely materialistic philosophy, or Descartes in the separation of faith and reason by the theory of dualism.

In contrast with the disturbance of faith by science was the increased knowledge of the Bible and interest in religious thought resulting from the publication of the King James Version in 1611. The way in which the biblical phraseology and ideas permeated the thought of the entire century is revealed by the literature of the period. It molds the style of many of the writers in prose, accounting for the sonorous tones of Sir Thomas Browne, Jeremy Taylor, and Milton; it becomes the substance and form of the graphic allegories

[2] Lines 290–92.

of Bunyan; it stirs the poets to epic conceptions—*Christ's Victory and Triumph, The Apollyonists, Davideis, Paradise Lost, Paradise Regained;* it bears fruit in a drama conceived in the classical mold, *Samson Agonistes,* and in a great satire, *Absalom and Achitophel;* and it is the inspiration of the lyric poets—Drummond, Wither, Donne, Herbert, Vaughan, Traherne, Crashaw, Quarles, and Herrick.

Gradually the mind worked its way out of the first reaction of gloom, which led to skepticism and on the one hand and to blind faith and retreat into mysticism on the other, and became aware that the new theory of the universe was a stupendous challenge to a broader view and not a destructive attack on faith. A creator who could conceive of the grandeur of an infinity of worlds and originate laws to give order to their motion was a greater god than a being who could conceive of only a limited universe. As man began to discover realms of knowledge of which he had previously been unaware, he saw that apparent lack of order in the world as he knew it might be attributable to man's restricted view and not to the plan. Perhaps there was a rational scheme of which man's puny mind could only dimly conceive. Late in the century Blackmore in his poem *The Creation* phrases the idea that if one could understand the entire system of worlds, faith would be strengthened rather than decreased:

> Would not this view convincing marks impart
> Of perfect prudence and stupendous art?

The idea of ordered systems of worlds was paralleled in the realm of creatures by a revival of the ancient conception of a "scale of nature" or "chain of being." No one species could ascend beyond its link in the chain or usurp the realm of the other, nor could the vegetable world encroach upon the animal. Evidence for such a law lay in the theory that without its existence chaos would prevail.

In this way man once more adjusted himself to the natural world, but he could not find his old complacence. His mental vision had been expanded by the new light it had received, and with enthusiasm and unremitting effort the intellectual leaders set out to explore the powers of the mind and to increase knowledge and understanding. It had become evident that the way to reach truth was through greater accuracy in observations and that to be accurate one must have adequate tools for measurement. The invention of the barometer, thermometer, air pump, and pendulum clock marks other steps of progress in science. Indeed, Robert Hooke, one of the members of the Royal Society, thought it might be possible to gain all knowledge through instruments; and man's ability to invent and discover did appear to be unlimited.

It soon became evident that more could be accomplished through a combination of efforts, and by 1645 a group of interested men were collaborating in their attempt to advance scientific knowledge. This group was known as the "Invisible College." It met first in London during the time of the greatest disturbance of university life in the civil war period, and later divided upon the return of some of the members of the group to Oxford. The London group is associated with Gresham College and forms the nucleus of the Royal Society, which was finally chartered in 1663. By the formal organization of the Royal Society public recognition was made of the national need of co-operation in furthering knowledge. Through correspondence and the visits of foreign scientists co-operation was, indeed, made international. Experiments were performed, inventions demonstrated, and data accumulated; and a careful record of all proceedings was kept in the *Philosophical Transactions*.

As the century advanced it became apparent that scientific principles and laws could be applied to practical affairs. The principle of accuracy and exactness was evidenced even in speech and writing. The Royal Society cultivated "a close, naked, natural way of speaking; positive expressions; clear senses; a native easiness; bringing all things as near the mathematical plainness as they can." Bishop Wilkins, a member of the Society, even attempted to find a symbolic language which would be as exact as is notation in mathematics. The fundamental postulate that certain causes inevitably produce certain results was applied to the study of governments; the laws of statistics were applied by Sir William Petty to population and trade; and the principle of balance, by Harrington to property.

The search for truth was carried over into the realm of human nature, and the study of man's mind and attitudes originated. Types of character were analyzed in the *Character Books* and portrayed by Jonson on the stage. History was interpreted through personality by Bacon in his *Henry VII*. Biographical writing became popular, and the carefully ascertained facts of a person's life were seen to be as essential to the understanding of his nature as was the close noting of his manners and eccentricities which made the more vivid portrait. Anthony Wood's facts and Aubrey's anecdotes were both important; and the blending of the two types of material by Walton marks a notable advance in biographical writing. Lyric writers studied and described the emotions. The old conventional pattern of the chivalrous code and idealistic love between man and woman was ruthlessly destroyed by Donne. He analyzed the actual emotions of love, laying bare the diversity of moods: cynicism and idealism, sensuality and purity, gaiety and despair, self-giving and grasping dominance—all are set forth in his poems. He and all the other religious poets of the age also portrayed such emotional states as resulted from the conflict between doubt and faith or the lure of sin and the desire of the soul for God.

The critical temper of mind was also focused upon the traditional conceptions of the Bible and of history. Spinoza in 1670 argued in his *Tractatus Theologico-politicus* that the miracles of the Old Testament could be explained as the workings of laws that it was possible to determine. Father Simon in *Histoire critique du Vieux Testament* attacked the reliability of Scriptural text. Both works were known in England; the latter was translated into English in 1682 and stimulated Dryden to write *Religio Laici*. In history the attempt to sift fact from legend led into zealous research in the antiquities of Britain. The fabulous account of the settlement of Britain by Brutus, descendant of Æneas, and of the incredible exploits of its heroes, including Arthur, was discarded. The monuments of Britain, old coins, old burial urns, old manuscripts—all could throw light on the past and help to separate truth from fiction. The Antiquarian Society, like the Royal Society, shows the appreciation of co-operative effort. Manuscripts were collected and transcribed; scholars in their enthusiasm frequently worked thirteen and fourteen hours a day at copying materials. Courteous exchange of valuable manuscripts and of transcriptions was made with foreign scholars. The generosity of the great collector of manuscript material is illustrated by the hospitality of Sir Robert Cotton, which made available his library for the constant use of scholars.

One of the most far-reaching results of the new realism was the conflict which immediately originated between authority and freedom. Cromwell's words, "Bethink you that you may be mistaken," might be used as a motto for the intellectuals. Intellectual life had long been based upon the authority of books and abstract theory, not upon the actualities of experience. The method employed by the medieval schoolmen to arrive at truth was the method of deduction from some general principle assumed to be true, but not tested for its truth by observation of fact. Such a method led to emphasis on a process of reasoning founded upon opinion, and often amounted to no more than the spinning out of words. Though Bacon admired the ancients, he saw that truth could be reached only after the mind had been liberated from the bondage of blind acceptance of the principles set up by the ancient writers, particularly Aristotle, and of the method of syllogistic reasoning perfected by the medieval schoolmen. Like Sir Thomas Browne in his *Vulgar Errors,* Bacon set out to meet the "Goliath and Giant Authority." Men should not make the ancients their dictators, he said, for "knowledge derived from Aristotle will at most rise no higher than the knowledge of Aristotle." Authority, he held, should be tested by reason and experiment; one should not be satisfied merely with theoretical arguments; but with a critical temper of mind, a spirit of inquiry, and a willingness to defer judgment over a period of time, one should observe things as they are and base opinion upon facts, not words. Bacon began a controversy over the relative value of the ancients and the moderns, which centered at first in the fields of science and philosophy but later in the century extended into the realm of literature.

One phase of the conflict between the ancients and the moderns in literature found expression in the new criticism, which went back to the ancients for models and standards. The establishment of the neo-classical rules is not due solely to French influence; there is a continuous movement toward a norm from Sidney, through Ben Jonson, to Dryden. This movement is in part an effort to gain the sophistication of maturity. The setting up of social codes, the development of satire, the critical temper of the age, the growing rationalism, the influence of scientific thought—all these contribute to the changing style in literature. The Jacobean and Caroline literature was considered too unrestrained. It was individual and emotional; freedom of expression led to violation of good taste; and imagination and fancy were not sufficiently curbed. Experimentation in verse forms had produced such oddities as stanzas shaped to form altars, crosses, and wings. Waller in his poem on the Earl of Roscommon's translation of Horace expresses the reaction against the literature of the first half of the century:

> Though poets may of inspiration boast,
> Their rage, ill-governed, in the clouds is lost.

The literary world became as weary of such exuberance as
the political world of violence, and in both realms there arose
the desire for stability. Early in the century Ben Jonson
had shown in *Timber* that the classical writers had many
valuable suggestions for the English. He pointed the way
to the improvement of English literature when he told Drummond that the study of Quintilian would correct the defects of his writing. The scientific point of view also in-
fluenced literature: regular and dependable laws had been
discovered in nature, and it was thought that laws of composition might be discovered in literature. The only field of
research was in the writing of past ages. Jonson does not,
however, advocate the "rules" drawn from the medieval
interpretation of Aristotle, but a return to the primary
sources. These are to be followed "as guides, not commanders," for "we have our own experience, which, if we will use
and apply, we have better means to pronounce." In Dryden's
Essay of Dramatic Poesy the relative values of ancient and
modern literature are left balanced. Dryden advocated the
analytical study of literature as it is and advanced the idea
that although conformity to law generally improved literature, sometimes violation of law, as in the case of Shakespeare, was compensated by other qualities. But even Dryden
felt with many others of his age that Shakespeare could be
improved, and illustrated his theory by adapting *Antony
and Cleopatra*. He did not depreciate native English genius
but felt that it would gain by conforming to certain basic
laws. He also urged the merits of rhyme on the ground that
it acted as a restraint to an over-luxuriant fancy, for he
felt that the overflow of the romanticists needed to be limited
by the bounds of the closed couplet.

The literary quarrel over the ancients and moderns was
not, however, limited to criticism; it found expression again

in Sir William Temple's *An Essay upon the Ancient and Modern Learning* (1690) and in Swift's *Battle of the Books* (1704), which took the discussion over into the eighteenth century.

Milton saw that freedom must be given also to the expression of thought and wrote his magnificent *Areopagitica*, protesting the act to re-establish the censorship of the press in 1643. His plea for the freedom of the press is one in principle with his constant plea for liberty—social, intellectual, religious, or political. In this work he establishes the principle upon which the more specialized arguments may be based: "Give me the liberty to know, to utter, and to argue freely, according to conscience, above all liberties." In a glowing defense of man's reason and the cause of truth he argues for freedom of intellectual activity as a foundation for national progress.

In education there was also a definite break with authority —the authority of the medieval scholastic system. Bacon was the first to see that there should be a humanitarian ideal back of learning, and in both *The Advancement of Learning* and the *New Atlantis* he sets forth the ideal that the "gift of reason" is for "the use and benefit of mankind" and that knowledge is "a rich storehouse for the glory of the Creator, and the relief of man's estate." Cowley reiterates this aim in his *Proposition for the Advancement of Experimental Philosophy*. Milton turns the humanistic ideal definitely toward the academic system, defining "a complete and generous education" as "that which fits a man to perform justly, skilfully, and magnanimously all the offices, both private and public, of peace and war."

Music was affected by its release from the authority of the church. When the Puritans forbade the use of music in the church, composers who had looked on music as primarily the handmaid of religion began to concentrate their attention upon the development of secular music. The Puritans had no quarrel with music itself; they opposed the elaborate church music as they did the richly carved high altars, and saw to it that both disappeared. But England was still a singing nation, Puritan no less than Cavalier. It was a Puritan parson in Jonson's *Epicœne* who "sat up late of night, singing catches"; Cromwell himself had an organ, and engaged an orchestra of forty-eight pieces to play when his daughter married.[3] Vocal solos became more popular, and the musical settings for the excellent lyrics of the time were carefully fitted to the metrical pattern. During the Commonwealth much music was published, and in 1657 the Puritan Council appointed a Committee for the Advancement of Music.[4] By the Restoration, English music was ready to profit by contact with French music. The break with traditional religious concepts, and the skeptical and intellectual attitude made impossible the old mystical expression which had characterized the music of worship. Music also became more intellectual, with more emphasis on structure and less on emotion. The experimental spirit of the age led to much experimentation in music, and many advances were made. There was great activity in the development of musical instruments, the laws of vibration were studied, and innovations in musical theory were promoted. Even Mr. Pepys entertained himself by inventing "a better theory of musique than hath yet been abroad." Purcell, in whom the new music of the century culminated, not only tried all the known forms of music but also developed other forms. The emphasis upon definiteness and clarity of pattern in music reveals the same temper of mind that is shown by precision in science and mathematics or by neat exactness in literary expression.

This conflict between authority and freedom took place not only in literature, the press, education, and music, but also in the civil, religious, and philosophical ideas. King James I had come to England claiming full power by the

[3] Scholes, *The Puritans and Music,* p. 5.
[4] *Ibid.,* pp. 282–86.

"Divine Right of Kings." He was "as God" to his subjects
and claimed to hold over them the power of life and death.
To the people this authority seemed a contradiction of their
old laws and personal rights; they held that the law was
supreme and that the king contracted with his subjects to
see that the law was carried out. In the attempt to establish
the precedent of early times, scholars and lawyers turned to
a study of the Common Law. Many of the documents, however, were in Anglo-Saxon, and through long neglect that
language had been completely lost. The restoration of the
vocabulary and grammar is one of the most thrilling of all
the miracles of literary achievement. From the likeness of
Anglo-Saxon words to the Dutch and from the use of familiar
materials, such as the Lord's Prayer and the Ten Commandments, or of the *Æneid* "Scottished," an understanding of
the language finally emerged. Parliament, convinced by this
study that supreme authority was vested in the law, set out
to maintain the rights of the people; and the rebellion was on.

As in all periods of war, the conflict had its impact upon
the writers. The reactions were of as many different sorts as
there were different temperaments, making a vivid cross
section of human response. Suckling is the man of action.
He drops his pen and is off to join the Scottish expedition,
lavishing his wealth on the equipment of his troop in order
to make a brave show before the enemy. Waller, on the other
hand, works with "covert guile," fomenting a plot within
the capital itself in the hope of restoring it to the king. Down
in Devonshire Herrick is apparently insensible to the great
upheaval that is going on; and when the Puritan forces eject
him from his parish, he hastens joyfully to London to see his
poems through the press. Wither, though he had enjoyed
the patronage of Princess Elizabeth, seems never to have been
a whole-hearted Royalist and swings over to Cromwell's
side, sells all that he has to aid the cause, and becomes a captain in the Parliamentary forces. Cowley goes to France
with the Queen's Party and devotes himself to dangerous

secret negotiations. Milton gives up his carefully planned literary program and consecrates his talent and rare scholarship to writing in liberty's defense, even though he recognizes that such writing is done, as he says, with his left hand. Of such men we might well say, "Not of an age, but for all time."

Diametrically opposed to the idea of the sovereignty of the law and the responsibility of the king in maintaining his part of the governmental contract is the idea set forth by Thomas Hobbes in 1651 in the *Leviathan*. To him the social contract does not mean mutual responsibility but the delegation, once and for all, of authority to a supreme power. To attain peace and security, the people must focus in the king all authority, both civil and religious, and merge all individual rights in the rights of this all-powerful state or *Leviathan* so established. Certainly Hobbes's theory seemed ratified by the failure of the Commonwealth. Hobbes held that man's nature is naturally evil and that the only check upon it is external law. Milton's explanation for the failure of the Commonwealth, however, is that the nation had not learned that true freedom lay in self-control through the dominance of the power of reason. The removal of external authority therefore led to the substitution of license for liberty. *Paradise Lost* is the literary interpretation of this age. Here Milton shows that true liberty in "right reason dwells," and that without the guidance of reason "all the upstart passions rise," snatching the reins of government in the individual life and bringing about a state of anarchy. Outer authority, he says, is only an indication of the loss of inner authority, the dominance of the rational. Others find an explanation for the chaotic conditions in the rise of the middle class and its insistence upon social equality, an advance which broke the order sustained by the "chain of being." The failure of the Commonwealth necessitated the Restoration, and it seemed that once more authority and the upper classes were dominant. But a nation that had beheaded a king could depose a king; and when the old conflict between authority and freedom was augmented by the fear of Catholicism and its implication of authority in religion, James II had to flee the kingdom. Meanwhile Locke added the support of his great name to the social contract theory, arguing that the supremacy lay in the will of the people. When William of Orange consummated the bloodless revolution in 1688, the modern nation had already arisen and the major source of power lay in Parliament.

The Parliamentarians, who had fought to gain freedom from the authority of the king, fought also for liberty in religious beliefs and practices. They believed that men had a right to think for themselves in religion; but having overthrown the authority of the church, they themselves would have shown the very intolerance they had put down had not Cromwell restrained them. Under Cromwell general liberty of worship was sustained, including that of the Jews; intolerance was shown only to the Catholics, who represented the power of authority. This breadth of thought was not maintained after the Restoration, and Charles II introduced strict laws against the Dissenters. It was not until the Act of Toleration in 1689 that the separation of the church and the state advocated by Milton really came into being. Locke's *Letter Concerning Toleration* is another landmark in the development of modern thought, in its logical distinctions between the provinces of civil government and religion. Beginning with 1689, freedom of worship was granted to all sects except the much-feared Catholics and the "heretical" Unitarians.

When we turn to the conflict between authority and freedom in philosophy, it is again Bacon who hurls the challenge. The first step in the advancement of thought is to rid oneself of all the prepossessions which arise from one's natural predisposition, whether racial or individual, from society and the accepted use of words, and from the accepted systems of philosophy. These he calls the Idols. Slowly, by the inductive method, one may then build up reality. Bacon, however, did not try to enter the theological realm. He kept the regions of reason and faith clearly separate, and so there could be no conflict; the end of reason was knowledge, but the end of faith was wonder. Hobbes, on the other hand, recognized only that to which the senses could testify. The only things which were real were the material. These realities were governed by mechanical laws which could be calculated and understood through the study of mathematics. Descartes, the great French philosopher who shaped much of English thought, started, like Bacon, with the principle that one should doubt all things. He conceded a dual reality of matter and the soul, both of which could be rationally understood. In England much sympathy for the philosophy of Descartes and much opposition to that of Hobbes were found in the group called the Cambridge Platonists. They reconciled the duality of matter and spirit by giving reason the control over the lower realms. Reason is something more than the "Inner Light" of the Quakers or the "Witness of the indwelling Spirit" of the Puritans: it is the very spirit of God, found not in inspired revelation but in a moral law which should be the guiding principle of life. "To follow Reason is to follow God" is the summary of the faith of the Cambridge Platonists as stated by one of their number, John Smith. This belief found realistic expression in a life of positive goodness, recognized as more important than faith in any creed. Milton saw in this rational choice of the good a substitute for the state of innocent goodness in the Garden of Eden, a "Paradise within thee, happier far," and recognized as the "true wayfaring Christian" the one who could distinguish between good and evil and choose good even when his natural desires made evil pleasing to him. Locke approached even more nearly the modern point of view. He broke entirely with traditional knowledge and opinion and set forth the idea that all one can really know is what he learns through experience and his own intellectual effort.

Tools with which to work, freedom from tradition and authority, and confidence in intellectual power were the gifts of this century to mankind. With these in his possession he caught the vision of progress. It is difficult for the modern age to conceive of a time when man looked back to the days of ancient Greece and Rome as the period of perfection and felt that since then the world had been plunging on a downward career toward ultimate destruction. Such, however, was the belief until the changing thought of the seventeenth century prepared the ground for the conception of continuous development. To earlier centuries the increasing age of the world meant only growing remoteness from the vigor of youth. This idea had been fostered by the portrayal of the golden age in classical literature, and it was popularized through the revival of this literature during the Renaissance. The pastorals of Renaissance England are full of it, and Spenser's poetry shows how much it had become a part of the thought of the age. The Christian picture of the state of innocence before the fall of man became colored by the classical representation of the golden age and gained great popularity in Puritan England. The high point of its expression is in the beautiful portrayal of life in the Garden of Eden in *Paradise Lost*. The Puritans held that the process of degeneration had gone on steadily since the fall and would terminate in the destruction of the world. From the ashes would arise like the phœnix (one of the favorite figures of the seventeenth century) a new heaven and a new earth— a golden age to be anticipated in the future.

When James I was welcomed to the throne of England, the poets and pageant-makers used the idea that now Astræa would return to earth and a new golden age would be ushered in. There were no remarkable changes, however, and it was soon apparent that after all it was only the "rusty iron age." To men who accepted the idea that they lived in the iron age and that they were not the equals of the ancients, there naturally came the doubt as to whether nature was still capable of producing men with as great ability, either physical or mental, as those of the past. Old tombs were opened and the bones measured, an experiment which established the fact that men had decreased in physical size. The result was that many believed that nature was losing her power and that not only was man degenerating but also that the universe was diminishing, and even that the very plants and animals were becoming smaller than in previous ages. The controversy over the decay of nature was so current in the reign of James I and the early years of Charles I that the question became the subject of books and was used for disputations in the universities. Bishop Goodman in 1616 wrote a book entitled *The Fall of Man, or the Corruption of Nature Proved by Natural Reason,* which was answered by George Hakewill in 1627 with *An Apologie or Declaration of the Power and Providence of God in the World.* Hakewill pointed out that belief in the Providence of God was irreconcilable with belief in the decay of nature. In the following year the subject of the decay of nature was used for disputation at Cambridge; and Milton, in writing the poetical treatment of the subject which was distributed among the audience, *Naturam Non Pati Senium,* argued on the negative.

With the growth of the new science it became apparent that new truths were constantly being reached. Discoveries and inventions were enabling man to attain heights that he had scarcely yet dreamed of. These were marshaled as proof that man was advancing beyond the achievements of the past. There also arose a sense of greater surety, for the laws of nature were found to be invariable and dependable, so that nature could be counted on to carry on her processes without alteration. In the light of the view that knowledge was to be used to meet human needs, man saw that through his own powers he could improve conditions, physical and social, and literally build a "new Jerusalem in England's green and pleasant land."

It was with exhilaration that the giant intellectuals at-

tempted to prove themselves equal to the challenge of progress. There was an intensity of eagerness about their work
and a spirit of co-operation in a great task that, together with
unusual gifts of genius, proved sufficient to meet the demands that arose. With enthusiasm these men set out to
enlarge their own mental horizons: Bacon, perceiving that
"the sovereignty of man lieth hid in knowledge," reached
forth to take all knowledge for his province; Crashaw wrote
of the "large drafts of intellectual day"; and Donne acknowledged a "hydroptic, immoderate desire of human learning."
In *The Harmony of the World* Kepler expressed the thankful exultation characteristic of these workers: "That . . .
for which I have devoted the best part of my life to astronomical contemplations—at length I have brought to light, and
recognized its truth beyond my most sanguine expectations."
Traherne sums up the new idea: "From the centre to the
utmost bounds of the everlasting hills all is Heaven before
God, and full of treasure: and he that walks like God in the
midst of them is blessed." [5]

Looking at the progress of this century, one questions
why these developments could not have come in the other
great age of scientific progress, the period between Pythagoras and Plato in Greece. The seventeenth century, however, fulfilled certain conditions necessary for further advance. There was a change in the type of reasoning: the
Greeks turned to the philosophical inquiry of *why* things
happen; the seventeenth century studied the more objective
question of *how* things happen. Theory was, therefore, re-
placed by experiment. A convenient and quick system of
notation to use in making astronomical computations or in
interpreting other phenomena, a system which Greek mathematics had not provided, was developed; and, finally, instruments which made possible more accurate observations
were produced. The extraordinary contribution of the century to the history of scientific thought lies back of all the

[5] *Centuries of Meditations,* IV, no. 37.

progress in the period and was made possible by the achievements of such men as Copernicus, Galileo, Bacon, Harvey, Kepler, Torricelli, Boyle, and Newton. Throwing off the restraining bondage of authority of all sorts and co-operating in organized effort to increase human knowledge, the leaders in thought used the new tools for accuracy and the new standards of precise thought so effectively that they created the idea of progress and challenged succeeding centuries to move forward in invention, discovery, and thought.

Francis Bacon 1561-1626

FEW FACTS of Bacon's early life are known. His father, Sir Nicholas Bacon, Lord Keeper of the Great Seal, lived at York House on the Strand when in the city and near St. Albans when in the country. At the age of twelve Bacon was admitted with his elder brother Anthony to Trinity College, Cambridge. He did not take a degree, however, but entered Gray's Inn to study law on June 27, 1576. Not long after, probably early in the following year, he went to Paris to join Sir Amias Paulet, the new Ambassador to France, and remained in France until his father's death in 1579. Upon his return to England he continued his study at Gray's Inn and was admitted as utter barrister in 1582. In 1584 he was elected to Parliament and entered upon his long public career.

For years he made little progress in spite of many appeals to his mother's powerful relations, Lord Burleigh and Robert Cecil, Burleigh's son and successor. In the latter part of Elizabeth's reign, however, he became a member of her "learned counsel," and he was among the three hundred knighted in that broad gesture made by James I on the eve of his coronation. It was under James I that he received advancement. This is best shown by the close sequence of appointments: Solicitor General, 1607; Attorney General, 1613; Privy Councillor, 1616; Lord Keeper, 1617; Lord Chancellor, 1618. He was made Baron Verulam in 1618, also, and Viscount St. Albans in 1621.

In true Elizabethan manner Fortune's wheel suddenly turned. Whatever the truth of Bacon's intention in the acceptance of bribes, he was convicted and a heavy penalty set. Although the penalty was greatly modified, Bacon was never allowed to sit in Parliament again. He retired to the family estate and turned his energies to the completion of the great work which he had first announced at thirty-one in a letter to Lord Burleigh.

He had already published parts of this work: the *Advancement of Learning* in 1605 and the *Novum Organum* in 1620. *De Augmentis Scientiarum*, a Latin version of the *Advancement of Learning*, followed in 1623, and many portions of the enormous project were left among his papers. Other works of this period are the *History of Henry VII*, 1622; the *New Atlantis*, 1624; and the completed or third edition of the *Essays*, 1625, the first edition having appeared in 1597. The *Sylva Sylvarum* was published posthumously in 1627.

Knowledge of Bacon's writings is too often limited to his essays, and yet the magnificent summary of the state of learning in his own day, the point from which his own work was to proceed, is a far more important work. *Novum Organum,* written and rewritten until the style is the perfect medium for the thought, is scarcely known at all by the general reader, but it is this which Coleridge ranks among "the three great works since the introduction of Christianity." It contains Bacon's leading ideas: the unity of knowledge, the relation of knowledge to practical purposes, the need for experiment, and a suggested method. In these major works we find embodied Bacon's ideal of serving his country, mankind, and religion through the unremitting search for truth. Known best for establishing the inductive method in scientific study, Bacon is also the greatest philosopher of the time. His ideas, powerful in themselves, gain strength through his mastery of a clear and eloquent prose style which does not attempt to reach over into the realm of poetry.

ESSAYS OR COUNSELS, CIVIL AND MORAL

Of Death

MEN fear death as children fear to go in the dark; and as that natural fear in children is increased with tales, so is the other. Certainly, the contemplation of death as the wages of sin and passage to another world, is holy and religious; but the fear of it as tribute due unto nature, is weak. Yet in religious meditations there is sometimes mixture of vanity and of superstition. You shall read in some of the friars' books of mortification that a man should think with himself what the pain is if he have but his finger's-end pressed or tortured, and thereby imagine what the pains of death are, when the whole body is corrupted and dissolved; when many times death passeth with less pain than the torture of a limb; for the most vital parts are not the quickest of sense. And by him that spake only as a philosopher and natural man it was well said: *Pompa mortis magis terret, quam mors ipsa.*[1] Groans and convulsions and a discolored face, and friends weeping, and blacks and obsequies and the like, show death terrible. It is worthy the observing that there is no passion in the mind of man so weak but it mates and masters the fear of death; and therefore death is no such terrible enemy when a man hath so many attendants about him that can win the combat of him. Revenge triumphs over death, love slights it, honor aspireth to it, grief flieth to it, fear pre-occupateth it; nay, we read after Otho the emperor had slain himself, pity, which is the tenderest of affections, provoked many to die out of mere compassion to their sovereign, and as the truest sort of followers. Nay, Seneca adds niceness and satiety: *Cogita quamdiu eadem feceris; mori velle, non tantum fortis, aut miser, sed etiam fastidiosus potest.*[2] A man would die, though he were neither

---

[1] *It is the accompaniments of death that are frightful rather than death itself.* (Seneca, *Epistles,* 24.)

[2] *Ibid.,* 77.

valiant nor miserable, only upon a weariness to do the same
thing so oft over and over. It is no less worthy to observe,
how little alteration in good spirits the approaches of death
make; for they appear to be the same men till the last instant. Augustus Cæsar died in a compliment, *Livia conjugi
nostri memor, vive et vale;* [3] Tiberius in dissimulation, as
Tacitus saith of him, *Jam Tiberium vires et corpus, non
dissimulatio, deserebant;* [4] Vespasian in a jest, sitting upon
the stool, *Ut puto Deus fio;* [5] Galba with a sentence, *Feri,
si ex re sit populi Romani,* [6] holding forth his neck; Septimius
Severus in dispatch, *Adeste, si quid mihi restat agendum;* [7]
and the like. Certainly the Stoics bestowed too much cost
upon death, and by their great preparations made it appear
more fearful. Better saith he, *Qui finem vitæ extremum inter
munera ponat naturæ.* [8] It is as natural to die as to be born,
and to a little infant perhaps the one is as painful as the
other. He that dies in an earnest pursuit is like one that is
wounded in hot blood, who for the time scarce feels the hurt;
and therefore, a mind fixed and bent upon somewhat that is
good, doth avert the dolors of death. But above all, believe
it, the sweetest canticle is Nunc Dimittis, when a man hath
obtained worthy ends and expectations. Death hath this
also, that it openeth the gate to good fame and extinguisheth
envy, *Extinctus amabitur idem.* [9]

[3] *Farewell, Livia, and forget not the days of our marriage.* (Suetonius,
Augustus, ch. 99.)
[4] *His powers of body left Tiberius, not his dissimulation.* (Tacitus,
Annals, VI. 50.)
[5] *I think I am becoming a God.* (Suetonius, *Vespasian,* ch. 23.)
[6] *Strike, if it be for the good of Rome.* (Tacitus, *History,* I. 41.)
[7] *Make haste, if there is anything more for me to do.* (Dio Cassius, *History of Rome,* LXXVI. 17.)
[8] *Who accounts the close of life as one of the benefits of nature.* (Juvenal,
Satires, X. 358.)
[9] *When he is dead the same man (who was envied when alive) shall be
loved.* (Horace, *Epistles,* II. i. 14.)

Of Adversity

It was an high speech of Seneca (after the manner of the Stoics), that the good things which belong to prosperity are to be wished; but the good things that belong to adversity are to be admired: *Bona rerum secundarum, optabilia; adversarum mirabilia.*[1] Certainly, if miracles be the command over nature, they appear most in adversity. It is yet a higher speech of his than the other (much too high for a heathen): It is true greatness to have in one the frailty of a man and the security of a God, *Vere magnum habere fragilitatem hominis, securitatem Dei.*[2] This would have done better in poesy, where transcendences are more allowed. And the poets, indeed, have been busy with it; for it is, in effect, the thing which is figured in that strange fiction of the ancient poets, which seemeth not to be without mystery; nay, and to have some approach to the state of a Christian: that Hercules, when he went to unbind Prometheus, by whom human nature is represented, sailed the length of the great ocean in an earthen pot or pitcher; lively describing Christian resolution, that saileth in the frail bark of the flesh through the waves of the world. But to speak in a mean, the virtue of prosperity is temperance; the virtue of adversity is fortitude, which in morals is the most heroical virtue. Prosperity

is the blessing of the Old Testament; adversity is the blessing of the New, which carrieth the greater benediction and the clearer revelation of God's favor. Yet even in the Old Testament, if you listen to David's harp, you shall hear as many hearselike airs as carols; and the pencil of the Holy Ghost hath labored more in describing the afflictions of Job than the felicities of Solomon. Prosperity is not without many fears and distastes; and adversity is not without comforts and hopes. We see in needleworks and embroideries, it is

---

[1] *Epistles,* 56. [2] *Ibid.,* 53.

more pleasing to have a lively work upon a sad and solemn ground, than to have a dark and melancholy work upon a lightsome ground: judge, therefore, of the pleasure of the heart by the pleasure of the eye. Certainly, virtue is like precious odors, most fragrant when they are incensed or crushed; (for prosperity doth best discover vice, but adversity doth best discover virtue.)

Of Great Place

MEN in great place are thrice servants: servants of the sovereign or state, servants of fame, and servants of business. So as they have no freedom, neither in their persons, nor in their actions, nor in their times. It is a strange desire, to seek power and lose liberty, or to seek power over others and to lose power over a man's self. The rising unto place is laborious, and by pains men come to greater pains; and it is sometimes base, and by indignities men come to dignities. The standing is slippery, and the regress is either a downfall or at least an eclipse, which is a melancholy thing: *Cum non sis qui fueris, non esse cur velis vivere.*[1] Nay, retire men cannot when they would, neither will they when it were reason; but are impatient of privateness, even in age and sickness, which require the shadow; like old townsmen, that will be still sitting at their street door, though thereby they offer age to scorn. Certainly, great persons had need to borrow other men's opinions to think themselves happy; for if they judge by their own feeling, they cannot find it; but if they think with themselves what other men think of them, and that other men would fain be as they are, then they are happy, as it were by report; when perhaps they find the contrary within. (For they are the first that find their own griefs, though they be the last that find their own faults.)

[1] *When a man feels he is no longer what he was, he loses all his interest in life.* (Cicero, *Ep. Fam.*, VII. 3.)

Certainly, men in great fortunes are strangers to themselves, and while they are in the puzzle of business they have no time to tend their health, either of body or mind. *Illi mors gravis incubat, qui notus nimis omnibus, ignotus moritur sibi.*[2] In place there is license to do good and evil, whereof the latter is a curse; for in evil the best condition is not to will, the second not to can. But power to do good is the true and lawful end of aspiring; for good thoughts (though God accept them) yet towards men are little better than good dreams, except they be put in act; and that cannot be without power and place, as the vantage and commanding ground. Merit and good works is the end of man's motion, and conscience of the same is the accomplishment of man's rest; for if a man can be partaker of God's theater, he shall likewise be partaker of God's rest. *Et conversus Deus, ut aspiceret opera quæ fecerunt manus suæ, vidit quod omnia essent bona nimis;*[3] and then the sabbath. In the discharge of thy place set before thee the best examples, for imitation is a globe of precepts. And after a time set before thee thine own example; and examine thyself strictly, whether thou didst not best at first. Neglect not also the examples of those that have carried themselves ill in the same place; not to set off thyself by taxing their memory, but to direct thyself what to avoid. Reform, therefore, without bravery, or scandal of former times and persons; but yet set it down to thyself, as well to create good precedents as to follow them. Reduce things to the first institution, and observe wherein and how they have degenerate; but yet ask counsel of both times; of the ancient time what is best, and of the latter time what is fittest. Seek to make thy course regular, that men may know beforehand what they may expect; but be not too positive and peremptory, and express thyself

[2] *It is a sad fate for a man to die too well known to everybody else, and still unknown to himself.* (Seneca, *Thyestes,* II. 401.)
[3] *And God turned to look upon the works which his hands had made and saw that all were very good.* (Genesis 1:31.)

well when thou digressest from thy rule. Preserve the right of thy place, but stir not questions of jurisdiction; and rather assume thy right in silence and *de facto,* than voice it with claims and challenges. Preserve likewise the rights of inferior places, and think it more honor to direct in chief than to be busy in all. Embrace and invite helps and advices touching the execution of thy place, and do not drive away such as bring thee information as meddlers, but accept of them in good part. The vices of authority are chiefly four: delays, corruption, roughness, and facility. For delays, give easy access, keep times appointed, go through with that which is in hand, and interlace not business but of necessity. For corruption, do not only bind thine own hands or thy servants' hands from taking, but bind the hands of suitors also from offering. For integrity used doth the one; but integrity professed and with a manifest detestation of bribery, doth the other. And avoid not only the fault, but the suspicion. Whosoever is found variable and changeth manifestly, without manifest cause, giveth suspicion of corruption. Therefore, always when thou changest thine opinion or course, profess it plainly and declare it, together with the reasons that move thee to change; and do not think to steal it. A servant or a favorite, if he be inward, and no other apparent cause of esteem, is commonly thought but a by-way to close corruption. For roughness, it is a needless cause of discontent; severity breedeth fear, but roughness breedeth hate. Even reproofs from authority ought to be grave, and not taunting. As for facility, it is worse than bribery; for bribes come but now and then; but if importunity or idle respects lead a man, he shall never be without. As Solomon saith, *To respect persons is not good, for such a man will transgress for a piece of bread.*[4] It is most true that was anciently spoken, *A place showeth the man;* and it showeth some to the better and some to the worse. *Omnium consensu capax imperii,*

[4] Prov. 28:21.

nisi imperasset,[5] saith Tacitus of Galba; but of Vespasian he saith, *Solus imperantium Vespasianus mutatus in melius:* [6] though the one was meant of sufficiency, the other of manners and affection. It is an assured sign of a worthy and generous spirit, whom honor amends. For honor is, or should be, the place of virtue; and as in nature things move violently to their place and calmly in their place, so virtue in ambition is violent, in authority settled and calm. All rising to great place is by a winding stair; and if there be factions, it is good to side a man's self whilst he is in the rising, and to balance himself when he is placed. Use the memory of thy predecessor fairly and tenderly; for if thou dost not, it is a debt will sure be paid when thou art gone. If thou have colleagues, respect them, and rather call them when they look not for it, than exclude them when they have reason to look to be called. Be not too sensible or too remembering of thy place in conversation and private answers to suitors; but let it rather be said, *When he sits in place he is another man.*

Of Travel

TRAVEL, in the younger sort, is a part of education; in the elder, a part of experience. He that traveleth into a country before he hath some entrance into the language, goeth to school, and not to travel. That young men travel under some tutor or grave servant, I allow well; so that he be such a one that hath the language, and hath been in the country before; whereby he may be able to tell them what things are worthy to be seen in the country where they go, what acquaintances they are to seek, what exercises or discipline the place yieldeth; for else young men shall go hooded,

[5] *A man whom everybody would have thought fit for empire, if he had not been emperor.* (Tacitus, *History*, I. 49.)

[6] *He was the only man whom the possession of empire changed for the better. (Ibid.,* I. 50.)

and look abroad little. It is a strange thing that in sea voyages, where there is nothing to be seen but sky and sea, men should make diaries; but in land travel, wherein so much is to be observed, for the most part they omit it; as if chance were fitter to be registered than observation. Let diaries, therefore, be brought in use. The things to be seen and observed are: the courts of princes, specially when they give audience to ambassadors; the courts of justice, while they sit and hear causes; and so of consistories ecclesiastic; the churches and monasteries, with the monuments which are therein extant; the walls and fortifications of cities and towns; and so the havens and harbors; antiquities and ruins; libraries; colleges, disputations, and lectures, where any are; shipping and navies; houses and gardens of state and pleasure near great cities; armories, arsenals, magazines, exchanges, burses, warehouses; exercises of horsemanship, fencing, training of soldiers, and the like; comedies, such whereunto the better sort of persons do resort; treasuries of jewels and robes; cabinets and rarities; and to conclude, whatsoever is memorable in the places where they go. After all which the tutors or servants ought to make diligent inquiry. As for triumphs, masks, feasts, weddings, funerals, capital executions, and such shows, men need not to be put in mind of them; yet are they not to be neglected. If you will have a young man to put his travel into a little room, and in a short time to gather much, this you must do. First, as was said, he must have some entrance into the language before he goeth; then he must have such a servant, or tutor, as knoweth the country, as was likewise said. Let him carry with him also some card, or book, describing the country where he traveleth, which will be a good key to his inquiry. Let him keep also a diary. Let him not stay long in one city or town, more or less as the place deserveth, but not long: nay, when he stayeth in one city or town, let him change his lodging from one end and part of town to another, which is a great adamant of acquaintance. Let him sequester himself from the company of his countrymen, and diet in such places where there is good company of the nation where he traveleth. Let him, upon his removes from one place to another, procure recommendation to some person of quality residing in the place whither he removeth, that he may use his favor in those things he desireth to see or know. Thus he may abridge his travel with much profit. As for the acquaintance which is to be sought in travel, that which is most of all profitable is acquaintance with the secretaries and employed men of ambassadors; for so in traveling in one country he shall suck the experience of many. Let him also see and visit eminent persons in all kinds which are of great name abroad, that he may tell how the life agreeth with the fame. For quarrels, they are with care and discretion to be avoided. They are commonly for mistresses, healths, place, and words. And let a man beware how he keepeth company with choleric and quarrelsome persons, for they will engage him into their own quarrels. When a traveler returneth home, let him not leave the countries where he hath traveled altogether behind him, but maintain a correspondence by letters with those of his acquaintance which are of most worth. And let his travel appear rather in his discourse than in his apparel or gesture; and in his discourse let him be rather advised in his answers than forward to tell stories. And let it appear that he doth not change his country manners for those of foreign parts, but only prick in some flowers of that he hath learned abroad into the customs of his own country.

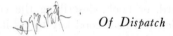

Of Dispatch

AFFECTED dispatch is one of the most dangerous things to business that can be; it is like that which the physicians call predigestion, or hasty digestion, which is sure to fill the body full of crudities, and secret seeds of diseases. Therefore measure not dispatch by the times of sitting, but by the advancement of the business. And as in races it is not the large stride or high lift that makes the speed, so in business the keeping close to the matter and not taking of it too much at once, procureth dispatch. It is the care of some, only to come off speedily for the time, or to contrive some false periods of business, because they may seem men of dispatch. But it is one thing to abbreviate by contracting, another by cutting off; and business so handled at several sittings or meetings goeth commonly backward and forward in an unsteady manner. I knew a wise man that had it for a byword, when he saw men hasten to a conclusion, *Stay a little, that we may make an end the sooner.*

On the other side, true dispatch is a rich thing. For time is the measure of business, as money is of wares; and business is bought at a dear hand where there is small dispatch. The Spartans and Spaniards have been noted to be of small dispatch: *Mi venga la muerte de Spagna;* Let my death come from Spain; for then it will be sure to be long in coming.

Give good hearing to those that give the first information in business; and rather direct them in the beginning than interrupt them in the continuance of their speeches: for he that is put out of his own order will go forward and backward, and be more tedious while he waits upon his memory than he could have been if he had gone on in his own course. But sometimes it is seen that the moderator is more troublesome than the actor.

Iterations are commonly loss of time. But there is no such gain of time as to iterate often the state of the question; for it chaseth away many a frivolous speech as it is coming forth. Long and curious speeches are as fit for dispatch as a robe or mantle with a long train is for a race. Prefaces, and passages, and excusations, and other speeches of reference to the person, are great wastes of time; and though they seem to proceed of modesty, they are bravery. Yet beware of being too material when there is any impediment of obstruction in men's wills; for pre-occupation of mind ever requireth preface of speech, like a fomentation to make the unguent enter.

Above all things, order and distribution, and singling out of parts, is the life of dispatch; so as the distribution be not too subtle: for he that doth not divide will never enter well into business; and he that divideth too much will never come out of it clearly. To choose time is to save time; and an unseasonable motion is but beating the air. There be three parts of business: the preparation, the debate or examination, and the perfection. Whereof, if you look for dispatch, let the middle only be the work of many, and the first and last the work of few. The proceeding upon somewhat conceived in writing doth for the most part facilitate dispatch: for, though it should be wholly rejected, yet that negative is more pregnant of direction than an indefinite; as ashes are more generative than dust.

Of Discourse

SOME in their discourse desire rather commendation of wit in being able to hold all arguments, than of judgment in discerning what is true; as if it were a praise to know what might be said, and not what should be thought. Some have certain commonplaces and themes wherein they are good, and want variety; which kind of poverty is for the most part tedious, and when it is once perceived, ridiculous. The honorablest part of talk is to give the occasion, and again to moderate and pass to somewhat else; for then a man leads the dance. It is good in discourse and speech of conversation to vary and intermingle speech of the present occasion with arguments, tales with reasons, asking of questions with telling of opinions, and jest with earnest; for it is a dull thing to tire, as we say now, to jade, anything too far. As for jest, there be certain things which ought to be privileged from it—namely, religion, matters of state, great persons, any man's present business of importance, and any case that deserveth pity. Yet there be some that think their wits have been asleep, except they dart out somewhat that is piquant and to the quick; that is a vein which would be bridled.

Parce, puer, stimulis, et fortius utere loris.[1]

And, generally, men ought to find the difference between saltness and bitterness. Certainly he that hath a satirical vein, as he maketh others afraid of his wit, so he had need be afraid of others' memory. He that questioneth much shall learn much, and content much; but especially if he apply his questions to the skill of the persons whom he asketh; for he shall give them occasion to please themselves in speaking, and himself shall continually gather knowledge. But let his questions not be troublesome, for that is fit for a poser; and let him be sure to leave other men their turns to speak. Nay, if there be any that would reign and take up all the time, let him find means to take them off, and to bring others on; as musicians use to do with those that dance too long galliards. If you dissemble sometimes your knowledge of that you are thought to know, you shall be thought another time to know that you know not. Speech of a man's self ought to be seldom, and well chosen. I knew one was wont to say in scorn, *He must needs be a wise man, he speaks so much of himself.* And there is but one case wherein a man may commend himself with good grace, and that is in commending virtue to another; especially if it be such a virtue whereunto himself pretendeth. Speech of touch towards others should be sparingly used; for discourse ought to be as a field, without coming home to any man. I knew two noblemen of the west part of England, whereof the one was given to scoff, but kept ever royal cheer in his house; the other would ask of those that had been at the other's table, *Tell truly, was there never*

[1] *Be gentle with the spurs and handle the reins more firmly.* (Ovid, *Metamorphoses*, II. 127.)

a flout or dry blow given? To which the guest would answer, *Such and such a thing passed.* The lord would say, *I thought he would mar a good dinner.* Discretion of speech is more than eloquence; and to speak agreeably to him with whom we deal is more than to speak in good words or in good order. A good continued speech, without a good speech of interlocution, shows slowness; and a good reply or second speech, without a good settled speech, showeth shallowness and weakness. As we see in beasts, that those that are weakest in the course are yet nimblest in the turn; as it is betwixt the greyhound and the hare. To use too many circumstances ere one come to the matter is wearisome; to use none at all, is blunt.

Of Youth and Age

A MAN that is young in years may be old in hours, if he have lost no time. But that happeneth rarely. Generally, youth is like the first cogitations, not so wise as the second, for there is a youth in thoughts as well as in ages. And yet the invention of young men is more lively than that of old, and imaginations stream into their minds better and, as it were, more divinely. Natures that have much heat and great and violent desires and perturbations, are not ripe for action till they have passed the meridian of their years; as it was with Julius Cæsar and Septimius Severus; of the latter of whom it is said, *Juventutem egit erroribus, imo furoribus plenam;* and yet he was the ablest emperor, almost, of all the list. But reposed natures may do well in youth, as it is seen in Augustus Cæsar, Cosmus Duke of Florence, Gaston de Foix, and others. On the other side, heat and vivacity in age is an excellent composition for business. Young men are fitter to invent than to judge, fitter for execution than for counsel, and fitter for new projects than for settled business; for the experience of age, in things that fall within the compass of it, directeth them, but in new things abuseth them.

The errors of young men are the ruin of business; but the errors of aged men amount to but this, that more might have been done, or sooner.

Young men, in the conduct and manage of actions, embrace more than they can hold; stir more than they can quiet; fly to the end without consideration of the means and degrees; pursue some few principles which they have chanced upon absurdly; care not to innovate, which draws unknown inconveniences; use extreme remedies at first; and, that which doubleth all errors, will not acknowledge or retract them, like an unready horse that will neither stop nor turn. Men of age object too much, consult too long, adventure too little, repent too soon, and seldom drive business home to the full period, but content themselves with a mediocrity of success. Certainly it is good to compound employments of both; for that will be good for the present, because the virtues of either age may correct the defects of both; and good for succession, that young men may be learners, while men in age are actors; and, lastly, good for externe accidents, because authority followeth old men, and favor and popularity youth. But, for the moral part, perhaps, youth will have the pre-eminence, as age hath for the politic. A certain rabbin, upon the text, *Your young men shall see visions, and your old men shall dream dreams,* inferreth that young men are admitted nearer to God than old, because vision is a clearer revelation than a dream. And, certainly, the more a man drinketh of the world, the more it intoxicateth; and age doth profit rather in the powers of understanding than in the virtues of the will and affections. There be some have an over-early ripeness in their years, which fadeth betimes: these are, first, such as have brittle wits, the edge whereof is soon turned; such as was Hermogenes the rhetorician, whose books are exceeding subtle, who afterwards waxed stupid. A second sort is of those that have some natural dispositions which have better grace in youth than in age; such as is a fluent and luxuriant speech, which becomes youth well, but not age. So Tully saith of

Hortensius, *Idem manebat, neque idem decebat.* The third is of such as take too high a strain at the first, and are magnanimous more than tract of years can uphold; as was Scipio Africanus, of whom Livy saith in effect, *Ultima primis cedebant.*

Of Studies

STUDIES serve for delight, for ornament, and for ability. Their chief use for delight is in privateness and retiring; for ornament, is in discourse; and for ability, is in the judgment and disposition of business. For expert men can execute, and perhaps judge of particulars, one by one; but the general counsels, and the plots and marshaling of affairs, come best from those that are learned. To spend too much time in studies is sloth; to use them too much for ornament is affectation; to make judgment wholly by their rules is the humor of a scholar. They perfect nature, and are perfected by experience; for natural abilities are like natural plants, that need pruning by study; and studies themselves do give forth directions too much at large, except they be bounded in by experience. Crafty men contemn studies, simple men admire them, and wise men use them, for they teach not their own use; but that is a wisdom without them, and above them, won by observation. Read not to contradict and confute, nor to believe and take for granted, nor to find talk and discourse, but to weigh and consider. Some books are to be tasted, others to be swallowed, and some few to be chewed and digested; that is, some books are to be read only in parts; others to be read, but not curiously; and some few to be read wholly, and with diligence and attention. Some books also may be read by deputy and extracts made of them by others, but that would be only in the less important arguments and the meaner sort of books; else distilled books are like common distilled waters, flashy things. Reading maketh a full man, conference a ready man, and writing an exact man. And therefore, if a man write little, he had need have a great memory; if he confer little, he had need have a present wit; and if he read little, he had need have more cunning, to seem to know that he doth not. Histories make men wise; poets, witty; the mathematics, subtle; natural philosophy, deep; moral, grave; logic and rhetoric, able to contend. *Abeunt studia in mores.* Nay, there is no stond or impediment in the wit but may be wrought out by fit studies, like as diseases of the body may have appropriate exercises. Bowling is good for the stone and reins, shooting for the lungs and breast, gentle walking for the stomach, riding for the head, and the like. So if a man's wit be wandering, let him study the mathematics; for in demonstrations, if his wit be called away never so little, he must begin again. If his wit be not apt to distinguish or find differences, let him study the schoolmen, for they are *Cymini sectores.* If he be not apt to beat over matters and to call up one thing to prove and illustrate another, let him study the lawyer's cases. So every defect of the mind may have a special receipt.

From THE ADVANCEMENT OF LEARNING [1]

The First Book

. . . THEREFORE I did conclude with myself that I could not
make unto your Majesty a better oblation than of some treatise tending to that end, whereof the sum will consist of these
two parts: the former concerning the excellency of learning
and knowledge, and the excellency of the merit and true glory
in the augmentation and propagation thereof; the latter what
the particular acts and works are which have been embraced
and undertaken for the advancement of learning, and again
what defects and undervalues I find in such particular acts:
to the end that though I cannot positively or affirmatively
advise your Majesty, or propound unto you framed particulars, yet I may excite your princely cogitations to visit the
excellent treasure of your own mind, and thence to extract
particulars for this purpose agreeable to your magnanimity
and wisdom.

In the entrance to the former of these, to clear the way,
and as it were to make silence to have the true testimonies
concerning the dignity of learning to be better heard without the interruption of tacit objections, I think good to
deliver it from the discredits and disgraces which it hath
received; all from ignorance, but ignorance severally dis-
guised: appearing sometimes in the zeal and jealousy of divines, sometimes in the severity and arrogancy of politiques,
and sometimes in the errors and imperfections of learned
men themselves.

I hear the former sort say that knowledge is of those things
which are to be accepted of with great limitation and caution; that the aspiring to overmuch knowledge was the
original temptation and sin whereupon ensued the fall of

[1] Text: 1605, first edition, The First Book, beginning paragraph 3, and
omitting The Survey of Knowledge from the creation through the time
of Julius Cæsar.

man; that knowledge hath in it somewhat of the serpent, and therefore where it entereth into a man it makes him swell—*Scientia inflat;* [2] that Solomon gives a censure, *That there is no end of making books, and that much reading is weariness of the flesh;* [3] and again in another place, *That in spacious knowledge there is much contristation, and that he that increaseth knowledge increaseth anxiety;* [4] that Saint Paul gives a caveat, *That we be not spoiled through vain philosophy;* [5] that experience demonstrates how learned men have been arch-heretics, how learned times have been inclined to atheism, and how the contemplation of second causes doth derogate from our dependence upon God, who is the first cause.

To discover then the ignorance and error of this opinion and the misunderstanding in the grounds thereof, it may well appear these men do not observe or consider that it was not the pure knowledge of nature and universality, a knowledge by the light whereof man did give names unto other creatures in Paradise as they were brought before him, according unto their proprieties, which gave the occasion to the fall; but it was the proud knowledge of good and evil, with an intent in man to give law unto himself and to depend no more upon God's commandments, which was the form of the temptation. Neither is it any quantity of knowledge, how great soever, that can make the mind of man to swell; for nothing can fill, much less extend the soul of man, but God and the contemplation of God; and therefore Solomon, speaking of the two principal senses of inquisition, the eye and the ear, affirmeth that *the eye is never satisfied with seeing, nor the ear with hearing;* [6] and if there be no fulness, then is the continent greater than the content: so of knowledge itself, and the mind of man, whereto the senses are but reporters, he defineth likewise in these words, placed after that calendar

[2] I Cor. 8:1.   [3] *Eccles.* 12:12.
[4] *Eccles.* 1:18.   [5] Col. 2:8.
[6] Eccles. 1:8.

or ephemerides which he maketh of the diversities of times
and seasons for all actions and purposes; and concludeth
thus: *God hath made all things beautiful, or decent, in the
true return of their seasons: Also he hath placed the world
in man's heart, yet cannot man find out the work which
God worketh from the beginning to the end:* [7] declaring not
obscurely, that God hath framed the mind of man as a mirror or glass capable of the image of the universal world, and
joyful to receive the impression thereof, as the eye joyeth to
receive light; and not only delighted in beholding the variety
of things and vicissitude of times, but raised also to find out
and discern the ordinances and decrees, which throughout
all those changes are infallibly observed. And although he
doth insinuate that the supreme or summary law of nature,
which he calleth *The work which God worketh from the beginning to the end,* is not possible to be found out by man;
yet that doth not derogate from the capacity of the mind, but
may be referred to the impediments, as of shortness of life,
ill conjunction of labors, ill tradition of knowledge over
from hand to hand, and many other inconveniences whereunto the condition of man is subject. For that nothing parcel
of the world is denied to man's inquiry and invention he doth
in another place rule over, when he saith, *The spirit of man
is as the lamp of God, wherewith he searcheth the inwardness
of all secrets.* [8] If then such be the capacity and receipt of
the mind of man, it is manifest that there is no danger at all
in the proportion or quantity of knowledge, how large soever,
lest it should make it swell or out-compass itself; no, but it
is merely the quality of knowledge, which be it in quantity
more or less, if it be taken without the true corrective thereof,
hath in it some nature of venom or malignity, and some effects of that venom, which is ventosity or swelling. This corrective spice, the mixture whereof maketh knowledge so
sovereign, is charity, which the apostle immediately addeth
to the former clause: for so he saith, *Knowledge bloweth up,*

[7] Eccles. 3:2.   [8] Prov. 20:27.

but charity buildeth up; [9] not unlike unto that which he delivereth in another place: *If I spake* (saith he) *with the tongues of men and angels, and had not charity, it were but as a tinkling cymbal;* [10] not but that it is an excellent thing to speak with the tongues of men and angels, but because if it be severed from charity, and not referred to the good of men and mankind, it hath rather a sounding and unworthy glory than a meriting and substantial virtue. And as for that censure of Solomon, concerning the excess of writing and reading books, and the anxiety of spirit which redoundeth from knowledge; and that admonition of Saint Paul, *That we be not seduced by vain philosophy;* [11] let those places be rightly understood, and they do indeed excellently set forth the true bounds and limitations whereby human knowledge is confined and circumscribed; and yet without any such contracting or coarctation, but that it may comprehend all the universal nature of things. For these limitations are three: the first, *That we do not so place our felicity in knowledge, as we forget our mortality:* the second, *That we make application of our knowledge, to give ourselves repose and contentment, and not distaste or repining:* the third, *That we do not presume by the contemplation of nature to attain to the mysteries of God.* For as touching the first of these, Solomon doth excellently expound himself in another place of the same book, where he saith: *I saw well that knowledge recedeth as far from ignorance as light doth from darkness; and that the wise man's eyes keep watch in his head, whereas the fool roundeth about in darkness: but withal I learned, that the same mortality involveth them both.* [12] And for the second, certain it is, there is no vexation or anxiety of mind which resulteth from knowledge otherwise than merely by accident; for all knowledge and wonder (which is the seed of knowledge) is an impression of pleasure in itself: but when men fall to framing conclusions out of their knowl-

9 I Cor. 8:1.   10 I Cor. 13:1.
11 Col. 2:8.   12 Eccles. 2:13.

edge, applying it to their particular, and ministering to themselves thereby weak fears or vast desires, there groweth
that carefulness and trouble of mind which is spoken of:
for then knowledge is no more *lumen siccum,* whereof
Heraclitus the profound said, *Lumen siccum optima
anima;* [13] but it becometh *lumen madidum,* or *maceratum,*
being steeped and infused in the humors of the affections.
And as for the third point, it deserveth to be a little stood
upon and not to be lightly passed over: for if any man shall
think by view and inquiry into these sensible and material
things to attain that light whereby he may reveal unto himself the nature or will of God, then indeed is he spoiled by
vain philosophy; for the contemplation of God's creatures
and works produceth (having regard to the works and
creatures themselves) knowledge, but (having regard to
God) no perfect knowledge, but wonder, which is broken
knowledge. And therefore it was most aptly said by one of
Plato's school,[14] *That the sense of man carrieth a resemblance with the sun, which (as we see) openeth and revealeth
all the terrestrial globe; but then again it obscureth and
concealeth the stars and celestial globe: so doth the sense
discover natural things, but it darkeneth and shutteth up
divine.* And hence it is true that it hath proceeded that divers
great learned men have been heretical, whilst they have
sought to fly up to the secrets of the Deity by the waxen
wings of the senses. And as for the conceit that too much
knowledge should incline a man to atheism, and that the
ignorance of second causes should make a more devout dependence upon God, which is the first cause; first, it is good
to ask the question which Job asked of his friends, *Will you
lie for God, as one man will do for another, to gratify him?* [15]
For certain it is that God worketh nothing in nature but by
second causes; and if they would have it otherwise believed,

---

[13] "The dry light is the best soul"; *lumen siccum* is contrasted with "a
light saturated with moisture."
[14] Philo Judæus.   [15] Job 13:7.

it is mere imposture, as it were in favor towards God, and
nothing else but to offer to the author of truth the unclean
sacrifice of a lie. But further, it is an assured truth and a
conclusion of experience, that a little or superficial knowledge of philosophy may incline the mind of man to atheism,
but a further proceeding therein doth bring the mind back
again to religion. For in the entrance of philosophy, when
the second causes, which are next unto the senses, do offer
themselves to the mind of man, if it dwell and stay there,
it may induce some oblivion of the highest cause; but when
a man passeth on further, and seeth the dependence of
causes, and the works of Providence, then, according to the
allegory of the poets, he will easily believe that the highest
link of nature's chain must needs be tied to the foot of Jupiter's chair. To conclude therefore, let no man upon a weak
conceit of sobriety or an ill-applied moderation think or
maintain, that a man can search too far, or be too well
studied in the book of God's word, or in the book of God's
works, divinity or philosophy; but rather let men endeavor
an endless progress or proficience in both; only let men beware that they apply both to charity, and not to swelling;
to use, and not to ostentation; and again, that they do not
unwisely mingle or confound these learnings together.

And as for the disgraces which learning receiveth from
politiques, they be of this nature: that learning doth soften
men's minds, and makes them more unapt for the honor and
exercise of arms; that it doth mar and pervert men's dispositions for matter of government and policy, in making
them too curious and irresolute by variety of reading, or
too peremptory or positive by strictness of rules and axioms,
or too immoderate and overweening by reason of the greatness of examples, or too incompatible and differing from the
times by reason of the dissimilitude of examples; or at
least that it doth divert men's travails from action and business, and bringeth them to a love of leisure and privateness;
and that it doth bring into states a relaxation of discipline,

whilst every man is more ready to argue than to obey and execute. Out of this conceit, Cato, surnamed the Censor, one of the wisest men indeed that ever lived, when Carneades the philosopher came in embassage to Rome, and that the young men of Rome began to flock about him, being allured with the sweetness and majesty of his eloquence and learning, gave counsel in open senate that they should give him his dispatch with all speed, lest he should infect and enchant the minds and affection of the youth, and at unawares bring in an alteration of the manners and customs of the state. Out of the same conceit or humor did Virgil, turning his pen to the advantage of his country and the disadvantage of his own profession, make a kind of separation between policy and government and between arts and sciences, in the verses so much renowned, attributing and challenging the one to the Romans, and leaving and yielding the other to the Grecians: *Tu regere imperio populos, Romane, memento, Hæ tibi erunt artes, &c.*[16] So likewise we see that Anytus, the accuser of Socrates, laid it as an article of charge and accusation against him that he did with the variety and power of his discourses and disputations withdraw young men from due reverence to the laws and customs of their country; and that he did profess a dangerous and pernicious science, which was to make the worse matter seem the better, and to suppress truth by force of eloquence and speech.

But these and the like imputations have rather a countenance of gravity than any ground of justice; for experience doth warrant that both in persons and in times there hath been a meeting and concurrence in learning and arms, flourishing and excelling in the same men and the same ages. For as for men, there cannot be a better nor the like instance as of that pair, Alexander the Great and Julius Cæsar the dictator; whereof the one was Aristotle's scholar in philosophy, and the other was Cicero's rival in eloquence; or if

---

[16] *Æneid,* vi. 851–52. Spedding translates: "Be thine, O Rome, with arts of government to rule the nations."

any man had rather call for scholars that were great
generals than generals that were great scholars, let him
take Epaminondas the Theban, or Xenophon the Athenian;
whereof the one was the first that abated the power of Sparta,
and the other was the first that made way to the overthrow
of the monarchy of Persia. And this concurrence is yet more
visible in times than in persons, by how much an age is
greater object than a man. For both in Egypt, Assyria, Persia,
Græcia, and Rome, the same times that are most renowned
for arms are likewise most admired for learning; so that the
greatest authors and philosophers and the greatest captains
and governors have lived in the same ages. Neither can it
otherwise be: for as in man the ripeness of strength of the
body and mind cometh much about an age, save that the
strength of the body cometh somewhat the more early, so
in states, arms, and learning, whereof the one correspondeth
to the body, the other to the soul of man, have a concurrence or near sequence in times.

And for matter of policy and government, that learning
should rather hurt than enable thereunto is a thing very
improbable: we see it is accounted an error to commit a
natural body to empiric physicians, which commonly have
a few pleasing receipts whereupon they are confident and
adventurous, but know neither the causes of diseases, nor
the complexions of patients, nor peril of accidents, nor the
true method of cures: we see it is a like error to rely upon
advocates or lawyers, which are only men of practice and
not grounded in their books, who are many times easily surprised when matter falleth out besides their experience, to
the prejudice of the causes they handle: so by like reason it
cannot be but a matter of doubtful consequence if states
be managed by empiric statesmen, not well mingled with
men grounded in learning. But contrariwise, it is almost without instance contradictory that ever any government was
disastrous that was in the hands of learned governors. For
howsoever it hath been ordinary with politique men to ex-

tenuate and disable learned men by the names of *pedantes;*
yet in the records of time it appeareth in many particulars
that the governments of princes in minority (notwithstanding the infinite disadvantage of that kind of state) have
nevertheless excelled the government of princes of mature
age, even for that reason which they seek to traduce, which
is, that by that occasion the state hath been in the hands
of *pedantes:* for so was the state of Rome for the first five
years, which are so much magnified, during the minority of
Nero, in the hands of Seneca, a *pedanti:* so it was again,
for ten years space or more, during the minority of Gordianus
the younger, with great applause and contentation in the
hands of Misitheus,[17] a *pedanti:* so was it before that, in
the minority of Alexander Severus,[18] in like happiness, in
hands not much unlike, by reason of the rule of the women,
who were aided by the teachers and preceptors. Nay, let a
man look into the government of the bishops of Rome, as
by name into the government of Pius Quintus [19] and Sextus
Quintus [20] in our times, who were both at their entrance
esteemed but as pedantical friars, and he shall find that
such popes do greater things, and proceed upon truer principles of estate than those which have ascended to the papacy
from an education and breeding in affairs of estate and
courts of princes; for although men bred in learning are perhaps to seek in points of convenience and accommodating
for the present, which the Italians call *ragioni di stato,*
whereof the same Pius Quintus could not hear spoken with
patience, terming them inventions against religion and the
moral virtues; yet on the other side, to recompense that,
they are perfect in those same plain grounds of religion,
justice, honor, and moral virtue, which if they be well and
watchfully pursued, there will be seldom use of those other,

[17] Gordianus married the daughter of Misitheus.
[18] Alexander Severus was seventeen when he succeeded to the throne
after Elagabalus, his cousin, was murdered, 222.
[19] Pius V, Pope, 1565–72.
[20] Sixtus V, succeeded Gregory XIII, 1585, and ruled five years.

no more than of physic in a sound or well-dieted body. Neither
can the experience of one man's life furnish examples and
precedents for the events of one man's life. For as it happeneth sometimes that the grandchild, or other descendant,
resembleth the ancestor more than the son, so many times
occurrences of present times may sort better with ancient
examples than with those of the later or immediate times;
and lastly, the wit of one man can no more countervail learning than one man's means can hold way with a common purse.

And as for those particular seducements or indispositions
of the mind for policy and government, which learning is
pretended to insinuate; if it be granted that any such thing
be, it must be remembered withal, that learning ministereth
in every of them greater strength of medicine or remedy
than it offereth cause of indisposition or infirmity. For if by
a secret operation it make men perplexed and irresolute,
on the other side by plain precept it teacheth them when
and upon what ground to resolve; yea, and how to carry
things in suspense without prejudice, till they resolve. If
it make men positive and regular, it teacheth them what
things are in their nature demonstrative, and what are con-
jectural; and as well the use of distinctions and exceptions,
as the latitude of principles and rules. If it mislead by dis-
proportion or dissimilitude of examples, it teacheth men
the force of circumstances, the errors of comparisons, and
all the cautions of application; so that in all these it doth
rectify more effectually than it can pervert. And these medicines it conveyeth into men's minds much more forcibly by
the quickness and penetration of examples. For let a man
look into the errors of Clement the Seventh, so lively described by Guicciardine,[21] who served under him, or into
the errors of Cicero, painted out by his own pencil in his
Epistles to Atticus,[22] and he will fly apace from being ir-

---

[21] Guicciardini, Italian historian, 1483–1540. See *Hist.*, xvi. 5, for description of weakness of Pope Clement VII.
[22] *Epist. to Atticus*, xvi. 7.

resolute. Let him look into the error of Phocion,[23] and he will beware how he be obstinate or inflexible. Let him but read the fable of Ixion, and it will hold him from being vaporous or imaginative. Let him look into the errors of Cato the Second,[24] and he will never be one of the Antipodes, to tread opposite to the present world.

And for the conceit that learning should dispose men to leisure and privateness and make men slothful; it were a strange thing if that which accustometh the mind to a perpetual motion and agitation should induce slothfulness: whereas contrariwise it may be truly affirmed, that no kind of men love business for itself but those that are learned; for other persons love it for profit, as an hireling that loves the work for the wages; or for honor, as because it beareth them up in the eyes of men and refresheth their reputation, which otherwise would wear; or because it putteth them in mind of their fortune, and giveth them occasion to pleasure and displeasure; or because it exerciseth some faculty wherein they take pride, and so entertaineth them in good humor and pleasing conceits toward themselves; or because it advanceth any other their ends. So that as it is said of untrue valors that some men's valors are in the eyes of them that look on, so such men's industries are in the eyes of others, or at least in regard of their own designments; only learned men love business as an action according to nature, as agreeable to health of mind as exercise of body, taking pleasure in the action itself, and not in the purchase: so that of all men they are the most indefatigable, if it be towards any business which can hold or detain their mind.

And if any man be laborious in reading and study and yet idle in business and action, it groweth from some weakness of body or softness of spirit, such as Seneca speaketh of: *Quidam tam sunt umbratiles, ut putent in turbido esse quic-*

---

[23] Phocion, an Athenian general, condemned for treason, 317 B.C.
[24] *Epist. to Atticus*, ii. 1. Cato supported the Roman republic, and when his party was defeated by Cæsar, committed suicide, 46 B.C.

quid in luce est,[25] and not of learning. Well may it be that
such a point of a man's nature may make him give himself
to learning, but it is not learning that breedeth any such
point in his nature.

And that learning should take up too much time or leisure;
I answer, the most active or busy man that hath been or
can be, hath (no question) many vacant times of leisure,
while he expecteth the tides and returns of business (except he be either tedious and of no dispatch, or lightly and
unworthily ambitious to meddle in things that may be better
done by others), and then the question is but how those
spaces and times of leisure shall be filled and spent: whether
in pleasures or in studies; as was well answered by Demosthenes to his adversary, Æschines, that was a man given
to pleasure, and told him *That his orations did smell of
the lamp: Indeed* (said Demosthenes) *there is a great difference between the things that you and I do by lamplight.*[26]
So as no man need doubt that learning will expulse business,
but rather it will keep and defend the possession of the mind
against idleness and pleasure, which otherwise at unawares
may enter to the prejudice of both.

Again, for that other conceit that learning should under-
mine the reverence of laws and government, it is assuredly
a mere depravation and calumny without all shadow of truth.
For to say that a blind custom of obedience should be a
surer obligation than duty taught and understood, it is to
affirm that a blind man may tread surer by a guide than a
seeing man can by a light. And it is without all controversy
that learning doth make the minds of men gentle, generous,
amiable,[27] and pliant to government; whereas ignorance
makes them churlish, thwart, and mutinous: and the evi-

[25] Seneca, *Epistles,* i. 3. Spedding translates: "There are some men so
fond of the shade, that they think they are in trouble whenever they are
in the light."

[26] Plutarch (*Demosthenes,* viii. 2) tells this story of Pytheas, not
Æschines.

[27] Some copies print "maniable," and this is, no doubt, the correct word.

dence of time doth clear this assertion, considering that the most barbarous, rude, and unlearned times have been most subject to tumults, seditions, and changes.

And as to the judgment of Cato the Censor, he was well punished for his blasphemy against learning, in the same kind wherein he offended; for when he was past threescore years old, he was taken with an extreme desire to go to school again, and to learn the Greek tongue, to the end to peruse the Greek authors; which doth well demonstrate that his former censure of the Grecian learning was rather an affected gravity, than according to the inward sense of his own opinion. And as for Virgil's verses, though it pleased him to brave the world in taking to the Romans the art of empire and leaving to others the arts of subjects; yet so much is manifest that the Romans never ascended to that height of empire till the time they had ascended to the height of other arts. For in the time of the two first Cæsars, which had the art of government in greatest perfection, there lived the best poet, Virgilius Maro; the best historiographer, Titus Livius; the best antiquary, Marcus Varro; and the best, or second orator, Marcus Cicero, that to the memory of man are known. As for the accusation of Socrates, the time must be remembered when it was prosecuted; which was under the Thirty Tyrants,[28] the most base, bloody, and envious persons that have governed; which revolution of state was no sooner over, but Socrates, whom they had made a person criminal, was made a person heroical, and his memory accumulate with honors divine and human; and those discourses of his which were then termed corrupting of manners, were after acknowledged for sovereign medicines of the mind and manners, and so have been received ever since till this day. Let this therefore serve for answer to politiques, which in their humorous severity, or in their feigned gravity, have presumed to throw imputations upon learning; which redargution nevertheless (save that we

[28] The Committee of Thirty which ruled Athens, 404–403 B.C.

know not whether our labors may extend to other ages) were
not needful for the present, in regard of the love and reverence
towards learning which the example and countenance of
two so learned princes, Queen Elizabeth and your Majesty,
being as Castor and Pollux, *lucida sidera,* stars of excellent
light and most benign influence, hath wrought in all men of
place and authority in our nation.

Now therefore we come to that third sort of discredit or
diminution of credit that groweth unto learning from learned
men themselves, which commonly cleaveth fastest: it is
either from their fortune, or from their manners, or from
the nature of their studies. For the first, it is not in their
power; and the second is accidental; the third only is proper
to be handled: but because we are not in hand with true
measure, but with popular estimation and conceit, it is not
amiss to speak somewhat of the two former. The derogations
therefore which grow to learning from the fortune or condition of learned men are either in respect of scarcity of means,
or in respect of privateness of life and meanness of employments.

Concerning want, and that it is the case of learned men
usually to begin with little and not to grow rich so fast as
other men, by reason they convert not their labors chiefly
to lucre and increase; it were good to leave the common place
in commendation of poverty to some friar to handle, to whom
much was attributed by Machiavel in this point, when he
said, *That the kingdom of the clergy had been long before
at an end, if the reputation and reverence towards the poverty of friars had not borne out the scandal of the superfluities and excesses of bishops and prelates.*[29] So a man might
say that the felicity and delicacy of princes and great persons
had long since turned to rudeness and barbarism, if the poverty of learning had not kept up civility and honor of life;
but without any such advantages, it is worthy the observation what a reverent and honored thing poverty of fortune

[29] *Discorsi sulle Deche di Tito Livio,* iii. 1.

was for some ages in the Roman state, which nevertheless was a state without paradoxes. For we see what Titus Livius saith in his introduction: *Cæterum aut me amor negotii suscepti fallit, aut nulla unquam respublica nec major, nec sanctior, nec bonis exemplis ditior fuit; nec in quam tam seræ avaritia luxuriaque immigraverint; nec ubi tantus ac tam diu paupertati ac parsimoniæ honos fuerit.*[30] We see likewise, after that the state of Rome was not itself but did degenerate, how that person that took upon him to be counselor to Julius Cæsar after his victory where to begin his restoration of the state, maketh it of all points the most summary to take away the estimation of wealth: *Verum hæc et omnia mala pariter cum honore pecuniæ desinent; si neque magistratus, neque alia vulgo cupienda, venalia erunt.*[31] To conclude this point, as it was truly said, that *Rubor est virtutis color,* though sometime it come from vice; so it may be fitly said that *Paupertas est virtutis fortuna,* though sometimes it may proceed from misgovernment and accident. Surely Solomon hath pronounced it both in censure, *Qui festinat ad divitias non erit insons;*[32] and in precept, *Buy the truth, and sell it not; and so of wisdom and knowledge:*[33] judging that means were to be spent upon learning, and not learning to be applied to means. And as for the privateness or obscureness (as it may be in vulgar estimation accounted) of life of contemplative men, it is a theme so common to extol a private life, not taxed with sensuality and sloth, in comparison and to the disadvantage of a civil life, for safety, liberty, pleasure, and dignity, or at least freedom from indignity, as no man handleth it but

[30] Livy, *Præc.*, ii. Spedding translates: "That if affection for his subject did not deceive him, there was never any state in the world either greater or purer or richer in good examples; never any into which avarice and luxury made their way so late; never any in which poverty and frugality were for so long a time held in so great honor."

[31] Pseudo Sallust, *Epist, ad Cæs.*, i. Spedding translates: "But these and all other evils (he says) will cease as soon as the worship of money ceases; which will come to pass when neither magistracies nor other things that are objects of desire to the vulgar shall be to be had for money."

[32] Prov. 28:22.   [33] Prov. 23:23.

handleth it well; such a consonancy it hath to men's conceits in the expressing, and to men's consents in the allowing.
This only I will add, that learned men forgotten in states,
and not living in the eyes of men, are like the images of
Cassius and Brutus in the funeral of Junia; of which not
being represented, as many others were, Tacitus saith, *Eo
ipso præfulgebant, quod non visebantur.*[34]

And for meanness of employment, that which is most
traduced to contempt is that the government of youth is
commonly allotted to them; which age, because it is the
age of least authority, it is transferred to the disesteeming
of those employments wherein youth is conversant, and
which are conversant about youth. But how unjust this
traducement is (if you will reduce things from popularity of
opinion to measure of reason) may appear in that we see
men are more curious what they put into a new vessel than
into a vessel seasoned, and what mold they lay about a
young plant than about a plant corroborate;[35] so as the
weakest terms and times of all things use to have the best
applications and helps. And will you hearken to the Hebrew
rabbins? *Your young men shall see visions, and your old
men shall dream dreams;*[36] say they youth is the worthier
age, for that visions are nearer apparitions of God than
dreams? And let it be noted that howsoever the condition
of life of *Pedantes* hath [37] been scorned upon theaters, as
the ape of tyranny, and that the modern looseness or negligence hath taken no due regard to the choice of schoolmasters and tutors; yet the ancient wisdom of the best times
did always make a just complaint that states were too busy
with their laws and too negligent in point of education: which
excellent part of ancient discipline hath been in some sort
revived of late times by the colleges of the Jesuits, of whom,

---

[34] *Annals,* iii. 76. Spedding translates: "They outshone the others because of the very fact that they were not seen." Junia was the wife of
Cassius and sister of Brutus.
[35] A plant full-grown.   [36] Joel 2:28.
[37] The edition of 1630 reads "conditions . . . have."

although in regard of their superstition I may say, *Quo meliores, eo deteriores;*[38] yet in regard to this, and some other points concerning human learning and moral matters, I may say, as Agesilaus said to his enemy Pharnabazus, *Talis quum sis, utinam noster esses.*[39] And thus much touching the discredits drawn from the fortunes of learned men.

As touching the manners of learned men, it is a thing personal and individual: and no doubt there be amongst them, as in other professions, of all temperatures: but yet so as it is not without truth which is said, that *Abeunt studia in mores,*[40] studies have an influence and operation upon the manners of those that are conversant in them.

But upon an attentive and indifferent review, I for my part cannot find any disgrace to learning can proceed from the manners of learned men; not inherent to them as they are learned; except it be a fault (which was the supposed fault of Demosthenes, Cicero, Cato the Second, Seneca, and many more) (that because the times they read of are commonly better than the duties practiced, they contend sometimes too far to bring things to perfection, and to reduce the corruption of manners to honesty of precepts or examples of too great height.) And yet hereof they have caveats enough in their own walks. For Solon, when he was asked whether he had given his citizens the best laws, answered wisely, *Yea of such as they would receive:* and Plato, finding that his own heart could not agree with the corrupt manners of his country, refused to bear place or office; saying, *That a man's country was to be used as his parents were, that is, with humble persuasions, and not with contestations.*[41] And Cæsar's counselor put in the same caveat, *Non ad vetera instituta revocans quæ jampridem corruptis moribus ludibrio sunt:*[42] and Cicero noteth this error directly in Cato

[38] Diog. Laert. *Plato*, vi. 46. [39] Plato, *Ages*, xii. 5.
[40] Ovid, *Epist.*, xv. 83. [41] Plato, *Epist.*, vii. 331.
[42] Pseudo Sallust. *Epist. ad Cæs.*, i. Spedding translates: "Not to attempt to bring things back to the original institution now that by reason of the corruption of manners the ancient simplicity and purity had fallen into contempt."

the Second, when he writes to his friend Atticus: *Cato optime sentit, sed nocet interdum reipublicæ; loquitur enim tanquam in republica Platonis, non tanquam in fæce Romuli.*[43] And the same Cicero doth excuse and expound the philosophers for going too far and being too exact in their prescripts, when he saith, *Isti ipsi præceptores virtutis et magistri videntur fines officiorum paulo longius quam natura vallet protulisse, ut cum ad ultimum animo contendissemus, ibi tamen, ubi oportet, consisteremus:*[44] and yet himself might have said, *Monitis sum minor ipse meis;*[45] for it was his own fault, though not in so extreme a degree.

Another fault likewise much of this kind hath been incident to learned men; which is, that they have esteemed the preservation, good, and honor of their countries or masters before their own fortunes or safeties. For so saith Demosthenes unto the Athenians: *If it please you to note it, my counsels unto you are not such whereby I should grow great amongst you, and you become little amongst the Grecians; but they be of that nature, as they are sometimes not good for me to give, but are always good for you to follow.*[46] And so Seneca, after he had consecrated that *Quinquennium Neronis* to the eternal glory of learned governors, held on his honest and loyal course of good and free counsel, after his master grew extremely corrupt in his government. Neither can this point otherwise be; for learning endueth men's minds with a true sense of the frailty of their persons, the casualty of their fortunes, and the dignity of their soul and vocation: so that it is impossible for them to esteem that any greatness of their own fortune can be a true or worthy end of their being and ordainment; and therefore are de-

---

[43] Cicero, *Atticus*, ii. 1. 8. Spedding translates: "Cato means excellently well, but he does hurt sometimes to the state; for he talks as if it were Plato's republic that we are living in, and not the dregs of Romulus."

[44] Cicero, *Pro Muræna*, 31. Spedding translates: "That they had set the points of duty somewhat higher than nature would bear, meaning belike to allow for shortcomings, and that our endeavors aiming beyond the mark and falling short, should light at the right place."

[45] Ovid, *Ars Amat.*, ii. 548.   [46] *De Chersonese*, xvi.

sirous to give their account to God, and so likewise to their masters under God (as kings and the states that they serve) in these words, *Ecce tibi lucrefeci,* and not *Ecce mihi lucrefeci:* whereas the corrupter sort of mere politiques, that have not their thoughts established by learning in the love and apprehension of duty, nor never look abroad into universality, do refer all things to themselves, and thrust themselves into the center of the world, as if all lines should meet in them and their fortunes; never caring in all tempests what becomes of the ship of estates, so they may save themselves in the cockboat of their own fortune: whereas men that feel the weight of duty and know the limits of self-love, use to make good their places and duties, though with peril; and if they stand in seditious and violent alterations, it is rather the reverence which many times both adverse parts do give to honesty, than any versatile advantage of their own carriage. But for this point of tender sense and fast obligation of duty, which learning doth indue the mind withal, howsoever fortune may tax it and many in the depth of their corrupt principles may despise it, yet it will receive an open allowance, and therefore needs the less disproof or excusation.

Another fault incident commonly to learned men, which may be more probably defended than truly denied, is that they fail sometimes in applying themselves to particular persons, which want of exact application ariseth from two causes: the one, because the largeness of their mind can hardly confine itself to dwell in the exquisite observation or examination of the nature and customs of one person, for it is a speech for a lover, and not for a wise man, *Satis magnum alter alteri theatrum sumus.*[47] Nevertheless I shall yield that he that cannot contract the sight of his mind as well as disperse and dilate it wanteth a great faculty. But there is a second cause, which is no inability but a rejection upon

[47] Seneca. *Epist.,* i. 7. 11. attributes this to Epicurus. Spedding translates: "Each is to other a theatre large enough."

choice and judgment. For the honest and just bounds of
observation by one person upon another, extend no further
but to understand him sufficiently, whereby not to give him
offense, or whereby to be able to give him faithful counsel,
or whereby to stand upon reasonable guard and caution in
respect of a man's self. But to be speculative into another
man to the end to know how to work him, or wind him, or
govern him, proceedeth from a heart that is double and
cloven, and not entire and ingenuous; which as in friendship it is want of integrity, so towards princes or superiors
is want of duty. For the custom of the Levant, which is that
subjects do forbear to gaze or fix their eyes upon princes,
is in the outward ceremony barbarous, but the moral is
good: for men ought not by cunning and bent observations
to pierce and penetrate into the hearts of kings, which the
Scripture hath declared to be inscrutable.

There is yet another fault (with which I will conclude
this part) which is often noted in learned men, that they
do many times fail to observe decency and discretion in their
behavior and carriage, and commit errors in small and ordinary points of action; so as the vulgar sort of capacities
do make a judgment of them in greater matters by that
which they find wanting in them in smaller. But this consequence doth oft deceive men, for which I do refer them
over to that which was said by Themistocles, arrogantly and
uncivilly, being applied to himself out of his own mouth,
but being applied to the general state of this question,
pertinently and justly; when being invited to touch a lute,
he said *He could not fiddle, but he could make a small town
a great state.* So no doubt many may be well seen in the
passages of government and policy, which are to seek in
little and punctual occasions. I refer them also to that which
Plato said of his master Socrates, whom he compared to the
gallipots of apothecaries, which on the outside had apes
and owls and antiques, but contained within sovereign and
precious liquors and confections; acknowledging that to an

external report, he was not without superficial levities and deformities, but was inwardly replenished with excellent virtues and powers. And so much touching the point of manners of learned men.

But in the meantime I have no purpose to give allowance to some conditions and courses base and unworthy, wherein divers professors of learning have wronged themselves and gone too far; such as were those trencher philosophers, which in the later age of the Roman state were usually in the houses of great persons, being little better than solemn parasites; of which kind, Lucian maketh a merry description of the philosopher that the great lady took to ride with her in her coach, and would needs have him carry her little dog, which he doing officiously and yet uncomely, the page scoffed and said, *That he doubted the philosopher of a Stoic would turn to be a Cynic.*[48] But above all the rest, the gross and palpable flattery whereunto many not unlearned have abased and abused their wits and pens, turning (as Du Bartas saith) [49] Hecuba into Helena, and Faustina into Lucretia, hath most diminished the price and estimation of learning. Neither is the *moderne* [50] dedications of books and writing, as to patrons, to be commended: for that books (such as are worthy the name of books) ought to have no patrons but truth and reason. And the ancient custom was to dedicate them only to private and equal friends, or to entitle the books with their names; or if to kings and great persons, it was to some such as the argument of the book was fit and proper for: but these and the like courses may deserve rather reprehension than defense.

Not that I can tax or condemn the morigeration [51] or application of learned men to men in fortune. For the answer was good that Diogenes made to one that asked him

---

[48] *De Mercede Conductis,* 33, 34. "Cynic" means "dog-like."
[49] See Du Bartas, *Bethulian's Rescue.*
[50] The correction in the Errata; the text has "moral," and later editions have continued the error.
[51] "Obsequiousness."

in mockery, *How it came to pass that philosophers were the followers of rich men, and not rich men of philosophers?* He answered soberly, and yet sharply, *Because the one sort knew what they had need of, and the other did not.* And of the like nature was the answer which Aristippus made, when having a petition to Dionysius and no ear given to him, he fell down at his feet; whereupon Dionysius stayed and gave him the hearing and granted it; and afterward some person tender on the behalf of philosophy, reproved Aristippus that he would offer the profession of philosophy such an indignity, as for a private suit to fall at a tyrant's feet: but he answered, *It was not his fault, but it was the fault of Dionysius, that had his ears in his feet.*[52] Neither was it accounted weakness but discretion in him that would not dispute his best with Adrianus Cæsar; excusing himself, *That it was reason to yield to him that commanded thirty legions.*[53] These and the like applications and stooping to points of necessity and convenience cannot be disallowed; for though they may have some outward baseness, yet in a judgment truly made, they are to be accounted submissions to the occasion and not to the person.

Now I proceed to those errors and vanities which have intervened amongst the studies themselves of the learned, which is that which is principal and proper to the present argument; wherein my purpose is not to make a justification of the errors, but by a censure and separation of the errors to make a justification of that which is good and sound, and to deliver that from the aspersion of the other. For we see that it is the manner of men to scandalize and deprave that which retaineth the state and virtue, by taking advantage upon that which is corrupt and degenerate: as the heathens in the primitive church used to blemish and taint the Christians with the faults and corruptions of

[52] Aristippus, Greek Philosopher, 435?–356? B.C. Dionysius, tyrant of Syracuse, 430?–367? B.C.

[53] The reference is to a Greek philosopher, Favorinus, and the story is found in *Vita Adriani,* 15, by Spartianus.

heretics. But nevertheless I have no meaning at this time to make any exact animadversion of the errors and impediments in matters of learning which are more secret and remote from vulgar opinion, but only to speak unto such as do fall under or near unto a popular observation.

There be therefore chiefly three vanities in studies, whereby learning hath been most traduced. For those things we do esteem vain which are either false or frivolous, those which either have no truth or no use; and those persons we esteem vain which are either credulous or curious; and curiosity is either in matter or words, so that in reason as well as in experience there fall out to be these three distempers (as I may term them) of learning: the first, fantastical learning; the second, contentious learning; and the last, delicate learning; vain imaginations, vain altercations, and vain affections; and with the last I will begin. Martin Luther, conducted (no doubt) by an higher Providence, but in discourse of reason finding what a province he had undertaken against the Bishop of Rome and the degenerate traditions of the church, and finding his own solitude, being no ways aided by the opinions of his own time, was enforced to awake all antiquity and to call former times to his succors to make a party against the present time; so that the ancient authors, both in divinity and in humanity, which had long time slept in libraries, began generally to be read and revolved. This by consequence did draw on a necessity of a more exquisite travail in the languages original, wherein those authors did write, for the better understanding of those authors and the better advantage of pressing and applying their words. And thereof grew again a delight in their manner of style and phrase, and an admiration of that kind of writing; which was much furthered and precipitated by the enmity and opposition that the propounders of those primitive but seeming new opinions had against the schoolmen; who were generally of the contrary part, and whose writings were altogether in a different style and form; taking

liberty to coin and frame new terms of art to express their
own sense, and to avoid circuit of speech, without regard to
the pureness, pleasantness, and (as I may call it) lawfulness
of the phrase or word. And again, because the great labor
then was with the people (of whom the Pharisees were wont
to say, *Execrabilis ista turba, quœ non novit legem*),[54] for
the winning and persuading of them, there grew of necessity in chief price and request eloquence and variety of discourse, as the fittest and forciblest access into the capacity
of the vulgar sort: so that these four causes concurring, the
admiration of ancient authors, the hate of the schoolmen,
the exact study of languages, and the efficacy of preaching,
did bring in an affectionate study of eloquence and copy of
speech, which then began to flourish. This grew speedily to
an excess; for men began to hunt more after words than
matter, and more after the choiceness of the phrase, and the
round and clean composition of the sentence, and the sweet
falling of the clauses, and the varying and illustration of
their works with tropes and figures than after the weight
of matter, worth of subject, soundness of argument, life of
invention, or depth of judgment. Then grew the flowing and
watery vein of Osorius,[55] the Portugal bishop, to be in price.
Then did Sturmius [56] spend such infinite and curious pains
upon Cicero the orator, and Hermogenes the rhetorician,
besides his own books of Periods and Imitation, and the like.
Then did Carr of Cambridge and Ascham with their lectures and writings almost deify Cicero and Demosthenes,
and allure all young men that were studious unto that delicate and polished kind of learning. Then did Erasmus take
occasion to make the scoffing echo, *Decem annos consumpsi
in legendo Cicerone;* [57] and the echo answered in Greek
One, Asine. Then grew the learning of the schoolmen to be

[54] John 7:49.
[55] Osorius, *d.* 1580. Ascham, in the *Scholemaster* criticizes his style.
[56] Sturmius, 1507–1589, was a professor at Paris and at Strassburg.
[57] Erasmus, *Colloq. Echo.*, x. 541. The *one* in *Cicerone* is the Greek word
for "ass."

utterly despised as barbarous. In sum, the whole inclination and bent of those times was rather towards copy than weight.

Here therefore [is] the first distemper of learning, when men study words and not matter; whereof, though I have represented an example of late times, yet it hath been and will be *secundum majus et minus* in all time. And how is it possible but this should have an operation to discredit learning, even with vulgar capacities, when they see learned men's works like the first letter of a patent or limned book, which though it hath large flourishes, yet it is but a letter? It seems to me that Pygmalion's frenzy is a good emblem or portraiture of this vanity: for words are but the images of matter; and except they have life of reason and invention, to fall in love with them is all one as to fall in love with a picture.

But yet notwithstanding it is a thing not hastily to be condemned, to clothe and adorn the obscurity even of philosophy itself with sensible and plausible elocution. For hereof we have great examples in Xenophon, Cicero, Seneca, Plutarch, and of Plato also in some degree; and hereof likewise there is great use: for surely, to the severe inquisition of truth and the deep progress into philosophy, it is some hindrance; because it is too early satisfactory to the mind of man, and quencheth the desire of further search, before we come to a just period. But then if a man be to have any use of such knowledge in civil occasions, of conference, counsel, persuasion, discourse, or the like, then shall he find it prepared to his hands in those authors which write in that manner. But the excess of this is so justly contemptible, that as Hercules, when he saw the image of Adonis, Venus' minion, in a temple, said in disdain, *Nil sacri est ;* so there is none of Hercules' followers in learning, that is, the more severe and laborious sort of inquirers into truth, but will despise those delicacies and affectations, as indeed capable of no divineness. And thus much of the first disease or distemper of learning.

The second, which followeth, is in nature worse than the

former; for as substance of matter is better than beauty of
words, so contrariwise vain matter is worse than vain words:
wherein it seemeth the reprehension of Saint Paul was not
only proper for those times, but prophetical for the times
following; and not only respective to divinity, but extensive
to all knowledge: *Devita profanas vocum novitates, et op-
positiones falsi nominis scientiæ.*[58] For he assigneth two
marks and badges of suspected and falsified science: the
one, the novelty and strangeness of terms; the other, the
strictness of positions, which of necessity doth induce oppositions, and so questions and altercations. Surely, like as
many substances in nature which are solid do putrefy and
corrupt into works, so it is the property of good and sound
knowledge to putrefy and dissolve into a number of subtle,
idle, unwholesome, and (as I may term them) vermiculate
questions, which have indeed a kind of quickness and life
of spirit, but no soundness of matter or goodness of quality.
This kind of degenerate learning did chiefly reign amongst
the schoolmen, who having sharp and strong wits, and abundance of leisure, and small variety of reading, but their wits
being shut up in the cells of a few authors (chiefly Aristotle
their dictator) as their persons were shut up in the cells of
monasteries and colleges, and knowing little history, either
of nature or time, did out of no great quantity of matter and
infinite agitation of wit spin out unto us those laborious webs
of learning which are extant in their books. For the wit and
mind of man, if it work upon matter, which is the contem-
plation of the creatures of God, worketh according to the
stuff and is limited thereby; but if it work upon itself, as
the spider worketh his web, then it is endless, and brings
forth indeed cobwebs of learning, admirable for the fineness
of thread and work, but of no substance or profit.

This same unprofitable subtility or curiosity is of two
sorts: either in the subject itself that they handle, when it

[58] I Tim. 6:20. Spedding translates: "Shun profane novelties of terms
and oppositions of science falsely so called."

is a fruitless speculation or controversy (whereof there are
no small number both in divinity and philosophy), or in the
manner or method of handling of a knowledge, which amongst
them was this: upon every particular position or assertion
to frame objections, and to those objections, solutions; which
solutions were for the most part not confutations, but distinctions: whereas indeed the strength of all sciences is, as
the strength of the old man's faggot, in the bond. For the
harmony of a science, supporting each part the other, is
and ought to be the true and brief confutation and suppression of all the smaller sort of objections. But, on the other
side, if you take out every axiom, as the sticks of the faggot, one by one, you may quarrel with them and bend them
and break them at your pleasure: so that as was said of
Seneca, *Verborum minutiis rerum frangit pondera,*[59] so a
man may truly say of the schoolmen, *Quæstionum minutiis
scientiarum frangunt soliditatem.*[60] For were it not better
for a man in a fair room to set up one great light, or branching candlestick of lights, than to go about with a small watch
candle into every corner? And such is their method, that
rests not so much upon evidence of truth, proved by arguments, authorities, similitudes, examples, as upon particular
confutations and solutions of every scruple, cavillation, and
objection; breeding for the most part one question as fast
as it solveth another; even as in the former resemblance,
when you carry the light into one corner, you darken the
rest; so that the fable and fiction of Scylla seemeth to be
a lively image of this kind of philosophy or knowledge;
which was transformed into a comely virgin for the upper
parts, but then *Candida succinctam latrantibus inguina
monstris:*[61] so the generalities of the schoolmen are for a
while good and proportionable; but then when you descend

[59] Quintilian, 10. 1. Spedding translates: "That he broke up the weight
and mass of the matter by verbal points and quiddities."
[60] Spedding translates: "They broke up the solidity and coherency of
the sciences by the minuteness and niceness of their questions."
[61] Virgil, *Eclogues,* vi. 75. Spedding translates: "There were barking
monsters all about her loins."

into their distinctions and decisions, instead of a fruitful womb for the use and benefit of man's life, they end in monstrous altercations and barking questions. So as it is not possible but this quality of knowledge must fall under popular contempt, the people being apt to contemn truth upon occasion of controversies and altercations, and to think they are all out of their way which never meet; and when they see such digladiation about subtilities, and matter of no use or moment, they easily fall upon that judgment of Dionysius of Syracusa. *Verba ista sunt senum otiosorum.*

Notwithstanding, certain it is that if those schoolmen to their great thirst of truth and unwearied travail of wit had joined variety and universality of reading and contemplation, they had proved excellent lights, to the great advancement of all learning and knowledge; but as they are, they are great undertakers indeed, and fierce with dark keeping. But as in the inquiry of the divine truth, their pride inclined to leave the oracle of God's word and to vanish in the mixture of their own inventions, so in the inquisition of nature they ever left the oracle of God's works and adored the deceiving and deformed images which the unequal mirror of their own minds or a few received authors or principles did represent unto them. And thus much for the second disease of learning.

For the third vice or disease of learning, which concerneth deceit or untruth, it is of all the rest the foulest; as that which doth destroy the essential form of knowledge, which is nothing but a representation of truth: for the truth of being and the truth of knowing are one, differing no more than the direct beam and the beam reflected. This vice therefore brancheth itself into two sorts: delight in deceiving and aptness to be deceived; imposture and credulity; which, although they appear to be of a diverse nature, the one seeming to proceed of cunning and the other of simplicity, yet certainly they do for the most part concur: for, as the verse noteth,

Percontatorem fugito, nam garrulus idem est,[62]

an inquisitive man is a prattler; so upon the like reason a credulous man is a deceiver: as we see it in fame, that he that will easily believe rumors, will as easily augment rumors and add somewhat to them of his own; which Tacitus wisely noteth, when he saith, *Fingunt simul creduntque:* [63] so great an affinity hath fiction and belief.

This facility of credit and accepting or admitting things weakly authorized or warranted is of two kinds according to the subject: for it is either a belief of history (as the lawyers speak, matter of fact), or else of matter of art and opinion. As to the former, we see the experience and inconvenience of this error in ecclesiastical history, which hath too easily received and registered reports and narrations of miracles wrought by martyrs, hermits, or monks of the desert, and other holy men, and their relics, shrines, chapels, and images: which though they had a passage for a time by the ignorance of the people, the superstitious simplicity of some, and the politic toleration of others, holding them but as divine poesies; yet after a period of time, when the mist began to clear up, they grew to be esteemed but as old wives' fables, impostures of the clergy, illusions of spirits, and badges of Antichrist, to the great scandal and detriment of religion.

So in natural history we see there hath not been that choice and judgment used as ought to have been; as may appear in the writings of Plinius, Cardanus,[64] Albertus,[65] and divers of the Arabians, being fraught with much fabulous matter, a great part not only untried, but notoriously untrue, to the great derogation of the credit of natural philosophy with the grave and sober kind of wits. Wherein the

---

[62] Horace, *Epist.*, i. 18. 69.   [63] Tacitus, *Annals,* v. 10.

[64] Cardan, famous Italian physician of the sixteenth century, interested in science and astrology.

[65] Albertus Magnus, bishop of Ratisbon, thirteenth century, writer of natural history.

wisdom and integrity of Aristotle is worthy to be observed, that, having made so diligent and exquisite a history of living creatures, hath mingled it sparingly with any vain or feigned matter; and yet on the other side hath cast all prodigious narrations which he thought worthy the recording into one book; excellently discerning that matter of manifest truth, such whereupon observation and rule was to be built, was not to be mingled or weakened with matter of doubtful credit; and yet again that rarities and reports that seem uncredible are not to be suppressed or denied to the memory of men.

And as for the facility of credit which is yielded to arts and opinions, it is likewise of two kinds: either when too much belief is attributed to the arts themselves, or to certain authors in any art. The sciences themselves which have had better intelligence and confederacy with the imagination of man than with his reason are three in number: astrology, natural magic, and alchemy, of which sciences, nevertheless, the ends or pretences are noble. For astrology pretendeth to discover that correspondence or concatenation which is between the superior globe and the inferior; natural magic pretendeth to call and reduce natural philosophy from variety of speculations to the magnitude of works; and alchemy pretendeth to make separation of all the unlike parts of bodies which in mixtures of nature are incorporate. But the derivations and prosecutions to these ends, both in the theories and in the practices, are full of error and vanity; which the great professors themselves have sought to veil over and conceal by enigmatical writings, and referring themselves to auricular traditions and such other devices to save the credit of impostures. And yet surely to alchemy this right is due, that it may be compared to the husbandman whereof Æsop makes the fable, that when he died, told his sons that he had left unto them gold buried under ground in his vineyard; and they digged over all the ground, and gold they found none; but by reason of their stirring and digging the mold about the roots of their vines, they had a great vintage the year following: so assuredly the search and stir to make gold hath brought to light a great number of good and fruitful inventions and experiments, as well for the disclosing of nature as for the use of man's life.

And as for the overmuch credit that hath been given unto authors in sciences, in making them dictators, that their words should stand, and not consuls [66] to give advice; the damage is infinite that sciences have received thereby, as the principal cause that hath kept them low, at a stay without growth or advancement. For hence it hath comen that in arts mechanical the first deviser comes shortest, and time addeth and perfecteth; but in sciences the first author goeth furthest, and time leaseth and corrupteth. So we see, artillery, sailing, printing, and the like were grossly managed at the first, and by time accommodated and refined: but contrariwise, the philosophies and sciences of Aristotle, Plato, Democritus, Hippocrates, Euclides, Archimedes, of most vigor at the first, and by time degenerate and imbased; whereof the reason is no other, but that in the former many wits and industries have contributed in one; and in the latter many wits and industries have been spent about the wit of someone, whom many times they have rather depraved than illustrated. For as water will not ascend higher than the level of the first springhead from whence it descendeth, so knowledge derived from Aristotle and exempted from liberty of examination will not rise again higher than the knowledge of Aristotle. And therefore although the position be good, *Oportet discentem credere,* yet it must be coupled with this, *Oportet edoctum judicare;* for disciples do owe unto masters only a temporary belief and a suspension of their own judgment till they be fully instructed, and not an absolute resignation or perpetual captivity: and there-

[66] So given in "Errata"; the text has "counsels"; editions 1629 and 1633 print "consuls," but the error has been repeated in later editions.

fore, to conclude this point, I will say no more, but so let great authors have their due, as time, which is the author of authors, be not deprived of his due, which is further and further to discover truth. Thus have I gone over these three diseases of learning; besides the which there are some other rather peccant humors than formed diseases, which nevertheless are not so secret and intrinsic but that they fall under a popular observation and traducement, and therefore are not to be passed over.

The first of these is the extreme affecting of two extremities: the one antiquity, the other novelty; wherein it seemeth the children of Time do take after the nature and malice of the father. For as he devoureth his children, so one of them seeketh to devour and suppress the other; while antiquity envieth there should be new additions, and novelty cannot be content to add but it must deface: surely the advice of the prophet is the true direction in this matter, *State super vias antiquas, et videte quænam sit via recta et bona et ambulate in ea.*[67] Antiquity deserveth that reverence, that men should make a stand thereupon and discover what is the best way; but when the discovery is well taken, then to make progression. And to speak truly, *Antiquitas sæculi juventus mundi.* These times are the ancient times, when the world is ancient, and not those which we account ancient *ordine retrogrado,* by a computation backward from ourselves.

Another error induced by the former is a distrust that anything should be now to be found out which the world should have missed and passed over so long time; as if the same objection were to be made to time that Lucian [68] maketh to Jupiter and other the heathen gods; of which he wondereth that they begot so many children in old time and begot none in his time; and asketh whether they were become septuagenary, or whether the law *Pappia,* made against old men's marriages, had restrained them. So it seemeth men

[67] Jeremiah 6:16. [68] Lucian, Greek satirical writer.

doubt lest time is become past children and generation; wherein contrariwise we see commonly the levity and un-constancy of men's judgments, which till a matter be done, wonder that it can be done; and as soon as it is done, wonder again that it was no sooner done: as we see in the expedi-tion of Alexander into Asia, which at first was prejudged as a vast and impossible enterprise; and yet afterwards it pleaseth Livy to make no more of it than this, *Nil aliud quam bene ausus vana contemnere.*[69] And the same hap-pened to Columbus in the western navigation. But in in-tellectual matters it is much more common; as may be seen in most of the propositions of Euclid, which till they be demonstrate, they seem strange to our assent; but being demonstrate, our mind accepteth of them by a kind of re-lation (as the lawyers speak) as if we had known them be-fore.

Another error, that hath also some affinity with the former, is a conceit that of former opinions or sects, after variety and examination, the best hath still prevailed and suppressed the rest; so as if a man should begin the labor of a new search, he were but like to light upon somewhat formerly rejected, and by rejection brought into oblivion: as if the multitude, or the wisest for the multitude's sake, were not ready to give passage rather to that which is popular and superficial than to that which is substantial and profound; for the truth is, that time seemeth to be of the nature of a river or stream, which carrieth down to us that which is light and blown up, and sinketh and drowneth that which is weighty and solid.

Another error, of a diverse nature from all the former, is the over-early and peremptory reduction of knowledge into arts and methods; from which time commonly sciences re-ceive small or no augmentation. But as young men, when they knit and shape perfectly, do seldom grow to a further

[69] Livy, ix. 17. Spedding translates: "It was but taking courage to despise vain apprehensions."

stature, so knowledge, while it is in aphorisms and observations, it is in growth: but when it once is comprehended in exact methods, it may perchance be further polished and illustrated and accommodated for use and practice; but it increaseth no more in bulk and substance.

Another error, which doth succeed that which we last mentioned, is that after the distribution of particular arts and sciences, men have abandoned universality or *philosophia prima;* which cannot but cease and stop all progression. For no perfect discovery can be made upon a flat or a level; neither is it possible to discover the more remote and deeper parts of any science, if you stand but upon the level of the same science, and ascend not to a higher science.

Another error hath proceeded from too great a reverence, and a kind of adoration of the mind and understanding of man; by means whereof men have withdrawn themselves too much from the contemplation of nature and the observations of experience, and have tumbled up and down in their own reason and conceits. Upon these intellectualists, which are notwithstanding commonly taken for the most sublime and divine philosophers, Heraclitus gave a just censure, saying, *Men sought truth in their own little worlds, and not in the great and common world;* for they disdain to spell, and so by degrees to read in the volume of God's works; and contrariwise by continual meditation and agitation of wit do urge and as it were invocate their own spirits to divine and give oracles unto them, whereby they are deservedly deluded.

Another error that hath some connection with this latter is that men have used to infect their meditations, opinions, and doctrines with some conceits which they have most admired, or some sciences which they have most applied; and given all things else a tincture according to them, utterly untrue and unproper. So hath Plato intermingled his philosophy with theology, and Aristotle with logic, and the second school of Plato, Proclus and the rest, with the math-

ematics. For these were the arts which had a kind of primogeniture with them severally. So have the alchemists
made a philosophy out of a few experiments of the furnace;
and Gilbertus, our countryman, hath made a philosophy out
of the observations of a loadstone.[70] So Cicero, when, re-
citing the several opinions of the nature of the soul, he found
a musician that held the soul was but a harmony, saith
pleasantly, *Hic ab arte sua non recessit, &c.* But of these
conceits Aristotle speaketh seriously and wisely when he
saith, *Qui respiciunt ad pauca de facili pronunciant.*

Another error is an impatience of doubt and haste to assertion without due and mature suspension of judgment.
For the two ways of contemplation are not unlike the two
ways of action commonly spoken of by the ancients: the
one plain and smooth in the beginning, and in the end im-
passable; the other rough and troublesome in the entrance,
but after a while fair and even: so it is in contemplation; if
a man will begin with certainties, he shall end in doubts; but
if he will be content to begin with doubts, he shall end in
certainties.

Another error is in the manner of the tradition and delivery of knowledge, which is for the most part magistral
and peremptory, and not ingenuous and faithful; in a sort
as may be soonest believed, and not easiliest examined. It
is true that in compendious treatises for practice that form
is not to be disallowed: but in the true handling of knowledge, men ought not to fall either on the one side into the
vein of Velleius the Epicurean, *Nil tam metuens, quam ne
dubitare aliqua de re videretur;* [71] nor on the other side into
Socrates his ironical doubting of all things; but to propound
things sincerely with more or less asseveration, as they stand
in a man's own judgment proved more or less.

Other errors there are in the scope that men propound

---

[70] William Gilbert, author of *De Magnete,* 1600.
[71] Cicero, *De Natura Deorum,* i. 8. 18. Spedding translates: "Who feared
nothing so much as seeming to be in doubt about anything."

to themselves, whereunto they bend their endeavors; for whereas the more constant and devote kind of professors of any science ought to propound to themselves to make some additions to their science, they convert their labors to aspire to certain second prizes: as to be a profound interpreter or commenter, to be a sharp champion or defender, to be a methodical compounder or abridger, and so the patrimony of knowledge cometh to be sometimes improved, but seldom augmented.

But the greatest error of all the rest is the mistaking or misplacing of the last or furthest end of knowledge. For men have entered into a desire of learning and knowledge, sometimes upon a natural curiosity and inquisitive appetite; sometimes to entertain their minds with variety and delight; sometimes for ornament and reputation; and sometimes to enable them to victory of wit and contradiction; and most times for lucre and profession; and seldom sincerely to give a true account of their gift of reason, to the benefit and use of men: as if there were sought in knowledge a couch, whereupon to rest a searching and restless spirit; or a terrace, for a wandering and variable mind to walk up and down with a fair prospect; or a tower of state, for a proud mind to raise itself upon; or a fort or commanding ground, for strife and contention; or a shop, for profit and sale; and not a rich storehouse for the glory of the Creator and the relief of man's estate. But this is that which will indeed dignify and exalt knowledge, if contemplation and action may be more nearly and straitly conjoined and united together than they have been; a conjunction like unto that of the two highest planets, Saturn, the planet of rest and contemplation, and Jupiter, the planet of civil society and action. Howbeit, I do not mean, when I speak of use and action, that end before-mentioned of the applying of knowledge to lucre and profession; for I am not ignorant how much that diverteth and interrupteth the prosecution and advancement of knowledge, like unto the golden ball thrown before Atalanta, which while she goeth aside and stoopeth to take up, the race is hindered,

Declinat cursus, aurumque volubile tollit.[72]

Neither is my meaning, as was spoken of Socrates, to call philosophy down from heaven to converse upon the earth; that is, to leave natural philosophy aside, and to apply knowledge only to manners and policy. But as both heaven and earth do conspire and contribute to the use and benefit of man, so the end ought to be, from both philosophies to separate and reject vain speculations and whatsoever is empty and void, and to preserve and augment whatsoever is solid and fruitful; that knowledge may not be as a courtesan, for pleasure and vanity only, or as a bond-woman, to acquire and gain to her master's use; but as a spouse, for generation, fruit, and comfort.

Thus have I described and opened, as by a kind of dissection, those peccant humors (the principal of them) which have not only given impediment to the proficience of learning, but have given also occasion to the traducement thereof: wherein if I have been too plain, it must be remembered, *fidelia vulnera amantis, sed dolosa oscula malignantis.*[73] This I think I have gained, that I ought to be the better believed in that which I shall say pertaining to commendation; because I have proceeded so freely in that which concerneth censure. And yet I have no purpose to enter into a laudative of learning, or to make a hymn to the Muses (though I am of opinion that it is long since their rites were duly celebrated), but my intent is, without varnish or amplification justly to weigh the dignity of knowledge in the balance with other things, and to take the true value thereof by testimonies and arguments divine and human. . . .[74]

It were too long to go over the particular remedies which

---

[72] Ovid, *Metamorphoses,* x. 667.
[73] Prov. 27:6. "The wounds of a friend are faithful, but the kisses of an enemy are deceitful."
[74] The general survey of knowledge which follows is omitted.

learning doth minister to all the diseases of the mind, sometimes purging the ill humors, sometimes opening obstruc-
tions, sometimes helping digestion, sometimes increasing appetite, sometimes healing the wounds and exulcerations
thereof, and the like; and therefore I will conclude with that
which hath *rationem totius;* which is, that it disposeth the
constitution of the mind not to be fixed or settled in the defects thereof, but still to be capable and susceptible of growth
and reformation. For the unlearned man knows not what it is
to descend into himself, or to call himself into account, nor
the pleasure of that *Suavissima vita, indies sentire se fieri
meliorem*: [75] the good parts he hath, he will learn to show to
the full and use them dexterously, but not much to increase
them: the faults he hath, he will learn how to hide and color
them, but not much to amend them; like an ill mower that
mows on still, and never whets his scythe: whereas with the
learned man it fares otherwise, that he doth ever intermix
the correction and amendment of his mind with the use and
employment thereof. Nay further in general and in sum, certain it is that *veritas* and *bonitas* differ but as the seal and
print; for truth prints goodness, and they be the clouds of
error, which descend in the storms of passions and perturbations.

From moral virtue let us pass on to matter of power and
commandment, and consider whether in right reason there be
any comparable with that wherewith knowledge investeth
and crowneth man's nature. We see the dignity of the commandment is according to the dignity of the commanded:
to have commandment over beasts, as herdsmen have, is a
thing contemptible; to have commandment over children, as
schoolmasters have, is a matter of small honor; to have
commandment over galley-slaves, is a disparagement, rather
than an honor. Neither is the commandment of tyrants much
better, over people which have put off the generosity of their

[75] Probably from Xenophon, *Memor.,* i. 6. 8. Spedding translates: "To
feel himself each day a better man than he was the day before."

minds: and therefore it was ever holden that honors in free monarchies and commonwealths had a sweetness more than in tyrannies; because the commandment extendeth more over the wills of men, and not only over their deeds and services. And therefore when Virgil putteth himself forth to attribute to Augustus Cæsar the best of human honors, he doth it in these words:

> *Victorque volentes*
> *Per populos, dat irua, viamque affectat Olympo:* [76]

But yet the commandment of knowledge is yet higher than the commandment over the will; for it is a commandment over the reason, belief, and understanding of man, which is the highest part of the mind, and giveth law to the will itself. For there is no power on earth, which setteth up a throne or chair of estate in the spirits and souls of men, and in their cogitations, imaginations, opinions, and beliefs, but knowledge and learning. And therefore we see the detestable and extreme pleasure that arch-heretics and false prophets and impostors are transported with, when they once find in themselves that they have a superiority in the faith and conscience of men; so great, as if they have once tasted of it, it is seldom seen that any torture or persecution can make them relinquish or abandon it. But as this is that which the author of Revelation calleth the depth or profoundness of Satan, so by argument of contraries, the just and lawful sovereignty over men's understanding, by face of truth rightly interpreted, is that which approacheth nearest to the similitude of the divine rule.

As for fortune and advancement, the beneficence of learning is not so consigned to give fortune only to states and commonwealths, as it doth not likewise give fortune to particular persons. For it was well noted long ago that Homer hath given more men their livings than either Sylla or Cæsar or

[76] *Georgics,* iv. 561. Spedding translates:
"Moving in conquest onward, at his will
To willing peoples he gives laws, and shapes
Through worthiest deeds on earth his course to heaven."

Augustus ever did, notwithstanding their great largesses and donatives and distributions of lands to so many legions. And no doubt it is hard to say whether arms or learning have advanced greater numbers. And in case of sovereignty, we see that if arms or descent have carried away the kingdom, yet learning hath carried the priesthood, which ever hath been in some competition with empire.

Again, for the pleasure and delight of knowledge and learning, it far surpasseth all other in nature: for shall the pleasures of the affections so exceed the senses, as much as the obtaining of desire or victory exceedeth song, or a dinner? and must not of consequence, the pleasures of the intellect or understanding exceed the pleasures of the affections? we see in all other pleasures there is satiety; [77] and after they be used, their verdure [78] departeth; which showeth well they be but deceits of pleasure, and not pleasures; and that it was novelty which pleased, and not the quality. And therefore we see that voluptuous men turn friars, and ambitious princes turn melancholy. But of knowledge there is no satiety, but satisfaction and appetite are perpetually interchangeable; and therefore appeareth to be good in itself simply, without fallacy or accident. Neither is that pleasure of small efficacy and contentment to the mind of man which the poet Lucretius describeth elegantly,

Suave mari magno, turbantibus æquora ventis: &c

It is a view of delight (saith he) to stand or walk upon the shore side, and to see a ship tossed with tempest upon the sea; or to be in a fortified tower and to see two battles join upon a plain. But it is a pleasure incomparable for the mind of man to be settled, landed, and fortified in the certainty of truth; and from thence to descry and behold the errors, perturbations, labors, and wanderings up and down of other men.[79]

---

[77] "Sacietie" is the form in the text.
[78] In 1605, 1629, and 1633 the word was "verdour."
[79] Lucretius, *De Rerum Natura,* ii. 1–10.

Lastly, leaving the vulgar arguments, that by learning man excelleth man in that wherein man excelleth beasts; that by learning man ascendeth to the heavens and their motions, where in body he cannot come; and the like; let us conclude with the dignity and excellency of knowledge and learning in that whereunto man's nature doth most aspire, which is immortality or continuance; for to this tendeth generation, and raising of houses and families; to this, buildings, foundations, and monuments; to this tendeth the desire of memory, fame and celebration; and in effect the strength of all other human desires. We see then how far the monuments of wit and learning are more durable than the monuments of power or of the hands. For have not the verses of Homer continued twenty-five hundred years or more, without the loss of a syllable or letter; during which time infinite palaces, temples, castles, cities, have been decayed and demolished? It is not possible to have the true pictures or statuaes [80] of Cyrus, Alexander, Cæsar, no nor of the kings or great personages of much later years; for the originals cannot last, and the copies cannot but leese of the life and truth. But the images of men's wits and knowledges remain in books, exempted from the wrong of time and capable of perpetual renovation. Neither are they fitly to be called images, because they generate still, and cast their seeds in the minds of others, provoking and causing infinite actions and opinions in succeeding ages. So that if the invention of the ship was thought so noble, which carrieth riches and commodities from place to place, and consociateth the most remote regions in participation of their fruits, how much more are letters to be magnified, which as ships pass through the vast seas of time, and make ages so distant to participate of the wisdom, illuminations, and inventions, the one of the other? Nay further, we see some of the philosophers which were least divine, and most immersed in the senses, and denied generally the immortality of the soul, yet came to this point, that whatsoever motions the spirit of man could act and

---

[80] "Statuaes" is the old form of the word.

perform without the organs of the body, they thought might remain after death; which were only those of the understanding, and not of the affection; so immortal and incorruptible a thing did knowledge seem unto them to be. But we, that know by divine revelation that not only the understanding but the affections purified, not only the spirit but the body changed, shall be advanced to immortality, do disclaim in these rudiments of the senses. But it must be remembered, both in this last point, and so it may likewise be needful in other places, that in probation of the dignity of knowledge or learning, I did in the beginning separate divine testimony from human, which method I have pursued, and so handled them both apart.

Nevertheless I do not pretend, and I know it will be impossible for me by any pleading of mine, to reverse the judgment, either of Æsop's cock, that preferred the barley-corn before the gem; or of Midas, that being chosen judge between Apollo, president of the Muses, and Pan, god of the flocks, judged for plenty; or of Paris, that judged for beauty and love against wisdom and power, or of Agrippina, *occidat matrem, modo imperet,* that preferred empire with any condition never so detestable; or of Ulysses, *qui vetulam prætulit immortalitati,* being a figure of those which prefer custom and habit before all excellency; or of a number of the like popular judgments. For these things [must] [81] continue as they have been: but so will that also continue whereupon learning hath ever relied, and which faileth not: *Justificata est sapientia a filiis suis.*

[81] "Must" is added in the "Errata."

From NOVUM ORGANUM [1]

[*Idols*]

XXXVIII

THE IDOLS [2] and false notions which are now in possession
of the human understanding, and have taken deep root
therein, not only so beset men's minds that truth can hardly
find entrance, but even after entrance obtained, they will
again in the very instauration of the sciences meet and
trouble us, unless men being forewarned of the danger fortify
themselves as far as may be against their assaults.

XXXIX

There are four classes of idols which beset men's minds.
To these for distinction's sake I have assigned names—
calling the first class *Idols of the Tribe;* the second, *Idols
of the Cave ;* the third, *Idols of the Market-place ;* the fourth,
Idols of the Theater.

XL

The formation of ideas and axioms by true induction is
no doubt the proper remedy to be applied for the keeping
off and clearing away of idols. To point them out, however,
is of great use; for the doctrine of idols is to the interpretation of nature what the doctrine of the refutation of sophisms is to common logic.

---

[1] Text: Works, edited by James Spedding and Robert Leslie Ellis. 15
vols. (Boston, 1843), Vol. VIII, 76–91, 99.
[2] The meaning here is "phantoms."

XLI

The *Idols of the Tribe* have their foundation in human nature itself, and in the tribe or race of men. For it is a false assertion that the sense of man is the measure of things. On the contrary, all perceptions as well of the sense as of the mind are according to the measure of the individual and not according to the measure of the universe. And the human understanding is like a false mirror, which, receiving rays irregularly, distorts and discolors the nature of things by mingling its own nature with it.

XLII

The *Idols of the Cave* are the idols of the individual man. For everyone (besides the errors common to human nature in general) has a cave or den of his own, which refracts and discolors the light of nature; owing either to his own proper and peculiar nature; or to his education and conversation with others; or to the reading of books, and the authority of those whom he esteems and admires; or to the differences of impressions, accordingly as they take place in a mind preoccupied and predisposed or in a mind indifferent and settled; or the like. So that the spirit of man (according as it is meted out to different individuals) is in fact a thing variable and full of perturbation, and governed as it were by chance. Whence it was well observed by Heraclitus that men look for sciences in their own lesser worlds, and not in the greater or common world.

XLIII

There are also idols formed by the intercourse and association of men with each other, which I call *Idols of the Market-place*, on account of the commerce and consort of men there. For it is by discourse that men associate; and words are imposed according to the apprehension of the vulgar. And therefore the ill and unfit choice of words wonderfully obstructs the understanding. Nor do the definitions or explanations wherewith in some things learned men are wont to guard and defend themselves, by any means set the matter right. But words plainly force and overrule the understanding, and throw all into confusion and lead men away into numberless empty controversies and idle fancies.

XLIV

Lastly, there are idols which have immigrated into men's minds from the various dogmas of philosophies, and also from wrong laws of demonstration. These I call *Idols of the Theater;* because in my judgment all the received systems are but so many stage-plays, representing worlds of their own creation after an unreal and scenic fashion. Nor is it only of the systems now in vogue, or only of the ancient sects and philosophies, that I speak; for many more plays of the same kind may yet be composed and in like artificial manner set forth; seeing that errors the most widely different have nevertheless causes for the most part alike. Neither again do I mean this only of entire systems, but also of many principles and axioms in science, which by tradition, credulity, and negligence, have come to be received.

But of these several kinds of idols I must speak more largely and exactly, that the understanding may be duly cautioned.

XLV

The human understanding is of its own nature prone to suppose the existence of more order and regularity in the world than it finds. And though there be many things in nature which are singular and unmatched, yet it devises for them parallels and conjugates and relatives which do not exist. Hence the fiction that all celestial bodies move in perfect circles; spirals and dragons being (except in name) utterly rejected. Hence too the element of fire with its orb is brought in, to make up the square with the other three which the sense perceives. Hence also the ratio of density of the so-called elements is arbitrarily fixed at ten to one. And so on of other dreams. And these fancies affect not dogmas only, but simple notions also.

XLVI

The human understanding when it has once adopted an opinion (either as being the received opinion or as being agreeable to itself) draws all things else to support and agree with it. And though there be a greater number and weight of instances to be found on the other side, yet these it either neglects and despises, or else by some distinction sets aside and rejects; in order that by this great and pernicious predetermination the authority of its former conclusions may remain inviolate. And therefore it was a good answer that was made by one who when they showed him hanging in a temple a picture of those who had paid their vows as having escaped shipwreck, and would have him say whether he did not now acknowledge the power of the gods—"Ay," asked he again, "but where are they painted that were drowned after their vows?" And such is the way of all superstition,

whether in astrology, dreams, omens, divine judgments, or
the like; wherein men having a delight in such vanities, mark
the events where they are fulfilled, but where they fail,
though this happen much oftener, neglect and pass them by.
But with far more subtlety does this mischief insinuate itself into philosophy and the sciences; in which the first conclusion colors and brings into conformity with itself all that
come after, though far sounder and better. Besides, inde-
pendently of that delight and vanity which I have described,
it is the peculiar and perpetual error of the human intellect
to be more moved and excited by affirmatives than by nega-
tives; whereas it ought properly to hold itself indifferently
disposed towards both alike. Indeed, in the establishment
of any true axiom, the negative instance is the more forcible
of the two.

XLVII

The human understanding is moved by those things most
which strike and enter the mind simultaneously and suddenly, and so fill the imagination; and then it feigns and
supposes all other things to be somehow, though it cannot
see how, similar to those few things by which it is surrounded. But for that going to and fro to remote and heterogeneous instances, by which axioms are tried as in the
fire, the intellect is altogether slow and unfit, unless it be
forced thereto by severe laws and overruling authority.

XLVIII

The human understanding is unquiet; it cannot stop or
rest, and still presses onward, but in vain. Therefore it is
that we cannot conceive of any end or limit to the world,
but always as of necessity it occurs to us that there is something beyond. Neither again can it be conceived how eternity

has flowed down to the present day; for that distinction which is commonly received of infinity in time past and in time to come can by no means hold; for it would thence follow that one infinity is greater than another, and that infinity is wasting away and tending to become finite. The like subtlety arises touching the infinite divisibility of lines, from the same inability of thought to stop. But this inability interferes more mischievously in the discovery of causes: for although the most general principles in nature ought to be held merely positive, as they are discovered, and cannot with truth be referred to a cause; nevertheless, the human understanding being unable to rest still seeks something prior in the order of nature. And then it is that in struggling towards that which is further off, it falls back upon that which is more nigh at hand; namely, on final causes: which have relation clearly to the nature of man rather than to the nature of the universe, and from this source have strangely defiled philosophy. But he is no less an unskilled and shallow philosopher who seeks causes of that which is most general, than he who in things subordinate and subaltern omits to do so.

XLIX

The human understanding is no dry light, but receives an infusion from the will and affections; whence proceed sciences which may be called "sciences as one would." For what a man had rather were true he more readily believes. Therefore he rejects difficult things from impatience of research; sober things, because they narrow hope; the deeper things of nature, from superstition; the light of experience, from arrogance and pride, lest his mind should seem to be occupied with things mean and transitory; things not commonly believed, out of deference to the opinion of the vulgar. Numberless in short are the ways, and sometimes imperceptible, in which the affections color and infect the understanding.

L

But by far the greatest hindrance and aberration of the human understanding proceeds from the dullness, incompetency, and deceptions of the senses; in that things which strike the sense outweigh things which do not immediately strike it, though they be more important. Hence it is that speculation commonly ceases where sight ceases; insomuch that of things invisible there is little or no observation. Hence all the working of the spirits enclosed in tangible bodies lies hid and unobserved of men. So also all the more subtle changes of form in the parts of coarser substances (which they commonly call alteration, though it is in truth local motion through exceedingly small spaces) is in like manner unobserved. And yet unless these two things just mentioned be searched out and brought to light, nothing great can be achieved in nature, as far as the production of works is concerned. So again the essential nature of our common air, and of all bodies less dense than air (which are very many) is almost unknown. For the sense by itself is a thing infirm and erring; neither can instruments for enlarging or sharpening the senses do much; but all the truer kind of interpretation of nature is effected by instances and experiments fit and apposite; wherein the sense decides touching the experiment only, and the experiment touching the point in nature and the thing itself.

LI

The human understanding is of its own nature prone to abstractions and gives a substance and reality to things which are fleeting. But to resolve nature into abstractions is less to our purpose than to dissect her into parts; as did the school of Democritus, which went further into nature than the rest. Matter rather than forms should be the object of our attention, its configurations and changes of configuration, and simple action, and law of action or motion; for forms are figments of the human mind, unless you will call those laws of action forms.

LII

Such then are the idols which I call *Idols of the Tribe;* and which take their rise either from the homogeneity of the substance of the human spirit, or from its preoccupation, or from its narrowness, or from its restless motion, or from an infusion of the affections, or from the incompetency of the senses, or from the mode of impression.

LIII

The *Idols of the Cave* take their rise in the peculiar constitution, mental or bodily, of each individual; and also in education, habit, and accident. Of this kind there is a great number and variety; but I will instance those the pointing out of which contains the most important caution, and which have most effect in disturbing the clearness of the understanding.

LIV

Men become attached to certain particular sciences and speculations, either because they fancy themselves the authors and inventors thereof, or because they have bestowed the greatest pains upon them and become most habituated to them. But men of this kind, if they betake themselves to philosophy and contemplations of a general character, distort and color them in obedience to their former fancies; a thing especially to be noticed in Aristotle, who made his natural philosophy a mere bondservant to his logic, thereby rendering it contentious and well nigh useless. The race of chemists again out of a few experiments of the furnace have built up a fantastic philosophy, framed with reference to a few things; and Gilbert also, after he had employed himself most laboriously in the study and observation of the loadstone, proceeded at once to construct an entire system in accordance with his favorite subject.

LV

There is one principal and, as it were, radical distinction between different minds, in respect of philosophy and the sciences, which is this: that some minds are stronger and apter to mark the differences of things, others to mark their resemblances. The steady and acute mind can fix its contemplations and dwell and fasten on the subtlest distinctions: the lofty and discursive mind recognizes and puts together the finest and most general resemblances. Both kinds however easily err in excess, by catching the one at gradations, the other at shadows.

LVI

There are found some minds given to an extreme admiration of antiquity, others to an extreme love and appetite for novelty; but few so duly tempered that they can hold the mean, neither carping at what has been well laid down by the ancients, nor despising what is well introduced by the moderns. This however turns to the great injury of the sciences and philosophy; since these affectations of antiquity and novelty are the humors of partisans rather than judgments; and truth is to be sought for not in the felicity of any age, which is an unstable thing, but in the light of nature and experience, which is eternal. These factions therefore must be abjured, and care must be taken that the intellect be not hurried by them into assent.

LVII

Contemplations of nature and of bodies in their simple form break up and distract the understanding, while contemplations of nature and bodies in their composition and configuration overpower and dissolve the understanding: a distinction well seen in the school of Leucippus and Democritus as compared with the other philosophies. For that school is so busied with the particles that it hardly attends to the structure; while the others are so lost in admiration of the structure that they do not penetrate to the simplicity of nature. These kinds of contemplation should therefore be alternated and taken by turns; that so the understanding may be rendered at once penetrating and comprehensive, and the inconveniences above mentioned, with the idols which proceed from them, may be avoided.

LVIII

Let such then be our provision and contemplative prudence for keeping off and dislodging the *Idols of the Cave,* which grow for the most part either out of the predominance of a favorite subject, or out of an excessive tendency to compare or to distinguish, or out of partiality for particular ages, or out of the largeness or minuteness of the objects contemplated. And generally let every student of nature take this as a rule,—that whatever his mind seizes and dwells upon with peculiar satisfaction is to be held in suspicion, and that so much the more care is to be taken in dealing with such questions to keep the understanding even and clear.

LIX

But the *Idols of the Market-place* are the most troublesome of all: idols which have crept into the understanding through the alliances of words and names. For men believe that their reason governs words; but it is also true that words react on the understanding; and this it is that has rendered philosophy and the sciences sophistical and inactive. Now words, being commonly framed and applied according to the capacity of the vulgar, follow those lines of division which are most obvious to the vulgar understanding. And whenever an understanding of greater acuteness or a more diligent observation would alter those lines to suit the true divisions of nature, words stand in the way and resist the change. Whence it comes to pass that the high and formal discussions of learned men end oftentimes in disputes about words and names; with which (according to the use and wisdom of the mathematicians) it would be more prudent to begin, and so by means of definitions reduce them to order. Yet even definitions cannot cure this evil in dealing with natural and material things; since the definitions themselves consist of words, and those words beget others: so that it is necessary to recur to individual instances, and those in due series and order; as I shall say presently when I come to the method and scheme for the formation of notions and axioms.

LX

The idols imposed by words on the understanding are of two kinds. They are either names of things which do not exist (for as there are things left unnamed through lack of observation, so likewise are there names which result from fantastic suppositions and to which nothing in reality responds), or they are names of things which exist, but yet confused and ill-defined, and hastily and irregularly derived from realities. Of the former kind are Fortune, the Prime Mover, Planetary Orbits, Element of Fire, and like fictions which owe their origin to false and idle theories. And this class of idols is more easily expelled, because to get rid of them it is only necessary that all theories should be steadily rejected and dismissed as obsolete.

But the other class, which springs out of a faulty and unskillful abstraction, is intricate and deeply rooted. Let us take for example such a word as *humid;* and see how far the several things which the word is used to signify agree with each other; and we shall find the word *humid* to be nothing else than a mark loosely and confusedly applied to denote a variety of actions which will not bear to be reduced to any constant meaning. For it both signifies that which easily spreads itself round any other body; and that which in itself is indeterminate and cannot solidize; and that which readily yields in every direction; and that which easily divides and scatters itself; and that which easily unites and collects itself; and that which readily flows and is put in motion; and that which readily clings to another body and wets it; and that which is easily reduced to a liquid, or being solid easily melts. Accordingly when you come to apply the word,—if you take it in one sense, flame is humid; if in another, air is not humid; if in another, fine dust is humid; if in another, glass is humid. So that it is easy to see that the notion is taken by abstraction only from water and common and ordinary liquids, without any due verification.

There are however in words certain degrees of distortion and error. One of the least faulty kinds is that of names of substances, especially of lowest species and well-deduced (for the notion of *chalk* and of *mud* is good, of *earth* bad);

a more faulty kind is that of actions, as *to generate, to corrupt, to alter;* the most faulty is of qualities (except such
as are the immediate objects of the sense), as *heavy, light,
rare, dense,* and the like. Yet in all these cases some notions
are of necessity a little better than others, in proportion to
the greater variety of subjects that fall within the range
of the human sense.

LXI

But the *Idols of the Theater* are not innate, nor do they
steal into the understanding secretly, but are plainly impressed and received into the mind from the play-books of
philosophical systems and the perverted rules of demonstration. To attempt refutations in this case would be merely inconsistent with what I have already said: for since we agree
neither upon principles nor upon demonstrations, there is
no place for argument. And this is so far well, inasmuch as
it leaves the honor of the ancients untouched. For they are
no wise disparaged—the question between them and me
being only as to the way. For as the saying is, the lame man
who keeps the right road outstrips the runner who takes a
wrong one. Nay, it is obvious that when a man runs the wrong
way, the more active and swift he is the further he will go
astray.

But the course I propose for the discovery of sciences is
such as leaves but little to the acuteness and strength of
wits, but places all wits and understandings nearly on a
level. For as in the drawing of a straight line or perfect
circle, much depends on the steadiness and practice of the
hand, if it be done by aim of hand only, but if with the aid
of rule or compass, little or nothing; so is it exactly with my
plan. But though particular confutations would be of no
avail, yet touching the sects and general divisions of such
systems I must say something; something also touching the
external signs which show that they are unsound; and finally

something touching the causes of such great infelicity and of such lasting and general agreement in error; that so the access to truth may be made less difficult, and the human understanding may the more willingly submit to its purgation and dismiss its idols.

LXII

Idols of the Theater, or of systems, are many, and there can be and perhaps will be yet many more. For were it not that now for many ages men's minds have been busied with religion and theology; and were it not that civil governments, especially monarchies, have been averse to such novelties, even in matters speculative; so that men labor therein to the peril and harming of their fortunes,—not only unrewarded, but exposed also to contempt and envy; doubtless there would have arisen many other philosophical sects like to those which in great variety flourished once among the Greeks. For as on the phenomena of the heavens many hypotheses may be constructed, so likewise (and more also) many various dogmas may be set up and established on the phenomena of philosophy. And in the plays of this philosophical theater you may observe the same thing which is found in the theater of the poets, that stories invented for the stage are more compact and elegant, and more as one would wish them to be, than true stories out of history.

In general, however, there is taken for the material of philosophy either a great deal out of a few things, or a very little out of many things; so that on both sides philosophy is based on too narrow a foundation of experiment and natural history, and decides on the authority of too few cases. For the rational school of philosophers snatches from experience a variety of common instances, neither duly ascertained nor diligently examined and weighed, and leaves all the rest to meditation and agitation of wit.

There is also another class of philosophers, who having bestowed much diligent and careful labor on a few experiments, have thence made bold to educe and construct systems; wresting all other facts in a strange fashion to conformity therewith.

And there is yet a third class, consisting of those who out of faith and veneration mix their philosophy with theology and traditions; among whom the vanity of some has gone so far aside as to seek the origin of sciences among spirits and genii. So that this parent stock of errors—this false philosophy—is of three kinds; the sophistical, the empirical, and the superstitious. . . .

LXVIII

So much concerning the several classes of idols, and their equipage: all of which must be renounced and put away with a fixed and solemn determination, and the understanding thoroughly freed and cleansed; the entrance into the kingdom of man, founded on the sciences, being not much other than the entrance into the kingdom of heaven, whereinto none may enter except as a little child.

John Donne   1572-1631

THROUGH his mother's side of the family Donne could trace his ancestry back to Sir Thomas More. The family was Catholic, and some members of it, including Donne's brother, had suffered persecution for their faith. Because of his religion Donne himself was unable to take a degree at either Oxford or Cambridge, though he studied at both, and he went on to London to study law at Lincoln's Inn. At some time, possibly before entering Lincoln's Inn, he traveled on the Continent.[1]

Meanwhile Donne's father had died, leaving his son a comfortable inheritance. This soon vanished in a gay waste of both money and life which years of repentance could never quite dim in his mind. His emotional life is revealed in the poetry which belongs to this period, but there was also time for equally intense study. A broad survey of the contemporary books of law is indicated by the law imagery which permeated all his writing.[2] Donne also made a comparative study of the Catholic and Anglican beliefs in an effort to find a rational foundation for a personal faith.

This chapter of his life was concluded when he joined Essex in the expeditions to Cadiz and to the Azores. Upon his return to England it was necessary for him to earn his own living, and he was fortunate in being recommended by Sir Henry Wotton as secretary to Sir Thomas Egerton, Lord Keeper of the Great Seal.

Here he met Lady Egerton's niece, Anne More, who had been established as hostess for her uncle following Lady Egerton's death. A secret marriage to Anne in 1601 led to Donne's imprisonment and the loss of his position. From the

---

[1] John Sparrow, "The Date of Donne's Travels," *A Garland for John Donne,* ed. by Theodore Spencer (Cambridge, Mass., 1931), pp. 131–32.

[2] An extensive study of this subject has been made by R. L. Hickey and will be published later.

prison there came the brief, expressive note to Anne: "John Donne, Anne Donne, Undone."

After Donne's release there was a long period of dependence upon relatives and patrons while Donne sought court preferment. His early study of divinity enabled him to assist Bishop Morton in his arguments against the Catholics, and the Bishop valued his learning so highly that he offered Donne a position in the church. Donne felt, however, that his life had been such that he could not take Holy Orders and so declined this offer.

Finally, when poverty and sickness in his family had led Donne to a mood of despair, Anne's father agreed upon a dowry to be paid as an allowance. Further good fortune came with the writing of a funeral elegy on the first anniversary of the death of Sir Robert Drury's young daughter. Donne and his family were now given a comfortable home with the new patron. Later when Sir Robert asked Donne to accompany him and his wife to the Continent, Donne wrote his exquisite farewells to Anne, "Sweetest love, I do not go," and "A Valediction Forbidding Mourning." A moving account of this separation is narrated in Walton's *Life of Donne*.

Donne's continued effort to secure court preferment led to nothing, for the king had determined to secure his services for the church. It was only after further study of divinity and a long battle with his conscience that Donne finally entered the church in 1615. Security and advancement came with this step. He became the chaplain of James I and at the king's request was granted an honorary degree from Cambridge. He was made divinity reader at Lincoln's Inn, and in 1621 was appointed Dean of St. Paul's.

Anne had lived only two years after Donne made his decision. The subject of death, which had always held a morbid interest for him, now preoccupied his mind. Walton tells how he posed for his portrait wrapped in a shroud and how "Death's Duel" was in reality his own funeral sermon.

The many sermons afford the best representation of Donne's prose style. Donne divides his text into all its possible parts, analyzing each through a process of reasoning that is intricate and often subtle. To illustrate his points he may use a striking image which is elaborated until comparisons are exhausted, as in the simile of the world as a sea, or he may bring out a hidden likeness through a brief metaphor, as in "Time is a short parenthesis in a long period." In prose as in poetry, one finds paradox, antithesis, hyperbole, and rhetorical question; and meets with the abrupt shock of some startling turn of idea or phrase. But the voice of authority speaks in the sermons, and the church Fathers are marshaled to support the arguments. Climax is employed in both the parts and the whole, and the reader feels intellectually and emotionally spent when some great sentence, such as the one on damnation in Sermon LXXVI, moves to an almost unbearable height, or when the lift of Donne's eloquence finally subsides in the cadence of the closing sentence.

The secret of Donne's strangely moving power is not, however, in his eloquence; it lies in the fact that Donne, never at peace with himself, becomes the fusion of audience and preacher, and the soul-searching is emotional and intense because Donne is probing into his own soul.

From DEVOTIONS UPON EMERGENT OCCASIONS [1]

XI. *Meditation*

Nobilibusque trahunt, a cincto corde, venenum, succis et gemmis, et quæ generosa, ministrant ars et natura instillant.

They use cordials to keep the venom and malignity of the disease from the heart.

WHENCE CAN we take a better argument, a clearer demonstration, that all the greatness of this world is built upon opinion of others and hath in itself no real being nor power of subsistence, than from the heart of man? It is always in action and motion, still busy, still pretending to do all, to furnish all the powers and faculties with all that they have; but if an enemy dare rise up against it, it is the soonest endangered, the soonest defeated of any part. The brain will hold out longer than it, and the liver longer than that; they will endure a siege; but an unnatural heat, a rebellious heat, will blow up the heart like a mine in a minute. But howsoever, since the heart hath the birthright and primogeniture, and that it is nature's eldest son in us, the part which is first born to life in man, and that the other parts, as younger brethren and servants in this family, have a dependence upon it, it is reason that the principal care be had of it, though it be not the strongest part, as the eldest is oftentimes not the strongest of the family. And since the brain and liver and heart hold not a triumvirate in man, a sovereignty equally shed upon them all, for his well-being, as the four elements do for his very being, but the heart alone is in the principality and in the throne as king, the rest as subjects, though in eminent place and office, must contribute to that, as children to their parents, as all persons to all kinds of superiors,

[1] Text: 1624, first edition, compared with 1626, third edition (both editions in the British Museum).

though oftentimes those parents, or those superiors, be not
of stronger parts than themselves that serve and obey them
that are weaker; neither doth this obligation fall upon us
by second dictates of nature, by consequences and conclusions arising out of nature, or derived from nature, by discourse (as many things bind us even by the law of nature,
and yet not by the primary law of nature; as all laws of
propriety in that which we possess are of the law of nature,
which law is, *To give every one his own,* and yet in the
primary law of nature there was no propriety, no *meum* and
tuum, but an universal community over all; so the obedience of superiors is the law of nature, and yet in the primary
law of nature there was no superiority, no magistracy); but
this contribution of assistance of all to the sovereign, of all
parts of the heart, is from the very first dictates of nature,
which is, in the first place, to have care of our own preservation, to look first to ourselves; for therefore doth the physician intermit the present care of the brain or liver because
there is a possibility that they may subsist though there
be not a present and a particular care had of them, but there
is no possibility that they can subsist if the heart perish:
and so when we seem to begin with others in such assistances,
indeed we do begin with ourselves, and we ourselves are
principally in our contemplation; and so all these officious
and mutual assistances are but complements towards others,
and our true end is ourselves. And this is the reward of the
pains of kings: sometimes they need the power of law, to
be obeyed; and when they seem to be obeyed voluntarily,
they who do it, do it for their own sakes. O how little a thing
is all the greatness of man, and through how false glasses
doth he make shift to multiply it and magnify it to himself!
And yet this is also another misery of this king of man, the
heart, which is appliable to the kings of this world, great
men, that the venom and poison of every pestilential disease
directs itself to the heart, affects that (pernicious affection),
and the malignity of ill men is also directed upon the great-

est and the best; and not only greatness, but goodness looses
the vigor of being an antidote, or cordial, against it. And as
the noblest and most generous cordials that nature or art
afford, or can prepare, if they be often taken and made
familiar, become no cordials, nor have any extraordinary
operation, so the greatest cordial of the heart, patience, if
it be much exercised, exalts the venom and the malignity of
the enemy, and the more we suffer, the more we are insulted
upon. When God had made this earth of nothing, it was but
a little help that he had, to make other things of this earth:
nothing can be nearer nothing than this earth; and yet how
little of this earth is the greatest man! He thinks he treads
upon the earth that all is under his feet, and the brain that
thinks so is but the earth; his highest region, the flesh that
covers that, is but earth; and even the top of that, that
wherein so many Absaloms take so much pride, is but a
bush growing upon that turf of earth. How little of the
world is the earth! And yet that is all that man hath or is.
How little of man is the heart! And yet it is all by which he
is; and this continually subject, not only to foreign poisons
conveyed by others, but to intestine poisons, bred in ourselves by pestilential sicknesses. O who, if before he had a
being, he could have sense of this misery, would buy a being
here upon these conditions?

XI. *Prayer* [2]

O ETERNAL and most gracious God, who in thy upper house,
the heavens, though there be many mansions, yet art alike,
and equally in every mansion; but here in thy lower house,
though thou fillest all, yet art otherwise in some rooms
thereof than in others; otherwise in thy church than in my
chamber, and otherwise in thy sacraments than in my prayers,

---

[2] Each *Devotion* consists of a *Meditation,* an *Expostulation,* and a
Prayer.

so thou be always present and always working in every room
of this thy house, my body, yet I humbly beseech thee to
manifest always a more effectual presence in my heart than
in the other offices. Into the house of thine anointed, disloyal
persons, traitors, will come; into thy house, the church,
hypocrites and idolaters will come; into some rooms of this
thy house, my body, temptations will come, infections will
come; but be my heart thy bedchamber, O my God, and
thither let them not enter. Job made a covenant with his
eyes, but not his making of that covenant, but thy dwelling
in his heart, enabled him to keep that covenant. Thy son
himself had *a sadness in his soul to death,* and he had a
reluctation, a deprecation of death in the approaches thereof;
but he had his cordial too, *Yet not my will, but thine be
done.* And as thou hast not delivered us, thine adopted sons,
from these infectious temptations, so neither hast thou delivered us over to them, nor withheld thy cordials from us.
I was baptized in thy cordial, water, against original sin;
and I have drunk of thy cordial, blood, for my recovery from
actual and habitual sin, in the other sacrament. Thou, O
Lord, who hast imprinted all medicinal virtues, which are in
all creatures, and hast made even the flesh of vipers to assist
in cordials, art able to make this present sickness, everlasting health; this weakness, everlasting strength; and this
very dejection and faintness of heart, a powerful cordial.
When thy blessed Son cried out to thee, *My God, my God,
why hast thou forsaken me?* thou didst reach out thy hand
to him; but not to deliver his sad soul, but to receive his holy
soul; neither did he longer desire to hold it of thee, but to
recommend it to thee. I see thine hand upon me now, O
Lord, and I ask not why it comes, what it intends; whether
thou wilt bid it stay still in this body for some time, or bid
it meet thee this day in Paradise, I ask not, not in a wish,
not in a thought: infirmity of nature, curiosity of mind, are
temptations that offer; but a silent and absolute obedience
to thy will, even before I know it, is my cordial. Preserve

that to me, O my God, and that will preserve me to thee; that when thou hast catechised me with affliction here, I may take a greater degree and serve thee in a higher place in thy kingdom of joy and glory. AMEN.

XIV. *Meditation*

Idque notant criticis, medici evenisse diebus.

The physicians observe these accidents to have fallen upon the critical days.

I WOULD not make man worse than he is, nor his condition more miserable than it is. But could I though I would? As a man cannot flatter God nor overpraise him, so a man cannot injure man nor undervalue him. Thus much must necessarily be presented to his remembrance, that those false happinesses which he hath in this world have their times and their seasons and their critical days; and they are judged and denominated according to the times when they befall us. What poor elements are our happinesses made of if time, time which we can scarce consider to be anything, be an essential part of our happiness! All things are done in some place; but if we consider place to be no more but the next hollow superficies of the air, alas! how thin and fluid a thing is air, and how thin a film is a superficies, and a superficies of air! All things are done in time too; but if we consider time to be but the measure of motion, and howsoever it may seem to have three stations, past, present, and future, yet the first and last of these are not (one is not now, and the other is not yet) and that which you call *present* is not now the same that it was when you began to call it so in this line (before you sound that word *present* or that monosyllable *now*, the present and the now is past). If this imaginary half-nothing, time, be of the essence of our happinesses, how can they be thought durable? Time is not so;

how can they be thought to be? Time is not so; not so considered in any of the parts thereof. If we consider eternity, into that, time never entered; eternity is not an everlasting flux of time, but time is a short parenthesis in a long period; and eternity had been the same as it is, though time had never been. If we consider, not eternity, but perpetuity; not that which had no time to begin in, but which shall outlive time and be, when time shall be no more, what a minute is the life of the durablest creature compared to that! and what a minute is man's life in respect of the sun's or of a tree! and yet how little of our life is occasion, opportunity to receive good in; and how little of that occasion do we apprehend and lay hold of! How busy and perplexed a cobweb is the happiness of man here, that must be made up with a watchfulness to lay hold upon occasion, which is but a little piece of that which is nothing, time! And yet the best things are nothing without that. Honors, pleasures, possessions presented to us out of time, in our decrepit and distasted and unapprehensive age, lose their office and lose their name; they are not honors to us that shall never appear nor come abroad into the eyes of the people to receive honor from them who give it; nor pleasures to us who have lost our sense to taste them; nor possessions to us who are departing from the possession of them. Youth is their critical day; that judges them, that denominates them, that inanimates and informs them, and makes them honors and pleasures and possessions; and when they come in an unapprehensive age, they come as a cordial when the bell rings out, as a pardon when the head is off. We rejoice in the comfort of fire, but does any man cleave to it at midsummer? We are glad of the freshness and coolness of a vault, but does any man keep his Christmas there? or are the pleasures of the spring acceptable in autumn? If happiness be in the season or in the climate, how much happier then are birds than men, who can change the climate and accompany and enjoy the same season ever.

XVII. *Meditation*

Nunc lento sonitu dicunt, morieris

Now this bell tolling softly for another, says to me, Thou must die.

PERCHANCE he for whom this bell tolls may be so ill as that he knows not it tolls for him; and perchance I may think myself so much better than I am, as that they who are about me and see my state may have caused it to toll for me, and I know not that. The church is catholic, universal, so are all her actions; all that she does belongs to all. When she baptizes a child, that action concerns me; for that child is thereby connected to that body which is my head too, and ingrafted into that body whereof I am a member. And when she buries a man, that action concerns me: all mankind is of one author and is one volume; when one man dies, one chapter is not torn out of the book, but translated into a better language; and every chapter must be so translated. God employs several translators; some pieces are translated by age, some by sickness, some by war, some by justice; but God's hand is in every translation, and his hand shall bind up all our scattered leaves again for that library where every book shall lie open to one another. As therefore the bell that rings to a sermon calls not upon the preacher only, but upon the congregation to come, so this bell calls us all; but how much more me, who am brought so near the door by this sickness. There was a contention as far as a suit (in which piety and dignity, religion and estimation, were mingled) which of the religious orders should ring to prayers first in the morning; and it was determined that they should ring first that rose earliest. If we understand aright the dignity of this bell that tolls for our evening prayer, we would be glad to make it ours by rising early, in that application, that it might be ours as well as his whose indeed it is. The bell doth toll for him that thinks it doth; and though it intermit again, yet from that minute that that occasion wrought upon him, he is united to God. Who casts not up his eye to the sun when it rises? but who takes off his eye from a comet when that breaks out? Who bends not his ear to any bell which upon any occasion rings? but who can remove it from that bell which is passing a piece of himself out of this world? No man is an island, entire of itself; every man is a piece of the continent, a part of the main. If a clod be washed away by the sea, Europe is the less, as well as if a promontory were, as well as if a manor of thy friend's or of thine own were. Any man's death diminishes me because I am involved in mankind, and therefore never send to know for whom the bell tolls; it tolls for thee. Neither can we call this a begging of misery or a borrowing of misery, as though we were not miserable enough of ourselves but must fetch in more from the next house, in taking upon us the misery of our neighbors. Truly it were an excusable covetousness if we did; for affliction is a treasure, and scarce any man hath enough of it. No man hath affliction enough that is not ma- tured and ripened by it and made fit for God by that afflic- tion. If a man carry treasure in bullion, or in a wedge of gold, and have none coined into current money, his treasure will not defray him as he travels. Tribulation is treasure in the nature of it, but it is not current money in the use of it, except we get nearer and nearer our home, heaven, by it. Another man may be sick too, and sick to death, and this affliction may lie in his bowels as gold in a mine and be of no use to him; but this bell that tells me of his affliction digs out and applies that gold to me, if by this consideration of another's danger I take mine own into contemplation and so secure myself by making my recourse to my God, who is our only security.

SERMONS

Sermon LXXX

Preached at the Funerals of Sir William Cokayne
Knight, Alderman of London, *December* 12, 1626.[1]

Lord, if thou hadst been here, my brother had not died.
—JOHN 11:21.

GOD MADE the first marriage, and man made the first divorce;
God married the body and soul in the creation, and man
divorced the body and soul by death through sin, in his fall.
God doth not admit, not justify, not authorize such superinductions upon such divorces, as some have imagined: that
the soul departing from one body should become the soul
of another body, in a perpetual revolution and transmigration of souls through bodies, which hath been the giddiness
of some philosophers to think; or that the body of the dead
should become the body of an evil spirit, that the spirit
might at his will and to his purposes inform and inanimate
that dead body; God allows no such superinductions, no
such second marriages upon such divorces by death, no such
disposition of soul or body, after their dissolution by death.
But because God hath made the band of marriage indissoluble but by death, farther than man can die, this divorce
cannot fall upon man; as far as man is immortal, man is
a married man still, still in possession of a soul, and a body
too; and man is forever immortal in both: immortal in his
soul by preservation, and immortal in his body by reparation in the resurrection. For, though they be separated *à
thoro et mensa,* from bed and board, they are not divorced;
though the soul be at the table of the Lamb, in glory, and
the body but at the table of the serpent, in dust; though the
soul be *in lecto florido,* in that bed which is always green,

[1] Text: 1640, first edition. This sermon provides an excellent example of
division of a text, and of climax, of balance and parallelism, of quotation,
allusion, and figurative writing—all characteristic of Donne.

in an everlasting spring, in *Abraham's Bosom;* and the body but in that green bed, whose covering is but a yard and a half of turf, and a rug of grass, and the sheet but a winding sheet, yet they are not divorced: they shall return to one another again, in an inseparable re-union in the resurrection. To establish this assurance of a resurrection in us, God does sometimes in this life that which he hath promised for the next; that is, he gives a resurrection to life after a bodily death here. God hath made two testaments, two wills; and in both he hath declared his power, and his will, to give this new life after death, in this world. To the widow's son of Zarephtha,[2] he bequeaths new life; and to the Shunamite's son,[3] he gives the same legacy, in the Old Testament. In the New Testament, to the widow of Nain's son,[4] he bequeaths new life; and to Jairus's daughter [5] he gives the same legacy: and out of the surplusage of his inexhaustible estate, out of the overflowing of his power, he enables his executors to do as he did; for Peter gives Dorcas this resurrection, too.[6] Divers examples hath he given us of the resurrection of every particular man, in particular resurrections; such as we have named; and one of the general resurrection, in the resurrection of Christ himself; for, in him, we all rose; for he was all in all; *con-vivificavit,* says the apostle; and *considere nos fecit, God hath quickened us* [7] (all us; not only St. Paul and his Ephesians, but all) and *God hath raised us,* and *God hath made us to sit together in heavenly places, in Christ Jesus.* They that are not fallen yet by any actual sin (children newly baptized) are risen already in him; and they that are not dead yet, nay, not alive yet, not yet born, have a resurrection in him, who was not only the Lamb slain from the beginning, but from before all beginnings was risen, too; and all that shall ever have part in the second resurrection are risen with him from that time. Now, next to that great prophetical action, that type of the general resurrection

[2] I Kings 17. [3] II Kings 4. [4] Luke 7:11.
[5] Matt. 9:25. [6] Acts 9:40. [7] Ephesians 2:5.

in the resurrection of Christ, the most illustrious evidence of the resurrection of particular men is this resuscitation of Lazarus; whose sister Martha, directed by faith, and yet transported by passion, seeks to entender and mollify, and supple him to impressions of mercy and compassion, who was himself the mold in which all mercy was cast, nay, the substance of which all mercy does consist, Christ Jesus, with this imperfect piece of devotion, which hath a tincture of faith, but is deeper dyed in passion, *Lord, if thou hadst been here, my brother had not died.*

This text which you hear, Martha's single words, complicated with this text which you see, the dead body of this our brother, makes up between them this body of instruction for the soul: first, that there is nothing in this world perfect; and then, that such as it is, there is nothing constant, nothing permanent. We consider the first, that there is nothing perfect in the best things, in spiritual things; even Martha's devotion and faith hath imperfections in it; and we consider the other, that nothing is permanent in temporal things; riches prosperously multiplied, children honorably bestowed, additions of honor and titles fairly acquired, places of command and government justly received and duly executed; all testimonies, all evidences of worldly happiness, have a dissolution, a determination in the death of this, and of every such man: there is nothing, no spiritual thing, perfect in this world; nothing, no temporal thing, permanent and durable; and these two considerations shall be our two parts; and then, these the branches from these two roots; first, in the first we shall see in general the weakness of man's best actions; and secondly, more particularly, the weaknesses in Martha's actions; and yet, in a third place, the easiness, the propenseness, the largeness, of God's goodness toward us, in the acceptation of our imperfect sacrifices; for Christ does not refuse, nor discourage Martha, though her action have these imperfections; and in this largeness of his mercy, which is the end of all, we shall end this part. And in our

second, that as in spiritual things nothing is perfect, so in
temporal things nothing is permanent, we shall, by the same
three steps as in the former, look first upon the general consideration, the fluidness, the transitoriness of all such temporal things; and then, consider it more particularly, in
God's master-piece, amongst mortal things, the body of man,
that even that flows into putrefaction; and then lastly, return to that in which we determined the former part, the
largeness of God's goodness to us, in affording even to man's
body, so dissolved into putrefaction, an incorruptible and a
glorious state. So have you the frame set up, and the rooms
divided; the two parts, and the three branches of each; and
to the furnishing of them, with meditations fit for this occasion, we pass now.

In entering upon the first branch of our first part, that
in spiritual things nothing is perfect, we may well afford a
kind of spiritual nature to knowledge; and how imperfect
is all our knowledge! What one thing do we know perfectly?
Whether we consider arts, or sciences, the servant knows but
according to the proportion of his master's knowledge in that
art, and the scholar knows but according to the proportion
of his master's knowledge in that science; young men mend
not their sight by using old men's spectacles, and yet we look
upon nature, but with Aristotle's spectacles, and upon the
body of man, but with Galen's, and upon the frame of the
world, but with Ptolemy's spectacles. Almost all knowledge
is rather like a child that is embalmed to make a mummy than
that is nursed to make a man; rather conserved in the stature of the first age, than grown to be greater; and if there
be any addition to knowledge, it is rather a new knowledge,
than a greater knowledge; rather a singularity in a desire
of proposing something that was not known at all before,
than an improving, an advancing, a multiplying of former
inceptions; and by that means no knowledge comes to be
perfect. One philosopher thinks he is dived to the bottom,
when he says he knows nothing but this, that he knows noth-

ing; and yet another thinks that he hath expressed more
knowledge than he, in saying that he knows not so much as
that, that he knows nothing. St. Paul found that to be all
knowledge, to know Christ; and Mahomet thinks himself
wise therefore, because he knows not, acknowledges not
Christ, as St. Paul does. Though a man knew not that every
sin casts another shovel of brimstone upon him in hell, yet
if he knew that every riotous feast cuts off a year, and every
wanton night seven years of his seventy in this world, it
were some degree towards perfection in knowledge. He that
purchases a manor, will think to have an exact survey of the
land; but who thinks of taking so exact a survey of his conscience, how that money was got that purchased that manor?
We call that a man's means, which he hath; but that is
truly his means, what way he came by it. And yet how few
are there (when a state comes to any great proportion) that
know that; that know what they have, what they are worth?
We have seen great wills dilated into glorious uses and into
pious uses, and then too narrow an estate to reach to it;
and we have seen wills, where the testator thinks he hath
bequeathed all, and he hath not known half his own worth.
When thou knowest a wife, a son, a servant, a friend no
better, but that that wife betrays thy bed, and that son
thine estate, and that servant thy credit, and that friend thy
secret, what canst thou say thou knowest? But we must not
insist upon this consideration of knowledge; for, though
knowledge be of a spiritual nature, yet it is but as a terrestrial
spirit, conversant upon earth; spiritual things, of a more
rarefied nature than knowledge, even faith itself and all that
grows from that in us, falls within this rule which we have in
hand, that even in spiritual things nothing is perfect.

We consider this therefore *in credendis,* in things that we
are bound to believe, there works our faith; and then, *in
petendis,* in things that we are bound to pray for, there
works our hope; and lastly, *in agendis,* in things that we
are bound to do, and there works our charity; and there is

nothing in any of these three perfect. When you remember
who they were that made that prayer, *Domine adauge,* that
the apostles themselves prayed, that their faith might receive an increase, *Lord increase our faith,*[8] you must necessarily second that consideration with a confession that no
man's faith is perfect. When you hear Christ so often up-
braid, sometimes whole congregations, with that *Modicæ
fidei, O ye of little faith;*[9] and sometimes his disciples alone,
with the same reproach, *Modicæ fidei, O ye of little faith;*[10]
when you may be perplexed with the variety of opinions
amongst the ancient interpreters, whether Christ spoke but
to the incredulous Jews, or to his own disciples, when he
said, *O faithless and perverse generation, how long shall I
be with you? how long shall I suffer you?*[11] (for many interpreters go one way, and many the other); and when you
may be cleared without any color of perplexity, that to
whomsoever Christ spoke in that place, he spoke plainly
to his own disciples when he said, *Because of your unbelief
you cannot do this;*[12] in which disciples of his, he denies
also that there is such a proportion of faith as a grain of
mustard seed, can ye place a perfectness of faith in any?
When the apostle takes knowledge of the good estate and condition of the Thessalonians and gave God thanks for *their
works of faith,* for *their labors of love,* for their *patience of
hope, in our Lord Jesus Christ,*[13] does he conclude them to be
perfect? No, for after this he says, *Night and day we pray exceedingly, that we may perfect that which is lacking in your
faith.*[14] And after this he sees the fruit of those prayers, *We
are bound to thank God always, because your faith groweth
exceedingly;*[15] still, at the best, it is but a growing faith, and
it may be better. There are men that are said to be *rich in
faith;*[16] men that are come from the *weak and beggarly elements of Nature, or of the Law,*[17] to the knowledge of the

[8] Luke 17:5. [9] Matt. 6:30. [10] Matt. 8:26.
[11] Matt. 17:17. [12] Matt. 17:20. [13] I Thess. 1:2.
[14] I Thess. 3:10. [15] II Thess. 1:3. [16] James 2:5.
[17] Gal. 4:9.

precious and glorious gospel, and so are *rich in faith,* enriched, improved by faith. These are men that *abound in faith;* [18] that is, in comparison of the emptiness of other men, or of their own emptiness before they embraced the gospel, they abound now; but still it is, *As God hath given the measure of faith to every man;* [19] not as of his manna, a certain measure, and an equal measure, and a full measure to every man; no man hath such a measure of faith as that he needs no more, or that he may not lose at least some of that. When Christ speaks so doubtfully, *When the Son of man cometh, shall he find faith upon earth?* [20] Any faith in any man? If the Holy Ghost be come into this presence, into this congregation, does he find faith in any? A perfect faith he does not.

Deceive not yourselves then, with that new charm and flattery of the soul, that if once you can say to yourselves you have faith, you need no more, or that you shall always keep that alive; the apostle says, *All boasting,* that is, all confidence, *is excluded; By what law?* says he, *by the law of faith,*[21] not by faith, but by the law of faith; there is a law of faith; a rule that ordinates, and regulates our faith; by which law and rule the apostle calls upon us to examine ourselves whether we be in the faith or no; [22] not only by the internal motions and private inspirations of his blessed spirit, but by the law and the rule, which he hath delivered to us in the gospel. The king's pardon flows from his mere grace, and from his breast; but we must have the writing and the seal, that we may plead it: so does faith from God; but we must see it ourselves and show it to others, or else we do not observe the law of faith. *Abraham received the seal of the righteousness of faith,*[23] says the apostle; he had an outward testimony to proceed by; and then Abraham became an outward testimony and rule to the faithful, *Walk in the steps of the faith of Abraham,* says that apostle in that place; not a faith conceived only, but a faith which you saw, the faith of Abraham;

[18] II Cor. 8:7.   [19] Rom. 12:3.   [20] Luke 18:8.
[21] Rom. 3:27.   [22] II Cor. 13:5.   [23] Rom. 4:11.

for, so the apostle proposing to us the example of other men says, *Their faith follow you*,[24] not faith in general, but their faith. So that it is not enough to say, I feel the inspiration of the Spirit of God, he infuses faith, and faith infused cannot be withdrawn; but, as there is a law of faith, and a practice of faith, a rule of faith, and an example of faith, apply thyself to both, regulate thy faith by the rule, that is, the word, and by example, that is, believe those things which the saints of God have constantly and unanimely believed to be necessary to salvation: the word is the law and the rule, the church is the practice and the precedent that regulates thy faith; and if thou make imaginary revelations and inspirations thy law, or the practice of sectaries thy precedent, thou dost but call fancy and imagination by the name of reason and understanding, and opinion by the name of faith, and singularity and schism by the name of communion of saints. (The law of thy faith is that that that thou believest, be universal, catholic, believed by all; and then, that the application be particular, to believe that as Christ died sufficiently for all, so he died effectually for thee.) And of this effectual dying for thee, there arises an evidence from thyself, in thy conformity to him; thy conformity consists in this, that thou art willing to live according to his gospel, and ready to die for him, that died for thee. For till a man have resisted unto blood, he cannot know experimentally what degrees towards perfection his faith hath; and though he may conceive in himself a holy purpose to die for Christ, yet till he have died for Christ, or died in Christ, that is, as long as we are in this valley of temptations, there is nothing, no not in spiritual things, not in faith itself, perfect.

It is not *in credendis,* in our embracing the object of faith; we do not that perfectly; it is not *in petendis,* in our directing our prayers faithfully neither; we do not that: our faith is not perfect, nor our hope is not perfect; for, so argues the apostle, *Ye ask, and receive not, because ye ask amiss;* [25] you cannot

[24] Heb. 13:7.   [25] James 4:3.

hope constantly, because you do not pray aright: and to
make a prayer a right prayer, there go so many essential circumstances as that the best man may justly suspect his best
prayer: for since prayer must be of faith, prayer can be but
so perfect as the faith is perfect; and the imperfections of the
best faith we have seen. Christ hath given us but a short
prayer, and yet we are weary of that. Some of the old heretics
of the primitive church abridged that prayer, and some of our
later schismatics have annihilated, evacuated that prayer:
the Cathari [26] then left out that one petition, *dimitte nobis,
Forgive us our trespasses,* for they thought themselves so
pure as that they needed no forgiveness; and our new men
leave out the whole prayer, because the same spirit that spake
in Christ speaks in their extemporal prayers, and they can
pray as well as Christ could teach them. And (to leave those
whom we are bound to leave, those old heretics, those new
schismatics), which of us ever, ever says over that short
prayer with a deliberate understanding of every petition as
we pass, or without deviations, and extravagances of our
thoughts, in that half-minute of our devotion? We have not
leisure to speak of the abuse of prayer in the Roman Church,
where they will antedate and postdate their prayers: say tomorrow's prayers today, and today's prayers tomorrow, if
they have other uses and employments of the due time between; where they will trade, and make merchandise of
prayers by way of exchange, my man shall fast for me, and I
will pray for my man; or my attorney and proxy shall pray
for us both, at my charge; nay, where they will play for
prayers, and the loser must pray for both; to this there belongs but a holy scorn, and I would fain pass it over quickly.
But when we consider with a religious seriousness the manifold weaknesses of the strongest devotions in time of prayer,
it is a sad consideration. I throw myself down in my chamber,
and I call in, and invite God and his angels thither, and
when they are there, I neglect God and his angels for the

[26] Various sects which arose during the Middle Ages were called Cathari.

noise of a fly, for the rattling of a coach, for the whining of
a door; I talk on in the same posture of praying, eyes lifted
up, knees bowed down, as though I prayed to God; and if
God or his angels should ask me, when I thought last of God
in that prayer, I cannot tell: sometimes I find that I had
forgot what I was about; but when I began to forget it, I
cannot tell. A memory of yesterday's pleasures, a fear of
tomorrow's dangers, a straw under my knee, a noise in mine
ear, a light in mine eye, an anything, a nothing, a fancy, a
chimera in my brain, troubles me in my prayer. So certainly
is there nothing, nothing in spiritual things, perfect in this
world.

Not *in credendis,* in things that belong to faith; not *in
petendis,* in things that belong to hope; nor *in agendis,* in
things that belong to action, to works, to charity, there is
nothing perfect there neither. (I would be loath to say, that
every good work is a sin; that were to say, that every deformed or disordered man were a beast, or that every corrupt
meat were poison; it is not utterly so; not so altogether; but
it is so much towards it, as that there is no work of ours so
good, as that we can look for thanks at God's hand for that
work; no work, that hath not so much ill mingled with it
as that we need not cry God mercy for that work) There was
so much corruption in the getting, or so much vainglory in
the bestowing, as that no man builds an hospital, but his
soul lies, though not dead, yet lame in that hospital; no man
mends a highway, but he is, though not drowned, yet mired
in that way; no man relieves the poor, but he needs relief for
that relief. In all those works of charity, the world that hath
benefit by them is bound to confess and acknowledge a goodness, and to call them good works; but the man that does
them, and knows the weakness of them, knows they are not
good works. It is possible to art, to purge a peccant humor
out of a sick body; but not possible to raise a dead body to
life. God, out of my confession of the impurity of my best
actions, shall vouchsafe to take off his eyes from that im-

purity, as though there were none; but no spiritual thing in us, not faith, not hope, not charity, have any purity, any perfection in themselves; which is the general doctrine we proposed at first; and our next consideration is, how this weakness appears in the action, and in the words of Martha in our text, *Lord, if thou hadst been here, my brother had not died.*

Now lest we should attribute this weakness, only to weak persons upon whom we had a prejudice, to Martha alone, we note to you first, that her sister Mary, to whom in the whole story very much is ascribed, when she comes to Christ, comes also in the same voice of infirmity, *Lord, if thou hadst been here, my brother had not died.* No person so perfect, that hath not of these imperfections; both these holy sisters, howsoever there might be differences of degrees in their holiness, have imperfections in all three, in the consideration of their faith, and their hope, and their charity; though in all three they had also, and had both, good degrees toward perfection. Look first upon their faith; they both say, *Lord, if thou hadst been here, our brother had not died.* We cannot say so to any consultation, to any college of physicians; not to a Chiron, to an Æsculapius,[27] to a god of physic, could any man say, if you had been here, my friend had not died; though surely there be much assistance to be received from them, whom God hath endowed with knowledge to that purpose. And yet there was a weakness in these sisters in that they said but so, and no more to Christ. They thought Christ to be the best amongst good men, but yet they were not come to the knowledge that he was God. Martha says, *I know, that even now, whatsoever thou askest of God, God will give it thee;* but she does not know him to be God himself. I do not here institute a confutation, but here and everywhere I lament the growth and insinuation of that pestilent heresy of Socinianism; that Christ was a holy, a thrice-holy

[27] Chiron in Greek mythology was a centaur skilled in medicine and Æsculapius was the Roman god of medicine.

man, an unreproachable, an irreprehensible, an admirable,
and incomparable man; a man to whom he that should equal
any other man, were worse than a devil; a man worthy to
be called God in a far higher sense than any magistrate, any
king, any prophet; but yet he was no God, say they, no Son
of God; a redeemer by way of good example; but no redeemer by way of equivalent satisfaction, say those heretics.
St. Paul says, *He is an atheist, that is without Christ;* [28] and
he is as much an atheist still that pretends to receive Christ,
and not as God; for if the receiving of Christ must redeem
him from being an atheist, there can no other way be imagined, but by receiving him as God, for that only, and no
other good opinion of Christ, overcomes and removes his
atheism. After the last day, whatsoever is not heaven, is
hell; he that then shall be where the sun is now (if he be not
then in heaven) shall be as far from heaven as if he were
where the center of the earth is now; he that confesses not
all Christ, confesses no Christ. *Horribile dictu, dicam tamen,*
says St. Augustine in another case; there belongs a holy
trembling to the saying of it, yet I must say it, *If Christ were
not God, he was a devil that durst say he was God.* This then
was one weakness in these sisters' faith, that it carried them
not up to the consideration of Christ as God; and then another rose out of that, that they insisted so much, relied so
much, upon his corporal and personal presence, and promised
themselves more from that, than he had ever given them
ground for; which was that which Christ diverted Mary
from, when after his resurrection manifesting himself to
her, and she flying unto him with that impatient zeal, and
that impetuous devotion, *Rabboni, Master, my master,* Christ
said to her, *Touch me not, for I am not ascended to my
Father;* [29] that is, Dwell not upon this passionate consideration of my bodily, and personal presence, but send thy
thoughts, and thy reverence, and thy devotion, and thy holy
amorousness up, whither I am going, to the right hand of my

[28] Ephes. 2:12.   [29] John 20:16.

Father, and consider me, contemplate me there. St. Peter had another holy distemper of another kind, upon the personal presence of Christ; he was so astonished at his presence in the power of a miracle, that he fell down at his feet, and said, *Depart from me, for I am a sinful man, O Lord*.[30] These sisters longed for him, and St. Peter longed as much to be delivered of him, both out of weakness and error. So is it an error and a weakness to attribute too much, or too little to Christ's presence in his sacraments, or other ordinances. To imprison Christ in *opere operato,* to conclude him so, as that where that action is done, Christ must necessarily be, and necessarily work, this is to say weakly with these sisters, *Lord, if thou hadst been here, our brother had not died*. As long as we are present at thine ordinance, thou art present with us. But to banish Christ from those holy actions, and to say that he is no otherwise present, or works no otherwise in those actions, than in other times and places, this is to say with Peter, in his astonishment, *Exi à me Domine, O Lord depart from me;* it is enough that thy sacrament be a sign; I do not look that it should be a seal, or a conduit of grace; this is the danger, this is the distemper, to ascribe too much, or too little to God's visible ordinances and institutions, either to say with those holy sisters, *Lord, if thou hadst been here, our brother had not died;* if we have a sacrament, if we have a sermon, all is well, we have enough; or else with Peter, *Exi à me,* leave me to myself, to my private motions, to my bosom inspirations, and I need no church-work, no sermons, no sacraments, no such assistances.

So there was weakness in their faith; there was so too in their hope, in their confidence in Christ, and in their manner of expressing it. For they did not go to him when their brother was sick, but sent. Nicodemus came in person for his sick soul;[31] and the centurion in person, for his sick servant;[32]

---

[30] Luke 5:8.
[31] John 3:1.
[32] Matt. 8:8.

and Jairus in person, for his sick daughter; [33] and the woman
with the bloody issue in person, for her sick self. These sisters did but send, but piously, and reverently; their messenger was to say to Christ, not Lazarus, not *our brother,* but
he whom thou lovest, is sick; and they left this intimation
to work upon Christ; but that was not enough, we must
bring Christ and our necessities nearer together than so.
There is good instruction in the several expressings of Christ's
curings of Peter's mother in the Evangelists. St. Mark says,
They told him of her; [34] and St. Luke says, *They brought
him up to her;* and St. Matthew says, *He saw her, and took
her by the hand.* I must not wrap up all my necessities in
general terms in my prayers, but descend to particulars;
for this places my devotion upon particular considerations
of God, to consider him in every attribute, what God hath
done for me in power, what in wisdom, what in mercy; which
is a great assistance, and establishing, and propagation of
devotion. As it is a degree of unthankfulness, to thank God
too generally, and not to delight to insist upon the weight,
and measure, and proportion, and the goodness of every particular mercy; so is it an irreverent, and inconsiderate thing,
not to take my particular wants into my thoughts, and into
my prayers, that so I may take a holy knowledge that I
have nothing, nothing but from God, and by prayer. And as
God is an accessible God, as he is his own master of requests,
and is ever open to receive thy petitions, in how small a
matter soever: for is he an inexhaustible God, he can give
infinitely, and an indefatigable God, he cannot be pressed
too much. Therefore hath Christ given us a parable of getting
bread at midnight by importunity, [35] and not otherwise;
and another of a judge that heard the widow's cause by importunity, [36] and not otherwise; and not a parable, but a
history, and a history of his own, of a woman of Canaan, [37]
that overcame him in the behalf of her daughter, by im-

[33] Matt. 9:20.　　　[34] Mark 1:30.　　　[35] Luke 11:5.
[36] Luke 18:7.　　　[37] Matt. 15:21.

portunity; when, but by importunity, she could not get so much as an answer, as a denial at his hands. Pray personally, rely not upon dead nor living saints; thy mother the church prays for thee, but pray for thyself too; she can open her bosom and put the breast to thy mouth, but thou must draw and suck for thyself. Pray personally, and pray frequently; David had many stationary times of the day, and night too, to pray in. Pray frequently, and pray fervently; God took it not ill, at David's hands, to be awaked, and to be called up, as though he were asleep at our prayers, and to be called upon, *to pull his hand out of his bosom,* as though he were slack in relieving our necessities. This was a weakness in those sisters, that they solicited not Christ in person; still get as near God as you can; and that they declared not their case particularly; it is not enough to pray, nor to confess in general terms; and, that they pursued not their prayer earnestly, thoroughly; it is not enough to have prayed once; Christ does not only excuse, but enjoin importunity.

And then a weakness there was in their charity too, even towards their dead brother. To lament a dead friend is natural, and civil; and he is the deader of the two, the verier carcass, that does not so. But inordinate lamentation implies a suspicion of a worse state in him that is gone; and if I do believe him to be in heaven, deliberately, advisedly to wish him here that is in heaven is an uncharitable desire. For, for me to say, he is preferred by being where he is, but I were better if he were again where I am, were such an indisposition as if the prince's servant should be loath to see his master king because he should not hold the same place with him, being king, as he did when he was prince. Not to hope well of him that is gone is uncharitableness; and at the same time, when I believe him to be better, to wish him worse is uncharitableness too. And such weaknesses were in those holy and devout sisters of Lazarus; which establishes our conclusion, there is nothing in this world, no not in spiritual things, not in knowledge, not in faith, not in hope, not in charity, perfect. But yet, for all these imperfections, Christ doth not refuse, nor chide, but cherish their piety, which is also another circumstance in that part.

There is no form of building stronger than an arch, and yet an arch hath declinations, which even a flat roof hath not; the flat roof lies equal in all parts; the arch declines downwards in all parts, and yet the arch is a firm supporter. Our devotions do not the less bear us upright in the sight of God because they have some declinations toward natural affections; God doth easilier pardon some neglectings of his grace when it proceeds out of a tenderness, or may be excused out of good nature, than any presuming upon his grace. If a man do depart in some actions from an exact obedience of God's will, upon infirmity, or human affections, and not a contempt, God passes it over oftentimes. For, when our Saviour Christ says, *Be pure as your Father in heaven is pure,* that is a rule for our purity, but not a measure of our purity; it is that we should be pure so, not that we should be so pure as our Father in heaven. When we consider that weakness that went through the apostles, even to Christ's ascension, that they looked for a temporal kingdom, and for preferment in that; when we consider that weakness in the chief of them, St. Peter, at the Transfiguration, when, as the text says, *He knew not what to say;* [38] when we consider the weakness of his action, that for fear of death, he renounced the Lord of life, and denied his master; when in this very story, when Christ said that Lazarus was alseep, and that he would go to awaken him, they could understand it so impertinently as that Christ should go such a journey, to come to the waking of a man asleep at that time when he spoke; all these infirmities of theirs multiply this consolation upon us: that though God look upon the inscription, he looks upon the metal too; though he look that his image should be preserved in us, he looks in what earthen vessels this image is put, and put by his own hand; and though he

[38] Mark 9:6.

hate us in our rebellions, yet he pities us in our grievances; though he would have us better, he forsakes us not for every degree of illness. There are three great dangers in this consideration of perfectness and purity; first, to distrust of God's mercy, if thou find not this purity in thyself and this perfectness; and then to presume upon God, nay upon thine own right, in an overvaluing of thine own purity and perfectness; and again, to condemn others, whom thou wilt needs think less pure or perfect than thyself. Against this diffidence in God, to think ourselves so desperately impure as that God will not look upon us; and this presumption in God, to think ourselves so pure as that God is bound to look upon us; and this uncharitableness towards others, to think none pure at all that are not pure our way; Christ arms us by his example, he receives these sisters of Lazarus, and accomplishes as much as they desired, though there were weaknesses in their faith, in their hope, in their charity, expressed in that imperfect speech, *Lord, if thou hadst been here, my brother had not died:* for there is nothing, not in spiritual things perfect. This we have seen out of the text we have heard; and now out of the text which we see, we shall see the rest, that as in spiritual things, there is nothing perfect, so in temporal, there is nothing permanent.

I need not call in new philosophy,[39] that denies a settledness, an acquiescence in the very body of the earth, but makes the earth to move in that place, where we thought the sun had moved; I need not that help, that the earth itself is in motion, to prove this, that nothing upon earth is permanent; the assertion will stand of itself, till some man assign me some instance, something that a man can rely upon, and find permanent. Consider the greatest bodies upon earth, the monarchies, objects which one would think destiny might stand and stare at, but not shake; consider the smallest bodies

[39] Cf. "First Anniversary," ll. 205–8, "The new philosophy calls all in doubt."

upon earth, the hairs of our head, objects which one would think destiny would not observe, or could not discern; and yet, destiny (to speak to a natural man), and God (to speak to a Christian), is no more troubled to make a monarchy ruinous than to make a hair gray. Nay, nothing needs be done to either, by God or destiny; a monarchy will ruin, as a hair will grow gray, of itself. In the elements themselves, of which all sub-elementary things are composed, there is no acquiescence, but a vicissitudinary transmutation into one another; air condensed becomes water, a more solid body, and air rarefied becomes fire, a body more disputable, and inapparent. It is so in the conditions of men too: a merchant condensed, kneaded and packed up in a great estate, becomes a lord; and a merchant rarefied, blown up by a perfidious factor, or by a riotous son, evaporates into air, into nothing, and is not seen. And if there were anything permanent and durable in this world, yet we got nothing by it, because howsoever that might last in itself, yet we could not last to enjoy it; if our goods were not amongst movables, yet we ourselves are: if they could stay with us, yet we cannot stay with them; which is another consideration in this part.

The world is a great volume, and man the index of that book; even in the body of man you may turn to the whole world; this body is an illustration of all nature; God's recapitulation of all that he had said before, in his *fiat lux,* and *fiat firmamentum,* and in all the rest, said or done, in all the six days. Propose this body to thy consideration in the highest exaltation thereof, as it is the temple of the Holy Ghost: nay, not in a metaphor, or comparison of a temple, or any other similitudinary thing, but as it was really and truly the very body of God, in the person of Christ; and yet this body must wither, must decay, must languish, must perish. When Goliah had armed and fortified this body, and Jezebel had painted and perfumed this body, and Dives had pampered and larded this body, as God said to Ezekiel, when he brought him to the dry bones, *Fili hominis, son of man, dost thou think these bones can live?* [40] they said in their hearts to all the world, Can these bodies die? And they are dead. Jezebel's dust is not amber, nor Goliah's dust *terra sigillata,* medicinal; nor does the serpent, whose meat they are both, find any better relish in Dives' dust than in Lazarus's. But as in our former part, where our foundation was, that in nothing, no spiritual thing, there was any perfectness, which we illustrated in the weaknesses of knowledge, and faith, and hope, and charity, yet we concluded that for all those defects, God accepted those their religious services; so in this part, where our foundation is, that nothing in temporal things is permanent, as we have illustrated that, by the decay of that which is God's noblest piece in nature, the body of man; so we shall also conclude that, with this goodness of God, that for all this dissolution, and putrefaction, he affords this body a resurrection.

The Gentiles, and their poets, describe the sad state of death so, *nox una obeunda,* that it is one everlasting night; to them, a night; but to a Christian, it is *dies mortis,* and *dies resurrectionis,* the day of death and the day of resurrection; we die in the light, in the sight of God's presence, and we rise in the light, in the sight of his very essence. Nay, God's corrections, and judgments upon us in this life, are still expressed so, *dies visitationis,* still it is a day, though a day of visitation; and still we may discern God to be in the action. The Lord of Life was the first that named death; *Morte morieris,* says God, Thou shalt die the death.[41] I do the less fear, or abhor death, because I find it in his mouth; even a malediction hath a sweetness in his mouth; for there is a blessing wrapped up in it; a mercy in every correction, a resurrection upon every death. When Jezebel's beauty, exalted to that height which it had by art, or higher than that, to that height which it had in her own opinion, shall be infinitely multiplied upon every body; and as God shall know

[40] Ezekiel 37:3.   [41] Gen. 2:17.

no man from his own son, so as not to see the very righteousness of his own son upon that man; so the angels shall know
no man from Christ, so as not to desire to look upon that
man's face, because the most deformed wretch that is there,
shall have the very beauty of Christ himself; so shall Goliah's
armor, and Dives' fullness, be doubled and redoubled upon
us, and everything that we can call good shall first be infinitely exalted in the goodness, and then infinitely multiplied in the proportion, and again infinitely extended in the
duration. And since we are in an action of preparing this dead
brother of ours to that state (for the funeral is the Easter-
eve, the burial is the depositing of that man for the resurrection), as we have held you with doctrine of mortification,
by extending the text, from Martha to this occasion; so shall
we dismiss you with consolation by a like occasional inverting
the text, from passion in Martha's mouth, *Lord, if thou
hadst been here, my brother had not died,* to joy in ours,
Lord, because thou wast here, our brother is not dead.

The Lord was with him in all these steps; with him in his
life; with him in his death; he is with him in his funerals,
and he shall be with him in his resurrection; and therefore,
because the Lord was with him, our brother is not dead. He
was with him in the beginning of his life, in this manifestation, that though he were of parents of a good, of a great
estate, yet his possibility and his expectation from them did
not slacken his own industry; which is a canker that eats
into, nay, that hath eat up many a family in this city, that
relying wholly upon what the father hath done, the son does
nothing for himself. And truly, it falls out too often that he
that labors not for more, does not keep his own. God imprinted in him an industrious disposition, though such hopes
from such parents might have excused some slackness; and
God prospered his industry so, as that when his father's
estate came to a distribution by death, he needed it not.
God was with him, as with David in a dilation, and then
in a repletion; God enlarged him, and then he filled him;

he gave him a large and a comprehensive understanding,
and with it, a public heart; and such as perchance in his
way of education, and in our narrow and contracted times,
in which every man determines himself in himself and scarce
looks farther, it would be hard to find many examples of
such largeness. You have, I think, a phrase of driving a
trade; and you have, I know, a practice of driving away trade
by other use of money; and you have lost a man that drove a
great trade, the right way in making the best use of our
home commodity. To fetch in wine, and spice, and silk is
but a drawing of trade; the right driving of trade is to vent
our own outward; and yet, for the drawing in of that which
might justly seem most behooveful, that is, of arts and manufactures to be employed upon our own commodity within the
kingdom, he did his part diligently, at least, if not vehemently, if not passionately. This city is a great theater, and
he acted great and various parts in it; and all well; and when
he went higher (as he was often heard in parliaments, at
council tables, and in more private accesses to the late king
of ever-blessed memory), as, for that comprehension of those
businesses, which he pretended to understand, no man doubts,
for no man lacks arguments and evidences of his ability
therein, so for his manner of expressing his intentions, and
digesting and uttering his purposes, I have sometimes heard
the greatest master of language and judgment which these
times, or any other did, or do, or shall give (that good and
great king of ours), say of him, that he never heard any man
of his breeding handle businesses more rationally, more
pertinently, more elegantly, more persuasively; and when his
purpose was to do a grace to a preacher of very good abilities
and good note in his own chapel, I have heard him say that
his language, and accent, and manner of delivering himself
was like this man. This man hath God accompanied all his
life; and by performance thereof seems to have made that
covenant with him, which he made to Abraham, *Multiplicabo*

te vehementer, I will multiply thee exceedingly.[42] He multiplied his estate so, as was fit to endow many and great children; and he multiplied his children so, both in their number and in their quality, as they were fit to receive a great estate. God was with him all the way, in a pillar of fire, in the brightness of prosperity, and in the pillar of clouds too, in many dark and sad and heavy crosses; so great a ship required a great ballast, so many blessings, many crosses; and he had them and sailed on his course the steadier for them; the cloud as well as the fire was a pillar to him; his crosses as well as his blessings established his assurance in God; and so, in all the course of his life, *The Lord was here,* and therefore *our brother is not dead;* not dead in the evidences and testimonies of life, for he, whom the world hath just cause to celebrate, for things done when he was alive, is alive, is alive still in their celebration.

The Lord was here, that is, with him at his death too. He was served with the process here in the city, but his cause was heard in the country; here he sickened, there he languished, and died there. In his sickness there, those that assisted him are witnesses of his many expressings of a religious and a constant heart towards God, and of his pious joining with them, even in the holy declaration of kneeling, then, when they, in favor of his weakness, would dissuade him from kneeling. I must not defraud him of this testimony from myself, that into this place where we are now met, I have observed him to enter with much reverence, and compose himself in this place with much declaration of devotion. And truly it is that reverence, which those persons who are of the same rank that he was in the city, that reverence that they use in this place when they come hither is that that makes us, who have now the administration of this choir, glad that our predecessors but a very few years before our time (and not before all our times neither) admitted

[42] Gen. 17:2.

these honorable and worshipful persons of this city to sit in this choir, so as they do upon Sundays: the church receives an honor in it; but the honor is more in their reverence than in their presence, though in that too: and they receive an honor, and an ease in it; and therefore they do piously towards God, and prudently for themselves, and gratefully towards us, in giving us, by their reverent comportment here, so just occasion of continuing that honor and that ease to them here, which to less reverent and unrespective persons, we should be less willing to do. To return to him in his sickness; he had but one day's labor, and all the rest were Sabbaths, one day in his sickness he converted to business, thus: he called his family and friends together; thankfully he acknowledged God's manifold blessings, and his own sins as penitently; and then, to those who were to have the disposing of his estate, jointly with his children, he recommended his servants, and the poor, and the hospitals, and the prisons, which, according to his purpose, have been all taken into consideration; and after this (which was his valediction to the world), he seemed always loath to return to any worldly business. His last commandment to wife and children was Christ's last commandment to his spouse, the church, in the apostles, *To love one another*. He blessed them, and the estate devolved upon them, unto them: and by God's grace shall prove as true a prophet to them in that blessing as he was to himself when in entering his last bed, two days before his death, he said, *Help me off with my earthly habit, and let me go to my last bed*. Where, in the second night after, he said. *Little know ye what pain I feel this night, yet I know, I shall have joy in the morning:* and in that morning he died. The form in which he implored his Saviour, was evermore, towards his end, this, *Christ Jesus, which died on the cross, forgive me my sins; He have mercy upon me:* and his last and dying words were the repetition of the name of Jesus; and when he had not strength to utter that name distinctly and perfectly, they might hear it from within him, as from a man afar off; even then, when his hollow and remote naming of Jesus was rather a certifying of them that he was with his Jesus than a prayer that he might come to him. And so *The Lord was here,* here with him in his death; and because *the Lord was here, our brother is not dead;* not dead in the eyes and ears of God; for as the blood of Abel speaks yet, so doth the zeal of God's saints; and their last prayers (though we hear them not) God continues still; and they pray in heaven, as the martyrs under the altar, even till the resurrection.

He is with him now too; here in his funerals, burial, and Christian burial, and solemn burial are all evidences, and testimonies of God's presence. God forbid we should conclude, or argue an absence of God, from the want of solemn burial, or Christian burial, or any burial; but neither must we deny it to be an evidence of his favor and presence, where he is pleased to afford these. So God makes that the seal of all his blessings to Abraham, *That he should be buried in a good age;* [43] God established Jacob with that promise, *That his son Joseph should have care of his funerals;* [44] and Joseph does cause his servants, *the physicians, to embalm him, when he was dead.* [45] Of Christ it was prophesied, *That he should have a glorious burial;* [46] and therefore Christ interprets well that profuse and prodigal piety of the woman that poured out the ointment upon him, *That she did it to bury him;* [47] and so shall Joseph of Arimathea be ever celebrated, for his care in celebrating Christ's funerals. If we were to send a son, or a friend, to take possession of any place in court, or foreign parts, we would send him out in the best equipage: let us not grudge to set down our friends, in the ante-chamber of heaven, the grave, in as good manner, as without vaingloriousness, and wastefulness we may; and, in inclining them, to whom that care belongs, to express that care as they do this day, *The Lord is with him,* even in this

[43] Gen. 15:15.   [44] Gen. 46:4.   [45] Gen. 50:2.
[46] Isa. 11:10.   [47] Matt. 26:12.

funeral; and because *The Lord is here, our brother is not dead;* not dead in the memories and estimation of men.

And lastly, that we may have God present in all his manifestations, *He that was, and is, and is to come,* was with him, in his life and death, and is with him in this holy solemnity, and shall be with him again in the resurrection. God says to Jacob, *I will go down with thee into Egypt, and I will also surely bring thee up again.*[48] God goes down with a good man into the grave, and will surely bring him up again. When? The angel promised to return to Abraham and Sarah, for the assurance of the birth of Isaac, *according to the time of life;*[49] that is, in such time as by nature a woman may have a child. God will return to us in the grave, *according to the time of life;* that is, in such time as he, by his gracious decree, hath fixed for the resurrection. And in the meantime, no more than the Godhead departed from the dead body of our Saviour in the grave, doth his power and his presence depart from our dead bodies in that darkness; but that which Moses said to the whole congregation, I say to you all, both to you that hear me and to him that does not, *All ye that did cleave unto the Lord your God are alive, every one of you, this day;*[50] even he, whom we call dead, is alive this day. In the presence of God, we lay him down; in the power of God, he shall rise; in the person of Christ, he is risen already. And so into the same hands that have received his soul, we commend his body; beseeching his blessed Spirit, that as our charity inclines us to hope confidently of his good estate, our faith may assure us of the same happiness in our own behalf; and that for all our sakes, but especially for his own glory, he will be pleased to hasten the consummation of all, in that kingdom which that Son of God hath purchased for us, with the inestimable price of his incorruptible blood. AMEN.

[48] Gen. 46:4.   [49] Gen. 18:10.
[50] Deut. 4:4.

FROM *Sermon LXXII* [1]

THE WORLD is a sea in many respects and assimilations. It is a sea as it is subject to storms and tempests; every man (and every man is a world) [2] feels that. And then it is never the shallower for the calmness, the sea is as deep, there is as much water in the sea, in a calm as in a storm; we may be drowned in a calm and flattering fortune, in prosperity, as irrecoverably as in a wrought sea, in adversity; so the world is a sea. It is a sea as it is bottomless to any line which we can sound it with and endless to any discovery that we can make of it. The purposes of the world, the ways of the world, exceed our consideration; but yet we are sure the sea hath a bottom, and sure that it hath limits that it cannot overpass; the power of the greatest in the world, the life of the happiest in the world, cannot exceed those bounds which God hath placed for them; so the world is a sea. It is a sea as it hath ebbs and floods and no man knows the true reason of those floods and those ebbs. All men have changes and vicissitudes in their bodies (they fall sick) and in their estates (they grow poor) and in their minds (they become sad) at which changes (sickness, poverty, sadness) themselves wonder, and the cause is wrapped up in the purpose and judgment of God only, and hid even from them that have them; and so the world is a sea. It is a sea as the sea affords water enough for all the world to drink, but such water as will not quench the thirst. The world affords conveniences enow to satisfy nature, but these increase our thirst with drinking, and our desire grows and enlarges itself with our abundance, and though we sail in a full sea, yet we lack water; so the world is a sea. It is a sea if we consider the inhabitants. In the sea the greater fish devour

---

[1] Text: *LXXX Sermons,* 1640.

[2] This is Donne's favorite figure of the microcosm. In this old mediaeval concept the body of man was supposed to repeat in detail all the physical characteristics of the universe.

the less; and so do the men of this world, too. And as fish, when they mud themselves, have no hands to make themselves clean, but the current of the waters must work that; so have the men of this world no means to clean themselves from those sins which they have contracted in the world, of themselves, till a new flood, waters of repentance drawn up and sanctified by the Holy Ghost, work that blessed effect in them.

All these ways the world is a sea, but especially is it a sea in this respect, that the sea is no place of habitation, but a passage to our habitations. So the apostle expresses the world, "Here we have no continuing city, but we seek one to come"; [3] we seek it not here, but we seek it whilst we are here, else we never find it. Those are the two great works which we are to do in this world: first to know that this world is not our home, and then to provide us another home whilst we are in this world. Therefore the prophet says, "Arise and depart, for this is not your rest." [4] Worldly men that have no farther prospect promise themselves some rest in this world ("Soul, thou hast much goods laid up for many years, take thine ease, eat, drink, and be merry," says the rich man),[5] but this is not your rest; indeed no rest; at least not yours. You must depart, depart by death, before ye come to that rest; but then you must arise before you depart; for except ye have a resurrection to grace here before you depart, you shall have no resurrection to glory in the life to come when you are departed.

FROM *Sermon LXXVI* [6]

"It is a fearful thing to fall into the hands of the living God"; [7] but to fall out of the hands of the living God is a horror beyond our expression, beyond our imagination.

[3] Heb. 13:14. [4] Micah 2:10. [5] Luke 12:19.
[6] Text: 1640. [7] Heb. 10:31.

That God should let my soul fall out of his hand into a
'bottomless pit and roll an unremovable stone upon it and
leave it to that which it finds there (and it shall find that
there which it never imagined till it came thither) and never
think more of that soul, never have more to do with it; that
of that providence of God that studies the life of every weed
and worm and ant and spider and toad and viper there should
never, never any beam flow out upon me; that that God who
looked upon me when I was nothing and called me when I
was not, as though I had been, out of the womb and depth
of darkness, will not look upon me now, when though a miserable and banished and damned creature, yet I am his creature still and contribute something to his glory even in my
damnation; that that God who hath often looked upon me
in my foulest uncleanness and when I had shut out the eye
of day, the sun, and the eye of the night, the taper, and the
eyes of all the world with curtains and windows and doors
did yet see me and see me in mercy by making me see that
he saw me and sometimes brought me to a present remorse
and (for that time) to a forbearing of that sin, should so
turn himself from me to his glorious saints and angels as that
no saint nor angel nor Christ Jesus himself should ever pray
him to look towards me, never remember him that such a
soul there is; that that God who hath so often said to my
soul, *Quare morieris?* why wilt thou die? and so often sworn
to my soul, *Vivit Dominus,* as the Lord liveth, I would not
have thee die but live, will neither let me die nor let me live,
but die an everlasting life and live an everlasting death; that
that God who, when he could not get into me by standing
and knocking, by his ordinary means of entering, by his
word, his mercies, hath applied his judgments and hath
shaked the house, this body, with agues and palsies, and set
this house on fire with fevers and calentures, and frighted the
master of the house, my soul, with horrors and heavy apprehensions and so made an entrance into me; that that God
should frustrate all his own purposes and practices upon

me and leave me and cast me away as though I had cost him
nothing; that this God at last should let this soul go away
as a smoke, as a vapor, as a bubble; and that then this soul
cannot be a smoke, a vapor, nor a bubble but must lie in
darkness as long as the Lord of light is light itself, and never
spark of that light reach to my soul; what Tophet is not
paradise, what brimstone is not amber, what gnashing is not
a comfort, what gnawing of the worm is not a tickling, what
torment is not a marriage-bed to this damnation, to be se-
cluded eternally, eternally, eternally from the sight of God?

FROM *Sermon XLIX* [8]

A HOUSE is not clean, though all the dust be swept together,
if it lie still in a corner within doors; a conscience is not
clean by having recollected all her sins in the memory, for
they may fester there and gangrene even to desperation till
she have emptied them in the bottomless sea of the blood
of Christ Jesus and the mercy of his Father by this way of
confession. But a house is not clean neither, though the dust
be thrown out, if there hang cobwebs about the walls in
how dark corners soever. A conscience is not clean, though
the sins brought to our memory by this examination be cast
upon God's mercy and the merits of his Son by confession,
if there remain in me but a cobweb, a little, but a sinful delight in the memory of those sins which I had formerly committed. How many men sin over the sins of their youth again
in their age by a sinful delight in remembering those sins
and a sinful desire that their bodies were not past them! How
many men sin over some sins but imaginarily (and yet
damnably) a hundred times, which they never sinned actually at all, by filling their imaginations with such thoughts
as these, how would I be revenged of such an enemy, if I
were in such a place of authority! How easily could I over-

[8] Text: *Fifty Sermons*, 1649.

throw such a wasteful young man and compass his land, if I had but money to feed his humors! Those sins which we have never been able to do actually to the harm of others we do as hurtfully to our own souls by a sinful desire of them and a sinful delight in them.

FROM *Sermon XXV* [9]

Erimus sicut angeli, says Christ, "There we shall be as angels." The knowledge which I have by nature shall have no clouds; here it hath. That which I have by grace shall have no reluctation, no resistance; here it hath. That which I have by revelation shall have no suspicion, no jealousy; here it hath. Sometimes it is hard to distinguish between a respiration from God and a suggestion from the devil. There our curiosity shall have this noble satisfaction, we shall know how the angels know by knowing as they know. We shall not pass from author to author as in a grammar school, nor from art to art as in an university; but as that general which knighted his whole army, God shall create us all doctors in a minute. That great library, volumes of the books of creatures, shall be taken away, quite away; no more nature; those reverend manuscripts written with God's own hand, the Scriptures themselves, shall be taken away, quite away; no more preaching, no more reading of Scriptures. And that great school-mistress, experience and observation, shall be removed; no new thing to be done, and in an instant I shall know more than they all could reveal unto me. I shall know not only as I know already that a bee-hive, that an ant-hill, is the same book in *decimo sexto* as a kingdom is in folio, that a flower that lives but a day is an abridgement of that king that lives out his threescore-and-ten years; but I shall know too that all these ants and bees and flowers and kings and kingdoms, howsoever they

[9] Text: 1660.

may be examples and comparisons to one another, yet they are all as nothing, altogether nothing, less than nothing, infinitely less than nothing to that which shall then be the subject of my knowledge, for it is the knowledge of the glory of God.

Sermon XXVI: Death's Duel [1]

*And unto God the Lord belong the issues of death
(from death).*—PSALM 68 : 20

BUILDINGS stand by the benefit of their foundations that sustain them, support them; and of their buttresses that comprehend them, embrace them; and of their contignations that knit and unite them. The foundation suffers them not to sink; the buttresses suffer them not to swerve; the contignation and knitting suffer them not to cleave. The body of our building is in the former part of this verse; it is this: *He that is our God, is the God of salvation; ad salutes,* of salvations in the plural, so it is in the original; the God that gives us spiritual and temporal salvation too. But of this building, the foundation, the buttresses, the contignation are in this part of the verse which constitutes our text, and in the three diverse acceptations of the words amongst our expositors, *Unto God the Lord belong the issues of death.* For, first the foundation of this building (that our God is the God of all salvations) is laid in this, *That unto this God the Lord belong the issues of death;* that is, it is his power to give us an issue and deliverance, even then when we are brought to the jaws and teeth of death, and to the lips of that whirlpool, the grave; and so in this acceptation, this *exitus mortis,* this issue of death is *liberatio à morte,* a deliverance from death;

---

[1] Text: *X Sermons,* ed. by Geoffrey Keynes from *XXVI Sermons,* (1660), XXVI. London, Nonesuch Press, 1923, pp. 145–58. This sermon was called "the author's own funeral sermon." For the circumstances of its delivery see Walton's *Life of Donne.*

and this is the most obvious and most ordinary acceptation of these words, and that upon which our translation lays hold, *the issues from death*. And then, secondly, the buttresses, that comprehend and settle this building; that *He that is our God is the God of salvation* are thus raised; *Unto God the Lord belong the issues of death,* that is, the disposition and manner of our death, what kind of issue and transmigration we shall have out of this world, whether prepared or sudden, whether violent or natural, whether in our perfect senses, or shaked and disordered by sickness; there is no condemnation to be argued out of that, no judgment to be made upon that, for howsoever they die, *precious in his sight is the death of his saints,* and with him are the issues of death, the ways of our departing out of this life are in his hands; and so, in this sense of the words, this *exitus mortis,* the issue of death, is *liberatio in morte,* a deliverance in death; not that God will deliver us from dying but that he will have a care of us in the hour of death, of what kind soever our passage be; and in this sense, and acceptation of the words, the natural frame and contexture doth well and pregnantly administer unto us. And then lastly, the contignation and knitting of this building, that *He that is our God is the God of all salvation,* consists in this, *Unto this God the Lord belong the issues of death,* that is, that this God the Lord, having united and knit both natures in one, and being God, having also come into this world in our flesh, he could have no other means to save us, he could have no other issue out of this world, nor return to his former glory, but by death. And so in this sense, this *exitus mortis,* the issue of death, is *liberatio per mortem,* a deliverance by death, by the death of this God our Lord, Christ Jesus; and this is St. Augustine's acceptation of the words, and those many and great persons that have adhered to him. In all these three lines then, we shall look upon these words, first, as the God of power, the Almighty Father, rescues his servants from the jaws of death; and then, as the God of mercy, the

glorious Son, rescued us by taking upon himself the issue
of death; and then (between these two) as the God of comfort, the Holy Ghost, rescues us from all discomfort by his
blessed impressions beforehand, that what manner of death
soever be ordained for us, yet this *exitus mortis,* shall be
introitus in vitam, our issue in death, shall be an entrance
into everlasting life. And these three considerations, our
deliverance *à morte, in morte, per mortem,* from death, in
death, and by death, will abundantly do all the offices of
the foundation, of the buttresses, of the contignation of
this our building, that *He that is our God, is the God of all
salvation,* because *Unto this God the Lord belong the issues
of death.*

First, then, we consider this *exitus mortis,* to be *liberatio
à morte;* that with *God the Lord are the issues of death,*
and therefore in all our deaths, and deadly calamities of
this life we may justly hope of a good issue from him; and
all our periods and transitions in this life, are so many passages from death to death. Our very birth, and entrance into
this life, is *exitus à morte,* an issue from death; for in our
mother's womb we are dead, so as that we do not know we
live; not so much as we do in our sleep; neither is there in
the grave so close or so putrid a prison as the womb would
be to us if we stayed in it beyond our time, or died there
before our time. In the grave the worms do not kill us: we
breed and feed and then kill those worms which we ourselves
produced. In the womb the dead child kills the mother that
conceived it and is a murderer, nay, a parricide, even after
it is dead. And if we be not dead so in the womb, so as that
being dead, we kill her that gave us our first life, our life of
vegetation, yet we are dead so as David's idols are dead;
in the womb we have eyes and see not, ears and hear not.[2]
There in the womb we are fitted for works of darkness, all
the while deprived of light; and there, in the womb, we are
taught cruelty, by being fed with blood; and may be damned

[2] Psalm 115:6.

though we be never born. Of our very making in the womb, David says, *I am wonderfully and fearfully made,*[3] and *Such knowledge is too excellent for me,*[4] for *Even that is the Lord's doing, and it is wonderful in our eyes,*[5] *Ipse fecit nos, It is he that hath made us, and not we ourselves,*[6] no, nor our parents neither. *Thy hands have made me, and fashioned me round about,* says Job; [7] and (as the original word is) *Thou hast taken pains about me;* and yet says he, *Thou dost destroy me:* though I be the master-piece of the greatest Master (man is so), yet if thou do no more for me, if thou leave me where thou madest me, destruction will follow. The womb, which should be the house of life, becomes death itself, if God leave us there. That which God threatens so often, the shutting of the womb, is not so heavy nor so discomfortable a curse in the first as in the latter shutting; not in the shutting of barrenness, as in the shutting of weakness, when *children are come to the birth and there is not strength to bring forth.*[8] It is the exaltation of misery to fall from a near hope of happiness. And in that vehement imprecation the prophet expresses the height of God's anger, *Give them, O Lord, what wilt thou give them? Give them a miscarrying womb.*[9] Therefore as soon as we are men (that is, inanimated, quickened in the womb), though we cannot ourselves, our parents have reason to say in our behalf, *Wretched man that he is, who shall deliver him from this body of death?* [10] for, even the womb is the body of death, if there be no deliverer. It must be he that said to Jeremy, *Before I formed thee I knew thee, and before thou camest out of the womb I sanctified thee.*[11] We are not sure that there was no kind of ship nor boat to fish in, nor to pass by, till God prescribed Noah that absolute form of the ark; that word which the Holy Ghost by Moses uses for the ark is common to all kinds of boats, *thebah;* and is the same word that Moses uses for

---

[3] Psalm 139:14.   [4] Psalm 139:6.   [5] Psalm 118:23.
[6] Psalm 100:3.   [7] Job 10:8.   [8] Isa. 37:3.
[9] Hosea 9:14.   [10] Rom. 7:24.   [11] Jer. 1:5.

the boat that he was exposed in,[12] that his mother laid him
in an ark of bulrushes. But we are sure that Eve had no mid-
wife when she was delivered of Cain; therefore she might
well say, *Possedi virum à Domino*,[13] I have gotten a man
from the Lord, wholly entirely from the Lord: it is the Lord
that hath enabled me to conceive, the Lord hath infused a
quickening soul into that conception, the Lord hath brought
into the world that which himself hath quickened; without
all this might Eve say, my body had been but the house of
death, and *Domini Domini sunt exitus mortis,* To God the
Lord belong the issues of death.

But then this *exitus à morte,* is but *introitus in mortem;*
this issue, this deliverance from that death, the death of
the womb, is an entrance, a delivering over to another death,
the manifold deaths of this world. We have a winding-sheet
in our mother's womb, that grows with us from our conception, and we come into this world wound up in that winding-
sheet; for we come to seek a grave. And as prisoners, discharged of actions, may lie for fees, so when the womb hath
discharged us, yet we are bound to it by cords of flesh, by
such a string as that we cannot go thence, nor stay there.
We celebrate our own funeral with cries, even at our birth,
as though our three-score and ten years of life were spent
in our mother's labor, and our circle made up in the first
point thereof. We beg one baptism with another, a sacrament of tears; and we come into a world that lasts many
ages, but we last not. *In domo Patris* (says our blessed Saviour, speaking of heaven) *multæ mansiones*,[14] there are
many, and mansions, divers and durable; so that if a man
cannot possess a martyr's house (he hath shed no blood for
Christ), yet he may have a confessor's; he hath been ready
to glorify God, in the shedding of his blood. And if a woman
cannot possess a virgin's house (she hath embraced the holy
state of marriage), yet she may have a matron's house; she
hath brought forth, and brought up children in the fear of

[12] Exod. 2:3.   [13] Gen. 4:1.   [14] John 14:2.

God. *In domo Patris,* In my Father's house, in heaven, there
are many mansions, but here upon earth, *The Son of Man
hath not where to lay his head,*[15] says he himself. No: *terram dedit filiis hominum.* How then hath God given this
earth to the sons of men? He hath given them earth for their
materials, to be made of earth; and he hath given them
earth for their grave and sepulture, to return and resolve to
earth; but not for their possession. *Here we have no continuing city;* [16] nay, no cottage that continues; nay, no we, no
persons, no bodies that continue. Whatsoever moved St.
Hierome to call the journeys of the Israelites in the wilderness, mansions, the word (the word is *nasang*) signifies but
a journey, but a peregrination: even the Israel of God hath
no mansions, but journeys, pilgrimages in this life. By that
measure did Jacob measure his life to Pharaoh, *The days of
the years of my pilgrimage.*[17] And though the apostle would
not say, *morimur,* That whilst we are in the body we are
dead, yet he says *peregrinamur,* Whilst we are in the body,
we are but in a pilgrimage, and we are absent from the Lord.[18]
He might have said dead; for this whole world is but an universal churchyard, but one common grave; and the life and
motion that the greatest persons have in it, is but the shaking
of buried bodies in their graves by an earthquake. That which
we call life, is but *hebdomada mortium,* a week of deaths,
seven days, seven periods of our life spent dying; a dying
seven times over, and there is an end. Our birth dies in infancy, and our infancy dies in youth, and our youth and
the rest die in age; and age also dies, and determines all.
Nor do all these, youth out of infancy, or age out of youth,
arise so, as a phœnix out of the ashes of another phœnix
formerly dead, but as a wasp, or a serpent out of carrion,
or as a snake out of dung; our youth is worse than our infancy, and our age worse than our youth; our youth is hungry
and thirsty after those sins which our infancy knew not,

[15] Matt. 8:20.   [16] Heb. 13:14.   [17] Gen. 47:9.
[18] II Cor. 5:6.

and our age is sorry and angry that it cannot pursue those sins which our youth did. And besides, all the way so many deaths, that is, so many deadly calamities accompany every condition and every period of this life, as that death itself would be an ease to them that suffer them. Upon this sense does Job wish that God had not given him an issue from the first death, from the womb: *Wherefore hast thou brought me forth out of the womb? O that I had given up the ghost, and no eye had seen me; I should have been, as though I had not been.*[19]

And not only the impatient Israelites in their murmuring, (*Would to God we had died by the hand of the Lord in the land of Egypt*),[20] but Elijah himself, when he fled from Jezebel, and went for his life, as that text says, under the juniper tree, requested that he might die, and said, *It is enough, now O Lord take away my life.*[21] So Jonah testifies his impatience, nay, his anger towards God himself; *Now O Lord take I beseech thee my life from me, for it is better for me to die than to live.*[22] And when God asked him, *Dost thou well to be angry for this?* and after (about the gourd), *Dost thou well to be angry for that?* he replies, *I do well to be angry even unto death.* How much worse a death than death, is this life, which so good men would so often change for death! But if my case be St. Paul's case, *Quotidie morior,* That I die daily, that something heavier than death fall upon me every day; if my case be David's case, *Tota die mortificamur,* All the day long we are killed, that not only every day, but every hour of the day, something heavier than death falls upon me: though that be true of me, *Conceptus in peccatis,* I was shapen in iniquity, and in sin did my mother conceive me[23] (there I died one death), though that be true of me, *Natus filius iræ,* I was born, not only the child of sin, but the child of the wrath of God for sin, which is a heavier death, yet *Domini Domini sunt exitus mortis,* with God the Lord are

[19] Job 10:18, 19.   [20] Exod. 16:3.   [21] I Kings 19:4.
[22] Jonah 4:3.   [23] Psalm 51:5.

the issues of death; and after a Job, and a Joseph, and a Jeremy, and a Daniel, I cannot doubt of a deliverance; and if no other deliverance conduce more to his glory, and my good, yet *He hath the keys of death,*[24] and he can let me out at that door, that is, deliver me from the manifold deaths of this world, the *omni die,* and the *tota die,* the every day's death, and every hour's death, by that one death, the final dissolution of body and soul, the end of all.

But then, is that the end of all? Is that dissolution of body and soul, the last death that the body shall suffer? (for of spiritual deaths we speak not now); it is not. Though this be *exitus à morte,* it is *introitus in mortem;* though it be an issue from the manifold deaths of this world, yet it is an entrance into the death of corruption, and putrefaction, and vermiculation, and incineration, and dispersion, in, and from the grave, in which every dead man dies over again. It was a prerogative peculiar to Christ, not to die this death, not to see corruption. What gave him this privilege? Not Joseph's great proportions of gums and spices, that might have preserved his body from corruption and incineration, longer than he needed it, longer than three days; but yet would not have done it forever. What preserved him then? Did his exemption, and freedom from original sin, preserve him from this corruption and incineration? it is true, that original sin hath induced this corruption and incineration upon us. If we had not sinned in Adam, mortality had not put on immortality (as the apostle speaks),[25] nor corruption had not put on incorruption, but we had had our transmigration from this to the other world without any mortality, any corruption at all. But yet since Christ took sin upon him, so far as made him mortal, he had it so far too as might have made him see this corruption and incineration, though he had no original sin in himself. What preserved him then? Did the hypostatical union of both natures, God and man, preserve his flesh from this corruption, this incineration? 'Tis true

[24] Rev. 1:18.   [25] I Cor. 15:53.

that this was a most powerful embalming: to be embalmed
with the divine nature itself, to be embalmed with eternity,
was able to preserve him from corruption and incineration
forever: and he was embalmed so, embalmed with the divine
nature, even in his body, as well as in his soul; for the Godhead, the divine nature, did not depart, but remained still
united to his body in the grave. But yet for all this powerful
embalming, this hypostatical union of both natures, we see,
Christ did die; and for all this union which made him God
and man, he became no man, for the union of the body and
soul makes the man, and he, whose soul and body are separated by death (as long as that state lasts), is (properly)
no man. And therefore as in him the dissolution of body and
soul was no dissolution of the hypostatical union, so there
is nothing constrains us to say that though the flesh of Christ
had seen corruption and incineration in the grave, this had
been any dissolving of the hypostatical union; for the divine nature, the Godhead, might have remained with all
the elements and principles of Christ's body, as well as it
did with the two constitutive parts of his person, his body
and soul. This incorruption then was not in Joseph's gums
and spices; nor was it in Christ's innocency and exemption
from original sin; nor was it (that is, it is not necessary to
say it was) in the hypostatical union. But this incorruptible-
ness of his flesh is most conveniently placed in that, *non
dabis, Thou wilt not suffer thy Holy One to see corruption.*[26]
We look no further for causes or reasons in the mysteries of
our religion, but to the will and pleasure of God. Christ
himself limited his inquisition in that; *Ita est,* Even so,
Father, for it seemed good in thy sight.[27] Christ's body did
not see corruption, therefore, because God had decreed that
it should not. The humble soul (and only the humble soul
is the religious soul) rests himself upon God's purposes and
his decrees; but then, it is upon those purposes and decrees
of God, which he hath declared and manifested; not such as

---

[26] Psalm 16:10.   [27] Matt. 11:26.

are conceived and imagined in ourselves, though upon some probability, some verisimilitude. So, in our present case, Peter proceeded in his sermon at Jerusalem,[28] and so Paul in his at Antioch; they preached Christ to be risen without having seen corruption, not only because God hath decreed it, but because he had manifested that decree in his prophet. Therefore does St. Paul cite by special number the second Psalm for that decree, and therefore both St. Peter and St. Paul cite that place in the sixteenth Psalm; for when God declares his decree and purpose in the express word of his prophet, or when he declares it in the real execution of the decree, then he makes it ours, then he manifests it to us. And therefore as the mysteries of our religion are not the objects of our reason, but by faith we rest in God's decree and purpose (it is so, O God, because it is thy will it should be so), so God's decrees are ever to be considered in the manifestation thereof. All manifestation is either in the Word of God, or in the execution of the decree; and when these two concur and meet, it is the strongest demonstration that can be: when therefore I find those marks of adoption and spiritual filiation, which are delivered in the Word of God, to be upon me; when I find that real execution of his good purpose upon me, as that actually I do live under the obedience, and under the conditions which are evidences of adoption and spiritual filiation, then, and so long as I see these marks, and live so, I may safely comfort myself in a holy certitude, and a modest infallibility of my adoption. Christ determines himself in that, the purpose of God; because the purpose of God was manifest to him: St. Peter and St. Paul determine themselves in those two ways of knowing the purpose of God, the Word of God before the execution of the decree in the fulness of time. It was prophesied before, said they, and it is performed now: Christ is risen without seeing corruption.

Now this which is so singularly peculiar to him, that his

[28] Acts 2:31; 13:35.

flesh should not see corruption, at his second coming, his coming to judgment, shall be extended to all that are then alive, their flesh shall not see corruption; because (as the apostle says, and says as a secret, as a mystery, *Behold I show you a mystery*) *we shall not all sleep,* that is, not continue in the state of the dead in the grave, *but we shall all be changed.*[29] In an instant we shall have a dissolution, and in the same instant a redintegration, a recompacting of body and soul; and that shall be truly a death, and truly a resurrection, but no sleeping, no corruption. But for us, who die now, and sleep in the state of the dead, we must all pass this posthume death, this death after death, nay, this death after burial, this dissolution after dissolution, this death of corruption and putrefaction, or vermiculation and incineration, of dissolution and dispersion, in, and from the grave. When those bodies which have been the children of royal parents, and the parents of royal children, must say with Job, *To corruption, Thou art my father, and to the worm, Thou art my mother and my sister.*[30] Miserable riddle, when the same worm must be my mother, and my sister, and myself. Miserable incest, when I must be married to mine own mother and sister, beget and bear that worm, which is all that miserable penury, when my mouth shall be filled with dust, and the worm shall feed, and feed sweetly upon me.[31] When the ambitious man shall have no satisfaction if the poorest alive tread upon him, nor the poorest receive any contentment, in being made equal to princes, for they shall be equal but in dust. One dieth at his full strength, being wholly at ease, and in quiet, and another dies in bitterness of his soul, and never eats with pleasure; but they lie down alike in the dust, and the worm covers them.[32] The worm covers them in Job, and in Esai, it covers them, and is spread under them (the worm is spread under thee, and the worm covers thee). There is the mats and the carpet that lie under; and there is the state and

[29] I Cor. 15:51.   [30] Job 17:14.   [31] Job 24:20.
[32] Job 29:23, 25, 26.

canopy that hangs over the greatest of the sons of men. Even these bodies that were the temples of the Holy Ghost, come to this dilapidation, to ruin, to rubbish, to dust: even the Israel of the Lord, and Jacob himself had no other specification, no other denomination but that *vermis Jacob,* Thou worm of Jacob.[33] Truly, the consideration of this posthume death, this death after the burial, that after God with whom are the issues of death, hath delivered me from the death of the womb, by bringing me into the world, and from the manifold deaths of the world, by laying me in the grave, I must die again, in an incineration of this flesh, and in a dispersion of that dust; that all that monarch that spread over many nations alive, must in his dust lie in a corner of that sheet of lead, and there but so long as the lead will last: and that private and retired man, that thought himself his own forever, and never came forth, must in the dust of the grave be published, and (such are the revolutions of graves), be mingled in his dust, with the dust of every highway, and of every dunghill, and swallowed in every puddle and pond; this is the most inglorious and contemptible vilification, the most deadly and peremptory nullification of man, that we can consider. God seems to have carried the declaration of his power to a great height, when he sets the prophet Ezekiel in the valley of dry bones, and says, *Son of man, can these dry bones live?* [34] as though it had been impossible; and yet they did; the Lord laid sinews upon them, and flesh, and breathed into them, and they did live. But in that case there were bones to be seen; something visible, of which it might be said, Can this, this live? but in this death of incineration and dispersion of dust, we see nothing that we can call that man's. If we say, Can this dust live? perchance it cannot. It may be the mere dust of the earth which never did live, nor never shall; it may be the dust of that man's worms which did live, but shall no more; it may be the dust of another man that concerns not him of whom it is asked. The

---

[33] Isa. 14:11.   [34] Ezek. 37:1–10.

death of incineration and dispersion is to natural reason the
most irrevocable death of all; and yet *Domini Domini sunt
exitus mortis, Unto God the Lord belong the issues of death,*
and by recompacting this dust into the same body, and re-
animating the same body with the same soul, he shall in a
blessed and glorious resurrection give me such an issue from
this death as shall never pass into any other death, but establish me in a life that shall last as long as the Lord of life
himself. And so have you that that belongs to the first acceptation of these words (*Unto God the Lord belong the
issues of death*): that though from the womb to the grave,
and in the grave itself, we pass from death to death, yet, as
Daniel speaks, The Lord our God is able to deliver us, and
he will deliver us. And so we pass to our second accommodation of these words (*Unto God the Lord belong the issues
of death*), that it belongs to God, and not to man, to pass
a judgment upon us at our death, or to conclude a derelic-
tion on God's part, upon the manner thereof.

Those indications which physicians receive, and those
presagitions which they give for death or recovery in the
patient, they receive, and they give, out of the grounds and
rules of their art: but we have no such rule or art to ground
a presagition of spiritual death, and damnation upon any
such indication as we see in any dying man: we see often
enough to be sorry, but not to despair; for the mercies of
God work momentanely, in minutes: and many times insensibly to bystanders, or any other than the party departing, and we may be deceived both ways: we use to comfort
ourselves in the death of a friend, if it be testified that he
went away like a lamb, that is, with any reluctation; but
God knows, that may have been accompanied with a dangerous damp and stupefaction, and insensibility of his present
state. Our blessed Saviour admitted colluctations with death,
and a sadness even in his soul to death, and an agony even
to a bloody sweat in his body, and expostulations with God,
and exclamations upon the cross. He was a devout man, who

upon his death-bed, or death-turf (for he was a hermit) said, *Septuaginta annis Domino servivisti, et mori times?* Hast thou served a good Master three-score and ten years, and now art thou loath to go into his presence? yet Hilarion was loath. He was a devout man (a hermit) that said that day he died, *Cogitate hodie cœpisse servire Domino, et hodie finiturum,* Consider this to be the first day's service that ever thou didst thy Master, to glorify him in a Christianly and constant death; and if thy first day be thy last day too, how soon dost thou come to receive thy wages; yet Barlaam could have been content to have stayed longer for it; make no ill conclusion upon any man's loathness to die. And then, upon violent deaths inflicted, as upon malefactors, Christ hath forbidden us by his own death to make any ill conclusion; for his own death had those impressions in it; he was reputed, he was executed as a malefactor, and no doubt many of them that concurred to his death did believe him to be so. Of sudden deaths there are scarce examples to be found in Scriptures, upon good men; for death in battle cannot be called sudden death: but God governs not by examples, but by rules; and therefore make no ill conclusions upon sudden death; nor upon distempers neither, though perchance accompanied with some words of diffidence and distrust in the mercies of God. The tree lies as it falls, 'tis true; but yet it is not the last stroke that fells the tree; nor the last word, nor last gasp that qualifies the soul. Still pray we for a peaceable life, against violent deaths, and for time of repentance against sudden deaths, and for sober and moderate assurance against distempered and diffident deaths, but never make ill conclusion upon persons overtaken with such deaths. *Domini Domini sunt exitus mortis,* To God the Lord belong the issues of death, and he received Samson, who went out of this world in such a manner (consider it actively, consider it passively; in his own death, and in those whom he slew with himself) as was subject to interpretation hard enough; yet the Holy Ghost hath moved

St. Paul to celebrate Samson, in his great catalogue,[35] and so doth all the church. Our critical day is not the very day of our death, but the whole course of our life: I thank him that prays for me when my bell tolls; but I thank him much more that catechises me, or preaches to me, or instructs me how to live, *fac hoc et vives,* there's my security; the mouth of the Lord hath spoken it, *Do this and thou shalt live.* But though I do it yet I shall die too, die a bodily, a natural death; but God never mentions, never seems to consider that death, the bodily, the natural death. God doth not say, Live well, and thou shalt die well; well, that is an easy, a quiet death; but live well here, and thou shalt live well forever. As the first part of the sentence pieces well with the last, and never respects, never hearkens after the parenthesis that comes between, so doth a good life here, flow into an eternal life, without any consideration what manner of death we die. But whether the gate of my prison be opened with an oiled key (by a gentle and preparing sickness), or the gate be hewed down, by a violent death, or the gate be burnt down by a raging and frantic fever; a gate into heaven I shall have; for from the Lord is the course of my life, and with God the Lord are the issues of death; and farther we carry not this second acceptation of the words, as the issue of death is *liberatio in morte,* God's care that the soul be safe, what agony soever the body suffer in the hour of death; but pass to our third and last part; as this issue of death is *liberatio per mortem,* a deliverance by the death of another, by the death of Christ.

Sufferentiam Job audiistis et vidistis finem Domini, says St. James 5:11. You have heard of the patience of Job, says he; all this while, you have done that: for in every man, calamitous, miserable man, a Job speaks. *Now see the end of the Lord,* saith that apostle, which is not that end which he proposed to himself (salvation to us), nor the end which he proposes to us (conformity to him), but, *See the end of*

[35] Heb. 11.

the Lord, says he, the end that the Lord himself came to, death, and a painful, and a shameful death. But why did he die? and why die so? *Quia Domini Domini sunt exitus mortis* (as St. Augustine interpreting this text, answers that question),[36] because to this God our Lord belonged these issues of death; *Quid aperticus diceretur?* says he there; What can be more obvious, more manifest, than this sense of these words? In the former part of the verse it is said, *He that is our God is the God of salvation; Deus salvos faciendi,* so he reads it, The God that must save us; Who can that be, saith he, but Jesus? For therefore that name was given him, because he was to save us:[37] And to this Jesus, saith he, this Saviour, belong the issues of death, *Nec oportuit eum de hac vita alios exitus habere, quam mortis,* Being come into this life in our mortal nature, he could not go out of it any other way than by death. *Ideo dictum* (saith he), therefore it is said, *To God the Lord belong the issues of death; Ut ostenderetur moriendo nos salvos facturum,* to show that his way to save us was to die. And from this text doth St. Isidore prove that Christ was truly man (which as many sects of heretics denied, as that he was truly God) because to him, though he were *Dominus Dominus* (as the text doubles it), God the Lord, yet to him, to God the Lord belonged the issues of death. *Oportuit eum pati,* more cannot be said than Christ himself saith of himself, *These things Christ ought to suffer;*[38] he had no other way but by death. So then, this part of our sermon must necessarily be a passion sermon, since all his life was a continual passion, all our Lent may well be a continual Good Friday; Christ's painful life took off none of the pains of his death; he felt not the less then, for having felt so much before; nor will anything that shall be said before, lessen, but rather enlarge your devotion to that which shall be said of his passion, at the time of the due solemnization thereof. Christ bled not

[36] *De Civitate Dei,* lib. xvii; c. xviii.   [37] Matt. 1:21.
[38] Luke 24:26.

a drop the less at last, for having bled at his circumcision before, nor will you shed a tear the less then, if you shed some now. And therefore be now content to consider with me, how to this *God the Lord belonged the issues of death.*

That God the Lord, the Lord of life could die, is a strange contemplation; that the Red Sea could be dry; that the sun could stand still; that an oven could be seven times its heat and not burn; that lions could be hungry and not bite, is strange, miraculously strange; but super-miraculous, that God could die: but that God would die, is an exaltation of that; but, even of that also, it is a super-exaltation, that God should die, must die; and *non exitus* (saith Augustine) God the Lord had no issue but by death, and *oportuit pati* (saith Christ himself), all this Christ ought to suffer, was bound to suffer. *Deus ultionum Deus,* saith David, God is the God of revenges; he would not pass over the sin of man unrevenged, unpunished. But then, *Deus ultionum libere egit* (says that place), The God of revenges works freely; he punishes, he spares whom he will; and would he not spare himself? He would not. *Dilectio fortis mortus,*[39] Love is as strong as death; stronger; it drew in death, that naturally was not welcome. *Si possibile* (saith Christ), *If it be possible, let this cup pass,* when his love, expressed in a former decree with his Father, had made it impossible. Many waters quench not love;[40] Christ tried many; he was baptized out of his love, and his love determined not there; he wept over Jerusalem out of his love, and his love determined not there; he mingled blood with water in his agony, and that determined not his love; he wept pure blood, all his blood, at all his eyes, at all his pores; in his flagellations, and thorns; to the Lord our God belonged the issues of blood; and these expressed, but these did not quench his love.

He would not spare, he would not spare himself; there was nothing more free, more voluntary, more spontaneous

[39] Cant. 8:6.   [40] *Ibid.,* 7.

than the death of Christ; 'tis true, *libere egit,* he died voluntarily; but yet, when we consider the contract that had passed between his Father and him, there was an *oportuit,* a kind of necessity upon him: all this Christ ought to suffer; and when shall we date this obligation, this *oportuit,* this necessity, when shall we say it began? Certainly this decree by which Christ was to suffer all this was an eternal decree; and was there anything before that that was eternal? Infinite love, eternal love; be pleased to follow this home, and to consider it seriously, that what liberty soever we can conceive in Christ to die, or not to die, this necessity of dying, this decree is as eternal as that liberty; and yet how small a matter made he of this necessity, and this dying? His Father calls it but a bruise, and but a bruising of his heel (*The serpent shall bruise his heel*),[41] and yet that was, that the serpent should practice and compass his death. Himself calls it but a baptism, as though he were to be the better for it; *I have a baptism to be baptized with;*[42] and he was in pain till it was accomplished; and yet this baptism was his death. The Holy Ghost calls it joy (*For the joy which was set before him, he endured the cross*),[43] which was not a joy of his reward after his passion, but a joy that filled him even in the midst of those torments, and arose from them. When Christ calls his passion *calicem,* a cup, and no worse (*Can ye drink of my cup*),[44] he speaks not odiously, not with detestation of it; indeed it was a cup; *salus mundo,* a health to all the world; and *quid retribuem,* says David, *What shall I render unto the Lord?*[45] Answer you with David, *Accipiam calicem,* I will take the cup of salvation. Take that, that cup of salvation his passion, if not into your present imitation, yet into your present contemplation, and behold how that the Lord who was God yet could die, would die, must die for your salvation.

[41] Gen. 3:15. [42] Luke 12:50. [43] Heb. 12:2.

[44] Matt. 20:22. [45] Psalm 116:12.

That Moses and Elias talked with Christ in the transfiguration both St. Matthew and St. Mark [46] tell us; but what
they talked of, only St. Luke; [47]*Dicebant excessum ejus,* says
he; they talked of his decease, of his death, which was to
be accomplished at Jerusalem. The word is of his Exodus,
the very word of our text, *Exitus,* his issue by death. Moses,
who in his Exodus had prefigured this issue of our Lord, and
in passing Israel out of Egypt through the Red Sea, had
foretold in that actual prophecy Christ's passing of mankind through the sea of his blood, and Elias, whose Exodus,
and issue out of this world, was a figure of Christ's ascension, had no doubt a great satisfaction in talking with our
blessed Lord, *De excessu ejus,* of the full consummation of
all this in his death, which was to be accomplished at Jerusalem. Our meditation of his death should be more visceral,
and affect us more, because it is of a thing already done. The
ancient Romans had a certain tenderness, and detestation
of the name of death; they would not name death, no not
in their wills; there they would not say, *Si mori contingat,*
but *Si quid humanitas contingat,* not if or when I die, but
when the course of nature is accomplished upon me. To us,
that speak daily of the death of Christ (he was crucified,
dead, and buried), can the memory or the mention of our
death be irksome or bitter? There are in these latter times
amongst us, that name death freely enough, and the death
of God, but in blasphemous oaths and execrations. Miserable men, who shall therefore be said never to have named
Jesus, because they have named him too often; and therefore hear Jesus say, *Nescivi vos,* I never knew you; because
they made themselves too familiar with him. Moses and
Elias talked with Christ of his death only in a holy and joyful sense of the benefit which they and all the world were to
receive by it. Discourses of religion should not be out of
curiosity, but of edification. And then they talked with
Christ of his death, at that time when he was at the greatest

[46] Matt. 17:3; Mark 9:4.   [47] Luke 9:31.

height of glory that ever he admitted in this world; that is his transfiguration. And we are afraid to speak to the great men of this world of their death, but nourish in them a vain imagination of immortality and immutability. But *bonum est nobis esse hic* (as St. Peter said there), It is good to dwell here, in this consideration of his death, and therefore transfer we our tabernacle (our devotion), through some of these steps, which God the Lord made to his issue of death, that day.

Take in his whole day, from the hour that Christ ate the passover upon Thursday, to the hour in which he died the next day. Make this present day, that day in thy devotion, and consider what he did, and remember what you have done. Before he instituted and celebrated the sacrament (which was after the eating of the passover), he proceeded to the act of humility, to wash his disciples' feet; even Peter's, who for a while resisted him. In thy preparation to the holy and blessed sacrament, hast thou with a sincere humility sought a reconciliation with all the world, even with those who have been averse from it, and refused that reconciliation from thee? If so (and not else), thou hast spent that first part, of this his last day, in a conformity with him. After the sacrament, he spent the time till night in prayer, in preaching, in psalms. Hast thou considered that a worthy receiving of the sacrament consists in a continuation of holiness after, as well as in a preparation before? If so, thou hast therein also conformed thyself to him: so Christ spent his time till night. At night he went into the garden to pray, and he prayed *prolixus;* he spent much time in prayer.[48] How much? because it is literally expressed that he prayed there three several times, and that returning to his disciples after his first prayer, and finding them asleep, said, *Could ye not watch with me one hour?* [49] It is collected that he spent three hours in prayer. I dare scarce ask thee whither thou wentest, or how thou disposedst of thyself, when it

[48] Luke 22:40–45.   [49] Matt. 26:40.

grew dark and after, last night. If that time were spent in
a holy recommendation of thyself to God, and a submission
of thy will to his, then it was spent in conformity to him.
In that time, and in those prayers were his agony and bloody
sweat. I will hope that thou didst pray; but not every ordinary and customary prayer, but prayer actually accompanied with shedding of tears, and dispositively, in a readiness to shed blood for his glory in necessary cases, puts thee
into a conformity with him. About midnight he was taken
and bound with a kiss. Art thou not too conformable to
him in that? Is not that too literally, too exactly thy case?
At midnight to have been taken, and bound with a kiss?
From thence he was carried back to Jerusalem; first to An-
nas, then to Caiaphas, and (as late as it was) there he was examined, and buffeted, and delivered over to the custody of
those officers, from whom he received all those irrisions,
and violences, the covering of his face, the spitting upon his
face, the blasphemies of words, and the smartness of blows
which the gospel mentions. In which compass fell that *gal-
licinium,* that crowing of the cock, which called Peter to his
repentance. How thou passedst all that time last night, thou
knowest. If thou didst anything then that needed Peter's
tears, and hast not shed them, let me be thy cock: do it now;
now thy Master (in the unworthiest of his servants) looks
back upon thee, do it now. Betimes in the morning, as soon
as it was day, the Jews held a council in the high priest's
house, and agreed upon their evidence against him, and then
carried him to Pilate, who was to be his judge. Didst thou
accuse thyself when thou wakedst this morning, and wast
thou content to admit even false accusations, that is, rather
to suspect actions to have been sin which were not, than to
smother and justify such as were truly sins? Then thou
spentest that hour in conformity to him. Pilate found no evidence against him; and therefore to ease himself, and to
pass a compliment upon Herod, tetrarch of Galilee, who
was at that time at Jerusalem (because Christ being a Gal-

ilean, was of Herod's jurisdiction), Pilate sent him to Herod;
and rather as a madman than a malefactor, Herod remanded
him with scorns to Pilate to proceed against him; and this
was about eight of the clock. Hast thou been content to come
to this inquisition, this examination, this agitation, this criba-
tion, this pursuit of thy conscience, to sift it, to follow it
from the sins of thy youth to the present sins, from the sins
of thy bed to the sins of thy board, and from the substance
to the circumstance of thy sins? That is time spent like thy
Saviour's. Pilate would have saved Christ by using the privilege of the day in his behalf, because that day one prisoner
was to be delivered; but they chose Barabbas. He would
have saved him from death, by satisfying their fury, with
inflicting other torments upon him, scourging, and crown-
ing with thorns, and loading him with many scornful and
ignominious contumelies; but this redeemed him not; they
pressed a crucifying. Hast thou gone about to redeem thy
sin, by fasting, by alms, by disciplines, and mortifications,
in the way of satisfaction to the justice of God? That will
not serve, that's not the right way. We press an utter crucifying of that sin that governs thee, and that conforms thee
to Christ. Towards noon Pilate gave judgment; and they
made such haste to execution, as that by noon he was upon
the cross. There now hangs that sacred body upon the cross,
re-baptized in his own tears and sweat, and embalmed in
his own blood alive. There are those bowels of compassion,
which are so conspicuous, so manifested, as that you may
see them through his wounds. There those glorious eyes grew
faint in their light, so as the sun, ashamed to survive them,
departed with his light too. And there that Son of God, who
was never from us, and yet had now come a new way unto
us, in assuming our nature, delivers that soul which was
never out of his Father's hands, into his Father's hands, by
a new way, a voluntary emission thereof; for though to *this
God our Lord belong these issues of death,* so that, considered in his own contract, he must necessarily die; yet at

no breach, nor battery which they had made upon his sacred
body, issues his soul, but *emisit*, he gave up the ghost: and
as God breathed a soul into the first Adam, so this second
Adam breathed his soul into God, into the hands of God.
There we leave you in that blessed dependency, to hang upon
him, that hangs upon the cross. There bathe in his tears, there
suck at his wounds, and lie down in peace in his grave, till
he vouchsafe you a resurrection, and an ascension into that
kingdom which he hath purchased for you, with the inestimable price of his incorruptible blood. AMEN.

BEN JONSON was the posthumous son of a minister and
a high-spirited mother of Scots borderland ancestry. His
stepfather, who was a bricklayer, allowed Ben to attend
Westminster School, where the great Camden was headmaster, but later required his help in bricklaying and did
not send him to the university. It is said that Ben always
had a book in his pocket, and his great learning and literary
productions finally won degrees for him at both universities.

There are interesting stories of his joining the military
forces in Flanders. Between the return from Flanders and
his connection with Henslowe's company of players the
events of his life are vague. We know that he married, but
we do not know with any certainty how he maintained himself and his wife. There are references which indicate that
he was a strolling player; [1] but soon he was known as a
playwright and was creating the "humor comedy," a type
in which the characters are built around the dominance of
one of the four humors of medieval physiology. For many
years he was alternately in prison for "slanderous matter"
or at the height of success. He showed intense loyalty to his
fellow-playwrights, and yet a quarrel with Gabriel Spencer,
an actor in Henslowe's company, resulted in a duel in which
he killed Spencer. The story of the playwrights' presenting
each other on the stage in "The War of the Theatres" is a
familiar one; it was the severity of the ridicule of Jonson
which turned him from the writing of comedies to the production of his two Roman tragedies, *Sejanus* and *Catiline*.
A period of membership in the Catholic church and a five-
year estrangement from his wife are chapters in Jonson's
private life which need not concern us here.

With the accession of James I, Jonson became the writer
of masques for the court, and some of his most delicate

---

[1] *Ben Jonson. The Man and His Work,* ed. by C. H. Herford and Percy
Simpson (Oxford, 1925–   ). To be completed in 10 vols. Vol. I. 13–14.

poetry appears in these spectacular productions. Collaborating with him were the greatest men of the time in their respective fields: Inigo Jones as the architect for the staging, Alfonso Ferrabosco as musician, and Thomas Giles as master of the dance.

Jonson's vigorous personality and the perfection of his art attracted many young playwrights and poets into the "Tribe of Ben." They gathered around him in the famous Apollo Room of the Devil's Tavern, met together in the Mermaid, and held the "lyric feasts" sung by Herrick in many another tavern. The range of friendships was, however, broader than this happy group: Shakespeare acted in *Every Man in His Humour;* Sir Robert Cotton welcomed him to his great library; Lucy, Countess of Bedford, entertained him at Twickenham in that brilliant company which included Donne; Sir Robert Sidney made him at home at Penshurst; and William Drummond was his host at Hawthornden when Jonson made his remarkable walking tour to Scotland.

Many excellent critical comments made during the visit at Hawthornden were set down by Drummond, but Jonson's chief critical work is contained in his commonplace book, *Timber, or Discoveries.* The source of much of this material is in ancient authors, but Jonson's assimilation of it and the expression of his own critical principles hold an important place in the development of neo-classicism.

In the later years of James's reign Jonson was superseded at court, and with the king's death he was neglected. He was paralyzed in 1628 and almost forgotten by the public. It is true that he was made City Chronologer in that year and later was pensioned by Charles I, but his income was insufficient. He wrote more plays, but they were not the success that his earlier plays had been. Only the young satellites remained loyal then; but when he died, a throng followed him to a grave in Westminster Abbey.

TIMBER: OR DISCOVERIES MADE UPON MEN AND MATTER [1]

Natura non effœta

I CANNOT think Nature is so spent and decayed that she can bring forth nothing worth her former years. She is always the same, like herself; and when she collects her strength is abler still. Men are decayed, and studies; she is not.

Non nimium credendum antiquitati

I KNOW nothing can conduce more to letters than to examine the writings of the ancients and not to rest in their sole authority, or take all upon trust from them provided the plagues of judging and pronouncing against them be away: such as are envy, bitterness, precipitation, impudence, and scurrile scoffing. For to all the observations of the ancients we have our own experience, which if we will use and apply, we have better means to pronounce. It is true they opened the gates, and made the way that went before us, but as guides, not commanders: *non domini nostri, sed duces fuere.* Truth lies open to all; it is no man's several. *Patet omnibus veritas, nondum est occupata; multum ex illa etiam futuris relictum* [2] *est.*

Censura de Poetis

NOTHING in our age, I have observed, is more preposterous than the running judgments upon poetry and poets, when we shall hear those things commended and cried up for the best writings, which a man would scarce vouchsafe to wrap any wholesale drug in; he would never light his tobacco

---

1 Text: From *Works* (1640), Vol. II (1641).
2 First edition reads *relicta.*

with them. And those men almost named for miracles, who are yet so vile, that if a man should go about to examine and correct them, he must make all they have done but one blot. Their good is so entangled with their bad, as forcibly one must draw on the other's death with it. A sponge dipped in ink will do all.

> *Comitetur Punica librum*
> *Spongia.*

Et paulò post,

> *Non possunt . . . multæ, una litura potest.*[3]
> —Mart. 1.4. epig. 10.

Yet their vices have not hurt them; nay, a great many they have profited, for they have been loved for nothing else. And this false opinion grows strong against the best men, if once it take root with the ignorant. Cestius in his time was preferred to Cicero, so far as the ignorant durst. They learned him without book and had him often in their mouths; but a man cannot imagine that thing so foolish or rude but will find and enjoy an admirer; at least, a reader or spectator. The puppets are seen now in despight of the players. Heath's *Epigrams* and the Skuller's poems [4] have their applause. There are never wanting that dare prefer the worst preachers, the worst pleaders, the worst poets: not that the better have left to write or speak better, but that they that hear them judge worse; *non illi pejus dicunt, sed hi corruptius judicant.* Nay, if it were put to the question of the Water-rhymer's works against Spenser's, I doubt not but that they would find more suffrages, because the most favor common vices, out of a prerogative the vulgar have to lose their judgments and like that which is naught.

Poetry in this latter age hath proved but a mean mistress to such as have wholly addicted themselves to her, or given

---

[3] "Let a Punic sponge accompany the book." . . . "no number of erasures will amend it; one general wiping out is necessary."

[4] John Taylor, the Water-Poet, 1580–1653.

their names up to her family. They who have but saluted her on the by, and now and then tendered their visits, she hath done much for, and advanced in the way of their own professions (both the *law* and the *gospel*) beyond all they could have hoped or done for themselves, without her favor. Wherein she doth emulate the judicious but preposterous bounty of the time's grandees, who accumulate all they can upon the parasite or freshman in their friendship, but think an old client or honest servant bound by his place to write and starve.

Indeed, the multitude commend writers as they do fencers or wrestlers, who if they come in robustiously and put for it with a deal of violence are received for the braver fellows; when many times their own rudeness is a cause of their disgrace, and a slight touch of their adversary gives all that boisterous force the foil. But in these things the unskilful are naturally deceived, and judging wholly by the bulk, think rude things greater than polished, and scattered more numerous than composed. Nor think this only to be true in the sordid multitude but the neater sort of our gallants, for all are the multitude, only they differ in clothes, not in judgment or understanding.

De Shakespeare nostrat[i]

I REMEMBER the players have often mentioned it as an honor to Shakespeare, that in his writing (whatsoever he penned) he never blotted out a line. My answer hath been, "Would he had blotted a thousand!" which they thought a malevolent speech. I had not told posterity this, but for their ignorance, who chose that circumstance to commend their friend by wherein he most faulted; and to justify mine own candor (for I loved the man, and do honor his memory on this side idolatry as much as any). He was, indeed, honest, and of an open and free nature; had an excellent fancy, brave notions, and gentle expressions, wherein he flowed with that facility that sometime it was necessary he should be stopped. *Sufflaminandus erat,* as Augustus said of Haterius.[5] His wit was in his own power; would the rule of it had been so too. Many times he fell into those things could not escape laughter, as when he said in the person of Cæsar, one speaking to him, "Cæsar, thou dost me wrong." [6] He replied, "Cæsar did never wrong but with just cause"; and such like, which were ridiculous. But he redeemed his vices with his virtues. There was ever more in him to be praised than to be pardoned.

De stilo, et optimo scribendi genere

For a man to write well, there are required three necessaries: to read the best authors, observe the best speakers, and much exercise of his own style. In style, to consider what ought to be written, and after what manner, he must first think and excogitate his matter, then choose his words, and examine the weight of either. Then take care, in placing and ranking both matter and words, that the composition be comely; and to do this with diligence and often. No matter how slow the style be at first, so it be labored and accurate; seek the best, and be not glad of the forward conceits or first words that offer themselves to us, but judge of what we invent, and order what we approve. Repeat often what we have formerly written; which beside that it helps the consequence, and makes the juncture better, it quickens the heat of imagination, that often cools in the time of setting down, and gives it new strength, as if it grew lustier by the going back. As we see in the contention of leaping,

[5] See Seneca *Exc. Controv.* 4; *Proœm.* 7: "Tanta erat illi velocitas orationis, ut vitium fieret. Itaque divus Augustus optime dixit: 'Haterius noster sufflaminandus est!'" Haterius was a rhetorician at the time of Augustus.

[6] *Julius Cæsar,* III. 1.

they jump farthest that fetch their race largest; or, as in throwing a dart or javelin, we force back our arms to make our loose the stronger. Yet, if we have a fair gale of wind, I forbid not the steering out of our sail, so the favor of the gale deceive us not. For all that we invent doth please us in the conception or birth, else we would never set it down. But the safest is to return to our judgment, and handle over again those things the easiness of which might make them justly suspected. So did the best writers in their beginnings; they imposed upon themselves care and industry; they did nothing rashly: they obtained first to write well, and then custom made it easy and a habit. By little and little their matter showed itself to them more plentifully; their words answered, their composition followed; and all, as in a well-order family, presented itself in the place. So that the sum of all is: ready writing makes not good writing, but good writing brings on ready writing. Yet, when we think we have got the faculty, it is even then good to resist it, as to give a horse a check sometimes with a bit, which doth not so much stop his course as stir his mettle. Again, whither a man's genius is best able to reach, thither it should more and more contend, lift, and dilate itself; as men of low stature raise themselves on their toes, and so ofttimes get even, if not eminent. Besides, as it is fit for grown and able writers to stand of themselves, and work with their own strength, to trust and endeavor by their own faculties, so it is fit for the beginner and learner to study others and the best. For the mind and memory are more sharply exercised in comprehending another man's things than our own; and such as accustom themselves and are familiar with the best authors shall ever and anon find somewhat of them in themselves, and in the expression of their minds, even when they feel it not, be able to utter something like theirs, which hath an authority above their own. Nay, sometimes it is the reward of a man's study, the praise of quoting another man fitly; and though a man be more prone and able for one kind of writing than another, yet he must exercise all. For as in an instrument, so in style, there must be a harmony and consent of parts.

Præcipiendi modi

I TAKE this labor in teaching others, that they should not be always to be taught, and I would bring my precepts into practice, for rules are ever of less force and value than experiments. Yet with this purpose, rather to show the right way to those that come after than to detect any that have slipped before by error; and I hope it will be more profitable, for men do more willingly listen, and with more favor, to precept than reprehension. Among diverse opinions of an art, and most of them contrary in themselves, it is hard to make election; and therefore, though a man cannot invent new things after so many, he may do a welcome work yet to help posterity to judge rightly of the old. But arts and precepts avail nothing except nature be beneficial and aiding. And therefore these things are no more written to a dull disposition than rules of husbandry to a barren soil. No precepts will profit a fool, no more than beauty will the blind or music the deaf. As we should take care that our style in writing be neither dry nor empty, we should look again that it be not winding, or wanton with far-fetched descriptions: either is a vice. But that is worse which proceeds out of want than which riots out of plenty. The remedy of fruitfulness is easy, but no labor will help the contrary; I will like and praise some things in a young writer, which yet if he continue in, I cannot but justly hate him for the same. There is a time to be given all things for maturity, and that even your country husbandman can teach, who to a young plant will not put a pruning knife because it seems to fear the iron, as not able to admit the scar. No more would I tell a green writer all his faults, lest I should make

him grieve and faint and at last despair. For nothing doth
more hurt than to make him so afraid of all things as he
can endeavor nothing. Therefore youth ought to be instructed
betimes, and in the best things; for we hold those longest
we take soonest: as the first scent of a vessel lasts, and that
tinct the wool first receives. Therefore a master should
temper his own powers and descend to the others' infirmity.
If you pour a glut of water upon a bottle, it receives little
of it; but with a funnel and by degrees, you shall fill many
of them and spill little of your own: to their capacity they
will all receive and be full. And as it is fit to read the best
authors to youth first, so let them be of the openest and
clearest, as Livy before Sallust, Sidney before Donne: and
beware of letting them taste Gower or Chaucer at first, lest
falling too much in love with antiquity, and not apprehending the weight, they grow rough and barren in language only.
When their judgments are firm and out of danger, let them
read both the old and the new; but no less take heed that
their new flowers and sweetness do not as much corrupt as
the other's dryness and squalor, if they choose not carefully.
Spenser, in affecting the ancients, writ no language: yet
I would have him read for his matter, but as Virgil read
Ennius. The reading of Homer and Virgil is counseled by
Quintilian as the best way of informing youth and confirming man. For, besides that the mind is raised with the
height and sublimity of such a verse, it takes spirit from the
greatness of the matter and is tincted with the best things.
Tragic and lyric poetry is good too, and comic with the best,
if the manners of the reader be once in safety. In the Greek
poets, as also in Plautus, we shall see the economy and disposition of poems better observed than in Terence, and the
later, who thought the sole grace and virtue of their fable,
the sticking in of sentences, as ours do the forcing in of jests.

Falsa querela fugienda [7]

WE SHOULD not protect our sloth with the patronage of difficulty. It is a false quarrel against nature, that she helps understanding but in a few, when the most part of mankind are inclined by her thither if they would take the pains, no less than birds to fly, horses to run, etc.: which if they lose, it is through their own sluggishness, and by that means become her prodigies, not her children. I confess, nature in children is more patient of labor in study than in age; for the sense of the pain, the judgment of the labor is absent: they do not measure what they have done. And it is the thought and consideration that affects us more than the weariness itself. Plato was not content with the learning that Athens could give him, but sailed into Italy for Pythagoras's knowledge: and yet not thinking himself sufficiently informed, went into Egypt to the priests, and learned their mysteries. He labored; so must we. Many things may be learned together and performed in one point of time, as musicians exercise their memory, their voice, their fingers, and sometime their head and feet at once. And so a preacher in the invention of matter, election of words, composition of gesture, look, pronunciation, motion, useth all these faculties at once. And if we express this variety together, why should not divers studies, at divers hours delight, when the variety is able alone to refresh and repair us? As when a man is weary of writing, to read; and then again of reading, to write. Wherein howsoever we do many things, yet are we (in a sort) still fresh to what we begin: we are recreated with change, as the stomach is with meats. But some will say, this variety breeds confusion, and makes that either we lose all, or hold no more than the last. Why do we not then persuade husbandmen that they should not till the

---

[7] This is a Jonsonian version of Quintilian, *Institutes,* i, lines 1 and 2.

land, help it with marl, lime, and compost; plant hop-gardens, prune trees, look to bee-hives, rear sheep and other cattle, all at once? It is easier to do many things and continue, than to do one thing long.

Præcepta elementaria

It is not the passing through these learnings that hurts us, but the dwelling and sticking about them. To descend to those extreme anxieties and foolish cavils of grammarians is able to break a wit in pieces, being a work of manifold misery and vainness, to be *elementarii senes*. Yet even letters are, as it were, the bank of words and restore themselves to an author as the pawns of language: but talking and eloquence are not the same: to speak and to speak well are two things. A fool may talk, but a wise man speaks; and out of the observation, knowledge, and use of things, many writers perplex their readers and hearers with mere nonsense. Their writings need sunshine. Pure and neat language I love, yet plain and customary. A barbarous phrase hath often made me out of love with good sense, and doubtful writing hath racked me beyond my patience. The reason why a poet is said that he ought to have all knowledge, is that he should not be ignorant of the most, especially of those he will handle. And indeed when the attaining of them is possible, it were a sluggish and base thing to despair. For frequent imitation of anything becomes a habit quickly. If a man should prosecute as much as could be said of everything, his work could find no end.

Poeta

What is a poet?

A poet is that which by the Greeks is called κατ᾽ ἐξοχήν, ὁ Ποιητής, a maker, or a feigner: his art, an art of imitation

or feigning; expressing the life of a man in fit measure, numbers, and harmony, according to Aristotle: from the word
ποιεῖν, which signifies to make or feign. Hence he is called
a poet, not he which writeth in measure only, but that feign-
eth and formeth a fable, and writes things like the truth.
For the fable and fiction is (as it were) the form and soul
of any poetical work or poem.

Poema

What mean you by a poem?

A POEM is not alone any work, or composition of the
poet's in many or few verses; but even one alone verse sometimes makes a perfect poem. As when Æneas hangs up, and
consecrates the arms of Abas, with this inscription:

> *Æneas hac de Danais victoribus arma.*
> —Virgil, *Æneid.* III.

And calls it a poem or *carmen*. Such are those in Martial.

> *Omnia, Castor, emis : sic fiet, ut omnia vendas,*

and

> *Pauper videri Cinna vult, et est pauper.*
> —Martial. lib. 8. epig. 19.[8]

So were Horace his Odes called *Carmina;* his lyric, songs.
And Lucretius designs a whole book in his sixth:

> *Quod in primo quoque carmine claret.*

And anciently all the oracles were called *carmina;* or whatever sentence was expressed, were it much, or little, it was
called an epic, dramatic, lyric, elegiac, or epigrammatic poem.

---

[8] "You are now buying everything, Castor; the time will come when
you will sell everything"; "Cinna wishes to seem a pauper, and is a
pauper."

Poesis

But, how differs a poem from what we call poesy?

A POEM, as I have told you, is the work of a poet; the end and fruit of his labor and study. Poesy is his skill or craft of making: the very fiction itself, the reason, or form of the work. And these three voices differ as the thing done, the doing, and the doer; the thing feigned, the feigning, and the feigner; so the poem, the poesy, and the poet. Now, the poesy is the habit or the art; nay rather the queen of arts, which had her original from heaven, received thence from the Hebrews and had in prime estimation with the Greeks, transmitted to the Latins and all nations that possessed civility. The study of it (if we will trust Aristotle) offers to mankind a certain rule and pattern of living well and happily; disposing us to all civil offices of society. If we will believe Tully, it nourisheth and instructeth our youth, delights our age, adorns our prosperity, comforts our adversity, entertains us at home, keeps us company abroad, travels with us, watches, divides the times of our earnest and sports, shares in our country recesses and recreations; insomuch as the wisest and best learned have thought her the absolute mistress of manners and nearest of kin to virtue. And whereas they entitle philosophy to be a rigid and austere poesy, they have (on the contrary) styled poesy a dulcet and gentle philosophy, which leads on and guides us by the hand to action, with a ravishing delight and incredible sweetness. But before we handle the kinds of poems with their special differences, or make court to the art itself, as a mistress, I would lead you to the knowledge of our poet, by a perfect information what he is, or should be by nature, by exercise, by imitation, by study; and so bring him down through the disciplines of grammar, logic, rhetoric, and the ethics, adding somewhat out of all, peculiar to himself and worthy of your admiration or reception.

First, we require in our poet or maker (for that title our language affords him elegantly with the Greek) a goodness of natural wit. For whereas all other arts consist of doctrine and precepts, the poet must be able by nature and instinct to pour out the treasure of his mind, and as Seneca saith, *Aliquando secundum Anacreontem insanire jucundum esse:* by which he understands the poetical rapture. And according to that of Plato, *Frustra poeticas fores sui compos pulsavit.* And, of Aristotle, *Nullum magnum ingenium sine mixtura dementiæ fuit. Nec potest grande aliquid, et supra cæteros loqui, nisi mota mens.* Then it riseth higher, as by a divine instinct, when it contemns common and known conceptions. It utters somewhat above a mortal mouth. Then it gets aloft and flies away with his rider whither before it was doubtful to ascend. This the poets understood by their Helicon, Pegasus, or Parnassus; and this made Ovid to boast:

> *Est deus in nobis; agitante calescimus illo:*
> *Sedibus ætheris spiritus ille venit.*

And Lipsius to affirm, *Scio, poetam neminem præstantem fuisse, sine parte quadam uberiore divinæ auræ.* And hence it is that the coming up of good poets (for I mind not *mediocres* or *imos*) is so thin and rare among us. Every beggarly corporation affords the state a mayor or two bailiffs yearly; but *solus rex, aut poeta, non quotannis nascitur.*

To this perfection of nature in our poet we require exercise of those parts, and frequent. If his wit will not arrive suddenly at the dignity of the ancients, let him not yet fall out with it, quarrel, or be over hastily angry, offer to turn it away from study, in a humor; but come to it again upon better cogitation, try another time with labor. If then it succeed not, cast not away the quills yet, nor scratch the wainscot, beat not the poor desk, but bring all to the forge and file again; turn it anew. There is no statute law of the kingdom bids you be a poet against your will, or the first quarter; if it comes in a year or two, it is well. The common

rhymers pour forth verses, such as they are (*ex tempore*);
but there never comes from them one sense worth the life
of a day. A rhymer and a poet are two things. It is said of
the incomparable Virgil that he brought forth his verses
like a bear and after formed them with licking. Scaliger,
the father, writes it of him that he made a quantity of verses
in the morning which afore night he reduced to a less number. But that which Valerius Maximus hath left recorded
of Euripides, the tragic poet, his answer to Alcestis, another
poet, is as memorable as modest; who when it was told to
Alcestis that Euripides had in three days brought forth but
three verses, and those with some difficulty and throes, Alcestis, glorying he could with ease have sent forth a hundred
in the space, Euripides roundly replied, "Like enough. But
here is the difference: thy verses will not last those three
days, mine will to all time." Which was as to tell him he
could not write a verse. I have met many of these rattles
that made a noise and buzzed. They had their hum, and no
more. Indeed, things wrote with labor deserve to be so read,
and will last their age.

The third requisite in our poet or maker is imitation, to
be able to convert the substance or riches of another poet
to his own use. To make choice of one excellent man above
the rest, and so to follow him till he grow very he, or so
like him as the copy may be mistaken for the principal. Not
as a creature that swallows what it takes in, crude, raw, or
undigested; but that feeds with an appetite, and hath a
stomach to concoct, divide, and turn all into nourishment.
Not to imitate servilely, as Horace saith, and catch at vices
for virtue, but to draw forth out of the best and choicest
flowers, with the bee, and turn all into honey, work it into
one relish and savor; make our imitation sweet; observe
how the best writers have imitated and follow them: how
Virgil and Statius have imitated Homer; how Horace,
Archilochus; how Alcæus and the other lyrics; and so of
the rest.

But that which we especially require in him is an exactness of study and multiplicity of reading, which maketh a full man, not alone enabling him to know the history or argument of a poem and to report it, but so to master the matter and style as to show he knows how to handle, place, or dispose of either with elegancy when need shall be. And not think he can leap forth suddenly a poet by dreaming he hath been in Parnassus, or having washed his lips (as they say) in Helicon. There goes more to his making than so. For to nature, exercise, imitation, and study, art must be added to make all these perfect.[9] And though these challenge to themselves much in the making up of our maker, it is art only can lead him to perfection, and leave him there in possession, as planted by her hand. . . .

To judge of poets is only the faculty of poets; and not of all poets, but the best. *Nemo infælicius de poetis judicavit quam qui de poetis scripsit.* But some will say, critics are a kind of tinkers, that make more faults than they mend ordinarily. See their diseases and those of grammarians. It is true, many bodies are the worse for meddling with; and the multitude of physicians hath destroyed many sound patients with their wrong practice. But the office of a true critic or censor is, not to throw by a letter anywhere, or damn not an innocent syllable, but lay the words together and amend them; judge sincerely of the author and his matter, which is the sign of solid and perfect learning in a man. . . .

[9] In the margin is, *Ars Coron.* for *ars coronat opus.*

Robert Burton　　　　　1576-1639

The Anatomy of Melancholy is evidence that a single book may win immortality for a man. The popularity of the one book to which Burton devoted his life has continued for three centuries in spite of a title appealing mainly to the seventeenth century, when all kinds of anatomies were being printed. It had eight editions in the seventeenth century; six of these contain Burton's own additions and corrections, though the sixth is a posthumous edition. This popularity was renewed and increased in the nineteenth century, and among those delighting in the book were Coleridge, Lamb, and Byron.

The home of the Burtons was Lindley in Leicestershire, and there Robert Burton was born in 1576. He followed his brother at Brasenose College, Oxford, in 1593, was elected student of Christ Church College in 1599, where he held the position of tutor, and later he took orders. Although he did not gain church preferment, he became Vicar of St. Thomas' in Oxford and was presented with the living of Segrave by Lord Berkeley.

A bachelor "penned up most part in my study," Burton lived a life easily sketched as to its external events; but who can do justice to the life of thought and to the inimitable mind which is Burton's? He lived in an age when men wrote out of libraries, but no writer has put together more books to make one than did Burton. He says, "It is all mine, and none mine," and as a good scholar he gives most of his references. It matters little to our modern feebleness that he quotes in Latin and Greek, for he either translates or paraphrases, or recklessly heaps up synonyms which leave the reader without doubt of the meaning though often breathless from the scope of his own language.

When Burton chose his subject, he chose one that covered all fields and would be of universal appeal, for (as he

shows) melancholy springs not only from the follies of mankind but also from its virtues; and one section bears the
heading "God a Cause." Furthermore, many books had been
written on the subject, and he had read them; and he was
also acquainted with melancholy from personal experience.
He was from a family in which this strain recurred, and his
procedure was that of modern psychiatry, for he says, "I
writ of melancholy by being busy to avoid melancholy."

Burton found his model in Democritus and wrote under
the name of Democritus Junior; yet in his analysis of the
discrepancy between pretense and reality he might have been
writing for the present century: "so many Christians, yet
so few imitators of Christ, so much science, so little conscience."

The spatial limitations of Burton's experience were of
little significance. Though he did not visit the continent as
did most of the learned men of the seventeenth century, he
had his "cards and maps" and was acquainted with the world.
For friends he had the wide range provided by a university
town, from Chancellor to admiring student. For amusement
he watched the crowds or listened to the bargemen swear at
their work on the river. For constant companions he had
his books and could say as Coleridge did, "Mine the converse
deep to hold with all the glorious sons of old."

THE ANATOMY OF MELANCHOLY [1]

FROM *Democritus Junior to the Reader*

. . . WHEN HIPPOCRATES was now come to Abdera,[2] the people of the city came flocking about him, some weeping, some entreating of him that he would do his best. After some little repast, he went to see Democritus, the people following him, whom he found (as before) in his garden in the suburbs all alone, "sitting upon a stone under a plane tree, without hose or shoes, with a book on his knees, cutting up several beasts, and busy at his study." The multitude stood gazing round about to see the congress. Hippocrates, after a little pause, saluted him by his name, whom he resaluted, ashamed almost that he could not call him likewise by his, or that he had forgot it. Hippocrates demanded of him what he was doing: he told him that he was "busy in cutting up several beasts, to find out the cause of madness and melancholy." Hippocrates commended his work, admiring his happiness and leisure. And why, quoth Democritus, have not you that leisure? Because, replied Hippocrates, domestical affairs hinder, necessary to be done for ourselves, neighbors, friends; expenses, diseases, frailties and mortalities which happen; wife, children, servants, and such businesses which deprive us of our time. At this speech Democritus profusely laughed (his friends and the people standing by, weeping in the meantime, and lamenting his madness). Hippocrates asked the reason why he laughed. He told him at the vanities and the fopperies of the time: to see men so empty of all virtuous actions, to hunt so far after gold, having no end of ambition; to take such infinite pains for a little glory, and to be favored of men; to make such deep mines into the earth for gold, and many times to find noth-

---

[1] Text: 1651, sixth edition. This is the text which contains Burton's final additions and revisions.

[2] The account is given by Hippocrates in his "Epistle to Damogetus."

ing, with loss of their lives and fortunes. Some to love dogs, others horses, some to desire to be obeyed in many provinces, and yet themselves will know no obedience. Some to love their wives dearly at first, and after a while to forsake and hate them; begetting children, with much care and cost for their education, yet when they grow to man's estate, to despise, neglect, and leave them naked to the world's mercy. Do not these behaviors express their intolerable folly? When men live in peace, they covet war, detesting quietness, deposing kings, and advancing others in their stead, murdering some men to beget children of their wives. How many strange humors are in men! When they are poor and needy, they seek riches; and when they have them, they do not enjoy them, but hide them under ground, or else wastefully spend them. O wise Hippocrates, I laugh at such things being done, but much more when no good comes of them, and when they are done to so ill purpose. There is no truth or justice found amongst them, for they daily plead one against another, the son against the father and the mother, brother against brother, kindred and friends of the same quality; and all this for riches, whereof after death they cannot be possessors. And yet notwithstanding they will defame and kill one another, commit all unlawful actions, contemning God and men, friends and country. They make great account of many senseless things, esteeming them as a great part of their treasure, statues, pictures, and such like movables, dear bought, and so cunningly wrought as nothing but speech wanteth in them, and yet they hate living persons speaking to them. Others affect difficult things; if they dwell on firm land, they will remove to an island, and thence to land again, being no way constant to their desires. They commend courage and strength in wars, and let themselves be conquered by lust and avarice; they are, in brief, as disordered in their minds, as Thersites was in his body.[3] And now, methinks, O most worthy Hippocrates, you should not reprehend my

---

[3] Thersites was squint-eyed, lame, and a hunchback. *Iliad,* II. 212.

laughing, perceiving so many fooleries in men; for no man
will mock his own folly, but that which he seeth in a second,
and so they justly mock one another. The drunkard calls
him a glutton whom he knows to be sober. Many men love
the sea, others husbandry; briefly, they cannot agree in
their own trades and professions, much less in their lives
and actions.

When Hippocrates heard these words so readily uttered,
without premeditation, to declare the world's vanity, full of
ridiculous contrariety, he made answer that necessity compelled men to many such actions, and divers wills ensuing
from divine permission, that we might not be idle, being
nothing is so odious to them as sloth and negligence. Besides, men cannot foresee future events, in this uncertainty
of human affairs; they would not so marry if they could fore-
tell the causes of their dislike and separation; or parents,
if they knew the hour of their children's death, so tenderly
provide for them; or an husbandman sow, if he thought
there would be no increase; or a merchant adventure to sea,
if he foresaw shipwreck; or be a magistrate, if presently
to be deposed. Alas, worthy Democritus, every man hopes
the best, and to that end he doth it, and therefore no such
cause, or ridiculous occasion of laughter.

Democritus hearing this poor excuse laughed again aloud,
perceiving he wholly mistook him, and did not well understand what he had said concerning perturbations and tranquillity of the mind. Insomuch that if men would govern
their actions by discretion and providence, they would not
declare themselves fools as now they do, and he should have
no cause of laughter; but (quoth he) they swell in this life
as if they were immortal and demigods, for want of understanding. It were enough to make them wise if they would
but consider the mutability of this world and how it wheels
about, nothing being firm and sure. He that is now above,
tomorrow is beneath; he that sate on this side today, tomorrow is hurled on the other: and not considering these

matters, they fall into many inconveniences and troubles,
coveting things of no profit, and thirsting after them, tumbling headlong into many calamities. So that if men would
attempt no more than what they can bear, they should lead
contented lives, and learning to know themselves, would
limit their ambition; they would perceive then that nature
hath enough without seeking such superfluities and unprofitable things, which bring nothing with them but grief and
molestation. As a fat body is more subject to diseases, so
are rich men to absurdities and fooleries, to many casualties and cross inconveniences. There are many that take no
heed what happeneth to others by bad conversation, and
therefore overthrow themselves in the same manner through
their own fault, not foreseeing dangers manifest. These are
things (O more than mad, quoth he) that give me matter of
laughter, by suffering the pains of your impieties, as your
avarice, envy, malice, enormous villainies, mutinies, unsati-
able desires, conspiracies, and other incurable vices; besides
your dissimulation and hypocrisy, bearing deadly hatred
one to the other, and yet shadowing it with a good face, flying out into all filthy lusts and transgressions of all laws,
both of nature and civility. Many things which they have
left off, after a while they fall to again, husbandry, navigation; and leave again, fickle and inconstant as they are. When
they are young, they would be old; and old, young. Princes
commend a private life; private men itch after honor: a magistrate commends a quiet life; a quiet man would be in his
office, and obeyed as he is: and what is the cause of all this,
but that they know not themselves? Some delight to destroy,
one to build, another to spoil one country to enrich another
and himself. In all these things they are like children, in
whom is no judgment or counsel, and resemble beasts, saving that beasts are better than they, as being contented with
nature. When shall you see a lion hide gold in the ground,
or a bull contend for better pasture? When a boar is thirsty,
he drinks what will serve him, and no more; and when his

belly is full, he ceaseth to eat: but men are immoderate in both; as in lust, they covet carnal copulation at set times; men always, ruinating thereby the health of their bodies. And doth it not deserve laughter to see an amorous fool torment himself for a wench; weep, howl for a misshapen slut, a dowdy sometimes, that might have his choice of the finest beauties? Is there any remedy for this in physic? I do not anatomize and cut up these poor beasts to see these distempers, vanities, and follies; yet such proof were better made on man's body, if my kind nature would endure it; who from the hour of his birth is most miserable, weak and sickly: when he sucks, he is guided by others; when he is grown great, practiceth unhappiness and is sturdy; and when old, a child again, and repenteth him of his life past. And here being interrupted by one that brought books, he fell to it again, that all were mad, careless, stupid. To prove my former speeches, look into courts or private houses. Judges give judgment according to their own advantage, doing manifest wrong to poor innocents to please others. Notaries alter sentences, and for money lose their deeds. Some make false moneys; others counterfeit false weights. Some abuse their parents, yea corrupt their own sisters; others make long libels and pasquils, defaming men of good life, and extol such as are lewd and vicious. Some rob one, some another: magistrates make laws against thieves and are the veriest thieves themselves. Some kill themselves, others despair, not obtaining their desires. Some dance, sing, laugh, feast and banquet, whilst others sigh, languish, mourn, and lament, having neither meat, drink, nor clothes. Some prank up their bodies, and have their minds full of execrable vices. Some trot about to bear false witness and say anything for money; and though judges know of it, yet for a bribe they wink at it and suffer false contracts to prevail against equity. Women are all day a-dressing to pleasure other men abroad, and go like sluts at home, not caring to please their own husbands whom they should. Seeing men are so fickle, so sottish, so intemperate, why should not I laugh at those to whom folly seems wisdom, will not be cured, and perceive it not?

It grew late: Hippocrates left him; and no sooner was he come away, but all the citizens came about flocking, to know how he liked him. He told them in brief that notwithstanding those small neglects of his attire, body, diet, the world had not a wiser, a more learned, a more honest man, and they were much deceived to say that he was mad.

Thus Democritus esteemed of the world in his time, and this was the cause of his laughter: and good cause he had.

> *Olim jure quidem, nunc plus Democrite ride;*
> *Quin rides? vita hæc nunc mage ridicula est.*

Never so much cause of laughter as now, never so many fools and madmen. 'Tis not one Democritus will serve turn to laugh in these days; we have now need of a "Democritus to laugh at Democritus"; one jester to flout at another, one fool to fleer at another: a great stentorian Democritus, as big as that Rhodian Colossus. For now, as Salisburiensis [4] said in his time, *totus mundus histrionem agit,* the whole world plays the fool; we have a new theater, a new scene, a new comedy of errors, a new company of personate actors, *volupiæ sacra* (as Calcagninus willingly feigns in his Apologues) are celebrated all the world over, where all the actors were madmen and fools, and every hour changed habits or took that which came next. He that was a mariner today is an apothecary tomorrow; a smith one while, a philosopher another, in his *volupiæ ludis;* a king now with his crown, robes, scepter, attendants, by and by drove a loaded ass before him like a carter, etc. If Democritus were alive now, he should see strange alterations, a new company of counterfeit vizards, whifflers, Cuman asses, maskers, mummers, painted puppets, outsides, fantastic shadows, gulls, monsters, giddy-heads, butterflies. And so many of them are indeed (if all

[4] *Policraticus,* lib. 3. cap. 8, è Petronius.

be true that I have read). For when Jupiter and Juno's wedding was solemnized of old, the gods were all invited to the feast, and many noble men besides: amongst the rest came Chrysalus, a Persian prince, bravely attended, rich in golden attires, in gay robes, with a majestical presence, but otherwise an ass. The gods, seeing him come in such pomp and state, rose up to give him place, *ex habitu hominem metientes;* but Jupiter perceiving what he was, a light, fantastic, idle fellow, turned him and his proud followers into butterflies: and so they continue still (for aught I know to the contrary), roving about in pied coats, and are called chrysalides by the wiser sort of men: that is, golden outsides, drones, flies, and things of no worth. Multitudes of such, etc.

> —*ubique invenies*
> *Stultos avaros, sycophantas prodigos.*

Many additions, much increase of madness, folly, vanity, should Democritus observe, were he now to travel or could get leave of Pluto to come see fashions, as Charon did in Lucian to visit our cities of Moronia Pia and Moronia Fælix: sure I think he would break the rim of his belly with laughing.

> *Si foret in terris rideret Democritus, seu,* etc.

A satirical Roman in his time,[5] thought all vice, folly, and madness were at a full sea, *Omne in præcipiti vitium stetit.*

Josephus the historian taxeth his countrymen Jews for bragging of their vices, publishing their follies, and that they did contend amongst themselves who should be most notorious in villainies;[6] but we flow higher in madness, far beyond them,

> *Mox daturi progeniem vitiosiorem,*

and the latter end (you know whose oracle it is) is like to be worse. 'Tis not to be denied, the world alters every day,

---

[5] Juvenal.
[6] Josephus, *De bello Jud.*, lib. 8. c. 11.

Ruunt urbes, regna transferuntur, etc. *variantur habitus, leges innovantur,* as Petrarch observes, we change language, habits, laws, customs, manners, but not vices, not diseases, not the symptoms of folly and madness; they are still the same. And as a river, we see, keeps the like name and place, but not water, and yet ever runs, *Labitur et labetur in omne volubilis ævum;* our times and persons alter, vices are the same, and ever will be; look how nightingales sang of old, cocks crowed, kine lowed, sheep bleated, sparrows chirped, dogs barked, so they do still; we keep our madness still, play the fools still, *nec dum finitus Orestes;* we are of the same humors and inclinations as our predecessors were; you shall find us all alike, much at one, we and our sons, *et nati natorum, et qui nascuntur ab illis.* And so shall our posterity continue to the last. But to speak of times present.

If Democritus were alive now, and should but see the superstition of our age, our religious madness, as Meteren [7] calls it, *Religiosam insaniam,* so many professed Christians, yet so few imitators of Christ; so much talk of religion, so much science, so little conscience; so much knowledge, so many preachers, so little practice; such variety of sects, such have and hold of all sides,—*obvia signis signa,* etc., such absurd and ridiculous traditions and ceremonies: if he should meet a Capuchin, a Franciscan, a pharisaical Jesuit, a man-serpent, a shave-crowned monk in his robes, a begging friar, or see their three-crowned sovereign lord the Pope, poor Peter's successor, *servus servorum Dei,* to depose kings with his foot, to tread on emperors' necks, make them stand bare-foot and bare-legged at his gates, hold his bridle and stirrup, etc. (O that Peter and Paul were alive to see this!); if he should observe a Prince creep so devoutly to kiss his toe, and those red-cap cardinals, poor parish priests of old, now princes' companions; what would he say? *Cælum ipsum petitur stultitia.* Had he met some of our devout pilgrims

[7] Emanuel Van Meteren, born in Antwerp 1535, fled to England, died 1612. He wrote a *History of the Low Countries;* see especially Book 8.

going barefoot to Jerusalem, our lady of Loretto, Rome, St.
Iago, St. Thomas' Shrine, to creep to those counterfeit and
maggot-eaten reliques; had he been present at a mass, and
seen such kissing of paxes, crucifixes, cringes, duckings, their
several attires and ceremonies, pictures of saints, indulgences,
pardons, vigils, fasting, feasts, crossing, knocking, kneeling
at *Ave-Marias*, bells, with many such,—*jucunda rudi spec-
tacula plebis*, praying in gibberish, and mumbling of beads.
Had he heard an old woman say her prayers in Latin, their
sprinkling of holy water, and going a procession,

> —*incedunt monachorum agmina mille,*
> *Quid memorem vexilla, cruces, idolaque culta,* etc.

their breviaries, bulls, hallowed beads, exorcisms, pictures,
curious crosses, fables, and baubles. Had he read the Golden
Legend, the Turks' Alcoran, or Jews' Talmud, the Rabbins'
Comments, what would he have thought? How dost thou
think he might have been affected? Had he more particularly
examined a Jesuit's life amongst the rest, he should have
seen an hypocrite profess poverty, and yet possess more goods
and lands than many princes, to have infinite treasures and
revenues; teach others to fast, and play the gluttons themselves, like the watermen that row one way and look another.
Vow virginity, talk of holiness, and yet indeed a notorious
bawd and famous fornicator, *lascivum pecus,* a very goat.
Monks by profession, such as give over the world and the
vanities of it, and yet a Machiavellian rout interested in all
manner of state: holy men, peace makers, and yet composed
of envy, lust, ambition, hatred, and malice; firebrands,
adulta patriæ pestis, traitors, assassins, *hac itur ad astra,*
and this is to supererogate, and merit heaven for themselves
and others. Had he seen on the adverse side, some of our
nice and curious schismatics in another extreme, abhor all
ceremonies, and rather lose their lives and livings than do
or admit anything Papists have formerly used, though in
things indifferent (they alone are the true Church, *sal ter-*

ræ, cum sint omnium insulsissimi). Formalists, out of fear
and base flattery, like so many weather-cocks turn round, a
rout of temporizers, ready to embrace and maintain all that
is or shall be proposed in hope of preferment: another Epicurean company, lying at lurch like so many vultures, watching for a prey of church goods, and ready to rise by the downfall of any: as Lucian said in like case, What dost thou think
Democritus would have done, had he been spectator of these
things?

Or had he but observed the common people follow like so
many sheep one of their fellows drawn by the horns over the
gap, some for zeal, some for fear, *quo se cunque rapit tem-
pestas,* to credit all, examine nothing, and yet ready to die
before they will abjure any of those ceremonies to which
they have been accustomed? others out of hypocrisy frequent sermons, knock their breasts, turn up their eyes, pretend zeal, desire reformation, and yet professed usurers,
gripers, monsters of men, harpies, devils in their lives, to express nothing less?

What would he have said to see, hear, and read so many
bloody battles, so many thousands slain at once, such streams
of blood able to turn mills: *unius ob noxam furiasque,* or
to make sport for princes, without any just cause, "for vain
titles (saith Austin), precedency, some wench, or such like
toy, or out of desire of domineering, vainglory, malice, revenge, folly, madness" (goodly causes all, *ob quas universus
orbis bellis et cædibus misceatur*), whilst statesmen themselves in the mean time are secure at home, pampered with
all delights and pleasures, take their ease and follow their
lusts, not considering what intolerable misery poor soldiers
endure, their often wounds, hunger, thirst, etc., the lamentable cares, torments, calamities, and oppressions that accompany such proceedings, they feel not, take no notice of
it. So wars are begun, by the persuasion of a few debauched,
hare-brain, poor, dissolute, hungry captains, parasitical fawn-
ers, unquiet Hotspurs, restless innovators, green-heads, to

satisfy one man's private spleen, lust, ambition, avarice, etc.; *tales rapiunt scelerata in prælia causæ. Flos hominum,* proper men, well proportioned, carefully brought up, able both in body and mind, sound, led like so many beasts to the slaughter in the flower of their years, pride, and full strength, without all remorse and pity, sacrificed to Pluto, killed up as so many sheep, for devils' food, 40,000 at once. At once, said I? that were tolerable, but these wars last always and for many ages; nothing so familiar as this hacking and hewing, massacres, murders, desolations—*ignoto cælum clangore remugit,* they care not what mischief they procure, so that they may enrich themselves for the present; they will so long blow the coals of contention, till all the world be consumed with fire. The siege of Troy lasted ten years, eight months; there died 870,000 Grecians, 670,000 Trojans at the taking of the city, and after were slain 276,000 men, women, and children, of all sorts. Cæsar killed a million, Mahomet the second Turk, 300,000 persons; Sicinius Dentatus fought in a hundred battles, eight times in single combat he overcame, had forty wounds before, was rewarded with 140 crowns, triumphed nine times for his good service. M. Sergius had 32 wounds; Scæva, the centurion, I know not how many; every nation had their Hectors, Scipios, Cæsars, and Alexanders. Our Edward the Fourth was in 26 battles afoot: and as they do all, he glories in it; 'tis related to his honor. At the siege of Jerusalem, 1,100,000 died with sword and famine. At the battle of Cannæ, 70,000 men were slain, as Polybius records, and as many at Battle Abbey with us; and 'tis no news to fight from sun to sun, as they did, as Constantine and Licinius, etc. At the siege of Ostend (the devil's academy) a poor town in respect, a small fort, but a great grave, 120,000 men lost their lives, besides whole towns, dorpes, and hospitals full of maimed soldiers; there were engines, fireworks, and whatsoever the devil could invent to do mischief with 2,500,000 iron bullets shot of 40 pounds weight, three or four millions of gold consumed. "Who (saith mine

author) can be sufficiently amazed at their flinty hearts,
obstinacy, fury, blindness, who without any likelihood of
good success, hazard poor soldiers, and lead them without
pity to the slaughter, which may justly be called the rage
of furious beasts, that run without reason upon their own
deaths": *quis malus genius, quæ furia, quæ pestis,* etc., what
plague, what fury brought so devilish, so brutish a thing
as war first into men's minds? Who made so soft and peaceable a creature, born to love, mercy, meekness, so to rave,
rage like beasts, and run on to their own destruction? how
may nature expostulate with mankind, *Ego te divinum animal finxi,* etc. I made thee an harmless, quiet, a divine creature: how may God expostulate, and all good men? Yet,
horum facta (as one condoles) [8] *tantum admirantur, et
heroum numero habent:* these are the brave spirits, the gallants of the world, these admired alone, triumph alone, have
statues, crowns, pyramids, obelisks to their eternal fame,
that immortal genius attends on them, *hac itur ad astra.*
When Rhodes was besieged, *fossæ urbis cadaveribus repletæ
sunt,* the ditches were full of dead carcasses: and as when the
said Solyman, great Turk, beleaguered Vienna, they lay level
with the top of the walls. This they made a sport of, and will
do it to their friends and confederates, against oaths, vows,
promises, by treachery or otherwise;—*dolus an virtus? quis
in hoste requirat?* leagues and laws of arms (*silent leges inter
arma*) for their advantage, *omnia jura, divina, humana,
proculcata plerumque sunt;* God's and men's laws are tram-
pled under foot, the sword alone determines all; to satisfy
their lust and spleen, they care not what they attempt, say,
or do, *Rara fides, probitasque viris qui castra sequuntur,*
nothing so common as to have "father fight against the son,
brother against brother, kinsman against kinsman, kingdom against kingdom, province against province, Christians
against Christians," *a quibus nec unquam cogitatione fuerunt
læsi,* of whom they never had offense in thought, word, or

---

[8] Erasmus.

deed. Infinite treasures consumed, towns burned, flourishing cities sacked and ruinated, *quodque animus meminisse horret,* goodly countries depopulated and left desolate, old inhabitants expelled, trade and traffic decayed, maids deflowered, *Virgines nondum thalamis jugatæ, et comis nondum positis ephæbi;* chaste matrons cry out with Andromache, *Concubitum mox cogar pati eius, qui interemit Hectorem,* they shall be compelled peradventure to lie with them that erst killed their husbands; to see rich, poor, sick, sound, lords, servants, *eodem omnes incommodo macti,* consumed all or maimed, etc., *et quicquid gaudens scelere animus audet, et perversa mens,* saith Cyprian,[9] and whatsoever torment, misery, mischief, hell itself, the devil, fury and rage can invent to their own ruin and destruction; so abominable a thing is war, as Gerbelius concludes, *adeo fœda et abominanda res est bellum, ex quo hominum cædes, vastationes,* etc., the scourge of God, cause, effect, fruit and punishment of sin, and not *tonsura humani generis,* as Tertullian calls it, but *ruina.* Had Democritus been present at the late civil wars in France, those abominable wars—*bellaque matribus detestata,* "where, in less than ten years, ten thousand men were consumed," saith Collignius, "20 thousand churches overthrown"; nay, the whole kingdom subverted (as Richard Dinoth adds). So many myriads of the commons were butchered up, with sword, famine, war, *tanto odio utrinque ut barbari ad abhorrendam lanienam obstupescerent,* with such feral hatred, the world was amazed at it: or at our late Pharsalian fields in the time of Henry the Sixth, betwixt the houses of Lancaster and York, a hundred thousand men slain, one writes; another, ten thousand families were rooted out, "that no man can but marvel," saith Comineus, "at that barbarous inhumanity, feral madness, committed betwixt

[9] Burton's sources in this description of war include Cyprian, Bishop of Carthage, c. 200–258, and sixteenth century historians of various countries: France (Collignius or Coligni, Dinoth, Scaliger), Italy (Barletius or Barlezio), Holland (Gallobelgicus), etc. Detailed notes would become ponderous.

men of the same nation, language, and religion." *Quis furor,
O cives?* "Why do the Gentiles so furiously rage," saith the
Prophet David, Psal. ii. 1. But we may ask, why do the
Christians so furiously rage? *Arma volunt, quare poscunt,
rapiuntque iuventus?* Unfit for Gentiles, much less for us
so to tyrannize, as the Spaniard in the West Indies that killed
up in 42 years (if we may believe Bartholomæus a Casa,
their own bishop) 12 millions of men, with stupendous and
exquisite torments; neither should I lie (said he) if I said
50 millions. I omit those French massacres, Sicilian even-
songs, the Duke of Alva's tyrannies, our gunpowder machinations, and that fourth fury, as one calls it, the Spanish
Inquisition, which quite obscures those ten persecutions—
sævit toto Mars impius orbe, is not this *mundus furiosus,*
a mad world, as he terms it, *insanum bellum?* are not these
mad men, as Scaliger concludes, *qui in prælio acerba morte,
insaniæ suæ memoriam pro perpetuo teste relinquunt pos-
teritati;* which leave so frequent battles, as perpetual memorials of their madness to all succeeding ages? Would this,
think you, have enforced our Democritus to laughter, or
rather made him turn his tune, alter his tone, and weep with
Heraclitus, or rather howl, roar, and tear his hair in commiseration, stand amazed; or as the poets feign, that Niobe
was for grief quite stupefied, and turned to a stone? I have
not yet said the worst, that which is more absurd and mad,
in their tumults, seditions, civil and unjust wars, *quod stulte
suscipitur, impie geritur, misere finitur,* such wars I mean;
for all are not to be condemned, as those fantastical Anabaptists vainly conceive. Our Christian tactics are all out
as necessary as the Roman *acies,* or Grecian *phalanx;* to be
a soldier is a most noble and honorable profession (as the
world is), not to be spared, they are our best walls and bul-
warks, and I do therefore acknowledge that of Tully to be
most true, "All our civil affairs, all our studies, all our pleading, industry, and commendation lies under the protection
of warlike virtues, and whensoever there is any suspicion

of tumult, all our arts cease"; wars are most behooveful, *et bellatores agricolis civitati sunt utiliores,* as Tyrius defends: and valor is much to be commended in a wise man; but they mistake most part, *auferre, trucidare, rapare, falsis nominibus virtutem vocant,* etc. ('twas Galgacus' observation in Tacitus), they term theft, murder, and rapine, virtue by a wrong name; rapes, slaughters, massacres, etc., *jocus et ludus,* are pretty pastimes, as Ludovicus Vives notes. "They commonly call the most hare-brain blood-suckers, strongest thieves, the most desperate villains, treacherous rogues, inhuman murderers, rash, cruel and dissolute caitiffs, courageous and generous spirits, heroical and worthy captains, brave men-at-arms, valiant and renowned soldiers, possessed with a brute persuasion of false honor," as Pontus Heuter in his Burgundian history complains. By means of which it comes to pass that daily so many voluntaries offer themselves, leaving their sweet wives, children, friends, for sixpence (if they can get it) a day, prostitute their lives and limbs, desire to enter upon breaches, lie sentinel, *perdue,* give the first onset, stand in the forefront of the battle, marching bravely on, with a cheerful noise of drums and trumpets, such vigor and alacrity, so many banners streaming in the air, glittering armors, motions of plumes, woods of pikes and swords, variety of colors, cost and magnificence as if they went in triumph, now victors to the Capitol, and with such pomp, as when Darius' army marched to meet Alexander at Issus. Void of all fear they run into imminent dangers, cannon's mouth, etc., *ut vulneribus suis ferrum hostium hebetent,* saith Barletius, to get a name of valor, honor and applause, which lasts not neither, for it is but a mere flash, this fame, and like a rose, *intra diem unum extinguitur,* 'tis gone in an instant. Of 15,000 proletaries slain in a battle, scarce fifteen are recorded in history, or one alone, the general perhaps, and after a while his and their names are likewise blotted out, the whole battle itself is forgotten. Those Grecian orators, *summa vi ingenii et eloquentiæ,* set out the renowned overthrows at *Thermopylæ, Salamis, Mara-thon, Mycale, Mantinea, Cheronœa, Platœa.* The Romans record their battle at Cannæ, and Pharsalian fields, but they do but record, and we scarce hear of them. And yet this supposed honor, popular applause, desire of immortality by this means, pride and vainglory spur them on many times rashly and unadvisedly to make away themselves and multitudes of others. Alexander was sorry, because there were no more worlds for him to conquer; he is admired by some for it, *animosa vox videtur, et regia,* 'twas spoken like a Prince; but as wise Seneca censures him, 'twas *vox iniquis-sima et stultissima,* 'twas spoken by a Bedlam fool; and that sentence which the same Seneca appropriates to his father Philip and him, I apply to them all, *Non minores fuere pestes mortalium quam inundatio, quam conflagratio, quibus,* etc., they did as much mischief to mortal men as fire and water, those merciless elements when they rage. Which is yet more to be lamented, they persuade them this hellish course of life is holy, they promise heaven to such as venture their lives *bello sacro,* and that by these bloody wars, as Persians, Greeks, and Romans of old, as modern Turks do now their commons to encourage them to fight, *ut cadant infeliciter,* "If they die in the field, they go directly to heaven, and shall be canonized for saints" (O diabolical invention!), put in the chronicles, *in perpetuam rei memoriam,* to their eternal memory: when as in truth, as some hold, it were much better (since wars are the scourge of God for sin, by which he punisheth mortal men's peevishness and folly) such brutish stories were suppressed, because *ad morum institutionem nihil habent,* they conduce not at all to manners or good life. But they will have it thus nevertheless, and so they put a note of "divinity upon the most cruel and pernicious plague of human kind," adore such men with grand titles, degrees, statues, images, honor, applaud, and highly reward them for their good service, no greater glory than to die in the field. So Africanus is extolled

by Ennius:[10] Mars, and Hercules, and I know not how many
besides of old, were deified; went this way to heaven, that
were indeed bloody butchers, wicked destroyers, and troublers of the world, prodigious monsters, hell-hounds, feral
plagues, devourers, common executioners of human kind, as
Lactantius truly proves, and Cyprian to Donat, such as
were desperate in wars, and precipitately made away themselves (like those Celts in Damascene, with ridiculous valor,
ut dedecorosum putarent muro ruenti se subducere, a disgrace to run away for a rotten wall, now ready to fall on
their heads), such as will not rush on a sword's point, or
seek to shun a cannon's shot, are base cowards, and no valiant
men. By which means, *Madet orbis mutuo sanguine,* the
earth wallows in her own blood, *Sævit amor ferri et scelerati
insania belli;* and for that, which if it be done in private,
a man shall be rigorously executed, "and which is no less
than murder itself; if the same fact be done in public in wars,
it is called manhood, and the party is honored for it."—
Prosperum et fœlix scelus, virtus vocatur.

We measure all as Turks do, by the event, and most part,
as Cyprian notes, in all our ages, countries, places, *sævitiæ
magnitudo impunitatem sceleris acquirit,* the foulness of the
fact vindicates the offender. One is crowned for that for
which another is tormented; *Ille crucem sceleris pretium
tulit, hic diadema,* made a knight, a lord, an earl, a great
duke (as Agrippa notes) for which another should have hung
in gibbets, as a terror to the rest,

> *—et tamen alter*
> *Si fecisset idem, caderet sub judice morum.*

A poor sheep-stealer is hanged for stealing of victuals, compelled peradventure by necessity of that intolerable cold,
hunger, and thirst, to save himself from starving; but a
great man in office may securely rob whole provinces, undo

---

[10] Quintus Ennius, 239–170 B.C. His *Annales* gave him the title of "the
Homer of Rome."

thousands, pill and poll, oppress *ad libitum,* flay, grind, tyrannize, enrich himself by spoils of the commons, be uncontrollable in his actions, and after all, be recompensed with turgent titles, honored for his good service, and no man dare find fault, or mutter at it.

How would our Democritus have been affected to see a wicked caitiff, or "fool, a very idiot, a fungus, a golden ass, a monster of men, to have many good men, wise men, learned men to attend upon him with all submission as an appendix to his riches, for that respect alone, because he hath more wealth and money, and to honor him with divine titles, and bombast epithets," to smother him with fumes and eulogies, whom they know to be a dizzard, a fool, a covetous wretch, a beast, etc., "because he is rich"? To see *sub exuviis leonis onagrum,* a filthy loathsome carcass, a Gorgon's head puffed up by parasites, assume this unto himself, glorious titles, in worth an infant, a Cuman ass, a painted sepulcher, an Egyptian temple! To see a withered face, a diseased, deformed, cankered complexion, a rotten carcass, a viperous mind, and Epicurean soul set out with orient pearls, jewels, diadems, perfumes, curious elaborate works, as proud of his clothes as a child of his new coats; and a goodly person, of an angel-like divine countenance, a saint, an humble mind, a meek spirit clothed in rags, beg, and now ready to be starved. To see a silly contemptible sloven in apparel, ragged in his coat, polite in speech, of a divine spirit, wise; another neat in clothes, spruce, full of courtesy, empty of grace, wit, talk nonsense.

To see so many lawyers, advocates, so many tribunals, so little justice; so many magistrates, so little care of the common good; so many laws, yet never more disorders; *tribunal litium segetem,* the tribunal a labyrinth, so many thousand suits in one court sometimes, so violently followed. To see *iniustissimum sæpe juri præsidentem, impium religioni, imperitissimum eruditioni, otiosissimum labori, monstrosum humanitati.* To see a lamb executed, a wolf pronounce sentence, *latro* arraigned, and *fur* sit on the bench, the judge severely punish others, and do worse himself, *eundem furtum facere et punire, rapinam plectere, quum sit ipse raptor.* Laws altered, misconstrued, interpreted *pro* and *con,* as the judge is made by friends, bribed, or otherwise affected as a nose of wax, good today, none tomorrow; or firm in his opinion, cast in his. Sentence prolonged, changed, *ad arbitrium iudicis,* still the same case, "one thrust out of his inheritance, another falsely put in by favor, false forged deeds or wills." *Incisæ leges negliguntur,* laws are made and not kept; or if put in execution, they be some silly ones that are punished. As put case it be fornication, the father will disinherit or abdicate his child, quite cashier him (out, villain, begone, come no more in my sight) ; a poor man is miserably tormented with loss of his estate perhaps, goods, fortunes, good name, forever disgraced, forsaken, and must do penance to the utmost; a mortal sin, and yet make the most of it, *nunquid aliud fecit,* saith Tranio in the poet,[11] *nisi quod faciunt summis nati generibus?* he hath done no more than what gentlemen usually do. *Neque novum, neque mirum, neque secus quam alii solent.* For in a great person, right worshipful sir, a right honorable grandee, 'tis not a venial sin, no, not a *peccadillo,* 'tis no offense at all, a common and ordinary thing, no man takes notice of it; he justifies it in public, and peradventure brags of it,

> *Nam quod turpe bonis, Titio, Seioque, decebat*
> *Crispinum.*

Many poor men, younger brothers, etc., by reason of bad policy and idle education (for they are likely brought up in no calling), are compelled to beg or steal, and then hanged for theft; than which, what can be more ignominious, *non minus enim turpe principi multa supplicia, quam medico multa funera,* 'tis the governor's fault. *Libentius verberant quam docent,* as schoolmasters do rather correct their pupils

[11] Plautus.

than teach them when they do amiss. "They had more need provide there should be no more thieves and beggars, as they ought with good policy, and take away the occasions, than let them run on, as they do to their own destruction: root out likewise those causes of wrangling, a multitude of lawyers, and compose controversies, *lites lustrales et seculares,* by some more compendious means." Whereas now for every toy and trifle they go to law, *mugit litibus insanum forum, et sævit invicem discordantium rabies,* they are ready to pull out one another's throats; and for commodity "to squeeze blood," saith Jerome, "out of their brother's heart," defame, lie, disgrace, backbite, rail, bear false witness, swear, forswear, fight and wrangle, spend their goods, lives, fortunes, friends, undo one another, to enrich an harpy advocate, that preys upon them both, and cries, *Eia Socrates, Eia Xantippe ;* or some corrupt judge, that like the kite in Æsop, while the mouse and frog fought, carried both away. Generally they prey one upon another as so many ravenous birds, brute beasts, devouring fishes, no medium, *omnes hic aut captantur aut captant ; aut cadavera quæ lacerantur, aut corvi qui lacerant,* either deceive or be deceived; tear others or be torn in pieces themselves; like so many buckets in a well, as one riseth another falleth, one's empty, another's full; his ruin is a ladder to the third; such are our ordinary proceedings. What's the market? A place, according to Anacharsis, wherein they cozen one another, a trap; nay, what's the world itself? A vast chaos, a confusion of manners, as fickle as the air, *domicilium insanorum,* a turbulent troop full of impurities, a mart of walking spirits, goblins, the theater of hypocrisy, a shop of knavery, flattery, a nursery of villainy, the scene of babbling, the school of giddiness, the academy of vice; a warfare, *ubi velis nolis pugnandum, aut vincas aut suc-cumbas,* in which kill or be killed; wherein every man is for himself, his private ends, and stands upon his own guard. No charity, love, friendship, fear of God, alliance, affinity, consanguinity, Christianity, can contain them, but if they be any ways offended, or that string of commodity be touched, they fall foul. Old friends become bitter enemies on a sudden for toys and small offenses, and they that erst were willing to do all mutual offices of love and kindness, now revile and persecute one another to death, with more than Vatinian hatred, and will not be reconciled. So long as they are behooveful, they love, or may bestead each other; but when there is no more good to be expected, as they do by an old dog, hang him up or cashier him: which Cato counts a great indecorum, to use men like old shoes or broken glasses, which are flung to the dunghill; he could not find in his heart to sell an old ox, much less to turn away an old servant: but they instead of recompense, revile him, and when they have made him an instrument of their villainy, as Bajazet the Second, Emperor of the Turks, did by Acomethes Bassa, made him away, or instead of reward, hate him to death, as Silius was served by Tiberius. In a word every man for his own ends. Our *summum bonum* is commodity, and the goddess we adore *Dea Moneta,* Queen Money, to whom we daily offer sacrifice, which steers our hearts, hands, affections, all: that most powerful goddess, by whom we are reared, depressed, elevated, esteemed the sole commandress of our actions, for which we pray, run, ride, go, come, labor, and contend as fishes do for a crumb that falleth into the water. It's not worth, virtue (that's *bonum theatrale*), wisdom, valor, learning, honesty, religion, or any sufficiency for which we are respected, but money, greatness, office, honor, authority; honesty is accounted folly; knavery, policy; men admired out of opinion, not as they are, but as they seem to be: such shifting, lying, cogging, plotting, counterplotting, temporizing, flattering, cozening, dissembling, "that of necessity one must highly offend God if he be conformable to the world, *Cretizare cum Crete,* or else live in contempt, disgrace and misery." One takes upon him temperance, holiness, another austerity, a third an affected kind of simplicity, whenas indeed he, and he, and he, and the rest are "hypocrites, ambidexters," outsides, so many turning pictures, a lion on the one side, a lamb on the other. How would Democritus have been affected to see these things!

To see a man turn himself into all shapes like a chameleon, or as Proteus, *omnia transformans sese in miracula rerum,* to act twenty parts and persons at once, for his advantage, to temporize and vary like Mercury the Planet, good with good, bad with bad; having a several face, garb, and character for everyone he meets; of all religions, humors, inclinations; to fawn like a spaniel, *mentitis et mimicis obsequiis,* rage like a lion, bark like a cur, fight like a dragon, sting like a serpent, as meek as a lamb, and yet again grin like a tiger, weep like a crocodile, insult over some, and yet others domineer over him, here command, there crouch, tyrannize in one place, be baffled in another, a wise man at home, a fool abroad to make others merry.

To see so much difference betwixt words and deeds, so many parasangs betwixt tongue and heart, men like stage-players act variety of parts, give good precepts to others, soar aloft, whilst they themselves grovel on the ground.

To see a man protest friendship, kiss his hand, *quem mallet truncatum videre,* smile with an intent to do mischief, or cozen him whom he salutes, magnify his friend unworthy with hyperbolical eulogiums; his enemy albeit a good man, to vilify and disgrace him, yea all his actions, with the utmost that liver and malice can invent.

To see a servant able to buy out his master, him that carries the mace more worth than the magistrate, which Plato, lib. 11, *De Leg.,* absolutely forbids, Epictetus abhors. A horse that tills the land fed with chaff, an idle jade have provender in abundance; him that makes shoes go barefoot himself, him that sells meat almost pined; a toiling drudge starve, a drone flourish.

To see men buy smoke for wares, castles built with fools' heads, men like apes follow the fashions in tires, gestures, actions: if the king laugh, all laugh;

Rides? majore cachinno
Concutitur, flet si lachrymas conspexit amici.

Alexander stooped, so did his courtiers; Alphonsus turned his head, and so did his parasites. Sabina Poppea, Nero's wife, wore amber-colored hair, so did all the Roman ladies in an instant; her fashion was theirs.

To see men wholly led by affection, admired and censured out of opinion without judgment: an inconsiderate multitude, like so many dogs in a village, if one bark all bark without a cause: as fortune's fan turns, if a man be in favor, or commanded by some great one, all the world applauds him; if in disgrace, in an instant all hate him, and as at the sun when he is eclipsed, that erst took no notice, now gaze and stare upon him.

To see a man wear his brains in his belly, his guts in his head, an hundred oaks on his back, to devour a hundred oxen at a meal, nay more, to devour houses and towns, or as those anthropophagi, to eat one another.

To see a man roll himself up like a snowball, from base beggary to right worshipful and right honorable titles, unjustly to screw himself into honors and offices; another to starve his genius, damn his soul to gather wealth, which he shall not enjoy, which his prodigal son melts and consumes in an instant.

To see the κακοζηλίαν of our times, a man bend all his forces, means, time, fortunes, to be a favorite's favorite's favorite, etc., a parasite's parasite's parasite, that may scorn the servile world as having enough already.

To see an hirsute beggar's brat that lately fed on scraps, crept and whined, crying to all and for an old jerkin ran on errands, now ruffle in silk and satin, bravely mounted, jovial and polite, now scorn his old friends and familiars, neglect his kindred, insult over his betters, domineer over all.

To see a scholar crouch and creep to an illiterate peasant for a meal's meat; a scrivener better paid for an obligation;

a falconer receive greater wages than a student; a lawyer get more in a day than a philosopher in a year, better reward for an hour, than a scholar for a twelvemonth's study; him that can paint Thais, play on a fiddle, curl hair, etc., sooner get preferment than a philologer or a poet.

To see a fond mother, like Æsop's ape, hug her child to death, a wittol wink at his wife's honesty, and too perspicuous in all other affairs; one stumble at a straw, and leap over a block; rob Peter, and pay Paul; scrape unjust sums with one hand, purchase great manors by corruption, fraud and cozenage, and liberally to distribute to the poor with the other, give a remnant to pious uses, etc. Penny wise, pound foolish; blind men judge of colors; wise men silent, fools talk; find fault with others, and do worse themselves; denounce that in public which he doth in secret; and which Aurelius Victor gives out of Augustus, severely censure that in a third, of which he is most guilty himself.

To see a poor fellow, or an hired servant venture his life for his new master that will scarce give him his wages at year's end; a country colone toil and moil, till and drudge for a prodigal idle drone, that devours all the gain, or lasciviously consumes with phantastical expenses; a noble man in a bravado to encounter death, and for a small flash of honor to cast away himself; a worldling tremble at an executor, and yet not fear hell-fire; to wish and hope for immortality, desire to be happy, and yet by all means avoid death, a necessary passage to bring him to it.

To see a foolhardy fellow like those old Danes, *qui decollari malunt quam verberari,* die rather than be punished, in a sottish humor embrace death with alacrity, yet scorn to lament his own sins and miseries, or his dearest friends' departures.

To see wise men degraded, fools preferred, one govern towns and cities, and yet a silly woman overrules him at home; command a province, and yet his own servants or children prescribe laws to him, as Themistocles' son did in

Greece; "What I will (said he) my mother will, and what my mother will, my father doth." To see horses ride in a coach, men draw it; dogs devour their masters; towers build masons; children rule; old men go to school; women wear the breeches; sheep demolish towns, devour men, etc. And in a word, the world turned upside downward. *O viveret Democritus!*

To insist in every particular were one of Hercules' labors, there's so many ridiculous instances, as motes in the sun. *Quantum est in rebus inane!* (How much vanity there is in things!) And who can speak of all? *Crimine ab uno disce omnes,* take this for a taste.

. . . . . .

FROM *Love Melancholy* [1]

PART III. sec. I. mem. 3

Charity

For as the soul doth rule the earthly mass,
And all the service of the body frame,
So love of soul doth love of body pass,
No less than perfect gold surmounts the meanest brass.[2]

A FAITHFUL friend is better than gold,[3] a medicine of misery, and an only possession; yet all this love of friends, all three loves put together, are little worth, if they proceed not from a true Christian illuminated soul, if it be not done for God's sake. *Though I had the gift of prophecy, spake with tongue of men and angels, though I feed the poor with all my goods, and give my body to be burned, and have not this love, it profiteth me nothing.* (I Cor. 13:1, 2, 3.) This

---

[1] Text: *The Anatomy of Melancholy,* 1621, first edition, Part III. sec. 1. mem. 3.

[2] Spenser, *Faerie Queene,* IV. 9. 2.

[3] Siracides, *Ecclesiasticus,* vii. 18.

is an all-apprehending love, love without an addition, love
κατ' ἐξοχὴν, love of God, and love of men. *The love of God
begets the love of man, and by this love of our neighbor, the
love of God is nourished and increased.*[4] By this happy union
of love, *all well-governed families and cities are combined,
the heavens annexed, and divine souls complicated, the world
itself composed, and all that is in it conjoined in God and
reduced to one.*[5] *This love causeth true and absolute virtues, the life and spirit and root of every virtuous action,
it finisheth prosperity, easeth adversity, corrects all natural
encumbrances,* inconveniences, sustained by faith and hope,
which with this our love make an indissoluble twist, a Gordian
knot, an equilateral triangle, *and yet the greatest of them
is love* (I Cor. 13 : 13), *which inflames our souls with a divine heat, and being so inflamed purgeth, and so purged elevates to God, makes an atonement and reconciles us unto
him. That other love infects the soul of man, this cleanseth;
that depresseth, this rears; that causeth cares and troubles,
this quietness of mind; this informs, that deforms our life;
that leads to repentance, this to heaven.*[6] For if once we be
truly linked and touched with this charity, we shall love
God above all, our neighbor as ourself, as we are enjoined
(Mark 12 : 31; Matt. 19 : 19), and perform all those duties
and exercise those operations of a good Christian.

*This love suffereth long, it is bountiful, it envieth not,
boasteth not itself, is not puffed up, it deceiveth not, it seeketh not his own things, is not provoked to anger, it think-
eth not evil, it rejoiceth not in iniquity, but in truth. It suffereth all things, believeth all things, hopeth all things* (I Cor.
13 : 4, 5, 6, 7); *it covereth all trespasses* (Prov. 10 : 12); *a
multitude of sins* (I Pet. 4 : 8); *it will defend the fatherless
and widow* (Isa. 1 : 17); *will seek no revenge or be mindful
of wrong* (Levit. 19 : 18); *will bring home his brother's ox*

---

[4] Greg. *Moralium*, Lib. VII. c. 24.
[5] Piccolomineus, grad. 7, cap. 27, "hoc felici amoris nodo ligantur
familiæ, civitates," etc.
[6] Bernard de Clairvaux.

if he go astray, as he is commanded (Deut. 22:1); *will re-sist evil, give to him that asketh, and not turn from him that borroweth, bless them that curse him, love his enemy* (Matt. 5); *bear his brother's burden* (Galat. 6:2). He will be hospitable, and distribute to the necessities of the saints; he will, if it be possible, have peace with all men, feed his enemy if he be hungry, if he be athirst give him drink, *he will make himself equal to them of the lower sort, rejoice with them that rejoice, weep with them that weep* (Rom. 12); he will speak truth to his neighbor, be courteous and tender-hearted, *forgiving others for Christ's sake, as God forgave him* (Eph. 4:32); *he will be like-minded* (Phil. 2:2), *of one judgment; be humble, meek, long suffering* (Colos. 3); *forbear, forget, and forgive* (12:13, 23), and what he doth shall be heartily done to God, and not to men; *be pitiful and courteous* (I Pet. 3), *seek peace and follow it.* He will love his brother, not in word and tongue, but in deed and truth (I John 3:18), *and he that loves God, Christ will love him that is begotten of him* (I John 5:1), etc. This should we willingly do, if we had a true touch of this charity, of this divine love, if we would perform this which we are en-joined, forget and forgive, and compose ourselves to those Christian laws of love.

> *O felix hominum genus,*
> *Si vestros animos amor*
> *Quo cœlum regitur regat.*[7]

Angelical souls, how blessed, how happy should we be, how might we triumph over the devil, and have another heaven upon earth!

But this we cannot do; and which is the cause of all our woes, miseries, discontent, melancholy, and want of this char-ity. We do *invicem angariare,* contemn, insult, vex, torture, molest and hold one another's nose to the grindstone hard,

---

[7] Boethius, lib. 2, met. 8, "O happy race of men, did but love which rules the heavens rule your souls!"

provoke, rail, scoff, calumniate, challenge, hate (hard-hearted, implacable, malicious, peevish, inexorable as we are) to satisfy our lust or private spleen, for toys, trifles, and impertinent occasions, spend ourselves, goods, friends, fortunes, to be revenged on our adversary, to ruin him and his. 'Tis all our study, our practice and business, how to plot mischief, mine and countermine, defend and offend, ward ourselves, injure others, hurt all; as if we were born to do mischief, and that with such eagerness and bitterness, with such rancor, malice, rage, and fury, we prosecute our intended designs, that neither affinity or consanguinity, love or fear of God or men can contain us: no satisfaction, no composition will be accepted, no offices will serve, no submission; though he shall upon his knees as Sarpedon did to Glaucus in Homer, acknowledging his error, yield himself with tears in his eyes, beg his pardon, we will not relent, forgive, or pardon, till we have confounded him and his, *made dice of his bones* as they say, see him rot in prison, friends, followers, *et omne invisum genus,* rooted him out and all his posterity. Monsters of men as we are, dogs, wolves, tigers, bulls, bears, fiends and devils, we do not only contend, oppress, and tyrannize ourselves, but as so many fire-brands we set on, and animate others; our whole life is a perpetual combat, a conflict, a set battle, a snarling fit. *Eris dea* is settled in our tents, *Omnia de lite,* opposing wit to wit, wealth to wealth, strength to strength, fortunes to fortunes, friends to friends, as at a sea-fight, we turn our broad-sides, or two millstones with continual attrition, we fire ourselves, or break another's back, and both are ruined and consumed in the end. Miserable wretches as we are, to fat and enrich ourselves, we care not how we get it, how many thousands we undo, whom we oppress, by whose ruin and downfall we arise, whom we injure, fatherless children, widows, common societies, to satisfy our own private lust. And though we have myriads, abundance of wealth and treasure (pitiless, merciless, remorseless as we are, and un-

charitable in the highest degree), and our poor brother in
need, sickness, and in great extremity, and now ready to
be starved for want of food, we had rather as the fox told
the ape, his tail should sweep the ground still, than cover
his buttocks; rather spend it idly, consume it with dogs,
hawks, hounds, unnecessary buildings, apparel, ingurgitate,
or let it be lost, than they should have part of it; rather take
from him that little which he hath than relieve him.

Or like the dog in the manger, neither use it ourselves,
nor let others make use of it, or enjoy it; part with nothing
while we live; and for want of disposing our household, and
setting things in order, set all the world together by the ears
after our death. Poor Lazarus lies, howling at his gates for
a few crumbs, he only seeks chippings, offals; let him roar
and howl, famish and eat his own flesh, he respects him not.
A poor decayed friend and kinsman of his sets upon him by
the way in all his jollity, and runs begging bareheaded by
him, conjuring by those former bonds of friendship, alliance,
consanguinity, etc., uncle, cousin, brother, father,

> *Per ego has lachrymas dextramque tuam te*
> *Si quidquam de te merui, fuit aut tibi quidquam*
> *Dulce meum, miserere mei.*[8]

Show some pity for Christ's sake, pity a sick man, an old
man; he cares not, ride on: pretend sickness, inevitable loss
of limbs, goods, plead suretyship and shipwreck, fires, common calamities, show thy wants and imperfections.

> *Et si per sanctum juratus dicat Osirim,*
> *Credite, non ludo, crudeles tollite claudum,*[9]

Swear, protest, take God and all his angels to witness, *quære
peregrinum*, he is not touched with it, *pauper ubique, iacet*,
ride on, he takes no notice of it. Put up a supplication to

[8] By these tears, by thy right hand I beseech thee, if ever I did thee a
service or gave thee pleasure, pity me.
[9] And if he swear by Osiris, "I jest not, believe me, be not so cruel, pick
up a lame man."

him in the name of a thousand orphans, an hospital, a spital, a prison, as he goes by, they cry out to him for aid, ride on, *surdo narras,* he cares not, let them eat stones, devour themselves with vermin, rot in their own dung, he cares not. Show him a decayed haven, a bridge, a school, a fortification, etc., or some public good; ride on; good your worship, your honor, for God's sake, for your country's sake, etc., ride on. But show him a roll wherein his name shall be registered in golden letters, and his bounty commended to all posterity, his arms set up, and his devices to be seen, and then peradventure he will stay and contribute; or if thou canst thunder upon him, as Papists do, with satisfactory and meritorious works, or persuade him by this means he shall save his soul out of hell, and free it from purgatory, then in all likelihood he will listen and stay; or that he have no children, no near kinsman, heir, he cares for at least, or cannot well tell how and where to bestow his possessions (for carry them with him he cannot), it may be then he will build some school or hospital in his life, or be induced to give liberally to pious uses after his death. For I dare boldly say that vainglory, that opinion of merit, and this inforced necessity, when they know not otherwise how to leave them, or what better to do with them, is the main cause of most of our good works. I will not say this to derogate from any good man's charitable devotion, or bounty in this kind, or censure any good work; no doubt there be many sanctified, heroical, and worthy-minded men, that out of true zeal and for virtue's sake (divine spirits), that out of commiseration and pity extend their liberality, and, as much as in them lies, do good to all men, clothe the naked, feed the hungry, comfort the sick and needy, relieve all, forget and forgive injuries, as true charity requires; yet most part there is *simulatum quid,* a deal of hypocrisy in this kind, much default and defect. As Cosmo de Medici, that rich citizen of Florence, confessed to a near friend of his, that would know of him why he built so many public and magnificent buildings, and bestowed so liberally on scholars, not that he loved learning more than others, "but to eternize his own name, to be immortal by the benefit of scholars; for when his friends were dead, walls decayed, and all inscriptions gone, books would remain to the world's end." Vainglory and emulation (as to most men) was the cause efficient, and to be a trumpeter of his own fame was his sole intent, so to do good that all the world may take notice of it. Such for the most part is the charity of our times, such our bene-factors, *Mæcenates* and patrons. Show me amongst so many myriads a truly devout, a right, honest, upright, meek, humble, a patient, innocuous, innocent, a merciful, a lov-ing, a charitable man. *Probus quis nobiscum vivit?* Show me a Caleb, or a Joshua. He that shall examine this iron age wherein we live, where charity is cold, *et jam terras Astræa reliquit,* and the devil loose, and see one man vilify and in-sult over his brother, as if he were an innocent, oppress, tyrannize, prey upon, torture him, vex, gall, torment and crucify him, starve him, where is charity? to see men swear and forswear, lie and bear false witness, to advantage them-selves, prejudice others, hazard goods, lives, fortunes, to be revenged on their enemies, men so unspeakable in their lusts, unnatural in malice, such bloody designments, Italian blas-pheming, Spanish renouncing, etc., where is charity? He that shall see so many lawsuits, such endless contentions, such plotting, undermining, so much money spent with such eager-ness and fury, every man for himself, his own ends, the devil for all; so many distressed souls, such lamentable complaints, so many factions, conspiracies, seditions, such grudging, re-pining, discontent, so much emulation, envy, so many brawls, quarrels, monomachies, etc., where is charity? to see and read of such cruel wars, tumults, uproars, bloody battles, so many men slain, so many cities ruinated, etc. (for what else is the subject of all our stories almost, but bills, bows, and guns), so many murders and massacres, etc., where is charity? To see men wholly devote to God, churchmen, professed divines, holy men, "to make the trumpet of the gospel the trumpet of war," a company of hell-born Jesuits, and fiery-spirited friars, *facem præferre* to all seditions; as so many firebrands set all the world by the ears (I say nothing of their contentions and railing books, whole ages spent in writing one against another, and that with such virulency and bitterness *Bionæis sermonibus et sale nigro*) and by their bloody inquisitions that in thirty years Bale [10] saith consumed 39 princes, 148 earls, 235 barons, 14,755 commons; worse than those ten persecutions, where is charity? He that shall observe and see these things may say to them as Cato to Cæsar, *credo quæ de inferis dicuntur falsa existimas,* sure I think thou art of opinion there is neither heaven nor hell. Let them pretend religion, zeal, make what shows they will, give alms, peacemakers, frequent sermons, if we may guess the tree by the fruit, they are no better than hypocrites, epicures, atheists, with the *fool in their hearts they say there is no God* [Psalm 13 : 1]. 'Tis no marvel then if being so uncharitable, hardhearted, as we are, we have so frequent and so many discontents, such melancholy fits, so many bitter pangs, mutual discords, all in a combustion, often complaints, so common grievances, general mischiefs, so many pestilences, wars, uproars, losses, deluges, fires, inundations, God's vengeance and all the plagues of Egypt come upon us, since we are so uncharitable one towards another, so respectless of God, and our neighbors, and by our crying sins pull these miseries upon our own heads. If we had any sense or feeling of these things, sure we should not go on as we do, in such irregular courses, practice all manner of impieties; our whole carriage would not be so averse from God. If a man would but consider, when he is in the midst and full career of such prodigious and uncharitable actions, how displeasing they are in God's sight, how noxious to himself, as Solomon told Joab (I Kings 2), *the Lord shall*

[10] John Bale, 1495–1563, often called "bilious Bale," a vehement anti-Catholic preacher and writer.

bring this blood upon their heads (Prov. 1: 27) : *sudden desolation and destruction shall come like a whirlwind upon them: affliction, anguish; the reward of his hand shall be given him* (Isa. 3: 11), etc.; *they shall fall into the pit they have digged for others* [Psalm 7: 15], and when they are scraping, tyrannizing, getting, wallowing in their wealth, *This night, O fool, I will take away thy soul* [St. Luke 12: 20], what a severe account they must make, and how gracious on the other side a charitable man is in God's eyes, *haruit sibi gratiam* (Matt. 5: 7) : *blessed are the merciful for they shall obtain mercy;* he that lendeth to the *poor gives to God,* and how it shall be restored to them again [Prov. 19: 17]; *how by their patience and long suffering they shall heap coals on their enemies' heads* (Rom. 12), *and he that followeth after righteousness and mercy shall find righteousness and glory* [Prov. 21: 21]. Surely they would check themselves, curb in their unnatural, inordinate affections, agree amongst themselves, abstain from doing evil, amend their lives and learn to do good. *Behold how comely and good a thing it is for brethren to live together in union: it is like the precious ointment,* etc. [Psalm 133]. How odious to contend one with the other. *Miseri quid luctatiunculis hisce volumus? ecce mors supra caput est, et supremum illud tribunal, ubi et dicta et facta nostra examinanda sunt: Sapiamus!* Why do we contend and vex one another? behold death is over our heads, and we must shortly give account of all our uncharitable words and actions: think upon it, and be wise.[11]

[11] Lipsius.

Sir Thomas Overbury　1581-1613

Sir Thomas Overbury took his A.B. degree at Queen's College, Oxford, and went on to London to study law in the Middle Temple. He became a friend of the king's favorite, Robert Carr, who was later Earl of Somerset, and being introduced at court was soon made servitor-in-ordinary to James I. He was knighted in 1608. He was on the Continent for a time and, upon his return, was in high favor. Later he became involved in Carr's intrigue with the wife of the Earl of Essex. Through his influence over the king, Carr, now Earl of Somerset, arranged the nullification of the marriage of the Countess and Essex and then married the Countess.

During all of this intrigue Overbury played his hand too high and lost favor on all sides. He was imprisoned in the Tower, where over a period of five months by some mysterious plan he was given slow poison in food and medicine so that he died. He was buried in the Tower; but his death becoming known, suspicion was aroused and many people were investigated. The case dragged on, and in 1616 Somerset was judged guilty of murder. He was finally released in 1622, but the case was never fully solved.

Overbury's sensational death created a great demand for his writings. *The Wife*, a long poem which he had written in the hope of persuading Somerset not to marry the Countess, was published in 1614 and was in such great demand that it had a second edition the same year. In the second edition twenty-two prose characters by Overbury and others were included. A number of editions followed, and by the end of the century there were eighty-three characters. It had then become impossible to identify authorship except in a few cases.[1]

The "characters," like Ben Jonson's "humors," were based on some dominant trait and represent a typical person, oc-

[1] See W. J. Paylor, *The Overburian Characters,* Oxford, 1936.

cupation, or age. This type of writing is as old as the thirty-
first chapter of Proverbs and the Greek characters of Theophrastus. In England Overbury's predecessor was Joseph
Hall, whose *Characters of Virtues and Vices* was published
in 1608. Overbury put the emphasis upon cleverness, both
in style and in the selection of details to depict a character;
and his work had great influence upon the development of
this type of writing in England.

Bishop Hall — first one of
write Character writing. Popular
of 19th cu. Ben Johnson is comedy
of Hamour, and a revival of
character writing.
Earle is polish, sentence, and 1818th
restoration Swift and is 17. And
Overbury the while Shakespeare is wit.

SIR THOMAS OVERBURY HIS WIFE . . .
NEW NEWS AND DIVERS MORE CHARACTERS [1]

A Courtier

To ALL men's thinking is a man, and to most men the finest: all things else are defined by the understanding, but this by the senses; but his surest mark is, that he is to be found only about princes. He smells; and putteth away much of his judgment about the situation of his clothes. He knows no man that is not generally known. His wit, like the marigold, openeth with the sun, and therefore he riseth not before ten of the clock. He puts more confidence in his words than meaning, and more in his pronunciation than his words. Occasion is his Cupid, and he hath but one receipt of making love. He follows nothing but inconstancy, admires nothing but beauty, honors nothing but fortune. Loves nothing. The sustenance of his discourse is news, and his censure, like a shot, depends upon the charging. He is not, if he be out of court, but fish-like breathes destruction if out of his own element. Neither his motion or aspect are regular, but he moves by the upper spheres and is the reflection of higher substances.

If you find him not here, you shall in Paul's, with a pick-tooth in his hat, a cape cloak, and a long stocking.

A Wise Man

Is THE truth of the true definition of man, that is, a reasonable creature. His disposition alters, he alters not. He hides himself with the attire of the vulgar; and in indifferent things is content to be governed by them. He looks according to nature, so goes his behavior. His mind enjoys a con-

[1] Text: 1616, ninth impression augmented.

tinual smoothness: so cometh it, that his consideration is
always at home. He endures the faults of all men silently,
except his friends, and to them he is the mirror of their
actions: by this means his peace cometh not from fortune,
but himself. He is cunning in men, not to surprise but keep
his own, and beats off their ill affected humors no otherwise
than ·if they were flies. He chooseth not friends by the
subsidy-book, and is not luxurious after acquaintance. He
maintains the strength of his body, not by delicacies, but
temperance; and his mind by giving it pre-eminence over
his body. He understands things not by their form, but qualities; and his comparisons intend not to excuse, but to provoke him higher. He is not subject to casualties, for fortune
hath nothing to do with the mind, except those drowned in
the body: but he hath divided his soul from the case of his
soul, whose weakness he assists no otherwise than commisera-
tively, not that it is his, but that it is. He is thus and will
be thus; and lives subject neither to time nor his frailties,
the servant of virtue, and by virtue the friend of the highest.

A Good Wife

Is A man's best movable, a scion incorporate with the
stock, bringing sweet fruit; one that to her husband is more
than a friend, less than trouble: an equal with him in the
yoke. Calamities and troubles she shares alike; nothing
pleaseth her that doth not him. She is relative in all; and he
without her, but half himself. She is his absent hands, eyes,
ears, and mouth: his present and absent all. She frames her
nature unto his howsoever: the hyacinth follows not the
sun more willingly. Stubbornness and obstinacy are herbs
that grow not in her garden. She leaves tattling to the gos-
sips of the town, and is more seen than heard. Her household
is her charge; her care to that makes her seldom non-resident.
Her pride is but to be cleanly, and her thrift not to be prodi-

gal. By her discretion she hath children, not wantons; a
husband without her is a misery in man's apparel: none but
she hath an aged husband, to whom she is both a staff and
a chair. To conclude, she is both wise and religious, which
makes her all this.

A Puritan

Is A diseased piece of Apocrypha: bind him to the Bible,
and he corrupts the whole text; ignorance, and fat feed are
his founders; his nurses, railing, rabies, and round breeches;
his life is but a borrowed blast of wind, for between two
religions, as between two doors, he is ever whistling. Truly
whose child he is, is yet unknown, for willingly his faith
allows no father: only thus far his pedigree is found, Brag-
ger and he flourished about a time first; his fiery zeal keeps
him continually costive, which withers him into his own
translation, and till he eat a Schoolman, he is hide-bound;
he ever prays against non-residents, but is himself the greatest discontinuer, for he never keeps near his text: anything
that the law allows, but marriage, and March-beer, he mur-
murs at; what it disallows and holds dangerous, makes him
a discipline. Where the gate stands open, he is ever seeking
a stile; and where his learning ought to climb, he creeps
through; give him advice, you run into *traditions,* and urge
a modest course, he cries out *councils.* His greatest care is
to condemn obedience, his last care to serve God handsomely
and cleanly; he is now become so cross a kind of teaching,
that should the church enjoin clean shirts, he were lousy;
more sense than single prayers is not his, nor more in those
than still the same petitions: from which he either fears
a learned faith, or doubts God understands not at first hearing. Show him a ring, he runs back like a bear; and hates
square dealing as allied to caps; a pair of organs blow him
out of the parish and are the only clyster pipes to cool him.

Where the meat is best, there he confutes most, for his arguing is but the efficacy of his eating: good bits he holds breeds
good positions, and the Pope he best concludes against in
plum-broth. He is often drunk, but not as we are, temporally;
nor can his sleep then cure him, for the fumes of his ambition make his very soul reel, and that small beer that should
allay him (silence) keeps him more surfeited, and makes his
heat break out in private houses; women and lawyers are
his best disciples, the one next fruit, longs for forbidden
doctrine, the other to maintain forbidden titles, both which
he sows amongst them. Honest he dare not be, for that loves
order; yet if he can be brought to ceremony, and made but
master of it, he is converted.

A Fair and Happy Milkmaid [2]

Is A country wench, that is so far from making herself
beautiful by art, that one look of hers is able to put all
face-physic out of countenance. She knows a fair look is but
a dumb orator to commend virtue, therefore minds it not.
All her excellencies stand in her so silently as if they had
stolen upon her without her knowledge. The lining of her
apparel (which is herself) is far better than outsides of tissue: for though she be not arrayed in the spoil of the silk-
worm, she is decked in innocence, a far better wearing. She
doth not, with lying long abed, spoil both her complexion
and conditions; nature hath taught her too immoderate sleep
is rust to the soul; she rises therefore with chanticleer, her
dame's cock, and at night makes the lamb her curfew. In
milking a cow, and straining the teats through her fingers,
it seems that so sweet a milk-press makes the milk the
whiter, or sweeter; for never came almond glove or aromatic
ointment on her palm to taint it. The golden ears of corn
fall and kiss her feet when she reaps them, as if they wished

[2] Probably by John Webster.

to be bound and led prisoners by the same hand that felled them. Her breath is her own, which scents all the year long of June, like a new-made haycock. She makes her hand hard with labor, and her heart soft with pity; and when winter evenings fall early (sitting at her merry wheel), she sings a defiance to the giddy wheel of fortune. She doth all things with so sweet a grace, it seems ignorance will not suffer her to do ill, being her mind is to do well. She bestows her year's wages at next fair; and in choosing her garments, counts no bravery in the world like decency. The garden and bee-hive are all her physic and chirurgery, and she lives the longer for it. She dares go alone, and unfold sheep in the night, and fears no manner of ill, because she means none: yet to say truth, she is never alone, for she is still accompanied with old songs, honest thoughts, and prayers, but short ones; yet they have their efficacy, in that they are not palled with ensuing idle cogitations. Lastly, her dreams are so chaste that she dare tell them; only a Friday's dream is all her superstition: that she conceals for fear of anger. Thus lives she, and all her care is she may die in the springtime, to have store of flowers stuck upon her winding-sheet.

A Roaring Boy

His LIFE is a mere counterfeit patent, which, nevertheless, makes many a country justice tremble. Don Quixote's water mills are still Scotch bagpipes to him. He sends challenges by word of mouth, for he protests (as he is a gentleman and a brother of the sword) he can neither write nor read. He hath run through divers parcels of land and great houses, beside both the counters. If any private quarrel happen among our great courtiers, he proclaims the business, that's the word, the *business;* as if the united forces of the Romish Catholics were making up for Germany. He cheats young gulls that are newly come to town; and when the keeper of the ordinary blames him for it, he answers him in his own profession, that a woodcock must be plucked ere he be dressed. He is a superior to brothels, and in them is a more unlawful reformer of vice than prentices on Shrove-Tuesday. He loves his friend as a counselor at law loves the velvet breeches he was first made barrister in: he'll be sure to wear him threadbare ere he forsake him. He sleeps with a tobacco pipe in his mouth; and his first prayer in the morning is, he may remember whom he fell out with overnight. Soldier he is none, for he cannot distinguish between onion feed and gunpowder; if he have worn it in his hollow tooth for the toothache, and so come to the knowledge of it, that's all. The tenure by which he holds his means is an estate at will; and that's borrowing. Landlords have but four quarter-days; but he three hundred and odd. He keeps very good company; yet is a man of no reckoning, and when he goes not drunk to bed, he is very sick next morning. He commonly dies like Anacreon, with a grape in his throat; or Hercules, with fire in his marrow. And I have heard of some (that have escaped hanging) begged for anatomies, only to deter men from taking tobacco.

A Phantastic

An Improvident Young Gallant

THERE IS a confederacy between him and his clothes, to be made a puppy; view him well, and you'll say his gentry fits as ill upon him, as if he had bought it with his penny. He hath more places to send money to than the devil hath to send his spirits; and to furnish each mistress would make him run beside his wits, if he had any to lose. He accounts bashfulness the wickedest thing in the world, and therefore studies impudence. If all men were of his mind, all honesty would be out of fashion: he withers his clothes on the stage, as a salesman is forced to do his suits in Birching-Lane; and when the play is done, if you mark his rising, 'tis with a kind of walking epilogue between the two candles, to know if his suit may pass for current; he studies by the discretion of his barber to frizzle like a baboon: three such would keep three the nimblest barbers in the town from ever having leisure to wear net garters, for when they have to do with him, they have many irons in the fire. He is traveled, but to little purpose; only went over for a squirt, and came back again, yet never the more mended in his conditions because he carried himself along with him: a scholar he pretends himself, and says he hath sweated for it; but the truth is, he knows Cornelius far better than Tacitus: his ordinary sports are cock fights; but the most frequent, horse races, from whence he comes home dry-foundered; thus when his purse hath cast her calf, he goes down into the country, where he is brought to milk and white cheese like the Switzers.

What a Character Is

IF I MUST speak the schoolmaster's language, I will confess that character comes from this infinite mood χαρά ξω, that signifieth to engrave, or make a deep impression. And for that cause, a letter (as A, B) is called a character.

Those elements which we learn first, leaving a strong seal in our memories.

Character is also taken from an Egyptian hieroglyphic, for an impress, or short emblem; in little comprehending much.

To square out a character by our English level, it is a picture (real or personal) quaintly drawn, in various colors, all of them heightened by one shadowing.

It is a quick and soft touch of many strings, all shutting up in one musical close; it is wit's descant on any plain song.

HOBBES, "poet and philosopher of Malmesbury," [1] is said
to have loved the book shops better than the lecture halls
when he was a student at Magdalen Hall, Oxford; nevertheless he took an A.B. degree in February 1608. He became
tutor to the eldest son of William Cavendish, only two years
younger than himself, and accompanied him on the usual
grand tour of the Continent. This trip vitalized his interest
in learning, and during the eighteen years he was in the
Cavendish home he seriously undertook to broaden his own
knowledge. He also found his way into literary circles, becoming the friend of such men as Bacon, Ben Jonson, and
Edward Herbert of Cherbury.

After the death of his first pupil, Hobbes undertook two
more tutorships, during each of which he was again on the
Continent. The most lasting effects on Hobbes were his first
acquaintance with the work of Euclid and association with
some of the leading European thinkers, who stimulated his
interest in philosophy.

He returned to an England torn by political conflict. His
The Elements of Law, National and Politique, advancing
the theory of social compact, was published in 1640, and he
became alarmed for himself when Laud and Strafford were
sent to the Tower. Fleeing to France, he spent eleven years
with the exiled group in Paris. He was tutor in mathematics
to Prince Charles, and was associated with Marsenne, the
friend of Descartes. It was during this time that he wrote
his anonymous "Objections" to Descartes' *Meditations* and
Dioptrique. The *De Cive* (1642), in which he stresses the
necessity for the subordination of the church to the state,
and the *Leviathan* (1651) belong also to this period. From
the latter, which Burnet calls "a very wicked book with a

[1] Preface to Sylvæ (1685), *Essays of John Dryden,* ed. W. P. Ker. 2 vols.
(Oxford, 1926) I, 259.

very strange title," arose suspicion of disloyalty so that he was barred from the Court circle. Attacks on the papacy endangered him among the French, and so it was necessary for him to return to England and make his submission to the Commonwealth. He then entered upon controversial subjects of less danger, arguing with the younger scientific men at Oxford concerning mathematics and physics.

After the Restoration he was again recognized by Charles II, but this fact did not save him from being under suspicion when the question arose as to whose wickedness brought down upon London the plague and the fire. After 1666 Hobbes was not allowed to publish anything for a number of years. The translation of first the *Odyssey* and then the *Iliad* belong to his old age.

CHAPTER XVII

Of the Causes, Generation, and Definition of a Commonwealth

THE FINAL cause, end, or design of men (who naturally love liberty and dominion over others) in the introduction of that restraint upon themselves (in which we see them live in commonwealths) is the foresight of their own preservation and of a more contented life thereby; that is to say, of getting themselves out from that miserable condition of war, which is necessarily consequent (as hath been shown) to the natural passions of men, when there is no visible power to keep them in awe and tie them by fear of punishment to the performance of their covenants, and observation of those laws of nature set down in the fourteenth and fifteenth chapters.

The end of Commonwealth, particular security:

Chap. 13.

For the laws of nature (as justice, equity, modesty, mercy, and, in sum, doing to others as we would be done to) of themselves, without the terror of some power to cause them to be observed, are contrary to our natural passions that carry us to partiality, pride, revenge, and the like. And covenants, without the sword, are but words, and of no strength to secure a man at all. Therefore, notwithstanding the laws of nature (which everyone hath then kept when he has the will to keep them, when he can do it safely), if there be no power erected or not great enough for our security, every man will, and may lawfully rely on his own strength and art for caution against all other men. And in all places where men have lived by small families, to rob and spoil one another has been a trade, and so far from being reputed against the law of nature, that the greater spoils they gained, the greater was their honor;

Which is not to be had from the law of nature:

[1] Text: 1651, first edition.

and men observed no other laws therein but the laws of honor: that is, to abstain from cruelty, leaving to men their lives, and instruments of husbandry. And as small families did then, so now do cities and kingdoms, which are but greater families, (for their own security) enlarge their dominions, upon all pretenses of danger and fear of invasion or assistance that may be given to invaders, endeavor as much as they can to subdue, or weaken their neighbors by open force and secret arts, for want of other caution, justly; and are remembered for it in after ages with honor.

Nor from the conjunction of a few men or families:

Nor is it the joining together of a small number of men that gives them this security, because, in small numbers, small additions on the one side or the other make the advantage of strength so great as is sufficient to carry the victory, and therefore gives encouragement to an invasion. The multitude sufficient to confide in for our security is not determined by any certain number, but by comparison with the enemy we fear; and is then sufficient when the odds of the enemy is not of so visible and conspicuous moment to determine the event of war as to move him to attempt.

Nor from a great multitude, unless directed by one judgment:

And be there never so great a multitude, yet if their actions be directed according to their particular judgments and particular appetites, they can expect thereby no defense nor protection, neither against a common enemy nor against the injuries of one another. For being distracted in opinions concerning the best use and application of their strength, they do not help, but hinder one another; and reduce their strength by mutual opposition to nothing: whereby they are easily not only subdued by a very few that agree together; but also when there is no common enemy, they make war upon each other for their particular interests. For if we could suppose a great multitude of men to consent in the observation of justice and other laws of nature, without a common power to keep them all in awe, we might as well suppose all mankind to do the same; and then there neither would be, nor need to be, any civil government or commonwealth at all, because there would be peace without subjection.

Nor is it enough for the security which men desire *And that* should last all the time of their life that they be governed *continually.* and directed by one judgment for a limited time, as in one battle or one war. For though they obtain a victory by their unanimous endeavor against a foreign enemy, yet afterwards, when either they have no common enemy, or he that by one part is held for an enemy is by another part held for a friend, they must needs by the difference of their interests dissolve, and fall again into a war amongst themselves.

It is true that certain living creatures, as bees and ants, *Why certain* live sociably one with another (which are therefore by *creatures* Aristotle numbered amongst political creatures), and yet *without rea-* have no other direction than their particular judgments *son, or* and appetites; nor speech, whereby one of them can *speech, do* signify to another what he thinks expedient for the com- *neverthe-* mon benefit; and therefore some man may perhaps desire *less live* to know why mankind cannot do the same. To which I *in society,* answer: *without any* *coercive* First, that men are continually in competition for honor *power.* and dignity, which these creatures are not; and consequently amongst men there ariseth on that ground envy and hatred and finally war; but amongst these not so.

Secondly, that amongst these creatures the common good differeth not from the private; and being by nature inclined to their private, they procure thereby the common benefit. But man, whose joy consisteth in comparing himself with other men, can relish nothing but what is eminent.

Thirdly, that these creatures, having not (as man) the use of reason, do not see nor think they see any fault in the administration of their common business; whereas amongst men, there are very many that think themselves wiser, and abler to govern the public better than the rest; and these strive to reform and innovate, one this way, another that way, and thereby bring it into distraction and civil war.

Fourthly, that these creatures, though they have some use of voice in making known to one another their desires and other affections, yet they want that art of words by which some men can represent to others that which is good in the likeness of evil, and evil in the likeness of good, and augment or diminish the apparent greatness of good and evil; discontenting men and troubling their peace at their pleasure.

Fifthly, irrational creatures cannot distinguish between injury and damage; and therefore as long as they be at ease, they are not offended with their fellows: whereas man is then most troublesome when he is most at ease; for then it is that he loves to show his wisdom, and control the actions of them that govern the commonwealth.

Lastly, the agreement of these creatures is natural; that of men is by covenant only, which is artificial: and therefore it is no wonder if there be somewhat else required (besides covenant) to make their agreement constant and lasting; which is a common power to keep them in awe and to direct their actions to the common benefit.

The genera-tion of a common-wealth.

The only way to erect such a common power as may be able to defend them from the invasion of foreigners and the injuries of one another, and thereby to secure them in such sort as that by their own industry and by the fruits of the earth they may nourish themselves and live contentedly, is to confer all their power and strength upon one man, or upon one assembly of men, that may reduce all their wills, by plurality of voices, unto one will: which is as much as to say, to appoint one man, or assembly of men, to bear their person; and everyone to own and acknowledge himself to be author of whatsoever he that so beareth their person shall act, or cause to be acted, in those things which concern the common peace and safety; and therein to submit their wills, everyone to his will, and their judgments, to his judgment. This is more than consent or concord; it is a real unity of them all, in one and the same person, made by covenant of every man with every man, in such manner as if every man should say to every man, *I authorize and give up my right of governing myself to this man, or to this assembly of men, on this condition, that thou give up thy right to him, and authorize all his actions in like manner.* This done, the multitude so united in one person is called a commonwealth, in Latin *civitas.* This is the generation of that great leviathan, or rather (to speak more reverently) of that *mortal god,* to which we owe under the *immortal God,* our peace and defense. For by this authority, given him by every particular man in the commonwealth, he hath the use of so much power and strength conferred on him that by terror thereof he is enabled to conform the wills of them all to peace at home and mutual aid against their enemies abroad. And in him consisteth the essence of the commonwealth; which (to define it) is *one person, of whose acts a great multitude, by mutual covenants one with another, have made themselves every one the author, to the end he may use the strength and means of them all as he shall think expedient, for their peace and common defense.* *The definition of a commonwealth.*

And he that carrieth this person is called sovereign, and said to have *sovereign power;* and everyone besides, his subject. *Sovereign, and subject, what.*

The attaining to this sovereign power is by two ways. One, by natural force; as when a man maketh his children to submit themselves and their children to his government, as being able to destroy them if they refuse; or by war subdueth his enemies to his will, giving them their lives on that condition. The other is when men agree amongst themselves to submit to some man, or assembly of men, voluntarily, on confidence to be protected by him against all others. This latter may be called a political commonwealth, or commonwealth by *institution;* and the former, a commonwealth by *acquisition.* And first, I shall speak of a commonwealth by institution. . . .

CHAPTER XIX

Of the Several Kinds of Commonwealth by Institution and of Succession to the Sovereign Power

The different forms of commonwealths but three.

THE DIFFERENCE of commonwealths consisteth in the difference of the sovereign, or the person representative of all and everyone of the multitude. And because the sovereignty is either in one man or in an assembly of more than one; and into that assembly either every man hath right to enter or not everyone, but certain men distinguished from the rest, it is manifest there can be but three kinds of commonwealth. For the representative must needs be one man, or more; and if more, then it is the assembly of all, or but of a part. When the representative is one man, then is the commonwealth a monarchy; when an assembly of all that will come together, then it is a democracy, or popular commonwealth; when an assembly of a part only, then it is called an aristocracy. Other kind of commonwealth there can be none; for either one, or more, or all, must have the sovereign power (which I have shown to be indivisible) entire.

Tyranny and oligarchy, but different names of monarchy and aristocracy.

There be other names of government in the histories and books of policy, as tyranny and oligarchy; but they are not the names of other forms of government, but of the same forms misliked. For they that are discontented under monarchy call it tyranny; and they that are displeased with aristocracy call it oligarchy: so, also, they which find themselves grieved under a democracy call it

anarchy (which signifies want of government); and yet
I think no man believes that want of government is any
new kind of government; nor by the same reason ought
they to believe that the government is of one kind when
they like it, and another when they mislike it or are oppressed by the governors.

It is manifest that men who are in absolute liberty, *Subordinate*
may, if they please, give authority to one man to repre- *representa-*
sent them everyone; as well as give such authority to *tives dan-*
any assembly of men whatsoever; and consequently may *gerous.*
subject themselves, if they think good, to a monarch as
absolutely as to any other representative. Therefore,
where there is already erected a sovereign power, there
can be no other representative of the same people, but
only to certain particular ends, by the sovereign limited.
For that were to erect two sovereigns; and every man to
have his person represented by two actors, that by opposing one another, must needs divide that power, which
(if men will live in peace) is indivisible; and thereby
reduce the multitude into the condition of war, contrary
to the end for which all sovereignty is instituted. And
therefore as it is absurd to think that a sovereign assembly, inviting the people of their dominion to send up their
deputies with power to make known their advice or desires, should therefore hold such deputies, rather than
themselves, for the absolute representative of the people;
so it is absurd, also, to think the same in a monarchy. And
I know not how this so manifest a truth should of late
be so little observed; that in a monarchy, he that had
the sovereignty from a descent of 600 years was alone
called sovereign, had the title of majesty from every one
of his subjects, and was unquestionably taken by them
for their king, was notwithstanding never considered as
their representative; that name without contradiction
passing for the title of those men, which at his command
were sent up by the people to carry their petitions, and

give him (if he permitted it) their advice. Which may serve as an admonition for those that are the true and absolute representative of a people, to instruct men in the nature of that office, and to take heed how they admit of any other general representation upon any occasion whatsoever, if they mean to discharge the trust committed to them.

Comparison of monarchy with sovereign assemblies.

The difference between these three kinds of commonwealth consisteth not in the difference of power, but in the difference of convenience or aptitude to produce the peace and security of the people; for which end they were instituted. And to compare monarchy with the other two, we may observe: first, that whosoever beareth the person of the people or is one of the assembly that bears it beareth also his own natural person. And though he be careful in his politic person to procure the common interest, yet he is more, or no less careful to procure the private good of himself, his family, kindred, and friends; and for the most part, if the public interest chance to cross the private, he prefers the private; for the passions of men are commonly more potent than their reason. From whence it follows that where the public and private interest are most closely united, there is the public most advanced. Now in monarchy, the private interest is the same with the public. The riches, power, and honor of a monarch arise only from the riches, strength, and reputation of his subjects. For no king can be rich, nor glorious, nor secure, whose subjects are either poor, or contemptible, or too weak through want or dissension to maintain a war against their enemies: whereas in a democracy or aristocracy the public prosperity confers not so much to the private fortune of one that is corrupt or ambitious as doth many times a perfidious advice, a treacherous action, or a civil war.

Secondly, that a monarch receiveth counsel of whom, when, and where he pleaseth; and consequently may hear

the opinion of men versed in the matter about which he
deliberates, of what rank or quality soever, and as long
before the time of action and with as much secrecy as he
will. But when a sovereign assembly has need of counsel,
none are admitted but such as have a right thereto from
the beginning, which for the most part are of those who
have been versed more in the acquisition of wealth than
of knowledge; and are to give their advice in long discourses, which may and do commonly excite men to action, but not govern them in it. For the understanding is
by the flame of the passions, never enlightened, but
dazzled; nor is there any place or time wherein an assembly can receive counsel with secrecy, because of their
own multitude.

Thirdly, that the resolutions of a monarch are subject
to no other inconstancy than that of human nature; but
in assemblies, besides that of nature, there ariseth an inconstancy from the number. For the absence of a few
that would have the resolution, once taken, continue firm
(which may happen by security, negligence, or private
impediments), or the diligent appearance of a few of the
contrary opinion, undoes today all that was concluded
yesterday.

Fourthly, that a monarch cannot disagree with himself out of envy, or interest; but an assembly may, and
that to such a height as may produce a civil war.

Fifthly, that in monarchy there is this inconvenience:
that any subject, by the power of one man, for the enriching of a favorite or flatterer, may be deprived of all
he possesseth; which I confess is a great and inevitable
inconvenience. But the same may as well happen where
the sovereign power is in an assembly: for their power
is the same; and they are subject to evil counsel and to
be seduced by orators, as a monarch by flatterers; and
becoming one another's flatterers, serve one another's
covetousness and ambition by turns. And whereas the

favorites of monarchs are few, and they have none else to advance but their own kindred; the favorites of an assembly are many, and the kindred much more numerous than of any monarch. Besides, there is no favorite of a monarch which cannot as well succor his friends as hurt his enemies; but orators, that is to say, favorites of sovereign assemblies, though they have great power to hurt, have little to save. For to accuse requires less eloquence (such is man's nature) than to excuse; and condemnation, than absolution more resembles justice.

Sixthly, that it is an inconvenience in monarchy, that the sovereignty may descend upon an infant, or one that cannot discern between good and evil; and consisteth in this, that the use of his power must be in the hand of another man, or of some assembly of men, which are to govern by his right and in his name, as curators and protectors of his person and authority. But to say there is inconvenience in putting the use of the sovereign power into the hand of a man, or an assembly of men, is to say that all government is more inconvenient than confusion and civil war. And therefore all the danger that can be pretended must arise from the contention of those that for an office of so great honor and profit may become competitors. To make it appear that this inconvenience proceedeth not from that form of government we call monarchy, we are to consider that the precedent monarch hath appointed who shall have the tuition of his infant successor, either expressly by testament, or tacitly by not controlling the custom in that case received: and then such inconvenience (if it happen) is to be attributed, not to the monarchy, but to the ambition and injustice of the subjects; which in all kinds of government where the people are not well instructed in their duty and the rights of sovereignty is the same. Or else the prece-

dent monarch hath not at all taken order for such tuition; and then the law of nature hath provided this sufficient rule, that the tuition shall be in him that hath
by nature most interest in the preservation of the authority of the infant, and to whom least benefit can accrue by his death or diminution. For seeing every man
by nature seeketh his own benefit and promotion, to put
an infant into the power of those that can promote themselves by his destruction or damage is not tuition but
treachery. So that sufficient provision being taken against
all just quarrel about the government under a child, if
any contention arise to the disturbance of the public peace,
it is not to be attributed to the form of monarchy, but
to the ambition of subjects and ignorance of their duty.
On the other side, there is no great commonwealth, the
sovereignty whereof is in a great assembly, which is not,
as to consultations of peace, and war, and making of laws,
in the same condition as if the government were in a
child. For as a child wants the judgment to dissent from
counsel given him and is thereby necessitated to take the
advice of them, or him, to whom he is committed: so an
assembly wanteth the liberty to dissent from the counsel
of the major part, be it good or bad. And as a child has
need of a tutor, or protector, to preserve his person and
authority: so also (in great commonwealths) the sovereign
assembly, in all great dangers and troubles, have need
of *custodes libertatis;* that is of dictators, protectors of
their authority, which are as much as temporary monarchs; to whom for a time they may commit the entire
exercise of their power, and have (at the end of that time)
been oftener deprived thereof than infant kings by their
protectors, regents, or any other tutors. . . .

CHAPTER XXI

Of the Liberty of Subjects

LIBERTY, or freedom, signifieth, properly, the absence of opposition (by opposition I mean external impediments of motion), and may be applied no less to irrational and inanimate creatures than to rational. For whatsoever is so tied or environed as it cannot move but within a certain space, which space is determined by the opposition of some external body, we say it hath not liberty to go further. And so of all living creatures whilst they are imprisoned or restrained with walls or chains; and of the water whilst it is kept in banks or vessels, that otherwise would spread itself into a larger space, we use to say they are not at liberty to move in such manner as without those external impediments they would. But when the impediment of motion is in the constitution of the thing itself, we use not to say it wants the liberty, but the power, to move, as when a stone lieth still, or a man is fastened to his bed by sickness.

What it is to be free. And according to this proper and generally received meaning of the word, a FREE MAN *is he that in those things which by his strength and wit he is able to do is not hindered to do what he has a will to.* But when the words *free* and *liberty* are applied to anything but *bodies*, they are abused; for that which is not subject to motion is not subject to impediment: and therefore, when 'tis said (for example) the way is free, no liberty of the way is signified, but of those that walk in it without stop. And when we say a gift is free, there is not meant any liberty of the gift, but of the giver, that was not bound by any law or covenant to give it. So when we *speak freely*, it is not the liberty of voice or pronunciation, but of the man, whom no law hath obliged to speak otherwise than he did. Lastly, from the use of the word *free will*, no liberty can be inferred of the will, desire, or inclination, but the liberty of the man; which consisteth in this, that he finds no stop in doing what he has the will, desire, or inclination to do.

Fear and liberty are consistent; as when a man throweth his goods into the sea for *fear* the ship should sink, he doth it nevertheless very willingly, and may refuse to do it if he will: it is therefore the action of one that was *free*: so a man sometimes pays his debt only for *fear* of imprisonment, which because nobody hindered him from detaining was the action of a man at *liberty*. And generally all actions which men do in commonwealths for *fear* of the law are actions which the doers had *liberty* to omit.

Fear and liberty consistent.

Liberty and *necessity* are consistent; as in the water that hath not only *liberty*, but a *necessity* of descending by the channel; so likewise in the actions which men voluntarily do: which, because they proceed from their will, proceed from *liberty*; and yet because every act of man's will, and every desire, and inclination proceedeth from some cause, and that from another cause, in a continual chain (whose first link is in the hand of God the first of all causes), they proceed from *necessity*. So that to him that could see the connection of those causes, the *necessity* of all men's voluntary actions would appear manifest. And therefore God, that seeth and disposeth all things, seeth also that the *liberty* of man in doing what he will is accompanied with the *necessity* of doing that which God will, and no more nor less. For though men may do many things which God does not command, nor is therefore author of them; yet they can have no passion, nor appetite to anything of which appetite God's will is not the cause. And did not his will assure the *necessity* of man's will, and consequently of all that on man's will dependeth, the *liberty* of men would be a contradiction

Liberty and necessity consistent.

and impediment to the omnipotence and *liberty* of God. And this shall suffice (as to the matter in hand) of that natural liberty, which only is properly called *liberty*.

Artificial bonds, or covenants.

But as men, for the attaining of peace and conservation of themselves thereby, have made an artificial man, which we call a commonwealth; so also have they made artificial chains, called *civil laws,* which they themselves, by mutual covenants, have fastened at one end to the lips of that man, or assembly, to whom they have given the sovereign power; and at the other end to their own ears. These bonds in their own nature but weak, may nevertheless be made to hold by the danger, though not by the difficulty, of breaking them.

Liberty of subjects consisteth in liberty from covenants.

In relation to these bonds only it is that I am to speak now of the *liberty* of *subjects.* For seeing there is no commonwealth in the world wherein there be rules enough set down for the regulating of all the actions and words of men (as being a thing impossible), it followeth necessarily that in all kinds of actions by the laws pretermitted, men have the liberty of doing what their own reasons shall suggest for the most profitable to themselves. For if we take liberty in the proper sense for corporal liberty, that is to say, freedom from chains and prison, it were very absurd for men to clamor as they do for the liberty they so manifestly enjoy. Again, if we take liberty for an exemption from laws, it is no less absurd for men to demand as they do, that liberty by which all other men may be masters of their lives. And yet as absurd as it is, this is it they demand; not knowing that the laws are of no power to protect them, without a sword in the hands of a man or men to cause those laws to be put in execution. The liberty of a subject lieth therefore only in those things which in regulating their actions, the sovereign hath pretermitted: such as is the liberty to buy, and sell, and otherwise contract with one another; to choose their own abode, their own diet, their own trade of life, and institute their children as they themselves think fit, and the like.

Nevertheless, we are not to understand that by such liberty the sovereign power of life and death is either abolished or limited. For it has been already shown that nothing the sovereign representative can do to a subject, on what pretense soever, can properly be called injustice or injury, because every subject is author of every act the sovereign doth; so that he never wanteth right to any thing, otherwise than as he himself is the subject of God and bound thereby to observe the laws of nature. And therefore it may, and doth, often happen in commonwealths that a subject may be put to death by the command of the sovereign power, and yet neither do the other wrong: as when Jephtha caused his daughter to be sacrificed; [2] in which, and the like cases, he that so dieth had liberty to do the action for which he is nevertheless without injury put to death. And the same holdeth also in a sovereign prince that putteth to death an innocent subject. For though the action be against the law of nature as being contrary to equity (as was the killing of Uriah by David),[3] yet it was not an injury to Uriah, but to God. Not to Uriah, because the right to do what he pleased was given him by Uriah himself; and yet to God, because David was God's subject, and prohibited all iniquity by the law of nature. Which distinction, David himself, when he repented the fact, evidently confirmed, saying, *To thee only have I sinned*. In the same manner, the people of Athens, when they banished the most potent of their commonwealth for ten years, thought they committed no injustice; and yet they never questioned what crime he had done, but what hurt he would do: nay, they commanded the banishment of they knew not whom; and every citizen bringing his oyster shell into the market place, written with the name of him he desired should be

Liberty of the subject consistent with the unlimited power of the sovereign.

[2] Judges 11:30–40.   [3] II Sam. 11.

banished, without actually accusing him, sometimes banished an Aristides for his reputation of justice; and sometimes a scurrilous jester, as Hyperbolus, to make a jest of it. And yet a man cannot say, the sovereign people of Athens wanted right to banish them, or an Athenian the liberty to jest or to be just.

The liberty which writers praise is the liberty of sovereigns, not of private men.

The liberty whereof there is so frequent and honorable mention in the histories and philosophy of the ancient Greeks and Romans, and in the writings and discourse of those that from them have received all their learning in the politics, is not the liberty of particular men, but the liberty of the commonwealth; which is the same with that which every man then should have, if there were no civil laws nor commonwealth at all. And the effects of it also be the same. For as amongst masterless men there is perpetual war of every man against his neighbor; no inheritance to transmit to the son, nor to expect from the father; no propriety of goods or lands; no security, but a full and absolute liberty in every particular man: so in states and commonwealths not dependent on one another, every commonwealth (not every man) has an absolute liberty to do what it shall judge (that is to say, what that man, or assembly that representeth it, shall judge) most conducing to their benefit. But withal, they live in the condition of a perpetual war, and upon the confines of battle, with their frontiers armed and cannons planted against their neighbors round about. The Athenians and Romans were free, that is, free commonwealths: not that any particular men had the liberty to resist their own representative, but that their representative had the liberty to resist or invade other people. There is written on the turrets of the city of Lucca in great characters at this day, the word LIBERTAS; yet no man can thence infer that a particular man has more liberty or immunity from the service of the commonwealth there than in Constantinople. Whether a commonwealth be monarchical or popular, the freedom is still the same.

But it is an easy thing for men to be deceived by the specious name of liberty; and for want of judgment to distinguish, mistake that for their private inheritance and birthright which is the right of the public only. And when the same error is confirmed by the authority of men in reputation for their writings on this subject, it is no wonder if it produce sedition and change of government. In these western parts of the world we are made to receive our opinions concerning the institution and rights of commonwealths, from Aristotle, Cicero, and other men, Greeks and Romans, that living under popular states, derived those rights not from the principles of nature, but transcribed them into their books out of the practice of their own commonwealths, which were popular; as the grammarians describe the rules of language out of the practice of the time; or the rules of poetry out of the poems of Homer and Virgil. And because the Athenians were taught (to keep them from desire of changing their government) that they were free men, and all that lived under monarchy were slaves, therefore Aristotle puts it down in his *Politics* (*lib. 6 cap. 2*), *In democracy, liberty is to be supposed: for 'tis commonly held that no man is free in any other government*. And as Aristotle, so Cicero and other writers have grounded their civil doctrine on the opinions of the Romans, who were taught to hate monarchy, at first, by them that having deposed their sovereign shared amongst them the sovereignty of Rome, and afterwards by their successors. And by reading of these Greek and Latin authors, men from their childhood have gotten a habit (under a false show of liberty) of favoring tumults, and of licentious controlling the actions of their sovereigns; and again of controlling those controllers, with the effusion of so much blood as I think I may truly say, there was never anything so dearly bought as these western parts have bought the learning of the Greek and Latin tongues.

Liberty of subjects, how to be measured.

To come now to the particulars of the true liberty of a subject, that is to say, what are the things, which though commanded by the sovereign, he may nevertheless, without injustice, refuse to do; we are to consider what rights we pass away when we make a commonwealth; or (which is all one) what liberty we deny ourselves by owning all the actions (without exception) of the man or assembly we make our sovereign. For in the act of our submission, consisteth both our obligation and our liberty; which must therefore be inferred by arguments taken from thence, there being no obligation on any man which ariseth not from some act of his own; for all men equally are by nature free. And because such arguments must either be drawn from the express words, *I authorize all his actions,* or from the intention of him that submitteth himself to his power (which intention is to be understood by the end for which he so submitteth), the obligation, and liberty of the subject is to be derived either from those words (or others equivalent), or else from the end of the institution of sovereignty; namely, the peace of the subjects within themselves, and their defense against a common enemy. . . .

Izaak Walton was born in Staffordshire and probably had little schooling. His wide acquaintance with literature came from his own reading and his friendships with many learned men, both divines and poets. He was early apprenticed to an ironmonger in London and after a short time had his own shop in Fleet Street. He became a member and vestryman at the neighboring church, St. Dunstan's in the West, where Donne was vicar. Here he formed a lasting friendship with Donne, and through Donne with Sir Henry Wotton and other prominent people.

It was for Wotton that he collected materials for a prefatory Life to a volume of Donne's Sermons, but after Wotton's death he fortunately undertook the biography himself. He also wrote brief biographies of Wotton, Richard Hooker, George Herbert, and Bishop Sanderson, all of which show him a master of portraiture, in spite of the fact that his characters take on much of the personality of the biographer.

In 1626 he married a descendant of Archbishop Cranmer. His seven children died in their infancy, and in 1640 his wife also died. Six years later he married the half sister of Bishop Ken, but outlived her by more than twenty years. These personal sorrows were borne quietly, and did not break the serenity of spirit which characterized the man. Some time after the death of his second wife, Walton was invited by George Morley, Bishop of Winchester, to make his home at the Bishop's Palace, and he lived the remainder of his long life in Winchester.

A city man who was in love with the country, Walton wrote an English prose pastoral which is unsurpassed. From this book one would never know that he had lived in the center of the stirring events and the expanding world of the seventeenth century, for here is only rural England quietly beautiful in the spring.

THE LIFE OF DR. JOHN DONNE [1]

MASTER JOHN DONNE was born in London in the year 1573,[2] of good and virtuous parents: and though his own learning and other multiplied merits may justly appear sufficient to dignify both himself and his posterity, yet the reader may be pleased to know that his father was masculinely and lineally descended from a very ancient family in Wales, where many of his name now live, that deserve, and have great reputation in that country.

By his mother he was descended of the family of the famous and learned Sir Thomas More, sometime Lord Chancellor of England: as also, from that worthy and laborious Judge Rastall, who left posterity the vast statutes of the law of this nation most exactly abridged.

He had his first breeding in his father's house, where a private tutor had the care of him, until the tenth year of his age; and in his eleventh year was sent to the university of Oxford, having at that time a good command both of the French and Latin tongue. This, and some other of his remarkable abilities, made one then give this censure of him: that this age had brought forth another Picus Mirandula, of whom story says, that he was rather born than made wise by study.

There he remained for some years in Hart Hall, having, for the advancement of his studies, tutors of several sciences to attend and instruct him, till time made him capable, and his learning expressed in public exercises declared him worthy, to receive his first degree in the schools; which he forbore by advice from his friends, who, being for their religion of the Romish persuasion, were conscionably averse

---

[1] Text: 1675, fourth edition. This *Life* was first prefixed to the 1640 edition of Donne's Sermons and was later revised and enlarged. It presents a highly idealized picture of Donne, without the violent contradictions that made up his nature.

[2] The time of his birth is now established at 1571/2.

to some parts of the oath that is always tendered at those times, and not to be refused by those that expect the titulary honor of their studies.

About the fourteenth year of his age, he was transplanted from Oxford to Cambridge; where, that he might receive nourishment from both soils, he stayed till his seventeenth year; all which time he was a most laborious student, often changing his studies, but endeavoring to take no degree, for the reasons formerly mentioned.

About the seventeenth year of his age he was removed to London, and then admitted into Lincoln's Inn with an intent to study the law; where he gave great testimonies of his wit, his learning, and of his improvement in that profession which never served him for other use than an ornament and self-satisfaction.

His father died before his admission into this society; and, being a merchant, left him his portion in money. (It was £3,000.) His mother, and those to whose care he was committed, were watchful to improve his knowledge, and to that end appointed him tutors both in the mathematics and in all the other liberal sciences, to attend him. But with these arts, they were advised to instill into him particular principles of the Romish Church; of which those tutors professed, though secretly, themselves to be members.

They had almost obliged him to their faith; having for their advantage, besides many opportunities, the example of his dear and pious parents, which was a most powerful persuasion and did work much upon him, as he professeth in his preface to his *Pseudo-Martyr,* a book of which the reader shall have some account in what follows.

He was now entered into the eighteenth year of his age; and at that time had betrothed himself to no religion that might give him any other denomination than a Christian. And reason and piety had both persuaded him that there could be no such sin as schism if an adherence to some visible church were not necessary.

About the nineteenth year of his age, he, being then un-resolved what religion to adhere to, and considering how much it concerned his soul to choose the most orthodox, did therefore (though his youth and health promised him a long life), to rectify all scruples that might concern that, pres-ently lay aside all study of the law, and of all other sciences that might give him a denomination; and begun seriously to survey and consider the body of divinity, as it was then controverted betwixt the Reformed and the Roman Church. And, as God's blessed Spirit did then awaken him to the search, and in that industry did never forsake him (they be his own words [3]), so he calls the same Holy Spirit to wit-ness this protestation: that in that disquisition and search he proceeded with humility and diffidence in himself, and by that which he took to be the safest way, namely, frequent prayers and an indifferent affection to both parties; and indeed, Truth had too much light about her to be hid from so sharp an inquirer; and he had too much ingenuity not to acknowledge he had found her.

Being to undertake this search, he believed the Cardinal Bellarmine to be the best defender of the Roman cause, and therefore betook himself to the examination of his reasons. The cause was weighty, and willful delays had been inex-cusable both towards God and his own conscience: he there-fore proceeded in this search with all moderate haste, and about the twentieth year of his age, did show the then Dean of Gloucester (whose name my memory hath now lost) all the Cardinal's works marked with many weighty observa-tions under his own hand; which works were bequeathed by him at his death as a legacy to a most dear friend.

About a year following he resolved to travel; and the Earl of Essex going first the Cadiz, and after, the Island voy-ages, the first *anno* 1596, the second 1597, he took the ad-vantage of those opportunities, waited upon his lordship,

[3] In his Preface to *Pseudo-Martyr.*

and was an eyewitness of those happy and unhappy employments.

But he returned not back into England, till he had stayed some years, first in Italy and then in Spain, where he made many useful observations of those countries, their laws and manner of government, and returned perfect in their languages.

The time that he spent in Spain was, at his first going into Italy, designed for traveling to the Holy Land, and for viewing Jerusalem and the sepulcher of our Saviour. But at his being in the furthest part of Italy, the disappointment of company, or of a safe convoy, or the uncertainty of returns of money into those remote parts, denied him that happiness, which he did often occasionally mention with a deploration.

Not long after his return into England, that exemplary pattern of gravity and wisdom, the Lord Ellesmere, then Keeper of the Great Seal, the Lord Chancellor of England, taking notice of his learning, languages, and other abilities, and much affecting his person and behavior, took him to be his chief secretary, supposing and intending it to be an introduction to some more weighty employment in the state; for which, his lordship did often protest, he thought him very fit.

Nor did his lordship in this time of Master Donne's attendance upon him account him to be so much his servant as to forget he was his friend; and to testify it, did always use him with much courtesy, appointing him a place at his own table, to which he esteemed his company and discourse to be a great ornament.

He continued that employment for the space of five years, being daily useful, and not mercenary to his friends. During which time, he (I dare not say unhappily) fell into such a liking, as (with her approbation) increased into a love with a young gentlewoman that lived in that family, who was niece to the Lady Ellesmere and daughter to Sir George More, then Chancellor of the Garter and Lieutenant of the Tower.

Sir George had some intimation of it and, knowing prevention to be a great part of wisdom, did therefore remove her with much haste, from that to his own house at Lothesley, in the County of Surrey; but too late, by reason of some faithful promises which were so interchangeably passed as never to be violated by either party.

These promises were only known to themselves; and the friends of both parties used much diligence and many arguments to kill or cool their affections to each other; but in vain, for love is a flattering mischief that hath denied aged and wise men a foresight of those evils that too often prove to be the children of that blind father; a passion, that carries us to commit errors with as much ease as whirlwinds remove feathers, and begets in us an unwearied industry to the attainment of what we desire. And such an industry did, notwithstanding much watchfulness against it, bring them secretly together (I forbear to tell the manner how) and at last to a marriage too, without the allowance of those friends whose approbation always was and ever will be necessary to make even a virtuous love become lawful.

And that the knowledge of their marriage might not fall like an unexpected tempest on those that were unwilling to have it so; and that pre-apprehensions might make it the less enormous when it was known, it was purposely whispered into the ears of many that it was so, yet by none that could affirm it. But, to put a period to the jealousies of Sir George (doubt often begetting more restless thoughts than the certain knowledge of what we fear) the news was, in favor to Mr. Donne and with his allowance, made known to Sir George, by his honorable friend and neighbor Henry, Earl of Northumberland; but it was to Sir George so immeasurably unwelcome, and so transported him that, as though his passion of anger and inconsideration might exceed theirs of love and error, he presently engaged his sister, the Lady Ellesmere, to join with him to procure her lord to discharge Mr. Donne of the place he held under his lordship. This request was followed with violence; and though Sir George were remembered that errors might be over punished and desired therefore to forbear till second considerations might clear some scruples, yet he became restless until his suit was granted and the punishment executed. And though the Lord Chancellor did not, at Mr. Donne's dismission, give him such a commendation as the great Emperor Charles the Fifth did of his Secretary Eraso, when he presented him to his son and successor, Philip the Second, saying, "That in his Eraso, he gave to him a greater gift than all his estate, and all the kingdoms which he then resigned to him": yet the Lord Chancellor said, "He parted with a friend, and such a secretary as was fitter to serve a king than a subject."

Immediately after his dismission from his service, he sent a sad letter to his wife, to acquaint her with it: and after the subscription of his name, wrote,

John Donne, Anne Donne, Un-done;

and God knows it proved too true; for this bitter physic of Mr. Donne's dismission was not enough to purge out all Sir George's choler; for he was not satisfied till Mr. Donne and his sometime com-pupil in Cambridge, that married him, namely, Samuel Brooke, who was after Doctor in Divinity, and Master of Trinity College, and his brother Mr. Christopher Brooke, sometime Mr. Donne's chamber-fellow in Lincoln's Inn, who gave Mr. Donne his wife and witnessed the marriage, were all committed to three several prisons.

Mr. Donne was first enlarged, who neither gave rest to his body or brain nor to any friend in whom he might hope to have an interest until he had procured an enlargement for his two imprisoned friends.

He was now at liberty, but his days were still cloudy:

and being past these troubles, others did still multiply upon
him; for his wife was, to her extreme sorrow, detained from
him; and though with Jacob he endured not a hard service
for her, yet he lost a good one and was forced to make good
his title, and to get possession of her by a long and restless
suit in law; which proved troublesome and sadly chargeable
to him, whose youth, and travel, and needless bounty had
brought his estate into a narrow compass.

It is observed, and most truly, that silence and submission are charming qualities, and work most upon passionate
men; and it proved so with Sir George; for these and a general report of Mr. Donne's merits, together with his winning
behavior, which, when it would entice, had a strange kind
of elegant irresistible art: these and time had so dispas-
sionated Sir George that as the world had approved his
daughter's choice, so he also could not but see a more than
ordinary merit in his new son; and this at last melted him
into so much remorse (for love and anger are so like agues
as to have hot and cold fits; and love in parents, though
it may be quenched, yet is easily rekindled and expires not
till death denies mankind a natural heat) that he labored
his son's restoration to his place; using to that end both his
own and his sister's power to her lord; but with no success;
for his answer was, "That though he was unfeignedly sorry
for what he had done, yet it was inconsistent with his place
and credit, to discharge and readmit servants at the request
of passionate petitioners."

Sir George's endeavor for Mr. Donne's readmission was
by all means to be kept secret: for men do more naturally
reluct for errors, than submit to put on those blemishes that
attend their visible acknowledgment. But, however, it was
not long before Sir George appeared to be so far reconciled
as to wish their happiness, and not to deny them his paternal
blessing, but yet refused to contribute any means that might
conduce to their livelihood.

Mr. Donne's estate was the greatest part spent in many

and chargeable travels, books, and dear-bought experience:
he out of all employment that might yield a support for
himself and wife, who had been curiously and plentifully
educated; both their natures generous, and accustomed to
confer, and not to receive, courtesies: these and other considerations, but chiefly that his wife was to bear a part in
his sufferings, surrounded him with many sad thoughts and
some apparent apprehensions of want.

But his sorrows were lessened and his wants prevented
by the seasonable courtesy of their noble kinsman, Sir Francis Wolly, of Pirford in Surrey, who intreated them to a
cohabitation with him; where they remained with much
freedom to themselves, and equal content to him, for some
years; and as their charge increased (she had yearly a
child) so did his love and bounty.

It hath been observed by wise and considering men that
wealth hath seldom been the portion, and never the mark
to discover good people; but that Almighty God, who disposeth all things wisely, hath of his abundant goodness denied it (he only knows why) to many whose minds he hath
enriched with the greater blessings of knowledge and virtue,
as the fairer testimonies of his love to mankind: and this
was the present condition of this man of so excellent erudi-
tion and endowments, whose necessary and daily expenses
were hardly reconcilable with his uncertain and narrow
estate. Which I mention, for that at this time there was
a most generous offer made him for the moderating of his
worldly cares, the declaration of which shall be the next
employment of my pen.

God hath been so good to his church as to afford it in every
age some such men to serve at his altar as have been piously
ambitious of doing good to mankind; a disposition that is
so like to God himself that it owes itself only to Him who
takes a pleasure to behold it in His creatures. These times [4]
he did bless with many such, some of which still live to be

[4] 1648.

patterns of apostolical charity and of more than human patience. I have said this because I have occasion to mention one of them in my following discourse; namely, Dr. Morton, the most laborious and learned Bishop of Durham; one that God hath blessed with perfect intellectuals and a cheerful heart at the age of 94 years (and is yet living): one that in his days of plenty had so large a heart as to use his large revenue to the encouragement of learning and virtue, and is now (be it spoken with sorrow) reduced to a narrow estate, which he embraces without repining; and still shows the beauty of his mind by so liberal a hand as if this were an age in which tomorrow were to care for itself. I have taken a pleasure in giving the reader a short, but true character of this good man, my friend, from whom I received this following relation.—He sent to Mr. Donne, and intreated to borrow an hour of his time for a conference the next day. After their meeting, there was not many minutes passed before he spake to Mr. Donne to this purpose: "Mr. Donne, the occasion of sending for you is to propose to you what I have often revolved in my own thought since I last saw you: which, nevertheless, I will not declare but upon this condition, that you shall not return me a present answer, but forbear three days and bestow some part of that time in fasting and prayer; and after a serious consideration of what I shall propose, then return to me with your answer. Deny me not, Mr. Donne; for it is the effect of a true love, which I would gladly pay as a debt due for yours to me."

This request being granted, the doctor expressed himself thus:

"Mr. Donne, I know your education and abilities; I know your expectation of a state-employment; and I know your fitness for it; and I know too the many delays and contingencies that attend court-promises: and let me tell you that my love, begot by our long friendship and your merits, hath prompted me to such an inquisition after your present temporal estate as makes me no stranger to your necessities; which I know to be such as your generous spirit could not bear if it were not supported with a pious patience. You know I have formerly persuaded you to waive your court-hopes, and enter into holy orders; which I now again persuade you to embrace, with this reason added to my former request: The king hath yesterday made me Dean of Gloucester, and I am also possessed of a benefice, the profits of which are equal to those of my deanery; I will think my deanery enough for my maintenance (who am, and resolved to die, a single man) and will quit my benefice, and estate you in it (which the Patron is willing I shall do) if God shall incline your heart to embrace this motion. Remember, Mr. Donne, no man's education or parts make him too good for this employment, which is to be an ambassador for the God of glory; that God, who by a vile death opened the gates of life to mankind. Make me no present answer but remember your promise and return to me the third day with your resolution."

At the hearing of this, Mr. Donne's faint breath and perplexed countenance gave a visible testimony of an inward conflict: but he performed his promise, and departed without returning an answer till the third day; and then his answer was to this effect:

"My most worthy and most dear friend, since I saw you, I have been faithful to my promise, and have also meditated much of your great kindness, which hath been such as would exceed even my gratitude; but that it cannot do; and more I cannot return you; and I do that with an heart full of humility and thanks, though I may not accept of your offer: but, sir, my refusal is not for that I think myself too good for that calling, for which kings, if they think so, are not good enough; nor for that my education and learning, though not eminent, may not, being assisted with God's grace and humility, render me in some measure fit for it: but I dare make so dear a friend as you are, my confessor: some irregularities of my life have been so visible to some men, that though I have, I thank God, made my peace with him by penitential resolutions against them, and by the assistance of his grace banished them my affections; yet this, which God knows to be so, is not so visible to man as to free me from their censures, and it may be that sacred calling from a dishonor. And besides, whereas it is determined by the best of casuists that God's glory should be the first end, and a maintenance the second motive to embrace that calling; and though each man may propose to himself both together, yet the first may not be put last without a violation of conscience, which he that searches the heart will judge. And truly my present condition is such that if I ask my own conscience whether it be reconcilable to that rule, it is at this time so perplexed about it that I can neither give myself nor you an answer. You know, sir, who says, 'Happy is that man whose conscience doth not accuse him for that thing which he does.' To these I might add other reasons that dissuade me; but I crave your favor that I may forbear to express them, and thankfully decline your offer."

This was his present resolution; but the heart of man is not in his own keeping, and he was destined to this sacred service by a higher hand, a hand so powerful as at last forced him to a compliance: of which I shall give the reader an account before I shall give a rest to my pen.

Mr. Donne and his wife continued with Sir Francis Wolly till his death: a little before which time, Sir Francis was so happy as to make a perfect reconciliation betwixt Sir George and his forsaken son and daughter; Sir George conditioning by bond to pay to Mr. Donne 800*l.* at a certain day, as a portion with his wife, or 20*l.* quarterly for their maintenance, as the interest for it, till the said portion was paid.

Most of those years that he lived with Sir Francis, he studied the civil and canon laws; in which he acquired such

a perfection as was judged to hold proportion with many
who had made that study the employment of their whole life.

Sir Francis being dead and that happy family dissolved,
Mr. Donne took for himself a house in Mitcham, near to
Croydon in Surrey, a place noted for good air and choice
company: there his wife and children remained; and for
himself he took lodgings in London, near to Whitehall,
whither his friends and occasions drew him very often, and
where he was as often visited by many of the nobility and
others of this nation, who used him in their counsels of
greatest consideration, and with some rewards for his better subsistence.

Nor did our own nobility only value and favor him, but
his acquaintance and friendship was sought for by most ambassadors of foreign nations, and by many other strangers,
whose learning or business occasioned their stay in this nation.

He was much importuned by many friends to make his
constant residence in London; but he still denied it, having settled his dear wife and children at Mitcham, and near
some friends that were bountiful to them and him; for they,
God knows, needed it; and that you may the better now
judge of the then present condition of his mind and fortune,
I shall present you with an extract collected out of some
few of his many letters.

———"And the reason why I did not send an answer to
your last week's letter, was, because it then found me under
too great a sadness; and at present 'tis thus with me: There
is not one person, but myself, well of my family: I have already lost half a child, and, with that mischance of hers, my
wife has fallen into such a discomposure as would afflict
her too extremely but that the sickness of all her other
children stupefies her: of one of which, in good faith, I have
not much hope: and these meet with a fortune so ill-provided
for physic, and such relief, that if God should ease us with

burials, I know not how to perform even that: but I flatter myself with this hope that I am dying too; for I cannot waste faster than by such griefs. As for,————

From my hospital at Mitcham.

Aug. 10. JOHN DONNE."

Thus he did bemoan himself: and thus in other letters.

————"For we hardly discover a sin when it is but an omission of some good, and no accusing act: with this or the former I have often suspected myself to be overtaken; which is with an over-earnest desire of the next life: and though I know it is not merely a weariness of this, because I had the same desire when I went with the tide and enjoyed fairer hopes than I now do; yet I doubt worldly troubles have increased it: 'tis now spring, and all the pleasures of it displease me; every other tree blossoms, and I wither: I grow older, and not better; my strength diminisheth, and my load grows heavier; and yet I would fain be or do something; but that I cannot tell what, is no wonder in this time of my sadness; for to choose is to do; but to be no part of any body is as to be nothing: and so I am, and shall so judge myself, unless I could be so incorporated into a part of the world, as by business to contribute some sustentation to the whole. This I made account; I began early, when I understood the study of our laws; but was diverted by leaving that, and embracing the worst voluptuousness, an hydroptic immoderate desire of human learning and languages: beautiful ornaments indeed to men of great fortunes, but mine was grown so low as to need an occupation; which I thought I entered well into, when I subjected myself to such a service as I thought might exercise my poor abilities: and there I stumbled, and fell too; and now I am become so little, or such a nothing, that I am not a subject good enough for one of my own letters.— Sir, I fear my

present discontent does not proceed from a good root, that
I am so well content to be nothing, that is, dead. But, sir,
though my fortune hath made me such, as that I am rather
a sickness or a disease of the world than any part of it,
and therefore neither love it, nor life; yet I would gladly
live to become some such thing as you should not repent
loving me: sir, your own soul cannot be more zealous for
your good than I am; and God, who loves that zeal in me,
will not suffer you to doubt it: you would pity me now if
you saw me write, for my pain hath drawn my head so much
awry, and holds it so, that my eye cannot follow my pen.
I therefore receive you into my prayers with mine own weary
soul and commend myself to yours. I doubt not but next
week will bring you good news, for I have either mending
or dying on my side: but, if I do continue longer thus, I
shall have comfort in this, that my blessed Saviour in exercising his justice upon my two worldly parts, my fortune
and my body, reserves all his mercy for that which most
needs it, my soul! which is, I doubt, too like a porter that
is very often near the gate and yet goes not out. Sir, I profess to you truly that my loathness to give over writing now
seems to myself a sign that I shall write no more.————

Your poor friend, and

God's poor patient,

Sept. 7.   JOHN DONNE."

By this you have seen a part of the picture of his narrow
fortune and the perplexities of his generous mind; and thus
it continued with him for almost two years, all which time
his family remained constantly at Mitcham; and to which
place he often retired himself, and destined some days to
a constant study of some points of controversy betwixt the
English and Roman Church, and especially those of supremacy and allegiance: and to that place and such studies,
he could willingly have wedded himself during his life: but

the earnest persuasion of friends became at last to be so powerful as to cause the removal of himself and family to London, where Sir Robert Drury, a gentleman of a very noble estate and a more liberal mind assigned him and his wife an useful apartment in his own large house in Drury Lane, and not only rent free, but was also a cherisher of his studies, and such a friend as sympathized with him and his in all their joys and sorrows.

At this time of Mr. Donne's and his wife's living in Sir Robert's house, the Lord Hay was by King James sent upon a glorious embassy to the then French King Henry the Fourth; and Sir Robert put on a sudden resolution to accompany him to the French Court, and to be present at his audience there. And Sir Robert put on as sudden a resolution, to subject Mr. Donne to be his companion in that journey. And this desire was suddenly made known to his wife, who was then with child, and otherways under so dangerous a habit of body as to her health that she professed an unwillingness to allow him any absence from her, saying, "Her divining soul boded her some ill in his absence"; and therefore desired him not to leave her. This made Mr. Donne lay aside all thoughts of the journey and really to resolve against it. But Sir Robert became restless in his persuasions for it; and Mr. Donne was so generous as to think he had sold his liberty when he received so many charitable kindnesses from him, and told his wife so; who did therefore, with an unwilling-willingness, give a faint consent to the journey, which was proposed to be but for two months; for about that time they determined their return. Within a few days after this resolve, the ambassador, Sir Robert, and Mr. Donne, left London; and were the twelfth day got all safe in Paris. Two days after their arrival there, Mr. Donne was left alone in that room in which Sir Robert, and he, and some other friends had dined together. To this place Sir Robert returned within half an hour; and as he left, so he found Mr. Donne alone; but in

such an ecstasy, and so altered as to his looks as amazed Sir
Robert to behold him; insomuch that he earnestly desired
Mr. Donne to declare what had befallen him in the short
time of his absence. To which Mr. Donne was not able to
make a present answer: but, after a long and perplexed
pause, did at last say, "I have seen a dreadful vision since
I saw you: I have seen my dear wife pass twice by me
through this room, with her hair hanging about her shoulders
and a dead child in her arms: this I have seen since I saw
you." To which Sir Robert replied, "Sure, sir, you have slept
since I saw you; and this is the result of some melancholy
dream, which I desire you to forget, for you are now awake."
To which Mr. Donne's reply was: "I cannot be surer that
I now live, than that I have not slept since I saw you: and
am as sure, that at her second appearing, she stopped, and
looked me in the face, and vanished." —Rest and sleep
had not altered Mr. Donne's opinion the next day: for he
then affirmed this vision with a more deliberate, and so confirmed a confidence, that he inclined Sir Robert to a faint
belief that the vision was true. It is truly said that desire
and doubt have no rest, and it proved so with Sir Robert;
for he immediately sent a servant to Drury House, with a
charge to hasten back and bring him word whether Mrs.
Donne were alive; and, if alive, in what condition she was
as to her health. The twelfth day the messenger returned
with this account: that he found and left Mrs. Donne very
sad and sick in her bed; and that, after a long and dangerous labor, she had been delivered of a dead child. And, upon
examination, the abortion proved to be the same day and
about the very hour that Mr. Donne affirmed he saw her
pass by him in his chamber.

This is a relation that will beget some wonder, and it well
may; for most of our world are at present possessed with
an opinion that visions and miracles are ceased. And, though
it is most certain that two lutes, being both strung and tuned
to an equal pitch, and then one played upon, the other that

is not touched being laid upon a table at a fit distance will
(like an echo to a trumpet) warble a faint audible harmony
in answer to the same tune; yet many will not believe there
is any such thing as a sympathy of souls; and I am well
pleased that every reader do enjoy his own opinion. But if
the unbelieving will not allow the believing reader of this
story a liberty to believe that it may be true; then I wish
him to consider, many wise men have believed that the
ghost of Julius Cæsar did appear to Brutus, and that both
St. Austin, and Monica his mother, had visions in order to
his conversion. And though these and many others (too
many to name) have but the authority of human story, yet
the incredible reader may find in the sacred story [5] that
Samuel did appear to Saul even after his death (whether
really or not, I undertake not to determine). And Bildad,
in the Book of Job, says these words: [6] "A spirit passed before my face; the hair of my head stood up; fear and trembling came upon me, and made all my bones to shake."
Upon which words I will make no comment, but leave them
to be considered by the incredulous reader; to whom I will
also commend this following consideration: that there be
many pious and learned men that believe our merciful God
hath assigned to every man a particular guardian angel to
be his constant monitor and to attend him in all his dangers,
both of body and soul. And the opinion that every man hath
his particular angel may gain some authority by the relation of St. Peter's miraculous deliverance out of prison,[7]
not by many, but by one angel. And this belief may yet gain
more credit by the reader's considering that when Peter
after his enlargement knocked at the door of Mary the
mother of John, and Rhoda, the maid-servant, being surprised with joy that Peter was there, did not let him in,
but ran in haste and told the disciples (who were then and
there met together) that Peter was at the door; and they,
not believing it, said she was mad: yet, when she again af-

[5] I Sam. 28:14.   [6] Job 4:13–16.   [7] Acts 12:7–10, 13–15.

firmed it, though they then believed it not, yet they concluded, and said, "It is his angel."

More observations of this nature, and inferences from them, might be made to gain the relation a firmer belief: but I forbear, lest I, that intended to be but a relater, may be thought to be an engaged person for the proving what was related to me; and yet I think myself bound to declare that, though it was not told me by Mr. Donne himself, it was told me (now long since) by a person of honor, and of such intimacy with him that he knew more of the secrets of his soul than any person then living: and I think he told me the truth; for it was told with such circumstances and such asseveration that (to say nothing of my own thoughts) I verily believe he that told it me did himself believe it to be true.

I forbear the reader's farther trouble as to the relation and what concerns it, and will conclude mine with commending to his view a copy of verses given by Mr. Donne to his wife at the time that he then parted from her. And I beg leave to tell that I have heard some critics, learned both in languages and poetry, say that none of the Greek or Latin poets did ever equal them. . . .[8]

I return from my account of the vision to tell the reader that both before Mr. Donne's going into France, at his being there, and after his return, many of the nobility and others that were powerful at court were watchful and solicitous to the king for some secular employment for him. The king had formerly both known and put a value upon his company, and had also given him some hopes of a state-employment; being always much pleased when Mr. Donne attended him, especially at his meals, where there were usually many deep discourses of general learning and very often friendly disputes or debates of religion betwixt His Majesty and those divines whose places required their at-

[8] The poem, "A Valediction Forbidding to Mourn," was printed here by Walton.

tendance on him at those times: particularly the Dean of
the Chapel, who then was Bishop Montague (the publisher
of the learned and eloquent works of His Majesty) and the
most Reverend Doctor Andrewes the late learned Bishop of
Winchester, who was then the king's almoner.

About this time there grew many disputes that concerned
the Oath of Supremacy and Allegiance, in which the king
had appeared, and engaged himself by his public writings
now extant: and His Majesty discoursing with Mr. Donne
concerning many of the reasons which are usually urged
against the taking of those oaths, apprehended such a validity
and clearness in his stating the questions, and his answers to
them, that His Majesty commanded him to bestow some
time in drawing the arguments into a method, and then to
write his answers to them; and, having done that, not to
send, but be his own messenger and bring them to him. To
this he presently and diligently applied himself, and within
six weeks brought them to him under his own handwriting,
as they be now printed; the book bearing the name of
Pseudo-Martyr, printed *anno* 1610.

When the king had read and considered that book, he
persuaded Mr. Donne to enter into the ministry; to which,
at that time, he was, and appeared, very unwilling, apprehending it (such was his mistaking modesty) to be too
weighty for his abilities: and though His Majesty had
promised him a favor, and many persons of worth mediated
with His Majesty for some secular employment for him
(to which his education had apted him), and particularly
the Earl of Somerset when in his greatest height of favor;
who being then at Theobald's with the king, where one of
the clerks of the council died that night, the Earl posted a
messenger for Mr. Donne to come to him immediately, and
at Mr. Donne's coming, said, "Mr. Donne, to testify the
reality of my affection, and my purpose to prefer you, stay
in this garden till I go up to the king, and bring you word
that you are clerk of the council: doubt not my doing this,

for I know the king loves you, and know the king will not
deny me." But the king gave a positive denial to all requests, and, having a discerning spirit, replied, "I know Mr.
Donne is a learned man, has the abilities of a learned divine, and will prove a powerful preacher; and my desire
is to prefer him that way, and in that way I will deny you
nothing for him." After that time, as he professeth,[9] "the
king descended to a persuasion, almost to a solicitation, of
him to enter into sacred orders": which, although he then
denied not, yet he deferred it for almost three years. All
which time he applied himself to an incessant study of textual
divinity, and to the attainment of a great perfection in the
learned languages, Greek and Hebrew.

In the first and most blessed times of Christianity, when
the clergy were looked upon with reverence, and deserved
it, when they overcame their opposers by high examples of
virtue, by a blessed patience and long suffering, those only
were then judged worthy the ministry whose quiet and meek
spirits did make them look upon that sacred calling with
an humble adoration and fear to undertake it; which indeed requires such great degrees of humility, and labor, and
care, that none but such were then thought worthy of that
celestial dignity. And such only were then sought out and
solicited to undertake it. This I have mentioned because
forwardness and inconsideration could not in Mr. Donne,
as in many others, be an argument of insufficiency or unfit-
ness; for he had considered long, and had many strifes within
himself concerning the strictness of life and competency
of learning required in such as enter into sacred orders; and
doubtless, considering his own demerits, did humbly ask
God with St. Paul, "Lord, who is sufficient for these things?"
and with meek Moses, "Lord, who am I?" And sure, if he
had consulted with flesh and blood, he had not for these
reasons put his hand to that holy plow. But God, who is
able to prevail, wrestled with him, as the angel did with

---

[9] In his book of *Devotions*.

Jacob, and marked him; marked him for his own; marked
him with a blessing, a blessing of obedience to the motions
of his blessed spirit. And then, as he had formerly asked
God with Moses, "Who am I?" so now, being inspired with
an apprehension of God's particular mercy to him, in the
king's and other solicitations of him, he came to ask King
David's thankful question, "Lord, who am I, that thou art
so mindful of me?" [10] So mindful of me as to lead me for
more than forty years through this wilderness of the many
temptations and various turnings of a dangerous life; so
merciful to me as to move the learnedest of kings to descend
to move me to serve at the altar; so merciful to me as at
last to move my heart to embrace this holy motion! Thy
motions I will and do embrace: and I now say with the
blessed Virgin, "Be it with thy servant as seemeth best in
thy sight": and so, blessed Jesus, I do take the cup of salvation and will call upon thy name and will preach thy gospel.

Such strifes as these St. Austin had, when St. Ambrose
endeavored his conversion to Christianity; with which he
confesseth he acquainted his friend Alipius. Our learned
author (a man fit to write after no mean copy) did the like.
And declaring his intentions to his dear friend Dr. King,
then Bishop of London, a man famous in his generation
and no stranger to Mr. Donne's abilities (for he had been
chaplain to the Lord Chancellor at the time of Mr. Donne's
being his lordship's secretary), that reverend man did re-
receive the news with much gladness; and, after some expressions of joy, and a persuasion to be constant in his pious
purpose, he proceeded with all convenient speed to ordain
him first deacon, and then priest not long after.

Now the English Church had gained a second St. Austin;
for I think none was so like him before his conversion, none
so like St. Ambrose after it: and if his youth had the infirmities of the one, his age had the excellencies of the other;
the learning and holiness of both.

[10] Psalm 8:4. "What is man, that thou art mindful of him?"

And now all his studies, which had been occasionally diffused, were all concentered in divinity. Now he had a new calling, new thoughts, and a new employment for his wit and eloquence. Now, all his earthly affections were changed into divine love; and all the faculties of his own soul were engaged in the conversion of others: in preaching the glad tidings of remission to repenting sinners and peace to each troubled soul. To these he applied himself with all care and diligence: and now such a change was wrought in him that he could say with David, "O how amiable are thy tabernacles, O Lord God of Hosts!" [11] Now he declared openly, "That when he required a temporal, God gave him a spiritual blessing." And that "he was now gladder to be a doorkeeper in the House of God, than he could be to enjoy the noblest of all temporal employments."

Presently after he entered into his holy profession, the king sent for him, and made him his Chaplain in Ordinary, and promised to take a particular care for his preferment.

And though his long familiarity with scholars and persons of greatest quality was such as might have given some men boldness enough to have preached to any eminent auditory; yet his modesty in this employment was such that he could not be persuaded to it, but went, usually accompanied with some one friend, to preach privately in some village not far from London; his first sermon being preached at Paddington. This he did till His Majesty sent and appointed him a day to preach to him at Whitehall; and, though much were expected from him, both by His Majesty and others, yet he was so happy (which few are) as to satisfy and exceed their expectations: preaching the Word so, as showed his own heart was possessed with those very thoughts and joys that he labored to distill into others: a preacher in earnest; weeping sometimes for his auditory, sometimes with them; always preaching to himself, like an angel from a cloud, but in none; carrying some, as St. Paul

[11] Psalm 84:4.

was, to heaven in holy raptures, and enticing others by a sacred art and courtship to amend their lives: here picturing a vice so as to make it ugly to those that practiced it; and a virtue so as to make it beloved, even by those that loved it not; and all this with a most particular grace and an unexpressible addition of comeliness.

There may be some that may incline to think (such indeed as have not heard him) that my affection to my friend hath transported me to an immoderate commendation of his preaching. If this meets with any such, let me entreat, though I will admit many, yet that they will receive a double witness for what I say; it being attested by a gentleman of worth (Mr. Chidley, a frequent hearer of his sermons) in part of a Funeral Elegy writ by him on Dr. Donne, and is a known truth, though it be in verse.

> ————Each altar had his fire————
> He kept his love, but not his object; wit
> He did not banish, but transplanted it;
> Taught it both time and place, and brought it home
> To piety, which it doth best become.
> For say, had ever pleasure such a dress?
> Have you seen crimes so shap'd, or loveliness
> Such as his lips did clothe religion in?
> Had not reproof a beauty passing sin?
> Corrupted nature sorrow'd that she stood
> So near the danger of becoming good.
> And, when he preach'd, she wish'd her ears exempt
> From piety, that had such pow'r to tempt.
> How did his sacred flattery beguile
> Men to amend?————

More of this, and more witnesses, might be brought; but I forbear and return.

That summer, in the very same month in which he entered into sacred orders and was made the king's chaplain, His

Majesty, then going his progress, was entreated to receive
an entertainment in the University of Cambridge: and Mr.
Donne attending His Majesty at that time, His Majesty
was pleased to recommend him to the University, to be
made Doctor in Divinity: Doctor Harsnett (after Archbishop of York) was then vice-chancellor, who, knowing
him to be the author of that learned book the *Pseudo-Martyr*,
required no other proof of his abilities, but proposed it to
the University, who presently assented, and expressed a gladness that they had such an occasion to entitle him to be
theirs.

His abilities and industry in his profession were so eminent, and he so known and so beloved by persons of quality,
that within the first year of his entering into sacred orders,
he had fourteen advowsons of several benefices presented
to him: but they were in the country, and he could not leave
his beloved London, to which place he had a natural inclination, having received both his birth and education in
it and there contracted a friendship with many whose conversation multiplied the joys of his life: but an employment
that might affix him to that place would be welcome, for he
needed it.

Immediately after his return from Cambridge, his wife
died, leaving him a man of a narrow, unsettled estate, and
(having buried five) the careful father of seven children
then living, to whom he gave a voluntary assurance never
to bring them under the subjection of a step-mother; which
promise he kept most faithfully, burying with his tears all
his earthly joys in his most dear and deserving wife's grave,
and betook himself to a most retired and solitary life.

In this retiredness, which was often from the sight of his
dearest friends, he became crucified to the world and all
those vanities, those imaginary pleasures that are daily acted
on that restless stage; and they were as perfectly crucified
to him. Nor is it hard to think (being passions may be both
changed and heightened by accidents) but that that abundant

affection which once was betwixt him and her, who had long
been the delight of his eyes, and the companion of his youth;
her, with whom he had divided so many pleasant sorrows
and contented fears, as common people are not capable
of; not hard to think but that she being now removed by
death, a commeasurable grief took a full possession of him
as joy had done; and so indeed it did; for now his very soul
was elemented of nothing but sadness; now grief took so
full a possession of his heart as to leave no place for joy:
if it did, it was a joy to be alone, where, like a pelican in
the wilderness, he might bemoan himself without witness
or restraint, and pour forth his passions like Job in the days
of his affliction: "Oh that I might have the desire of my
heart! Oh that God would grant the thing that I long for." [12]
For then, as the grave is become her house, so I would hasten
to make it mine also; that we two might there make our
beds together in the dark. Thus, as the Israelites sat mourning by the rivers of Babylon when they remembered Sion,
so he gave some ease to his oppressed heart by thus venting
his sorrows: thus he began the day and ended the night;
ended the restless night and began the weary day in lamentations. And thus he continued, till a consideration of his new
engagements to God, and St. Paul's "Woe is me, if I preach
not the gospel" dispersed those sad clouds that had then
benighted his hopes, and now forced him to behold the light.

His first motion from his house was to preach where his
beloved wife lay buried (in St. Clement's Church, near Temple Bar, London) and his text was a part of the Prophet
Jeremy's *Lamentation:* "Lo, I am the man that hath seen
affliction." [13]

And indeed his very words and looks testified him to be
truly such a man; and they, with the addition of his sighs and
tears, expressed in his sermon, did so work upon the affections of his hearers as melted and molded them into a com-
panionable sadness; and so they left the congregation: but

---

[12] Job 6:8.   [13] Lamentations 3:1.

then their houses presented them with objects of diversion; and his presented him with nothing but fresh objects of sorrow, in beholding many helpless children, a narrow fortune, and a consideration of the many cares and casualties that attend their education.

In this time of sadness he was importuned by the grave benchers of Lincoln's Inn (who were once the companions and friends of his youth) to accept of their lecture, which by reason of Dr. Gataker's removal from thence was then void; of which he accepted, being most glad to renew his intermitted friendship with those whom he so much loved, and where he had been a Saul, though not to persecute Christianity or to deride it, yet in his irregular youth to neglect the visible practice of it; there to become a Paul and preach salvation to his beloved brethren.

And now his life was a shining light among his old friends; now he gave an ocular testimony of the strictness and regularity of it; now he might say, as St. Paul adviseth his Corinthians, "Be ye followers of me, as I follow Christ, and walk as ye have me for an example"; [14] not the example of a busybody, but of a contemplative, a harmless, an humble, and an holy life and conversation.

The love of that noble society was expressed to him many ways; for, besides fair lodgings that were set apart and newly furnished for him with all necessaries, other courtesies were also daily added; indeed so many, and so freely, as if they meant their gratitude should exceed his merits: and in this love-strife of desert and liberality, they continued for the space of two years, he preaching faithfully and constantly to them, and they liberally requiting him. About which time the Emperor of Germany died, and the Palsgrave, who had lately married the Lady Elizabeth, the king's only daughter, was elected and crowned King of Bohemia, the unhappy beginning of many miseries in that nation.

[14] I Cor. 4:16.

King James, whose motto, *Beati pacifici,* did truly speak the very thoughts of his heart, endeavored first to prevent, and after to compose, the discords of that discomposed state: and, amongst other his endeavors, did then send the Lord Hay, Earl of Doncaster, his ambassador to those unsettled princes; and, by a special command from His Majesty, Dr. Donne was appointed to assist and attend that employment to the princes of the Union; for which the Earl was most glad, who had always put a great value on him, and taken a great pleasure in his conversation and discourse: and his friends at Lincoln's Inn were as glad; for they feared that his immoderate study and sadness for his wife's death would, as Jacob said, "make his days few," and, respecting his bodily health, "evil" too: [15] and of this there were many visible signs.

At his going, he left his friends of Lincoln's Inn, and they him, with many reluctations: for, though he could not say as St. Paul to his Ephesians, "Behold, you, to whom I have preached the kingdom of God, shall from henceforth see my face no more"; yet he, believing himself to be in a consumption, questioned, and they feared it: all concluding that his troubled mind, with the help of his unintermitted studies, hastened the decays of his weak body. But God, who is the God of all wisdom and goodness, turned it to the best; for this employment (to say nothing of the event of it) did not only divert him from those too serious studies and sad thoughts, but seemed to give him a new life by a true occasion of joy, to be an eye-witness of the health of his most dear and most honored mistress, the Queen of Bohemia, in a foreign nation; and to be a witness of that gladness which she expressed to see him: who, having formerly known him a courtier, was much joyed to see him in a canonical habit, and more glad to be an ear-witness of his excellent and powerful preaching.

About fourteen months after his departure out of England, he returned to his friends of Lincoln's Inn, with his sorrows

[15] Gen. 47:9.

moderated and his health improved; and there betook himself to his constant course of preaching.

About a year after his return out of Germany, Dr. Carey was made Bishop of Exeter, and by his removal the deanery of St. Paul's being vacant, the king sent to Dr. Donne and appointed him to attend him at dinner the next day. When His Majesty was sat down, before he had eat any meat, he said after his pleasant manner, "Dr. Donne, I have invited you to dinner; and, though you sit not down with me, yet I will carve to you of a dish that I know you love well; for, knowing you love London, I do therefore make you Dean of St. Paul's; and, when I have dined, then do you take your beloved dish home to your study, say grace there to yourself, and much good may it do you."

Immediately after he came to his deanery, he employed workmen to repair and beautify the chapel; suffering, as holy David once vowed, "his eyes and temples to take no rest, till he had first beautified the house of God." [16]

The next quarter following, when his father-in-law, Sir George More (whom time had made a lover and admirer of him), came to pay to him the conditioned sum of twenty pounds, he refused to receive it; and said (as good Jacob did, when he heard his beloved son Joseph was alive, "It is enough"): "You have been kind to me and mine: I know your present condition is such as not to abound, and I hope mine is, or will be such as not to need it: I will therefore receive no more from you upon that contract"; and in testimony of it freely gave him up his bond.

Immediately after his admission into his deanery, the vicarage of St. Dunstan in the West, London, fell to him by the death of Dr. White, the advowson of it having been given to him long before by his honorable friend Richard Earl of Dorset, then the patron, and confirmed by his brother the late deceased Edward, both of them men of much honor.

By these, and another ecclesiastical endowment which fell

[16] Psalm 132:4.

to him about the same time, given to him formerly by the Earl of Kent, he was enabled to become charitable to the poor, and kind to his friends, and to make such provision for his children that they were not left scandalous as relating to their or his profession and quality.

The next parliament, which was within that present year, he was chosen Prolocutor to the Convocation, and about that time was appointed by His Majesty, his most gracious master, to preach very many occasional sermons, as at St. Paul's Cross and other places. All which employments he performed to the admiration of the representative body of the whole clergy of this nation.

He was once, and but once, clouded with the king's displeasure, and it was about this time; which was occasioned by some malicious whisper, who had told His Majesty that Dr. Donne had put on the general humor of the pulpits, and was become busy in insinuating a fear of the king's inclining to popery, and a dislike of his government; and particularly for the king's then turning the evening lectures into catechising, and expounding the prayer of our Lord, and of the belief and commandments. His Majesty was the more inclinable to believe this, for that a person of nobility and great note, betwixt whom and Dr. Donne there had been a great friendship, was at this very time discarded the court (I shall forbear his name, unless I had a fairer occasion) and justly committed to prison; which begot many rumors in the common people, who in this nation think they are not wise unless they be busy about what they understand not, and especially about religion.

The king received this news with so much discontent and restlessness that he would not suffer the sun to set and leave him under this doubt, but sent for Dr. Donne and required his answer to the accusation; which was so clear and satisfactory that the king said, "he was right glad he rested no longer under the suspicion." When the king had said this, Doctor Donne kneeled down and thanked His Majesty, and protested his answer was faithful, and free from all collusion, and therefore "desired that he might not rise till, as in like cases he always had from God, so he might have from His Majesty, some assurance that he stood clear and fair in his opinion." At which the king raised him from his knees with his own hands, and "protested that he believed him; and that he knew he was an honest man, and doubted not but that he loved him truly." And, having thus dismissed him, he called some lords of his council into his chamber, and said with much earnestness, "My Doctor is an honest man; and, my lords, I was never better satisfied with an answer than he hath now made me; and I always rejoice when I think that by my means he became a divine."

He was made dean the fiftieth year of his age; and in his fifty-fourth year a dangerous sickness seized him, which inclined him to a consumption: but God, as Job thankfully acknowledged, preserved his spirit and kept his intellectuals as clear and perfect as when that sickness first seized his body; but it continued long and threatened him with death, which he dreaded not.

In this distemper of body, his dear friend, Dr. Henry King (then chief residenciary of that church, and late Bishop of Chichester), a man generally known by the clergy of this nation, and as generally noted for his obliging nature, visited him daily; and observing that his sickness rendered his recovery doubtful, he chose a seasonable time to speak to him to this purpose.

"Mr. Dean, I am, by your favor, no stranger to your temporal estate, and you are no stranger to the offer lately made us for the renewing a lease of the best prebend's corps belonging to our church; and you know 'twas denied, for that our tenant being very rich, offered to fine at so low a rate as held not proportion with his advantages: but I will either raise him to an higher sum, or procure that the other residenciaries shall join to accept of what was offered; one of these, I can and will by your favor do without delay, and without any trouble either to your body or mind: I beseech you to accept of my offer, for I know it will be a considerable addition to your present estate, which I know needs it."

To this, after a short pause, and raising himself upon his bed, he made this reply:

"My most dear friend, I most humbly thank you for your many favors, and this in particular; but in my present condition I shall not accept of your proposal; for doubtless there is such a sin as sacrilege; if there were not, it could not have a name in Scripture: and the primitive clergy were watchful against all appearances of that evil; and indeed then all Christians looked upon it with horror and detestation, judging it to be even an open defiance of the power and providence of Almighty God and a sad presage of a declining religion. But instead of such Christians, who had selected times set apart to fast and pray to God for a pious clergy, which they then did obey, our times abound with men that are busy and litigious about trifles and church ceremonies, and yet so far from scrupling sacrilege that they make not so much as a *quære* what it is: but I thank God I have; and dare not now upon my sickbed, when Almighty God hath made me useless to the service of the church, make any advantages out of it. But if he shall again restore me to such a degree of health as again to serve at his altar, I shall then gladly take the reward which the bountiful benefactors of this church have designed me; for God knows my children and relations will need it. In which number, my mother (whose credulity and charity has contracted a very plentiful to a very narrow estate) must not be forgotten. But Dr. King, if I recover not, that little worldly estate that I shall leave behind me (that very little when divided into eight parts) must, if you deny me not so charitable a favor, fall into your hands, as my most faithful friend and executor; of whose care and justice I make no more doubt than of God's blessing, on that which I have conscientiously collected for them; but it shall not be augmented on my sickbed; and this I declare to be my unalterable resolution."

The reply to this was only a promise to observe his request.

Within a few days his distempers abated; and as his strength increased, so did his thankfulness to Almighty God, testified in his most excellent book of *Devotions*, which he published at his recovery; in which the reader may see the most secret thoughts that then possessed his soul, paraphrased and made public: a book, that may not unfitly be called a sacred picture of spiritual ecstasies, occasioned and appliable to the emergencies of that sickness; which book, being a composition of meditations, disquisitions, and prayers, he wrote on his sickbed; herein imitating the holy patriarchs, who were wont to build their altars in that place where they had received their blessings.

This sickness brought him so near to the gates of death, and he saw the grave so ready to devour him, that he would often say, his recovery was supernatural: but that God that then restored his health, continued it to him till the fifty-ninth year of his life: and then, in August 1630, being with his eldest daughter, Mrs. Harvey, at Abury Hatch in Essex, he there fell into a fever, which, with the help of his constant infirmity (vapors from the spleen) hastened him into so visible a consumption that his beholders might say, as St. Paul of himself, "He dies daily"; and he might say with Job, "My welfare passeth away as a cloud, the days of my affliction have taken hold of me, and weary nights are appointed for me." [17]

Reader, this sickness continued long, not only weakening, but wearying him so much, that my desire is he may now take some rest; and that before I speak of his death, thou wilt not think it an impertinent digression to look back with me upon some observations of his life, which whilst a gentle slumber gives rest to his spirits, may, I hope, not unfitly exercise thy consideration.

[17] Job 30:15–17.

His marriage was the remarkable error of his life; an error, which, though he had a wit able and very apt to maintain paradoxes, yet he was very far from justifying it; and though his wife's competent years and other reasons might be justly urged to moderate severe censures, yet he would occasionally condemn himself for it: and doubtless it had been attended with an heavy repentance, if God had not blessed them with so mutual and cordial affections as in the midst of their sufferings made their bread of sorrow taste more pleasantly than the banquets of dull and low-spirited people.

The recreations of his youth were poetry, in which he was so happy as if nature and all her varieties had been made only to exercise his sharp wit and high fancy; and in these pieces which were facetiously composed and carelessly scattered (most of them being written before the twentieth year of his age) it may appear by his choice metaphors that both nature and all the arts joined to assist him with their utmost skill.

It is a truth that in his penitential years, viewing some of those pieces that had been loosely (God knows, too loosely) scattered in his youth, he wished they had been abortive, or so short-lived that his own eyes had witnessed their funerals: but, though he was no friend to them, he was not so fallen out with heavenly poetry as to forsake that; no, not in his declining age; witnessed then by many divine sonnets and other high, holy, and harmonious composures. Yea, even on his former sickbed he wrote this heavenly hymn, expressing the great joy that then possessed his soul, in the assurance of God's favor to him when he composed it:

An Hymn
To God the Father

Wilt thou forgive that sin where I begun,
    Which was my sin, though it were done before?
Wilt thou forgive that sin through which I run,
    And do run still, though still I do deplore?
When thou hast done, thou hast not done,
                    For I have more.

Wilt thou forgive that sin, which I have won
    Others to sin, and made my sin their door?
Wilt thou forgive that sin which I did shun
    A year or two, but wallow'd in a score?
When thou hast done, thou hast not done,
                    For I have more.

I have a sin of fear, that when I've spun
    My last thread, I shall perish on the shore;
But swear by thy self, that at my death thy Son
    Shall shine as he shines now, and heretofore;
And having done that, thou hast done,
                    I fear no more.

I have rather mentioned this hymn, for that he caused
it to be set to a most grave and solemn tune and to be often
sung to the organ by the choristers of St. Paul's Church in
his own hearing, especially at the evening service; and at
his return from the customary devotions in that place, did
occasionally say to a friend, "The words of this hymn have
restored to me the same thoughts of joy that possessed my
soul in my sickness when I composed it. And, O the power
of church-music! that harmony added to this hymn has
raised the affections of my heart and quickened my graces

of zeal and gratitude; and I observe that I always return
from paying this public duty of prayer and praise to God,
with an unexpressible tranquillity of mind and a willingness
to leave the world."

After this manner did the disciples of our Saviour, and the
best of Christians in those ages of the church nearest to
his time, offer their praises to Almighty God. And the reader
of St. Augustine's life may there find, that towards his dissolution he wept abundantly that the enemies of Christianity
had broke in upon them and profaned and ruined their
sanctuaries; and because their public hymns and lauds were
lost out of their churches. And after this manner have many
devout souls lifted up their hands and offered acceptable
sacrifices unto Almighty God, where Dr. Donne offered his,
and now lies buried.

But now, Oh Lord! how is that place become desolate! [18]

Before I proceed further, I think fit to inform the reader
that not long before his death he caused to be drawn a figure
of the body of Christ extended upon an anchor, like those
which painters draw when they would present us with the
picture of Christ crucified on the cross: his varying no
otherwise, than to affix him not to a cross, but to an anchor,
the emblem of hope; this he caused to be drawn in little,
and then many of those figures thus drawn to be engraven
very small in heliotropium stones and set in gold; and of
these he sent to many of his dearest friends, to be used as
seals, or rings, and kept as memorials of him and of his affection to them.

His dear friends and benefactors, Sir Henry Goodyere
and Sir Robert Drury, could not be of that number; nor
could the Lady Magdalen Herbert, the mother of George
Herbert, for they had put off mortality and taken possession
of the grave before him: but Sir Henry Wotton, and Dr.
Hall, the then late deceased Bishop of Norwich, were; and
so were Dr. Duppa, Bishop of Salisbury, and Dr. Henry

[18] 1656.

King, Bishop of Chichester, lately deceased: men, in whom there was such a commixture of general learning, of natural eloquence, and Christian humility that they deserve a commemoration by a pen equal to their own, which none have exceeded.

And in this enumeration of his friends, though many must be omitted, yet that man of primitive piety, Mr. George Herbert, may not; I mean that George Herbert who was the author of *The Temple, or Sacred Poems and Ejaculations,* a book in which, by declaring his own spiritual conflicts, he hath comforted and raised many a dejected and discomposed soul and charmed them into sweet and quiet thoughts; a book, by the frequent reading whereof, and the assistance of that spirit that seemed to inspire the author, the reader may attain habits of peace and piety and all the gifts of the Holy Ghost and heaven: and may, by still reading, still keep those sacred fires burning upon the altar of so pure a heart as shall free it from the anxieties of this world and keep it fixed upon things that are above. Betwixt this George Herbert and Dr. Donne there was a long and dear friendship, made up by such a sympathy of inclinations that they coveted and joyed to be in each other's company; and this happy friendship was still maintained by many sacred endearments. . . .[19]

I return to tell the reader that, besides the verses to his dear Mr. Herbert, and that hymn that I mentioned to be sung in the choir of St. Paul's Church, he did also shorten and beguile many sad hours by composing other sacred ditties; and he wrote an hymn on his deathbed, which bears this title:

[19] Here Walton quotes the poem which Donne sent with one of his seals and Herbert's reply.

An Hymn to God,
My God, in My Sickness
March 23, 1630

Since I am coming to that holy room,
  Where, with thy quire of saints, for evermore
I shall be made thy music, as I come
  I tune my instrument here at the door,
  And what I must do then, think here before.

Since my physicians by their loves are grown
  Cosmographers; and I their map, who lie
Flat on this bed . . .

So, in his purple wrapt, receive me, Lord!
  By these his thorns, give me his other crown:
And as to other souls I preached thy word,
  Be this my text, my sermon to mine own,
  "That he may raise, therefore the Lord throws down."

If these fall under the censure of a soul whose too much
mixture with earth makes it unfit to judge of these high
raptures and illuminations, let him know that many holy
and devout men have thought the soul of Prudentius to be
most refined, when, not many days before his death, "he
charged it to present his God each morning and evening
with a new and spiritual song"; justified by the example
of King David and the good King Hezekiah, who, upon the
renovation of his years paid his thankful vows to Almighty
God in a royal hymn, which he concludes in these words;
"The Lord was ready to save; therefore I will sing my songs
to the stringed instruments all the days of my life in the
temple of my God." [20]

[20] Isa. 38:20.

The latter part of his life may be said to be a continued study; for as he usually preached once a week, if not oftener, so after his sermon he never gave his eyes rest till he had chosen out a new text, and that night cast his sermon into a form and his text into divisions; and the next day betook himself to consult the Fathers, and to commit his meditations to his memory, which was excellent. But upon Saturday he usually gave himself and his mind a rest from the weary burthen of his week's meditations, and usually spent that day in visitation of friends, or some other diversions of his thoughts; and would say, "that he gave both his body and mind that refreshment that he might be enabled to do the work of the day following, not faintly, but with courage and cheerfulness."

Nor was his age only so industrious, but in the most unsettled days of his youth, his bed was not able to detain him beyond the hour of four in a morning; and it was no common business that drew him out of his chamber till past ten; all which time was employed in study, though he took great liberty after it. And if this seem strange, it may gain a belief by the visible fruits of his labors; some of which remain as testimonies of what is here written: for he left the resultance of 1400 authors, most of them abridged and analyzed with his own hand; he left also six score of his sermons, all written with his own hand, also an exact and laborious treatise concerning self-murder, called _Biathanatos_, wherein all the laws violated by that act are diligently surveyed and judiciously censured: a treatise written in his younger days, which alone might declare him then not only perfect in the civil and canon law, but in many other such studies and arguments as enter not into the consideration of many that labor to be thought great clerks, and pretend to know all things.

Nor were these only found in his study, but all businesses that passed of any public consequence, either in this or any of our neighbor nations, he abbreviated either in Latin or in the language of that nation, and kept them by him for useful memorials. So he did the copies of divers letters and cases of conscience that had concerned his friends, with his observations and solutions of them; and divers other businesses of importance, all particularly and methodically digested by himself.

He did prepare to leave the world before life left him, making his will when no faculty of his soul was damped or made defective by pain or sickness, or he surprised by a sudden apprehension of death: but it was made with mature deliberation, expressing himself an impartial father, by making his children's portions equal; and a lover of his friends, whom he remembered with legacies fitly and discreetly chosen and bequeathed. I cannot forbear a nomination of some of them; for methinks they be persons that seem to challenge a recordation in this place; as namely, to his brother-in-law, Sir Thomas Grimes, he gave that striking clock, which he had long worn in his pocket; to his dear friend and executor, Dr. King (late Bishop of Chichester), that model of gold of the Synod of Dort, with which the States presented him at his last being at the Hague; and the two pictures of Padre Paulo and Fulgentio, men of his acquaintance when he traveled Italy, and of great note in that nation for their remarkable learning. To his ancient friend Dr. Brooke (that married him), Master of Trinity College in Cambridge, he gave the picture of the Blessed Virgin and Joseph. To Dr. Winniff who succeeded him in the deanery he gave a picture called the Skeleton. To the succeeding dean, who was not then known, he gave many necessaries of worth, and useful for his house; and also several pictures and ornaments for the chapel, with a desire that they might be registered, and remain as a legacy to his successors. To the Earls of Dorset and Carlisle he gave several pictures, and so he did to many other friends: legacies given rather to express his affection than to make any addition to their estates. But unto the poor he was full of charity, and unto many others, who by his constant and long continued bounty might entitle themselves to be his alms-people: for all these he made provision, and so largely, as, having then six children living, might to some appear more than proportionable to his estate. I forbear to mention any more, lest the reader may think I trespass upon his patience: but I will beg his favor, to present him with the beginning and end of his will.

"In the name of the blessed and glorious Trinity, Amen. I, John Donne, by the mercy of Christ Jesus and by the calling of the Church of England, priest, being at this time in good health and perfect understanding (praised be God therefore), do hereby make my last will and testament in manner and form following:

"First, I give my gracious God an entire sacrifice of body and soul, with my most humble thanks for that assurance which his blessed Spirit imprints in me now of the salvation of the one and the resurrection of the other; and for that constant and cheerful resolution, which the same spirit hath established in me, to live and die in the religion now professed in the Church of England. In expectation of that resurrection, I desire my body may be buried (in the most private manner that may be) in that place of St. Paul's Church, London, that the now residenciaries have at my request designed for that purpose, etc. And this my last will and testament, made in the fear of God (whose mercy I humbly beg, and constantly rely upon in Jesus Christ) and in perfect love and charity with all the world (whose pardon I ask, from the lowest of my servants, to the highest of my superiors) written all with my own hand, and my name subscribed to every page, of which there are five in number.

Sealed December 13, 1630.

Nor was this blessed sacrifice of charity expressed only at his death, but in his life also, by a cheerful and frequent visitation of any friend whose mind was dejected or his for-

tune necessitous; he was inquisitive after the wants of prisoners and redeemed many from thence that lay for their
fees or small debts; he was a continual giver to poor scholars,
both of this and foreign nations. Besides what he gave with
his own hand, he usually sent a servant, or a discreet and
trusty friend, to distribute his charity to all the prisons
in London at all the festival times of the year, especially
at the birth and resurrection of our Saviour. He gave an
hundred pounds at one time to an old friend, whom he had
known live plentifully and by a too liberal heart and carelessness become decayed in his estate; and when the receiving of it was denied, by the gentleman's saying, "He wanted
not"; for the reader may note that as there be some spirits
so generous as to labor to conceal and endure a sad poverty
rather than expose themselves to those blushes that attend
the confession of it, so there be others to whom nature and
grace have afforded such sweet and compassionate souls
as to pity and prevent the distresses of mankind; which
I have mentioned because of Dr. Donne's reply, whose answer was, "I know you want not what will sustain nature,
for a little will do that; but my desire is that you, who in
the days of your plenty have cheered and raised the hearts
of so many of your dejected friends, would now receive this
from me and use it as a cordial for the cheering of your
own": and upon these terms it was received. He was an
happy reconciler of many differences in the families of his
friends and kindred (which he never undertook faintly;
for such undertakings have usually faint effects) and they
had such a faith in his judgment and impartiality that he
never advised them to anything in vain. He was, even to
her death, a most dutiful son to his mother, careful to provide for her supportation, of which she had been destitute,
but that God raised him up to prevent her necessities; who
having sucked in the religion of the Roman Church with her
mother's milk, spent her estate in foreign countries to en-

joy a liberty in it, and died in his house but three months before him.

And to the end it may appear how just a steward he was of his Lord and Master's revenue, I have thought fit to let the reader know that after his entrance into his deanery, as he numbered his years, he, at the foot of a private account, to which God and his angels were only witnesses with him, computed first his revenue; then what was given to the poor, and other pious uses; and lastly, what rested for him and his; and having done that, he then blessed each year's poor remainder with a thankful prayer. . . .[21]

But I return from my long digression.

We left the author sick in Essex, where he was forced to spend much of that winter, by reason of his disability to remove from that place; and having never, for almost twenty years, omitted his personal attendance on His Majesty in that month in which he was to attend and preach to him; nor having ever been left out of the roll and number of Lent preachers, and there being then (in January, 1630) a report brought to London, or raised there, that Dr. Donne was dead, that report gave him occasion to write the following letter to a dear friend.

"Sir,

"This advantage you and my other friends have by my frequent fevers, that I am so much the oftener at the gates of heaven; and this advantage by the solitude and close imprisonment that they reduce me to after, that I am so much the oftener at my prayers, in which I shall never leave out your happiness; and I doubt not, among his other blessings, God will add some one to you for my prayers. A man would almost be content to die (if there were no other benefit in death) to hear of so much sorrow and so much good testimony from good men as I (God be blessed for it) did upon

---

[21] Here Walton quotes several prayers in Latin.

the report of my death: yet I perceive it went not through all; for one writ to me, that some (and he said of my friends) conceived I was not so ill as I pretended, but withdrew myself to live at ease, discharged of preaching. It is an unfriendly, and, God knows, an ill-grounded interpretation; for I have always been sorrier when I could not preach than any could be they could not hear me. It hath been my desire, and God may be pleased to grant it, that I might die in the pulpit; if not that, yet that I might take my death in the pulpit, that is, die the sooner by occasion of those labors. Sir, I hope to see you presently after Candlemas; about which time will fall my Lent sermon at court, except my Lord Chamberlain believe me to be dead, and so leave me out of the roll: but as long as I live, and am not speechless, I would not willingly decline that service. I have better leisure to write than you to read, yet I would not willingly oppress you with too much letter. God so bless you and your son, as I wish to

Your poor friend and servant
in Christ Jesus,
J. DONNE."

Before that month ended, he was appointed to preach upon his old constant day, the first Friday in Lent: he had notice of it, and had in his sickness so prepared for that employment that as he had long thirsted for it, so he resolved his weakness should not hinder his journey; he came therefore to London some few days before his appointed day of preaching. At his coming thither, many of his friends (who with sorrow saw his sickness had left him but so much flesh as did only cover his bones) doubted his strength to perform that task and did therefore dissuade him from undertaking it, assuring him, however, it was like to shorten his life: but he passionately denied their requests, saying "he would not doubt that that God, who in so many weaknesses had assisted him with an unexpected strength, would now withdraw it in his last employment; professing an holy ambition to perform that sacred work." And when, to the amazement of some beholders, he appeared in the pulpit, many of them thought he presented himself not to preach mortification by a living voice, but mortality by a decayed body and a dying face. And doubtless many did secretly ask that question in Ezekiel,[22] "Do these bones live? or, can that soul organize that tongue, to speak so long time as the sand in that glass will move towards its center, and measure out an hour of this dying man's unspent life? Doubtless it cannot." And yet, after some faint pauses in his zealous prayer, his strong desires enabled his weak body to discharge his memory of his preconceived meditations, which were of dying; the text being, "To God the Lord belong the issues from death." [23] Many that then saw his tears, and heard his faint and hollow voice, professing they thought the text prophetically chosen and that Dr. Donne had preached his own funeral sermon.

Being full of joy that God had enabled him to perform this desired duty, he hastened to his house; out of which he never moved, till, like St. Stephen, "he was carried by devout men to his grave."

The next day after his sermon, his strength being much wasted and his spirits so spent as indisposed him to business or to talk, a friend that had often been a witness of his free and facetious discourse asked him, "Why are you sad?" To whom he replied, with a countenance so full of cheerful gravity as gave testimony of an inward tranquillity of mind and of a soul willing to take a farewell of this world, and said:

"I am not sad; but most of the night past I have entertained myself with many thoughts of several friends that have left me here, and are gone to that place from which they shall not return; and that within a few days I also shall go hence and be no more seen. And my preparation

---

[22] Chap. 37:3.   [23] Psalm 68:20.

for this change is become my nightly meditation upon my bed, which my infirmities have now made restless to me. But at this present time, I was in a serious contemplation of the providence and goodness of God to me; to me, who am less than the least of his mercies: and looking back upon my life past, I now plainly see it was his hand that prevented me from all temporal employment and that it was his will I should never settle nor thrive till I entered into the ministry; in which I have now lived almost twenty years (I hope to his glory) and by which, I most humbly thank him, I have been enabled to requite most of those friends which showed me kindness when my fortune was very low, as God knows it was: and as it hath occasioned the expression of my gratitude, I thank God most of them have stood in need of my requital. I have lived to be useful and comfortable to my good father-in-law, Sir George More, whose patience God hath been pleased to exercise with many temporal crosses; I have maintained my own mother, whom it hath pleased God after a plentiful fortune in her younger days to bring to great decay in her very old age. I have quieted the consciences of many that have groaned under the burthen of a wounded spirit, whose prayers I hope are available for me. I cannot plead innocency of life, especially of my youth; but I am to be judged by a merciful God, who is not willing to see what I have done amiss. And though of myself I have nothing to present to him but sins and misery, yet I know he looks not upon me now as I am of myself, but as I am in my Saviour, and hath given me, even at this present time, some testimonies by his Holy Spirit, that I am of the number of his elect: I am therefore full of inexpressible joy, and shall die in peace."

I must here look so far back as to tell the reader that at his first return out of Essex, to preach his last sermon, his old friend and physician, Dr. Fox, a man of great worth, came to him to consult his health; and after that a sight of him and some queries concerning his distempers, he told

him, "That by cordials, and drinking milk twenty days together, there was a probability of his restoration to health";
but he passionately denied to drink it. Nevertheless, Dr.
Fox, who loved him most entirely wearied him with solicitations, till he yielded to take it for ten days; at the end of
which time he told Dr. Fox, "He had drunk it more to satisfy him, than to recover his health; and that he would not
drink it ten days longer upon the best moral assurance of
having twenty years added to his life; for he loved it not;
and was so far from fearing death, which to others is the
king of terrors, that he longed for the day of his dissolution."

It is observed that a desire of glory or commendation is
rooted in the very nature of man; and that those of the
severest and most mortified lives, though they may become
so humble as to banish self-flattery, and such weeds as naturally grow there; yet they have not been able to kill this
desire of glory, but that like our radical heat, it will both
live and die with us; and many think it should do so; and we
want not sacred examples to justify the desire of having our
memory to outlive our lives; which I mention, because Dr.
Donne, by the persuasion of Dr. Fox, easily yielded at this
very time to have a monument made for him; but Dr. Fox
undertook not to persuade him how, or what monument it
should be; that was left to Dr. Donne himself.

A monument being resolved upon, Dr. Donne sent for a
carver to make for him in wood the figure of an urn, giving
him directions for the compass and height of it; and to bring
with it a board, of the just height of his body. These being
got, then without delay a choice painter was got to be in
readiness to draw his picture, which was taken as followeth.
Several charcoal fires being first made in his large study,
he brought with him into that place his winding-sheet in
his hand, and having put off all his clothes, had this sheet
put on him, and so tied with knots at his head and feet,
and his hands so placed as dead bodies are usually fitted to
be shrouded and put into their coffin or grave. Upon this

urn he thus stood with his eyes shut and with so much of
the sheet turned aside as might show his lean, pale, and
death-like face, which was purposely turned towards the
east, from whence he expected the second coming of his and
our Saviour Jesus. In this posture he was drawn at his just
height; and when the picture was fully finished, he caused
it to be set by his bedside, where it continued and became
his hourly object till his death, and was then given to his
dearest friend and executor Dr. Henry King, then chief residenciary of St. Paul's, who caused him to be thus carved
in one entire piece of white marble, as it now stands in that
church; and by Dr. Donne's own appointment, these words
were to be affixed to it as an epitaph:

JOHANNES DONNE
Sac. Theol. Profess.

Post varia studia quibus ab annis tenerrimis
fideliter, nec infeliciter incubuit,
instinctu et impulsu Sp. Sancti, monitu
et hortatu

REGIS JACOBI, *ordines sacros*
amplexus, anno sui Jesu, 1614, et suæ ætatis 42,
decanatu hujus ecclesiæ indutus 27,
Novembris, 1621,

exutus morte ultimo die Martii, 1631,
hic licet in occiduo cinere aspicit eum
cujus nomen est Oriens.

And now, having brought him through the many labyrinths and perplexities of a various life, even to the gates
of death and the grave; my desire is, he may rest till I
have told my reader that I have seen many pictures of him

in several habits and at several ages and in several postures; and I now mention this, because I have seen one picture of him, drawn by a curious hand, at his age of eighteen, with his sword, and what other adornments might then suit with the present fashions of youth and the giddy gaieties of that age; and his motto then was—

> How much shall I be changed,
> Before I am changed!

And if that young and his now dying picture were at this time set together, every beholder might say, "Lord! how much is Dr. Donne already changed, before he is changed!" And the view of them might give my reader occasion to ask himself with some amazement, "Lord! how much may I also, that am now in health, be changed before I am changed; before this vile, this changeable body shall put off mortality!" and therefore to prepare for it. But this is not written so much for my reader's memento as to tell him that Dr. Donne would often in his private discourses, and often publicly in his sermons, mention the many changes both of his body and mind; especially of his mind from a vertiginous giddiness; and would as often say, "His great and most blessed change was from a temporal to a spiritual employment"; in which he was so happy, that he accounted the former part of his life to be lost; and the beginning of it to be from his first entering into sacred orders and serving his most merciful God at his altar.

Upon Monday, after the drawing this picture, he took his last leave of his beloved study; and, being sensible of his hourly decay, retired himself to his bed-chamber; and that week sent at several times for many of his most considerable friends, with whom he took a solemn and deliberate farewell, commending to their consideration some sentences useful for the regulation of their lives; and then dismissed them, as good Jacob did his sons, with a spiritual benediction. The Sunday following, he appointed his servants, that

if there were any business yet undone that concerned him
or themselves, it should be prepared against Saturday next;
for after that day he would not mix his thoughts with anything that concerned this world; nor ever did; but, as Job,
so he "waited for the appointed day of his dissolution."

And now he was so happy as to have nothing to do but
to die, to do which he stood in need of no longer time; for
he had studied it long and to so happy a perfection that in
a former sickness he called God to witness,[24] "He was that
minute ready to deliver his soul into his hands, if that minute
God would determine his dissolution." In that sickness he
begged of God the constancy to be preserved in that estate
forever; and his patient expectation to have his immortal
soul disrobed from her garment of mortality makes me confident that he now had a modest assurance that his prayers
were then heard and his petition granted. He lay fifteen days
earnestly expecting his hourly change; and in the last hour
of his last day, as his body melted away and vapored into
spirit, his soul having, I verily believe, some revelation
of the beatifical vision, he said, "I were miserable if I might
not die"; and after those words, closed many periods of his
faint breath by saying often, "Thy kingdom come, thy will
be done." His speech, which had long been his ready and
faithful servant, left him not till the last minute of his life,
and then forsook him, not to serve another master (for who
speaks like him) but died before him; for that it was then
become useless to him that now conversed with God on
earth as angels are said to do in heaven, only by thoughts
and looks. Being speechless, and seeing heaven by that illumination by which he saw it, he did, as St. Stephen, "look
steadfastly into it, till he saw the Son of Man standing at
the right hand of God his Father"; [25] and being satisfied
with this blessed sight, as his soul ascended and his last
breath departed from him, he closed his own eyes; and then

[24] In his book of *Devotions* written then.
[25] Acts 7:55.

disposed his hands and body into such a posture as required not the least alteration by those that came to shroud him.

Thus variable, thus virtuous was the life: thus excellent, thus exemplary was the death of this memorable man.

He was buried in that place of St. Paul's Church which he had appointed for that use some years before his death; and by which he passed daily to pay his public devotions to Almighty God (who was then served twice a day by a public form of prayer and praises in that place): but he was not buried privately, though he desired it; for, besides an unnumbered number of others, many persons of nobility, and of eminency for learning, who did love and honor him in life, did show it at his death by a voluntary and sad attendance of his body to the grave, where nothing was so remarkable as a public sorrow.

To which place of his burial some mournful friends repaired, and, as Alexander the Great did to the grave of the famous Achilles, so they strowed his with an abundance of curious and costly flowers; which course, they (who were never yet known) continued morning and evening for many days, not ceasing, till the stones that were taken up in that church to give his body admission into the cold earth (now his bed or rest) were again by the mason's art so leveled and firmed as they had been formerly, and his place of burial undistinguishable to common view.

The next day after his burial, some unknown friend, some one of the many lovers and admirers of his virtue and learning, wrote this epitaph with a coal on the wall over his grave:

> Reader! I am to let thee know,
> Donne's body only lies below;
> For, could the grave his soul comprise,
> Earth would be richer than the skies!

Nor was this all the honor done to his reverend ashes; for, as there be some persons that will not receive a reward for that for which God accounts himself a debtor, persons that

dare trust God with their charity and without a witness; so
there was by some grateful unknown friend that thought
Dr. Donne's memory ought to be perpetuated, an hundred
marks sent to his faithful friends [26] and executors, towards
the making of his monument. It was not for many years
known by whom; but after the death of Dr. Fox, it was
known that it was he that sent it; and he lived to see as lively
a representation of his dead friend as marble can express:
a statue indeed so like Dr. Donne, that (as his friend Sir
Henry Wotton hath expressed himself) "It seems to breathe
faintly, and posterity shall look upon it as a kind of artificial
miracle."

He was of stature moderately tall; of a straight and
equally-proportioned body, to which all his words and actions gave an unexpressible addition of comeliness.

The melancholy and pleasant humor were in him so con-
tempered that each gave advantage to the other, and made
his company one of the delights of mankind.

His fancy was unimitably high, equaled only by his great
wit; both being made useful by a commanding judgment.

His aspect was cheerful, and such as gave a silent testimony of a clear knowing soul, and of a conscience at peace
with itself.

His melting eye showed that he had a soft heart, full of
noble compassion; of too brave a soul to offer injuries and
too much a Christian not to pardon them in others.

He did much contemplate (especially after he entered into
his sacred calling) the mercies of Almighty God, the immortality of the soul, and the joys of heaven: and would
often say in a kind of sacred ecstasy—"Blessed be God that
he is God, only and divinely like himself."

He was by nature highly passionate, but more apt to reluct
at the excesses of it. A great lover of the offices of humanity,
and of so merciful a spirit that he never beheld the miseries
of mankind without pity and relief.

[26] Dr. King and Dr. Montford.

He was earnest and unwearied in the search of knowledge, with which his vigorous soul is now satisfied, and employed in a continual praise of that God that first breathed it into his active body: that body, which once was a temple of the Holy Ghost and is now become a small quantity of Christian dust:

But I shall see it reanimated.

Feb. 15, 1639.   I. W.

From THE COMPLETE ANGLER,

OR THE CONTEMPLATIVE MAN'S RECREATION [1]

First Day, Chapter I

A Conference betwixt an Angler, a Falconer, and a Hunter, each commending his Recreation

PISCATOR, VENATOR, AUCEPS

PISCATOR. You are well overtaken, gentlemen; a good morning to you both; I have stretched my legs up Tottenham Hill to overtake you, hoping your business may occasion you towards Ware, whither I am going this fine, fresh May morning.

VENATOR. Sir, I for my part shall almost answer your hopes, for my purpose is to drink my morning's draught at the Thatched House in Hoddesdon; and I think not to rest till I come thither, where I have appointed a friend or two to meet me: but for this gentleman that you see with me, I know not how far he intends his journey; he came so lately into my company that I have scarcely had time to ask him the question.

AUCEPS. Sir, I shall by your favor bear you company as far as Theobald's,[2] and there leave you; for then I turn up to a friend's house, who mews a hawk for me, which I now long to see.

VEN. Sir, we are all so happy as to have a fine, fresh, cool morning, and I hope we shall each be the happier in the others' company. And, gentlemen, that I may not lose yours, I shall either abate or amend my pace to enjoy it, knowing

---

[1] Text: 1676, fifth edition, the last in Walton's lifetime, with Walton's revisions and expansions.
[2] Theobald's, built by Lord Cecil Burleigh, was about twelve miles from London.

that (as the Italians say) "good company in a journey makes the way seem the shorter."

Auc. It may do so, sir, with the help of good discourse, which, methinks, we may promise from you, that both look and speak so cheerfully: and for my part I promise you, as an invitation to it, that I will be as free and openhearted as discretion will allow me to be with strangers.

Ven. And, sir, I promise the like.

Pisc. I am right glad to hear your answers; and in confidence you speak the truth, I shall put on a boldness to ask you, sir, whether business or pleasure caused you to be so early up, and walk so fast; for this other gentleman hath declared he is going to see a hawk, that a friend mews for him.

Ven. Sir, mine is a mixture of both, a little business and more pleasure; for I intend this day to do all my business, and then bestow another day or two in hunting the otter, which a friend that I go to meet tells me is much pleasanter than any other chase whatsoever; howsoever I mean to try it, for tomorrow morning we shall meet a pack of otter-dogs of noble Mr. Sadler's upon Amwell Hill, who will be there so early that they intend to prevent the sun rising.

Pisc. Sir, my fortune has answered my desires, and my purpose is to bestow a day or two in helping to destroy some of those villainous vermin: for I hate them perfectly, because they love fish so well, or rather, because they destroy so much; indeed so much that in my judgment, all men that keep otter-dogs ought to have pensions from the king to encourage them to destroy the breed of those base otters, they do so much mischief.

Ven. But what say you to the foxes of the nation; would not you as willingly have them destroyed? for doubtless they do as much mischief as otters do.

Pisc. Oh, sir, if they do, it is not so much to me and my fraternity, as those base vermin the otters do.

Auc. Why, sir, I pray, of what fraternity are you, that you are so angry with the poor otters?

Pisc. I am, sir, a brother of the angle, and therefore an enemy to the otter: for you are to note, that we anglers all love one another, and therefore do I hate the otter both for my own and their sakes who are of my brotherhood.

Ven. And I am a lover of hounds; I have followed many a pack of dogs many a mile, and heard many merry hunts-men make sport and scoff at anglers.

Auc. And I profess myself a falconer, and have heard many grave, serious men pity them, it is such a heavy, con-temptible, dull recreation.

Pisc. You know, gentlemen, it is an easy thing to scoff at any art or recreation; a little wit, mixed with ill nature, confidence, and malice, will do it; but though they often venture boldly, yet they are often caught, even in their own trap, according to that of Lucian, the father of the family of scoffers.

> Lucian, well-skilled in scoffing, this hath writ,
> Friend, that's your folly, which you think your wit:
> This you vent oft, void both of wit and fear,
> Meaning another, when yourself you jeer.

If to this you add what Solomon says of scoffers, that they are an abomination to mankind, let him that thinks fit scoff on, and be a scoffer still; but I account them enemies to me and all that love virtue and angling.

And for you that have heard many grave, serious men pity anglers; let me tell you, sir, there be many men that are by others taken to be serious and grave men, whom we contemn and pity. Men that are taken to be grave, because nature hath made them of a sour complexion; money-getting men, that spend all their time, first in getting, and next, in anxious care to keep it; men that are condemned to be rich, and then always busy or discontented: for these poor-rich-men, we anglers pity them perfectly, and stand in no need to bor-row their thoughts to think ourselves so happy. No, no, sir, we enjoy a contentedness above the reach of such dispositions, and as the learned and ingenuous Montaigne [3] says like himself, freely, "When my cat and I entertain each other with mutual apish tricks, as with playing with a garter, who knows but that I make my cat more sport than she makes me? Shall I conclude her to be simple, that has her time to begin or refuse to play as freely as I myself have? Nay, who knows but that it is a defect of my not understanding her language (for doubtless cats talk and reason with one another) that we agree no better: and who knows but that she pities me for being no wiser than to play with her, and laughs and censures my folly for making sport with her, when we two play together." Thus freely speaks Montaigne concerning cats; and I hope I may take as great a liberty to blame any man, and laugh at him, too, let him be never so grave, that hath not heard what anglers can say in the justification of their art and recreation; which I may again tell you, is so full of pleasure that we need not borrow their thoughts, to think ourselves happy.

VEN. Sir, you have almost amazed me; for though I am no scoffer, yet I have (I pray let me speak it without offense) always looked upon anglers as more patient and more simple men than I fear I shall find you to be.

PISC. Sir, I hope you will not judge my earnestness to be impatience: and for my simplicity, if by that you mean a harmlessness, or that simplicity which was usually found in the primitive Christians, who were, as most anglers are, quiet men, and followers of peace; men that were so simply wise as not to sell their consciences to buy riches, and with them vexation and a fear to die; if you mean such simple men as lived in those times when there were fewer lawyers; when men might have had a lordship safely conveyed to them in a piece of parchment no bigger than your hand, though several sheets will not do it safely in a wiser age; I say, sir, if you take us anglers to be such simple men as I have spoken of, then myself and those of my profession will be glad to

[3] In *Apology for Raymond Sebond*. See Florio's *Montaigne*, ch. 12.

be so understood: but if by simplicity you meant to express
a general defect in those that profess and practice the excellent art of angling, I hope in time to disabuse you, and
make the contrary appear so evidently, that if you will but
have patience to hear me, I shall remove all the anticipa-
tions that discourse, or time, or prejudice, have possessed you
with against that laudable and ancient art; for I know it
is worthy the knowledge and practice of a wise man.

But, gentlemen, though I be able to do this, I am not
so unmannerly as to engross all the discourse to myself;
and, therefore, you two having declared yourselves, the one
to be a lover of hawks, the other of hounds, I shall be most
glad to hear what you can say in the commendation of that
recreation which each of you love and practice; and having
heard what you can say, I shall be glad to exercise your attention with what I can say concerning my own recreation
and art of angling, and by this means, we shall make the
way seem the shorter; and if you like my motion, I would
have Mr. Falconer begin.

Auc. Your motion is consented to with all my heart, and
to testify it, I will begin as you have desired me.

And first, for the element that I use to trade in, which is
the air, an element of more worth than weight, an element
that doubtless exceeds both the earth and water; for though
I sometimes deal in both, yet the air is more properly mine,
I and my hawks use that most, and it yields us most recreation; it stops not the high-soaring of my noble generous
falcon; in it she ascends to such an height, as the dull eyes
of beasts and fish are not able to reach to; their bodies are
too gross for such high elevations; in the air my troops of
hawks soar up on high, and when they are lost in the sight
of men, then they attend upon and converse with gods; therefore I think my eagle is so justly styled Jove's servant in
ordinary: and that very falcon that I am now going to see
deserves no meaner a title, for she usually in her flight en-
dangers herself, like the son of Dædalus, to have her wings

scorched by the sun's heat, she flies so near it, but her mettle makes her careless of danger; for she then heeds nothing, but makes her nimble pinions cut the fluid air, and so makes her highway over the steepest mountains and deepest rivers, and in her glorious career looks with contempt upon those high steeples and magnificent palaces which we adore and wonder at; from which height I can make her descend by a word from my mouth (which she both knows and obeys) to accept of meat from my hand, to own me for her master, to go home with me, and be willing the next day to afford me the like recreation.

And more; this element of air which I profess to trade in, the worth of it is such, and it is of such necessity, that no creature whatsoever—not only those numerous creatures that feed on the face of the earth, but those various creatures that have their dwelling within the waters, every creature that hath life in its nostrils, stands in need of my element. The waters cannot preserve the fish without air, witness the not breaking of ice in an extreme frost; the reason is, for that if the inspiring and expiring organ of any animal be stopped, it suddenly yields to nature, and dies. Thus necessary is air to the existence, both of fish and beasts, nay, even to man himself; that air, or breath of life, with which God at first inspired mankind, he, if he wants it, dies presently, becomes a sad object to all that loved and beheld him, and in an instant turns to putrefaction.

Nay more, the very birds of the air, those that be not hawks, are both so many and so useful and pleasant to mankind that I must not let them pass without some observations. They both feed and refresh him; feed him with their choice bodies, and refresh him with their heavenly voices: I will not undertake to mention the several kinds of fowl by which this is done, and his curious palate pleased by day, and which with their very increments afford him a soft lodging by night. These I will pass by, but not those little nimble musicians of the air, that warble forth their curious ditties with which nature furnished them to the shame of art.

As first the lark, when she means to rejoice, to cheer herself and those that hear her; she then quits the earth, and sings as she ascends higher into the air, and having ended her heavenly employment, grows then mute and sad, to think she must descend to the dull earth, which she would not touch but for necessity.

How do the blackbird and throstle with their melodious voices bid welcome to the cheerful spring, and in their fixed months warble forth such ditties as no art or instrument can reach to!

Nay, the smaller birds also do the like in their particular seasons, as namely the laverock, the titlark, the little linnet, and the honest robin, that loves mankind both alive and dead.

But the nightingale, another of my airy creatures, breathes such sweet loud music out of her little instrumental throat that it might make mankind to think miracles are not ceased. He that at midnight, when the very laborer sleeps securely, should hear (as I have very often) the clear airs, the sweet descants, the natural rising and falling, the doubling and redoubling of her voice, might well be lifted above earth, and say, "Lord, what music hast thou provided for the saints in heaven, when thou affordest bad men such music on earth!"

And this makes me less to wonder at the many aviaries in Italy, or at the great charge of Varro's aviary, the ruins of which are yet to be seen in Rome, and is still so famous there that it is reckoned for one of those notables which men of foreign nations either record, or lay up in their memories when they travel.

This for the birds of pleasure, of which very much more might be said. My next shall be of birds of political use; I think 'tis not to be doubted that swallows have been taught to carry letters betwixt two armies; but 'tis certain that when the Turks besieged Malta or Rhodes (I now remember not which 'twas) pigeons are then related to carry and re-carry letters; and Mr. Sandys, in his "Travels," [4] relates it to be done betwixt Aleppo and Babylon. But if that be disbelieved, it is not to be doubted that the dove was sent out of the ark by Noah, to give him notice of land, when to him all appeared to be sea, and the dove proved a faithful and comfortable messenger. And for the sacrifices of the law, a pair of turtle-doves or young pigeons were as well accepted as costly bulls and rams. And when God would feed the prophet Elijah (I Kings 17:46), after a kind of miraculous manner, he did it by ravens, who brought him meat morning and evening. Lastly, the Holy Ghost, when it descended visibly upon our Saviour, did it by assuming the shape of a dove. And, to conclude this part of my discourse, pray remember these wonders were done by birds of the air, the element in which they, and I, take so much pleasure.

There is also a little contemptible winged creature, an inhabitant of my aerial element, namely the laborious bee, of whose prudence, policy, and regular government of their own commonwealth I might say much, as also of their several kinds, and how useful their honey and wax is both for meat and medicines to mankind; but I will leave them to sweet labor, without the least disturbance, believing them to be all very busy at this very time amongst the herbs and flowers that we see nature puts forth this May morning.

And now to return to my hawks, from whom I have made too long a digression; you are to note, that they are usually distinguished into two kinds; namely, the long-winged, and the short-winged hawk: of the first kind, their be chiefly in use amongst us in this nation,

> The gerfalcon and jerkin,
> The falcon and tassel-gentle,
> The laner and laneret,
> The bockerel and bockeret,

[4] George Sandys, 1615, p. 269.

The saker and sacaret,
The merlin and jack merlin,
The hobby and jack.
There is the stelletto of Spain,
The blood-red rook from Turkey,
The waskite from Virginia:
And there is of short-winged hawks,
The eagle and iron,
The goshawk and tercel,
The sparhawk and musket,
The French pye of two sorts;
These are reckoned hawks of note and worth, but we have
also of inferior rank,
The stanyel, the ringtail,
The raven, the buzzard,
The forked kite, the bald buzzard,
The hen-driver, and others that I forbear to name.

Gentlemen, if I should enlarge my discourse to the observation of the eires, the brancher, the ramish hawk, the
haggard, and the two sorts of lentners, and then treat of
their several aeries, their mewings, rare order of casting, and
the renovation of their feathers; their reclaiming, dieting,
and then come to their rare stories of practice; I say, if I
should enter into these, and many other observations that I
could make, it would be much, very much pleasure to me;
but lest I should break the rules of civility with you, by taking up more than the proportion of time allotted to me, I
will here break off and entreat you, Mr. Venator, to say what
you are able in the commendation of hunting, to which you
are so much affected; and if time will serve, I will beg your
favor for a further enlargement of some of those several heads
of which I have spoken. But no more at present.

VEN. Well, sir, and now I will take my turn, and will first
begin with a commendation of earth, as you have done most
excellently of the air; the earth being that element upon
which I drive my pleasant, wholesome, hungry trade. The

earth is a solid, settled element; an element most universally beneficial both to man and beast: to men who have their several recreations upon it, as horse-races, hunting, sweet smells, pleasant walks: the earth feeds man, and all those several beasts that both feed him, and afford him recreation. What pleasure doth man take in hunting the stately stag, the generous buck, the wild boar, the cunning otter, the crafty fox, and the fearful hare! And if I may descend to lower game, what pleasure is it sometimes with gins to betray the very vermin of the earth: as namely, the fichat, the fulimart, the ferret, the pole-cat, the moldwarp, and the like creatures that live upon the face and within the bowels of the earth. How doth the earth bring forth herbs, flowers, and fruits, both for physic and the pleasure of mankind! and above all, to me at least, the fruitful vine, of which when I drink moderately, it clears my brain, cheers my heart, and sharpens my wit. How could Cleopatra have feasted Mark Antony with eight wild boars roasted whole at one supper, and other meat suitable, if the earth had not been a bountiful mother? But to pass by the mighty elephant, which the earth breeds and nourisheth, and descend to the least of creatures, how doth the earth afford us a doctrinal example in the little pismire, who in the summer provides and lays up her winter provision, and teaches man to do the like! The earth feeds and carries those horses that carry us. If I would be a prodigal of my time and your patience, what might I not say in commendation of the earth? That puts limits to the proud and raging sea, and by that means preserves both man and beast, that it destroys them not, as we see it daily doth those that venture upon the sea, and are there ship-wrecked, drowned, and left to feed haddocks; when we that are so wise as to keep ourselves on earth, walk, and talk, and live, and eat, and drink, and go a-hunting: of which recreation I will say a little, and then leave Mr. Piscator to the commendation of angling.

Hunting is a game for princes and noble persons; it hath

been highly prized in all ages; it was one of the qualifications that Xenophon bestowed on his Cyrus, that he was a hunter of wild beasts. Hunting trains up the younger nobility to the use of manly exercises in their riper age. What more manly exercise than hunting the wild boar, the stag, the buck, the fox, or the hare? How doth it preserve health, and increase strength and activity!

And for the dogs that we use, who can commend their excellency to that height which they deserve? How perfect is the hound at smelling, who never leaves or forsakes his first scent, but follows it through so many changes and varieties of other scents, even over, and in the water, and into the earth! What music doth a pack of dogs then make to any man, whose heart and ears are so happy as to be set to the tune of such instruments! How will a right greyhound fix his eye on the best buck in the herd, single him out, and follow him, and him only, through a whole herd of rascal game, and still know and then kill him! For my hounds, I know the language of them, and they know the language and meaning of one another, as perfectly as we know the voices of those with whom we discourse daily.

I might enlarge myself in the commendation of hunting, and of the noble hound especially, as also of the docibleness of dogs in general; and I might make many observations of land-creatures, that for composition, order, figure, and constitution approach nearest to the completeness and understanding of man; especially of those creatures which Moses in the Law permitted to the Jews (which have cloven hoofs and chew the cud), which I shall forbear to name, because I will not be so uncivil to Mr. Piscator as not to allow him time for the commendation of angling, which he calls an art; but doubtless 'tis an easy one: and Mr. Auceps, I doubt we shall hear a watery discourse of it, but I hope 'twill not be a long one.

Auc. And I hope so too, though I fear it will.

Pisc. Gentlemen, let not prejudice possess you. I confess

my discourse is like to prove suitable to my recreation, calm
and quiet; we seldom take the name of God into our mouths,
but it is either to praise him, or to pray to him; if others
use it vainly in the midst of their recreations, so vainly as
if they meant to conjure, I must tell you, it is neither our
fault nor our custom; we protest against it. But, pray remember, I accuse nobody; for as I would not make a "watery discourse," so I would not put too much vinegar into it;
nor would I raise the reputation of my own art by the diminution or ruin of another's. And so much for the prologue to
what I mean to say.

And now for the water, the element that I trade in. The
water is the eldest daughter of the creation, the element
upon which the Spirit of God did first move, the element
which God commanded to bring forth living creatures abundantly; and without which, those that inhabit the land,
even all creatures that have breath in their nostrils, must
suddenly return to putrefaction. Moses, the great lawgiver
and chief philosopher, skilled in all the learning of the Egyptians, who was called the friend of God, and knew the mind
of the Almighty, names this element the first in the creation: this is the element upon which the spirit of God did
first move; and is the chief ingredient in the creation: many
philosophers have made it to comprehend all the other elements, and most allow it the chiefest in the mixtion of all
living creatures.

There be that profess to believe that all bodies are made
of water, and may be reduced back again to water only; they
endeavor to demonstrate it thus:

Take a willow (or any like speedy-growing plant) newly
rooted in a box or barrel of earth, weigh them altogether
exactly when the trees begin to grow, and then weigh them
altogether after the tree is increased from its first rooting,
to weigh an hundred pound weight more than when it was
first rooted and weighed; and you shall find this augment
of the tree to be without the diminution of one drachm weight

of the earth. Hence they infer this increase of wood to be from water or rain, or from dew, and not to be from any other element. And they affirm they can reduce this wood back again to water; and they affirm also, the same may be done in any animal or vegetable. And this I take to be a fair testimony of the excellency of my element of water.

The water is more productive than the earth. Nay, the earth hath no fruitfulness without showers or dews; for all the herbs and flowers, and fruit, are produced and thrive by water; and the very minerals are fed by streams that run under ground, whose natural course carries them to the tops of many high mountains, as we see by several springs breaking forth on the tops of the highest hills; and this is also witnessed by the daily trial and testimony of several miners.

Nay, the increase of those creatures that are bred and fed in the water are not only more and more miraculous, but more advantageous to man, not only for the lengthening of his life, but for the preventing of sickness; for 'tis observed by the most learned physicians, that the casting off of Lent, and other fish-days (which hath not only given the lie to so many learned, pious, wise founders of colleges, for which we should be ashamed) hath doubtless been the chief cause of those many putrid, shaking, intermitting agues, unto which this nation of ours is now more subject than those wiser countries that feed on herbs, salads, and plenty of fish; of which it is observed in story that the greatest part of the world now do. And it may be fit to remember that Moses (Lev. 11:9, Deut. 14:9) appointed fish to be the chief diet for the best commonwealth that ever yet was.

And it is observable, not only that there are fish, as namely the whale, three times as big as the mighty elephant that is so fierce in battle, but that the mightiest feasts have been of fish. The Romans, in the height of their glory, have made fish the mistress of all their entertainments; they have had music to usher in their sturgeons, lampreys, and mullets, which they would purchase at rates rather to be wondered at than believed. He that shall view the writings of Macrobious [5] or Varro [6] may be confirmed and informed of this, and of the incredible value of their fish and fish-ponds.

But, gentlemen, I have almost lost myself, which I confess I may easily do in this philosophical discourse; I met with most of it very lately, and I hope happily, in a conference with a most learned physician, Dr. Wharton,[7] a dear friend, that loves both me and my art of angling. But, however, I will wade no deeper in these mysterious arguments, but pass to such observations as I can manage with more pleasure and less fear of running into error. But I must not yet forsake the waters, by whose help we have so many known advantages.

And, first to pass by the miraculous cures of our known baths, how advantageous is the sea for our daily traffic, without which we could not now subsist! How does it not only furnish us with food and physic for the bodies, but with such observations for the mind as ingenious persons would not want!

How ignorant we would have been of the beauty of Florence, of the monuments, urns, and rarities that yet remain in, and near unto old and new Rome (so many as it is said will take up a year's time to view, and afford to each of them but a convenient consideration) and, therefore, it is not to be wondered at, that so learned and devout a father as St. Jerome, after his wish to have seen Christ in the flesh, and to have heard St. Paul preach, makes his third wish, to have seen Rome in her glory; and that glory is not yet all lost, for what pleasure is it to see the monuments of Livy, the choicest of the historians; of Tully, the best of orators; and to see the bay trees that now grow out of the very tomb of Virgil! These, to have any that love learning, must be pleasing. But what pleasure is it to a devout Christian to see there the humble house in which St. Paul was content to dwell, and

---

[5] Aurelius Macrobius, 4th century. See Hakewill's *Apology*, Bk. 4, s. 6, p. 434.
[6] Marcus Terentius Varro, a contemporary of Cicero.
[7] Dr. Thomas Wharton, first mentioned in this edition.

to view the many rich statues that are made in honor of his memory! nay, to see the very place in which St. Peter and he lie buried together! These are in Rome and near to Rome. And how much more doth it please the pious curiosity of a Christian to see that place on which the blessed Saviour of the world was pleased to humble himself, and take our nature upon him, and to converse with men: and to see Mount Sion, Jerusalem, and the very sepulcher of our Lord Jesus! How may it beget and heighten the zeal of a Christian to see the devotions that are daily paid to him at that place! Gentlemen, lest I forget myself, I will stop here, and remember you that but for my element of water, the inhabitants of this poor island must remain ignorant that such things ever were, or that any of them have yet a being.

Gentlemen, I might both enlarge and lose myself in such like arguments. I might tell you that Almighty God is said to have spoken to a fish, but never to a beast; that he hath made a whale a ship, to carry and set his prophet, Jonah, safe on the appointed shore. Of these I might speak, but I must in manners break off, for I see Theobald's House. I cry you mercy for being so long, and thank you for your patience.

Auc. Sir, my pardon is easily granted you: I except against nothing that you have said; nevertheless, I must part with you at this park-wall, for which I am very sorry; but I assure you, Mr. Piscator, I now part with you full of good thoughts, not only of yourself, but your recreation. And so, gentlemen, God keep you both.

Pisc. Well, now, Mr. Venator, you shall neither want time nor my attention to hear you enlarge your discourse concerning hunting.

Ven. Not I, sir: I remember you said that angling itself was of great antiquity, and a perfect art, and an art not easily attained to; and you have so won upon me in your former discourse, that I am very desirous to hear what you can say concerning those particulars.

Pisc. Sir, I did say so: and I doubt not but if you and I

did converse together but a few hours, to leave you possessed with the same high and happy thoughts that now possess me of it; not only of the antiquity of angling, but that it deserves commendations; and that it is an art, and an art worthy the knowledge and practice of a wise man.

VEN. Pray, sir, speak of them what you think fit, for we have yet five miles to the Thatched House; during which walk, I dare promise you, my patience and diligent attention shall not be wanting. And if you shall make that to appear which you have undertaken, first, that it is an art, and an art worth the learning, I shall beg that I may attend you a day or two a-fishing and that I may become your scholar and be instructed in the art itself which you so much magnify.

PISC. Oh, sir, doubt not but that angling is an art; is it not an art to deceive a trout with an artificial fly? a trout, that is more sharp-sighted than any hawk you have named, and more watchful and timorous than your high-mettled merlin is bold? and yet I doubt not to catch a brace or two tomorrow, for a friend's breakfast: doubt not, therefore, sir, but that angling is an art, and an art worth your learning. The question is rather, whether you be capable of learning it, for angling is somewhat like poetry, men are to be born so: I mean with some inclinations to it, though both may be heightened by discourse and practice; but he that hopes to be a good angler must not only bring an inquiring, searching, observing wit, but he must bring a large measure of hope and patience, and a love and propensity to the art itself; but having once got and practiced it, then doubt not but angling will prove to be so pleasant that it will prove to be, like virtue, a reward to itself.

VEN. Sir, I am now become so full of expectation that I long much to have you proceed, and in the order that you propose.

PISC. Then, first, for the antiquity of angling, of which I shall not say much, but only this: some say it is as ancient as Deucalion's flood; others, that Belus, who was the first inventor of godly and virtuous recreations, was the first inventor of angling; and some others say (for former times have had their disquisitions about the antiquity of it) that Seth, one of the sons of Adam, taught it to his sons, that by them it was derived to posterity; others say that he left it engraven on those pillars which he erected, and trusted to preserve the knowledge of the mathematics, music, and the rest of that precious knowledge, and those useful arts, which by God's appointment or allowance, and his noble industry, were thereby preserved from perishing in Noah's flood.

These, sir, have been the opinions of several men, that have possibly endeavored to make angling more ancient than is needful, or may well be warranted; but for my part, I shall content myself in telling you, that angling is much more ancient than the incarnation of our Saviour; for in the Prophet Amos mention is made of fish-hooks; and in the book of Job, which was long before the days of Amos (for that book is said to have been written by Moses), mention is made also of fish-hooks, which must imply anglers in those times.

But, my worthy friend, as I would rather prove myself a gentleman, by being learned and humble, valiant and inoffensive, virtuous and communicable, than by any fond ostentation of riches, or, wanting those virtues myself, boast that these were my ancestors; and yet I grant that where a noble and ancient descent and such merit meet in any man, it is a double dignification of that person; so if this antiquity of angling, which for my part I have not forced, shall like an ancient family be either an honor or an ornament to this virtuous art which I profess to love and practice, I shall be the gladder that I made an accidental mention of the antiquity of it; of which I shall say no more, but proceed to that just commendation which I think it deserves.

And for that I shall tell you, that in ancient times a debate hath risen, and it remains yet unresolved, whether the happiness of man in this world doth consist more in contemplation or action. Concerning which some have endeavored to maintain their opinion of the first by saying, that the nearer we mortals come to God by way of imitation, the more happy we are. And they say that God enjoys himself only, by a contemplation of his own infiniteness, eternity, power, and goodness, and the like. And upon this ground, many cloisteral men of great learning and devotion prefer contemplation before action. And many of the Fathers seem to approve this opinion, as may appear in their commentaries upon the words of our Saviour to Martha (Luke 10:41, 42).

And on the contrary, there want not men of equal authority and credit that prefer action to be the more excellent: as namely, experiments in physic, and the application of it, both for the ease and prolongation of man's life, by which each man is enabled to act and do good to others, either to serve his country, or do good to particular persons; and they say also, that action is doctrinal, and teaches both art and virtue, and is a maintainer of human society; and for these, and other like reasons, to be preferred before contemplation.

Concerning which two opinions I shall forbear to add a third by declaring my own, and rest myself contented in telling you, my very worthy friend, that both these meet together, and do most properly belong to the most honest, ingenuous, quiet, and harmless art of angling.

And first, I shall tell you what some have observed, and I have found to be a real truth, that the very sitting by the river's side is not only the quietest and fittest place for contemplation, but will invite an angler to it: and this seems to be maintained by the learned Peter du Moulin,[8] who in his discourse of the fulfilling of prophecies, observes, that when God intended to reveal any future events or high notions to his prophets, he then carried them either to the deserts, or the seashore, that having so separated them,

[8] Peter du Moulin, Chaplain to Charles II. *The Accomplishment of the Prophecies,* translated by J. Heath, Oxford, 1613.

from amidst the press of people and business, and the cares of the world, he might settle their mind in a quiet repose, and there make them fit for revelation.

And this seems also to be intimated by the children of Israel (Psalm 137), who having in a sad condition banished all mirth and music from their pensive hearts, and having hung up their then mute harps upon the willow trees growing by the rivers of Babylon, sat down upon those banks, bemoaning the ruins of Sion and contemplating their own sad condition.

And an ingenious Spaniard [9] says, that "rivers and the inhabitants of the watery element were made for wise men to contemplate, and fools to pass by without consideration." And though I will not rank myself in the number of the first, yet give me leave to free myself from the last by offering to you a short contemplation, first of rivers, and then of fish; concerning which I doubt not but to give you many observations that will appear very considerable: I am sure they have appeared so to me, and made many an hour pass away more pleasantly, as I have sat quietly on a flowery bank by a calm river, and contemplated what I shall now relate to you.

And first concerning rivers; there be so many wonders reported and written of them, and of the several creatures that be bred and live in them, and those by authors of so good credit [10] that we need not to deny them an historical faith.

As namely of a river in Epirus, that puts out any lighted torch, and kindles any torch that was not lighted. Some waters being drunk, cause madness, some drunkenness, and

[9] John Valdesso. *The Hundred and Ten Considerations of Signor Valdesso,* translated by Nicolas Farrar, Oxford, 1638.

[10] Meric Casaubon, 1599–1671, *Of Credulity,* 1668; and John Tradescant, gardener to Charles I, whose collection of books and manuscripts was transmitted to Elias Ashmole and is now in the Ashmolean Museum, Oxford.

some laughter to death. The river Selarus in a few hours turns a rod or wand to stone: and our Camden mentions the like in England, and the like in Lochmere in Ireland. There is also a river in Arabia, of which all the sheep that drink thereof have their wool turned into a vermilion color. And one of no less credit than Aristotle tells us of a merry river, the river Elusina, that dances at the noise of music, for with music it bubbles, dances, and grows sandy, and so continues till the music ceases, but then it presently returns to its wonted calmness and clearness. And Camden tells us of a well near to Kirby in Westmoreland, that ebbs and flows several times every day; and he tells us of a river in Surrey (it is called Mole), that after it has run several miles, being opposed by hills, finds or makes itself a way under ground, and breaks out again so far off that the inhabitants thereabout boast, as the Spaniards do of their river Anus, that they feed divers flocks of sheep upon a bridge. And, lastly, for I would not tire your patience, one of no less authority than Josephus, that learned Jew, tells us of a river in Judea that runs swiftly all the six days of the week, and stands still and rests all their Sabbath. . . .

VEN. Sir, you have angled me on with much pleasure to the Thatched House; and I now find your words true, "That good company makes the way seem short"; for trust me, sir, I thought we had wanted three miles of this house till you showed it to me. But now we are at it, we'll turn into it, and refresh ourselves with a cup of drink and a little rest.

PISC. Most gladly, sir, and we'll drink a civil cup to all the otter hunters that are to meet you tomorrow.

VEN. That we will, sir, and to all the lovers of angling, too, of which number I am now willing to be one myself; for by the help of your good discourse and company, I have put on new thoughts both of the art of angling and of all that profess it. And if you will but meet me tomorrow at the time and place appointed and bestow one day with me and my friends in hunting the otter, I will dedicate the next two days to wait upon you; and we two will, for that time, do nothing but angle, and talk of fish and fishing.

Pisc. It is a match, sir; I'll not fail you, God willing, to be at Amwell Hill tomorrow morning before sun-rising.

(*End of first day*)

Third Day, Chap. IV

. . . And now you shall see me try my skill to catch a trout. And at my next walking, either this evening or tomorrow morning, I will give you direction how you yourself shall fish for him.

Ven. Trust me, master, I see now it is a harder matter to catch a trout than a chub; for I have put on patience, and followed you these two hours, and not seen a fish stir, neither at your minnow nor your worm.

Pisc. Well, scholar, you must endure worse luck sometime, or you will never make a good angler. But what say you now? There is a trout now, and a good one too, if I can but hold him; and two or three turns more will tire him. Now you see he lies still and the sleight is to land him; reach me the landing-net. So, sir, now he is mine own: what say you now, is not this worth all my labor and your patience?

Ven. On my word, master, this is a gallant trout; what shall we do with him?

Pisc. Marry! e'en eat him to supper: we'll go to my hostess from whence we came; she told me, as I was going out of door, that my brother Peter, a good angler and a cheerful companion, had sent word he would lodge there tonight, and bring a friend with him. My hostess has two beds, and I know you and I have the best; we'll rejoice with my brother Peter and his friend, tell tales, or sing ballads, or make a catch, or find some harmless sport to content us, and pass away a little time without offense to God or man.

VEN. A match, good master! let's go to that house, for the linen looks white, and smells of lavender, and I long to lie in a pair of sheets that smell so. Let's be going, good master, for I am hungry again, with fishing.

PISC. Nay, stay a little, good scholar, I caught my last trout with a worm; now, I will put on a minnow, and try a quarter of an hour about yonder trees for another; and so, walk towards our lodging. Look you, scholar, thereabout we shall have a bite presently, or not at all. Have with you, sir! o' my word I have hold of him. Oh! it is a great logger-headed chub; come, hang him upon that willow twig, and let's be going. But turn out of the way a little, good scholar, toward yonder high honeysuckle hedge; there we'll sit and sing, whilst this shower falls so gently upon the teeming earth, and gives yet a sweeter smell to the lovely flowers that adorn these verdant meadows.

Look! under that broad beech tree I sat down when I was last this way a-fishing. And the birds in the adjoining grove seemed to have a friendly contention with an echo, whose dead voice seemed to live in a hollow tree, near to the brow of that primrose-hill. There, I saw viewing the silver streams glide silently towards their center, the tempestuous sea; yet sometimes opposed by rugged roots and pebble-stones, which broke their waves, and turned them into foam. And some-times I beguiled time by viewing the harmless lambs; some leaping securely in the cool shade, whilst others sported themselves in the cheerful sun; and saw others craving comfort from the swollen udders of their bleating dams. As thus I sat, these and other sights had so fully possessed my soul with content that I thought, as the poet has happily expressed it,

I was for that time lifted above earth;
And possessed joys not promised in my birth.

As I left this place and entered into the next field, a second pleasure entertained me: 'twas a handsome milkmaid, that had not yet attained so much age and wisdom as to load her mind with any fears of many things that will never be, as too many men often do; but she cast away all care, and sung like a nightingale. Her voice was very good, and the ditty fitted for it: 'twas that smooth song which was made by Kit Marlowe, now at least fifty years ago. And the milkmaid's mother sung an answer to it, which was made by Sir Walter Raleigh in his younger days.

They were old-fashioned poetry, but choicely good; I think, much better than the strong lines that are now in fashion in this critical age. Look yonder! on my word, yonder they be a-milking again. I will give her the chub, and persuade them to sing those two songs to us.

God speed you, good woman! I have been a-fishing; and am going to Bleak Hall to my bed; and having caught more fish than will sup myself and my friend, I will bestow this upon you and your daughter, for I use to sell none.

Milk-w. Marry! God requite you, sir, and we'll eat it cheerfully. And if you come this way a-fishing two months hence, a grace of God, I'll give you a syllabub of new verjuice, in a new-made hay-cock, for it. And my Maudlin shall sing you one of her best ballads; for she and I both love all anglers, they be such honest, civil, quiet men. In the meantime will you drink a draught of red cow's milk? You shall have it freely.

Pisc. No, I thank you; but, I pray, do us a courtesy that shall stand you and your daughter in nothing, and yet we will think ourselves still something in your debt: it is but to sing us a song that was sung by your daughter when I last passed over this meadow, about eight or nine days since.

Milk-w. What song was it, I pray? Was it, "Come shepherds deck your herds"? or, "As at noon Dulcina rested"? or, "Phillida flouts me"? or, "Chevy Chase"? or, "Johnny Armstrong"? or, "Troy Town"?

Pisc. No, it is none of those; it is a song that your daughter sung the first part, and you sung the answer to it.

Milk-w. O, I know it now. I learned the first part in my golden age, when I was about the age of my poor daughter; and the latter part, which indeed fits me best now, but two or three years ago, when the cares of the world began to take hold of me: but you shall, God willing, hear them both; and sung as well as we can, for we both love anglers. Come Maudlin! sing the first part to the gentlemen, with a merry heart; and I'll sing the second, when you have done.

The Milkmaid's Song

Come live with me, and be my love;
And we will all the pleasures prove
That valleys, groves, or hills, or fields,
Or woods, and steepy mountains yields;

Where we will sit upon the rocks,
And see the shepherds feed our flocks,
By shallow rivers, to whose falls
Melodious birds sing madrigals.

And I will make thee beds of roses;
And, then, a thousand fragrant poesies;
A cap of flowers; and a kirtle,
Embroidered all with leaves of myrtle.

A gown made of the finest wool,
Which from our pretty lambs we pull;
Slippers, lined choicely for the cold,
With buckles of the purest gold;

A belt of straw and ivy buds,
With coral clasps, and amber studs.

And if these pleasures may thee move,
Come live with me, and be my love.

Thy silver dishes for thy meat
As precious as the gods do eat
Shall, on an ivory table, be
Prepared each day for thee and me.

The shepherd swains shall dance and sing,
For thy delight, each May morning.
If these delights thy mind may move,
Then live with me, and be my love.

VEN. Trust me, master, it is a choice song, and sweetly
sung by honest Maudlin. I now see it was not without
cause that our good Queen Elizabeth did so often wish herself a milkmaid all the month of May; because they are
not troubled with fears and cares, but sing sweetly all the
day and sleep securely all the night: and without doubt,
honest, innocent, pretty Maudlin does so. I'll bestow Sir
Thomas Overbury's milkmaid's wish upon her, "That she
may die in the spring; and being dead, may have good store
of flowers stuck round her winding-sheet." [11]

The Milkmaid's Mother's Answer

If all the world and love were young,
And truth in every shepherd's tongue,
These pretty pleasures might me move
To live with thee and be thy love.

But Time drives flocks from field to fold;
When rivers rage, and rocks grow cold,

[11] "Character of a Fair and Happy Milkmaid," in Overbury's *The Wife*
(no. 51), London, 1638.

Then Philomel becometh dumb;
And age complains of care to come.

The flowers do fade, and wanton fields
The wayward winter reckoning yields,
A honey tongue, a heart of gall,
Is fancy's spring, but sorrow's fall.

Thy gowns, thy shoes, thy beds of roses,
Thy cap, thy kirtle, and thy posies,
Soon break, soon wither, soon forgotten;
In folly ripe, in reason rotten.

The belt of straw, and ivy buds,
The coral clasps, and amber studs,
All these in me no means can move,
To come to thee, and be thy love.

What should we talk of dainties then,
Of better meat than's fit for men?
These are but vain: that's only good
Which God hath blest, and sent for food.

But could youth last, and love still breed;
Had joys no date, nor age no need;
Then those delights my mind might move,
To live with thee, and be thy love.

MOTHER. Well! I have done my song. But stay, honest anglers; for I will make Maudlin to sing you one short song more. Maudlin, sing that song that you sung last night, when young Coridon the shepherd played so purely on his oaten pipe to you and your cousin Betty.

MAUD. I will, mother.

I married a wife of late,
The more's my unhappy fate:
    I married her for love,
    As my fancy did me move,
And not for a worldly estate.

    But oh! the green sickness
    Soon changed her likeness;
And all her beauty did fail.
        But 'tis not so,
        With those that go,
        Through frost and snow,
        As all men know,
And carry the milking-pail.

Pisc. Well sung, good woman; I thank you. I'll give you another dish of fish one of these days, and then beg another song of you. Come, scholar! let Maudlin alone: do not offer to spoil her voice. Look! yonder comes mine hostess to call us to supper. How now! is my brother Peter come?

Hostess. Yes, and friend with him. They are both glad to hear that you are in these parts; and long to see you; and long to be at supper, for they be very hungry.

Fourth Day, Chap. XVI

Is of nothing, or that which is nothing worth

Pisc. My purpose was to give you some directions concerning Roach and Dace, and some other inferior fish, which make the angler excellent sport, for you know there is more pleasure in hunting the hare than in eating her: but I will forbear at this time to say any more, because you see yonder come our brother Peter and honest Coridon. But I will promise you, that as you and I fish and walk tomorrow towards London, if I have now forgotten anything that I can then remember, I will not keep it from you.

Well met, gentlemen; this is lucky that we meet so just together at this very door. Come, hostess, where are you? Is supper ready? Come, first give us a drink, and be as quick as you can, for I believe we are all very hungry. Well, brother Peter and Coridon, to you both! Come, drink, and then tell me what luck of fish: we two have caught but ten trouts, of which my scholar caught three; look! here's eight, and a brace we gave away; we have had a most pleasant day fishing and talking, and are returned home both weary and hungry; and now meat and rest will be pleasant.

PET. And Coridon and I have not had an unpleasant day, and yet I have caught but five trouts: for indeed we went to a good honest ale-house, and there we played at shovel-board half the day; all the time that it rained we were there, and as merry as they that fished. And I am glad we are now with a dry house over our heads, for hark how it rains and blows. Come, hostess, give us more ale, and our supper with what haste you may; and when we have supped, let us have your song, Piscator, and the catch that your scholar promised us, or else Coridon will be dogged.

PISC. Nay, I will not be worse than my word; you shall not want my song, and I hope I shall be perfect in it.

VEN. And I hope the like for my catch, which I have ready too: and therefore let's go merrily to supper, and then have a gentle touch at singing and drinking; but the last with moderation.

COR. Come, now for your song, for we have fed heartily. Come, hostess, lay a few more sticks on the fire; and now sing when you will.

PISC. Well then, here's to you Coridon; and now for my song.

> Oh! the gallant fisher's life
> It is the best of any;
> 'Tis full of pleasure, void of strife,

And 'tis beloved of many:
>Other joys
>Are but toys;
>Only this
>Lawful is;
>For our skill
>Breeds no ill,
But content and pleasure.

In a morning up we rise,
>Ere Aurora's peeping;
Drink a cup to wash our eyes,
>Leave the sluggard sleeping.
>>Then we go
>>To and fro,
>>With our knacks
>>At our backs,
>>To such streams
>>As the Thames,
If we have the leisure.

When we please to walk abroad
>For our recreation,
In the fields is our abode,
>Full of delectation:
>>Where in a brook
>>With a hook,
>>Or a lake,
>>Fish we take;
>>There we sit,
>>For a bit,
Till we fish entangle.

We have gentles in a horn,
>We have paste and worms too;
We can catch both night and morn,

Suffer rain and storms too.
> None do here
> Use to swear;
> Oaths do fray
> Fish away;
> We sit still,
> And watch our quill;
Fishers must not wrangle.

If the sun's excessive heat
> Make our bodies swelter,
To an osier hedge we get
> For a friendly shelter;
>> Where in a dike
>> Perch or pike,
>> Roach or dace,
>> We do chase,
>> Bleak or gudgeon
>> Without grudging;
We are still contented.

Or we sometimes pass an hour
> Under a green willow;
That defends us from a shower,
> Making earth our pillow;
>> Where we may
>> Think and pray,
>> Before death
>> Stops our breath:
>> Other joys
>> Are but toys,
And to be lamented.

> Jo. CHALKHILL

VEN. Well sung, master; this day's fortune and pleasure, and this night's company and song, do all make me more and

more in love with angling. Gentlemen, my master left me
alone for an hour this day, and I verily believe he retired
himself from talking with me that he might be so perfect in
this song; was it not, master?

PISC. Yes, indeed, for it is many years since I learned it;
and, having forgotten a part of it, I was forced to patch it
up by the help of mine own invention, who am not excellent at poetry, as my part of the song may testify: but of
that I will say no more, lest you should think I mean by dis-
commending it to beg your commendations of it. And therefore, without replications, let's hear your catch, scholar;
which I hope will be a good one, for you are both musical and
have a good fancy to boot.

VEN. Marry, and that you shall; and as freely as I would
have my honest master tell me some secrets of fish and fishing, as we walk and fish towards London tomorrow. But,
master, first let me tell you, that very hour which you were
absent from me, I sat down under a willow tree by the waterside, and considered what you had told me of the owner of
that pleasant meadow in which you then left me: that he
had a plentiful estate, and not a heart to think so; that he
had at this time many lawsuits depending, and that they
both damped his mirth and took up so much of his time and
thoughts that he himself had not leisure to take the sweet
content that I, who pretended no title to them, took in his
fields; for I could there sit quietly; and looking on the water,
see some fishes sport themselves in the silver streams, others
leaping at flies of several shapes and colors; looking on the
hills, I could behold them spotted with woods and groves;
looking down the meadows, could see here a boy gathering
lilies and lady-smocks, and there a girl cropping culverkeyes
and cowslips, all to make garlands suitable to this present
month of May: these and many other field flowers so perfumed the air that I thought this very meadow like that
field in Sicily of which Diodorus speaks, where the perfumes
arising from the place make all the dogs that hunt in it to

fall off and to lose their hottest scent. I say, as I thus sat, joying in my own happy condition, and pitying this poor rich man that owned this and many other pleasant groves and meadows about me, I did thankfully remember what my Saviour said, that the meek possess the earth,[12] or rather, they enjoy what the others possess and enjoy not: for anglers and meek, quiet-spirited men are free from those high, those restless thoughts, which corrode the sweets of life; and they, and they only, can say as the poet has happily expressed it:

Hail! blest estate of lowliness!
Happy enjoyments of such minds
As, rich in self-contentedness,
Can, like the reeds in roughest winds,
By yielding make that blow but small,
At which proud oaks and cedars fall.

There came also into my mind at that time, certain verses in praise of a mean estate and an humble mind; they were written by Phineas Fletcher, an excellent divine and an excellent angler, and the author of excellent *Piscatory Eclogues,* in which you shall see the picture of this good man's mind: and I wish mine to be like it.

No empty hopes, no courtly fears him fright,
No begging wants his middle fortunes bite,
But sweet content exiles both misery and spite.

His certain life, that never can deceive him,
Is full of thousand sweets and rich content;
The smooth-leaved beeches in the field receive him,
With coolest shade, till noon-tide's heat be spent:
His life is neither tossed in boisterous seas,
Or the vexatious world, or lost in slothful ease;
Pleased and full blessed he lives, when he his God can please.

[12] Matt. 5:5. See also Psalm 37:11.

His bed, more safe than soft, yields quiet sleeps,
While by his side his faithful spouse hath place,
   His little son into his bosom creeps,
   The lively picture of his father's face.
His humble house, or poor state ne'er torment him;
Less he could like, if less his God had lent him:
And when he dies, green turfs do for a tomb content him.

Gentlemen, these were a part of the thoughts that then possessed me; and I there made a conversion of a piece of an old catch, and added more to it, fitting them to be sung by us as anglers. Come, master, you can sing well; you must sing part of it as it is in this paper.

The Angler's Song

By Mr. Henry Lawes.

Man's life is but vain, for 'tis subject to pain,
   And sorrow, and short as a bubble;
'Tis a hodge-podge of business, and money, and care,
   And care, and money, and trouble.

But we'll take no care when the weather proves fair;
   Nor will we vex now though it rain;
We'll banish all sorrow, and sing till tomorrow,
   And angle and angle again.

PET. Aye marry, sir, this is music indeed; this has cheered my heart, and made me to remember six verses in praise of music, which I will speak to you instantly.

Music, miraculous rhetoric that speakest sense
Without a tongue, excelling eloquence;
With what ease might thy errors be excused
Wert thou as truly loved as th' art abused.
But though dull souls neglect, and some reprove thee,
I cannot hate thee, 'cause the angels love thee.

VEN. And the repetition of these last verses of music have called to my memory what Mr. Edmund Waller, a lover of the angle, says of love and music.

> Whilst I listen to thy voice,
>   Chloris, I feel my heart decay:
>   That powerful voice,
>   Calls my fleeting soul away;
> Oh! suppress that magic sound
> Which destroys without a wound.
>
> Peace, Chloris, peace, or singing die,
>   That together you and I
>   To heaven may go:
>   For all we know
> Of what the blessed do above
> Is that they sing and that they love.

PISC. Well remembered, brother Peter, these verses came seasonably, and we thank you heartily. Come, we will all join together, mine host and all, and sing my scholar's catch over again; and then each man drink the tother cup and to bed, and thank God we have a dry house over our heads.

PISC. Well now, good night to everybody.

PET. And so say I.

VEN. And so say I.

COR. Good night to you all, and I thank you.

The Fifth Day

PISC. Good morrow, brother Peter, and the like to you, honest Coridon. Come, my hostess says there's seven shillings to pay: let's each man drink a pot for his morning's draught, and lay down his two shillings, so that my hostess may not have occasion to repent herself of being so diligent, and using us so kindly.

PET. The motion is liked by everybody; and so, hostess, here's your money: we anglers are all beholding to you; it will not be long ere I'll see you again. And now, brother Piscator, I wish you and my brother your scholar a fair day and good fortune. Come, Coridon, this is our way.

Fifth Day, Chap. XXI

. . . . .

VEN. Well, master, these verses [13] be worthy to keep a room in every man's memory. I thank you for them; and I thank you for your many instructions, which, God willing, I will not forget. And as St. Austin in his *Confessions* (book iv. chap. 3) commemorates the kindness of his friend Vere-cundus, for lending him and his company a country house, because there they rested and enjoyed themselves free from the troubles of the world, so having had the like advantage both by your conversation and the art you have taught me, I ought ever to do the like: for indeed, your company and discourse have been so useful and pleasant, that I may truly say I have only lived since I enjoyed them and turned angler, and not before. Nevertheless, here I must part with you, here in this now sad place, where I was so happy as first to meet you: but I shall long for the ninth of May, for then I hope again to enjoy your beloved company at the appointed time and place. And now I wish for some somniferous po-tion that might force me to sleep away the intermitted time, which will pass away with me as tediously as it does with men in sorrow; nevertheless I will make it as short as I can, by my hopes and wishes. And my good master, I will not forget the doctrine which you told me Socrates taught his scholars, that they should not think to be honored so

[13] "Farewell to the Vanities of the World," Sir Henry Wotton (?).

much for being philosophers, as to honor philosophy by their virtuous lives. You advised me to the like concerning angling, and I will endeavor to do so, and to live like those many worthy men of which you made mention in the former part of your discourse. This is my firm resolution. And as a pious man advised his friend, that, to beget mortification, he should frequent churches, and view monuments and charnel-houses, and then and there consider how many dead bones Time had piled up at the gates of Death: so when I would beget content, and increase confidence in the power, and wisdom, and providence of almighty God, I will walk the meadows by some gliding stream, and there contemplate the lilies that take no care, and those very many other various little living creatures that are not only created, but fed, man knows not how, by the goodness of the God of Nature, and therefore trust in him. That is my purpose; and so, "Let everything that hath breath praise the Lord." [14] And let the blessing of St. Peter's Master be with mine.

Pisc. And all that are lovers of virtue; and dare trust in His providence, and be quiet, and go a-angling.

"STUDY TO BE QUIET."

—1 Thess. 4: 11.

[14] Psalm 101:6.

James Howell 1594(?)-1666

JAMES HOWELL was a Welshman, and his natural fancy and
quick sense of humor are delightfully revealed in his writings, especially in his best-known book, *Epistolæ Ho-Elianæ*
or *Familiar Letters*. He attended Jesus College, Oxford, and
several of his letters are addressed to the Principal of this
college, Dr. Francis Mansell. After receiving his degree, he
secured a position in Sir Robert Mansell's glassworks in
London. As agent for this business abroad, he was on the
Continent six years, but after this time he severed his connection with the glassworks.

He made a number of efforts to enter diplomatic service,
but was unsuccessful. Late in 1622, however, he was sent to
Madrid on a mission concerning the seizure of an English
vessel which belonged to the Turkey Company. While he
was negotiating this matter, Prince Charles and the Duke
of Buckingham came to the Spanish Court; and in a letter
to Captain Thomas Porter, Howell gives a delightful account of the wooing of the Infanta. Upon his return to England, he had no steady employment, but held several secre-
taryships. In 1627 he was elected member of Parliament
for Richmond, Yorkshire.

He finally became Clerk of the Privy Council, but was
suddenly imprisoned in the Fleet, whether for political reasons or for debt has never been settled. He remained in prison
eight or nine years, doing much of his writing during this
time. After the Restoration he was made the first Historiographer Royal, a position of which he was very proud.

Howell's allegorical writings survive as curiosities rather
than for any particular value. His *Instructions for Foreign
Travel*, however, is not only of historical significance as "the
earliest guide book in English," but growing out of his
own experience, it contains much good sense and is phrased
in an entertaining way. The *Familiar Letters* belong in the

category of essays and deserve more than Thackeray's appreciation of them as "artless prattle." Using the letter as
a literary device, Howell gives a vivid portrayal of places
and affairs which has the authentic ring of first-hand reporting.

EPISTOLÆ HO-ELIANÆ, FAMILIAR LETTERS [1]

Book I, Section I

LETTER I

[The Overbury Murder]

To my Father upon my first going beyond Sea

SIR,

I should be much wanting to myself, and to that obligation of duty, the Law of God and his handmaid Nature hath imposed upon me, if I should not acquaint you with the course and quality of my affairs and fortunes, especially at this time that I am upon point of crossing the seas to eat my bread abroad. Nor is it the common relation of a son that only induced me hereunto, but that most indulgent and costly care you have been pleased (in so extraordinary a manner) to have had of my breeding (though but one child of fifteen) by placing me in a choice methodical school [2] (so far distant from your dwelling) under a learned (though lashing) master; and by transplanting me thence to Oxford, to be graduated; and so holding me still up by the chin until I could swim without bladders. This patrimony of liberal education you have been pleased to endow me withal, I now carry along with me abroad, as a sure inseparable treasure; nor do I feel it any burden or incumbrance unto me at all. And what danger soever my person, or other things I have about me, do incur, yet I do not fear the losing of this, either by shipwreck, or pirates at sea, nor by robbers, or fire, or any other casualty ashore: and at my return to England, I hope at leastwise I shall do my endeavor, that you may find this patrimony improved somewhat to your comfort.

The main of my employment is from that gallant knight,

---

[1] Text: 1645, first edition.   [2] Hereford Free School.

332

Sir Robert Mansell,[3] who, with my Lord of Pembroke [4] and divers others of the prime lords of the court, have got the sole patent of making all sorts of glass with pit-coal, only to save those huge proportions of wood which were consumed formerly in the glass furnaces: and this business being of that nature, that the workmen are to be had from Italy, and the chief materials from Spain, France, and other foreign countries, there is need of an agent abroad for this use (and better than I have offered their service in this kind), so that I believe I shall have employment in all these countries before I return.

Had I continued still steward of the glass-house in Broad Street, where Captain Francis Bacon hath succeeded me, I should in a short time have melted away to nothing amongst those hot Venetians, finding myself too green for such a charge; therefore it hath pleased God to dispose of me now to a condition more suitable to my years, and that will, I hope, prove more advantageous to my future fortunes.

In this my peregrination, if I happen by some accident to be disappointed of that allowance I am to subsist by, I must make my address to you, for I have no other rendezvous to flee unto; but it shall not be, unless in case of great indigence.

Touching the news of the time: Sir George Villiers, the new favorite, tapers up apace and grows strong at court; his predecessor, the Earl of Somerset,[5] hath got a lease of ninety years for his life, and so hath his articulate lady, called so for articling against the frigidity and impotence of her former lord. She was afraid that Coke, the Lord Chief Justice (who had used such extraordinary art and industry in discovering all the circumstances of the poisoning of Overbury), would have made white broth of them, but that the prerogative kept them from the pot; yet the subservient instruments,

[3] Treasurer of the Navy, who became interested in glass-making.
[4] William Herbert, third Earl of Pembroke, was Chancellor of Oxford.
[5] Robert Carr, implicated in the poisoning of Overbury, but pardoned and released from the tower in 1625.

the lesser flies, could not break through, but lay entangled in the cobweb; amongst others, Mistress Turner, the first inventress of yellow starch, was executed in a cobweb lawn ruff of that color at Tyburn, and with her I believe that yellow starch, which so much disfigured our nation and rendered them so ridiculous and fantastic, will receive its funeral. Sir Gervas Elwaies, Lieutenant of the Tower, was made a notable example of justice and terror to all officers of trust; for being accessary, and that in a passive way only, to the murder, yet he was hanged on Tower Hill; and the caveat is very remarkable which he gave upon the gallows, that people should be very cautious how they make vows to heaven, for the breach of them seldom passes without a judgment, whereof he was a most ruthful example; for, being in the Low Countries, and much given to gaming, he once made a solemn vow (which he brake afterwards), that if he played above such a sum, he might be hanged. My Lord (William) of Pembroke did a most noble act, like himself; for the king having given him all Sir Gervas Elwaies' estate, which came to above 1000 pounds per annum, he freely bestowed it on the widow and her children.

The latter end of this week I am to go a shipboard, and first for the Low Countries. I humbly pray your blessing may accompany me in these my travels by land and sea, with a continuance of your prayers, which will be as so many good gales to blow me to safe port; for I have been taught, *that the parent's benedictions contribute very much, and have a kind of prophetic virtue to make the child prosperous.* In this opinion I shall ever rest,

Broad Street, London, 1 *March,* 1618.   Your dutiful son,

J.H.

Book I, Section I

LETTER XVI [6]

[Paris in the Seventeenth Century]

To Capt. Francis Bacon, from Paris

SIR,

I received two of yours in Rouen with the bills of exchange there enclosed; and according to your directions, I sent you those things which you wrote for.

I am now newly come to Paris, this huge magazine of men, the epitome of this large populous kingdom and rendezvous of all foreigners. The structures here are indifferently fair, though the streets generally foul all the four seasons of the year; which I impute first, to the position of the city being built upon an isle (the Isle of France, made so by the branching and serpentine course of the river of Seine), and having some of her suburbs seated high, the filth runs down the channel and settles in many places within the body of the city, which lieth upon a flat; as also for a world of coaches, carts, and horses of all sorts that go to and fro perpetually, so that sometimes one shall meet with a stop half a mile long of those coaches, carts, and horses that can move neither forward nor backward by reason of some sudden encounter of others coming a cross-way, so that often times it will be an hour or two before they can disentangle. In such a stop the great Henry was so fatally slain by Ravillac.[7] Hence comes it to pass that this town (for Paris is a town, a city, and a university) is always dirty, and 'tis such a dirt that by perpetual motion is beaten into such a thick black unctuous oil that where it sticks, no art can wash it off of

[6] Text: 1678, fifth edition.
[7] Ravaillac, a lay-Jesuit, murdered Henry IV on May 14, 1610. An account of the murder and the torture of Ravaillac is given from the report of an eye witness in Howell's letter.

some colors, insomuch that it may be no improper comparison to say, that an ill name is like the crot (the dirt) of
Paris, which is indelible; besides the stain this dirt leaves,
it also gives so strong a scent that it may be smelt many miles
off if the wind be in one's face as he comes from the fresh
air of the country. This may be one cause why the plague
is always in some corner or other of this vast city, which
may be called, as once Scythia was, *vagina populorum,* or
(as mankind was called by a great philosopher) a great
molehill of ants. Yet I believe this city is not so populous
as she seems to be, for her form being round (as the whole
kingdom is), the passengers wheel about and meet oftener
than they use to do in the long continued streets of London,
which makes London appear less populous than she is indeed; so that London for length (though not for latitude),
including Westminster, exceeds Paris, and hath in Michaelmas term more souls moving within her in all places. 'Tis
under one hundred years that Paris is become so sumptuous
and strong in buildings; for her houses were mean until a
mine of white stone was discovered hard by, which runs in
a continued vein of earth and is digged out with ease, being
soft, and is between a white clay and chalk at first; but being
pulleyed up, with the open air it receives a crusty kind of
hardness, and so becomes perfect freestone; and before it is
sent up from the pit they can reduce it to any form: of this
stone the Louvre, the king's palace, is built, which is a vast
fabric, for the gallery wants not much an Italian mile in
length, and will easily lodge 3,000 men; which some told
me was the end for which the last king made it so big, that
lying at the fag-end of this great mutinous city, if she perchance should rise, the king might pour out of the Louvre
so many thousand men unawares into the heart of her.

I am lodged here hard by the Bastile, because it is furthest off from those places where the English resort, for
I would go on to get a little language as soon as I could. In
my next I shall impart unto you what state-news France

affords; in the interim, and always, I am, your humble servant,

Paris, the 30 *of March,* 1620.   J.H.

Book I, Section II

LETTER VIII

[Description of a Great House]

To Dan. Caldwell, Esq; [8] *from the Lord Savage's
House in Long Melford*

MY DEAR DAN,
Though considering my former condition of life, I may now
be called a countryman, yet you cannot call me a rustic (as
you would imply in your letter) as long as I live in so civil
and noble a family, as long as I lodge in so virtuous and regular a house as any I believe in the land, both for economical
government, and the choice company, for I never saw yet
such a dainty race of children in all my life together; I never
saw yet such an orderly and punctual attendance of servants,
nor a great house so neatly kept; here one shall see no dog,
nor cat, nor cage to cause any nastiness within the body of
the house. The kitchen and gutters and other offices of noise
and drudgery are at the sag-end; there is a back gate for
beggars and the meaner sort of swains to come in at; the
stables butt upon the park, which for a cheerful rising
ground, for groves and browsings for the deer, for rivulets
of water may compare with any for its bigness in the whole
land; it is opposite to the front of the great house, whence
from the gallery one may see much of the game when they
are a-hunting. Now for the gardening and costly choice

[8] Friend made at Oxford University.

flowers, for ponds, for stately large walks, green and gravelly, for orchards and choice fruits of all sorts, there are few the like in England: here you have your Bon Christian pear and bergamot in perfection, your muscadel grapes in such plenty that there are some bottles of wine sent every year to the king; and one Dr. Daniel, a worthy gentleman hard by, who hath been long abroad, makes good store in his vintage. Truly this house of Long Melford, though it be not so great, yet it is so well compacted and contrived with such dainty conveniences every way that if you saw the landscape of it, you would be mightily taken with it, and it would serve for a choice pattern to build and contrive a house by. If you come this summer to your manor of Sheriff in Essex, you will not be far off hence; if your occasions will permit, it will be worth your coming hither, though it be only to see him, who would think it a short journey to go from St. David's Head to Dover Cliffs to see and serve you, were there occasion: If you would know who the same is, 'tis

20 *March*, 1619   Your J.H.

Book I, Section III

LETTER XVIII

[Wooing of the Infanta]

To Captain Thomas Porter

NOBLE CAPTAIN,

My last unto you was in Spanish, in answer to one of yours in the same language; and amongst that confluence of English gallants, which upon the occasion of His Highness being here, are come to this court, I fed myself with hopes a long while to have seen you, but I find now that these hopes were

imped with false feathers. I know your heart is here and
your best affections, therefore I wonder what keeps back
your person; but I conceive the reason to be that you intend to come like yourself, to come commander-in-chief
of one of the castles of the crown, one of the ships royal. If
you come so to this shore side, I hope you will have time to
come to the court. I have at any time a good lodging for you,
and my landlady is none of the meanest, and her husband
hath many good parts: I heard her setting him forth one day
and giving this character of him: *Mi marido ei buen musico,
buen esgrimido, buen escrivano, excellente arithmetico, salvo
que no multiplica* (my husband is a good musician, a good
fencer, a good horseman, a good penman, and an excellent
arithmetician, only he cannot multiply). For outward usage
there is all industry used to give the prince and his servants
all possible contentment, and some of the king's own servants
wait upon them at table in the palace, where I am sorry to
hear some of them jeer at the Spanish fare, and others use
slighting speeches and demeanor. There are many excellent
poems made here since the prince's arrival, which are too
long to couch in a letter, yet I will venture to send you this
one stanza of Lope de Vega:

> *Carlos Estuardo Soy*
> *Que siendo Amor mi guia*
> *Al cielo d'España voy*
> *Por ver mi Estrella Maria.*[9]

There are comedians once a week come to the palace,
where under a great canopy the queen and the Infanta sit in
the middle, our prince and Don Carlos on the queen's right
hand, the king and the little cardinal on the Infanta's left
hand. I have seen the prince have his eyes immovably fixed
upon the Infanta half-an-hour together in a thoughtful,

[9] Charles Stuart am I,
    Whom Love has guided afar;
    To this heaven of Spain I am come,
    To see Maria, my Star.

speculative posture, which sure would needs be tedious, unless affection did sweeten it; it was no handsome comparison of Olivares, that he watched her as a cat doth a mouse. Not long since the prince, understanding that the Infanta was used to go some mornings to the Casa de Campo, a summer house the king hath the other side the river, to gather May dew, he did rise betimes and went thither, taking your brother with him; they were let into the house and into the garden, but the Infanta was in the orchard; and there being a high partition-wall between and the door doubly bolted, the prince got on top of the wall and sprung down a great height, and so made towards her; but she, spying him first of all the rest, gave a shriek and ran back. The old marquis that was then her guardian came towards the prince and fell on his knees, conjuring His Highness to retire, in regard he hazarded his head if he admitted any to her company; so the door was opened, and he came out under that wall over which he had got in. I have seen him watch a long hour together in a close coach in the open street to see her as she went abroad. I cannot say that the prince did ever talk with her privately, yet publicly often, my Lord of Bristol being interpreter; but the king always sat hard by to overhear all. Our cousin Archy [10] hath more privilege than any, for he often goes with his fool's coat where the Infanta is with her *meninas* and ladies of honor, and keeps a-blowing and blustering amongst them, and flirts out what he list.

One day they were discoursing what a marvelous thing it was that the Duke of Bavaria with less than 15,000 men, after a long toilsome march, should dare to encounter the Palsgrave's army consisting of above 25,000, and to give them an utter discomfiture, and take Prague presently after. Whereunto Archy answered that he would tell them a stranger thing than that! Was it not a strange thing, quoth he, that in the year '88 there should come a fleet of 140 sails from

[10] Archy Armstrong was the Court Fool of James I.

Spain to invade England, and that ten of these could not go back to tell what became of the rest? By the next opportunity I will send you the Cordovan pockets and gloves you wrote for of Francisco Moreno's perfuming. So may my dear Captain live long and love his

Madrid, July 10, 1623   J.H.

Book I, Section IV

LETTER VIII

[Death of Sir Francis Bacon]

To Dr. Pritchard [11]

SIR,

Since I was beholden to you for your many favors in Oxford, I have not heard from you (*ne* γρὺ *quidem*); I pray let wonted correspondence be now revived and receive new vigor between us.

My Lord Chancellor Bacon is lately dead of a long languishing weakness; he died so poor that he scarce left money to bury him, which, though he had a great wit, did argue no great wisdom; it being one of the essential properties of a wise man to provide for the main chance. I have read that it had been the fortunes of all poets commonly to die beggars; but for an orator, a lawyer, and philosopher, as he was, to die so, 'tis rare. It seems that same fate befell him that attended Demosthenes, Seneca, and Cicero (all great men), of whom the two first fell by corruption. The fairest diamond may have a flaw in it, but I believe he died poor out of a contempt of the pelf of fortune, as also out of an excess of generosity; which appeared, as in divers other pas-

[11] Vice-principal of Jesus College, 1621.

sages, so once when the king had sent him a stag, he sent up for the underkeeper, and having drunk the king's health to him in a great silver-gilt bowl, he gave it to him for his fee.

He wrote a pitiful letter to King James not long before his death, and concludes, *Help me, dear sovereign lord and master, and pity me so far, that I who have been born to a bag, be not now in my age forced in effect to bear a wallet; nor I that desire to live to study, may be driven to study to live.* Which words, in my opinion, argued a little abjection of spirit, as his former letter to the prince did of profaneness; wherein he hoped that as the father was his creator the son will be his redeemer. I write not this to derogate from the noble worth of the Lord Viscount Verulam, who was a rare man, a man *reconditæ scientiæ et ad salutem literarum natus,* and I think the eloquentest that was born in this isle. They say he shall be the last Lord Chancellor, as Sir Edward Coke was the last Lord Chief Justice of England; for ever since they have been termed *Lord Chief Justices of the King's Bench:* so hereafter they shall be only *Keepers of the Great Seal,* which for title and office are deposable; but they say the Lord Chancellor's title is indelible.

I was lately at Gray's Inn with Sir Eubule, and he desired me to remember him to you, as I do also salute *meum Prichardum ex imis præcordiis, Vale* κεφαλή μοι προσφιλεσάτη.

Yours affectionately, while J.H.

London, 6 Jan. 1625.[12]

---

[12] New Style, 1626; yet still inconsistent in the reference to Bacon's death on April 9, 1626.

Book I, Section V

LETTER VII

[Murder of Buckingham]

*To the Right Hon. the Lady Scroop, Countess of Sunderland;
from Stamford*

MADAM,

I lay yesternight at the post-house at Stilton, and this morning betimes the postmaster came to my bed's head and told me the Duke of Buckingham was slain: my faith was not then strong enough to believe it, till an hour ago I met in the way with my Lord of Rutland (your brother) riding post towards London; it pleased him to alight and show me a letter, wherein there was an exact relation of all the circumstances of this sad tragedy.

Upon Saturday last, which was but next before yesterday, being Bartholomew eve, the Duke did rise up in a well-disposed humor out of his bed, and cut a caper or two; and being ready, and having been under the barber's hand (where the murderer had thought to have done the deed, for he was leaning upon the window all the while), he went to breakfast, attended by a great company of commanders, where Monsieur Soubize came to him, and whispered him in the ear that Rochelle was relieved; the Duke seemed to slight the news, which made some think that Soubize went away discontented. After breakfast, the Duke going out, Colonel Fryer stepped before him, and stopping him upon some business, Lieutenant Felton being behind, made a thrust with a common tenpenny knife over Fryer's arm at the Duke, which lighted so fatally that he slit his heart in two, leaving the knife sticking in the body. The Duke took out the knife and threw it away, and laying his hand on his sword, and drawing it half out, said, "The villain hath killed me" (meaning, as some think, Colonel Fryer), for there had been some difference 'twixt them; so reeling against a chimney, he fell down dead. The Duchess being with child, hearing the noise below, came in her night-gears from her bedchamber, which was in an upper room, to a kind of rail, and thence beheld him weltering in his own blood. Felton had lost his hat in the crowd, wherein there was a paper sewed, wherein he declared that the reason which moved him to this act was no grudge of his own, though he had been far behind for his pay, and had been put by his captain's place twice, but in regard he thought the Duke an enemy to the state, because he was branded in parliament; therefore what he did was for the public good of his country. Yet he got clearly down, and so might have gone to his horse, which was tied to a hedge hard by; but he was so amazed that he missed his way, and so struck into the pastry, where, although the cry went that some Frenchman had done it, he thinking the word was Felton, boldly confessed, 'twas he that had done the deed, and so he was in their hands. Jack Stamford [13] would have run at him, but he was kept off by Mr. Nicholas; so being carried up to a tower, Captain Mince tore off his spurs, and asking how he durst attempt such an act, making him believe the Duke was not dead, he answered boldly that he knew he was dispatched, for 'twas not he, but the hand of heaven that gave the stroke, and though his whole body had been covered over with armor of proof, he could not have avoided it. Captain Charles Price went post presently to the King four miles off, who being at prayers on his knees when it was told him, yet never stirred, nor was he disturbed a whit till all divine service was done. This was the relation, as far as my memory could bear, in my Lord of Rutland's letter, who willed me to remember him to your Ladyship, and tell you that he was going to comfort your niece (the Duchess) as fast as he could. And so I have sent the truth of this sad

[13] Servant of the Duke.

story to your Ladyship, as fast as I could by this post, because I cannot make that speed myself, in regard of some business I have to dispatch for my lord in the way: so I humbly take my leave, and rest

Your Ladyship's most dutiful servant, J.H.

Stamford, 5 Aug. 1628

Book I, Section V

LETTER XVI

[Jonson's Degrees of Madness]

To my Father, Mr. Ben Jonson

Father Ben, *nullum fit magnum ingenium sine mixtura dementiæ,* there's no great wit without some mixture of madness; so saith the philosopher: nor was he a fool who answered, *nec parvum sine mixtura stultitiæ,* nor small wit without some allay of foolishness. Touching the first, it is verified in you, for I find that you have been oftentimes mad: you were mad when you wrote your *Fox,* and madder when you wrote your *Alchemist;* you were mad when you wrote *Catiline,* and stark mad when you wrote *Sejanus;* but when you wrote your *Epigrams,* and the *Magnetic Lady,* you were not so mad; insomuch that I perceive there be degrees of madness in you. Excuse me that I am so free with you. The madness I mean is that divine fury, that heating and heightening spirit which Ovid speaks of,

Est Deus in nobis, agitante calescimus illo: that true enthusiasm which transports and elevates the souls of poets above the middle region of vulgar conceptions, and makes them soar up to heaven to touch the stars with their laureled heads, to walk in the Zodiac with Apollo himself, and command Mercury upon their errand.

I cannot yet light upon Dr. Davies' *Welsh Grammar;* [14] before Christmas I am promised one: so desiring you to look better hereafter to your charcoal fire and chimney,[15] which I am glad to be one that preserved it from burning, this being the second time that Vulcan hath threatened you, it may be because you have spoken ill of his wife, and been too busy with his horns; I rest

Your son, and contiguous

neighbor, J.H.

Westm., 27 Jun., 1629

Book I, Section VI

LETTER XLVII

[Howell's Arrest]

To the Earl of B.[ristol], from the Fleet

MY LORD,

I was lately come to London upon some occasions of mine own, and I had been divers times in Westminster Hall, where I conversed with many parliament men of my acquaintance; but one morning betimes there rushed into my chamber five armed men with swords, pistols, and bills, and told me they had a warrant from the Parliament for me. I desired to see their warrant, they denied it; I desired to see the date of it, they denied it; I desired to see my name in the warrant, they denied all; at last one of them pulled a greasy paper out of his pocket and showed me only three or four names subscribed, and no more; so they rushed presently into my closet and seized on all my papers and letters and anything that was manuscript; and many printed books they took also, and hurled all into a great hair trunk, which

---

[14] London, 1621.

[15] Jonson's house was burned, and many of his books and manuscripts were destroyed.

they carried away with them. I had taken a little physic that morning, and with very much ado, they suffered me to stay in my chamber with two guards upon me till the evening; at which time they brought me before the committee for examination, where I confess I found good respect; and being brought up to the Close Committee, I was ordered to be forthcoming till some papers of mine were perused, and Mr. Corbet was appointed to do it. Some days after, I came to Master Corbet, and he told me that he had perused them and could find nothing that might give offense; hereupon, I desired him to make a report to the House accordingly, which (as I was told) he did very fairly; yet such was my hard hap that I was committed to the Fleet, where I am now under close restraint: and, as far as I can see, I must lie at dead anchor in this Fleet a long time, unless some gentle gale blow thence to make me launch out. God's will be done, and amend the times, and make up these ruptures which threaten so much calamity. So I am

Your lordship's most faithful
(though now afflicted)
Fleet, 20 *Nov.*, 1643.   servitor, J.H.

Book I, Section VI

LETTER LVI

[A True Friend]

To Tho. Ham[mon], Esq:

SIR,

There is no such treasure as a true friend; it is a treasure far above that of St. Mark's in Venice, a treasure that is not liable to those casualties which others are liable to, as to plundering and burglary, to bankrupts and ill debtors, to firing and shipwrecks: for when one hath lost his fortunes by any of these disasters, he may recover them all in a true friend, who is always a sure and staple commodity. This is verified in you, who have stuck so close to me in these my pressures; like a glow-worm (the old emblem of true friendship) you have shined unto me in the dark: nor could you do good offices to any that wisheth you better; for I always loved you for the freedom of your genius, for those choice parts and fancies I found in you, which I confess, hath made me more covetous of your friendship than I use to be of others. And to deal clearly with you, one of my prime errands to this town (when this disaster fell upon me) was to see you.

God put a speedy period to these sad distempers; but this wish, as I was writing, did vanish in the impossibility of the thing, for I fear they are of a long continuance: so I pray God keep you, and comfort me, who am

The Fleet, 5 *May*, 1643.

Your true friend
to serve you, J.H.

Book I, Section VI

LETTER LVII

[The Value of Adversity]

To Phi. Warwick, Esquire

SIR,

The earth doth not always produce roses and lilies, but she brings forth also nettles and thistles: so the world affords us not always contentments and pleasure, but sometimes afflictions and trouble; *ut illa tribulos, sic iste tribulationes producit.* The sea is not more subject to contrary blasts, nor the surges thereof to tossings and tumblings, [than] the

actions of men are to encumbrances and crosses: the air is
not fuller of meteors than man's life is of miseries; but as
we find that it is not a clear sky but the clouds that drop
fatness, as the Holy Text tells us, so adversity is far more
fertile than prosperity: it useth to water and mollify the
heart, which is the center of our affections, and makes it produce excellent fruit, whereas the glaring sunshine of a continual prosperity would enharden and dry it up, and so make
it barren.

There is not a greater evidence of God's care and love to
his creature than affliction, for as a French author doth illustrate it by a familiar example: if two boys should be seen
to fight in the streets and a ring of people about them, one
of the standers-by parting them, lets the one go untouched,
but he falls a correcting the other, whereby the beholders
will infer that he is his child, or at least one whom he wisheth well unto. So the strokes of adversity which fall upon
us from heaven show that God is our Father as well as our
Creator. This makes this bitter cup of affliction become
nectar, and the bread of carefulness I now eat to be true am-
brosia unto me. This makes me esteem these walls wherein
I have been immured these thirty months to be no other
than a college of instruction unto me; and whereas Varro
said that the great world was but the house of little man,
I hold this Fleet to be one of the best lodgings in that house.

There is a people in Spain called *Los Pattuecos* who some
threescore and odd years since were discovered by the flight
of a hawk of the Duke of Alva's; this people, then all savage
(though they dwelt in the center of Spain, not far from To-
ledo, and are yet held to be part of those Aborigines that
Tubal Cain brought in), being hemmed in and imprisoned,
as it were, by a multitude of craggy huge mountains, thought
that behind those mountains there was no more earth: I
have been so habituated to this prison and accustomed to
the walls thereof so long that I might well be brought to
think that there is no other world behind them. And in my

extravagant imaginations I often compare this Fleet to Noah's Ark, surrounded with a vast sea, and huge deluge of calamities which hath overwhelmed this poor island. Nor although I have been so long aboard here, was I yet under hatches, for I have a cabin upon the upper deck, whence I breathe the best air the place affords; add hereunto that the society of Master Hopkins, the Warden, is an advantage to me, who is one of the knowingest and most civil gentlemen that I have conversed withal. Moreover, there are here some choice gentlemen who are my co-martyrs, for a prisoner and a martyr are the same thing, save that the one is buried before his death, and the other after.

God Almighty amend these times that make imprisonment to be preferred before liberty, it being more safe and desirable by some, though not by

Your affectionate servitor, J.H.

From the Fleet, 3 *Nov.,* 1645.

———

From INSTRUCTIONS FOR FOREIGN TRAVEL [1]

Section I

AMONGST THOSE many advantages which conduce to enrich the mind with variety of knowledge, to rectify [and ascertain] the judgment, and [to] compose outward manners, and build one up to the highest story of perfection, peregrination or foreign travel is none of the least.

But to be a sedentary traveler only, penned up between walls, and to stand poring all day upon a map, upon artificial globes and planispheres, upon imaginary circles and scales, is like him who thought to come to be a good fencer by looking on Agrippa's or Don Luis de Nervius' book-postures only: as also to run over and traverse the world by hearsay and traditional relation, with other men's eyes, and so take all things upon courtesy, is but a confused and imperfect kind of speculation, which leaveth but weak and distrustful notions behind it. In regard the ear is not so authentic a witness as the eye, by which as through a clear crystal casement, we discern the various works of art and nature, and in one instant comprehend half the whole universe in so small a room after so admirable a manner; I say the eye, having a more quick and immediate commerce and familiarity with the soul (being the principal of her *cinque ports* and her *sentinel*) [2] taketh in far deeper ideas, and so makes firmer and more lasting impressions, conveying the object more faithfully and clearly to the memory, where it remains afterward upon lasting record in particular topical notes, marks, and indelible characters. For though I confess with the Stagirite that hearing is the sense of learn-

[1] Text: English Reprints by Edward Arber, 1869, no. 16, a collation of the first edition, 1642, and the second, 1650. The additions from the 1650 text are silently incorporated except as indicated in the footnotes.

[2] The second edition reads: "being, as it were, her *sentinel,* or the principal of her *cinq ports.*"

ing (and of faith also, as the Holy Text tells me), yet the sight surpasseth it by many degrees in point of activity and excellency, if [3] you respect the curious workmanship with the delicateness of the organ, and the advantage of situation, being the readiest road to the heart and love's best intelligencer and usher. As also for the penetrative apprehension of the object, with the intuitive virtue and force of affection, it worketh inwardly, as we find upon good record that a herd of sheep conceived once by the strength of the eye, as likewise for the wonderful quickness of this sense,[4] which is such that it makes the effect oftentimes seem to fore-run the cause: as we see the lightning before we hear the thunder, though thunder be first in nature, being by the violent eruption it makes of the [5] cloud, the cause of such fulgurations. And hereunto that although one should read all the topographers that ever wrote of or anatomized a town or country, and mingle discourse with the most exact observers of the government thereof; and labor to draw and drain out of them all they possibly know or can remember; yet one's own ocular view and personal conversation will still find out something new and unpointed at by any other, either in the carriage [6] or the genius of the people, or in the policy and municipal customs of the country, or in the quality of the clime and soil, and so enable him to discourse more knowingly and confidently and with a kind of authority thereof, it being an act of parliament in force amongst all nations that one eye witness is of more validity than ten auricular.

Moreover, as everyone is said to abound with his own sense, and that among the race of mankind opinions and fancies are found to be as various as the several faces and voices, so in each individual man there is a differing faculty

[3] The second edition reads "whether."
[4] In the second edition the sentence continues, "moreover this sense hath the pre-eminence of all the rest for the wonderful quickness of its motion."
[5] The second edition reads "a."
[6] The second edition reads "behavior."

of observation, of judgment, of application, which makes
that everyone is best satisfied and most faithfully instructed
by himself; I do not mean solely by himself (for so he may
have a fool to his master) but books also, and conversation
with the dead must concur, for they are likewise good teachers and edify infinitely; yet the study of living men and a
collation of his own optic observations and judgment with
theirs, work much more strongly, and where these meet (I
mean the living and the dead) they perfect.

And indeed this is the prime use of peregrination, which
therefore may be not improperly called a moving academy, or
the true peripatetic school. This made Ulysses to be cried up
so much amongst the Greeks for their greatest and wisest
because he had traveled through many strange countries and
observed the manners of divers nations, having seen, as it
was said and sung of him, more cities than there were houses
in Athens, which was much in that green age of the world;
and the greatest of their emperors did use to glory in nothing
so often as that he had surveyed more land with his eye
than other kings could comprehend with their thoughts.

Amongst other people of the earth, islanders seems to stand
in most need of foreign travel, for they being cut off (as it
were) from the rest of the citizens of the world, have not
those obvious accesses and contiguity of situation, and other
advantages of society to mingle with those more refined nations whom learning and knowledge did first urbanize and
polish. And [7] as all other things by a kind of secret instinct
of nature follow the motion of the sun, so it is observed that
the arts and sciences which are the greatest helps to civility,
and all moral endowments, as well as intellectual, have
wheeled about and traveled in a kind of concomitant motion with that great luminary of heaven. They budded first
amongst the Brahmans and Gymnosophists in India; then
they blossomed amongst the Chaldeans and priests of Egypt,
whence they came down the Nile and crossed over to Greece,

[7] The second edition reads "now."

and there [8] they may be said to have borne ripe fruit, having taken such firm rooting and making so long a plantation
in Athens and elsewhere. Afterwards they found the way to
Italy, and thence they clambered over the Alpian hills to
visit Germany and France, whence the Britains with other
northwest nations of the lower world fetched them over;
and it is not improbable that the next flight they will make
will be to the savages of the new discovered world in America
and so turn 'round, and by this circular perambulation visit
the Levantines again.

Hence we see what a traveler learning hath been, having
in conformity of course been a kind of companion to Apollo
himself. And as the heavenly bodies are said to delight in
movement and perpetual circumgyration, wherein as Pythagoras, who by the Delphian oracle was pronounced the wisest
man that ever Greece bred, did hold there was a kind of
music and harmonious consent that issued out of this regular motion, which we cannot perceive because being born in
it, it is connatural to us, so it is observed to be the genius
of all active and generous spirits.

> *Quêis meliore luto finxit præcordia Titan.* [9]

To have been always transported with a desire of travel
and not to be bounded or confined within the shores and
narrow circumference of an island, without ever treading
any piece of the continent; whereas on the other side, mean
and vulgar spirits, whose souls soar no higher than their
sense, love to hover over home, lying still as it were at dead
anchor, moving no further than the length of the cable whereunto they are tied, not daring to lance out into the main to
see the wonders of the deep: such a one was he of whom
Claudian speaks, to have had his birth, breeding, and burial

[8] The second edition reads "where."
[9] The second edition translates:
> "Whom Titan with his gentle ray
> Hath molded of a finer clay."
Juvenal (Sat. 14, ll. 34–35) writes, *"Quibus arte benigna et meliore,* etc."

in one parish, whence he never had sallied out the whole
course of his life: such slow and sluggish spirits may be said
to be like snails or tortoises in their shells, crawling always
about their own home, or like the Cynic, shut up always in
a tub.

Amongst other nations of the world the English are observed to have gained much and improved themselves infinitely by voyaging both by land and sea, and of those four
Worthies who compassed about the terrestrial globe, I find
the major part of them were English; but the scope of this
discourse is to prescribe precepts for land travel only (for
the other requires another tract apart) and first,

A Jove principium—
Sic feret antennas aura fecunda tuas.[10]

[10] The second edition translates:
   "Begin with Jove, then an auspicious gale
   Will fill thy sails, and to safe harbor hale."

John Earle 1601(?)-1665

JOHN EARLE was born in York and received his university education at Oxford. There is some discrepancy in the records as to the date of entrance and the college he attended for undergraduate work. He received his M.A. in 1624 and was appointed fellow at Merton College. His observation of University types resulted in some of the best "Characters" which he wrote for the *Microcosmography,* first published in 1628. This popular volume brought Earle to the attention of people of prominence. He became proctor of the university in 1631 and afterwards was chaplain to the Chancellor, the Earl of Pembroke. Later he was appointed chaplain and tutor to the Prince of Wales.

Because of his loyalty to the king he was deprived of his property. He went to France to be with Charles II there and continued to serve as his chaplain. After the Restoration he was made successively dean of Westminster, bishop of Worcester, and bishop of Salisbury.

Earle is known for his moderation and the sweetness of his temper, though he could be sharp in attacking insincerity. His wit is without venom, however, and his keen perception of man's weakness is tempered by the warmth of his heart, so that in Clarendon's much-quoted words, "he was amongst the few excellent men who never had, nor ever could have an enemy." His characters have a universal quality which makes them as recognizable on campuses today as they were at Oxford in the seventeenth century.

MICROCOSMOGRAPHY [1]

A Child

IS A MAN in a small letter, yet the best copy of Adam before he tasted of Eve or the apple; and he is happy whose small practice in the world can only write this character. He is nature's fresh picture newly drawn in oil, which time, and much handling, dims and defaces. His soul is yet a white paper unscribbled with observations of the world, wherewith, at length, it becomes a blurred notebook. He is purely happy, because he knows no evil, nor hath made means by sin to be acquainted with misery. He arrives not at the mischief of being wise, nor endures evils to come by foreseeing them. He kisses and loves all, and, when the smart of the rod is past, smiles on his beater. Nature and his parents alike dandle him, and tice him on with a bait of sugar to a draught of wormwood. He plays yet, like a young prentice the first day, and is not come to his task of melancholy.[2] His hardest labor is his tongue, as if he were loath to use so deceitful an organ; and he is best company with it when he can but prattle. We laugh at his foolish sports, but his game is our earnest; and his drums, rattles, and hobbyhorses, but the emblems and mocking of man's business. His father hath writ him as his own little story, wherein he reads those days of his life that he cannot remember, and sighs to see what innocence he hath outlived. The elder he grows, he is a stair lower from God; and, like his first father, much worse in his breeches. He is the Christian's example, and the old man's fate;[3] the one imitates his pureness, and the other falls into his simplicity. Could he put off his body

---

[1] Text: 1628 (3rd edition in that year), except for last two characters from 1633 edition.

[2] The following sentence was added later: "All the language he speaks yet is tears, and they serve him well enough to express his necessity."

[3] In edition of 1628–29 "relapse" is substituted for "fate."

with his little coat, he had got eternity without a burden, and exchanged but one heaven for another.

A Young Raw Preacher

Is A BIRD not yet fledged, that hath hopped out of his nest to be chirping on a hedge, and will be straggling abroad at what peril soever. His backwardness in the university hath set him thus forward; for had he not truanted there, he had not been so hasty a divine. His small standing, and time, hath made him a proficient only in boldness, out of which and his tablebook he is furnished for a preacher. His collections of study are the notes of sermons, which, taken up at St. Mary's,[4] he utters in the country: and if he writes brachygraphy,[5] his stock is so much the better. His writing is more than his reading, for he reads only what he gets without book. Thus accomplished he comes down to his friends, and his first salutation is grace and peace out of the pulpit. His prayer is conceited, and no man remembers his college more at large. The pace of his sermon is a full career, and he runs wildly over hill and dale, till the clock stop him. The labor of it is chiefly in his lungs; and the only thing he had made of it himself is the faces. He takes on against the pope without mercy, and has a jest still in lavender for Bellarmine.[6] His action is all passion, and his speech interjections. He has an excellent faculty in bemoaning the people, and spits with a very good grace.[7] He will not draw his handkercher out of his place, nor blow his nose without discretion. His

[4] St. Mary's, built by King Alfred and rebuilt in the time of Henry VII, is still the church in which the public sermons are preached in the University.

[5] Shorthand, introduced into England in 1590, had become very popular.

[6] Robert Bellarmine, 1542–1621, Jesuit Cardinal. In later editions Earle continued the sentence: "yet he preaches heresy, if it comes in his way, though with a mind, I must needs say, very orthodox."

[7] The following sentence is added in later editions: "His style is compounded of twenty several men's; only his body imitates someone extraordinary."

commendation is, that he never looks upon book; and indeed he was never used to it. He preaches but once a year, though twice on Sunday; for the stuff is still the same, only the dressing a little altered. He has more tricks with a sermon than a tailor with an old cloak, to turn it, and piece it, and at last quite disguise it with a new preface. If he have waded farther in his profession, and would show reading of his own, his authors are postils, and his school-divinity a catechism. His fashion and demure habit gets him in with some town-precisian, and makes him a guest on Friday nights. You shall know him by his narrow velvet cape, and serge facing; and his ruff, next his hair, the shortest thing about him. The companion of his walk is some zealous tradesman, whom he astonishes with strange points, which they both understand alike. His friends and much painfulness may prefer him to thirty pounds a year, and this means to a chambermaid; with whom we leave him now in the bonds of wedlock: next Sunday you shall have him again.

A Downright Scholar

Is ONE that has much learning in the ore, unwrought and untried, which time and experience fashions and refines. He is good metal in the inside, though rough and unscoured without, and therefore hated of the courtier, that is quite contrary. The time has got a vein of making him ridiculous, and men laugh at him by tradition, and no unlucky absurdity but is put upon his profession, and done like a scholar. But his fault is only this, that his mind is too much taken up with his mind, and his thoughts not loaden with any carriage besides. He has not put on the quaint garb of the age, which is now become a man's total.[8] He has not humbled his meditations to the industry of compliment, nor afflicted his brain in an elaborate leg. His body is not set

[8] Later editions read instead of "total," "Imprimis and all the Item."

upon nice pins, to be turning and flexible for every motion, but his scrape is homely and his nod worse. He cannot kiss his hand and cry, "Madam," nor talk idly enough to bear her company. His smacking of a gentlewoman is somewhat too savory, and he mistakes her nose for her lip. A very woodcock would puzzle him in carving, and he wants the logic of a capon. He has not the glib faculty of sliding over a tale, but his words come squeamishly out of his mouth, and the laughter commonly before the jest. He names this word college too often, and his discourse beats too much on the university. The perplexity of mannerliness will not let him feed, and he is sharp set at an argument when he should cut his meat. He is discarded for a gamester at all games but one-and-thirty, and at tables [9] he reaches not beyond doublets. His fingers are not long and drawn out to handle a fiddle, but his fist clenched with the habit of disputing. He ascends a horse somewhat sinisterly, though not on the left side, and they both go jogging in grief together. He is exceedingly censured by the inns-of-court men, for that heinous vice, being out of fashion. He cannot speak to a dog in his own dialect, and understands Greek better than the language of a falconer. He has been used to a dark room, and dark clothes, and his eyes dazzle at a satin suit. The hermitage of his study has made him somewhat uncouth in the world, and men make him worse by staring on him. Thus is he ridiculous, and it continues with him for some quarter of a year out of the university. But practice him a little in men, and brush him o'er with good company, and he shall outbalance those glisterers, as far as a solid substance does a feather; or gold, gold-lace.

[9] This game is described in Strutt's *Sports and Pastimes,* but there is no mention of *"one-and-thirty."*

A She Precise Hypocrite

Is ONE in whom good women suffer, and have their truth
misinterpreted by her folly. She is one, she knows not what
herself if you ask her, but she is indeed one that has taken
a toy at the fashion of religion, and is enamored of the new-
fangle. She is a nonconformist in a close stomacher and ruff
of Geneva print,[10] and her purity consists much in her linen.
She has heard of the rag of Rome, and thinks it a very slut-
tish religion, and rails at the whore of Babylon for a very
naughty woman. She has left her virginity as a relic of
popery, and marries in her tribe without a ring. Her devotion at the church is much in the turning up of her eye, and
turning down the leaf in her book, when she hears named
chapter and verse. When she comes home, she commends
the sermon for the Scripture, and two hours. She loves preaching better than praying, and of preachers, lecturers; and
thinks the week day's exercise far more edifying than the
Sunday's. Her oftest gossipings are sabbath-day's journeys,
where (though an enemy to superstition) she will go in
pilgrimage five miles to a silenced minister, when there is
a better sermon in her own parish. She doubts of the virgin
Mary's salvation, and dares not saint her, but knows her own
place in heaven as perfectly as the pew she has a key to.
She is so taken up with faith she has no room for charity,
and understands no good works but what are wrought on
the sampler. She accounts nothing vices but superstition and
an oath, and thinks adultery a less sin than to swear *by my
truly*. She rails at other women by the names of Jezebel and
Delilah; and calls her own daughters Rebecca and Abigail,
and not Ann but Hannah. She suffers them not to learn on
the virginals, because of their affinity with organs, but is
reconciled to the bells for the chimes' sake, since they were

---

[10] The small ruff of the Puritans with its exact folds led to the comparison with the minute type used for printing in Geneva.

reformed to the tune of a psalm. She overflows so with the
Bible that she spills it upon every occasion, and will not
cudgel her maids without Scripture. It is a question whether
she is more troubled with the devil, or the devil with her:
she is always challenging and daring him, and her weapons
are spells no less potent than different, as being the sage
sentences of some of her own Sectaries.[11] Nothing angers her
so much as that women cannot preach, and in this point
only thinks the Brownist erroneous; but what she cannot
at the church she does at the table, where she prattles more
than any against sense and Antichrist, till a capon's wing
silence her. She expounds the priests of Baal, reading ministers, and thinks the salvation of that parish as desperate
as the Turk's. She is a main derider, to her capacity, of
those that are not her preachers, and censures all sermons
but bad ones. If her husband be a tradesman, she helps him
to customers, howsoever to good cheer, and they are a most
faithful couple at these meetings, for they never fail. Her
conscience is like others' lust, never satisfied, and you might
better answer Scotus than her scruples. She is one that thinks
she performs all her duties to God in hearing, and shows
the fruits of it in talking. She is more fiery against the maypole than her husband, and thinks she might do a Phineas
his act to break the pate of the fiddler. She is an everlasting
argument; but I am weary of her.

A Pretender to Learning

Is ONE that would make others more fools than himself,
for though he know nothing, he would not have the world
know so much. He conceits nothing in learning but the
opinion, which he seeks to purchase without it, though he
might with less labor cure his ignorance than hide it. He

---

[11] Later editions read, "weapon is the *Practice of Piety*."

is indeed a kind of scholar-mountebank, and his art our de-
lusion. He is tricked out in all the accouterments of learning, and at the first encounter none passes better. He is oftener
in his study than at his book, and you cannot pleasure him
better than to deprehend him. Yet he hears you not till
the third knock, and then comes out very angry, as interrupted. You find him in his slippers and a pen in his ear,
in which formality he was asleep. His table is spread wide
with some classic folio, which is as constant to it as the
carpet, and hath lain open in the same page this half year.[12]
His candle is always a longer sitter-up than himself, and
the boast of his window at midnight. He walks much alone
in the posture of meditation, and has a book still before
his face in the fields. His pocket is seldom without a Greek
Testament or Hebrew Bible, which he opens only in the
church, and that when some stander-by looks over. He has
his sentences for company, some scatterings of Seneca and
Tacitus, which are good upon all occasions. If he read anything in the morning, it comes up all at dinner; and as long
as that lasts, the discourse is his. He is a great plagiary of
tavern wit, and comes to sermons only that he may talk
of Austin. His parcels are the mere scrapings from company, yet he complains at parting what time he has lost.
He is wondrously capricious to seem a judgment, and lis-
tens with a sour attention to what he understands not. He
talks much of Scaliger, and Casaubon, and the Jesuits, and
prefers some unheardof Dutch name before them all. He has
verses to bring in upon these and these hints, and it shall
go hard but he will wind in his opportunity. He is critical
in a language he cannot construe, and speaks seldom under
Arminius in divinity. His business and retirement and caller-
away is his study, and he protests no delight to it comparable.
He is a great nomenclator of authors, which he had read in
general in the catalogue, and in particular in the title, and

[12] This sentence was originally after "He talks much of Scaliger . . ."

goes seldom so far as the dedication. He never talks of anything but learning, and learns all from talking. Three encounters with the same men pump him, and then he only puts in or gravely says nothing. He has taken pains to be an ass, though not to be a scholar, and is at length discovered and laughed at.

An University Don
(u)

Is a GENTLEMAN's follower cheaply purchased, for his own money has hired him. He is an inferior creditor of some ten shillings downwards, contracted for horse-hire, or perchance for drink, too weak to be put in suit, and he arrests your modesty. He is now very expensive of his time, for he will wait upon your stairs a whole afternoon, and dance attendance with more patience than a gentleman-usher. He is a sore beleaguerer of chambers, and assaults them sometimes with furious knocks; yet finds strong resistance commonly, and is kept out. He is a great complainer of scholars' loitering, for he is sure never to find them within, and yet he is the chief cause many times that makes them study. He grumbles at the ingratitude of men that shun him for his kindness, but indeed it is his own fault, for he is too great an upbraider. No man puts them more to their brain than he; and by shifting him off they learn to shift in the world. Some choose their rooms a purpose to avoid his surprisals, and think the best commodity in them his prospect. He is like a rejected acquaintance, hunts those that care not for his company; and he knows it well enough and yet will not keep away. The sole place to supply him is the buttery, where he takes grievous use upon your name, and he is one more wrought with good beer and rhetoric. He is a man of most unfortunate voyages, and no gallant walks the streets to less purpose.

A Drunkard [13]

Is one that will be a man tomorrow morning, but is now what you will make him, for he is in the power of the next man, and if a friend the better. One that hath let go himself from the hold and stay of reason, and lies open to the mercy of all temptations. No lust but finds him disarmed and fenceless, and with the least assault enters. If any mischief escape him, it was not his fault, for he was laid as fair for it as he could. Every man sees him, as Cham saw his father, the first of this sin, an uncovered man, and though his garment be on, uncovered; the secretest part of his soul lying in the nakedest manner visible: all his passions come out now, all his vanities, and those shamefuler humors which discretion clothes. His body becomes at last like a miry way, where the spirits are beclogged and cannot pass: all his members are out of office, and his heels do but trip up one another. He is a blind man with eyes, and a cripple with legs on. All the use he has of this vessel himself, is to hold thus much; for his drinking is but a scooping in of so many quarts, which are filled out into his body, and that filled out again into the room, which is commonly as drunk as he. Tobacco serves to air him after a washing, and is his only breath and breathing while. He is the greatest enemy to himself, and the next to his friend, and then most in the act of his kindness, for his kindness is but trying a mastery, who shall sink down first: and men come from him as a battle, wounded and bound up. Nothing takes a man off more from his credit, and business, and makes him more recklessly careless what becomes of all. Indeed he dares not enter on a serious thought, or if he do, it is such melancholy that it sends him to be drunk again.

[13] Text: 1633.

A Mere Complimental Man [14]

Is ONE to be held off still at the same distance you are now; for you shall have him but thus, and if you enter on him farther you lose him. Methinks Virgil well expresses him in those well-behaved ghosts that Æneas met with, that were friends to talk with, and men to look on, but if he grasped them, but air. He is one that lies kindly to you, and for good fashion's sake, and 'tis discourtesy in you to believe him. His words are so many fine phrases set together, which serve equally for all men, and are equally to no purpose. Each fresh encounter with a man puts him to the same part again, and he goes over to you what he said to him was last with him; he kisses your hands as he kissed his before, and is your servant to be commanded, but you shall intreat of him nothing. His proffers are universal and general, with exceptions against all particulars. He will do anything for you, but if you urge him to this, he cannot, or to that, he is engaged; but he will do anything. Promises he accounts but a kind of mannerly words, and in the expectation of your manners not to exact them; if you do, he wonders at your ill breeding, that cannot distinguish betwixt what is spoken and what is meant. No man gives better satisfaction at the first, and comes off more with the elegy of a kind gentleman, till you know him better; and then you know him for nothing. And commonly those most rail at him that have before most commended him. The best is, he cozens you in a fair manner, and abuses you with great respect.

[14] Text: 1633.

Owen Felltham 1602(?)-1668

FEW FACTS concerning the life of Owen Felltham have been found. We know that his parents lived in Mutford, Suffolk, and that at eighteen he published a collection of essays called *Resolves*. He added to these in later editions, always writing on subjects of broad interest and directing them toward the instruction of those whom he calls "the middle sort of people." He also wrote *A Brief Character of the Low Countries* and a volume of poetry entitled *Lusoria*. In the latter is his famous answer to Jonson's "Come, leave the loathèd stage."

It has been established [1] that he served, probably as steward, in the household of the Earl of Thomond at Great Billing, Northamptonshire, for about forty years and that he died at the London house of the Countess Dowager of Thomond in the Strand.

[1] F. S. Tupper, "New Facts Regarding Owen Felltham," *Modern Language Notes* (May, 1939), Vol. LIV, 199–201.

RESOLVES, DIVINE, MORAL, AND POLITICAL [1]

THE FIRST CENTURY

Of Resolution

WHAT A skein of ruffled silk is the uncomposed man! Every thing that but offers to even him entangles him more; as if, while you unbend him one way, he warpeth worse the other. He cannot but meet with variety of occasions, and every one of these entwines him in a deeper trouble. His ways are strewed with briars, and he bustles himself into his own confusion. Like a partridge in the net, he masks himself the more by the anger of his fluttering wing. Certainly, a good resolution is the most fortifying armor that a discreet man can wear. That can defend him against all the unwelcome shuffles that the poor rude world puts on him. Without this, like hot iron, he hisses at every drop that finds him. With this, he can be a servant as well as a lord, and have the same inward pleasantness in the quakes and shakes of fortune that he carries in her softest smiles. I confess biting penury has too strong talons for mud-walled man to grasp withal. Nature is importunate for necessities and will try all the engines of her wit and power rather than suffer her own destruction. But where she hath so much as she may live, resolution is the only marshal that can keep her in a decent order. That which puts the loose-woven mind into a whirling tempest is by the resolute seen, slighted, laughed at; with as much honor, more quiet, more safety. The world has nothing in it worthy a man's serious anger. The best way to perish discontentments is either not to see them, or convert them to a dimpling mirth. How endless will be the quarrels of a choleric man; and the contentments of him that is resolved to turn indignities into things to make sport withal!

[1] Text from the second edition, 1628.

'Tis sure, nothing but experience and collected judgment can make a man do this; but when he has brought himself unto it, how infinite shall he find his ease! It was Xantippe's [2] observation, that she ever found Socrates return with the same countenance that he went abroad withal. Lucan can tell us,

> *Fortunaque perdat*
> *Opposita virtute minas.*

> All Fortune's threats be lost,
> Where Virtue does oppose.

I wish no man so spiritless as to let all abuses press the dullness of a willing shoulder; but I wish him an able discretion to discern which are fit to be stirred in, and those to prosecute for no other end but to show the injury the more to virtue and dear Nature's justice than to himself. Every man should be equity's champion, because it is that eternal pillar whereon the world is founded. In high and mountained fortunes resolution is necessary to ensafe us from the thefts and wiles of prosperity, which steal us away, not only from ourselves but virtue: and for the most part, like a long peace, softly delivers us into impoverishing war. In the wane of fortune resolution is likewise necessary, to guard us from the discontents that usually assail the poor dejected man. For all the world will beat the man whom Fortune buffets. And unless by this he can turn off the blows, he shall be sure to feel the greatest burthen in his own sad mind. A wise man makes a trouble less by fortitude; but to a fool, it is heavier by his stooping to it. I would fain bring myself to that pass, that I might not make my happiness depend on another's judgment. But as I would never do anything dishonestly, so I would never fear the immaterial wind of censure when it is done. He that steers by that gale is ever in danger of wreck. Honesty is a warrant of far

---

[2] Wife of Socrates, famous for her nagging.

more safety than fame: I will never be ashamed of that
which bears her seal, as knowing it is only pride's being in
fashion that hath put honest humility out of countenance.
As for the crackers of the brain, the tongue-squibs, they
will die alone if I shall not revive them. The best way to
have them forgotten by others is first to forget them myself. This will keep myself in quiet, and, by a noble not-
caring, arrow the intender's bosom; who will ever fret most
when he finds his designs most frustrate. Yet in all these
I will something respect custom because she is magnified
in that world wherein I am one. But when she parts from
just reason, I shall rather displease her by parting than offend in her company. I would have all men set up their rest
for all things that this world can yield: yet so as they build
upon a surer foundation than themselves; otherwise, that
which should have been their foundation will surely cross
them, and that is God.

Of the Worship of Admiration

WHATSOEVER is rare and passionate carries the soul to the
thought of eternity, and by contemplation gives it some
glimpses of more absolute perfection than here it is capable
of. When I see the royalty of a state show, at some unwonted
solemnity, my thoughts present me something more royal
than this. When I see the most enchanting beauties that
earth can show me, I yet think, there is something far more
glorious: methinks I see a kind of higher perfection peep-
ing through the frailty of a face. When I hear the ravishing
strains of a sweet-tuned voice, married to the warbles of
the artful instrument, I apprehend by this a higher diapason;
and do almost believe I hear a little deity whispering through
the pory substance of the tongue. But this I can but grope
after. I can neither find nor say what it is. When I read a
rarely sententious man, I admire him to my own impatiency.

I cannot read some part of Seneca above two leaves together: he raises my soul to a contemplation, which sets
me a-thinking on more than I can imagine. So I am forced
to cast him by, and subside to an admiration. Such effects
works poetry, when it looks to towering virtues. It gives up
a man to raptures; and irradiates the soul with such high
apprehensions that all the glories which this world hath
hereby appear contemptible. Of which the soft-souled Ovid
gives a touch, when he complains the want.

> *Impetus ille sacer, qui vatum pectora nutrit,*
> *Qui prius in nobis esse solebat, abest.*

> That sacred vigor, which had wont alone
> To flame the poet's noble breast, is gone.

But this is, when these excellencies incline to gravity and
seriousness. For, otherwise, light airs turn us into spriteful
actions, which breathe away in a loose laughter, not leaving
half that impression behind them which serious considerations do. As if mirth were the excellency for the body, and
meditation for the soul. As if one were for the contentment
of this life; and the other, eyeing to that of the life to come.
All endeavors aspire to eminency; all eminencies do beget
an admiration. And this makes me believe that contemplative admiration is a large part of the worship of the Deity.
'Tis an adoration purely of the spirit; a more sublime bow-
ing of the soul to the Godhead. And this is it which that
Homer of philosophers avowed could bring a man to perfect
happiness, if to his contemplation he joined a constant imitation of God, in justice, wisdom, holiness. Nothing can
carry us so near to God and heaven as this. The mind can
walk beyond the sight of the eye; and (though in a cloud)
can lift us into heaven while we live. Meditation is the soul's
perspective glass: whereby, in her long remove, she discerneth
God as if he were nearer hand. I persuade no man to make
it his whole life's business. We have bodies, as well as souls.

And even this world, while we are in it, ought somewhat to be cared for. As those states are likely to flourish where execution follows sound advisements, so is man, when contemplation is seconded by action. Contemplation generates; action propagates. Without the first, the latter is defective; without the last, the first is but abortive and embrious. St. Bernard[3] compares contemplation to Rachel, which was the more fair; but action to Leah, which was the more fruitful.[4] I will neither always be busy and doing, nor ever shut up in nothing but thoughts. Yet that which some would call idleness, I will call the sweetest part of my life: and that is, my thinking. Surely, God made so many varieties in his creatures, as well for the inward soul as the outward senses; though he made them primarily for his own free-will and glory. He was a monk of an honester age, that being asked how he could endure that life without the pleasure of books, answered: The nature of the creatures was his library; wherein, when he pleased, he could muse upon God's deep oracles.

Of Idleness

THE IDLE man is the barrenest piece of earth in the orb. There is no creature that hath life, but is busied in some action for the benefit of the restless world. Even the most venomous and most ravenous things that are, have their commodities as well as their annoyances; and they are ever engaged in some action which both profiteth the world and continues them in their nature's courses. Even the vegetables, wherein calm nature dwells, have their turns and times in fructifying; they leaf, they flower, they seed. Nay, creatures quite inanimate are (some) the most laborious in their motion. With what a cheerful face the golden sun chariots

[3] St. Bernard of Clairvaux (1091–1103).
[4] Gen. 29.

through the rounding sky! How perpetual is the maiden moon in her just and horned mutations! The fire, how restless in his quick and catching flames! in the air, what transitions! and how fluctuous are the salted waves! Nor is the teeming earth weary after so many thousand years' productions! All which may tutor the couch-stretched man, and raise the modest red to showing through his unwashed face. Idleness is the most corrupting fly that can blow in any human mind. That ignorance is the most miserable which knows not what to do. The idle man is like the dumb jack in a virginal: [5] while all the other dance out a winning music, this, like a member out of joint, sullens the whole body with an ill disturbing laziness. I do not wonder to see some of our gentry grown (well-near) the lewdest men of our land; since they are, most of them, so muffled in a non-employment. 'Tis action that does keep the soul both sweet and sound; while lying still does rot it to an ordured noisomeness. Augustine imputes Esau's loss of the blessing partly to his slothfulness, that had rather receive meat than seek it. Surely, exercise is the fattening food of the soul, without which she grows lank and thinly-parted. That the followers of great men are so much debauched, I believe to be want of employment: for the soul, impatient of an absolute recess, for want of the wholesome food of business, preys upon the lewder actions. 'Tis true men learn to do ill by doing what is next it, nothing. I believe Solomon meant the field of the sluggard as well for the emblem of his mind as the certain index of his outward state. As the one is overgrown with thorns and briars, so is the other with vices and enormities. If any wonder how Egistus grew adulterate,[6] the exit of the verse will tell him,—*Desidiosus erat*. When one would brag the blessing of the Roman state, that since Carthage was razed and Greece subjected, they might now be happy, as

[5] The jack is the mechanism which lifts up and plucks the string when the key is pressed.

[6] In the *Agamemnon* of Æschylus, Ægisthus seduces Clytemnestra and murders Agamemnon.

having nothing to fear: says the best Scipio, "We now are most in danger: for while we want business, and have no foe to awe us, we are ready to drown in the mud of vice and slothfulness." How bright does the soul grow with use and negotiation! With what proportioned sweetness does that family flourish, where but one laborious guide steereth in an ordered course! When Cleanthes[7] had labored, and gotten some coin, he shows it his companions, and tells them that he now, if he will, can nourish another Cleanthes. Believe it, industry is never wholly unfruitful. If it bring not joy with the incoming profit, it will yet banish mischief from thy busied gates. There is a kind of good angel waiting upon diligence, that ever carries a laurel in his hand to crown her. Fortune, as they said of old, should not be prayed unto but with hands in motion. The bosomed fist beckons the approach of poverty, and leaves besides the noble head unguarded; but the lifted arm does frighten want, and is ever a shield to that noble director. How unworthy was that man of the world that never did aught, but only lived and died! Though Epaminondas[8] was severe, he was yet exemplary, when he found a soldier sleeping in his watch and ran him through with his sword; as if he would bring the two brothers, death and sleep, to a meeting: and when he was blamed for that, as cruelty, he says, he did but leave him as he found him, dead. It is none of the meanest happiness to have a mind that loves a virtuous exercise; 'tis daily rising to blessedness and contentation. They are idle divines that are not heavened in their lives above the unstudious man. Everyone shall smell of that he is busied in: as those that stir among perfumes and spices shall, when they are gone, have still a grateful odor with them: so, they that turn the leaves of the worthy writer cannot but retain a smack of their long-lived author. They converse with virtue's soul, which he that wrote did spread upon his lasting

[7] Cleanthes, Greek stoic philosopher, 300(?)–220(?) B.C.
[8] Epaminondas, a Theban general of praiseworthy character, c. 418–362.

paper. Every good line adds sinew to the virtuous mind;
and withal heals that vice which would be springing in it.
That I have liberty to do anything, I account it from the
favoring heavens. That I have a mind sometimes inclining
to use that liberty well, I think I may without ostentation
be thankful for it as a bounty of the Deity. Sure, I should be
miserable if I did not love this business in my vacancy. I
am glad of that leisure which gives me leisure to employ
myself. If I should not grow better for it, yet this benefit,
I am sure, would accrue me, I should both keep myself from
worse, and not have time to entertain the devil in.

Of Poets and Poetry

SURELY he was a little wanton with his leisure that first
invented poetry. 'Tis but a play which makes words dance
in the evenness of a cadency; yet without doubt, being a
harmony, it is nearer the mind than prose, for that itself
is a harmony in height. But the words being rather the
drossy part, conceit I take to be the principal. And here,
though it digresseth from truth, it flies above her, making
her more rare by giving curious raiment to her nakedness.
The name the Grecians gave the men that wrote thus, showed
how much they honored it; they called them "makers." And
had some of them had power to put their conceits in act,
how near would they have come to deity! And for the virtues of men, they rest not on the bare demeanor, but slide
into imagination; so proposing things above us, they kindle
the reader to wonder and imitation. And certainly, poets that
write thus Plato never meant to banish. His own practice
shows he excluded not all. He was content to hear An-
timachus [9] recite his poem, when all the herd had left him;
and he himself wrote both tragedies and other pieces. Perhaps he found them a little too busy with his gods; and he,

[9] Greek poet, at his height about 400 B.C., known for the epic *Thebais*.

being the first that made philosophy divine and rational, was modest in his own beginnings. Another name they had of honor, too, and that was "vates." Nor know I how to distinguish between the prophets and poets of Israel. What is Jeremiah's Lamentation but a kind of Sapphic elegy? David's Psalms are not only poems but songs, snatches and raptures of a flaming spirit. And this indeed I observe to the honor of poets; I never found them covetous or scrapingly base. The Jews had not two such kings in all their catalogue as Solomon and his father, poets both. There is a largeness in their souls beyond the narrowness of other men; and why may we not then think this may embrace more both of heaven and God? I cannot but conjecture this to be the reason that they, most of them, are poor; they find their minds so solaced with their own flights that they neglect the study of growing rich; and this, I confess again, I think turns them to vice and unmanly courses. Besides, they are for the most part mighty lovers of their palates, and this is known an impoverisher. Antigonus,[10] in the tented field, found Antagoras cooking of a conger himself. And they all are friends to the grape and liquor, though I think many, more out of a ductible nature and their love to pleasant company than their affection to the juice alone. They are all of free natures, and are the truest definition of that philosopher's man, which gives him *animal risibile.* Their grossest fault is that you may conclude them sensual, yet this does not touch them all. Ingenious for the most part they are. I know there be some rhyming fools; but what have they to do with poetry? When Sallust would tell us that Sempronia's wit was not ill, says he, *Potuit versus facere, et iocum movere:* She could make a verse and break a jest. Something there is in it more than ordinary in that it is all in such measured language as may be marred by reading. I laugh heartily at Philoxenus[11] his jest, who

[10] Antigonus, general of Alexander the Great, 382–301 B.C.
[11] Philoxenus of Cythera (435–380 B.C.).

passing by, and hearing some masons mis-sensing his lines (with their ignorant sawing of them), falls to breaking their bricks amain; they ask the cause, and he replies, they spoil his work, and he theirs. Certainly, a worthy poet is so far from being a fool that there is some wit required in him that shall be able to read him well; and without the true accent, numbered poetry does lose of the gloss. It was a speech becoming an able poet of our own, when a lord read his verses crookedly, and he beseeched his lordship not to murder him in his own lines. He that speaks false Latin breaks Priscian's head, but he that repeats a verse ill puts Homer out of joint. One thing commends it beyond oratory, it ever complieth to the sharpest judgments. He is the best orator that pleaseth all, even the crowd and clowns. But poetry would be poor that they should all approve of. If the learned and judicious like it, let the throng bray. These, when 'tis best, will like it the least. So they contemn what they understand not, and the neglected poet falls by want. Calpurnius makes one complain the misfortune,[12]

Frange, puer, calamos, et inanes desere Musas:
Et potius glandes, rubicundaque collige corna.
Duc ad mulctra greges, et lac venale per urbem
Non tacitus porta: Quid enim tibi fistula reddet,
Quo tutere famem? certe, mea carmina nemo
Præter ab his scopulis ventosa remurmurat Echo.

Boy, break thy pipes, leave, leave thy fruitless Muse:
Rather the mast and blood-red cornel choose.
Go lead thy flocks to milking; sell and cry
Milk through the city: what can learning buy,
To keep back hunger? None my verses mind,
But Echo, babbling from these rocks and wind.

[12] Roman bucolic poet, imitator of Theocritus, probably in the reign of Nero. *Eclogue,* IV. 23.

Two things are commonly blamed in poetry; nay, you take away that, if them; and these are lies and flattery. But I have told them in the worst words; for 'tis only to the shallow insight that they appear thus. Truth may dwell more clearly in an allegory or a moraled fable than in a bare narration. And for flattery, no man will take poetry literal; since in commendations it rather shows what men should be, than what they are. If this were not, it would appear uncomely. But we all know, hyperboles in poetry do bear a decency, nay, a grace along with them. The greatest danger that I find in it is, that it wantons the blood and imagination, as carrying a man in too high a delight. To prevent these, let the wise poet strive to be modest in his lines. First, that he dash not the gods; next, that he injure not chastity, nor corrupt the ear with lasciviousness. When these are declined, I think a grave poem the deepest kind of writing. It wings the soul up higher than the slacked pace of prose. Flashes that do follow the cup, I fear me, are too sprightly to be solid; they run smartly upon the loose for a distance or two, but then, being foul, they give in and tire. I confess I love the sober Muse and fasting; from the other, matter cannot come so clear but that it will be misted with the fumes of wine. Long poetry some cannot be friends withal; and indeed, it palls upon the reading. The wittiest poets have been all short and changing soon their subject, as Horace, Martial, Juvenal, Seneca and the two comedians. Poetry should be rather like a coranto, short and nimbly-lofty, than a dull lesson of a day long. Nor can it be but deadish, if distended; for when 'tis right, it centers conceit and takes but the spirit of things, and therefore foolish poesy is of all writing the most ridiculous. When a goose dances and a fool versifies, there is sport alike. He is twice an ass, that is a rhyming one. He is something the less unwise, that is unwise but in prose. If the subject be history or contexted fable, then I hold it better put in prose or blanks; for ordinary discourse never shows so well in meter as in the strain it may seem to be spoken in; the commendation is, to do it to the life, nor is this any other than poetry in prose. Surely, though the world think not so, he is happy to himself that can play the poet. He shall vent his passions by his pen, and ease his heart of their weight; and he shall often raise himself a joy in his raptures which no man can perceive but he. Sure Ovid found a pleasure in it, even when he wrote his *Tristia*. It gently delivers the mind of distempers, and works the thoughts to a sweetness in their searching conceit. I would not love it for a profession, and I would not want it for a recreation. I can make myself harmless, nay, amending mirth with it, while I should, perhaps, be trying of a worser pastime. And this I believe in it further, unless conversation corrupts his easiness, it lifts a man to nobleness, and is never in any rightly, but it makes him of a royal and capacious soul.

THE SECOND CENTURY

A Rule in Reading Authors

SOME MEN may read authors as our gentlemen use flowers, only for delight and smell, to please their fancy and refine their tongue. Others, like the bee, extract only the honey, the wholesome precepts; and this alone they bear away, leaving the rest, as little worth, of small value. In reading I will care for both, though for the last most; the one serves to instruct the mind, the other fits her to tell what she hath learned: pity it is they should be divided; he that hath worth in him, and cannot express it, is a chest, keeping a rich jewel, and the key lost. Concealing goodness is vice; virtue is better by being communicated. A good style with wholesome matter is a fair woman with a virtuous soul, which attracts the eyes of all. The good man thinks chastely and loves her beauty for her virtue, which he still thinks

more fair for dwelling in so fair an outside. The vicious man
hath lustful thoughts, and he would for her beauty fain
destroy her virtue; but coming to solicit his purpose, finds
such divine lectures from her angel's tongue, and those delivered with so sweet a pleasing modesty, that he thinks
virtue is dissecting her soul to him, to ravish man with a
beauty which he dreamed not of. So he could not curse himself for desiring that lewdly, which he hath learned since
only to admire and reverence. Thus he goes away better,
that came with an intent to be worse. Quaint phrases on a
good subject are baits to make an ill man virtuous; how
many vile men seeking these have found themselves con-
vertites! I may refine my speech without harm; but I will
endeavor more to reform my life. 'Tis a good grace both of
oratory or the pen to speak or write proper; but that is the
best work, where the Graces and the Muses meet.

Of Lamenting the Loss of Trifles

MANY have much lamented the loss of trifles, when they
might have gained by such damages, had they not with
them lost themselves: I mean, their quiet minds and patience.
Unwise so to debar themselves of rest, when their vexation
cannot yield them profit. If tears could either recover a
loss or recall time, then to weep were but to purpose; but
things past, though with prudence they may be corrected,
yet with greatest grief they cannot be recalled: make them
better we may, but to make them not to be at all requires
more than a human strength or a finite power. Actions once
done admit a correction, not a nullity. Although I will endeavor to amend what is gone by amiss, yet will I labor
never to grieve for anything past, but sin: and for that
always. A small loss shall never trouble me; neither shall
the greatest hindrance make my heart not mine own. He

spoke well, that said, "He which hath himself, hath lost nothing."

Good Name, how it is both the best and brittlest Thing that is

A GOOD name is, among all externals, both the best and most brittle blessing. If it be true, that *Difficilia quæ pulchra,* this is a fair beatitude. It is the hardest both to get and keep: like a glass of most curious workmanship, long a making, and broke in a moment. That which is not gained but by a continued habit of many virtues, is, by one short vicious action, lost for ever. Nay, if it could only vanish in this sort, it would then by many be kept untainted: if it could not be lost but upon certainties; if it were in our own keeping; or, if not in our own, in the hands of the wise and honest; how possible were it to preserve it pure! But, alas! this is the misery, that it rests upon probabilities, which, as they are hard to disprove, so they are ready to persuade: that it is in the hands of others, not ourselves; in the custody not of the discreet and good only, but also of fools, knaves, villains; who though they cannot make us worse to ourselves, yet how vile may they render us to others! To vindicate it from the tongues of these, there is no remedy but a constant careful discretion. I must not only be good, but not seem ill. Appearance alone, which in good is too little, is in evil too much. He is a wilful murderer of his own fame that willingly appears in the ill action he did not. It is not enough to be well lived, but well reported. When we know good fame a blessing, we may easily in the contrary discern a curse; whereof we are justly seized, while we labor not to avoid it. I will care as well to be thought honest, as to be so: my friends know me by the actions they see; strangers, by the things they hear: the agreement of both is the confirming of my goodness. The one is a good complexion, the other a good countenance: I deny not but they may be several; but they are then most graceful when both are seated together. It had been well spoken of Cæsar, if he had not put her away when, after trial and the crime cleared, he said, "Cæsar's wife should not only be free from sin, but from suspicion." An ill name may be free from dishonesty, but not from some folly. Though slanders rise from others, we ourselves oft give the occasion. The first best way to a good name is a good life; the next is a good behavior.

BROWNE AND MILTON, both born in Cheapside, were almost exact contemporaries. Browne, however, became an Oxford man and a Loyalist. He went to the Continent for three years of study in the field of medicine and, after spending some time at Montpellier and Padua, took his degree at Leyden. His return to England was about the time that Milton went to Horton; and by the time that Milton went on the Grand Tour, Browne had received his M.D. from Oxford, had written the *Religio Laici,* and had received an invitation to practice medicine in Norwich.

Browne lived in Norwich the remainder of his life undisturbed by private or public misfortunes. The wife he chose in 1641 was entirely compatible in spite of little vanities such as liking her shoes "eythar pinke or blew." He accepted the loss of six of his ten children as the way of the world in the seventeenth century, and though a Royalist in the midst of Puritans his only assistance to the king's cause was his refusal to contribute toward a fund for retaking Newcastle and his quiet encouragement to fellow Royalists to increase their numbers. His one reaction that showed his real concern came with the Restoration and his open rejoicing over Cromwell's being burned in effigy and the three gruesome heads displayed on Westminster Hall. His interest was in birth and death as he saw them among his patients and in matters of the past revealed in old books, or in the coins and urns which were plowed up in Norwich.

Browne's spiritual autobiography in *Religio Medici* is less stirring than Bunyan's, but none the less sincere for its serenity; perhaps it is more appealing by being more gentlemanly and polished. The *Vulgar Errors* delights us with its mixture of credulity and elaborate exposure, while the *Garden of Cyrus* with its reduction of all things to quincunxes astonishes us as much as it did Coleridge. But it is the

Urn-Burial over which we willingly linger, taking time to scrutinize each ancient object which escaped the funeral fire—the opal which perhaps inspired Browne or the wine so long buried in the earth. Browne himself lost his first enthusiasm for antiquarian information on urns and old funeral customs, and was soon swept into a moving prose poem on death. Where can we see more fully revealed the mature genius of Sir Thomas Browne than in Chapter V of this work? This is the chapter which George Saintsbury calls "the longest piece, perhaps, of absolutely sublime rhetoric to be found in the prose literature of the world." [1]

[1] *Cambridge History of English Literature*, VII. 242.

From HYDRIOTAPHIA;

URN-BURIAL, OR A DISCOURSE OF THE SEPULCHRAL
URNS LATELY FOUND IN NORFOLK [1]

CHAPTER III

PLASTERED AND whited sepulchers were anciently affected in
cadaverous and corrupted burials; and the rigid Jews were
wont to garnish the sepulchers of the righteous.[2] Ulysses,
in *Hecuba*,[3] cared not how meanly he lived, so he might find
a noble tomb after death. Great princes affected great monuments; and the fair and larger urns contained no vulgar
ashes, which makes that disparity in those which time dis-
covereth among us. The present urns were not of one capacity,
the largest containing above a gallon, some not much above
half that measure; nor all of one figure, wherein there is
no strict conformity in the same or different countries, observable from those represented by Casalius, Bosio, and
others, though all found in Italy; while many have handles,
ears, and long necks, but most imitate a circular figure, in
a spherical and round composure; whether from any mystery,
best duration, or capacity were but a conjecture. But the
common form with necks was a proper figure, making our
last bed like our first; nor much unlike the urns of our nativity while we lay in the nether part of the earth,[4] and inward vault of our microcosm. Many urns are red, these but
of a black color, somewhat smooth, and dully sounding,
which begat some doubt whether they were burnt, or only
baked in oven or sun, according to the ancient way in many
bricks, tiles, pots, and testaceous works; and, as the word
testa is properly to be taken, when occurring without addition and chiefly intended by Pliny, when he commendeth
bricks and tiles of two years old, and to make them in the

---

[1] Text: 1658, first edition.   [2] Matt. 23:27–29.
[3] Tragedy by Euripides.   [4] Psalm 63:9.

385

spring. Nor only these concealed pieces, but the open magnificence of antiquity, ran much in the artifice of clay. Hereof
the house of Mausolus was built, thus old Jupiter stood in the
Capitol, and the *statua* of Hercules, made in the reign of
Tarquinius Priscus,[5] was extant in Pliny's days. And such as
declined burning or funeral urns affected coffins of clay, according to the mode of Pythagoras, and way preferred by
Varro. But the spirit of great ones was above these circum-
scriptions, affecting copper, silver, gold, and porphyry urns,
wherein Severus lay, after a serious view and sentence on
that which should contain him. Some of these urns were
thought to have been silvered over, from sparklings in several pots, with small tinsel parcels; uncertain whether from
the earth, or the first mixture in them.

Among these urns we could obtain no good account of their
coverings; only one seemed arched over with some kind of
brickwork. Of those found at Buxton, some were covered
with flints, some, in other parts, with tiles; those at Yarmouth
Caster were closed with Roman bricks, and some have proper
earthen covers adapted and fitted to them. But in the Homeri-
cal urn of Patroclus, whatever was the solid tegument, we
find the immediate covering to be a purple piece of silk: and
such as had no covers might have the earth closely pressed
into them, after which disposure were probably some of these,
wherein we found the bones and ashes half mortared unto
the sand and sides of the urn, and some long roots of quich,
or dog's-grass, wreathed about the bones.

No lamps, included liquors, lachrymatories, or tear bottles
attended these rural urns, either as sacred unto the *manes,*
or passionate expressions of their surviving friends. While
with rich flames and hired tears, they solemnized their obsequies, and in the most lamented monuments made one part
of their inscriptions. Some find sepulchral vessels containing liquors, which time hath incrassated into jellies. For,
besides these lachrymatories, notable lamps, with vessels of

---

[5] Tarquinius Priscus, fifth king of Rome, died 578 B.C.

oils, and aromatical liquors, attended noble ossuaries; and some yet retaining a vinosity and spirit in them, which, if any have tasted, they have far exceeded the palates of antiquity. Liquors not to be computed by years of annual magistrates, but by great conjunctions and the fatal periods of kingdoms.[6] The draughts of consulary date were but crude unto these, and Opimian wine [7] but in the must unto them.

In sundry graves and sepulchers we meet with rings, coins, and chalices. Ancient frugality was so severe that they allowed no gold to attend the corpse but only that which served to fasten their teeth. Whether the opaline stone in this urn were burnt upon the finger of the dead, or cast into the fire by some affectionate friend, it will consist with either custom. But other incinerable substances were found so fresh that they could feel no singe from fire. These, upon view, were judged to be wood; but, sinking in water, and tried by the fire, we found them to be bone or ivory. In their hardness and yellow color they most resembled box, which, in old expressions, found the epithet of eternal, and perhaps in such conservatories might have passed uncorrupted.

That bay leaves were found green in the tomb of St. Humbert, after an hundred and fifty years, was looked upon as miraculous. Remarkable it was unto old spectators that the cypress of the temple of Diana lasted so many hundred years; the wood of the ark, and olive-rod of Aaron, were older at the captivity; but the cypress of the ark of Noah was the greatest vegetable antiquity, if Josephus were not deceived by some fragments of it in his days: to omit the moor logs and fir trees found underground in many parts of England; the undated ruins of winds, floods, or earthquakes, and which in Flanders still show from what quarter they fell, as generally lying in a northeast position.

But though we found not these pieces to be wood, according to first apprehensions, yet we missed not altogether of

---

[6] About five hundred years. (Plato)
[7] *Vinum Opimianum annorum centum.* (Petronius)

some woody substance; for the bones were not so clearly picked but some coals were found amongst them; a way to make wood perpetual, and a fit associate for metal, whereon was laid the foundation of the great Ephesian temple, and which were made the lasting tests of old boundaries and landmarks. Whilst we look on these, we admire not observations of coals found fresh after four hundred years. In a long-deserted habitation even egg-shells have been found fresh, not tending to corruption.

In the monument of King Childeric [8] the iron relics were found all rusty and crumbling into pieces; but our little iron pins, which fastened the ivory works, held well together and lost not their magnetical quality, though wanting a tenacious moisture for the firmer union of parts; although it could hardly be drawn into fusion, yet that metal soon submitteth unto rust and dissolution. In the brazen pieces we admired not the duration, but the freedom from rust and ill savor upon the hardest attrition; but now exposed unto the piercing atoms of air, in the space of a few months, they begin to spot and betray their green entrails. We conceive not these urns to have descended thus naked as they appear, or to have entered their graves without the old habit of flowers. The urn of Philopœmen [9] was so laden with flowers and ribbons that it afforded no sight of itself. The rigid Lycurgus allowed olive and myrtle. The Athenians might fairly except against the practice of Democritus to be buried up in honey, as fearing to embezzle a great commodity of their country, and the best of that kind in Europe. But Plato seemed too frugally politic, who allowed no larger monument than would contain four heroic verses, and designed the most barren ground for sepulture: though we cannot commend the goodness of that sepulchral ground which was set at no higher rate than

[8] King Childeric I, king of the Franks (c. 437–481); his tomb was discovered in 1653, and the arms, jewels, etc., which it contained aroused much interest.

[9] Philopœmen (253–184 B.C.), famous Greek general.

the mean salary of Judas. Though the earth had confounded the ashes of these ossuaries, yet the bones were so smartly burnt that some thin plates of brass were found half melted among them. Whereby we apprehend they were not of the meanest carcasses, perfunctorily fired, as sometimes in military, and commonly in pestilence, burnings; or after the manner of abject corpses, huddled forth and carelessly burnt, without the Esquiline Port at Rome; which was an affront continued upon Tiberius, while they but half burnt his body,[10] and in the amphitheater, according to the custom in notable malefactors; whereas Nero seemed not so much to fear his death as that his head should be cut off and his body not burnt entire.

Some, finding many fragments of skulls in these urns, suspected a mixture of bones; in none we searched was there cause of such conjecture, though sometimes they declined not that practice. The ashes of Domitian were mingled with those of Julia;[11] of Achilles with those of Patroclus. All urns contained not single ashes; without confused burnings they affectionately compounded their bones, passionately endeavoring to continue their living unions. And when distance of death denied such conjunctions, unsatisfied affections conceived some satisfaction to be neighbors in the grave, to lie urn by urn, and touch but in their *manes*. And many were so curious to continue their living relations that they contrived large and family urns, wherein the ashes of their nearest friends and kindred might successively be received, at least some parcels thereof, while their collateral memorials lay in minor vessels about them.

Antiquity held too light thoughts from objects of mortality, while some drew provocatives of mirth from anatomies, and jugglers showed tricks with skeletons; when fiddlers made not so pleasant mirth as fencers, and men could sit with

[10] Suetonius, in *Vita Tiberius*.
[11] Suetonius in *Vita Domitian*.

quiet stomachs, while hanging was played before them.[12] Old considerations made few mementoes by skulls and bones upon their monuments. In the Egyptian obelisks and hieroglyphical figures it is not easy to meet with bones. The sepulchral lamps speak nothing less than sepulture, and in their literal draughts prove often obscene and antic pieces. Where we find D.M.[13] it is obvious to meet with sacrificing pateras and vessels of libation upon old sepulchral monuments. In the Jewish hypogæum and subterranean cell at Rome, was little observable beside the variety of lamps and frequent draughts of the holy candlestick. In authentic draughts of Anthony and Jerome we meet with thigh bones and death's-heads; but the cemeterial cells of ancient Christians and martyrs were filled with draughts of Scripture stories; not declining the flourishes of cypress, palms, and olive, and the mystical figures of peacocks, doves, and cocks; but iterately affecting the portraits of Enoch, Lazarus, Jonas, and the vision of Ezekiel, as hopeful draughts, and hinting imagery of the resurrection, which is the life of the grave, and sweetens our habitations in the land of moles and pismires.

Gentile inscriptions precisely delivered the extent of men's lives, seldom the manner of their deaths, which history itself so often leaves obscure in the records of memorable persons. There is scarce any philosopher but dies twice or thrice in Laertius; nor almost any life without two or three deaths in Plutarch; which makes the tragical ends of noble persons more favorably resented by compassionate readers who find some relief in the election of such differences.

The certainty of death is attended with uncertainties, in time, manner, places. The variety of monuments hath often obscured true graves; and cenotaphs confounded sepulchers.

---

[12] Ἀγχώνην παίζειν. A barbarous pastime at feasts, when men stood upon a rolling globe with their necks in a rope, and a knife in their hands, ready to cut it when the stone was rolled away, wherein if they failed, they lost their lives to the laughter of the spectators. (Athenæus)

[13] Diis Manibus.

For beside their real tombs, many have found honorary and empty sepulchers. The variety of Homer's monuments made him of various countries. Euripides had his tomb in Africa, but his sepulture in Macedonia. And Severus found his real sepulcher in Rome, but his empty grave in Gallia.

He that lay in a golden urn eminently above the earth [14] was not like to find the quiet of these bones. Many of these urns were broken by a vulgar discoverer in hope of enclosed treasure. The ashes of Marcellus were lost above ground, upon the like account. Where profit hath prompted, no age hath wanted such miners; for which the most barbarous expilators found the most civil rhetoric: Gold once out of the earth is no more due unto it, what was unreasonably committed to the ground is reasonably resumed from it; let monuments and rich fabrics, not riches, adorn men's ashes. The commerce of the living is not to be transferred unto the dead; it is no injustice to take that which none complains to lose, and no man is wronged where no man is possessor. [15]

What virtue yet sleeps in this *terra damnata* and aged cinders, were petty magic to experiment. These crumbling relics and long fired particles superannuate such expectations: bones, hairs, nails, and teeth of the dead were the treasures of old sorcerers. In vain we revive such practices; present superstition too visibly perpetuates the folly of our forefathers, wherein unto old observation this island was so complete that it might have instructed Persia.

Plato's historian of the other world lies twelve days incorrupted, while his soul was viewing the large stations of the dead. How to keep the corpse seven days from corruption by anointing and washing, without exenteration, were an hazardable piece of art, in our choicest practice. How they made distinct separation of bones and ashes from fiery admixture, hath found no historical solution; though they

[14] Trajan.
[15] The commission of the Gothic King Theodoric for finding out sepulchral treasure. (Cassiodorus, var. 1. 4.)

seemed to make a distinct collection, and overlooked not Pyrrhus his toe. Some provision they might make by fictile vessels, coverings, tiles, or flat stones, upon and about the body (and in the same field, not far from these urns, many stones were found under ground), as also by careful separation of extraneous matter, composing and raking up the burnt bones with forks, observable in that notable lamp of Galvanus. Marlianus,[16] who had the sight of the *vas ustrinum* or vessel wherein they burnt the dead, found in the Esquiline field at Rome, might have afforded clearer solution. But their insatisfaction herein begat that remarkable invention in the funeral pyres of some princes, by incombustible sheets made with a texture of asbestos, incremable flax, or salamander's wool, which preserved their bones and ashes incommixed.

How the bulk of a man should sink into so few pounds of bones and ashes may seem strange unto any who considers not its constitution, and how slender a mass will remain upon an open and urging fire of the carnal composition. Even bones themselves, reduced into ashes, do abate a notable proportion, and consisting much of a volatile salt, when that is fired out, make a light kind of cinders; although their bulk be disproportionable to their weight when the heavy principle of salt is fired out and the earth almost only remaineth: observable in sallow, which makes more ashes than oak, and discovers the common fraud of selling ashes by measure and not by ponderation.

Some bones make best skeletons, some bodies quick and speediest ashes. Who would expect a quick flame from hydropical Heraclitus? The poisoned soldier when his belly brake put out two pyres in Plutarch. But in the plague of Athens, one private pyre served two or three intruders; and the Saracens burnt in large heaps by the king of Castile showed how little fuel sufficeth. Though the funeral pyre of Patroclus took up a hundred foot, a piece of an old boat

---

[16] *Romœ Typographia ex Marliano. Cap. de campo Esquilino.*

burnt Pompey; and if the burthen of Isaac were sufficient for an holocaust, a man may carry his own pyre.

From animals are drawn good burning lights, and good medicines against burning. Though the seminal humor seems of a contrary nature to fire, yet the body completed proves a combustible lump, wherein fire finds flame even from bones, and some fuel almost from all parts; though the metropolis of humidity [17] seems least disposed unto it, which might render the skulls of these urns less burnt than other bones. But all flies or sinks before fire almost in all bodies: when the common ligament is dissolved, the attenuable parts ascend, the rest subside in coal, calx, or ashes.

To burn the bones of the king of Edom [18] for lime seems no irrational ferity, but to drink of the ashes of dead relations,[19] a passionate prodigality. He that hath the ashes of his friend hath an everlasting treasure; where fire taketh leave, corruption slowly enters. In bones well burnt, fire makes a wall against itself; experimented in cupels, and tests of metals, which consist of such ingredients. What the sun compoundeth, fire analyzeth, not transmuteth. That devouring agent leaves almost always a morsel for the earth, whereof all things are but a colony; and which, if time permits, the mother element will have in their primitive mass again.

He that looks for urns and old sepulchral relics must not seek them in the ruins of temples, where no religion anciently placed them. These were found in a field, according to ancient custom, in noble or private burial; the old practice of the Canaanites, the family of Abraham, and the burying-place of Joshua, in the borders of his possessions; and also agreeable unto Roman practice to bury by highways, whereby their monuments were under eye: memorials of themselves, and mementos of mortality unto living passengers; whom the epitaphs of great ones were fain to beg to stay and look

[17] The brain. (Hippocrates)
[18] Amos 2:1.
[19] As Artemisia of her husband Mausolus. The tomb she had erected for him, the Mausoleum, was one of the Seven Wonders of the World.

upon them, a language though sometimes used, not so proper in church inscriptions. The sensible rhetoric of the dead, to exemplarity of good life, first admitted the bones of pious men and martyrs within church walls, which in succeeding ages crept into promiscuous practice: while Constantine was peculiarly favored to be admitted into the church porch, and the first thus buried in England was in the days of Cuthred.

Christians dispute how their bodies should lie in the grave. In urnal interment they clearly escaped this controversy. Though we decline the religious consideration, yet in cemeterial and narrower burying-places, to avoid confusion and cross-position, a certain posture were to be admitted: which even Pagan civility observed. The Persians lay north and south; the Megarians and Phœnicians placed their heads to the east; the Athenians, some think, towards the west, which Christians still retain. And Beda will have it to be the posture of our Saviour. That he was crucified with his face toward the west, we will not contend with tradition and probable account; but we applaud not the hand of the painter, in exalting his cross so high above those on either side: since hereof we find no authentic account in history, and even the crosses found by Helena pretend no such distinction from longitude or dimension.

To be knaved out of our graves, to have our skulls made drinking-bowls, and our bones turned into pipes, to delight and sport our enemies, are tragical abominations escaped in burning burials.

Urnal interments and burnt relics lie not in fear of worms, or to be an heritage for serpents. In carnal sepulture, corruptions seem peculiar unto parts; and some speak of snakes out of the spinal marrow. But while we suppose common worms in graves, 'tis not easy to find any there; few in churchyards above a foot deep, fewer or none in churches, though in fresh-decayed bodies. Teeth, bones, and hair give the most lasting defiance to corruption. In an hydropical body ten years buried in the churchyard, we met with a fat concretion, where the niter of the earth, and the salt and lixivious liquor of the body, had coagulated large lumps of fat into the consistence of the hardest Castile soap, whereof part remaineth with us. After a battle with the Persians, the Roman corpses decayed in a few days, while the Persian bodies remained dry and uncorrupted. Bodies in the same ground do not uniformly dissolve, nor bones equally molder; whereof in the opprobious disease we expect no long duration. The body of the Marquis of Dorset seemed sound and handsomely cereclothed, that after seventy-eight years was found uncorrupted.[20] Common tombs preserve not beyond powder: a firmer consistence and compage of parts might be expected from arefaction, deep burial, or charcoal. The greatest antiquities of mortal bodies may remain in petrified bones, whereof, though we take not in the pillar of Lot's wife, or metamorphosis of Ortelius,[21] some may be older than pyramids, in the petrified relics of the general inundation. When Alexander opened the tomb of Cyrus, the remaining bones discovered his proportion, whereof urnal fragments afford but a bad conjecture, and have this disadvantage of grave interments, that they leave us ignorant of most personal discoveries. For since bones afford not only rectitude and stability but figure unto the body, it is no impossible physiognomy to conjecture at fleshy appendencies, and after what shape the muscles and carnous parts might hang in their full consistencies. A full-spread *cariola* shows a well-shaped horse behind; handsome formed skulls give some analogy to fleshy resemblance. A critical view of bones makes a good distinction of sexes. Even color is not beyond conjecture, since it is hard to be deceived in the distinction of negroes' skulls. Dante's characters are to be found in skulls as well as faces. Hercules is not only known by his foot.

[20] The Marquis of Dorset was buried in 1530 and taken up in 1608. See Burton's *Description of Leicestershire*.
[21] In his map of Russia.

Other parts make out their comproportions and inferences upon whole or parts. And since the dimensions of the head measure the whole body, and the figure thereof gives conjecture of the principal faculties, physiognomy outlives ourselves and ends not in our graves.

Severe contemplators, observing these lasting relics, may think them good monuments of persons past, little advantage to future beings; and, considering that power which subdueth all things unto itself, that can resume the scattered atoms, or identify out of anything, conceive it superfluous to expect a resurrection out of relics: but the soul subsisting, other matter, clothed with due accidents, may salve the individuality. Yet the saints, we observe, arose from graves and monuments about the Holy City. Some think the ancient patriarchs so earnestly desired to lay their bones in Canaan, as hoping to make a part of that resurrection; and, though thirty miles from Mount Calvary, at least to lie in that region which should produce the first fruits of the dead. And if, according to learned conjecture, the bodies of men shall rise where the greatest relics remain, many are not like to err in the topography of their resurrection, though their bones or bodies be after translated by angels into the field of Ezekiel's vision,[22] or as some will order it, into the valley of judgment, or Jehosaphat.

CHAPTER IV

CHRISTIANS have handsomely glossed the deformity of death by careful consideration of the body and civil rites which take off brutal terminations: and though they conceived all reparable by a resurrection, cast not off all care of interment. And since the ashes of sacrifices burnt upon the altar of God were carefully carried out by the priests, and deposed in a clean field; since they acknowledged their bodies

[22] Ezek. 37:1–14.

to be the lodging of Christ, and temples of the Holy Ghost, they devolved not all upon the sufficiency of soul-existence; and therefore with long services and full solemnities, concluded their last exequies, wherein to all distinctions the Greek devotion seems most pathetically ceremonious.

Christian invention hath chiefly driven at rites, which speak hopes of another life and hints of a resurrection. And if the ancient Gentiles held not the immortality of their better part, and some subsistence after death, in several rites, customs, actions, and expressions, they contradicted their own opinions: wherein Democritus went high, even to the thought of a resurrection, as scoffingly recorded by Pliny. What can be more express than the expression of Phocylides? [23] Or who would expect from Lucretius a sentence of Ecclesiastes? [24] Before Plato could speak, the soul had wings in Homer, which fell not, but flew out of the body into the mansions of the dead; who also observed that handsome distinction of *Demas* and *Soma,* for the body conjoined to the soul, and body separated from it. Lucian spoke much truth in jest, when he said that part of Hercules which proceeded from Alcmena perished, that from Jupiter remained immortal. Thus Socrates was content that his friends should bury his body, so they would not think they buried Socrates; and, regarding only his immortal part, was indifferent to be burnt or buried. From such considerations, Diogenes might contemn sepulture, and, being satisfied that the soul could not perish, grow careless of corporal interment. The Stoics, who thought the souls of wise men had their habitation about the moon, might take slight account of subterraneous deposition; whereas the Pythagorean and transcorporating philosophers, who were to be often buried, held great care of their interment. And the Platonics rejected not a due care of the

[23] Phocylides (born *c.* 560 B.C.) was a Greek gnomic poet whose phrasing sometimes resembled passages in the Old Testament, especially in Ecclesiastes.

[24] Eccles. 12:7. "Then shall the dust return to the earth as it was." Lucretius: *Cedit enim retro de terra quod fuit ante in terram.*

grave, though they put their ashes to unreasonable expectations, in their tedious term of return and long set revolution.

Men have lost their reason in nothing so much as their religion, wherein stones and clouts make martyrs; and, since the religion of one seems madness unto another, to afford an account or rational of old rites requires no rigid reader. That they kindled the pyre aversely, or turning their face from it, was an handsome symbol of unwilling ministration. That they washed their bones with wine and milk; that the mother wrapped them in linen and dried them in her bosom, the first fostering part and place of their nourishment; that they opened their eyes towards heaven before they kindled the fire, as the place of their hopes or original, were no improper ceremonies. Their last valediction, thrice uttered by the attendants,[25] was also very solemn, and somewhat answered by Christians, who thought it too little if they threw not the earth thrice upon the interred body. That, in strewing their tombs, the Romans affected the rose; the Greeks amaranthus and myrtle: that the funeral pyre consisted of sweet fuel, cypress, fir, larix, yew, and trees perpetually verdant, lay silent expressions of their surviving hopes. Wherein Christians, who deck their coffins with bays, have found a more elegant emblem; for that it, seeming dead, will restore itself from the root, and its dry and exsuccous leaves resume their verdure again; which, if we mistake not, we have also observed in furze. Whether the planting of yew in churchyards hold not its original from ancient funeral rites, or as an emblem of resurrection from its perpetual verdure, may also admit conjecture.

They made use of music to excite or quiet the affections of their friends, according to different harmonies. But the secret and symbolical hint was the harmonical nature of the soul; which, delivered from the body, went again to enjoy the primitive harmony of heaven, from whence it first descended;

[25] *Vale, vale, vale nos te ordine quo natura permittet sequamur.*

which, according to its progress traced by antiquity, came down by Cancer, and ascended by Capricornus.

They burnt not children before their teeth appeared, as apprehending their bodies too tender a morsel for fire, and that their gristly bones would scarce leave separable relics after the pyral combustion. That they kindled not fire in their houses for some days after was a strict memorial of the late afflicting fire. And mourning without hope, they had an happy fraud against excessive lamentation, by a common opinion that deep sorrows disturb their ghosts.

That they buried their dead on their backs, or in a supine position, seems agreeable unto profound sleep, and common posture of dying; contrary to the most natural way of birth; nor unlike our pendulous posture, in the doubtful state of the womb. Diogenes was singular, who preferred a prone situation in the grave; and some Christians like neither, who decline the figure of rest, and make choice of an erect posture.

That they carried them out of the world with their feet forward, not inconsonant unto reason, as contrary unto the native posture of man, and his production first into it; and also agreeable unto their opinions, while they bid adieu unto the world, not to look again upon it; whereas Mahometans, who think to return to a delightful life again, are carried forth with their heads forward, and looking toward their houses.

They closed their eyes, as parts which first die or first discover the sad effects of death. But their iterated clamations to excitate their dying or dead friends, or revoke them unto life again, was a vanity of affection; as not presumably ignorant of the critical tests of death, by apposition of feather, glasses, and reflection of figures, which dead eyes represent not: which, however not strictly verifiable in fresh and warm cadavers, could hardly elude the test in corpses of four or five days.

That they sucked in the last breath of their expiring friends was surely a practice of no medical institution, but a loose opinion that the soul passed out that way, and a fondness of affection, from some Pythagorical foundation, that the spirit of one body passed into another, which they wished might be their own.

That they poured oil upon the pyre was a tolerable practice, while the intention rested in facilitating the ascension. But to place good omens in the quick and speedy burning, to sacrifice unto the winds for a dispatch in this office, was a low form of superstition.

The archimime, or jester, attending the funeral train and imitating the speeches, gesture, and manners of the deceased, was too light for such solemnities, contradicting their funeral orations and doleful rites of the grave.

That they buried a piece of money with them as a fee of the Elysian ferryman, was a practice full of folly. But the ancient custom of placing coins in considerable urns, and the present practice of burying medals in the noble foundations of Europe, are laudable ways of historical discoveries, in actions, persons, chronologies; and posterity will applaud them.

We examine not the old laws of sepulture, exempting certain persons from burial or burning. But hereby we apprehend that these were not the bones of persons planet-struck or burnt with fire from heaven; no relics of traitors to their country, self-killers, or sacrilegious malefactors; persons in old apprehension unworthy of the earth; condemned unto the Tartarus of hell, and bottomless pit of Pluto, from whence there was no redemption.

Nor were only many customs questionable in order to their obsequies, but also sundry practices, fictions, and conceptions, discordant or obscure, of their state and future beings. Whether unto eight or ten bodies of men to add one of a woman, as being more inflammable, and unctuously constituted for the better pyral combustion, were any rational practice; or whether the complaint of Periander's wife be tolerable, that wanting her funeral burning, she suffered intolerable cold in hell, according to the constitution of the infernal house of Pluto, wherein cold makes a great part of their tortures, it cannot pass without some question.

Why the female ghosts appear unto Ulysses, before the heroes and masculine spirits; why the Psyche or soul of Tiresias is of the masculine gender, who, being blind on earth, sees more than all the rest in hell; why the funeral suppers consisted of eggs, beans, smallage, and lettuce, since the dead are made to eat asphodels about the Elysian meadows; why, since there is no sacrifice acceptable, nor any propitiation for the covenant of the grave, men set up the deity of Morta, and fruitlessly adored divinities without ears, it cannot escape some doubt.

The dead seem all alive in the human Hades of Homer, yet cannot well speak, prophesy, or know the living, except they drink blood, wherein is the life of man. And therefore the souls of Penelope's paramours, conducted by Mercury, chirped like bats, and those which followed Hercules made a noise but like a flock of birds.

The departed spirits know things past and to come; yet are ignorant of things present. Agamemnon foretells what should happen unto Ulysses; yet ignorantly inquires what is become of his own son. The ghosts are afraid of swords in Homer; yet Sibylla tells Æneas in Virgil the thin habit of spirits was beyond the force of weapons. The spirits put off their malice with their bodies, and Cæsar and Pompey accord in Latin hell; yet Ajax, in Homer, endures not a conference with Ulysses: and Deiphobus appears all mangled in Virgil's ghosts, yet we meet with perfect shadows among the wounded ghosts of Homer.

Since Charon in Lucian applauds his condition among the dead, whether it be handsomely said of Achilles, that living contemner of death, that he had rather be a plowman's servant than emperor of the dead? How Hercules his soul is in hell, and yet in heaven; and Julius his soul in a star, yet seen by Æneas in hell? except the ghosts were but images and shadows of the soul, received in higher mansions, according to the ancient division of body, soul, and image, or *simulacrum* of them both. The particulars of future beings must needs be dark unto ancient theories, which Christian philosophy yet determines but in a cloud of opinions. A dialogue between two infants in the womb concerning the state of this world might handsomely illustrate our ignorance of the next, whereof methinks we yet discourse in Plato's den, and are but embryon philosophers.

Pythagoras escapes in the fabulous hell of Dante, among that swarm of philosophers, wherein whilst we meet with Plato and Socrates, Cato is to be found in no lower place than purgatory. Among all the set, Epicurus is most considerable, whom men make honest without an Elysium, who contemned life without encouragement of immortality, and making nothing after death, yet made nothing of the king of terrors.

Were the happiness of the next world as closely apprehended as the felicities of this, it were a martyrdom to live; and unto such as consider none hereafter, it must be more than death to die, which makes us amazed at those audacities that durst be nothing and return into their chaos again. Certainly such spirits as could contemn death, when they expected no better being after, would have scorned to live, had they known any. And therefore we applaud not the judgment of Machiavel, that Christianity makes men cowards, or that with the confidence of but half-dying, the despised virtues of patience and humility have abased the spirits of men, which Pagan principles exalted; but rather regulated the wildness of audacities, in the attempts, grounds, and eternal sequels of death; wherein men of the boldest spirits are often prodigiously temerarious. Nor can we extenuate the valor of ancient martyrs, who contemned death in the uncomfortable scene of their lives, and in their decrepit martyrdoms did probably lose not many months of their days, or parted with life when it was scarce worth the living. For (besides that long time past holds no consideration unto a slender time to come) they had no small disadvantage from the constitution of old age, which naturally makes men fearful; complexionally superannuated from the bold and courageous thoughts of youth and fervent years. But the contempt of death from corporal animosity promoteth not our felicity. They may sit in the orchestra, and noblest seats of heaven, who have held up shaking hands in the fire, and humanly contended for glory.

Meanwhile Epicurus lies deep in Dante's hell, wherein we meet with tombs enclosing souls which denied their immortalities. But whether the virtuous heathen, who lived better than he spake, or erring in the principles of himself, yet lived above philosophers of more specious maxims, lie so deep as he is placed, at least so low as not to rise against Christians, who believing or knowing that truth, have lastingly denied it in their practice and conversation, were a query too sad to insist on.

But all or most apprehensions rested in opinions of some future being, which, ignorantly or coldly believed, begat those perverted conceptions, ceremonies, sayings, which Christians pity or laugh at. Happy are they which live not in that disadvantage of time, when men could say little for futurity, but from reason: whereby the noblest minds fell often upon doubtful deaths, and melancholic dissolutions. With these hopes, Socrates warmed his doubtful spirits against that cold potion; and Cato, before he durst give the fatal stroke, spent part of the night in reading the Immortality of Plato, thereby confirming his wavering hand unto the animosity of that attempt.

It is the heaviest stone that melancholy can throw at a man to tell him he is at the end of his nature; or that there is no further state to come, unto which this seems progressional, and otherwise made in vain. Without this accomplishment, the natural expectation and desire of such a state were but a fallacy in nature; unsatisfied considerators would quarrel the justice of their constitutions, and rest content that

Adam had fallen lower; whereby, by knowing no other original, and deeper ignorance of themselves, they might have enjoyed the happiness of inferior creatures, who in tranquillity possess their constitutions, as having not the apprehension to deplore their own natures; and, being framed below the circumference of these hopes, or cognition of better being, the wisdom of God hath necessitated their contentment: but the superior ingredient and obscured part of ourselves, whereto all present felicities afford no resting contentment, will be able at last to tell us, we are more than our present selves, and evacuate such hopes in the fruition of their own accomplishments.

CHAPTER V

Now SINCE these dead bones have already outlasted the living ones of Methuselah, and in a yard underground, and thin walls of clay, outworn all the strong and specious buildings above it, and quietly rested under the drums and tramplings of three conquests; what prince can promise such diuturnity unto his relics, or might not gladly say,

Sic ego componi versus in ossa velim? [26]

Time, which antiquates antiquities, and hath an art to make dust of all things, hath yet spared these minor monuments.

In vain we hope to be known by open and visible conservatories, when to be unknown was the means of their continuation, and obscurity their protection. If they died by violent hands, and were thrust into their urns, these bones become considerable, and some old philosophers would honor them, whose souls they conceived most pure, which were thus snatched from their bodies, and to retain a stronger propension unto them; whereas they weariedly left a languishing

[26] "Thus when I am turned to bones, I should wish to be laid to rest." (Tibullus)

corpse, and with faint desires of reunion. If they fell by long
and aged decay, yet wrapped up in the bundle of time, they
fall into indistinction, and make but one blot with infants.
If we begin to die when we live, and long life be but a prolongation of death, our life is a sad composition; we live
with death, and die not in a moment. How many pulses made
up the life of Methuselah, were work for Archimedes: common counters sum up the life of Moses his man. Our days
become considerable, like petty sums, by minute accumula-
tions; where numerous fractions make up but small round
numbers; and our days of a span long make not one little
finger.[27]

If the nearness of our last necessity brought a nearer conformity unto it, there were a happiness in hoary hairs, and
no calamity in half-senses. But the long habit of living in-
disposeth us for dying; when avarice makes us the sport of
death, when even David grew politically cruel, and Solomon
could hardly be said to be the wisest of men. But many are
too early old, and before the date of age. Adversity stretch-
eth our days, misery makes Alcmena's nights,[28] and time
hath no wings unto it. But the most tedious being is that
which can unwish itself, content to be nothing, or never to
have been, which was beyond the malcontent of Job, who
cursed not the day of his life, but his nativity: content to
have so far been as to have a title to future being; although
he had lived here but in an hidden state of life, and as it
were an abortion.

What song the Sirens sang, or what name Achilles assumed
when he hid himself among women, though puzzling questions, are not beyond all conjecture. What time the persons
of these ossuaries entered the famous nations of the dead,
and slept with princes and counselors, might admit a wide
solution. But who were the proprietaries of these bones, or

[27] According to the ancient arithmetic of the hand wherein the little
finger of the right hand contracted signified an hundred. (Pierius in
Hieroglyph)
[28] One night as long as three.

what bodies these ashes made up, were a question above antiquarism; not to be resolved by man, nor easily perhaps by spirits, except we consult the provincial guardians, or tutelary observators. Had they made as good provision for their names as they have done for their relics, they had not so grossly erred in the art of perpetuation. But to subsist in bones, and be but pyramidally extant, is a fallacy in duration. Vain ashes, which in the oblivion of names, persons, times, and sexes, have found unto themselves a fruitless continuation, and only arise unto late posterity, as emblems of mortal vanities, antidotes against pride, vainglory, and madding vices. Pagan vainglories, which thought the world might last for ever, had encouragement for ambition; and, finding no Atropos unto the immortality of their names, were never damped with the necessity of oblivion. Even old ambitions had the advantage of ours, in the attempts of their vainglories, who, acting early and before the probable meridian of time, have by this time found great accomplishment of their designs, whereby the ancient heroes have already outlasted their monuments and mechanical preservations. But in this latter scene of time, we cannot expect such mummies unto our memories, when ambition may fear the prophecy of Elias,[29] and Charles the Fifth can never hope to live within two Methuselahs of Hector.

And therefore, restless inquietude for the diuturnity of our memories unto present considerations seems a vanity almost out of date, and superannuated piece of folly. We cannot hope to live so long in our names as some have done in their persons; one face of Janus holds no proportion unto the other. 'Tis too late to be ambitious. The great mutations of the world are acted, or time may be too short for our designs. To extend our memories by monuments, whose death we daily pray for, and whose duration we cannot hope, without injury to our expectations in the advent of the last day, were a contradiction to our beliefs. We whose generations

[29] That the world may last but six thousand years.

are ordained in this setting part of time are providentially taken off from such imaginations; and, being necessitated to eye the remaining particle of futurity, are naturally constituted unto thoughts of the next world, and cannot excusably decline the consideration of that duration, which maketh pyramids pillars of snow, and all that's past a moment.

Circles and right lines limit and close all bodies, and the mortal right-lined circle must conclude and shut up all. There is no antidote against the opium of time, which temporally considereth all things: our fathers find their graves in our short memories, and sadly tell us how we may be buried in our survivors. Gravestones tell truth scarce forty years. Generations pass while some trees stand, and old families last not three oaks. To be read by bare inscriptions like many in Gruter,[30] to hope for eternity by enigmatical epithets or first letters of our names, to be studied by antiquaries, who we were, and have new names given us like many of the mummies, are cold consolations unto the students of perpetuity, even by everlasting languages.

To be content that times to come should only know there was such a man, not caring whether they knew more of him, was a frigid ambition in Cardan; disparaging his horoscopal inclination and judgment of himself. Who cares to subsist like Hippocrates' patients, or Achilles' horses in Homer, under naked nominations, without deserts and noble acts, which are the balsam of our memories, the *entelechia* and soul of our subsistencies? To be nameless in worthy deeds exceeds an infamous history. The Canaanitish woman lives more happily without a name than Herodias with one. And who had not rather have been the good thief than Pilate?

But the iniquity of oblivion blindly scattereth her poppy, and deals with the memory of men without distinction to merit of perpetuity. Who can but pity the founder of the pyramids? Herostratus lives that burnt the temple of Diana; he is almost lost that built it. Time hath spared the epitaph

---

[30] Gruteri, *Inscriptiones Antiquæ.*

of Adrian's horse, confounded that of himself. In vain we
compute our felicities by the advantage of our good names,
since bad have equal durations, and Thersites is like to live
as long as Agamemnon. Who knows whether the best of
men be known, or whether there be not more remarkable
persons forgot than any that stand remembered in the known
account of time? [Without the favor of the everlasting register,] the first man had been as unknown as the last, and
Methuselah's long life had been his only chronicle.

Oblivion is not to be hired: the greater part must be content to be as though they had not been, to be found in the
register of God, not in the record of man. Twenty-seven
names make up the first story,[31] and the recorded names
ever since contain not one living century. The number of
the dead long exceedeth all that shall live. The night of time
far surpasseth the day, and who knows when was the equinox?
Every hour adds unto that current arithmetic, which scarce
stands one moment. And since death must be the *Lucina* of
life, and even Pagans could doubt whether thus to live were
to die; since our longest sun sets at right descensions, and
makes but winter arches, and therefore it cannot be long
before we lie down in darkness, and have our light in ashes;[32]
since the brother of death daily haunts us with dying mementos, and time that grows old in itself bids us hope no long
duration; diuturnity is a dream and folly of expectation.

Darkness and light divide the course of time, and oblivion
shares with memory a great part even of our living beings;
we slightly remember our felicities, and the smartest strokes
of affliction leave but short smart upon us. Sense endureth
no extremities, and sorrows destroy us or themselves. To
weep into stones are fables. Afflictions induce callosities;
miseries are slippery, or fall like snow upon us, which notwithstanding is no unhappy stupidity. To be ignorant of

[31] That is, before the flood.
[32] According to the custom of the Jews, who place a lighted wax candle
in a pot of ashes by the corpse. (Leo)

evils to come, and forgetful of evils past, is merciful provision in nature, whereby we digest the mixture of our few
and evil days, and, our delivered senses not relapsing into
cutting remembrances, our sorrows are not kept raw by
the edge of repetitions. A great part of antiquity contented
their hopes of subsistency with a transmigration of their
souls: a good way to continue memories, while having the
advantage of plural successions, they could not but act something remarkable in such variety of beings, and enjoying
the fame of their passed selves, make accumulation of glory
unto their last durations. Others, rather than be lost in the
uncomfortable night of nothing, were content to recede
into the common being, and make one particle of the public
soul of all things, which was no more than to return into
their unknown and divine original again. Egyptian ingenuity
was more unsatisfied, contriving their bodies in sweet consistencies, to attend the return of their souls. But all was
vanity, feeding the wind, and folly. The Egyptian mummies,
which Cambyses or time hath spared, avarice now consumeth.
Mummy is become merchandise, Mizraim cures wounds,
and Pharaoh is sold for balsams.

In vain do individuals hope for immortality, or any patent
from oblivion, in preservations below the moon; men have
been deceived even in their flatteries above the sun, and
studied conceits to perpetuate their names in heaven. The
various cosmography of that part hath already varied the
names of contrived constellations: Nimrod is lost in Orion,
and Osiris in the Dog Star. While we look for incorruption
in the heavens, we find they are but like the earth, durable
in their main bodies, alterable in their parts: whereof beside comets and new stars, perspectives begin to tell tales,
and the spots that wander about the sun, with Phæton's favor,
would make clear conviction.

There is nothing strictly immortal but immortality. Whatever hath no beginning may be confident of no end; all others
have a dependent being and within the reach of destruction;

which is the peculiar of that necessary essence that cannot destroy itself; and the highest strain of omnipotency, to be so powerfully constituted as not to suffer even from the power of itself. But the sufficiency of Christian immortality frustrates all earthly glory, and the quality of either state after death makes a folly of posthumous memory. God, who can only destroy our souls, and hath assured our resurrection, either of our bodies or names hath directly promised no duration. Wherein there is so much of chance that the boldest expectants have found unhappy frustration; and to hold long subsistence seems but a scape in oblivion. But man is a noble animal, splendid in ashes, and pompous in the grave, solemnizing nativities and deaths with equal luster, nor omitting ceremonies of bravery in the infamy of his nature.

Life is a pure flame, and we live by an invisible sun within us. A small fire sufficeth for life, great flames seemed too little after death, while men vainly affected precious pyres, and to burn like Sardanapalus; but the wisdom of funeral laws found the folly of prodigal blazes, and reduced undoing fires unto the rule of sober obsequies, wherein few could be so mean as not to provide wood, pitch, a mourner, and an urn.

Five languages secured not the epitaph of Gordianus. The man of God lives longer without a tomb than any by one, invisibly interred by angels, and adjudged to obscurity, though not without some marks directing human discovery. Enoch and Elias, without either tomb or burial, in an anomalous state of being, are the great examples of perpetuity, in their long and living memory, in strict account being still on this side death, and having a late part yet to act upon this stage of earth. If in the decretory term of the world we shall not all die but be changed, according to received translation, the last day will make but few graves; at least quick resurrections will anticipate lasting sepultures; some graves will be opened before they be quite closed, and Lazarus be no wonder. When many that feared to die shall groan that they can die but once, the dismal state is the second and living death, when life puts despair on the damned; when men shall wish the coverings of mountains, not of monuments, and annihilations shall be courted.

While some have studied monuments, others have studiously declined them; and some have been so vainly boisterous that they durst not acknowledge their graves, wherein Alaricus [33] seems most subtle, who had a river turned to hide his bones at the bottom. Even Sylla, that thought himself safe in his urn, could not prevent revenging tongues, and stones thrown at his monument. Happy are they whom privacy makes innocent, who deal so with men in this world that they are not afraid to meet them in the next; who, when they die, make no commotion among the dead, and are not touched with that poetical taunt of Isaiah.[34]

Pyramids, arches, obelisks were but the irregularities of vainglory, and wild enormities of ancient magnanimity. But the most magnanimous resolution rests in the Christian religion, which trampleth upon pride, and sits on the neck of ambition, humbly pursuing that infallible perpetuity unto which all others must diminish their diameters, and be poorly seen in angles of contingency.

Pious spirits who passed their days in raptures of futurity made little more of this world than the world that was before it, while they lay obscure in the chaos of pre-ordination, and night of their fore-beings. And if any have been so happy as truly to understand Christian annihilation, ecstasies, exolution, liquefaction, transformation, the kiss of the spouse, gustation of God, and ingression into the divine shadow, they have already had an handsome anticipation of heaven; the glory of the world is surely over, and the earth in ashes unto them.

To subsist in lasting monuments, to live in their produc-

[33] Alaric, Gothic conqueror (c. 370–410). The river Busento was temporarily turned aside while the interment was made in the river bed.
[34] Isa. 14:16.

tions, to exist in their names and predicament of chimeras, was large satisfaction unto old expectations, and made one part of their Elysiums. But all this is nothing in the metaphysics of true belief. To live indeed is to be again ourselves, which being not only an hope but an evidence in noble believers, 'tis all one to lie in St. Innocent's churchyard,[35] as in the sands of Egypt: ready to be anything, in the ecstasy of being ever, and as content with six foot as the *moles* of Adrianus.[36]

> —*Tabesne cadavera solvat,*
> *An rogus, haud refert.*
> Lucan [*Phars.* vii. 809.]

---

[35] In Paris where bodies soon consume.
[36] A stately Mausoleum or sepulchral pyle built by Adrianus in Rome, where now standeth the Castle of St. Angelo.

From THE GARDEN OF CYRUS,

OR THE QUINCUNX MYSTICALLY CONSIDERED [1]

CHAPTER V

To ENLARGE this contemplation unto all the mysteries and secrets accommodable unto this number were inexcusable Pythagorism, yet cannot omit the ancient conceit of five surnamed the number of justice; [2] as justly dividing between the digits and hanging in the center of nine, described by square numeration, which angularly divided will make the decussated number; and so agreeable unto the quincuncial ordination and rows divided by equality and just decorum in the whole com-plantation; and might be the original of that common game among us, wherein the fifth place is sovereign and carrieth the chief intention. The ancients wisely instructing youth, even in their recreations unto virtue, that is, early to drive at the middle point and central seat of justice.

Nor can we omit how agreeable unto this number an handsome division is made in trees and plants, since Plutarch and the ancients have named it the divisive number, justly dividing the entities of the world, many remarkable things in it, and also comprehending the general division of vegetables.[3] And he that considers how most blossoms of trees and greatest number of flowers consist of five leaves; and therein doth rest the settled rule of nature, so that in those which exceed there is often found, or easily made, a variety; may readily discover how nature rests in this number, which is indeed the first rest and pause of numeration in the fingers,

---

[1] Text: 1658, first edition.

[2] δίκη.

[3] Δένδρον, θάμνος, θρύγανον, πόα, *Arbor, frutex, suffrutex, herba,* and that fifth which comprehendeth the *fungi* and *tubera,* whether to be named Ἄσχιον or γύμνον, comprehending also *conferva marina salsa,* and sea-cords of so many yards' length.

the natural organs thereof. Nor in the division of the feet of perfect animals doth nature exceed this account. And even in the joints of feet, which in birds are most multiplied, surpasseth not this number; so progressionally making them out in many, that from five in the fore-claw she descendeth unto two in the hindemost; and so in four feet makes up the number of joints in the five fingers or toes of man.

Not to omit the quintuple section of a cone,[4] of handsome practice in ornamental garden plots, and in some way discoverable in so many works of nature: in the leaves, fruits, and seeds of vegetables, and scales of some fishes, so much considerable in glasses and the optic doctrine, wherein the learned may consider the crystalline humor of the eye in the cuttlefish and *loligo*.

He that forgets not how antiquity named this the conjugal or wedding number and made it the emblem of the most remarkable conjunction, will conceive it duly appliable unto this handsome economy, and vegetable combination; may hence apprehend the allegorical sense of that obscure expression of Hesiod,[5] and afford no improbable reason why Plato admitted his nuptial guests by fives, in the kindred of the married couple.[6]

And though a sharper mystery might be implied in the number of the five wise and foolish virgins which were to meet the Bridegroom, yet was the same agreeable unto the conjugal number, which ancient numerists made out by two and three, the first parity and imparity, the active and passive digits, the material and formal principles in generative societies. And not discordant even from the customs of the Romans, who admitted but five torches in their nuptial solemnities.[7] Whether there were any mystery or not implied, the most generative animals were created on this day, and had accordingly the largest benediction; and under

[4] *Elleipsis, parabola, hyperbola, circulus, triangulum.*
[5] πέμητας, *id est nuptias multas.* (Rhodig.)
[6] Plato, *De Leg.* 6.
[7] Plutarch, *Problem. Rom.* I.

a quintuple consideration wanton antiquity considered the circumstances of generation, while by this number of five they naturally divided the nectar of the fifth planet.

The same number in the Hebrew mysteries and cabalistical accounts was the character of generation,[8] declared by the letter *He,* the fifth in their alphabet; according to that cabalistical dogma, if Abram had not had this letter added unto his name, he had remained fruitless and without the power of generation: not only because hereby the number of his name attained two hundred forty-eight, the number of the affirmative precepts, but because as in created natures there is male and female, so in divine and intelligent productions, the mother of life and fountain of souls in cabalistical technology is called *Binah,* whose seal and character was *He.* So that being sterile before, he received the power of generation from that measure and mansion in the archetype, and was made conformable unto *Binah.* And upon such involved considerations, the ten[9] of Sarai was exchanged into five. If any shall look upon this as a stable number and fitly appropriable unto trees, as bodies of rest and station, he hath herein a great foundation in nature, who observing much variety in legs and motive organs of animals as two, four, six, eight, ten, twelve, fourteen, and more, hath passed over five and ten and assigned them unto none (or very few, as the *phalangium monstrosum Brasilianum, Clusii et Jac. de Laet. Cur. Poster. Americæ Descript.*), if perfectly described. And for the stability of this number, he shall not want the sphericity of its nature, which multiplied in itself will return into its own denomination and bring up the rear of the account. Which is also one of the numbers that make up the mystical name of God, which consisting of letters denoting the spherical numbers, ten, five, and six, emphatically sets forth the notion of Trismegistus, and that intelligible sphere which is the nature of God.[10]

---

[8] *Archang. Dog. Cabal.*   [9] *Jod* into *He.*
[10] Hermes Trismegistus, a mythical philosopher of Egypt.

Many expressions by this number occur in Holy Scripture, perhaps unjustly laden with mystical expositions and little concerning our order. That the Israelites were forbidden to eat the fruit of their new-planted trees before the fifth year was very agreeable unto the natural rules of husbandry: fruits being unwholesome and lash before the fourth or fifth year. In the second day or feminine part of five, there was added no approbation. For in the third or masculine day the same is twice repeated; and a double benediction enclosed both creations, whereof the one, in some part, was but an accomplishment of the other. That the trespasser was to pay a fifth part above the head or principal [11] makes no secret in this number, and implied no more than one part above the principal; which being considered in four parts, the additional forfeit must bear the name of a fifth. The five golden mice had plainly their determination from the number of princes: that five should put to flight an hundred might have nothing mystically implied, considering a rank of soldiers could scarce consist of a lesser number. Saint Paul had rather speak five words in a known, than ten thousand in an unknown tongue: that is as little as could well be spoken. A simple proposition consisting of three words and a complexed one not ordinarily short of five.

More considerable there are in this mystical account which we must not insist on. And therefore why the radical letters in the Pentateuch should equal the number of the soldiery of the tribes; why our Saviour in the wilderness fed five thousand persons with the five barley loaves, and again but four thousand with no less than seven of wheat? Why Joseph designed five changes of raiment unto Benjamin? and David took just five pebbles out of the brook against the pagan champion? We leave it unto arithmetical [12] divinity and theological explanation.

Yet if any delight in new problems, or think it worth the

---

[11] Lev. 6.

[12] τέσσαρα ἕν κε, four and one, or five. (Scalig.)

inquiry, whether the critical physician hath rightly hit the nominal notation of *quinque:* why the ancients mixed five or three, but not four parts of water unto their wine; and Hippocrates observed a fifth proportion in the mixture of water with milk, as in dysenteries and bloody fluxes. Under what abstruse foundation astrologers do figure the good or bad fate from our children in a good fortune, or the fifth house of their celestial schemes.[13] Whether the Egyptians described a star by a figure of five points with reference unto the five capital aspects,[14] whereby they transmit their influences, or abstruser considerations. Why the cabalistical doctors, who conceive the whole *sephiroth* or divine emanations to have guided the ten-stringed harp of David, whereby he pacified the evil spirit of Saul, in strict numeration do begin with the *perihypate meson,* or *si fa ut,* and so place the *tiphereth* answering C *sol fa ut,* upon the fifth string: or whether this number be oftener applied unto bad things and ends than good in Holy Scripture, and why? He may meet with abstrusities of no ready resolution.

If any shall question the rationality of that magic in the cure of the blind man by Serapis, commanded to place five fingers on his altar and then his hand on his eyes? Why since the whole comedy is primarily and naturally comprised in four parts,[15] and antiquity permitted not so many persons to speak in one scene, yet would not comprehend the same in more or less than five acts? Why amongst the sea-stars nature chiefly delighteth in five points? And since there are found some of no fewer than twelve, and some of seven and nine, there are few or none discovered of six or eight? If any shall inquire why the flowers of rue properly consist of four leaves, the first and third flower have five? Why since many flowers have one leaf or none,[16] as Scaliger will have it, divers three, and the greatest number consist of five di-

---

[13] Ἀγαθὴ τύχη, or *bona fortuna,* the name of the fifth house.
[14] Conjunct, opposite, sextile, trigonal, tetragonal.
[15] πρότασις, ἐπίτασις, κατάστασις, καταστροφή.
[16] *Unifolium, nullifolium.*

vided from their bottoms; there are yet so few of two: or why nature generally beginning or setting out with two opposite leaves at the root, doth so seldom conclude with that order and number at the flower? he shall not pass his hours in vulgar speculation.

If any shall further query why magnetical philosophy excludeth decussations, and needles transversely placed do naturally distract their verticities? Why geomancers do imitate the quintuple figure in their mother characters of acquisition and amission, etc., somewhat answering the figures in the lady or speckled beetle? With what equity chiromantical conjectures decry these decussations in the lines and mounts of the hand? What that decussated figure in the medal of Alexander the Great? Why the goddesses sit commonly cross-legged in ancient draughts, since Juno is described in the same as a venefical posture to hinder the birth of Hercules? If any shall doubt why at the Amphidromical feasts, on the fifth day after the child was born, presents were sent from friends, of polypuses and cuttlefishes? Why five must be only left in that symbolical mutiny among the men of Cadmus? Why Proteus in Homer, the symbol of the first matter, before he settled himself in the midst of his sea monsters, doth place them out by fives? Why the fifth year's ox was acceptable sacrifice unto Jupiter? Or why the noble Antoninus in some sense doth call the soul itself a rhombus? He shall not fall on trite or trivial disquisitions. And these we invent and propose unto acuter inquirers, nauseating crambe verities, and questions over-queried. Flat and flexible truths are beat out by every hammer, but Vulcan and his whole forge sweat to work out Achilles his armor. A large field is yet left unto sharper discerners to enlarge upon this order, to search out the *quaternios* and figured draughts of this nature, and moderating the study of names and mere nomenclature of plants, to erect generalities, disclose unobserved proprieties, not only in the vegetable shop, but the whole volume of nature; affording delightful truths, confirmable by sense and ocular observation, which seems to me the surest path to trace the labyrinth of truth. For though discursive inquiry and rational conjecture may leave handsome gashes and flesh wounds, yet without conjunction of this expect no mortal or dispatching blows unto error.

But the quincunx of heaven [17] runs low, and 'tis time to close the five ports of knowledge; we are unwilling to spin out our awaking thoughts into the phantasms of sleep, which often continueth precogitations, making cables of cobwebs and wildernesses of handsome groves. Besides Hippocrates [18] hath spoke so little and the oneirocritical masters [19] have left such frigid interpretations from plants that there is little encouragement to dream of paradise itself. Nor will the sweetest delight of gardens afford much comfort in sleep; wherein the dullness of that sense shakes hands with delectable odors, and though in the bed of Cleopatra,[20] can hardly with any delight raise up the ghost of a rose.

Night, which pagan theology could make the daughter of Chaos, affords no advantage to the description of order: although no lower than that mass can we derive its genealogy. All things began in order, so shall they end, and so shall they begin again; according to the ordainer of order and mystical mathematics of the city of heaven.

Though Somnus in Homer be sent to rouse up Agamemnon, I find no such effects in these drowsy approaches of sleep. To keep our eyes open longer were but to act our antipodes.[21] The huntsmen are up in America, and they are

[17] *Hyades*, near the horizon about midnight at that time.
[18] *De Insomniis.*
[19] Artemidorus and Apomazar.   [20] Strewed with roses.
[21] Of this passage Coleridge says, "Think you, my dear friend, that there ever was such a reason given before for going to bed at midnight;—to wit, that if we did not, we should be acting the part of our Antipodes! And then 'the huntsmen are up in America.'—What life, what fancy! Does the whimsical knight give us thus a dish of strong green tea and call it an opiate?" From a letter to Sarah Hutchinson sent with the book as a gift.— T. M. Raysor, *Coleridge's Miscellaneous Criticism*, p. 272.

already past their first sleep in Persia. But who can be drowsy at that hour which freed us from everlasting sleep? Or have slumbering thoughts at that time when sleep itself must end, and as some conjecture all shall awake again?

FULLER was born the same year as Milton and was also a Cambridge University man, though in residence at Queens' College until after he took his M.A. After that he was appointed a Fellow-commoner at Sidney-Sussex. In spite of the fact that this college was strongly Puritan, Fuller continued a moderate Royalist. Perhaps his knowledge of the Puritans, gained through this close association, increased his spirit of toleration which became increasingly evident throughout his life.

When there was a vacancy at St. Benet's church, Cambridge, Fuller was appointed by Corpus Christi College to the perpetual curacy of this church, and the following year (1631) his uncle, bishop of Salisbury, secured for him a prebendary in the Salisbury diocese. Although Fuller speaks of seventeen years in Cambridge, we know that in 1635 he held a position in the diocese of Bristol at Broadwandsor. He was not "formally sequestered," but he gave up this position, and settled in London, preaching at the Inns of Court and acting as curate of the Savoy. In London, partisanship ran high, and Fuller's moderation was not pleasing to either side. He therefore took refuge at Lincoln's College, Oxford, sustaining a great loss by his flight. The seventeen weeks spent at Oxford are often compared with the seventeen years at Cambridge.

Becoming more active among the Royalists, Fuller served as chaplain for one of the generals, Ralph Hopton. Finally, however, he was appointed by the king as chaplain to the infant Princess Henrietta and settled down quietly at Exeter, busying himself with his writing. When Exeter surrendered to Halifax, he returned to London, where he preached in various churches until he was prohibited. He was fortunate in holding several chaplaincies: first to the second Earl of Carlisle, who presented him with the curacy of Waltham

Abbey, and next to the first Earl of Berkeley, who secured for him the appointment to Cranford, near Hounslow. After the Restoration he was made chaplain to the king and resumed his lectures at the Savoy and also his former prebendary in the Salisbury diocese. During a visit to Salisbury the year following the Restoration he contracted a fever which was probably typhus fever, and returning to London, died of it.

History was Fuller's "velvet study," and even though he said that during the Civil War he "could not *live to study,* who did only *study to live,*" [1] he seems constantly to have collected materials for his works. In 1656 he published his enormous *Church History of Britain,* commenting that he had "written a book to Eternity." His other major work, *The History of the Worthies of England,* for which he had traveled all over England collecting data, was left unfinished, even though in his last illness he often called for his pen, ink, and books. This was later edited and published by the son of his first marriage. John had enjoyed the unusual privilege of seeing his father made doctor of divinity at Cambridge by royal command the same year he himself received his A.B. at Sidney-Sussex, and it is fitting that he was able to complete the work.

Fuller's works live not only because of the nature of his undertakings and his enormous research but also because of the humanity of the man and the charm of his style. His theory that "an ounce of mirth with the same degree of grace will serve God farther than a pound of sadness" [2] attracted a wide range of friends among his contemporaries and has continued to make him beloved in later centuries.

[1] *Appeal to Injured Innocence,* 1840, p. 317.
[2] *Worthies,* 1840, II, 55. Cf. II, 583.

THE HOLY STATE [1]

Of Memory

IT IS the treasure house of the mind, wherein the monuments thereof are kept and preserved. Plato makes it the mother of the Muses. Aristotle sets it one degree further, making experience the mother of arts, memory the parent of experience. Philosophers place it in the rear of the head; and it seems the mine of memory lies there, because there naturally men dig for it, scratching it when they are at a loss. This again is twofold: one, the simple retention of things; the other, a regaining them when forgotten.

1. *Brute creatures equal if not excel men in a bare retentive memory.* Through how many labyrinths of woods, without other clue of thread than natural instinct, doth the hunted hare return to her muce? [2] How doth the little bee, flying into several meadows and gardens, sipping of many cups, yet never intoxicated, through an ocean (as I may say) of air, steadily steer herself home, without help of card [3] or compass. But these cannot play an aftergame, and recover what they have forgotten, which is done by the mediation of discourse.

2. *Artificial memory is rather a trick than an art, and more for the gain of the teacher than profit of the learners.* Like the tossing of a pike, which is no part of the postures and motions thereof, and is rather for ostentation than use, to show the strength and nimbleness of the arm, and is often used by wandering soldiers as an introduction to beg. Understand it of the artificial rules which at this day are delivered by memory-mountebanks; for sure an art thereof may be made (wherein as yet the world is defective) and that

[1] Text: *The Holy State and the Profane State,* ed. by Maximilian Graff Walten. A facsimile of the first edition, 1642. 2 vols. (New York, 1938). *The Holy State* (Vol. II), pp. 174–76.

[2] Hiding place.

[3] Chart.

no more destructive to natural memory than spectacles are
to eyes, which girls in Holland wear from 12 years of age.
But till this be found out, let us observe these plain rules.

3. *First, soundly infix in thy mind what thou desirest to
remember*. What wonder is it if agitation of business jog
that out of thy head which was there rather tacked than fastened? Whereas those notions which get in by *violenta pos-
sessio* will abide there till *ejectio firma*, sickness or extreme
age, dispossess them. It is best knocking in the nail overnight, and clinching it the next morning.

4. *Overburden not thy memory to make so faithful a servant
a slave.* Remember Atlas was weary. Have as much reason
as a camel, to rise when thou hast thy full load. Memory,
like a purse, if it be over full that it cannot shut, all will
drop out of it. Take heed of a gluttonous curiosity to feed
on many things, lest the greediness of the appetite of thy
memory spoil the digestion thereof. Beza's [4] case was peculiar
and memorable; being above fourscore years of age he perfectly could say by heart any Greek chapter in St. Paul's
Epistles, or anything else which he had learnt long before,
but forgot whatsoever was newly told him; his memory like
an inn retaining old guests, but having no room to entertain
new.

5. *Spoil not thy memory with thine own jealousy, nor make
it bad by suspecting it.* How canst thou find that true which
thou wilt not trust? St. Augustine tells us of his friend Sim-
plicius, who being asked, could tell all Virgil's verses backward and forward, and yet the same party vowed to God,
that he knew not that he could do it till they did try him.
Sure there is concealed strength in men's memories, which
they take no notice of.

6. *Marshal thy notions into a handsome method*. One will
carry twice more weight trussed and packed up in bundles
than when it lies untowardly flapping and hanging about

[4] Theodore Beza, 1519–1605, theologian.

his shoulders. Things orderly fardeled up under heads are most portable.

7. *Adventure not all thy learning in one bottom, but divide it betwixt thy memory and thy notebooks.* He that with bias carries all his learning about him in his head will utterly be beggared and bankrupt, if a violent disease, a merciless thief, should rob and strip him. I know some have a commonplace against commonplace books, and yet perchance will privately make use of what publicly they declaim against. A commonplace book contains many notions in garrison, whence the owner may draw out an army into the field on competent warning.

8. *Moderate diet and good air preserve memory;* but what air is best I dare not define, when such great ones differ.[5] Some say a pure and subtle air is best, another commends a thick and foggy air. For the Pisans sited in the fens and marsh of Arnus have excellent memories, as if the foggy air were a cap for their heads.

9. *Thankfulness to God, for it continues the memory;* whereas some proud people have been visited with such oblivion that they have forgotten their own names. Staupitius, tutor to Luther, and a godly man, in a vain ostentation of his memory repeated Christ's genealogy (Matt. 1) by heart in his sermon; but being out about the captivity of Babylon, "I see," saith he, "God resisteth the proud," and so betook himself to his book. Abuse not thy memory to be sin's register, nor make advantage thereof for wickedness. Excellently Augustine, *Quidam vero pessimi memoria sunt mirabili, qui tanto pejores sunt, quanto minus possunt, quæ male cogitant, oblivisci.*[6]

---

5 "Plato, Aristotle, Tully." [Fuller's note]
6 "Some of the most wicked of mankind possess wonderful powers of memory; but they are such persons as become still worse, by their greater inability to forget the evil thoughts which have themselves conceived."

THE PROFANE STATE [1]

The Degenerous Gentleman

SOME WILL challenge this title of incongruity, as if those two words were so dissonant that a whole sentence cannot hold them; for sure where the gentleman is the root, degenerous cannot be the fruit. But if any quarrel with my words, Valerius Maximus shall be my champion, who styleth such, *Nobilia Portenta*. By Gentlemen we understand one whom the heralds (except they will deny their best records) must allow of ancient parentage. Such a one, when a child, being kept the devil's Nazarite that no razor of correction must come upon his head in his father's family, see what he proves in the process of time brought to extreme poverty. Herein we intend no invective glance on those pious gentlemen whose states are consumed through God's secret judgment, and none of the owner's visible default; only we meddle with such as by carelessness and riot cause their own ruin.

He goes to school to learn in jest and play in earnest. Now this gentleman, now that gentlewoman begs him a playday, and now the book must be thrown away that he may see the buck hunted. He comes to school late, departs soon, and the whole year with him (like the fortnight when Christmas day falls on a Tuesday) is all holidays and half-holidays. And as the poets feign of Thetis, that she drenched Achilles her son in the Stygian waters that he might not be wounded with any weapon, so cockering mothers enchant their sons to make them rod-free, which they do by making some golden circles in the hand of the schoolmaster: thus these two conjoining together make the indentures to bind the youth to eternal ignorance; yet perchance he may get some alms of learning, here a snap, there a piece of knowledge, but nothing to purpose.

[1] Text: *The Holy State and the Profane State,* ed. by Maximilian Graff Walten. A facsimile of the first edition, 1642. 2 vols. (New York, 1938). *The Profane State* (Vol. II), pp. 410–17.

His father's servingmen (which he counts no mean preferment) admit him into their society. Going to a drinking match, they carry him with them to enter him, and applaud his hopefulness, finding him vicious beyond his age. The butler makes him free (having first paid his fees accustomed) of his own father's cellar, and guesseth the profoundness of his young master's capacity by the depth of the whole-ones he fetcheth off.

Coming to the university, his chief study is to study nothing. What is learning but a cloakbag of books, cumbersome for a gentleman to carry? and the Muses fit to make wives for farmers' sons: perchance his own tutor, for the promise of the next living (which notwithstanding his promise he afterwards sells to another) contributes to his undoing, letting him live as he list: yea, perhaps his own mother (whilst his father diets him for his health with a moderate allowance) makes him surfeit underhand by sending him money. Thus whilst some complain that the university infected him, he infected the university, from which he sucked no milk but poisoned her nipples.

At the Inns of Court under pretense to learn law, he learns to be lawless, not knowing by his study so much as what an execution means till he learns it by his own dear experience. Here he grows acquainted with the *Roaring Boys,* I am afraid so called by a woeful prolepsis, here, for hereafter. What formerly was counted the chief credit of an orator, these esteem the honor of a swearer, pronunciation, to mouth an oath with a graceless grace. These (as David saith) *clothe themselves with curses as with a garment,* and therefore desire to be in the latest fashion both in their clothes and curses; these infuse all their skill into their young novice, who shortly proves such a proficient that he exceeds his masters in all kinds of vicious courses.

Through the mediation of a scrivener he grows acquainted with some great usurer. Nor is this youngster so ravenous, as the other is ready to feed him with money, sometimes with a courteous violence forcing on him more than he desires, provided the security be good, except the usurer be so valiant as to hazard the losing of a small hook to catch a great fish and will adventure to trust him, if his estate in hope be overmeasure, though he himself be under age. Now the greater part of the money he takes up is not for his own spending, but to pay the shot of other men's riot.

After his father's death he flies out more than ever before. Formerly he took care for means for his spending; now he takes care for spending for his means. His wealth is so deep a gulf no riot can ever sound the bottom of it. To make his guests drunk is the only seal of their welcome. His very meanest servant may be master of the cellar, and those who deserve no beer may command the best wine; such dancing by day, such masking by night, such roaring, such reveling, able to awake the sleeping ashes of his great-great-grandfather and to fright all blessing from his house.

Meantime the old sore of his London debts corrupts and festers. He is careless to take out the dead flesh or to discharge either principal or interest. Such small leaks are not worth the stopping or searching for till they be greater; he should undervalue himself to pay a sum before it grew considerable for a man of his estate. Nor can he be more careless to pay than the usurer is willing to continue the debt, knowing that his bands, like infants, battle best with sleeping.

Vacation is his vocation, and he scorns to follow any profession; and will not be confined to any laudable employment. But they who count a calling a prison shall at last make a prison their calling. He instills also his lazy principles into his children, being of the same opinion with the Neapolitan gentry, who stand so on the puntos of their honor that they prefer robbery before industry, and will rather suffer their daughter to make merchandise of her chastity than marry the richest merchant.

Drinking is one of the principal liberal sciences he pro-

fesseth. A most ungentle quality, fit to be banished to rogues and rags. It was anciently counted a Dutch vice, and swarmed most in the country. I remember a sad accident which happened to Fliolmus King of Gothland, who whilst a lord of misrule ruled in his court and both he and his servants were drunk, in mere merriment, meaning no harm, they took the king and put him in jest into a great vessel of beer, and drowned him in earnest.[2] But one [3] tells us that this ancient and habited vice is amongst the Dutch of late years much decreased: which if it be not, would it were. Sure our mariners observe that as the sea grows daily shallower and shallower on the shores of Holland and Zealand, so the channel of late waxeth deeper on the coasts of Kent and Essex. I pray God if drunkenness ebbs in Dutchland, it doth not flow in England and gain not in the Island what it loseth in the Continent. Yea some plead, when overwhelmed with liquor, that their thirst is but quenched: as well may they say that in Noah's flood the dust was but sufficiently allayed.

Gaming is another art he studies much, an enticing witch that hath caused the ruin of many. Hannibal said of Marcellus that *nec bonam nec malam fortunam ferre potest,*[4] he could be quiet neither conqueror nor conquered; thus such is the itch of play that gamesters neither winning nor losing can rest contented. One propounded this question, Whether men in ships on sea were to be accounted among the living or the dead, because there were but few inches betwixt them and drowning. The same scruple may be made of great gamesters, though their estate be never so great, whether they are to be esteemed poor or rich, there being but a few casts at dice betwixt a gentleman (in great game) and a beggar. Our gallant games deeply and makes no doubt

[2] Olaus Magnus, *Historia de Gentibus Septentrionalibus,* Rome, 1555, p. 531.
[3] Richard Verstegen, *Restitution of Decayed Intelligence,* 1628, p. 53.
[4] Livy, lib. 27. XIV. i. The original reads: *nec bonam nec malam ferre fortunam possit.*

in conscience to adventure advowsons, patronages, and church-livings in gaming. He might call to mind Sir Miles Partridge, who (as the soldiers cast lots for Christ his coat) played at dice for Jesus bells with King Henry the Eighth, and won them of him.[5] Thus he brought the bells to ring in his pocket, but the ropes afterwards catched about his neck, and for some offenses he was hanged in the days of King Edward the Sixth.

Then first he sells the outworks of his state, some straggling manor. Nor is he sensible of this sale, which makes his means more entire, as counting the gathering of such scattering rents rather burdensome than profitable. This he sells at half the value, so that the feathers will buy the goose and the wood will pay for the ground; with this money if he stops the hole to one creditor, by his prodigality he presently opens a wider gap to another.

By this time the long dormant usurer ramps for the payment of his money. The principal, the grandmother; and the use, the daughter; and the use upon use, the grandchild; and perchance a generation farther, hath swelled the debt to an incredible sum, for the satisfying whereof our gallant sells the moiety of his estate.

Having sold half his land he abates nothing of his expenses, but thinks five hundred pounds a year will be enough to maintain that for which a thousand pound was too little. He will not stoop till he falls, nor lessen his kennel of dogs till with Actæon he be eaten up with his own hounds.[6]

Being about to sink he catcheth at every rush to save himself. Perchance sometimes he snatcheth at the thistle of a project, which first pricks his hands and then breaks. Herein it may be he adventured on a matter wherein he had no skill himself (hoping by letting the Commonwealth blood to fill up his own veins again) and therefore trades

[5] "There were four bells, the greatest in London, hanging in a fair tower in Paul's Churchyard. Stowe's Survey of London, p. 357." [Fuller's note]
[6] Diana changed Actæon to a stag after he had surprised her at her bath.

with his partner's brains, as his partner with his purse, till both miscarry together; or else it may be he catcheth hold on the heel of another man who is in as dangerous a case as himself, and they embracing each other in mutual bands hasten their drowning together. His last manor he sells twice, to a country-gentleman, and a London-usurer, though the last, as having the first title, prevails to possess it: usurers herein being like unto foxes; they seldom take pains to dig any holes themselves, but earth in that which the foolish badger made for them, and dwell in the manors and fair houses which others havè built and provided.

Having lost his own legs, he relies on the staff of his kin-dred; first visiting them as an intermitting ague, but after-wards turns a quotidian, wearing their thresholds as bare as his own coat. At last he is as welcome as a storm; he that is abroad shelters himself from it, and he that is at home shuts the door. If he intrudes himself, yet some with their jeering tongues give him many a gird, but his brazen impudence feels nothing; and let him be armed on free-cost with the pot and the pipe, he will give them leave to shoot their flouts at him till they be weary. Sometimes he sadly paceth over the ground he sold, and is on fire with anger with himself for his folly, but presently quencheth it at the next alehouse.

Having undone himself, he sets up the trade to undo others. If he can but screw himself into the acquaintance of a rich heir, he rejoiceth as much at the prize as the Hollanders when they had intercepted the Plate-Fleet.[7] He tutors this young gamester in vice, leading him a more compendious way to his ruin than possibly he could find out of himself. And doth not the guide deserve good wages for his direction?

Perhaps he behaves himself so basely that he is degraded; the sad and solemn ceremonies whereof we may meet with in old presidents: but of them all, in my apprehension, none

[7] In 1628 the Dutch under Piet Hein intercepted the Spanish "Silver Fleet" with its great treasure.

should make deeper impression in an ingenuous soul than this one, that at the solemn degradation of a knight for high misdemeanor, the king and twelve knights more did put on mourning garments [8] as an emblem of sorrow for this injury to honor, that a man gentle by birth and blood, or honored by a prince's favor, should so far forget not only himself but his order, as to deserve so severe punishment.

His death is as miserable as his life hath been vicious. An hospital is the height he hopes to be advanced to; but commonly he dies not in so charitable a prison, but sings his last note in a cage. Nor is it impossible but that wanting land of his own he may encroach on the king's highway, and there, taking himself to be lord of the soil, seize on travelers as strays due unto him; and so the hangman give him a wreath more than he had in his arms before. If he dies at liberty in his pilgrimage betwixt the houses of his acquaintance, perhaps some well-disposed gentleman may pay for his burial and truly mourn at the funeral of an ancient family. His children, if any, must seek their fortunes the farther off because their father found his too soon, before he had wisdom to manage them. Within two generations his name is quite forgotten that ever any such was in the place, except some herald in his visitation pass by and chance to spell his broken arms in a church window. And then how weak a thing is gentry, than which (if it wants virtue) brittle glass is the more lasting monument?

We forbear to give an instance of a degenerous gentleman; would to God the world gave no examples of them. If any please to look into the forenamed Valerius Maximus, he shall there find the base son of Scipio Africanus, the conqueror of Hannibal and Afric, so ill imitating his father that for his viciousness he received many disgraceful repulses from the people of Rome, the fragrant smell of his father's memory making him to stink the more in their

---

[8] Markham's *Decades of Honour,* p. 76. Francis Markham (1565–1627). *The Booke of Honour: Five Decades of Epistles of Honour,* 1625.

nostrils; yea they forced him to pluck off from his finger a signet-ring, whereon the face of his father was engraven, as counting him unworthy to wear his picture who would not resemble his virtue.

ORNITHO-LOGIE [1]

The Phœnix

SIR, OR Mistress Phœnix, saith the Hawk, for I know not in what gender to address my language unto you, in whom both sexes are jumbled together, I desire to be informed of you, whether that be a truth or a long-lived common error, of the manner of your original from the ashes of your ancestor. If it be a truth, I stand ready with admiration to embrace and entertain it; if an error, I am resolved posterity shall no longer be deluded therewith. We live in an age of knowledge, the beams whereof have dispelled those mists of errors wherewith our forefathers were cheated into the belief of many impossibilities recommended unto them by tradition, as if the gray periwig of old age should command so much veneration from us that we should consign up our judgment to the implicit belief of anything which former ages have related. Deal therefore openly with me, and inform me the truth, whether your generation be thus by continuation of a miracle.

I cannot resolve you herein, saith the Phœnix, of the particulars of my extraction, which happened long before the register of my memory. Sure I am there are no other of my kind for me to couple with, which demonstrates the truth of that which is generally received. I confess men make use of me rather for a moral and an emblem to denote those things which are rare and seldom come to pass. Thus a Court Lord who will honestly pay all his debts is accounted a phœnix; a judge who will not suffer his conscience to be robbed by a bribe secretly proffered unto him as a phœnix; a great man who looks straight forward to the public good, not bound on either side with his own interest, is a phœnix. However, assure yourself that besides the morality that may be made thereof, I have, as you see, a real existence in na-

---

[1] *Ornitho-Logie,* 1655, pp. 21–27.

ture, and if any will take the pains to travel into Arabia to Mecca, he shall find my nest in a tree hanging there almost as artificially as doth the tomb of Mahomet bribed by an invisible loadstone into that miraculous posture thereof.

But now, saith the Hawk, suppose I should seize on you this night for my supper, whether do you think that the loss of your life would be so great a defect in nature that the whole universe would fare the worse for the same?

Undoubtedly it would, saith the Phœnix, for this is received for an undoubted maxim amongst philosophers, that if one whole kind or species of creatures be destroyed, the whole world would be ruined thereby, for every kind of creatures are so essential to the well being thereof that if any one of them be utterly destroyed, all the rest out of sympathy will decay.

I conceive not, saith the Hawk, that you are such a foundation stone in nature's building that the taking you away will hazard the whole architecture thereof. However, I am resolved to put it to the trial, be it but to gain knowledge by experiment. I know that Plato saith that "those are the happiest kingdoms, wherein either their kings are philosophers, or their philosophers are kings." Seeing therefore the history of nature is so necessary to an accomplished governor, I who desire all perfections in that kind will to satisfy my curiosity make proof thereof.

The Phœnix pleaded for herself the benefit of a proclamation of liberty to all for three days to come and go with safety, the Eagle smiling at her silly plea, informing her that such grants are to be kept no farther than they are consistent with the conveniency of those that grant them. Yet for the present the Phœnix was reprieved, because the Hawk's stomach lately gorged, had not as yet recovered his appetite to his supper.

———

THE HISTORY OF THE WORTHIES OF ENGLAND [1]

Anne Boleyn

ANNE BOLEYN, daughter of the Lord Thomas Boleyn, Earl of Wiltshire, was (as some of her honorable relations still surviving do conjecture) born in London, and became second wife to King Henry the Eighth. Indeed, he passionately affected her when but a lord's daughter, but did not marry her till she was a princess; created by him Marchioness of Pembroke, partly to make her the more proportionable match, and partly to try how she would become a coronet, before she wore a crown.

The papists much disparage her memory (malice will lie, or must be dumb), making all her wit to consist in boldness, her beauty in a French garb, and her modesty in a cunning coyness: whereas indeed she was a lady accomplished in body (was it likely King Henry would love what was not lovely?) and virtuous in mind, and, whilst a favorite of the king's, a favorer of all good men, and a great promoter of the gospel. The inconstancy of her husband's affections is conceived by most moderate men (what else soever was pretended) her chiefest crime and cause of her death, which happened *anno* 1536.

Ben Jonson [2]

BENJAMIN JONSON was born in this city. Though I cannot, with all my industrious inquiry, find him in his cradle, I can fetch him from his long coats. When a little child, he lived in Hartshorn Lane near Charing Cross, where his mother married a bricklayer for her second husband.

[1] Text: 1662, first edition.
[2] Fuller, *op. cit.*, "Benjamin Jonson."

He was first bred in a private school in Saint Martin's Church; then in Westminster School, witness his own epigram: [3]

> "Camden, most reverend head, to whom I
>   owe
> All that I am in arts, all that I know;
> How nothing's that to whom my country
>   owes
> The great renown and name wherewith she
>   goes," etc.

He was statutably admitted into Saint John's College in Cambridge (as many years after incorporated an honorary member of Christ Church in Oxford), where he continued but few weeks for want of further maintenance, being fain to return to the trade of his father-in-law. And let them blush not that have, but those who have not, a lawful calling. He helped in the new structure of Lincoln's Inn, when, having a trowel in his hand, he had a book in his pocket.

Some gentlemen, pitying that his parts should be buried under the rubbish of so mean a calling, did by their bounty manumise him freely to follow his own ingenious inclinations. Indeed his parts were not so ready to run of themselves as able to answer the spur; so that it may be truly said of him that he had an elaborate wit wrought out in his own industry. He would sit silent in a learned company, and suck in (besides wine) their several humors into his observation. What was ore in others, he was able to refine to himself.

He was paramount in the dramatic part of poetry, and taught the stage an exact conformity to the laws of comedians. His comedies were above the _volge_ (which are only tickled with downright obscenity), and took not so well at the first

---

[3] "To William Camden," Epigram 14. Camden was Headmaster of Westminster School.

stroke as at the rebound, when beheld the second time; yea, they will endure reading, and that with due commendation, so long as either ingenuity or learning are fashionable in our nation. If his later be not so spriteful and vigorous as his first pieces, all that are old will, and all that desire to be old should, excuse him therein.

He was not very happy in his children, and most happy in those which died first, though none lived to survive him. This he bestowed as part of an epitaph on his eldest son, dying in infancy: [4]

> Rest in soft peace; and ask'd, say here
> doth lie,
> Ben Jonson his best piece of poetry.

He died *anno Domini* 1638; and was buried about the belfry, in the abbey church at Westminster.

MANY WERE the wit-combats [5] betwixt him [Shakespeare] and Ben Jonson; which two I behold like a Spanish great galleon and an English man-of-war; Master Jonson (like the former) was built far higher in learning; solid, but slow, in her performances. Shakespeare, with the English man-of-war, lesser in bulk, but lighter in sailing, could turn with all tides, tack about, and take advantage of all winds, by the quickness of his wit and invention. He died *anno Domini* 1616, and was buried at Stratford-upon-Avon, the town of his nativity.

---

[4] "On My First Son," Epigram 45.
[5] Fuller, *op. cit.*, "William Shakespeare."

GOOD THOUGHTS IN BAD TIMES [1]

Personal Meditations

V

LORD, MY voice by nature is harsh and untunable, and it is vain to lavish any art to better it. Can my singing of psalms be pleasing to thy ears, which is unpleasant to my own? Yet though I cannot chant with the nightingale or chirp with the blackbird, I had rather chatter with the swallow, yea, rather croak with the raven, than be altogether silent. Hadst thou given me a better voice, I would have praised thee with a better voice. Now what my music wants in sweetness, let it have in sense, singing praises with understanding. Yea, Lord, create in me a new heart, therein to make melody, and I will be contented with my old voice until, in thy due time, being admitted into the choir of heaven, I have another, more harmonious, bestowed upon me.

XII

LORD, WHAT faults I correct in my son, I commit myself: I beat him for dabbling in the dirt, whilst my own soul doth wallow in sin; I beat him for crying to cut his own meat, yet am not myself contented with that state thy providence hath carved unto me; I beat him for crying when he is to go to sleep, and yet I fear I myself shall cry when thou callest me to sleep with my fathers. Alas! I am more childish than my child, and what I inflict on him I justly deserve to receive from thee; only here is the difference: I pray and desire that my correction on my child may do him good; it is in thy power, Lord, to effect that thy correction on me shall do me good.

[1] Text: 1662, but first published 1645. Fuller's humor and wit in his meditations should be compared with the tone of Donne's.

XVI

Lord, when I am to travel, I never use to provide myself till the very time; partly out of laziness, loath to be troubled till needs I must; partly out of pride, as presuming all necessaries for my journey will wait upon me at the instant. Some say this is scholars' fashion, and it seems by following it, I hope to approve myself to be one. However, it often comes to pass that my journey is finally stopped through the narrowness of the time to provide for it. Grant, Lord, that my confessed improvidence in temporal, may make me suspect my providence in spiritual matters. Solomon saith, man goeth to his long home.[2] Short preparation will not fit so long a journey. O let me not put it off to the last, to have my oil to buy when I am to burn it.[3] But let me so dispose of myself that when I am to die, I may have nothing to do but to die.

XXI

Lord, I confess this morning I remembered my breakfast but forgot my prayers. And as I have returned no praise, so thou mightst justly have afforded me no protection. Yet thou hast carefully kept me to the middle of this day, entrusted me with a new debt before I have paid the old score. It is now noon, too late for a morning, too soon for an evening sacrifice. My corrupt heart prompts me to put off my prayers till night; but I know it too well, or rather too ill, to trust it. I fear if till night I defer them, I shall forget them. Be pleased, therefore, now to accept them. Lord, let not a few hours the later make a breach; especially seeing (be it spoken not to excuse my negligence, but to implore thy pardon) a thousand years in thy sight are but as yester-

[2] Eccles. 12:5.
[3] See the parable of the wise and the foolish virgins, Matt. 25:1–13.

day.[4] I promise hereafter, by thy assistance, to bring forth fruit in due season. See how I am ashamed the sun should shine on me, who now newly start in the race of my devotions when he like a giant hath run more than half his course in the heavens.

[4] Psalm 59:4.

John Milton 1608-1674

MILTON, son of a scrivener on Bread Street, near St. Paul's Cathedral, had superior early training at St. Paul's School when that remarkable teacher, Alexander Gill, was headmaster. His schooling was also supplemented by tutors at home. In 1625 he entered Christ's College, Cambridge, receiving his A.B. in 1629 and his M.A. in 1632; but he was constantly irked by the narrow medieval curriculum. Soon after entering college, he had some trouble with his tutor and was suspended for a while. During his years at the university, however, he distinguished himself and his college by writing poetry, in both Latin and English, which continues to live.

The period of formal education was followed by five years of intense private study at Horton, the little village near London where his father was living in retirement. Finally his education was broadened by the "Grand Tour" on the Continent. Hearing of wars at home, Milton did not go on to Greece as he had planned, but from Naples began the return journey.

Peace had been made before he reached home, however, and establishing himself in London, he set up a small private school in his own home. For about twenty years he laid aside his poetic plans and devoted his abilities to writing in prose for religious, domestic, and civil liberty.

Meanwhile his private life was full of hardships. His impulsive marriage to the young Royalist, Mary Powell, had ended in her deserting him after about a month, and in his long consideration of divorce. The reconciliation three years later did not bring happiness, and her death in 1652 left him with three young daughters to care for. He became totally blind while writing the *Second Defense*. The dark days following have one period of light, the brief happy marriage with Katherine Woodcock in 1656. This, however, ended in double tragedy when both Katherine and her baby died.

After the Restoration Milton was heavily fined and had to live in hiding until the Act of Oblivion was passed. His difficult situation was somewhat alleviated by a marriage of convenience arranged with Elizabeth Minshull in 1663.

During the years of public and personal stress, Milton's promise to the nation to write something which it would "not willingly let die" was not forgotten. He turned to his long-deferred plans and produced the three great poems, *Paradise Lost, Paradise Regained,* and *Samson Agonistes.*

It is the time of public service when Milton was writing in "the cool element of prose" which particularly concerns us here. His first five pamphlets attacked the authority of the bishops and supported religious liberty. After Mary Powell returned to her family, he wrote four divorce pamphlets in which he presented the modern view that marriage may be dissolved on grounds of incompatibility. The results of his experiments in teaching were set down in a small tract written in 1644 at the request of Samuel Hartlib, a merchant who was interested in the improvement of education. In the same year he wrote his greatest piece of prose, the *Areopagitica,* an argument for the liberty of the press and freedom of speech, written in answer to the licensing act passed by Parliament the preceding year. The *Tenure of Kings and Magistrates,* published soon after the beheading of Charles I, was the first pamphlet in the cause of civil liberty, and was influential in his appointment as Latin Secretary for the Council of State. In this position he wrote not only the *Letters of State* but *Eikonoclastes,* the first and second *Defense of the English People,* and various pamphlets. After his blindness he was given an assistant, and in the comparative leisure following, he wrote the *History of Britain* and a theological work in Latin, *De Doctrina Christiana.*

Much of his prose is unpleasantly controversial and like

all the pamphlets of the time contains harsh personal attacks on the adversaries. The things which concern us today are the logical arguments, the modern views, the eloquent writing, and the autobiographical information. The Milton of the prose period is the same Milton that we see in the periods of poetic writing before and after it. He is the Renaissance scholar, full of allusions to classical literature, and able to handle his oratory in the Ciceronian manner. The high ideals are the same that we are familiar with in the great poems; and when he is expressing them, the prose takes on the quality of poetry. Finally, in prose as in poetry, whatever the subject, it is Milton himself upon whom the attention is focused.

From AN APOLOGY FOR SMECTYMNUUS [1]

I HAD MY time, readers, as others have who have good learning bestowed upon them, to be sent to those places where, the opinion was, it might soonest be obtained; and as the manner is, was not unstudied in those authors which are most commended. Whereof some were grave orators and historians, whose matter methought I loved indeed, but as my age then was, so I understood them; others were the smooth elegiac poets, whereof the schools are not scarce, whom both for the pleasing sound of their numerous writing, which in imitation I found most easy, and most agreeable to nature's part in me, and for their matter, which what it is, there be few who know not, I was so allured to read that no recreation came to me better welcome. For that it was then those years with me which are excused, though they be least severe, I may be saved the labor to remember ye. Whence having observed them to account it the chief glory of their wit, in that they were able to judge, to praise, and by that could esteem themselves worthiest to love those high perfections, which under one or other name they took to celebrate, I thought to myself by every instinct and presage of nature, which is not wont to be false, that what emboldened them to this task might with such diligence as they used embolden me; and that what judgment, wit, or elegance was my share would herein best appear and best value itself, by how much more wisely, and with more love of virtue I should choose (let rude ears be absent) the object of not unlike praises. For albeit these thoughts to some will seem virtuous and commendable, to others only pardonable, to a third sort perhaps idle; yet the mentioning of them now will end in serious.

[1] Text: Columbia edition of Milton's *Works*. (New York, 1931), Vol. III, 302–06. This pamphlet was edited by Harry Morgan Ayres. It was first issued in 1642.

Nor blame it, readers, in those years to propose to themselves such a reward as the noblest dispositions above other
things in this life have sometimes preferred: whereof not
to be sensible when good and fair in one person meet, argues
both a gross and shallow judgment, and withal an ungentle
and swainish breast. For by the firm settling of these persuasions, I became, to my best memory, so much a proficient
that if I found those authors anywhere speaking unworthy
things of themselves or unchaste of those names which before they had extolled, this effect it wrought on me, from
that time forward their art I still applauded, but the men
I deplored; and above them all preferred the two famous
renowners of Beatrice and Laura, who never write but
honor of them to whom they devote their verse, displaying
sublime and pure thoughts, without transgression. And long
it was not after when I was confirmed in this opinion, that
he who would not be frustrate of his hope to write well
hereafter in laudable things, ought himself to be a true poem,
that is a composition and pattern of the best and honorablest
things; not presuming to sing praises of heroic men, or famous cities, unless he have in himself the experience and practice of all that which is praiseworthy. These reasonings, together with a certain niceness of nature, an honest haughtiness, and self-esteem either of what I was or what I might
be (which let envy call pride), and lastly that modesty,
whereof though not in the title page, yet here I may be excused to make some beseeming profession, all these uniting
the supply of their natural aid together, kept me still above
those low descents of mind beneath which he must deject
and plunge himself that can agree to salable and unlawful
prostitutions.

Next (for hear me out now, readers, that I may tell ye
whither my younger feet wandered), I betook me among
those lofty fables and romances, which recount in solemn
cantos the deeds of knighthood founded by our victorious
kings, and from hence in renown all over Christendom. There

I read it in the oath of every knight that he should defend
to the expense of his best blood, if so befell him, the honor
and chastity of virgin or matron; from whence even then
I learned what a noble virtue chastity must be, to the defense
of which so many worthies, by such a dear adventure of
themselves, had sworn. And if I found in the story afterward, any of them, by word or deed, breaking that oath, I
judged it the same fault of the poet as that which is attributed
to Homer, to have written indecent things of the gods. Only
this my mind gave me, that every free and gentle spirit,
without that oath, ought to be born a knight, nor needed
to expect the gilt spur, or the laying of a sword upon his
shoulder to stir him up both by his counsel and his arms to
secure and protect the weakness of any attempted chastity.
So that even those books, which to many others have been
the fuel of wantonness and loose living, I cannot think how,
unless by divine indulgence, proved to me so many incite-
ments as you have heard to the love and steadfast observation of that virtue which abhors the society of the bordellos.
Thus from the laureate fraternity of poets, riper years and
the ceaseless round of studies led me to the shady spaces of
philosophy; but chiefly to the divine volumes of Plato and
his equal Xenophon: where if I should tell ye what I learned
of chastity and love, I mean of that which is truly so, whose
charming cup is only virtue, which she bears in her hand
to those who are worthy (the rest are cheated with a thick
intoxicating potion, which a certain sorceress, the abuser
of love's name, carries about) and how the first and chiefest
office of love ends in the soul, producing those happy twins
of her divine generation, knowledge and virtue, with such
abstracted sublimities as these, it might be worth your listening, readers, as I may one day hope to have ye in a still
time, when there shall be no chiding; not in these noises,
the adversary as ye know, barking at the door; or searching for me at the bordellos, where it may be he has lost
himself and raps up without pity the sage and rheumatic

old prelatess with all her young Corinthian laity to inquire for such a one.

Last of all, not in time, but as perfection is last, that care was ever had of me, with my earliest capacity, not to be negligently trained in the precepts of the Christian religion: this that I have hitherto related, hath been to show that though Christianity has been but slightly taught me, yet a certain reservedness of natural disposition and moral discipline, learnt out of the noblest philosophy, was enough to keep me in disdain of far less incontinences than this of the bordello. But having had the doctrine of holy Scripture unfolding those chaste and high mysteries, with timeliest care infused, that *the body is for the Lord and the Lord for the body,* thus also I argued to myself, that if unchastity in a woman, whom St. Paul terms the glory of man, be such a scandal and dishonor, then certainly in a man, who is both the image and glory of God, it must, though commonly not so thought, be much more deflowering and dishonorable; in that he sins both against his own body, which is the perfecter sex, and his own glory, which is in the woman; and, that which is worst, against the image and glory of God, which is in himself. Nor did I slumber over that place expressing such high rewards of ever accompanying the Lamb, with those celestial songs to others inapprehensible, but not to those who were not defiled with women, which doubtless means fornication; for marriage must not be called a defilement.

From THE REASON OF CHURCH GOVERNMENT URGED AGAINST PRELATY

Introduction to the Second Book [1]

How HAPPY were it for this frail and, as it may be truly called, mortal life of man, since all earthly things which have the name of good and convenient in our daily use are withal so cumbersome and full of trouble, if knowledge, yet which is the best and lightsomest possession of the mind, were as the common saying is, no burden, and that what it wanted of being a load to any part of the body, it did not with a heavy advantage overlay upon the spirit. For not to speak of that knowledge that rests in the contemplation of natural causes and dimensions, which must needs be a lower wisdom, as the object is low, certain it is that he who hath obtained in more than the scantest measure to know anything distinctly of God, and of his true worship, and what is infallibly good and happy in the state of man's life, what in itself evil and miserable, though vulgarly not so esteemed, he that hath obtained to know this, the only high valuable wisdom indeed, remembering also that God even to a strictness requires the improvement of these his entrusted gifts, cannot but sustain a sorer burden of the mind, and more pressing than any supportable toil or weight which the body can labor under; how and in what manner he shall dispose and employ those sums of knowledge and illumination which God hath sent him into this the world to trade with. And that which aggravates the burden more is that, having received amongst his allotted parcels certain precious truths of such an orient luster as no diamond can equal, which nevertheless he has in charge to put off at any cheap rate, yea, for nothing to them that will, the great merchants of this world, fearing that this course would soon discover and disgrace the

---

[1] Text: 1641, first edition.

false glitter of their deceitful wares wherewith they abuse the people, like poor Indians with beads and glasses, practice by all means how they may suppress the venting of such rarities and such a cheapness as would undo them and turn their trash upon their hands. Therefore by gratifying the corrupt desires of men in fleshly doctrines, they stir them up to persecute with hatred and contempt all those that seek to bear themselves uprightly in this their spiritual factory: which they foresee-ing, though they cannot but testify of truth and the excellence of that heavenly traffic which they bring, against what op-position or danger soever, yet needs must it sit heavily upon their spirits, that being in God's prime intention and their own, selected heralds of peace and dispensers of treasures inestimable without price to them that have no peace, they find in the discharge of their commission that they are made the greatest variance and offense, a very sword and fire both in house and city over the whole earth. This is that which the sad prophet Jeremiah laments, *Woe is me, my mother, that thou hast borne me a man of strife and contention.*[2] And al-though divine inspiration must certainly have been sweet to those ancient prophets, yet the irksomeness of that truth which they brought was so unpleasant to them that every-where they called it a burden. Yea, that mysterious book of Revelation, which the great Evangelist was bid to eat, as it had been some eye-brightening electuary of knowledge and foresight, though it were sweet in his mouth and in the learning, it was bitter in his belly; bitter in the denouncing. Nor was this hid from the wise poet Sophocles, who in that place of his tragedy where Tiresias is called to resolve King Œdipus in a matter which he knew would be grievous, brings him in bemoaning his lot, that he knew more than other men. For surely to every good and peaceable man it must in nature needs be a hateful thing to be the displeaser and molester of thousands; much better would it like him doubtless to be the messenger of gladness and contentment, which is his chief

[2] Jer. 15:10.

intended business to all mankind, but that they resist and oppose their own true happiness. But when God commands to take the trumpet and blow a dolorous or a jarring blast, it lies not in man's will what he shall say or what he shall conceal. If he shall think to be silent, as Jeremiah did, because of the reproach and derision he met with daily, and all his familiar friends watched for his halting [3] to be revenged on him for speaking the truth, he would be forced to confess as he confessed, *His word was in my heart as a burning fire shut up in my bones; I was weary with forbearing and could not stay:* [4] which might teach these times not suddenly to condemn all things that are sharply spoken or vehemently written, as proceeding out of stomach, virulence, and ill nature; but to consider rather that if the prelates have leave to say the worst that can be said and do the worst that can be done, while they strive to keep themselves to their great pleasure and commodity those things which they ought to render up, no man can be justly offended with him that shall endeavor to impart and bestow without any gain to himself those sharp but saving words which would be a terror, and a torment to him to keep back. For me, I have determined to lay up as the best treasure, and solace of a good old age, if God vouchsafe it me, the honest liberty of free speech from my youth, where I shall think it available in so dear a concernment as the Church's good. For if I be, either by disposition or what other cause, too inquisitive or suspicious of myself and mine own doings, who can help it? But this I foresee, that should the Church be brought under heavy oppression, and God have given me ability the while to reason against that man that should be the author of so foul a deed; or should she, by blessing from above on the industry and courage of faithful men, change this her distracted estate into better days without the least furtherance or contribution of those few talents, which God at that present had lent me: I foresee what stories I should hear within myself, all my life after, of discourage

[3] Jer. 20:10.   [4] Jer. 20:9.

and reproach. Timorous and ungrateful, the Church of God
is now again at the foot of her insulting enemies, and thou
bewailest. What matters it for thee, or thy bewailing? When
time was, thou couldst not find a syllable of all that thou hast
read or studied, to utter in her behalf. Yet ease and leisure
was given thee for thy retired thoughts, out of the sweat of
other men. Thou hadst the diligence, the parts, the language
of a man, if a vain subject were to be adorned or beautified;
but when the cause of God and his Church was to be pleaded,
for which purpose that tongue was given thee which thou
hast, God listened if he could hear thy voice among his zealous
servants, but thou wert dumb as a beast: from henceforward
be that which thine own brutish silence hath made thee. Or
else I should have heard on the other ear: Slothful, and ever
to be set light by, the Church hath now overcome her late
distresses after the unwearied labors of many her true servants that stood up in her defense; thou also wouldst take
upon thee to share amongst them of their joy: but wherefore
thou? Where canst thou show any word or deed of thine
which might have hastened her peace? Whatever thou dost
now talk, or write, or look is the alms of other men's active
prudence and zeal. Dare not now to say or do anything better
than thy former sloth and infancy; or if thou darest, thou
dost impudently to make a thrifty purchase of boldness to
thyself out of the painful merits of other men; what before
was thy sin is now thy duty to be, abject and worthless. These,
and such-like lessons as these, I know would have been my
matins duly, and my evensong. But now by this little diligence,
mark what a privilege I have gained with good men and saints
to claim my right of lamenting the tribulations of the Church,
if she should suffer, when others, that have ventured nothing
for her sake, have not the honor to be admitted mourners.
But if she lift up her drooping head and prosper, among those
that have something more than wished her welfare, I have
my charter and freehold of rejoicing to me and my heirs.
Concerning therefore this wayward subject against prelaty,

the touching whereof is so distasteful and disquietous to a
number of men, as by what hath been said I may deserve of
charitable readers to be credited, that neither envy nor gall
hath entered me upon this controversy, but the enforcement
of conscience only and a preventive fear lest the omitting of
this duty should be against me when I would store up to myself the good provision of peaceful hours; so, lest it should
be still imputed to me, as I have found it hath been, that
some self-pleasing humor of vainglory hath incited me to
contest with men of high estimation now while green years
are upon my head, from this needless surmisal I shall hope
to dissuade the intelligent and equal auditor, if I can but say
successfully that which in this exigent behooves me; although
I would be heard only, if it might be, by the elegant and
learned reader, to whom principally for a while I shall beg
leave I may address myself. To him it will be no new thing,
though I tell him that if I hunted after praise by the ostentation of wit and learning, I should not write thus out of mine
own season, when I have neither yet completed to my mind
the full circle of my private studies, although I complain not
of any insufficiency to the matter in hand; or were I ready to
my wishes, it were a folly to commit anything elaborately
composed to the careless and interrupted listening of these
tumultuous times. Next, if I were wise only to my own ends,
I would certainly take such a subject as of itself might catch
applause, whereas this hath all the disadvantages on the
contrary; and such a subject as the publishing whereof might
be delayed at pleasure, and time enough to pencil it over
with all the curious touches of art, even to the perfection of
a faultless picture: whenas in this argument the not deferring
is of great moment to the good speeding, that if solidity have
leisure to do her office, art cannot have much. Lastly, I
should not choose this manner of writing, wherein knowing
myself inferior to myself, led by the genial power of nature
to another task, I have the use, as I may account it, but of
my left hand. And though I shall be foolish in saying more

to this purpose, yet, since it will be such a folly as wisest men going about to commit, have only confessed and so committed, I may trust with more reason, because with more folly, to have courteous pardon. For although a poet, soaring in the high region of his fancies, with his garland and singing robes about him, might, without apology, speak more of himself than I mean to do; yet for me sitting here below in the cool element of prose, a mortal thing among many readers of no empyreal conceit, to venture and divulge unusual things of myself, I shall petition to the gentler sort, it may not be envy to me. I must say, therefore, that after I had for my first years, by the ceaseless diligence and care of my father, whom God recompense, been exercised to the tongues, and some sciences, as my age would suffer, by sundry masters and teachers, both at home and at the schools, it was found that whether aught was imposed me by them that had the overlooking, or betaken to of mine own choice in English or other tongue, prosing or versing, but chiefly by this latter, the style, by certain vital signs it had, was likely to live. But much latelier in the private academies of Italy, whither I was favored to resort, perceiving that some trifles which I had in memory, composed at under twenty or thereabout (for the manner is, that everyone must give some proof of his wit and reading there), met with acceptance above what was looked for; and other things, which I had shifted in scarcity of books and conveniences to patch up amongst them, were received with written encomiums, which the Italian is not forward to bestow on men of this side the Alps; I began thus far to assent both to them and divers of my friends here at home, and not less to an inward prompting which now grew daily upon me, that by labor and intent study (which I take to be my portion in this life), joined with the strong propensity of nature, I might perhaps leave something so written to aftertimes, as they should not willingly let it die. These thoughts at once possessed me, and these other: that if I were certain to write as men buy leases, for three lives and downward, there ought no regard be sooner had than to God's glory, by the honor and instruction of my country. For which cause, and not only for that I knew it would be hard to arrive at the second rank among the Latins, I applied myself to that resolution, which Ariosto followed against the persuasions of Bembo,[5] to fix all the industry and art I could unite to the adorning of my native tongue; not to make verbal curiosities the end, that were a toilsome vanity, but to be an interpreter and relater of the best and sagest things among mine own citizens throughout this island in the mother dialect. That what the greatest and choicest wits of Athens, Rome, or modern Italy, and those Hebrews of old did for their country, I, in my proportion, with this over and above, of being a Christian, might do for mine: not caring to be once named abroad, though perhaps I could attain to that, but content with these British islands as my world; whose fortune hath hitherto been, that if the Athenians, as some say, made their small deeds great and renowned by their eloquent writers, England hath had her noble achievements made small by the unskillful handling of monks and mechanics.

Time serves not now, and perhaps I might seem too profuse, to give any certain account of what the mind at home in the spacious circuits of her musing hath liberty to propose to herself, though of highest hope and hardest attempting: whether that epic form whereof the two poems of Homer, and those other two of Virgil and Tasso, are a diffuse, and the book of Job a brief model; or whether the rules of Aristotle herein are strictly to be kept, or nature to be followed, which in them that know art and use judgment is no transgression but an enriching of art; and lastly, what king or knight before the Conquest might be chosen, in whom to lay the pattern of a Christian hero. And as Tasso gave to a

[5] Cardinal Pietro Bembo, 1470–1547, scholar and writer in both Italian and Latin.

prince of Italy his choice whether he would command him to write of Godfrey's expedition against the Infidels, or Belisarius against the Goths, or Charlemain against the Lombards; if to the instinct of nature and the emboldening of art aught may be trusted, and that there be nothing adverse in our climate or the fate of this age, it haply would be no rashness, from an equal diligence and inclination, to present the like offer in our own ancient stories; or whether those dramatic constitutions, wherein Sophocles and Euripides reign, shall be found more doctrinal and exemplary to a nation. The Scripture also affords us a divine pastoral drama in the Song of Solomon, consisting of two persons and a double chorus, as Origen [6] rightly judges. And the Apocalypse of St. John is the majestic image of a high and stately tragedy, shutting up and intermingling her solemn scenes and acts with a sevenfold chorus of hallelujahs and harping symphonies: and this my opinion the grave authority of Pareus,[7] commenting that book, is sufficient to confirm. Or if occasion shall lead, to imitate those magnific odes and hymns, wherein Pindarus and Callimachus are in most things worthy, some others in their frame judicious, in their matter most an end faulty: but those frequent songs throughout the Law and Prophets beyond all these, not in their divine argument alone, but in the very critical art of composition, may be easily made appear over all the kinds of lyric poesy, to be incomparable. These abilities, wheresoever they be found, are the inspired gift of God, rarely bestowed, but yet to some (though most abuse) in every nation: and are of power, besides the office of a pulpit, to inbreed and cherish in a great people the seeds of virtue and public civility; to allay the perturbations of the mind and set the affections in right tune; to celebrate in glorious and lofty hymns the throne and equipage of God's Almightiness, and what he works and what he suffers to be wrought with high providence in

---

[6] Origen, 185(?)–254(?), of Alexandria, early Christian writer.
[7] David Pareus, 1548–1622. German theological writer.

his church; to sing victorious agonies of martyrs and saints, the deeds and triumphs of just and pious nations, doing valiantly through faith against the enemies of Christ; to deplore the general relapses of kingdoms and states from justice and God's true worship. Lastly, whatsoever in religion is holy and sublime, in virtue amiable or grave, whatsoever hath passion or admiration in all the changes of that which is called fortune from without, or the wily subtleties and refluxes of man's thoughts from within; all these things with a solid and treatable smoothness to paint out and describe. Teaching over the whole book of sanctity and virtue, through all the instances of example, with such delight to those especially of soft and delicious temper, who will not so much as look upon Truth herself, unless they see her elegantly dressed; that whereas the paths of honesty and good life appear now rugged and difficult, though they be indeed easy and pleasant, they would appear to all men both easy and pleasant, though they were rugged and difficult indeed. And what a benefit this would be to our youth and gentry, may be soon guessed by what we know of the corruption and bane which they suck in daily from the writings and interludes of libidinous and ignorant poetasters, who having scarce ever heard of that which is the main consistence of a true poem, the choice of such persons as they ought to introduce, and what is moral and decent to each one, do for the most part lay up vicious principles in sweet pills to be swallowed down, and make the taste of virtuous documents harsh and sour. But because the spirit of man cannot demean itself lively in this body without some recreating intermissions of labor and serious things, it were happy for the commonwealth, if our magistrates, as in those famous governments of old, would take into their care, not only the deciding of our contentious law-cases and brawls, but the managing of our public sports and festival pastimes; that they might be, not such as were authorized a while since, the provocations of drunkenness and lust, but such as may inure and harden our bodies by martial exercises to all warlike skill and performance; and may civilize, adorn, and make discreet our minds by the learned and affable meeting of frequent academies, and the procurement of wise and artful recitations, sweetened with eloquent and graceful enticements to the love and practice of justice, temperance, and fortitude, instructing and bettering the nation at all opportunities, that the call of wisdom and virtue may be heard everywhere, as Solomon saith: *She crieth without, she uttereth her voice in the streets, in the top of high places, in the chief concourse, and in the openings of the gates.*[8] Whether this may not be, not only in pulpits, but after another persuasive method, at set and solemn paneguries, in theaters, porches, or what other place or way may win most upon the people to receive at once both recreation and instruction, let them in authority consult. The thing which I had to say, and those intentions which have lived within me ever since I could conceive myself anything worth to my country, I return to crave excuse that urgent reason hath plucked from me, by an abortive and foredated discovery. And the accomplishment of them lies not but in a power above man's to promise; but that none hath by more studious ways endeavored, and with more unwearied spirit that none shall, that I dare almost aver of myself, as far as life and free leisure will extend; and that the land had once enfranchised herself from this impertinent yoke of prelaty, under whose inquisitorious and tyrannical duncery no free and splendid wit can flourish. Neither do I think it shame to covenant with any knowing reader, that for some few years yet I may go on trust with him toward the payment of what I am now indebted, as being a work not to be raised from the heat of youth or the vapors of wine, like that which flows at waste from the pen of some vulgar amorist or the trencher fury of a rhyming parasite; nor to be obtained by the invocation of dame Memory and her siren daughters; but by devout prayer to that eternal Spirit,

[8] Prov. 8:2–3.

who can enrich with all utterance and knowledge, and sends
out his seraphim, with the hallowed fire of his altar, to
touch and purify the lips of whom he pleases: to this must
be added industrious and select reading, steady observation,
insight into all seemly and generous arts and affairs; till
which in some measure be compassed, at mine own peril
and cost, I refuse not to sustain this expectation from as
many as are not loath to hazard so much credulity upon the
best pledges that I can give them. Although it nothing content me to have disclosed thus much beforehand, but that I
trust hereby to make it manifest with what small willingness
I endure to interrupt the pursuit of no less hopes than these,
and leave a calm and pleasing solitariness, fed with cheerful
and confident thoughts, to embark in a troubled sea of noises
and hoarse disputes, put from beholding the bright countenance of Truth in the quiet and still air of delightful studies,
to come into the dim reflection of hollow antiquities sold
by the seeming bulk, and there be fain to club quotations
with men whose learning and belief lies in marginal stuffings,
who when they have like good sumpters laid ye down their
horse-loads of citations and Fathers at your door, with a
rhapsody of who and who were bishops here or there, ye
may take off their packsaddles, their day's work is done,
and episcopacy, as they think, stoutly vindicated. Let any
gentle apprehension, that can distinguish learned pains from
unlearned drudgery, imagine what pleasure or profoundness
can be in this, or what honor to deal against such adversaries.
But were it the meanest under-service, if God by his secretary conscience enjoin it, it were sad for me if I should draw
back; for me especially, now when all men offer their aid
to help, ease, and lighten the difficult labors of the Church,
to whose service by the intentions of my parents and friends
I was destined of a child, and in mine own resolutions: till
coming to some maturity of years and perceiving what
tyranny had invaded the Church, that he who would take
orders must subscribe slave, and take an oath withal, which,

unless he took with a conscience that would retch, he must either straight perjure, or split his faith; I thought it better to prefer a blameless silence before the sacred office of speaking, bought and begun with servitude and forswearing. Howsoever, thus church-outed by the prelates, hence may appear the right I have to meddle in these matters, as before the necessity and constraint appeared.

———

From THE SECOND DEFENSE OF THE ENGLISH PEOPLE [1]

. . . I wish that I could with equal facility refute what this barbarous opponent has said of my blindness; but I cannot do it; and I must submit to the affliction. It is not so wretched to be blind, as it is not to be capable of enduring blindness. But why should I not endure a misfortune which it behooves everyone to be prepared to endure if it should happen; which may, in the common course of things, happen to any man; and which has been known to happen to the most distinguished and virtuous persons in history. Shall I mention those wise and ancient bards whose misfortunes the gods are said to have compensated by superior endowments, and whom men so much revered that they chose rather to impute their want of sight to the injustice of heaven than to their own want of innocence or virtue? What is reported of the augur Tiresias is well known, of whom Apollonius sung this in this Argonauts:

> To men he dared the will divine disclose,
> Nor feared what Jove might in his wrath impose.
> The gods assigned him age, without decay,
> But snatched the blessing of his sight away.

But God himself is truth, in propagating which, as men display a greater integrity and zeal, they approach nearer to the similitude of God and possess a greater portion of his love. We cannot suppose the Deity envious of truth or unwilling that it should be freely communicated to mankind. The loss of sight, therefore, which this inspired sage, who was so eager in promoting knowledge among men, sustained, cannot be considered as a judicial punishment. Or shall I mention those worthies who were as distinguished for wis-

[1] Text: *Defensio Secunda pro Populo Anglicano*, trans. by Robert Fellowes, 1806.

dom in the cabinet as for valor in the field? And first, Timoleon of Corinth, who delivered his city and all Sicily from the yoke of slavery; than whom there never lived in any age a more virtuous man or a more incorrupt statesman; next Appius Claudius, whose discreet counsels in the senate, though they could not restore sight to his own eyes, saved Italy from the formidable inroads of Pyrrhus; then Cæcilius Metellus the high priest, who lost his sight, while he saved, not only the city, but the palladium, the protection of the city, and the most sacred relics from the destruction of the flames. On other occasions Providence has indeed given conspicuous proofs of its regard for such singular exertions of patriotism and virtue; what, therefore, happened to so great and so good a man, I can hardly place in the catalogue of misfortunes. Why should I mention others of later times, as Dandolo of Venice, the incomparable Doge; or Boemar Zisca, the bravest of generals, and the champion of the cross; or Jerome Zanchius, and some other theologians of the highest reputation? For it is evident that the patriarch Isaac, than whom no man ever enjoyed more of the divine regard, lived blind for many years; and perhaps also his son Jacob, who was equally an object of the divine benevolence. And in short, did not our Saviour himself clearly declare that poor man whom he restored to sight had not been born blind either on account of his own sins or those of his progenitors? And with respect to myself, though I have accurately examined my conduct, and scrutinized my soul, I call thee, O God, the searcher of hearts, to witness that I am not conscious, either in the more early or in the later periods of my life, of having committed any enormity, which might deservedly have marked me out as a fit object for such a calamitous visitation. But since my enemies boast that this affliction is only a retribution for transgressions of my pen, I again invoke the Almighty to witness that I never at any time wrote anything which I did not think agreeable to truth, to justice, and to piety. This was my persuasion then, and I feel the same persuasion now. Nor was I ever prompted to such exertions by the influence of ambition, by the lust of lucre or of praise; it was only by the conviction of duty and the feeling of patriotism, a disinterested passion for the extension of civil and religious liberty. Thus, therefore, when I was publicly solicited to write a reply to the Defense of the royal cause, when I had to contend with the pressure of sickness, and with the apprehension of soon losing the sight of my remaining eye, and when my medical attendants clearly announced that if I did engage in the work, it would be irreparably lost, their premonitions caused no hesitation and inspired no dismay. I would not have listened to the voice even of Esculapius himself from the shrine of Epidauris, in preference to the suggestions of the heavenly monitor within my breast; my resolution was unshaken, though the alternative was either the loss of my sight or the desertion of my duty: and I called to mind those two destinies which the Oracle of Delphi announced to the son of Thetis:

> Two fates may lead me to the realms of night;
> If staying here, around Troy's wall I fight,
> To my dear home no more must I return;
> But lasting glory will adorn my urn.
> But, if I withdraw from the martial strife,
> Short is my fame, but long will be my life.
>
> —*Iliad,* ix.

I considered that many had purchased a less good by a greater evil, the meed of glory by the loss of life; but that I might procure great good by little suffering; that though I am blind, I might still discharge the most honorable duties, the performance of which, as it is something more durable than glory, ought to be an object of superior admiration and esteem; I resolved, therefore, to make the short interval of sight which was left me to enjoy, as beneficial as possible to the public interest. Thus it is clear by what motives I was governed in the measures which I took and the losses which

I sustained. Let then the calumniators of the divine goodness cease to revile or to make me the object of their superstitious imaginations. Let them consider that my situation,
such as it is, is neither an object of my shame or my regret,
that my resolutions are too firm to be shaken, that I am not
depressed by any sense of the divine displeasure; that, on
the other hand, in the most momentous periods, I have had
full experience of the divine favor and protection; and that,
in the solace and the strength which have been infused into
me from above, I have been enabled to do the will of God;
that I may oftener think on what he has bestowed than on
what he has withheld; that, in short, I am unwilling to exchange my consciousness of rectitude with that of any other
person; and that I feel the recollection a treasured store
of tranquillity and delight. But, if the choice were necessary, I would, sir, prefer my blindness to yours; yours is a
cloud spread over the mind, which darkens both the light
of reason and of conscience; mine keeps from my view only
the colored surfaces of things, while it leaves me at liberty
to contemplate the beauty and stability of virtue and of
truth. How many things are there besides which I would
not willingly see; how many which I must see against my
will; and how few which I feel any anxiety to see! There
is, as the apostle has remarked, a way of strength through
weakness. Let me then be the most feeble creature alive, as
long as that feebleness serves to invigorate the energies of my
rational and immortal spirit; as long as in that obscurity,
in which I am enveloped, the light of the divine presence
more clearly shines. Then, in proportion as I am blind,
I shall more clearly see. O! that I may thus be perfected
by feebleness and irradiated by obscurity! And, indeed, in
my blindness I enjoy in no inconsiderable degree the favor
of the Deity, who regards me with more tenderness and compassion in proportion as I am able to behold nothing but
himself. Alas! for him who insults me, who maligns and merits public execration! For the divine law not only shields

me from injury, but almost renders me too sacred to attack ;
not indeed so much from the privation of my sight, as from
the over-shadowing of those heavenly wings which seem to
have occasioned this obscurity ; and which, when occasioned,
He is wont to illuminate with an interior light, more precious
and more pure.

OF EDUCATION [1]

Letter to Master Samuel Hartlib

MASTER HARTLIB,

I am long since persuaded that to say or do aught worth memory and imitation, no purpose or respect should sooner move us than simply the love of God and of mankind. Nevertheless, to write now the reforming of education, though it be one of the greatest and noblest designs that can be thought on, and for the want whereof this nation perishes, I had not yet at this time been induced but by your earnest entreaties and serious conjurements; as having my mind for the present half diverted in the pursuance of some other assertions, the knowledge and the use of which cannot but be a great furtherance both to the enlargement of truth and honest living, with much more peace. Nor should the laws of any private friendship have prevailed with me to divide thus or transpose my former thoughts, but that I see those aims, those actions which have won you with me the esteem of a person sent hither by some good providence from a far country to be the occasion and the incitement of a great good to this island. And, as I hear, you have obtained the same repute with men of most approved wisdom, and some of highest authority among us; not to mention the learned correspondence which you hold in foreign parts, and the extraordinary pains and diligence which you have used in this matter both here and beyond the seas, either by the definite will of God so ruling, or the peculiar sway of nature, which also is God's working. Neither can I think that, so reputed and so valued as you are, you would, to the forfeit of your own discerning ability, impose upon me an unfit and over-ponderous argument; but that the satisfaction, which you profess to have received from those incidental discourses which we

[1] Text: 1644, first edition. I have followed Milton's paragraphing in spite of the length of the paragraphs.

have wandered into, hath pressed and almost constrained you into a persuasion, that what you require from me in this point, I neither ought nor can in conscience defer beyond this time, both of so much need at once, and so much opportunity to try what God hath determined. I will not resist, therefore, whatever it is either of divine or human obligement that you lay upon me; but will forthwith set down in writing, as you request me, that voluntary idea, which hath long in silence presented itself to me, of a better education, in extent and comprehension far more large, and yet of time far shorter and of attainment far more certain, than hath been yet in practice. Brief I shall endeavor to be; for that which I have to say, assuredly this nation hath extreme need should be done sooner than spoken. To tell you, therefore, what I have benefited herein among old renowned authors, I shall spare; and to search what many modern Januas and Didactics [2] more than ever I shall read, have projected, my inclination leads me not. But if you can accept of these few observations which have flowered off, and are, as it were, the burnishing of many studious and contemplative years altogether spent in the search of religious and civil knowledge, and such as pleased you so well in the relating, I here give you them to dispose of.

The end, then, of learning is to repair the ruins of our first parents by regaining to know God aright, and out of that knowledge to love him, to imitate him, to be like him, as we may the nearest by possessing our souls of true virtue, which being united to the heavenly grace of faith makes up the highest perfection. But because our understanding cannot in this body found itself but on sensible things, nor arrive so clearly to the knowledge of God and things invisible as by orderly conning over the visible and inferior creature, the same method is necessarily to be followed in all discreet teaching. And seeing every nation affords not experience and

[2] The reference is to two works by Comenius: *Janua Linguarum Reserata* and *Didactica Magna*.

tradition enough for all kind of learning, therefore we are chiefly taught the languages of those people who have at any time been most industrious after wisdom; so that language is but the instrument conveying to us things useful to be known. And though a linguist should pride himself to have all the tongues that Babel cleft the world into, yet if he have not studied the solid things in them, as well as the words and lexicons, he were nothing so much to be esteemed a learned man, as any yeoman or tradesman competently wise in his mother dialect only. Hence appear the many mistakes which have made learning generally so unpleasing and so unsuccessful. First, we do amiss to spend seven or eight years merely in scraping together so much miserable Latin and Greek as might be learned otherwise easily and delightfully in one year. And that which casts our proficiency therein so much behind is our time lost in too oft idle vacancies given both to schools and universities; partly in a preposterous exaction, forcing the empty wits of children to compose themes, verses, and orations, which are the acts of ripest judgment and the final work of a head filled by long reading and observing, with elegant maxims and copious invention. These are not matters to be wrung from poor striplings, like blood out of the nose, or the plucking of untimely fruit; besides the ill habit which they get of wretched barbarizing against the Latin and Greek idiom, with their untutored Anglicisms, odious to be read, yet not to be avoided without a well-continued and judicious conversing among pure authors, digested, which they scarce taste; whereas, if after some preparatory grounds of speech by their certain forms got into memory, they were led to the praxis thereof in some chosen short book lessoned thoroughly to them, they might then forthwith proceed to learn the substance of good things, and arts in due order, which would bring the whole language quickly into their power. This I take to be the most rational and most profitable way of learning languages, and whereby we may best hope to give account to God of our youth spent herein: and for the usual method of teaching arts, I deem it to be an old error of universities not yet well recovered from the scholastic grossness of barbarous ages, that, instead of beginning with arts most easy, and those be such as are most obvious to the sense, they present their young un-matriculated novices at first coming with the most intel-lective abstractions of logic and metaphysics: so that they, having but newly left those grammatic flats and shallows where they stuck unreasonably to learn a few words with lamentable construction, and now on the sudden transported under another climate, to be tossed and turmoiled with their unballasted wits in fathomless and unquiet deeps of con-troversy, do, for the most part, grow into hatred and con-tempt of learning, mocked and deluded all this while with ragged notions and babblements, while they expected worthy and delightful knowledge; till poverty or youthful years call them importunately their several ways, and hasten them with the sway of friends either to an ambitious and merce-nary, or ignorantly zealous divinity: some allured to the trade of law, grounding their purposes not on the prudent and heavenly contemplation of justice and equity, which was never taught them, but on the promising and pleasing thoughts of litigious terms, fat contentions, and flowing fees. Others betake them to state affairs, with souls so un-principled in virtue and true generous breeding that flattery, and court-shifts, and tyrannous aphorisms appear to them the highest points of wisdom, instilling their barren hearts with a conscientious slavery, if, as I rather think, it be not feigned. Others, lastly, of a more delicious and airy spirit, retire themselves, knowing no better, to the enjoyments of ease and luxury, living out their days in feast and jollity; which, indeed, is the wisest and safest course of all these, unless they were with more integrity undertaken. And these are the errors, and these are the fruits of mis-spending our prime youth at the schools and universities as we do, either in learning mere words, or such things chiefly as were better unlearned.

I shall detain you no longer in the demonstration of what we should not do, but straight conduct ye to a hillside, where I will point ye out the right path of a virtuous and noble education; laborious indeed at the first ascent, but else so smooth, so green, so full of goodly prospect and melodious sounds on every side, that the harp of Orpheus was not more charming. I doubt not but ye shall have more ado to drive our dullest and laziest youth, our stocks and stubs, from the infinite desire of such a happy nurture, than we have now to haul and drag our choicest and hopefulest wits to that asinine feast of sow-thistles and brambles which is commonly set before them, as all the food and entertainment of their tenderest and most docible age. I call, therefore, a complete and generous education, that which fits a man to perform justly, skillfully, and magnanimously all the offices, both private and public, of peace and war. And how all this may be done between twelve and one-and-twenty, less time than is now bestowed in pure trifling at grammar and sophistry, is to be thus ordered.

First, to find out a spacious house and ground about it fit for an academy, and big enough to lodge a hundred and fifty persons, whereof twenty or thereabout may be attendants, all under the government of one who shall be thought of desert sufficient, and ability either to do all or wisely to direct and oversee it done. This place should be at once both school and university, not needing a remove to any other house of scholarship, except it be some peculiar college of law or physic, where they mean to be practitioners; but as for those general studies which take up all our time from Lilly [3] to the commencing, as they term it, Master of Art, it should be absolute. After this pattern, as many edifices may

[3] Lilly's Latin Grammar used in all the schools. William Lilly, 1468(?)–1522, was headmaster of St. Paul's School.

be converted to this use as shall be needful in every city throughout the land, which would tend much to the increase of learning and civility everywhere. This number, less or more, thus collected, to the convenience of a foot-company or interchangeably two troops of cavalry, should divide their day's work into three parts, as it lies orderly: their studies, their exercise, and their diet.

For their studies: first, they should begin with the chief and necessary rules of some good grammar, either that now used, or any better; and while this is doing, their speech is to be fashioned to a distinct and clear pronunciation, as near as may be to the Italian, especially in the vowels. For we Englishmen, being far northerly, do not open our mouths in the cold air wide enough to grace a southern tongue; but are observed by all other nations to speak exceeding close and inward, so that to smatter Latin with an English mouth is as ill a hearing as law French. Next, to make them expert in the usefulest points of grammar, and withal to season them and win them early to the love of virtue and true labor, ere any flattering seducement or vain principle seize them wandering, some easy and delightful book of education would be read to them, whereof the Greeks have store, as Cebes,[4] Plutarch, and other Socratic discourses; but in Latin we have none of classic authority extant, except the two or three first books of Quintilian [5] and some select pieces elsewhere. But here the main skill and groundwork will be to temper them such lectures and explanations upon every opportunity, as may lead and draw them in willing obedience, inflamed with the study of learning and the admiration of virtue, stirred up with high hopes of living to be brave men and worthy patriots, dear to God and famous to all ages: that they may despise and scorn all their childish and ill-taught qualities, to delight in manly and liberal exercises; which he who hath the art and proper eloquence to catch

---

[4] Cebes was a disciple of Socrates.
[5] The *Institutio Oratoria* treats of education as well as of oratory.

them with, what with mild and effectual persuasions, and what with the intimation of some fear, if need be, but chiefly by his own example, might in a short space gain them to an incredible diligence and courage, infusing into their young breasts such an ingenuous and noble ardor as would not fail to make many of them renowned and matchless men. At the same time, some other hour of the day might be taught them the rules of arithmetic; and, soon after, the elements of geometry, even playing, as the old manner was. After evening repast till bed-time their thoughts would be best taken up in the easy grounds of religion and the story of Scripture. The next step would be to the authors of agriculture, Cato, Varro, and Columella, for the matter is most easy; and if the language be difficult, so much the better; it is not a difficulty above their years. And here will be an occasion of inciting and enabling them hereafter to improve the tillage of their country, to recover the bad soil, and to remedy the waste that is made of good; for this was one of Hercules' praises. Ere half these authors be read, which will soon be with plying hard and daily, they cannot choose but be masters of any ordinary prose: so that it will be then seasonable for them to learn in any modern author the use of the globes and all the maps, first with the old names and then with the new; or they might be then capable to read any compendious method of natural philosophy: and, at the same time, might be entering into the Greek tongue, after the same manner as was before prescribed in the Latin; whereby the difficulties of grammar being soon overcome, all the historical physiology of Aristotle and Theophrastus are open before them and, as I may say, under contribution. The like access will be to Vitruvius,[6] to Seneca's *Natural Questions*,[7] to Mela,[8] Celsus,[9] Pliny, or Solinus.[10] And hav-

---

[6] Author of *De Architectura*.
[7] A textbook of astronomy and meteorology.
[8] Mela, author of *De Chorographia*, a geographical work.
[9] Celsus, author of *De Medicina*.
[10] Solinus, editor of Pliny.

ing thus passed the principles of arithmetic, geometry, astronomy, and geography, with a general compact of physics, they may descend in mathematics to the instrumental science of trigonometry, and from thence to fortification, architecture, enginery, or navigation. And in natural philosophy they may proceed leisurely from the history of meteors, minerals, plants, and living creatures, as far as anatomy. Then also in course might be read to them out of some not tedious writer the institution of physic; that they may know the tempers, the humors, the seasons, and how to manage a crudity; which he who can wisely and timely do is not only a great physician to himself and to his friends, but also may at some time or other save an army by this frugal and expenseless means only, and not let the healthy and stout bodies of young men rot away under him for want of this discipline; which is a great pity, and no less a shame to the commander. To set forward all these proceedings in nature and mathematics, what hinders but that they may procure, as oft as shall be needful, the helpful experiences of hunters, fowlers, fishermen, shepherds, gardeners, apothecaries; and in other sciences, architects, engineers, mariners, anatomists; who, doubtless, would be ready, some for reward and some to favor such a hopeful seminary. And this will give them such a real tincture of natural knowledge as they shall never forget, but daily augment with delight. Then also those poets which are now counted most hard will be both facile and pleasant: Orpheus, Hesiod, Theocritus, Aratus, Nicander, Oppian, Dionysius; and, in Latin, Lucretius, Manilius, and the rural part of Virgil.

By this time, years and good general precepts will have furnished them more distinctly with that act of reason which in ethics is called *proairesis,* that they may with some judgment contemplate upon moral good and evil. Then will be required a special reinforcement of constant and sound indoctrinating to set them right and firm, instructing them more amply in the knowledge of virtue and the hatred of vice;

while their young and pliant affections are led through all
the moral works of Plato, Xenophon, Cicero, Plutarch, Laertius,[11] and those Locrian [12] remnants; but still to be reduced
in their nightward studies, wherewith they close the day's
work, under the determinate sentence of David or Solomon,
or the evangels and apostolic Scriptures. Being perfect in
the knowledge of personal duty, they may then begin the
study of economics. And either now or before this they may
have easily learned at any odd hour the Italian tongue. And
soon after, but with wariness and good antidote, it would
be wholesome enough to let them taste some choice comedies,
Greek, Latin, or Italian; those tragedies also that treat of
household matters, as *Trachiniæ, Alcestis*, and the like. The
next remove must be to the study of politics; to know the
beginning, end, and reasons of political societies, that they
may not, in a dangerous fit of the commonwealth, be such
poor, shaken, uncertain reeds, of such a tottering conscience
as many of our great counselors have lately shown themselves, but steadfast pillars of the state. After this they are
to dive into the grounds of law and legal justice, delivered
first and with best warrant by Moses; and, as far as human
prudence can be trusted, in those extolled remains of Grecian law-givers, Lycurgus, Solon, Zaleucus, Charondas; and
thence to all the Roman edicts and tables, with their Justinian; and so down to the Saxon and common laws of England and the statutes. Sundays also and every evening may
now be understandingly spent in the highest matters of theology and church history, ancient and modern; and ere this
time the Hebrew tongue at a set hour might have been
gained, that the Scriptures may be read in their own original;
whereto it would be no impossibility to add the Chaldee and
the Syrian dialect. When all these employments are well conquered, then will the choice histories, heroic poems, and
Attic tragedies of stateliest and most regal argument, with

[11] Diogenes Laertius, author of *Lives of the Philosophers*.
[12] Timæus of Locri, a Pythagorean philosopher.

all the famous political orations, offer themselves; which,
if they were not only read, but some of them got by memory,
and solemnly pronounced with right accent and grace, as
might be taught, would endue them even with the spirit
and vigor of Demosthenes or Cicero, Euripides or Sophocles.
And now, lastly, will be the time to read with them those
organic arts which enable men to discourse and write per-
spicuously, elegantly, and according to the fitted style of
lofty, mean, or lowly. Logic, therefore, so much as is useful,
is to be referred to this due place, with all her well-couched
heads and topics, until it be time to open her contracted
palm into a graceful and ornate rhetoric taught out of the
rule of Plato, Aristotle, Phalereus,[13] Cicero, Hermogenes,[14]
Loginus.[15] To which poetry would be made subsequent, or,
indeed, rather precedent, as being less subtle and fine, but
more simple, sensuous, and passionate; I mean not here the
prosody of a verse, which they could not but have hit on
before among the rudiments of grammar, but that sublime
art which in Aristotle's *Poetics,* in Horace, and the Italian
commentaries of Castelvetro, Tasso, Mazzoni, and others,
teaches what the laws are of a true epic poem, what of a
dramatic, what of a lyric, what decorum is, which is the
grand masterpiece to observe. This would make them soon
perceive what despicable creatures our common rhymers and
play-writers be; and show them what religious, what glorious and magnificent use might be made of poetry, both
in divine and human things. From hence, and not till now,
will be the right season of forming them to be able writers
and composers in every excellent matter, when they shall
be thus fraught with an universal insight into things. Or
whether they be to speak in Parliament or Council, honor
and attention would be waiting on their lips. There would
then also appear in pulpits other visages, other gestures, and

---

[13] Phalereus, an orator of Athens, author of *Elocution.*
[14] Hermogenes, Greek rhetorician whose works were used as textbooks.
[15] Longinus, Greek critic, author of *On the Sublime.*

stuff otherwise wrought than what we now sit under, oft-times to as great a trial of our patience as any other that they preach to us. These are the studies wherein our noble and our gentle youth ought to bestow their time in a disciplinary way from twelve to one-and-twenty, unless they rely more upon their ancestors dead than upon themselves living. In which methodical course it is so supposed they must proceed by the steady pace of learning onward, as at convenient times for memory's sake to retire back into the middle ward, and sometimes into the rear of what they have been taught, until they have confirmed and solidly united the whole body of their perfected knowledge, like the last embattling of a Roman legion. Now will be worth the seeing what exercises and what recreations may best agree and become those studies.

Their Exercise

THE COURSE of study hitherto briefly described is, what I can guess by reading, likest to those ancient and famous schools of Pythagoras, Plato, Isocrates, Aristotle, and such others, out of which were bred such a number of renowned philosophers, orators, historians, poets, and princes all over Greece, Italy, and Asia, besides the flourishing studies of Cyrene and Alexandria. But herein it shall exceed them, and supply a defect as great as that which Plato noted in the commonwealth of Sparta; whereas that city trained up their youth most for war, and these in their academies and Lyceum all for the gown, this institution of breeding which I here delineate shall be equally good both for peace and war. Therefore, about an hour and a half ere they eat at noon should be allowed them for exercise, and due rest afterwards; but the time for this may be enlarged at pleasure, according as their rising in the morning shall be early. The exercise which I commend first is the exact use of their

weapon, to guard, and to strike safely with edge or point;
this will keep them healthy, nimble, strong, and well in
breath, is also the likeliest means to make them grow large
and tall, and to inspire them with a gallant and fearless
courage, which, being tempered with seasonable lectures and
precepts to them of true fortitude and patience, will turn
into a native and heroic valor, and make them hate the
cowardice of doing wrong. They must be also practiced in
all the locks and gripes of wrestling, wherein Englishmen
were wont to excel, as need may often be in fight to tug, to
grapple, and to close. And this, perhaps, will be enough
wherein to prove and heat their single strength. The interim
of unsweating themselves regularly, and convenient rest before meat, may both with profit and delight be taken up in
recreating and composing their travailed spirits with the
solemn and divine harmonies of music heard or learned;
either while the skillful organist plies his grave and fancied
descant in lofty fugues, or the whole symphony with artful
and unimaginable touches adorn and grace the well-studied
chords of some choice composer; sometimes the lute or soft
organ-stop, waiting on elegant voices, either to religious,
martial, or civil ditties; which, if wise men and prophets
be not extremely out, have a great power over dispositions
and manners, to smooth and make them gentle from rustic
harshness and distempered passions. The like also would
not be inexpedient after meat, to assist and cherish nature
in her first concoction, and send their minds back to study
in good tune and satisfaction. Where having followed it close
under vigilant eyes until about two hours before supper, they
are, by a sudden alarum or watchword, to be called out to
their military motions, under sky or covert, according to the
season, as was the Roman wont; first on foot, then, as their
age permits, on horseback, to all the art of cavalry; that
having in sport, but with much exactness and daily muster,
served out the rudiments of their soldiership in all the skill
of embattling, marching, encamping, fortifying, besieging,

and battering, with all the helps of ancient and modern stratagems, tactics, and warlike maxims, they may, as it were out
of a long war, come forth renowned and perfect commanders
in the service of their country. They would not then, if they
were trusted with fair and hopeful armies, suffer them for
want of just and wise discipline to shed away from about
them like sick feathers, though they be never so oft supplied;
they would not suffer their empty and unrecruitable colonels
of twenty men in a company to quaff out or convey into
secret hoards, the wages of a delusive list and a miserable
remnant; yet in the meanwhile to be overmastered with a
score or two of drunkards, the only soldiery left about them,
or else to comply with all rapines and violences. No, certainly, if they knew aught of that knowledge that belongs
to good men or good governors, they would not suffer these
things. But to return to our own institute: besides these constant exercises at home, there is another opportunity of
gaining experience to be won from pleasure itself abroad;
in those vernal seasons of the year, when the air is calm and
pleasant, it were an injury and sullenness against nature not
to go out and see her riches and partake in her rejoicing with
heaven and earth. I should not, therefore, be a persuader
to them of studying much then, after two or three years
that they have well laid their grounds, but to ride out in
companies with prudent and staid guides to all the quarters
of the land, learning and observing all places of strength,
all commodities of building and of soil, for towns and tillage,
harbors, and ports for trade. Sometimes taking sea as far
as to our navy, to learn there also what they can in the
practical knowledge of sailing and of sea-fight. These ways
would try all their peculiar gifts of nature; and if there were
any secret excellence among them, would fetch it out and
give it fair opportunity to advance itself by, which could
not but mightily redound to the good of this nation, and
bring into fashion again those old admired virtues and excellencies, with far more advantage now in this purity of

Christian knowledge. Nor shall we then need the monsieurs of Paris to take our hopeful youth into their slight and prodigal custodies, and send them over back again transformed into mimics, apes, and kickshaws. But if they desire to see other countries at three or four and twenty years of age, not to learn principles, but to enlarge experience and make wise observation, they will by that time be such as shall deserve the regard and honor of all men where they pass, and the society and friendship of those in all places who are best and most eminent. And perhaps then other nations will be glad to visit us for their breeding, or else to imitate us in their own country.

Now, lastly, for their diet there cannot be much to say, save only that it would be best in the same house; for much time else would be lost abroad, and many ill habits got; and that it should be plain, healthful, and moderate, I suppose is out of controversy. Thus, Mr. Hartlib, you have a general view in writing, as your desire was, of that which at several times I had discoursed with you concerning the best and noblest way of education; not beginning, as some have done, from the cradle, which yet might be worth many considerations, if brevity had not been my scope. Many other circumstances also I could have mentioned; but this, to such as have the worth in them to make trial, for light and direction may be enough. Only I believe that this is not a bow for every man to shoot in that counts himself a teacher, but will require sinews almost equal to those which Homer gave Ulysses; yet I am withal persuaded that it may prove much more easy in the assay than it now seems at distance, and much more illustrious: howbeit not more difficult than I imagine, and that imagination presents me with nothing but very happy and very possible according to best wishes; if God have so decreed, and this age have spirit and capacity enough to apprehend.

———

AREOPAGITICA [1]

A Speech for the Liberty of Unlicensed Printing, to the Parliament of England

THEY, WHO to states and governors of the Commonwealth direct their speech, High Court of Parliament, or, wanting such access in a private condition, write that which they foresee may advance the public good; I suppose them, as at the beginning of no mean endeavor, not a little altered and moved inwardly in their minds: some with doubt of what will be the success, others with fear of what will be the censure; some with hope, others with confidence of what they have to speak. And me perhaps each of these dispositions, as the subject was whereon I entered, may have at other times variously affected; and likely might in these foremost expressions now also disclose which of them swayed most, but that the very attempt of this address thus made, and the thought of whom it hath recourse to, hath got the power within me to a passion, far more welcome than incidental to a preface. Which though I stay not to confess ere any ask, I shall be blameless, if it be no other than the joy and gratulation which it brings to all who wish and promote their country's liberty; whereof this whole discourse proposed will be a certain testimony, if not a trophy. For this is not the liberty which we can hope, that no grievance ever should arise in the Commonwealth: that let no man in this world expect; but when complaints are freely heard, deeply considered and speedily reformed, then is the utmost bound of civil liberty attained that wise men look for. To which if I now manifest by the very sound of this which

[1] Text: 1644, first edition. Since Milton indicates the structure of the essay by his paragraphing, his own divisions have been preserved in spite of the great length of some of them. As will be seen in the latter part of the essay, Milton can write short paragraphs when the topic can be briefly covered.

I shall utter, that we are already in good part arrived, and yet from such a steep disadvantage of tyranny and superstition grounded into our principles as was beyond the manhood of a Roman recovery, it will be attributed first, as is most due, to the strong assistance of God our deliverer; next to your faithful guidance and undaunted wisdom, Lords and Commons of England. Neither is it in God's esteem the diminution of his glory, when honorable things are spoken of good men and worthy magistrates; which if I now first should begin to do, after so fair a progress of your laudable deeds, and such a long obligement upon the whole realm to your indefatigable virtues, I might be justly reckoned among the tardiest, and the unwillingest of them that praise ye. Nevertheless, there being three principal things, without which all praising is but courtship and flattery: first, when that only is praised which is solidly worth praise; next, when greatest likelihoods are brought that such things are truly and really in those persons to whom they are ascribed; the other, when he who praises, by showing that such his actual persuasion is of whom he writes, can demonstrate that he flatters not; the former two of these I have heretofore endeavored, rescuing the employment from him who went about to impair your merits with a trivial and malignant encomium; [2] the latter as belonging chiefly to mine own acquittal, that whom I so extolled I did not flatter, hath been reserved opportunely to this occasion. For he who freely magnifies what hath been nobly done, and fears not to declare as freely what might be done better, gives ye the best covenant of his fidelity; and that his loyalest affection and his hope waits on your proceedings. His highest praising is not flattery, and his plainest advice is a kind of praising; for though I should affirm and hold by argument, that it would fare better with truth, with learning, and the Commonwealth, if one of your published Orders, which I should name,

[2] Bishop Joseph Hall in his *Humble Remonstrance to the High Court of Parliament*.

were called in; yet at the same time it could not but much redound to the luster of your mild and equal government, whenas private persons are hereby animated to think ye better pleased with public advice, than other statists have been delighted heretofore with public flattery. And men will then see what difference there is between the magnanimity of a triennial Parliament, and that jealous haughtiness of prelates and cabin counselors that usurped of late, whenas they shall observe ye in the midst of your victories and successes more gently brooking written exceptions against a voted Order than other courts, which had produced nothing worth memory but the weak ostentation of wealth, would have endured the least signified dislike at any sudden proclamation. If I should thus far presume upon the meek demeanor of your civil and gentle greatness, Lords and Commons, as what your published Order hath directly said, that to gainsay, I might defend myself with ease, if any should accuse me of being new or insolent, did they but know how much better I find ye esteem it to imitate the old and elegant humanity of Greece than the barbaric pride of a Hunnish and Norwegian stateliness. And out of those ages, to whose polite wisdom and letters we owe that we are not yet Goths and Jutlanders, I could name him who from his private house wrote that discourse to the Parliament of Athens,[3] that persuades them to change the form of democraty which was then established. Such honor was done in those days to men who professed the study of wisdom and eloquence, not only in their own country, but in other lands, that cities and signiories heard them gladly and with great respect, if they had aught in public to admonish the state. Thus did Dion Prusæus, a stranger and a private orator, counsel the Rhodians against a former edict; [4] and I abound

[3] Isocrates, 355 B.C., in the capacity of a private citizen presented a written address to the Areopagus. Milton follows his example in this address to Parliament and derives his title from the Areopagiticus of Isocrates. For another reference to Isocrates see Milton's sonnet to Lady Margaret Ley.
[4] Dion Prusæus, first century B.C.

with other like examples, which to set here would be superfluous. But if from the industry of a life wholly dedicated
to studious labors, and those natural endowments haply not
the worse for two-and-fifty degrees of northern latitude, so
much must be derogated as to count me not equal to any
of those who had this privilege, I would obtain to be thought
not so inferior, as yourselves are superior to the most of
them who received their counsel: and how far you excel
them, be assured, Lords and Commons, there can no greater
testimony appear than when your prudent spirit acknowledges and obeys the voice of reason, from what quarter soever it be heard speaking; and renders ye as willing to repeal any Act of your own setting forth, as any set forth
by your predecessors.

If ye be thus resolved, as it were injury to think ye were
not, I know not what should withhold me from presenting
ye with a fit instance wherein to show both that love of
truth which ye eminently profess, and that uprightness of
your judgment which is not wont to be partial to yourselves;
by judging over again that Order [5] which ye have ordained
to regulate printing: *that no book, pamphlet, or paper shall
be henceforth printed, unless the same be first approved and
licensed by such,* or at least one of such, as shall be thereto
appointed. For that part which preserves justly every man's
copy to himself, or provides for the poor, I touch not; only
wish they be not made pretenses to abuse and persecute
honest and painful men, who offend not in either of these
particulars. But that other clause of licensing books, which
we thought had died with his brother quadragesimal [6] and
matrimonial when the prelates expired,[7] I shall now attend
with such a homily, as shall lay before ye, first, the inventors
of it to be those whom ye will be loath to own; next, what
is to be thought in general of reading, whatever sort the

[5] The Order of June 14, 1643.
[6] Quadragesimal licenses were issued for eating white meats in Lent.
[7] The reference is to the bill of 1642 for the Exclusion of Bishops from
Parliament.

books be; and that this Order avails nothing to the suppressing of scandalous, seditious, and libelous books, which
were mainly intended to be suppressed. Last, that it will
be primely to the discouragement of all learning, and the
stop of truth, not only by disexercising and blunting our
abilities in what we know already, but by hindering and
cropping the discovery that might be yet further made, both
in religious and civil wisdom.

I deny not, but that it is of greatest concernment in the
church and Commonwealth, to have a vigilant eye how books
demean themselves, as well as men; and thereafter to confine, imprison, and do sharpest justice on them as malefactors:
for books are not absolutely dead things, but do contain a
potency of life in them to be as active as that soul was whose
progeny they are; nay, they do preserve as in a vial the
purest efficacy and extraction of that living intellect that
bred them. I know they are as lively and as vigorously productive as those fabulous dragon's teeth; and being sown
up and down, may chance to spring up armed men.[8] And
yet, on the other hand, unless wariness be used, as good almost kill a man as kill a good book: who kills a man kills
a reasonable creature, God's image; but he who destroys
a good book, kills reason itself, kills the image of God, as
it were, in the eye. Many a man lives a burden to the earth;
but a good book is the precious life-blood of a master spirit,
embalmed and treasured up on purpose to a life beyond life.
'Tis true, no age can restore a life, whereof perhaps there
is no great loss; and revolutions of ages do not oft recover
the loss of a rejected truth, for the want of which whole nations fare the worse. We should be wary, therefore, what
persecution we raise against the living labors of public men,
how we spill that seasoned life of man preserved and stored
up in books; since we see a kind of homicide may be thus
committed, sometimes a martyrdom, and if it extend to the
whole impression, a kind of massacre; whereof the execu-

[8] See the myth of Cadmus and the myth of Jason and the golden fleece.

tion ends not in the slaying of an elemental life, but strikes at that ethereal and fifth essence, the breath of reason itself, slays an immortality rather than a life. But lest I should be condemned of introducing license, while I oppose licensing, I refuse not the pains to be so much historical, as will serve to show what hath been done by ancient and famous commonwealths against this disorder, till the very time that this project of licensing crept out of the Inquisition, was catched up by our prelates, and hath caught some of our presbyters.

In Athens, where books and wits were ever busier than in any other part of Greece, I find but only two sorts of writings which the magistrate cared to take notice of: those either blasphemous and atheistical, or libelous. Thus the books of Protagoras [9] were by the judges of Areopagus commanded to be burnt, and himself banished the territory for a discourse begun with his confessing not to know *whether there were gods, or whether not*. And against defaming, it was agreed that none should be traduced by name, as was the manner of Vetus Comœdia, whereby we may guess how they censured libeling: and this course was quick enough, as Cicero writes, to quell both the desperate wits of other atheists, and the open way of defaming, as the event showed. Of other sects and opinions, though tending to voluptuousness and the denying of Divine Providence, they took no heed. Therefore we do not read that either Epicurus, or that libertine school of Cyrene,[10] or what the Cynic impudence uttered, was ever questioned by the laws. Neither is it recorded that the writings of those old comedians were suppressed, though the acting of them were forbid; and that Plato commended the reading of Aristophanes, the loosest of them all, to his royal scholar Dionysius, is commonly known, and may be excused, if holy Chrysostom, as is reported, nightly studied so much the same author and had

[9] Protagoras, 480–410 B.C.
[10] The Cyrenaic philosophers considered pleasure the highest good.

the art to cleanse a scurrilous vehemence into the style of
a rousing sermon. That other leading city of Greece, Lac-
edæmon, considering that Lycurgus their lawgiver was so
addicted to elegant learning as to have been the first that
brought out of Ionia the scattered works of Homer, and
sent the poet Thales [11] from Crete to prepare and mollify
the Spartan surliness with his smooth songs and odes, the
better to plant among them law and civility; it is to be
wondered how museless and unbookish they were, mind-
ing naught but the feats of war. There needed no licensing
of books among them, for they disliked all but their own
laconic apothegms, and took a slight occasion to chase
Archilochus [12] out of their city, perhaps for composing in
a higher strain than their own soldierly ballads and roundels
could reach to: or if it were for his broad verses, they were
not therein so cautious, but they were as dissolute in their
promiscuous conversing; whence Euripides affirms in *Andromache* that their women were all unchaste. Thus much
may give us light after what sort books were prohibited
among the Greeks. The Romans also, for many ages trained
up only to a military roughness, resembling most the Lac-
edæmonian guise, knew of learning little but what their
twelve Tables and the Pontific College with their augurs
and flamens taught them in religion and law, so unacquainted
with other learning that when Carneades and Critolaus,
with the Stoic Diogenes coming ambassadors to Rome, took
thereby occasion to give the city a taste of their philosophy,
they were suspected for seducers by no less a man than Cato
the Censor, who moved it in the Senate to dismiss them
speedily, and to banish all such Attic babblers out of Italy.
But Scipio and others of the noblest senators withstood him
and his old Sabine austerity; honored and admired the men;
and the Censor himself at last, in his old age, fell to the

[11] Thaletas, the poet from Crete, is meant. He flourished about 620 B.C.
[12] Archilochus, who flourished about 650 B.C., is supposed to have originated iambic meter as a suitable verse form for satiric poetry.

study of that whereof before he was so scrupulous. And yet at the same time, Nævius and Plautus, the first Latin comedians, had filled the city with all the borrowed scenes of Menander and Philemon. Then began to be considered there also what was to be done to libelous books and authors; for Nævius was quickly cast into prison for his unbridled pen, and released by the tribunes upon his recantation; we read also that libels were burnt, and the makers punished by Augustus. The like severity, no doubt, was used, if aught were impiously written against their esteemed gods. Except in these two points, how the world went in books, the magistrate kept no reckoning. And therefore Lucretius without impeachment versifies his Epicurism to Memmius, and had the honor to be set forth the second time by Cicero, so great a father of the commonwealth; although himself disputes against that opinion in his own writings. Nor was the satirical sharpness or naked plainness of Lucilius, or Catullus, or Flaccus, by any order prohibited. And for matters of state, the story of Titus Livius, though it extolled that part which Pompey held, was not therefore suppressed by Octavius Cæsar, of the other faction. But that Naso was by him banished in his old age for the wanton poems of his youth was but a mere covert of state over some secret cause: and besides, the books were neither banished nor called in. From hence we shall meet with little else but tyranny in the Roman empire, that we may not marvel if not so often bad as good books were silenced. I shall therefore deem to have been large enough, in producing what among the ancients was punishable to write, save only which, all other arguments were free to treat on.

By this time the emperors were become Christians, whose discipline in this point I do not find to have been more severe than what was formerly in practice. The books of those whom they took to be grand heretics were examined, refuted, and condemned in the general councils; and not till then were prohibited, or burnt, by authority of the em-

peror. As for the writings of heathen authors, unless they
were plain invectives against Christianity, as those of Por-
phyrius and Proclus,[13] they met with no interdict that can
be cited, till about the year 400, in a Carthaginian Council,
wherein bishops themselves were forbid to read the books
of Gentiles, but heresies they might read; while others long
before them, on the contrary, scrupled more the books of
heretics than of Gentiles. And that the primitive councils
and bishops were wont only to declare what books were not
commendable, passing no further, but leaving it to each
one's conscience to read or to lay by, till after the year 800,
is observed already by Padre Paolo, the great unmasker of
the Trentine Council. After which time the Popes of Rome,
engrossing what they pleased of political rule into their own
hands, extended their dominion over men's eyes, as they had
before over their judgments, burning and prohibiting to
be read what they fancied not; yet sparing in their censures,
and the books not many which they so dealt with: till
Martin the Fifth, by his bull, not only prohibited, but was
the first that excommunicated the reading of heretical books;
for about that time Wyckliffe and Huss, growing terrible,
were they who first drove the papal court to a stricter policy
of prohibiting. Which course Leo the Tenth and his successors followed, until the Council of Trent and the Spanish
Inquisition engendering together brought forth, or perfected,
those Catalogues and expurging Indexes, that rake through
the entrails of many an old good author with a violation
worse than any could be offered to his tomb. Nor did they
stay in matters heretical, but any subject that was not to
their palate, they either condemned in a Prohibition, or
had it straight into the new purgatory of an Index. To fill
up the measure of encroachment, their last invention was
to ordain that no book, pamphlet, or paper should be printed
(as if St. Peter had bequeathed them the keys of the press

[13] Porphyrus, A.D. 233(?)–304(?), and Proclus A.D. 410–485, were Neopla-
tonists.

also out of paradise) unless it were approved and licensed under the hands of two or three gluttonous friars. For example:

> Let the Chancellor Cini be pleased to see
> if in this present work be contained aught
> that may withstand the printing.
> > Vincent Rabatta, Vicar of Florence.

> I have seen this present work, and find nothing
> athwart the Catholic faith and good manners:
> in witness whereof I have given, etc.
> > Nicolò Cini, Chancellor of Florence.

> Attending the precedent relation, it is allowed
> that this present work of Davanzati may be
> printed.
> > Vincent Rabatta, etc.
> It may be printed, July 15.
> > Friar Simon Mompei d'Amelia, Chancellor
> > of the holy office in Florence.

Sure they have a conceit, if he of the bottomless pit had not long since broke prison, that this quadruple exorcism would bar him down. I fear their next design will be to get into their custody the licensing of that which they say Claudius intended, but went not through with. Vouchsafe to see another of their forms, the Roman stamp:

> Imprimatur, If it seem good to the reverend master
> of the holy palace.
> > Belcastro, Vicegerent.

> Imprimatur, Friar Nicolò Rodolphi, Master of the
> holy palace.

Sometimes five Imprimaturs are seen together dialogue-wise in the piazza of one title-page, complimenting and ducking each to other with their shaven reverences, whether the author, who stands by in perplexity at the foot of his epistle, shall to the press or to the sponge. These are the pretty responsories, these are the dear antiphonies, that so bewitched of late our prelates and their chaplains with the goodly echo they made; and besotted us to the gay imitation of a lordly Imprimatur, one from Lambeth House, another from the west end of Paul's; so apishly Romanizing, that the word of command still was set down in Latin; as if the learned grammatical pen that wrote it would cast no ink without Latin; or perhaps, as they thought, because no vulgar tongue was worthy to express the pure conceit of an Imprimatur; but rather, as I hope, for that our English, the language of men ever famous and foremost in the achievements of liberty, will not easily find servile letters enow to spell such a dictatory presumption English. And thus ye have the inventors and the original of book-licensing ripped up and drawn as lineally as any pedigree. We have it not, that can be heard of, from any ancient state, or polity, or church, nor by any statute left us by our ancestors elder or later; nor from the modern custom of any reformed city or church abroad; but from the most anti-Christian council and the most tyrannous Inquisition that ever inquired. Till then books were ever as freely admitted into the world as any other birth; the issue of the brain was no more stifled than the issue of the womb: no envious Juno sat cross-legged [14] over the nativity of any man's intellectual offspring; but if it proved a monster, who denies but that it was justly burnt, or sunk into the sea? But that a book, in worse condition than a peccant soul, should be to stand before a jury ere it be born to the world, and undergo yet in darkness the judgment of Radamanth and his colleagues,

[14] Juno sat cross-legged on the threshold muttering evil spells when Hercules, son of Jupiter and Alcmena, was born.

ere it can pass the ferry backward into light, was never heard
before, till that mysterious iniquity, provoked and troubled
at the first entrance of Reformation, sought out new limbos
and new hells wherein they might include our books also
within the number of their damned. And this was the rare
morsel so officiously snatched up, and so ill-favoredly imitated by our inquisiturient bishops, and the attendant minor-
ites their chaplains. That ye like not now these most certain
authors of this licensing order, and that all sinister intention
was far distant from your thoughts when ye were importuned
the passing it, all men who know the integrity of your actions,
and how ye honor truth, will clear ye readily.

But some will say, What though the inventors were bad,
the thing for all that may be good. It may so; yet if that
thing be no such deep invention, but obvious, and easy for
any man to light on, and yet best and wisest commonwealths
through all ages and occasions have forborne to use it, and
falsest seducers and oppressors of men were the first who
took it up, and to no other purpose but to obstruct and
hinder the first approach of Reformation; I am of those who
believe it will be a harder alchemy than Lullius [15] ever
knew, to sublimate any good use out of such an invention.
Yet this only is what I request to gain from this reason, that
it may be held a dangerous and suspicious fruit, as certainly it deserves, for the tree that bore it, until I can dissect
one by one the properties it has. But I have first to finish,
as was propounded, what is to be thought in general of
reading books, whatever sort they be, and whether be more
the benefit or the harm that thence proceeds?

Not to insist upon the examples of Moses, Daniel, and
Paul, who were skillful in all the learning of the Egyptians,
Chaldeans, and Greeks, which could not probably be without reading their books of all sorts, in Paul especially, who
thought it no defilement to insert into Holy Scripture the

---

[15] Raymond Lully, 1235–1313. His system, known as *Ars Lulliana,* was
famous in the fourteenth, fifteenth, and sixteenth centuries.

sentences of three Greek poets, and one of them a tragedian; the question was notwithstanding sometimes controverted among the primitive doctors, but with great odds on that side which affirmed it both lawful and profitable, as was then evidently perceived, when Julian the Apostate, and subtlest enemy to our faith, made a decree forbidding Christians the study of heathen learning; for, said he, they wound us with our own weapons, and with our own arts and sciences they overcome us. And indeed the Christians were put so to their shifts by this crafty means, and so much in danger to decline into all ignorance, that the two Apollinarii [16] were fain, as a man may say, to coin all the seven liberal sciences out of the Bible, reducing it into divers forms of orations, poems, dialogues, even to the calculating of a new Christian grammar. But, saith the historian Socrates, the providence of God provided better than the industry of Apollinarius and his son, by taking away that illiterate law with the life of him who devised it. So great an injury they then held it to be deprived of Hellenic learning; and thought it a persecution more undermining, and secretly decaying the Church, than the open cruelty of Decius or Diocletian. And perhaps it was the same politic drift that the devil whipped St. Jerome in a Lenten dream, for reading Cicero; or else it was a phantasm bred by the fever which had then seized him. For had an angel been his discipliner, unless it were for dwelling too much upon Ciceronianisms, and had chastised the reading, not the vanity, it had been plainly partial: first to correct him for grave Cicero, and not for scurrile Plautus, whom he confesses to have been reading not long before; next to correct him only, and let so many more ancient Fathers wax old in those pleasant and florid studies without the lash of such a tutoring apparition; insomuch that Basil teaches how some good use may be made of

[16] Apollinaris the Elder and his son, bishop of Laodicea, in Syria, changed the Old Testament into Homeric and Pindaric poetry and the New Testament into Platonic dialogues.

Margites, a sportful poem, not now extant, writ by Homer; and why not then of *Morgante,* an Italian romance much to the same purpose? But if it be agreed we shall be tried by visions, there is a vision recorded by Eusebius, far ancienter than this tale of Jerome to the nun Eustochium, and, besides, has nothing of a fever in it. Dionysius Alexandrinus was about the year 240 a person of great name in the church for piety and learning, who had wont to avail himself much against heretics by being conversant in their books; until a certain presbyter laid it scrupulously to his conscience, how he durst venture himself among those defiling volumes. The worthy man, loath to give offense, fell into a new debate with himself what was to be thought; when suddenly a vision sent from God (it is his own epistle that so avers it) confirmed him in these words: Read any books whatever come to thy hands, for thou are sufficient both to judge aright, and to examine each matter. To this revelation he assented the sooner, as he confesses, because it was answerable to that of the Apostle to the Thessalonians, Prove all things, hold fast that which is good.[17] And he might have added another remarkable saying of the same author: To the pure, all things are pure;[18] not only meats and drinks, but all kind of knowledge whether of good or evil; the knowledge cannot defile, nor consequently the books, if the will and conscience be not defiled. For books are as meats and viands are; some of good, some of evil substance; and yet God, in that unapocryphal vision, said without exception, Rise, Peter, kill and eat,[19] leaving the choice to each man's discretion. Wholesome meats to a vitiated stomach differ little or nothing from unwholesome; and best books to a naughty mind are not unappliable to occasions of evil. Bad meats will scarce breed good nourishment in the healthiest concoction; but herein the difference is of bad books, that they to a discreet and judicious reader serve in many respects to discover, to confute, to forewarn, and to illustrate. Whereof

[17] I Thess. 5:21.   [18] Titus 1:15.   [19] Acts 10:13.

what better witness can ye expect I should produce, than one of your own now sitting in Parliament, the chief of learned men reputed in this land, Mr. Selden; [20] whose volume of natural and national laws proves, not only by great authorities brought together, but by exquisite reasons and theorems almost mathematically demonstrative, that all opinions, yea errors, known, read, and collated, are of main service and assistance toward the speedy attainment of what is truest. I conceive, therefore, that when God did enlarge the universal diet of man's body, saving ever the rules of temperance, he then also, as before, left arbitrary the dieting and repasting of our minds; as wherein every mature man might have to exercise his own leading capacity. How great a virtue is temperance, how much of moment through the whole life of man! Yet God commits the managing so great a trust, without particular law or prescription, wholly to the demeanor of every grown man. And therefore when he himself tabled the Jews from heaven, that omer, which was every man's daily portion of manna, is computed to have been more than might have well sufficed the heartiest feeder thrice as many meals. For those actions which enter into a man, rather than issue out of him, and therefore defile not, God uses not to captivate under a perpetual childhood of prescription, but trusts him with the gift of reason to be his own chooser; there were but little work left for preaching, if law and compulsion should grow so fast upon these things which heretofore were governed only by exhortation. Solomon informs us that much reading is a weariness to the flesh; but neither he nor other inspired author tells us that such or such reading is unlawful: yet certainly had God thought good to limit us herein, it had been much more expedient to have told us what was unlawful than what was wearisome. As for the burning of those Ephesian books by St. Paul's converts, 'tis replied the books were magic, the Syriac so renders them. It was a private act, a voluntary act, and leaves us to a voluntary imitation: the men in

[20] John Selden, 1584–1654.

remorse burnt those books which were their own; the magistrate by this example is not appointed; these men practiced the books, another might perhaps have read them in some sort usefully. Good and evil we know in the field of this world grow up together almost inseparably; and the knowledge of good is so involved and interwoven with the knowledge of evil, and in so many cunning resemblances hardly to be discerned, that those confused seeds which were imposed on Psyche as an incessant labor to cull out and sort asunder, were not more intermixed. It was from out the rind of one apple tasted, that the knowledge of good and evil, as two twins cleaving together, leaped forth into the world. And perhaps this is that doom which Adam fell into of knowing good and evil, that is to say of knowing good by evil. As therefore the state of man now is, what wisdom can there be to choose, what continence to forbear without the knowledge of evil? He that can apprehend and consider vice with all her baits and seeming pleasures, and yet abstain, and yet distinguish, and yet prefer that which is truly better, he is the true wayfaring Christian. I cannot praise a fugitive and cloistered virtue, unexercised and unbreathed, that never sallies out and sees her adversary, but slinks out of the race where that immortal garland is to be run for, not without dust and heat. Assuredly we bring not innocence into the world, we bring impurity much rather; that which purifies us is trial, and trial is by what is contrary. That virtue therefore which is but a youngling in the contemplation of evil, and knows not the utmost that vice promises to her followers, and rejects it, is but a blank virtue, not a pure; her whiteness is but an excremental whiteness; which was the reason why our sage and serious poet Spenser (whom I dare be known to think a better teacher than Scotus or Aquinas), describing true temperance under the person of Guyon, brings him in with his palmer through the cave of Mammon and the bower of earthly bliss,[21] that he might see and know, and yet abstain. Since therefore the

[21] *The Faerie Queene,* Book II, Canto 7.

knowledge and survey of vice is in this world so necessary
to the constituting of human virtue, and the scanning of error
to the confirmation of truth, how can we more safely, and
with less danger, scout into the regions of sin and falsity
than by reading all manner of tractates and hearing all manner of reason? And this is the benefit which may be had of
books promiscuously read. But of the harm that may result
hence, three kinds are usually reckoned. First, is feared the
infection that may spread; but then all human learning and
controversy in religious points must remove out of the world,
yea, the Bible itself; for that ofttimes relates blasphemy
not nicely, it describes the carnal sense of wicked men not
unelegantly, it brings in holiest men passionately murmuring
against Providence through all the arguments of Epicurus:
in other great disputes it answers dubiously and darkly to
the common reader: and ask a Talmudist what ails the
modesty of his marginal Keri, that Moses and all the prophets
cannot persuade him to pronounce the textual Chetiv.[22] For
these causes we all know the Bible itself put by the papist
into the first rank of prohibited books. The ancientest Fathers must be next removed, as Clement of Alexandria, and
that Eusebian book of evangelic preparation, transmitting
our ears through a hoard of heathenish obscenities to receive the Gospel. Who finds not that Irenæus, Epiphanius,
Jerome, and others discover more heresies than they well
confute, and that oft for heresy which is the truer opinion?
Nor boots it to say for these, and all the heathen writers of
greatest infection, if it must be thought so, with whom is
bound up the life of human learning, that they writ in an
unknown tongue, so long as we are sure those languages are
known as well to the worst of men, who are both most able,
and most diligent to instill the poison they suck, first into
the courts of princes, acquainting them with the choicest
delights and criticisms of sin. As perhaps did that Petronius,

[22] The marginal annotations, or Keri, were to be read wherever the original text, or Chetiv, was offensive.

whom Nero called his arbiter, the master of his revels; and the notorious ribald of Arezzo,[23] dreaded and yet dear to the Italian courtiers. I name not him for posterity's sake, whom Harry the Eighth named in merriment his vicar of hell. By what compendious way all the contagion that foreign books can infuse will find a passage to the people far easier and shorter than an Indian voyage, though it could be sailed either by the north of Cataio eastward, or of Canada westward, while our Spanish licensing gags the English press never so severely. But on the other side that infection which is from books of controversy in religion is more doubtful and dangerous to the learned than to the ignorant; and yet those books must be permitted untouched by the licenser. It will be hard to instance where any ignorant man hath been ever seduced by papistical book in English, unless it were commended and expounded to him by some of that clergy: and indeed all such tractates, whether false or true, are as the prophecy of Isaiah was to the eunuch,[24] not to be understood without a guide. But of our priests and doctors how many have been corrupted by studying the comments of Jesuits and Sorbonists, and how fast they could transfuse that corruption into the people, our experience is both late and sad. It is not forgot, since the acute and distinct Arminius was perverted merely by the perusing of a nameless discourse written at Delft, which at first he took in hand to confute. Seeing, therefore, that those books, and those in great abundance, which are likeliest to taint both life and doctrine, cannot be suppressed without the fall of learning and of all ability in disputation, and that these books of either sort are most and soonest catching to the learned (from whom to the common people whatever is heretical or dissolute may quickly be conveyed), and that evil manners are as perfectly learnt without books a thousand other ways which cannot be stopped, and evil doctrine not with books can propagate, except a teacher guide, which he might also

[23] Pietro Aretino, 1492–1557.   [24] Acts 8:28–35.

do without writing, and so beyond prohibiting, I am not able to unfold how this cautelous enterprise of licensing can be exempted from the number of vain and impossible attempts. And he who were pleasantly disposed could not well avoid to liken it to the exploit of that gallant man who thought to pound up the crows by shutting his park gate. Besides another inconvenience, if learned men be the first receivers out of books and dispreaders both of vice and error, how shall the licensers themselves be confided in, unless we can confer upon them, or they assume to themselves above all others in the land, the grace of infallibility and uncorruptedness? And again, if it be true that a wise man, like a good refiner, can gather gold out of the drossiest volume, and that a fool will be a fool with the best book, yea or without book; there is no reason that we should deprive a wise man of any advantage to his wisdom, while we seek to restrain from a fool that which being restrained will be no hindrance to his folly. For if there should be so much exactness always used to keep that from him which is unfit for his reading, we should in the judgment of Aristotle not only, but of Solomon and of our Saviour, not vouchsafe him good precepts, and by consequence not willingly admit him to good books; as being certain that a wise man will make better use of an idle pamphlet, than a fool will do of Sacred Scripture. 'Tis next alleged we must not expose ourselves to temptations without necessity, and next to that, not employ our time in vain things. To both these objections one answer will serve, out of the grounds already laid, that to all men such books are not temptations, nor vanities; but useful drugs and materials wherewith to temper and compose effective and strong medicines, which man's life cannot want. The rest, as children and childish men, who have not the art to qualify and prepare these working minerals, well may be exhorted to forbear, but hindered forcibly they cannot be by all the licensing that sainted Inquisition could ever yet contrive: which is what I promised to deliver next, that this

order of licensing conduces nothing to the end for which it
was framed and hath almost prevented me by being clear
already while thus much hath been explaining. See the ingenuity of Truth, who, when she gets a free and willing hand,
opens herself faster than the pace of method and discourse
can overtake her. It was the task which I began with, to
show that no nation, or well-instituted state, if they valued
books at all, did ever use this way of licensing; and it might
be answered, that this is a piece of prudence lately discovered.
To which I return, that as it was a thing slight and obvious
to think on, so if it has been difficult to find out, there wanted
not among them long since who suggested such a course;
which they not following, leave us a pattern of their judgment that it was not the knowing, but the not approving,
which was the cause of their not using it. Plato, a man of
high authority, indeed, but least of all for his commonwealth,
in the book of his laws, which no city ever yet received, fed
his fancy with making many edicts to his airy burgomasters,
which they who otherwise admire him wish had been rather
buried and excused in the genial cups of an academic night-
sitting. By which laws he seems to tolerate no kind of learning but by unalterable decree, consisting most of practical
traditions, to the attainment whereof a library of smaller
bulk than his own dialogues would be abundant. And there
also enacts that no poet should so much as read to any
private man what he has written, until the judges and law-
keepers had seen it and allowed it. But that Plato meant
this law peculiarly to that commonwealth which he had
imagined, and to no other, is evident. Why was he not else
a lawgiver to himself, but a transgressor, and to be expelled
by his own magistrates, both for the wanton epigrams and
dialogues which he made and his perpetual reading of Sophron
Mimus [25] and Aristophanes, books of grossest infamy, and
also for commending the latter of them, though he were the

---

[25] Sophron Mimus, fifth century B.C., a writer of coarse but amusing
mimes.

malicious libeler of his chief friends, to be read by the tyrant Dionysius, who had little need of such trash to spend his time on? But that he knew this licensing of poems had reference and dependence to many other provisos there set down in his fancied republic, which in this world could have no place; and so neither he himself, nor any magistrate, or city ever imitated that course, which, taken apart from those other collateral injunctions, must needs be vain and fruitless. For if they fell upon one kind of strictness, unless their care were equal to regulate all other things of like aptness to corrupt the mind, that single endeavor they knew would be but a fond labor; to shut and fortify one gate against corruption, and be necessitated to leave others round about wide open. If we think to regulate printing, thereby to rectify manners, we must regulate all recreations and pastimes, all that is delightful to man. No music must be heard, no song be set or sung, but what is grave and Doric. There must be licensing dancers, that no gesture, motion, or deportment be taught our youth but what by their allowance shall be thought honest; for such Plato was provided of; it will ask more than the work of twenty licensers to examine all the lutes, the violins, and the guitars in every house; they must not be suffered to prattle as they do, but must be licensed what they may say. And who shall silence all the airs and madrigals that whisper softness in chambers? The windows also, and the balconies must be thought on; there are shrewd books, with dangerous frontispieces, set to sale; who shall prohibit them, shall twenty licensers? The villages also must have their visitors to inquire what lectures the bagpipe and the rebec reads even to the ballatry and the gamut of every municipal fiddler, for these are the countryman's *Arcadias*, and his Montemayors.[26] Next, what more national corruption, for which England hears ill abroad, than household gluttony: who shall be the rectors of our daily rioting? And

[26] Montemayor, 1520(?)–1561, was the author of a popular prose pastoral *Diana Enamorada*.

what shall be done to inhibit the multitudes that frequent
those houses where drunkenness is sold and harbored? Our
garments also should be referred to the licensing of some
more sober workmasters to see them cut into a less wanton
garb. Who shall regulate all the mixed conversation of our
youth, male and female together, as is the fashion of this
country; who shall still appoint what shall be discoursed,
what presumed, and no further? Lastly, who shall forbid
and separate all idle resort, all evil company? These things
will be, and must be; but how they shall be least hurtful,
how least enticing, herein consists the grave and governing
wisdom of a state. To sequester out of the world into At-
lantic and Utopian polities which never can be drawn into
use, will not mend our condition; but to ordain wisely as
in this world of evil, in the midst whereof God hath placed
us unavoidably. Nor is it Plato's licensing of books will do
this, which necessarily pulls along with it so many other
kinds of licensing as will make us both ridiculous and weary,
and yet frustrate; but those unwritten, or at least uncon-
straining laws of virtuous education, religious and civil nurture, which Plato there mentions as the bonds and ligaments
of the commonwealth, the pillars and the sustainers of every
written statute; these they be which will bear chief sway in
such matters as these, when all licensing will be easily eluded.
Impunity and remissness, for certain, are the bane of a
commonwealth; but here the great art lies, to discern in
what the law is to bid restraint and punishment, and in
what things persuasion only is to work. If every action which
is good or evil in man at ripe years were to be under pittance
and prescription and compulsion, what were virtue but a
name, what praise could be then due to well-doing, what
gramercy to be sober, just, or continent? Many there be that
complain of Divine Providence for suffering Adam to transgress; foolish tongues! when God gave him reason, he gave
him freedom to choose, for reason is but choosing; he had
been else a mere artificial Adam, such an Adam as he is in

the motions.[27] We ourselves esteem not of that obedience,
or love, or gift, which is of force: God therefore left him
free, set before him a provoking object, ever almost in his
eyes; herein consisted his merit, herein the right of his reward, the praise of his abstinence. Wherefore did he create
passions within us, pleasures round about us, but that these
rightly tempered are the very ingredients of virtue? They
are not skillful considerers of human things, who imagine to
remove sin by removing the matter of sin; for, besides that
it is a huge heap increasing under the very act of diminishing,
though some part of it may for a time be withdrawn from
some persons, it cannot from all, in such a universal thing
as books are; and when this is done, yet the sin remains entire. Though ye take from a covetous man all his treasure,
he has yet one jewel left, ye cannot bereave him of his
covetousness. Banish all objects of lust, shut up all youth
into the severest discipline that can be exercised in any
hermitage, ye cannot make them chaste that came not thither
so: such great care and wisdom is required to the right
managing of this point. Suppose we could expel sin by this
means; look how much we thus expel of sin, so much we
expel of virtue: for the matter of them both is the same;
remove that, and ye remove them both alike. This justifies
the high providence of God, who, though he commands us
temperance, justice, continence, yet pours out before us,
even to a profuseness, all desirable things, and gives us
minds that can wander beyond all limit and satiety. Why
should we then affect a rigor contrary to the manner of God
and of nature, by abridging or scanting those means, which
books freely permitted are, both to the trial of virtue and
the exercise of truth? It would be better done, to learn that
the law must needs be frivolous, which goes to restrain things,
uncertainly and yet equally working to good and to evil.
And were I the chooser, a dram of well-doing should be preferred before many times as much the forcible hindrance of

[27] In the puppet-shows.

evil-doing. For God sure esteems the growth and completing of one virtuous person more than the restraint of ten vicious. And albeit whatever thing we hear or see, sitting, walking, traveling, or conversing, may be fitly called our book, and is of the same effect that writings are, yet grant the thing to be prohibited were only books, it appears that this Order hitherto is far insufficient to the end which it intends. Do we not see, not once or oftener, but weekly, that continued court-libel against the Parliament and city,[28] printed, as the wet sheets can witness, and dispersed among us, for all that licensing can do? Yet this is the prime service a man would think, wherein this Order should give proof of itself. If it were executed, you'll say. But certain, if execution be remiss or blindfold now, and in this particular, what will it be hereafter and in other books? If then the Order shall not be vain and frustrate, behold a new labor, Lords and Commons, ye must repeal and proscribe all scandalous and unlicensed books already printed and divulged; after ye have drawn them up into a list, that all may know which are condemned, and which not; and ordain that no foreign books be delivered out of custody till they have been read over. This office will require the whole time of not a few overseers, and those no vulgar men. There be also books which are partly useful and excellent, partly culpable and pernicious; this work will ask as many more officials, to make expurgations and expunctions, that the commonwealth of learning be not damnified. In fine, when the multitude of books increase upon their hands, ye must be fain to catalogue all those printers who are found frequently offending, and forbid the importation of their whole suspected typography. In a word, that this your Order may be exact and not deficient, ye must reform it perfectly according to the model of Trent and Seville, which I know ye abhor to do. Yet though ye should con-

---

[28] The reference seems to be to John Birkenhead's *Mercurius Aulicus* (published 1642–1645), which supported the royalists and ridiculed the parliamentarians.

descend to this, which God forbid, the Order still would be but fruitless and defective to that end whereto ye meant it. If to prevent sects and schisms, who is so unread or so uncatechised in story, that hath not heard of many sects refusing books as a hindrance, and preserving their doctrine unmixed for many ages, only by unwritten traditions? The Christian faith, for that was once a schism, is not unknown to have spread all over Asia, ere any Gospel or Epistle was seen in writing. If the amendment of manners be aimed at, look into Italy and Spain, whether those places be one scruple the better, the honester, the wiser, the chaster, since all the inquisitional rigor that hath been executed upon books.

Another reason, whereby to make it plain that this Order will miss the end it seeks, consider by the quality which ought to be in every licenser. It cannot be denied but that he who is made judge to sit upon the birth or death of books, whether they may be wafted into this world or not, had need to be a man above the common measure, both studious, learned, and judicious; there may be else no mean mistakes in the censure of what is passable or not; which is also no mean injury. If he be of such worth as behooves him, there cannot be a more tedious and unpleasing journey-work, a greater loss of time levied upon his head, than to be made the perpetual reader of unchosen books and pamphlets, ofttimes huge volumes. There is no book that is acceptable unless at certain seasons; but to be enjoined the reading of that at all times, and in a hand scarce legible, whereof three pages would not down at any time in the fairest print, is an imposition which I cannot believe how he that values time and his own studies, or is of but a sensible nostril, should be able to endure. In this one thing I crave leave of the present licensers to be pardoned for so thinking; who doubtless took this office up, looking on it through their obedience to the Parliament, whose command perhaps made all things seem easy and unlaborious to them; but that this short trial hath wearied them out already, their own expressions and excuses to them who make so many journeys to solicit their license are testimony enough. Seeing therefore those who now possess the employment, by all evident signs wish themselves well rid of it; and that no man of worth, none that is not a plain unthrift of his own hours is ever likely to succeed them, except he mean to put himself to the salary of a press corrector; we may easily foresee what kind of licensers we are to expect hereafter, either ignorant, imperious, and remiss, or basely pecuniary. This is what I had to show, wherein this Order cannot conduce to that end whereof it bears the intention.

I lastly proceed from the no good it can do, to the manifest hurt it causes, in being first the greatest discouragement and affront that can be offered to learning, and to learned men. It was the complaint and lamentation of prelates, upon every least breath of a motion to remove pluralities, and distribute more equally church revenues, that then all learning would be forever dashed and discouraged. But as for that opinion, I never found cause to think that the tenth part of learning stood or fell with the clergy: nor could I ever but hold it for a sordid and unworthy speech of any churchman who had a competency left him. If therefore ye be loath to dishearten utterly and discontent, not the mercenary crew of false pretenders to learning, but the free and ingenuous sort of such as evidently were born to study, and love learning for itself, not for lucre or any other end but the service of God and of truth, and perhaps that lasting fame and perpetuity of praise which God and good men have consented shall be the reward of those whose published labors advance the good of mankind: then know, that so far to distrust the judgment and the honesty of one who hath but a common repute in learning, and never yet offended, as not to count him fit to print his mind without a tutor and examiner, lest he should drop a schism, or something of corruption, is the greatest displeasure and indignity to a free and knowing spirit that can be put upon him. What advantage is it to be a man over it is to be a boy at school, if we have only escaped the ferula to come under the fescue of an Imprimatur? If serious and elaborate writings, as if they were no more than the theme of a grammar-lad under his pedagogue, must not be uttered without the cursory eyes of a temporizing and extemporizing licenser? He who is not trusted with his own actions, his drift not being known to be evil, and standing to the hazard of law and penalty, has no great argument to think himself reputed in the commonwealth wherein he was born, for other than a fool or a foreigner. When a man writes to the world, he summons up all his reason and deliberation to assist him; he searches, meditates, is industrious, and likely consults and confers with his judicious friends; after all which done he takes himself to be informed in what he writes, as well as any that writ before him; if, in this the most consummate act of his fidelity and ripeness, no years, no industry, no former proof of his abilities can bring him to that state of maturity, as not to be still mistrusted and suspected, unless he carry all his considerate diligence, all his midnight watchings and expense of Palladian oil, to the hasty view of an unleisured licenser, perhaps much his younger, perhaps far his inferior in judgment, perhaps one who never knew the labor of bookwriting; and if he be not repulsed or slighted, must appear in print like a puny with his guardian, and his censor's hand on the back of his title to be his bail and surety that he is no idiot or seducer; it cannot be but a dishonor and derogation to the author, to the book, to the privilege and dignity of learning. And what if the author shall be one so copious of fancy, as to have many things well worth the adding come into his mind after licensing, while the book is yet under the press, which not seldom happens to the best and diligentest writers; and that perhaps a dozen times in one book? The printer dares not go beyond his licensed copy; so often then must the author trudge to his leave-giver, that those his new insertions may be viewed; and many a jaunt will be made, ere that licenser, for it must be the same man, can either be found, or found at leisure; meanwhile either the press must stand still, which is no small damage, or the author lose his accuratest thoughts, and send the book forth worse than he had made it, which to a diligent writer is the greatest melancholy and vexation that can befall. And how can a man teach with authority, which is the life of teaching; how can he be a doctor in his book as he ought to be, or else had better be silent, whenas all he teaches, all he delivers, is but under the tuition, under the correction of his patriarchal licenser to blot or alter what precisely accords not with the hide-bound humor which he calls his judgment? When every acute reader, upon the first sight of a pedantic license, will be ready with these like words to ding the book a quoit's distance from him: I hate a pupil teacher, I endure not an instructor that comes to me under the wardship of an overseeing fist. I know nothing of the licenser, but that I have his own hand here for his arrogance; who shall warrant me his judgment? The state, sir, replies the stationer, but has a quick return: The state shall be my governors, but not my critics; they may be mistaken in the choice of a licenser, as easily as this licenser may be mistaken in an author; this is some common stuff; and he might add from Sir Francis Bacon, that *such authorized books are but the language of the times.*[29] For though a licenser should happen to be judicious more than ordinary, which will be a great jeopardy of the next succession, yet his very office and his commission enjoins him to let pass nothing but what is vulgarly received already. Nay, which is more lamentable, if the work of any deceased author, though never so famous in his lifetime and even to this day, come to their hands for license to be printed, or reprinted, if there be found in his book one sentence of a venturous

---

[29] "On the Controversies of the Church," in *The Letters and the Life of Francis Bacon, Including All His Occasional Works,* ed. James Spedding. 7 vols. (London, 1890) Vol. I, p. 78.

edge, uttered in the height of zeal, and who knows whether it might not be the dictate of a divine spirit, yet not suiting with every low decrepit humor of their own, though it were Knox himself, the reformer of a kingdom, that spake it, they will not pardon him their dash: the sense of that great man shall to all posterity be lost, for the fearfulness or the presumptuous rashness of a perfunctory licenser. And to what an author this violence hath been lately done, and in what book of greatest consequence to be faithfully published, I could now instance but shall forbear till a more convenient season. Yet if these things be not resented seriously and timely by them who have the remedy in their power, but that such iron molds as these shall have authority to gnaw out the choicest periods of exquisitest books, and to commit such a treacherous fraud against the orphan remainders of worthiest men after death, the more sorrow will belong to that hapless race of men, whose misfortune it is to have understanding. Henceforth let no man care to learn, or care to be more than worldly wise; for certainly in higher matters to be ignorant and slothful, to be a common steadfast dunce, will be the only pleasant life, and only in request.

And as it is a particular disesteem of every knowing person alive, and most injurious to the written labors and monuments of the dead, so to me it seems an undervaluing and vilifying of the whole nation. I cannot set so light by all the invention, the art, the wit, the grave and solid judgment which is in England, as that it can be comprehended in any twenty capacities how good soever, much less that it should not pass except their superintendence be over it, except it be sifted and strained with their strainers, that it should be uncurrent without their manual stamp. Truth and understanding are not such wares as to be monopolized and traded in by tickets and statutes and standards. We must not think to make a staple commodity of all the knowledge in the land, to mark and license it like our broadcloth and our woolpacks. What is it but a servitude like that imposed by the Philistines,[30] not to be allowed the sharpening of our own axes and coulters, but we must repair from all quarters to twenty licensing forges? Had anyone written and divulged erroneous things and scandalous to honest life, misusing and forfeiting the esteem had of his reason among men, if after conviction this only censure were adjudged him, that he should never henceforth write but what were first examined by an appointed officer, whose hand should be annexed to pass his credit for him that now he might be safely read, it could not be apprehended less than a disgraceful punishment. Whence to include the whole nation, and those that never yet thus offended, under such a diffident and suspectful prohibition, may plainly be understood what a disparagement it is. So much the more, whenas debtors and delinquents may walk abroad without a keeper, but unoffensive books must not stir forth without a visible jailer in their title. Nor is it to the common people less than a reproach; for if we be so jealous over them as that we dare not trust them with an English pamphlet, what do we but censure them for a giddy, vicious, and ungrounded people; in such a sick and weak estate of faith and discretion as to be able to take nothing down but through the pipe of a licenser? That this is care or love of them, we cannot pretend, whenas, in those popish places where the laity are most hated and despised, the same strictness is used over them. Wisdom we cannot call it, because it stops but one breach of license, nor that neither: whenas those corruptions which it seeks to prevent break in faster at other doors which cannot be shut.

And in conclusion it reflects to the disrepute of our ministers also, of whose labors we should hope better, and of the proficiency which their flock reaps by them, than that after all this light of the Gospel which is, and is to be, and all this continual preaching, they should be still frequented with such an unprincipled, unedified and laic rabble, as that the whiff of every new pamphlet should stagger them out

[30] I Sam. 13:19-22.

of their catechism and Christian walking. This may have much reason to discourage the ministers when such a low conceit is had of all their exhortations, and the benefiting of their hearers, as that they are not thought fit to be turned loose to three sheets of paper without a licenser; that all the sermons, all the lectures preached, printed, vented in such numbers, and such volumes, as have now well-nigh made all other books unsalable, should not be armor enough against one single enchiridion, without the castle St. Angelo of an Imprimatur.

And lest some should persuade ye, Lords and Commons, that these arguments of learned men's discouragement at this your Order are mere flourishes, and not real, I could recount what I have seen and heard in other countries, where this kind of inquisition tyrannizes; when I have sat among their learned men, for that honor I had, and been counted happy to be born in such a place of philosophic freedom as they supposed England was, while themselves did nothing but bemoan the servile condition into which learning amongst them was brought; that this was it which had damped the glory of Italian wits; that nothing had been there written now these many years but flattery and fustian. There it was that I found and visited the famous Galileo,[31] grown old, a prisoner to the Inquisition, for thinking in astronomy otherwise than the Franciscan and Dominican licensers thought. And though I knew that England then was groaning loudest under the prelatical yoke, nevertheless I took it as a pledge of future happiness, that other nations were so persuaded of her liberty. Yet was it beyond my hope that those worthies were then breathing in her air, who should be her leaders to such a deliverance as shall never be forgotten by any revolution of time that this world hath to finish. When that was once begun, it was as little in my fear that what words of complaint I heard among learned men of other parts

[31] This was during his grand tour, 1638–1639. He reached Florence in the fall of 1638.

uttered against the Inquisition, the same I should hear by
as learned men at home, uttered in time of Parliament against
an order of licensing; and that so generally that, when I had
disclosed myself a companion of their discontent, I might
say, if without envy, that he whom an honest quæstorship
had endeared to the Sicilians was not more by them importuned against Verres,[32] than the favorable opinion which
I had among many who honor ye, and are known and respected by ye, loaded me with entreaties and persuasions
that I would not despair to lay together that which just
reason should bring into my mind, toward the removal of
an undeserved thraldom upon learning. That this is not
therefore the disburdening of a particular fancy, but the
common grievance of all those who had prepared their minds
and studies above the vulgar pitch to advance truth in others,
and from others to entertain it, thus much may satisfy. And
in their name I shall for neither friend nor foe conceal what
the general murmur is; that if it come to inquisitioning
again and licensing, and that we are so timorous of ourselves,
and so suspicious of all men, as to fear each book and the
shaking of every leaf, before we know what the contents
are; if some who but of late were little better than silenced
from preaching shall come now to silence us from reading,
except what they please, it cannot be guessed what is intended by some but a second tyranny over learning: and
will soon put it out of controversy that bishops and presbyters
are the same to us, both name and thing.[33] That those evils
of prelaty, which before from five or six and twenty sees
were distributively charged upon the whole people, will now
light wholly upon learning, is not obscure to us: whenas
now the pastor of a small unlearned parish on the sudden
shall be exalted archbishop over a large diocese of books,
and yet not remove, but keep his other cure, too, a mystical

[32] Cicero's orations are against the bad government of Verres.
[33] "New presbyter is but old priest writ large," the last line of "On the
New Forcers of Conscience under the Long Parliament."

pluralist. He who but of late cried down the sole ordination of every novice Bachelor of Art, and denied sole jurisdiction over the simplest parishioner, shall now at home
in his private chair assume both these over worthiest and
excellentest books and ablest authors that write them. This
is not, ye Covenants and Protestations that we have made,
this is not to put down prelaty; this is but to chop an episcopacy; this but to translate the Palace Metropolitan from
one kind of dominion into another; this is but an old canonical sleight of commuting our penance. To startle thus
betimes at a mere unlicensed pamphlet will after a while
be afraid of every conventicle, and a while after will make
a conventicle of every Christian meeting. But I am certain
that a state governed by the rules of justice and fortitude,
or a church built and founded upon the rock of faith and
true knowledge, cannot be so pusillanimous. While things
are yet not constituted in religion that freedom of writing
should be restrained by a discipline imitated from the prelates and learnt by them from the Inquisition, to shut us
up all again into the breast of a licenser, must needs give
cause of doubt and discouragement to all learned and religious men. Who cannot but discern the fineness of this
politic drift, and who are the contrivers; that while bishops
were to be baited down, then all presses might be open;
it was the people's birthright and privilege in time of Parliament, it was the breaking forth of light. But now the bishops
abrogated and voided out the church, as if our Reformation
sought no more but to make room for others into their seats
under another name, the episcopal arts begin to bud again,
the cruse of truth must run no more oil; liberty of printing
must be enthralled again under a prelatical commission of
twenty; the privilege of the people nullified; and, which is
worse, the freedom of learning must groan again, and to
her old fetters: all this the Parliament yet sitting. Although
their own late arguments and defenses against the prelates
might remember them that this obstructing violence meets

for the most part with an event utterly opposite to the end which it drives at: instead of suppressing sects and schisms, it raises them and invests them with a reputation. *The punishing of wits enhances their authority,* saith the Viscount St. Albans; and *a forbidden writing is thought to be a certain spark of truth that flies up in the faces of them who seek to tread it out.*[34] This Order, therefore, may prove a nursing-mother to sects, but I shall easily show how it will be a stepdame to truth: and first by disenabling us to the maintenance of what is known already.

Well knows he who uses to consider, that our faith and knowledge thrives by exercise, as well as our limbs and complexion. Truth is compared in Scripture to a streaming fountain; if her waters flow not in a perpetual progression, they sicken into a muddy pool of conformity and tradition. A man may be a heretic in the truth; and if he believe things only because his pastor says so, or the Assembly so determines, without knowing other reason, though his belief be true, yet the very truth he holds becomes his heresy. There is not any burden that some would gladlier post off to another than the charge and care of their religion. There be, who knows not that there be, of protestants and professors who live and die in as arrant an implicit faith as any lay papist of Loretto. A wealthy man, addicted to his pleasure and to his profits, finds religion to be a traffic so entangled, and of so many piddling accounts, that of all mysteries he cannot skill to keep a stock going upon that trade. What should he do? Fain he would have the name to be religious, fain he would bear up with his neighbors in that. What does he therefore, but resolves to give over toiling, and to find himself out some factor, to whose care and credit he may commit the whole managing of his religious affairs; some divine of note and estimation that must be. To him he adheres, resigns the whole warehouse of his religion, with all the locks and keys, into his custody; and indeed makes the

[34] Bacon, *op. cit.*

very person of that man his religion; esteems his associating with him a sufficient evidence and commendatory of his own piety. So that a man may say his religion is now no more within himself, but is become a dividual movable, and goes and comes near him, according as that good man frequents the house. He entertains him, gives him gifts, feasts him, lodges him; his religion comes home at night, prays, is liberally supped, and sumptuously laid to sleep, rises, is saluted, and after the malmsey, or some well-spiced brewage, and better breakfasted than He whose morning appetite would have gladly fed on green figs between Bethany and Jerusalem, his religion walks abroad at eight, and leaves his kind entertainer in the shop trading all day without his religion.

Another sort there be who, when they hear that all things shall be ordered, all things regulated and settled, nothing written but what passes through the custom-house of certain publicans that have the tonnaging and poundaging of all free-spoken truth, will straight give themselves up into your hands, make 'em and cut 'em out what religion ye please: there be delights, there be recreations and jolly pastimes that will fetch the day about from sun to sun, and rock the tedious year as in a delightful dream. What need they torture their heads with that which others have taken so strictly and so unalterably into their own purveying? These are the fruits which a dull ease and cessation of our knowledge will bring forth among the people. How goodly and how to be wished were such an obedient unanimity as this, what a fine conformity would it starch us all into! Doubtless a staunch and solid piece of framework, as any January could freeze together.

Nor much better will be the consequence even among the clergy themselves. It is no new thing never heard of before, for a parochial minister, who has his reward and is at his Hercules' pillars in a warm benefice, to be easily inclinable, if he have nothing else that may rouse up his studies, to finish his circuit in an English concordance and a topic folio, the gatherings and savings of a sober graduateship, a harmony and a catena; treading the constant round of certain common doctrinal heads, attended with the uses, motives, marks, and means; out of which, as out of an alphabet, or sol-fa, by forming and transforming, joining and disjoining variously, a little book-craft, and two hours' meditation, might furnish him unspeakably to the performance of more than a weekly charge of sermoning: not to reckon up the infinite helps of interlinearies, breviaries, synopses, and other loitering gear. But as for the multitude of sermons ready printed and piled up, on every text that is not difficult, our London trading St. Thomas in his vestry, and add to boot St. Martin and St. Hugh, have not within their hallowed limits more vendible ware of all sorts ready made: so that penury he never need fear of pulpit provision, having where so plenteously to refresh his magazine. But if his rear and flanks be not impaled, if his back door be not secured by the rigid licenser, but that a bold book may now and then issue forth and give the assault to some of his old collections in their trenches, it will concern him then to keep waking, to stand in watch, to set good guards and sentinels about his received opinions, to walk the round and counterround with his fellow inspectors, fearing lest any of his flock be seduced, who also then would be better instructed, better exercised and disciplined. And God send that the fear of this diligence, which must then be used, do not make us affect the laziness of a licensing church.

For if we be sure we are in the right, and do not hold the truth guiltily, which becomes not, if we ourselves condemn not our own weak and frivolous teaching, and the people for an untaught and irreligious gadding rout, what can be more fair than when a man judicious, learned, and of a conscience, for aught we know, as good as theirs that taught us what we know, shall not privily from house to house, which is more dangerous, but openly by writing publish to the

world what his opinion is, what his reasons, and wherefore
that which is now thought cannot be sound? Christ urged
it as wherewith to justify himself, that he preached in public;
yet writing is more public than preaching and more easy
to refutation, if need be, there being so many whose business
and profession merely it is to be the champions of truth;
which if they neglect, what can be imputed but their sloth,
or inability?

Thus much we are hindered and disinured by this course
of licensing, toward the true knowledge of what we seem
to know. For how much it hurts and hinders the licensers
themselves in the calling of their ministry, more than any
secular employment, if they will discharge that office as
they ought, so that of necessity they must neglect either the
one duty or the other, I insist not, because it is a particular,
but leave it to their own conscience how they will decide it
there.

There is yet behind of what I proposed to lay open, the
incredible loss and detriment that this plot of licensing puts
us to; more than if some enemy at sea should stop up all
our havens and ports and creeks, it hinders and retards
the importation of our richest merchandise, truth; nay, it
was first established and put in practice by anti-Christian
malice and mystery on set purpose to extinguish, if it were
possible, the light of Reformation, and to settle falsehood;
little differing from that policy wherewith the Turk up-
holds his Alcoran, by the prohibition of printing. 'Tis not
denied, but gladly confessed, we are to send our thanks and
vows to heaven louder than most of nations, for that great
measure of truth which we enjoy, especially in those main
points between us and the Pope, with his appurtenances the
prelates: but he who thinks we are to pitch our tent here,
and have attained the utmost prospect of reformation that
the mortal glass wherein we contemplate can show us, till
we come to beatific vision, that man by this very opinion
declares that he is yet far short of truth.

Truth indeed came once into the world with her Divine Master, and was a perfect shape most glorious to look on: but when he ascended, and his apostles after him were laid asleep, then straight arose a wicked race of deceivers, who, as that story goes of the Egyptian Typhon with his conspirators, how they dealt with the good Osiris,[35] took the virgin Truth, hewed her lovely form into a thousand pieces, and scattered them to the four winds. From that time ever since, the sad friends of Truth, such as durst appear, imitating the careful search that Isis made for the mangled body of Osiris, went up and down gathering up limb by limb, still as they could find them. We have not yet found them all, Lords and Commons, nor ever shall do, till her Master's second coming; he shall bring together every joint and member, and shall mold them into an immortal feature of loveliness and perfection. Suffer not these licensing prohibitions to stand at every place of opportunity, forbidding and disturbing them that continue seeking, that continue to do our obsequies to the torn body of our martyred saint. We boast our light; but if we look not wisely on the sun itself, it smites us into darkness. Who can discern those planets that are oft combust, and those stars of brightest magnitude that rise and set with the sun, until the opposite motion of their orbs bring them to such a place in the firmament where they may be seen evening or morning? The light which we have gained was given us, not to be ever staring on, but by it to discover onward things more remote from our knowledge. It is not the unfrocking of a priest, the unmitring of a bishop, and the removing him from off the Presbyterian shoulders, that will make us a happy nation. No, if other things as great in the church, and in the rule of life both economical and political, be not looked into and reformed, we have looked so long upon the blaze that Zuinglius and Calvin hath beaconed

[35] Typhon had cut the body of his brother Osiris into fourteen pieces and scattered them. Thirteen of these were found after tireless searching by the wife of Osiris, but the fourteenth had been eaten by the fish of the Nile.

up to us, that we are stark blind. There be who perpetually complain of schisms and sects, and make it such a calamity that any man dissents from their maxims. 'Tis their own pride and ignorance which causes the disturbing, who neither will hear with meekness, nor can convince; yet all must be suppressed which is not found in their syntagma.[36] They are the troublers, they are the dividers of unity, who neglect and permit not others to unite those dissevered pieces which are yet wanting to the body of Truth. To be still searching what we know not by what we know, still closing up truth to truth as we find it (for all her body is homogeneal and proportional), this is the golden rule in theology as well as in arithmetic, and makes up the best harmony in a church; not the forced and outward union of cold and neutral and inwardly divided minds.

Lords and Commons of England, consider what nation it is whereof ye are, and whereof ye are the governors: a nation not slow and dull, but of a quick, ingenious and piercing spirit, acute to invent, subtle and sinewy to discourse, not beneath the reach of any point, the highest that human capacity can soar to. Therefore the studies of learning in her deepest sciences have been so ancient and so eminent among us, that writers of good antiquity and ablest judgment have been persuaded that even the school of Pythagoras and the Persian wisdom took beginning from the old philosophy of this island. And that wise and civil Roman, Julius Agricola, who governed once here for Cæsar, preferred the natural wits of Britain before the labored studies of the French. Nor is it for nothing that the grave and frugal Transylvanian sends out yearly from as far as the mountainous borders of Russia, and beyond the Hercynian wilderness, not their youth, but their staid men, to learn our language and our theologic arts. Yet that which is above all this, the favor and the love of heaven, we have great argument to think in a peculiar manner propitious and propend-

[36] In their own beliefs.

ing towards us. Why else was this nation chosen before any other, that out of her, as out of Sion, should be proclaimed and sounded forth the first tidings and trumpet of Reformation to all Europe? And had it not been the obstinate perverseness of our prelates against the divine and admirable spirit of Wyckliffe, to suppress him as a schismatic and innovator, perhaps neither the Bohemian Huss and Jerome, no, nor the name of Luther or of Calvin, had been ever known: the glory of reforming all our neighbors had been completely ours. But now, as our obdurate clergy have with violence demeaned the matter, we are become hitherto the latest and backwardest scholars of whom God offered to have made us the teachers. Now once again by all concurrence of signs, and by the general instinct of holy and devout men, as they daily and solemnly express their thoughts, God is decreeing to begin some new and great period in his church, even to the reforming of Reformation itself; what does he then but reveal himself to his servants, and as his manner is, first to his Englishmen? I say, as his manner is, first to us, though we mark not the method of his counsels, and are unworthy. Behold now this vast city: a city of refuge, the mansion house of liberty, encompassed and surrounded with his protection; the shop of war hath not there more anvils and hammers waking, to fashion out the plates and instruments of armed justice in defense of beleaguered truth, than there be pens and heads there, sitting by their studious lamps, musing, searching, revolving new notions and ideas wherewith to present, as with their homage and their fealty, the approaching Reformation: others as fast reading, trying all things, assenting to the force of reason and convincement. What could a man require more from a nation so pliant and so prone to seek after knowledge? What wants there to such a towardly and pregnant soil, but wise and faithful laborers, to make a knowing people, a nation of prophets, of sages, and of worthies? We reckon more than five months yet to harvest; there need not be five weeks; had we but eyes to lift up, the fields

are white already. Where there is much desire to learn, there
of necessity will be much arguing, much writing, many
opinions; for opinion in good men is but knowledge in the
making. Under these fantastic terrors of sect and schism we
wrong the earnest and zealous thirst after knowledge and
understanding which God hath stirred up in this city. What
some lament of, we rather should rejoice at, should rather
praise this pious forwardness among men, to reassume the
ill-deputed care of their religion into their own hands again.
A little generous prudence, a little forbearance of one another, and some grain of charity might win all these dili-
gences to join, and unite in one general and brotherly search
after truth; could we but forgo this prelatical tradition of
crowding free consciences and Christian liberties into canons
and precepts of men. I doubt not, if some great and worthy
stranger should come among us, wise to discern the mold
and temper of a people, and how to govern it, observing the
high hopes and aims, the diligent alacrity of our extended
thoughts and reasonings in the pursuance of truth and freedom, but that he would cry out as Pyrrhus [37] did, admiring
the Roman docility and courage: If such were my Epirots,
I would not despair the greatest design that could be attempted, to make a church or kingdom happy. Yet these are
the men cried out against for schismatics and sectaries; as
if, while the temple of the Lord was building, some cutting,
some squaring the marble, others hewing the cedars, there
should be a sort of irrational men, who could not consider
there must be many schisms and many dissections made in
the quarry and in the timber, ere the house of God can be
built. And when every stone is laid artfully together, it cannot be united into a continuity, it can be but contiguous in
this world; neither can every piece of the building be of
one form; nay rather the perfection consists in this, that out
of many moderate varieties and brotherly dissimilitudes that
are not vastly disproportional, arises the goodly and the

[37] At the defeat of the Romans at Heraclea, 280 B.C.

graceful symmetry that commends the whole pile and structure. Let us therefore be more considerate builders, more
wise in spiritual architecture, when great reformation is
expected. For now the time seems come, wherein Moses the
great prophet may sit in heaven rejoicing to see that memorable and glorious wish of his fulfilled, when not only our
seventy elders, but all the Lord's people, are become prophets.
No marvel then though some men, and some good men too
perhaps, but young in goodness, as Joshua then was, envy
them. They fret, and out of their own weakness are in agony,
lest these divisions and subdivisions will undo us. The adversary again applauds, and waits the hour: when they have
branched themselves out, saith he, small enough into parties
and partitions, then will be our time. Fool! he sees not the
firm root out of which we all grow, though into branches;
nor will beware until he see our small divided maniples
cutting through at every angle of his ill-united and unwieldy
brigade. And that we are to hope better of all these supposed
sects and schisms, and that we shall not need that solicitude,
honest perhaps though over-timorous of them that vex in
this behalf, but shall laugh in the end at those malicious
applauders of our differences, I have these reasons to persuade me.

First, when a city shall be as it were besieged and blocked
about, her navigable river infested, inroads and incursions
round, defiance and battle oft rumored to be marching up
even to her walls and suburb trenches; that then the people,
or the greater part, more than at other times, wholly taken
up with the study of highest and most important matters to
be reformed, should be disputing, reasoning, reading, inventing, discoursing, even to a rarity and admiration, things
not before discoursed or written of, argues first a singular
goodwill, contentedness and confidence in your prudent foresight and safe government, Lords and Commons; and from
thence derives itself to a gallant bravery and well-grounded
contempt of their enemies, as if there were no small number

of as great spirits among us, as his was who, when Rome was
nigh besieged by Hannibal, being in the city, bought that
piece of ground at no cheap rate, whereon Hannibal himself
encamped his own regiment. Next, it is a lively and cheerful
presage of our happy success and victory. For as in a body,
when the blood is fresh, the spirits pure and vigorous, not
only to vital but to rational faculties, and those in the acutest
and the pertest operations of wit and subtlety, it argues in
what good plight and constitution the body is; so when the
cheerfulness of the people is so sprightly up, as that it has
not only wherewith to guard well its own freedom and safety,
but to spare, and to bestow upon the solidest and sublimest
points of controversy and new invention, it betokens us not
degenerated, nor drooping to a fatal decay, but casting off
the old and wrinkled skin of corruption to outlive these
pangs and wax young again, entering the glorious ways of
truth and prosperous virtue, destined to become great and
honorable in these latter ages. Methinks I see in my mind
a noble and puissant nation rousing herself like a strong man
after sleep, and shaking her invincible locks: methinks I
see her as an eagle mewing her mighty youth, and kindling
her undazzled eyes at the full mid-day beam; purging and
unscaling her long-abused sight at the fountain itself of
heavenly radiance; while the whole noise of timorous and
flocking birds, with those also that love the twilight, flutter
about, amazed at what she means, and in their envious gabble
would prognosticate a year of sects and schisms.

   What should ye do then, should ye suppress all this flowery
crop of knowledge and new light sprung up and yet springing
daily in this city? Should ye set an oligarchy of twenty en-
grossers over it, to bring a famine upon our minds again,
when we shall know nothing but what is measured to us by
their bushel? Believe it, Lords and Commons, they who
counsel ye to such a suppressing do as good as bid ye suppress yourselves; and I will soon show how. If it be desired
to know the immediate cause of all this free writing and free

speaking, there cannot be assigned a truer than your own mild and humane government. It is the liberty, Lords and Commons, which your own valorous and happy counsels have purchased us, liberty which is the nurse of all great wits; this is that which hath rarefied and enlightened our spirits like the influence of heaven; this is that which hath enfranchised, enlarged and lifted up our apprehensions degrees above themselves. Ye cannot make us now less capable, less knowing, less eagerly pursuing of the truth, unless ye first make yourselves, that made us so, less the lovers, less the founders of our true liberty. We can grow ignorant again, brutish, formal, and slavish, as ye found us; but you then must first become that which ye cannot be, oppressive, arbitrary and tyrannous, as they were from whom ye have freed us. That our hearts are now more capacious, our thoughts more erected to the search and expectation of greatest and exactest things, is the issue of your own virtue propagated in us; ye cannot suppress that unless ye reinforce an abrogated and merciless law, that fathers may despatch at will their own children. And who shall then stick closest to ye, and excite others? Not he who takes up arms for coat and conduct, and his four nobles of Danegelt.[38] Although I dispraise not the defense of just immunities, yet love my peace better, if that were all. Give me the liberty to know, to utter, and to argue freely according to conscience, above all liberties.

What would be best advised, then, if it be found so hurtful and so unequal to suppress opinions for the newness or the unsuitableness to a customary acceptance, will not be my task to say; I only shall repeat what I have learned from one of your own honorable number, a right noble and pious lord, who, had he not sacrificed his life and fortunes to the Church and Commonwealth, we had not now missed and bewailed a worthy and undoubted patron of this argument. Ye know him, I am sure; yet I for honor's sake, and may it

[38] A noble was 6s. 8d. Danegelt was a tax levied to protect the country from invasion by the Danes.

be eternal to him, shall name him, the Lord Brooke. He, writing of episcopacy and by the way treating of sects and schisms, left ye his vote, or rather now the last words of his dying charge, which I know will ever be of dear and honored regard with ye, so full of meekness and breathing charity, that next to His last testament, who bequeathed love and peace to His disciples, I cannot call to mind where I have read or heard words more mild and peaceful. He there exhorts us to hear with patience and humility those, however they be miscalled, that desire to live purely, in such a use of God's ordinances, as the best guidance of their conscience gives them, and to tolerate them, though in some disconformity to ourselves. The book itself will tell us more at large, being published to the world, and dedicated to the Parliament by him who, both for his life and for his death, deserves that what advice he left be not laid by without perusal.

And now the time in special is, by privilege to write and speak what may help to the further discussing of matters in agitation. The temple of Janus with his two controversial faces might now not unsignificantly be set open. And though all the winds of doctrine were let loose to play upon the earth, so Truth be in the field, we do injuriously by licensing and prohibiting to misdoubt her strength. Let her and Falsehood grapple; who ever knew Truth put to the worse in a free and open encounter? Her confuting is the best and surest suppressing. He who hears what praying there is for light and clearer knowledge to be sent down among us, would think of other matters to be constituted beyond the discipline of Geneva, framed and fabricked already to our hands. Yet when the new light which we beg for shines in upon us, there be who envy and oppose, if it come not first in at their casements. What a collusion is this, whenas we are exhorted by the wise man to use diligence, to seek for wisdom as for hidden treasures early and late, that another order shall enjoin us to know nothing but by statute? When a man hath been laboring the hardest labor in the deep mines of knowledge, hath furnished out his findings in all their equipage, drawn forth his reasons as it were a battle ranged, scattered and defeated all objections in his way, calls out his adversary into the plain, offers him the advantage of wind and sun, if he please, only that he may try the matter by dint of argument; for his opponents then to skulk, to lay ambushments, to keep a narrow bridge of licensing where the challenger should pass, though it be valor enough in soldiership, is but weakness and cowardice in the wars of Truth. For who knows not that Truth is strong, next to the Almighty? She needs no policies, nor stratagems, nor licensings to make her victorious; those are the shifts and the defenses that error uses against her power. Give her but room, and do not bind her when she sleeps, for then she speaks not true, as the old Proteus did, who spake oracles only when he was caught and bound, but then rather she turns herself into all shapes, except her own, and perhaps tunes her voice according to the time, as Micaiah did before Ahab,[39] until she be adjured into her own likeness. Yet is it not impossible that she may have more shapes than one. What else is all that rank of things indifferent, wherein Truth may be on this side or on the other, without being unlike herself? What but a vain shadow else is the abolition of those ordinances, that handwriting nailed to the cross? What great purchase is this Christian liberty which Paul so often boasts of? His doctrine is, that he who eats or eats not, regards a day or regards it not, may do either to the Lord. How many other things might be tolerated in peace, and left to conscience, had we but charity, and were it not the chief stronghold of our hypocrisy to be ever judging one another? I fear yet this iron yoke of outward conformity hath left a slavish print upon our necks; the ghost of a linen decency yet haunts us. We stumble and are impatient at the least dividing of one visible congregation from another, though it be not in fundamentals; and through our forwardness to suppress, and our

[39] I Kings 22.

backwardness to recover any enthralled piece of truth out of the gripe of custom, we care not to keep truth separated from truth, which is the fiercest rent and disunion of all. We do not see that, while we still affect by all means a rigid external formality, we may as soon fall again into a gross conforming stupidity, a stark and dead congealment of wood and hay and stubble, forced and frozen together, which is more to the sudden degenerating of a church than many subdichotomies of petty schisms. Not that I can think well of every light separation, or that all in a church is to be expected gold and silver and precious stones: it is not possible for man to sever the wheat from the tares, the good fish from the other fry; that must be the angels' ministry at the end of mortal things. Yet if all cannot be of one mind, as who looks they should be? this doubtless is more wholesome, more prudent, and more Christian that many be tolerated, rather than all compelled. I mean not tolerated popery and open superstition, which, as it extirpates all religious and civil supremacies, so itself should be extirpate, provided first that all charitable and compassionate means be used to win and regain the weak and the misled: that also which is impious or evil absolutely either against faith or manners, no law can possibly permit, that intends not to unlaw itself: but those neighboring differences, or rather indifferences, are what I speak of, whether in some point of doctrine or of discipline, which though they may be many, yet need not interrupt the unity of spirit, if we could but find among us the bond of peace. In the meanwhile, if anyone would write, and bring his helpful hand to the slow-moving reformation which we labor under, if Truth have spoken to him before others, or but seemed at least to speak, who hath so bejesuited us that we should trouble that man with asking license to do so worthy a deed? and not consider this, that if it come to prohibiting, there is not aught more likely to be prohibited than truth itself: whose first appearance to our eyes, bleared and dimmed with prejudice and custom,

is more unsightly and unplausible than many errors, even
as the person is of many a great man slight and contemptible
to see to. And what do they tell us vainly of new opinions,
when this very opinion of theirs, that none must be heard
but whom they like, is the worst and newest opinion of all
others; and is the chief cause why sects and schisms do so
much abound, and true knowledge is kept at distance from
us; besides yet a greater danger which is in it. For when
God shakes a kingdom with strong and heathful commotions
to a general reforming, 'tis not untrue that many sectaries
and false teachers are then busiest in seducing; but yet more
true it is, that God then raises to his own work men of rare
abilities, and more than common industry, not only to look
back and revise what hath been taught heretofore, but to
gain further and go on some new enlightened steps in the
discovery of truth. For such is the order of God's enlighten-
ing his church, to dispense and deal out by degrees his beam,
so as our earthly eyes may best sustain it. Neither is God
appointed and confined, where and out of what place these
his chosen shall be first heard to speak; for he sees not as
man sees, chooses not as man chooses, lest we should devote
ourselves again to set places, and assemblies, and outward
callings of men; planting our faith one while in the old Convocation house, and another while in the Chapel at Westminster; when all the faith and religion that shall be there
canonized is not sufficient without plain convincement, and
the charity of painful instruction to supple the least bruise
of conscience, to edify the meanest Christian, who desires
to walk in the spirit, and not in the letter of human trust,
for all the number of voices that can be there made; no,
though Harry the Seventh himself there, with all his liege
tombs about him, should lend them voices from the dead
to swell their number. And if the men be erroneous who appear to be the leading schismatics, what withholds us but
our sloth, our self-will, and distrust in the right cause, that
we do not give them gentle meetings and gentle dismissions,

that we debate not and examine the matter thoroughly with liberal and frequent audience; if not for their sakes, yet for our own? Seeing no man who hath tasted learning, but will confess the many ways of profiting by those who, not contented with stale receipts, are able to manage and set forth new positions to the world. And were they but as the dust and cinders of our feet, so long as in that notion they may yet serve to polish and brighten the armory of truth, even for that respect they were not utterly to be cast away. But if they be of those whom God hath fitted for the special use of these times with eminent and ample gifts, and those perhaps neither among the priests nor among the Pharisees; and we in the haste of a precipitant zeal shall make no distinction, but resolve to stop their mouths, because we fear they come with new and dangerous opinions, as we commonly forejudge them ere we understand them, no less than woe to us, while, thinking thus to defend the Gospel, we are found the persecutors.

There have been not a few since the beginning of this Parliament, both of the presbytery and others, who by their unlicensed books, to the contempt of an Imprimatur, first broke that triple ice clung about our hearts, and taught the people to see day; I hope that none of those were the persuaders to renew upon us this bondage which they themselves have wrought so much good by contemning. But if neither the check that Moses gave to young Joshua, nor the countermand which our Saviour gave to young John, who was so ready to prohibit those whom he thought unlicensed, be not enough to admonish our elders how unacceptable to God their testy mood of prohibiting is; if neither their own remembrance what evil hath abounded in the church by this let of licensing, and what good they themselves have begun by transgressing it, be not enough, but that they will persuade and execute the most Dominican part of the Inquisition over us, and are already with one foot in the stirrup so active at suppressing, it would be no unequal distribution in the first place to suppress the suppressors themselves: whom the change of their condition hath puffed up, more than their late experience of harder times hath made wise.

And as for regulating the press, let no man think to have the honor of advising ye better than yourselves have done in that Order published next before this,[40] that no book be printed, unless the printer's and the author's name, or at least the printer's be registered. Those which otherwise come forth, if they be found mischievous and libelous, the fire and the executioner will be the timeliest and the most effectual remedy that man's prevention can use. For this authentic Spanish policy of licensing books, if I have said aught, will prove the most unlicensed book itself within a short while; and was the immediate image of a Star Chamber decree to that purpose made in those very times when that Court did the rest of those pious works, for which she is now fallen from the stars with Lucifer. Whereby ye may guess what kind of state prudence, what love of the people, what care of religion or good manners there was at the contriving, although with singular hypocrisy it pretended to bind books to their good behavior. And how it got the upper hand of your precedent Order so well constituted before, if we may believe those men whose profession gives them cause to inquire most, it may be doubted there was in it the fraud of some old patentees and monopolizers in the trade of bookselling; who under pretense of the poor in their company not to be defrauded, and the just retaining of each man his several copy, which God forbid should be gainsaid, brought divers glozing colors to the House, which were indeed but colors, and serving to no end except it be to exercise a superiority over their neighbors; men who do not therefore labor in an honest profession to which learning is indebted, that they should be made other men's vassals. Another end is thought was aimed at by some of them in procuring by petition this Order, that, having power in their hands, ma-

[40] The licensing act of January 29, 1641/42.

lignant books might the easier scape abroad, as the event shows. But of these sophisms and elenchs of merchandise I skill not. This I know, that errors in a good government and in a bad are equally almost incident; for what magistrate may not be misinformed, and much the sooner, if liberty of printing be reduced into the power of a few? But to redress willingly and speedily what hath been erred, and in highest authority to esteem a plain advertisement more than others have done a sumptuous bribe, is a virtue (honored Lords and Commons) answerable to your highest actions, and whereof none can participate but greatest and wisest men.

Jeremy Taylor 1613-1667

Jeremy Taylor was born in Cambridge. After attending the famous Perse School for seven years, he was admitted to Caius College, Cambridge University, in 1626, about a year after Milton had enrolled at Christ's College. He continued in the University for nine years, remaining as fellow after taking his A.B. degree. In 1634 he proceeded Master of Arts. He had taken holy orders the preceding year, though he could not be ordained since the required age for ordination was twenty-four; but when he acted as substitute for a friend at St. Paul's, the congregation received him as "some young angel, newly descended from the visions of glory." He was handsome and eloquent; and Laud, recognizing his potential usefulness and his unusual ability, appointed him chaplain-in-ordinary to the king and used his personal authority to have him made a fellow of All Souls College, Oxford.

Taylor's first church appointment was to Uppingham, but with the impeachment of Laud and the outbreak of the Civil War, he joined the king's followers at Oxford and there began his controversial writing. When the king's forces left Oxford, Taylor seems to have become separated in some way, and we next hear of his being captured at the fall of Cardigan Castle in South Wales. When he was released, he found a new patron in the Earl of Carbery, who made him his chaplain and received him at his home, Golden Grove. Presumably Taylor's family joined him at some time here, but there is no definite information as to when they came to Wales.

He also taught in a "private academy" and spent much time in writing, though he felt greatly handicapped without a library. The most famous work of this period is *The Liberty of Prophesying*. Like Milton's *Areopagitica* it is an earnest defense of freedom of speech and expresses a new spirit of toleration. By widely divergent routes the Royalist and the Puritan had approached the same point of view. Taylor also felt that there was a broader foundation for religious peace than that offered by agreement upon common essentials; this was the acceptance of the church as "a company of men believing in Jesus Christ" without any restrictions being put upon their differing approaches to this position.

Other works followed, and at Lady Carbery's suggestion he began preparing an edition of his sermons, which, however, was not published until after her early death. One of the finest of all his sermons is the biographical elegy which he preached at her funeral. In it he portrays that "rare soul" who was "so hugely loving to oblige others, she was very unwilling to be in arrear to any upon the stock of courtesies and liberality."

Taylor sustained a double loss: Lady Carbery died in October, 1650, and in April, 1651, he wrote to a friend that he had "lately buried" his "dear wife." Out of this experience came that beautiful and moving book, *The Rule of Holy Dying,* in which the negation of death is relieved by the fresh beauty of nature imagery drawn from the quiet scene of Golden Grove. The immediate popularity of this work is indicated by the fact that twenty editions appeared before the end of the century.

The period of calm which Taylor had enjoyed at Golden Grove was now broken. He was often in London, but his writings brought down great criticism and he was imprisoned for a short time. Fortunately he had won the friendship of Evelyn, and through Evelyn had met other men of importance, so that he had friends who were able to assist him. In 1655 when he was returning to Wales, he was taken and imprisoned at Chepstow Castle. When he was released, he went to the home of Joanna Bridges, about twelve miles from Golden Grove, for on account of Taylor's activities Lord

Carbery had been prohibited from having a chaplain. It does not seem likely that Joanna was married to Taylor at this time; but she was the benefactress of his children, Lord Carbery having remarried, and at some time she became the second Mrs. Taylor.

Taylor had to meet new personal bereavements: he lost one son in 1656 and two others from smallpox in the following year. He became so depressed that he left Wales and lived in seclusion in London. Evelyn, concerned over his poverty, arranged a subscription among his friends for Taylor's relief and also suggested to Lord Conway that he take Taylor as Lecturer at Lisburn. In Lord Conway a new benefactor was found for Taylor, and Portmore, the Conway home, provided again a quiet retreat. Even after the Restoration, when Taylor was made Bishop of Down and Connor and was vice-chancellor of Dublin University, he continued to live at Portmore.

The Presbyterians in Ireland were predominant, and their enmity made life almost intolerable for Taylor. The tolerant liberal of *The Liberty of Prophesying* was forced by his position to use severe discipline with his insubordinate ministers, who preached against the episcopacy and planned to make it impossible for an Episcopalian bishop to control the diocese. Taylor wished to withdraw, but was not permitted to do so, and, suffering greatly in spirit and health under the difficult situation, died before he was fifty-five.

Though Taylor's work is primarily theological and often controversial, so that many of the ideas are outmoded, it lives for the great beauty of the prose. Taylor has been called the "Shakespeare of English prose"; but in imagery that appeals to the senses, in diction that is exact and beautiful, and in rhythms which give the effect of meter, his expanded similes and many other ornate passages deserve the name of prose poems. At times, particularly in the sermons, the ornate style gives over to a swift and concise simplicity

which presents a happy contrast. He is as much in command
of phrase and sentence, even when, in Coleridge's words,
they form a "thought-agglomerating flood," as he is of the
logical reasoning which they embody.

From THE RULE AND EXERCISES OF HOLY DYING [1]

Consideration of the Vanity and Shortness of Man's Life

A MAN is a bubble, said the Greek proverb; which Lucian represents with advantages and its proper circumstances, to this purpose; saying, that all the world is a storm, and men rise up in their several generations like bubbles descending *à Jove pluvio,* from God and the dew of heaven, from a tear and drop of man, from nature and Providence: and some of these instantly sink into the deluge of their first parent and are hidden in a sheet of water, having had no other business in the world but to be born that they might be able to die; others float up and down two or three turns and suddenly disappear and give their place to others; and they that live longest upon the face of the waters are in perpetual motion, restless and uneasy, and being crushed with the great drop of a cloud sink into flatness and a froth; the change not being great, it being hardly possible it should be more a nothing than it was before. So is every man: he is born in vanity and sin; he comes into the world like morning mushrooms, soon thrusting up their heads into the air and conversing with their kindred of the same production, and as soon they turn into dust and forgetfulness; some of them without any other interest in the affairs of the world but that they made their parents a little glad, and very sorrowful; others ride longer in the storm; it may be until seven years of vanity be expired, and then peradventure the sun shines hot upon their heads and they fall into the shades below, into the cover of death and darkness of the grave to hide them. But if the bubble stands the shock of a bigger

[1] Text: 1651, first edition.

drop, and outlives the chances of a child, of a careless nurse,
of drowning in a pail of water, of being overlaid by a sleepy
servant, or such little accidents, then the young man dances
like a bubble, empty and gay, and shines like a dove's neck,
or the image of a rainbow, which hath no substance, and
whose very imagery and colors are fantastical; and so he
dances out the gaiety of his youth, and is all the while in a
storm, and endures only because he is not knocked on the
head by a drop of bigger rain, or crushed by the pressure
of a load of indigested meat, or quenched by the disorder of
an ill-placed humor: and to preserve a man alive in the midst
of so many chances and hostilities is as great a miracle as
to create him; to preserve him from rushing into nothing,
and at first to draw him up from nothing were equally the
issues of an Almighty power. And therefore the wise men
of the world have contended who shall best fit man's condition with words signifying his vanity and short abode. Homer
calls a man "a leaf," the smallest, the weakest piece of a
short-lived, unsteady plant: Pindar calls him "the dream of
a shadow": another, "the dream of the shadow of smoke":
but St. James spake by a more excellent spirit, saying, "our
life is but a vapor," [2] viz., drawn from the earth by a celestial
influence; made of smoke, or the lighter parts of water,
tossed with every wind, moved by the motion of a superior
body, without virtue in itself, lifted up on high or left below,
according as it pleases the sun its foster-father. But it is
lighter yet. It is but "appearing"; a fantastic vapor, an apparition, nothing real; it is not so much as a mist, not the
matter of a shower, nor substantial enough to make a cloud;
but it is like Cassiopeia's chair, or Pelops' shoulder, [3] or the
circles of heaven, φαινόμενα, than which you cannot have a
word that can signify a verier nothing. And yet the expression
is one degree more made diminutive: a "vapor," and "fantastical," or a "mere appearance," and this but for a little
while neither; the very dream, the phantasm disappears in a

[2] James 4:14.   [3] Ovid, *Metamorphoses*, vi. 403.

small time, "like the shadow that departeth"; or "like a tale that is told"; or "as a dream when one awaketh." A man is so vain, so unfixed, so perishing a creature, that he cannot long last in the scene of fancy: a man goes off, and is forgotten, like the dream of a distracted person. The sum of all is this: that thou art a man, than whom there is not in the world any greater instance of heights and declensions, of lights and shadows, of misery and folly, of laughter and tears, of groans and death.

And because this consideration is of great usefulness and great necessity to many purposes of wisdom and the spirit; all the succession of time, all the changes in nature, all the varieties of light and darkness, the thousand thousands of accidents in the world, and every contingency to every man, and to every creature, does preach our funeral sermon, and calls us to look, and see how the old sexton Time throws up the earth, and digs a grave where we must lay our sins or our sorrows, and sow our bodies till they rise again in a fair, or in an intolerable eternity. Every revolution which the sun makes about the world divides between life and death; and death possesses both those portions by the next morrow; and we are dead to all those months which we have already lived, and we shall never live them over again: and still God makes little periods of our age. First, we change our world, when we come from the womb to feel the warmth of the sun. Then we sleep and enter into the image of death, in which state we are unconcerned in all the changes of the world: and if our mothers or our nurses die, or a wild boar destroy our vineyards, or our king be sick, we regard it not, but during that state are as disinterested as if our eyes were closed with the clay that weeps in the bowels of the earth. At the end of seven years our teeth fall and die before us, representing a formal prologue to the tragedy; and still every seven years it is odds but we shall finish the last scene: and when nature, or chance, or vice, takes our body in pieces, weakening some parts and loosing others, we taste the grave and the solemnities of our own funerals, first, in those parts that ministered to vice, and next in them that served for ornament, and in a short time even they that served for necessity become useless, and entangled like the wheels of a broken clock. Baldness is but a dressing to our funerals, the proper ornament of mourning, and of a person entered very far into the regions and possession of death: and we have many more of the same signification: gray hairs, rotten teeth, dim eyes, trembling joints, short breath, stiff limbs, wrinkled skin, short memory, decayed appetite. Every day's necessity calls for a reparation of that portion which death fed on all night, when we lay in his lap and slept in his outer chambers. The very spirits of a man prey upon the daily portion of bread and flesh, and every meal is a rescue from one death and lays up for another; and while we think a thought, we die; and the clock strikes, and reckons on our portion of eternity: we form our words with the breath of our nostrils, we have the less to live upon for every word we speak.

Thus nature calls us to meditate of death by those things which are the instruments of acting it; and God by all the variety of his providence makes us see death everywhere, in all variety of circumstances, and dressed up for all the fancies and the expectation of every single person. Nature hath given us one harvest every year, but death hath two: and the spring and the autumn send throngs of men and women to charnel-houses; and all the summer long men are recovering from their evils of the spring, till the dog-days come, and then the Sirian star makes the summer deadly; and the fruits of autumn are laid up for all the year's provision, and the man that gathers them eats and surfeits, and dies and needs them not, and himself is laid up for eternity; and he that escapes till winter only stays for another opportunity, which the distempers of that quarter minister to him with great variety. Thus death reigns in all the portions of our time. The autumn with its fruits provides disorders for us, and the winter's cold turns them into sharp diseases, and the spring brings

flowers to strew our hearse, and the summer gives green turf
and brambles to bind upon our graves. Calentures [4] and surfeit, cold and agues, are the four quarters of the year, and all
minister to death; and you can go no whither but you tread
upon a dead man's bones.

The wild fellow in Petronius [5] that escaped upon a broken
table from the furies of a shipwreck, as he was sunning himself upon the rocky shore, espied a man rolled upon his floating bed of waves, ballasted with sand in the folds of his
garment and carried by his civil enemy, the sea, towards the
shore to find a grave, and it cast him into some sad thoughts: [6]
that peradventure this man's wife in some part of the Continent, safe and warm, looks next month for the good man's
return; or, it may be, his son knows nothing of the tempest;
or his father thinks of that affectionate kiss, which still is
warm upon the good old man's cheek ever since he took a
kind farewell; and he weeps with joy to think how blessed he
shall be when his beloved boy returns into the circle of his
father's arms. These are the thoughts of mortals, this is the
end and the sum of all their designs: a dark night and an ill
guide, a boisterous sea and a broken cable, a hard rock and
a rough wind, dashed in pieces the fortune of a whole family,
and they that shall weep loudest for the accident are not yet
entered into the storm, and yet have suffered shipwreck. Then
looking upon the carcass, he knew it, and found it to be the
master of the ship, who the day before cast up the accounts of
his patrimony and his trade, and named the day when he
thought to be at home: see how the man swims who was so
angry two days since; his passions are becalmed with the
storm, his accounts cast up, his cares at an end, his voyage
done, and his gains are the strange events of death, which
whether they be good or evil, the men that are alive seldom
trouble themselves concerning the interest of the dead.

But seas alone do not break our vessel in pieces: every-

---

[4] Fevers. [5] *Satyricon,* cxv.
[6] The source of these "sad thoughts" is Seneca, *Epist.* ci. 6.

where we may be shipwrecked. A valiant general, when he is to reap the harvest of his crowns and triumphs, fights unprosperously, or falls into a fever with joy and wine, and changes his laurel into cypress, his triumphal chariot to a hearse; dying the night before he was appointed to perish in the drunkenness of his festival joys. It was a sad arrest of the loosenesses and wilder feasts of the French court, when their king Henry the Second was killed really by the sportive image of a fight. And many brides have died under the hands of paranymphs and maidens, dressing them for uneasy joy, the new and undiscerned chains of marriage: according to the sayings of Bensirah,[7] the wise Jew, "The bride went into her chamber, and knew not what should befall her there." Some have been paying their vows, and giving thanks for a prosperous return to their own house, and the roof hath descended upon their heads and turned their loud religion into the deeper silence of a grave. And how many teeming mothers have rejoiced over their swelling wombs, and pleased themselves in becoming the channels of blessing to a family; and the mid-wife hath quickly bound their heads and feet, and carried them forth to burial! Or else the birthday of an heir hath seen the coffin of the father brought into the house, and the divided mother hath been forced to travail twice, with a painful birth, and a sadder death.

There is no state, no accident, no circumstance of our life, but it hath been soured by some sad instance of a dying friend: a friendly meeting often ends in some sad mischance and makes an eternal parting: and when the poet Æschylus was sitting under the walls of his house, an eagle hovering over his bald head mistook it for a stone, and let fall his oyster, hoping there to break the shell, but pierced the poor man's skull.[8]

Death meets us everywhere, and is procured by every instrument and in all chances, and enters in at many doors:

[7] Ben Sira is the Hebrew title for Sirach, an Apocryphal book of wisdom.
[8] Pliny, *Natural History*, x. 3. 6–8.

by violence and secret influence, by the aspect of a star and the stink of a mist, by the emissions of a cloud and the meeting of a vapor, by the fall of a chariot and the stumbling at a stone, by a full meal or an empty stomach, by watching at the wine or by watching at prayers, by the sun or the moon, by a heat or a cold, by sleepless nights or sleeping days, by water frozen into the hardness and sharpness of a dagger, or water thawed into the floods of a river, by a hair or a raisin, by violent motion or sitting still, by severity or dissolution, by God's mercy or God's anger; by everything in providence and everything in manners, by everything in nature and everything in chance,

eripitur persona, manet res; [9]

we take pains to heap up things useful to our life, and get our death in the purchase; and the person is snatched away, and the goods remain. And all this is the law and constitution of nature; it is a punishment to our sins, the unalterable event of providence and the decree of heaven. The chains that confine us to this condition are strong as destiny, and immutable as the eternal laws of God.

I have conversed with some men who rejoiced in the death or calamity upon others, and accounted it as a judgment upon them for being on the other side, and against them in the contention; but within the revolution of a few months, the same man met with a more uneasy and unhandsome death: which when I saw, I wept, and was afraid; for I knew that it must be so with all men; for we also shall die, and end our quarrels and contentions by passing to a final sentence.

CHAPTER I, SECTION 2

This discourse will be useful if we consider and practice by the following rules and considerations respectively,—

[9] Lucretius, *De Rerum Natura*, iii. 58.

1. All the rich and all the covetous men in the world will perceive, and all the world will perceive for them, that it is but an ill recompense for all their cares, that by this time all that shall be left will be this, that the neighbors shall say he died a rich man: and yet his wealth will not profit him in the grave, but hugely swell the sad accounts of Dooms-day; and he that kills the Lord's people with unjust or ambitious wars for an unrewarding interest, shall have this character, that he threw away all the days of his life, that one year might be reckoned with his name and computed by his reign, or consulship; and many men by great labors and affronts, many indignities and crimes, labor only for a pompous epitaph, and a loud title upon their marble; whilst those into whose possessions their heirs or kindred are entered, are forgotten, and lie unregarded as their ashes, and without concernment or relation, as the turf upon the face of their grave. A man may read a sermon, the best and most passionate that ever man preached, if he shall but enter into the sepulchers of kings. In the same Escurial where the Spanish princes live in greatness and power, and decree war or peace, they have wisely placed a cemetery where their ashes and their glories shall sleep till time shall be no more; and where our kings have been crowned, their ancestors lay interred, and they must walk over their grandsire's head to take his crown. There is an acre sown with royal seed, the copy of the greatest change, from rich to naked, from ceiled roofs to arched coffins, from living like gods to die like men. There is enough to cool the flames of lust, to abate the heights of pride, to appease the itch of covetous desires, to sully and dash out the dissembling colors of a lustful, artificial, and imaginary beauty. There the warlike and the peaceful, the fortunate and the miserable, the beloved and the despised princes mingle their dust, and pay down their symbol of mortality, and tell all the world that when we die, our ashes shall be equal to kings, and our accounts easier, and our

pains or our crowns shall be less. To my apprehension it is a sad record which is left by Athenæus [10] concerning Ninus, the great Assyrian monarch, whose life and death is summed up in these words:

Ninus the Assyrian had an ocean of gold, and other riches more than the sand in the Caspian sea: he never saw the stars, and perhaps he never desired it; he never stirred up the holy fire among the Magi, nor touched his god with the sacred rod according to the laws; he never offered sacrifice, nor worshiped the deity, nor administered justice, nor spake to his people, nor numbered them; but he was most valiant to eat and drink, and having mingled his wines, he threw the rest upon the stones: this man is dead; behold his sepulcher, and now hear where Ninus is. Sometimes I was Ninus, and drew the breath of a living man, but now am nothing but clay. I have nothing but what I did eat and what I served to myself in lust (that was and is all my portion); the wealth with which I was esteemed blessed, my enemies meeting together shall bear away, as the mad Thyades [11] carry a raw goat. I am gone to hell; and when I went thither, I neither carried gold, nor horse, nor silver chariot. I that wore a miter am now a little heap of dust.

I know not anything that can better represent the evil condition of a wicked man, or a changing greatness. From the greatest secular dignity to dust and ashes, his nature bears him; and from thence to hell his sins carry him, and there he shall be forever under the dominion of chains and devils, wrath, and an intolerable calamity. This is the reward of an unsanctified condition, and a greatness ill gotten or ill administered.

· · · · · ·

[10] *Phœnix poeta Colophonius apud Athen.,* lib xii. cap. 40., p. 1186 (ed. 1827).
[11] The women who accompanied Bacchus, so called for their impetuousness.

5. Since we stay not here, being people but of a day's abode, and our age is like that of a fly and contemporary with a gourd, we must look somewhere else for an abiding city, a place in another country to fix our house in, whose walls and foundation is God, where we must find rest, or else be restless forever. For whatsoever ease we can have or fancy here is shortly to be changed into sadness or tediousness: it goes away too soon like the periods of our life; or stays too long like the sorrows of a sinner; its own weariness or a contrary disturbance is its load; or it is eased by its revolution into vanity and forgetfulness; and where either there is sorrow or an end of joy, there can be no true felicity; which because it must be had by some instrument and in some period of our duration, we must carry up our affections to the mansions prepared for us above, where eternity is the measure, felicity is the state, angels are the company, the Lamb is the light, and God is the portion and inheritance.

CHAPTER I, SECTION 3

Rules and spiritual arts of lengthening our days, and to take off the objection of a short life.

.   .   .   .

2. Neither must we think that the life of a man begins when he can feed himself or walk alone, when he can fight, or beget his like; for so he is contemporary with a camel, or a cow; but he is first a man when he comes to a certain, steady use of reason, according to his proportion, and when that is, all the world of men cannot tell precisely. Some are called at age at fourteen; some, at one-and-twenty, some, never; but all men, late enough; for the life of a man comes upon him slowly and insensibly. But as when the sun approaches towards the gates of morning, he first opens a little eye of heaven, and sends away the spirits of darkness, and gives light to a cock, and calls up the lark to matins,

and by and by gilds the fringes of a cloud and peeps over the
eastern hills, thrusting out his golden horns, like those which
decked the brows of Moses when he was forced to wear a
veil, because himself had seen the face of God; and still while
a man tells a story, the sun gets up higher, till he shows a
fair face and a full light, and then he shines one whole day,
under a cloud often, and sometimes weeping great and little
showers, and sets quickly: so is a man's reason and his life.
He first begins to perceive himself to see or taste, making
little reflections upon his actions of sense, and can discourse
of flies and dogs, shells and play, horses and liberty; but
when he is strong enough to enter into arts and little institutions, he is at first entertained with trifles and impertinent
things, not because he needs them, but because his understanding is no bigger; and little images of things are laid
before him, like a cock-boat to a whale, only to play withal:
but before a man comes to be wise, he is half dead with
gouts and consumptions, with catarrhs and aches, with sore
eyes, and a worn-out body: so that if we must reckon the
life of a man but by the accounts of his reason, he is long
before his soul be dressed; and he is not to be called a man
without a wise and an adorned soul, a soul at least furnished
with what is necessary towards his well-being: but by that
time his soul is thus furnished, his body is decayed; and
then you can hardly reckon him to be alive, when his body
is possessed by so many degrees of death.

[PROSE LYRICS]

[*The Rose*]

IT IS a mighty change that is made by the death of every person, and it is visible to us who are alive. Reckon but from the spritefulness of youth, and the fair cheeks and full eyes of childhood, from the vigorousness and strong flexure of the joints of five-and-twenty, to the hollowness and dead paleness, to the loathsomeness and horror of a three days' burial, and we shall perceive the distance to be very great and very strange. But so have I seen a rose newly springing from the clefts of its hood, and at first it was fair as the morning, and full with the dew of heaven, as a lamb's fleece; but when a ruder breath had forced open its virgin modesty, and dismantled its too youthful and unripe retirements, it began to put on darkness, and to decline to softness and the symptoms of a sickly age; it bowed the head, and broke its stalk, and at night having lost some of its leaves and all its beauty, it fell into the portion of weeds and outworn faces: the same is the portion of every man, and every woman . . .[1]

[*The Lark*]

FOR so have I seen a lark rising from his bed of grass and soaring upwards, singing as he rises, and hopes to get to heaven, and climb above the clouds; but the poor bird was beaten back with the loud sighings of an eastern wind, and his motion made irregular and unconstant, descending more at every breath of the tempest, than it could recover by the libration and frequent weighing of his wings, till the little creature was forced to sit down and pant, and stay till the storm was over; and then it made a prosperous flight, and did rise and sing, as if it had learned music and motion from

[1] *Holy Dying,* 1651, Chap. I. s. 2, pp. 10–11.

546

an angel as he passed sometimes through the air about his ministries here below; so is the prayers of a good man.[2]

[The Worm]

For as a worm creeping with her belly on the ground, with her portion and share of Adam's curse, lifts up its head to partake a little of the blessings of the air and opens the junctures of her imperfect body, and curls her little rings into knots and combinations, drawing up her tail to a neighborhood of the head's pleasure and motion; but still it must return to abide the fate of its own nature, and dwell and sleep upon the dust: so are the hopes of a mortal man; he opens his eyes and looks upon fine things at a distance, and shuts them again with weakness, because they are too glorious to behold; and the man rejoices because he hopes fine things are staying for him; but his heart aches because he knows there are a thousand ways to fail and miss of these glories; and though he hopes, yet he enjoys not; he longs, but he possesses not, and must be content with his portion of dust; and being *a worm and no man* must lie down in this position, before he can receive the end of his hopes, the salvation of his soul in the resurrection of the dead.[3]

[The Unfinished Building]

But so have I seen a fair structure begun with art and care and raised to half its stature, and then it stood still by the misfortune and negligence of the owner, and the rain descended and dwelt in its joints, and supplanted the contexture of its pillars, and having stood a while like the antiquated temple of a deceased oracle, it fell into a hasty age,

---

[2] *XXV Sermons,* Sermon V. ii. 1, pp. 61–2.
[3] *Sermon at the Funeral of the Archbishop of Armagh,* 3rd ed., 1663, p. 1.

and sunk upon its own knees, and so descended into ruin:
so is the imperfect, unfinished spirit of a man; it lays the
foundation of a holy resolution, and strengthens it with
vows and arts of persecutions, it raises up the walls, sacraments, and prayers, reading, and holy ordinances; and holy
actions begin with a slow motion, and the building stays,
and the spirit is weary, and the soul is naked, and exposed
to temptation, and in the days of storm takes in everything
that can do it mischief; and it is faint and sick, listless and
tired, and it stands till its own weight wearies the foundation, and then declines to death and sad disorder, being so
much the worse because it hath not only returned to its first
follies, but hath superadded unthankfulness and carelessness,
a positive neglect, and a despite of holy things, a setting a
low price to the things of God, lazinesses and wretchlessness
all which are evils superadded to the first state of coldness,
whither he is with all these loads and circumstances of death
easily revolved.[4]

[The Needle of a Compass]

BUT AS the needle of a compass, when it is directed to its
beloved star, at the first addresses waves on either side, and
seems indifferent in his courtship of the rising or declining
sun, and when it seems first determined to the north, stands
a while trembling, as if it suffered inconvenience in the first
fruition of its desires and stands not still in a full enjoyment
till after, first, a great variety of motion, and then an undisturbed posture: so is the piety and so is the conversion of
a man wrought by degrees and several steps of imperfection;
and at first our choices are wavering, convinced by the
grace of God and yet not persuaded; and then persuaded,
but not resolved; and then resolved, but deferring to begin;
and then beginning, but (as all beginnings are) in weakness

[4] *XXV Sermons,* 1653, Sermon XIII, p. 157.

and uncertainty; and we fly out often into huge indiscretions, and look back to Sodom, and long to return to Egypt; and when the storm is quite over we find little bubblings and unevennesses upon the face of the waters, we often weaken our own purposes by the returns of sin; and we do not call ourselves conquerors till by the long possession of virtues it is a strange and unusual, and therefore an uneasy and unpleasant thing to act a crime.[5]

[*The River*]

THE RIVER that runs slow and creeps by the banks, and begs leave of every turf to let it pass, is drawn into little hollownesses, and spends itself in smaller portions, and dies with diversion; but when it runs with vigorousness and a full stream, and breaks down every obstacle, making it even as its own brow, it stays not to be tempted by little avocations, and to creep into holes, but runs into the sea through full and useful channels: so is a man's prayer, if it moves on the feet of an abated appetite, it wanders into the society of every trifling accident, and stays at the corners of the fancy, and talks with every object it meets, and cannot arrive at heaven; but when it is carried upon the wings of passion and strong desires, a swift motion and hungry appetite, it passes on through all the intermedial regions of clouds, and stays not till it dwells at the foot of the throne, where mercy sits, and thence sends holy showers of refreshment.[6]

[*Repentance*]

REPENTANCE is like the sun, which enlightens not only the tops of the eastern hills, or warms the wall-fruits of Italy;

[5] *XXVIII Sermons*, 1651, Sermon XVII, p. 534.
[6] *XXV Sermons*, 1653, Sermon XIII, pp. 161–62.

it makes the little balsam tree to weep precious tears with staring upon its beauties; it produces rich spices in Arabia, and warms the cold hermit in his grot, and calls the religious man from his dorter [7] in all parts of the world where holy religion dwells; at the same time it digests the American gold, and melts the snows from the Riphæan mountains, because he darts his rays in every portion of the air, and the smallest atom that dances in the air is tied to a little thread of light, which by equal emanations fills all the capacities of every region: so is repentance. [8]

---

[7] "Dormitory," from the French *dortoir*.
[8] *Unum Necessarium*, 1655, p. 668.

From THE LIBERTY OF PROPHESYING [1]

The Epistle Dedicatory

·　·　·　·　·

THE SUM of the following discourses is nothing but the
sense of these words of Scripture: that since *we know in
part, and prophesy in part,* and that *now we see through a
glass darkly,*[2] we should not despise or contemn persons
not so knowing as ourselves, but *him that is weak in the
faith, we should receive, but not to doubtful disputations;* [3]
therefore certainly to charity, and not to vexations, not to
those which are the idle effects of impertinent wranglings.
And provided they keep close to the foundation, which is
faith and obedience, let them build upon this foundation
matter more or less precious; yet if the foundation be entire, they shall be saved with or without loss. And since we
profess ourselves servants of so meek a Master, and disciples
of so charitable an institute, *Let us walk worthy of the vocation wherewith we are called with all lowliness and meekness, with long suffering, forbearing one another in love;* [4]
for this is the best *endeavoring to keep the unity of the
Spirit,* when it is fast tied *in the bond of peace.* And although
it be a duty of Christianity that *we all speak the same thing,
that there be no divisions among us, but that we be perfectly
joined together in the same mind and in the same judgment;* [5]
yet this unity is to be estimated according to the unity of
faith, in things necessary, in matters of creed, and articles
fundamental: for as for other things, it is more to be wished
than to be hoped for; there are some *doubtful disputations,*
and in such *the scribe, the wise, the disputer of this world,*[6]
are most commonly very far from certainty, and many times
from truth. There are diversity of persuasions in matters

---

[1] Text: 1647, first edition, pp. 6–37.　　[2] I Cor. 13:9, 12.
[3] Rom. 14:1.　　[4] Ephes. 4:2, 3.　　[5] I Cor. 1:10.
[6] I Cor. 1:20.

adiaphorous, as meats and drinks, and holy days, etc., and both parties, the affirmative and the negative, affirm and deny with innocence enough; for the observer and he that observes not, intend both to God; and God is our common Master, we all fellow-servants, and not the judge of each other in matters of conscience or doubtful disputation; and every man that *hath faith must have it himself before God,*[7] but no man must either in such matters *judge his brother or set him at nought ;* but *let us follow after the things which make for peace, and things wherewith one may edify another ;* and the way to do this is not by knowledge, but by charity, *for knowledge puffeth up, but charity edifieth ;* [8] and since *there is not in every man the same knowledge, but the conscience of some are weak ;* [9] *as my liberty must not be judged of another man's weak conscience,*[10] so must not I please myself so much in my right opinion, but I must also take order that his *weak conscience be not offended or despised,* for no man must *seek his own* but *every man another's wealth :* and although we *must contend earnestly for the faith,*[11] yet *above all things we must put on charity which is the bond of perfectness.*[12] And therefore this contention must be with arms fit for the Christian warfare, *the sword of the Spirit, and the shield of faith, and preparation of the gospel of peace instead of shoes, and a helmet of salvation,*[13] but not with other arms, for a churchman must not be πληκτικὸς, *a striker,* for *the weapons of our warfare are not carnal* [14] but spiritual, and the persons that use them ought to be *gentle, and easy to be intreated,*[15] and we *must give an account of our faith to them that ask us with meekness and humility, for so is the will of God, that with well-doing ye may put to silence the ignorance of foolish men.*[16] These and thousands more to the same purpose are the doctrines of Christianity, whose sense and intendment I have prosecuted in the following dis-

[7] Rom. 14:22, 10, 19.   [8] I Cor. 8:1.   [9] I Cor. 8:7.
[10] I Cor. 10:29.   [11] Jude 3.   [12] Colos. 3:14
[13] Ephes. 6:15 ff.   [14] See II Cor. 10:4.   [15] James 3:17.
[16] I Peter 3:15; 2:15.

course, being very much displeased that so many opinions
and new doctrines are commenced among us, but more
troubled that every man that hath an opinion thinks his own
and other men's salvation is concerned in its maintenance,
but most of all that men should be persecuted and afflicted
for disagreeing in such opinions which they cannot with
sufficient grounds obtrude upon others necessarily, because
they cannot propound them infallibly, and because they have
no warrant from Scripture so to do. For if I shall tie other
men to believe my opinion because I think I have a place of
Scripture which seems to warrant it to my understanding,
why may he not serve up another dish to me in the same
dress, and exact the same task of me to believe the contradictory? And then since all the heretics in the world have offered
to prove their articles by the same means by which true
believers propound theirs, it is necessary that some separation either of doctrine or of persons be clearly made, and
that all pretenses may not be admitted, nor any just allegations be rejected; and yet that in some other questions,
whether they be truly or falsely pretended, if not evidently
or demonstratively, there may be considerations had to
the persons of men and to the laws of charity, more than
to the triumphing in any opinion or doctrine not simply necessary. Now because some doctrines are clearly not necessary,
and some are absolutely necessary, why may not the first
separation be made upon this difference, and articles necessary be only urged as necessary, and the rest left to men indifferently, as they were by the Scripture indeterminately?
And it were well if men would as much consider themselves
as the doctrines, and think that they may as well be deceived
by their own weakness as persuaded by the arguments of a
doctrine which other men, as wise, call inevident. For it is
a hard case that we shall think all papists and anabaptists
and sacramentaries to be fools and wicked persons: certainly
among all these sects there are very many wise men and
good men, as well as erring; and although some zeals are so

hot and their eyes so inflamed with their ardors that they do
not think their adversaries look like other men, yet certainly
we find by the results of their discourses and the transactions
of their affairs of civil society, that they are men that speak
and make syllogisms, and use reason, and read Scripture;
and although they do no more understand all of it than we
do, yet they endeavor to understand as much as concerns
them, even all that they can, even all that concerns repentance from dead works, and faith in our Lord Jesus Christ.
And therefore methinks this also should be another consideration distinguishing the persons, for if the persons be
Christians in their lives, and Christians in their profession,
if they acknowledge the eternal Son of God for their Master
and their Lord and live in all relations as becomes persons
making such professions, why then should I hate such persons
whom God loves and who love God, who are partakers of
Christ and Christ hath a title to them, who dwell in Christ
and Christ in them, because their understandings have not
been brought up like mine, have not had the same masters,
they have not met with the same books nor the same company, or have not the same interest, or are not so wise, or
else are wiser, that is (for some reason or other which I
neither do understand, nor ought to blame), have not the
same opinions that I have, and do not determine their school-
questions to the sense of my sect or interest?

But now I know beforehand that those men who will endure none but their own sect will make all manner of attempts against these purposes of charity and compliance,
and, say I or do what I can, will tell all their proselytes that
I preach indifferency of religion; that I say it is no matter
how we believe nor what they profess, but that they may
comply with all sects, and do violence to their own consciences; that they may be saved in all religions; and so
make way for a *colluvies* of heresies, and by consequence
destroy all religion. Nay, they will say worse than all this,
and but that I am not used to their phrases and forms of

declamation, I am persuaded I might represent fine tragedies beforehand. And this will be such an objection, that although I am most confident I shall make [17] apparent to be
as false and scandalous as the objectors themselves are
zealous and impatient; yet besides that I believe the objection will come where my answers will not come, or not
be understood, I am also confident that in defiance and in-
curiousness of all that I shall say, some men will persist
pertinaciously in the accusation, and deny my conclusion
in despite of me: well, but however I will try.

And first I answer, that whatsoever is against the foundation of faith or contrary to good life and the laws of obedience, or destructive to human society and the public and
just interests of bodies politic, is out of the limits of my question and does not pretend to compliance or toleration: so
that I allow no indifferency, nor any countenance to those
religions whose principles destroy government, nor to those
religions (if there be any such) that teach ill life; nor do I
think that anything will now excuse from belief of a fundamental article, except stupidity or sottishness and natural
inability. This alone is sufficient answer to this vanity, but
I have much more to say.

Secondly, the intendment of my discourse is, that permissions should be in questions speculative, indeterminable,
curious, and unnecessary, and that men should not make
more necessities than God made, which indeed are not many.
The fault I find, and seek to remedy, is that men are so dogmatical and resolute in their opinions, and impatient of
others' disagreeings in those things wherein is no sufficient
means of union and determination; but that men should let
opinions and problems keep their own forms, and not be
obtruded as axioms, nor questions in the vast collection of
the system of divinity be adopted into the family of faith:
and I think I have reason to desire this.

Thirdly, it is hard to say that he who would not have men

17 "it" is omitted.

put to death or punished corporally for such things, for which no human authority is sufficient either for cognizance or determination or competent for infliction, that he persuades to an indifferency when he refers to another judicatory which is competent, sufficient, infallible, just, and highly severe. No man or company of men can judge or punish our thoughts or secret purposes whilst they so remain, and yet it will be unequal to say that he who owns this doctrine preaches it lawful to men to think or purpose what they will. And so it is in matters of doubtful disputation (such as are the distinguishing articles of most of the sects of Christendom) : so it is in matters intellectual (which are not cognoscible by a secular power), in matters spiritual (which are to be discerned by spiritual authority which cannot make corporal inflictions), and in questions indeterminate (which are doubtfully propounded or obscurely, and therefore may be *in utramque partem* disputed or believed) ; for God alone must be Judge of these matters, who alone is Master of our souls, and hath a dominion over human understanding, and he that says this does not say that indifferency is persuaded, because God alone is Judge of erring persons.

Fourthly, no part of this discourse teaches or encourages variety of sects, and contradiction in opinions, but supposes them already in being; and therefore since there are, and ever were, and ever will be variety of opinions, because there is variety of human understandings and uncertainty in things, no man should be too forward in determining all questions, nor so forward in prescribing to others, nor invade that liberty which God hath left to us entire, by propounding many things obscurely, and by exempting our souls and understandings from all power externally compulsory: so that the restraint is laid upon men's tyranny, but no license given to men's opinions; they are not considered in any of the conclusions, but in the premises only, as an argument to exhort to charity. So that if I persuade a license of discrediting anything which God hath commanded us to be-

lieve, and allow a liberty where God hath not allowed it, let
it be shown, and let the objection press as hard as it can;
but to say that men are too forward in condemning where
God hath declared no sentence nor prescribed any rule is
to dissuade from tyranny, not to encourage licentiousness;
is to take away a license of judging, not to give a license of
dogmatizing what everyone please, or as may best serve
his turn. And for the other part of the objection:

Fifthly, this discourse is so far from giving leave to men
to profess anything though they believe the contrary, that
it takes order that no man shall be put to it, for I earnestly
contend that another man's opinion shall be no rule to mine,
and that my opinion shall be no snare and prejudice to myself; that men use one another so charitably and so gently
that no error or violence tempt men to hypocrisy, this very
thing being one of the arguments I use to persuade permissions, lest compulsion introduce hypocrisy and make sincerity troublesome and unsafe.

Sixthly, if men would not call all opinions by the name of
religion, and superstructures by the name of fundamental
articles, and all fancies by the glorious appellative of faith,
this objection would have no pretense or footing; so that
it is the disease of the men, not any cause that is ministered
by such precepts of charity that makes them perpetually
clamorous. And it would be hard to say that such physicians
are incurious of their patients, and neglectful of their health,
who speak against the unreasonableness of such empirics
that would cut off a man's head if they see but a wart upon
his cheek, or a dimple upon his chin, or any lines in his
face to distinguish him from another man: the case is altogether the same, and we may as well decree a wart to
be mortal as a various opinion in *re alioqui non necessaria*
to be capital and damnable.

For I consider that there are but few doctrines of Christianity that were ordered to be preached to all the world,
to every single person, and made a necessary article of his

explicit beliefs. Other doctrines which are all of them not simply necessary, are either such as are not clearly revealed, or such as are: if they be clearly revealed, and that I know so too, or may but for my own fault, I am not to be excused; but for this I am to be left to God's judgment, unless my fault be externally such as to be cognoscible and punishable in human judicatory: but then if it be not so revealed but that wise men and good men differ in their opinions, it is a clear case it is not *inter dogmata necessaria simpliciter,* and then it is certain I may therefore safely disbelieve it, because I may be safely ignorant of it: for if I may with innocence be ignorant, then to know it or believe it, is not simply obligatory; ignorance is absolutely inconsistent with such an obligation, because it is destructive and a plain negative to its performance, and if I do my honest endeavor to understand it and yet do not attain it, it is certain that is not obligatory to me so much as by accident, for no obligation can press the person of a man if it be impossible; no man is bound to do more than his best, no man is bound to have an excellent understanding, or to be infallible, or to be wiser than he can, for these are things that are not in his choice, and therefore not a matter of law, nor subject to reward and punishment; so that where ignorance of the article is not a sin, there disbelieving it in the right sense, or believing it in the wrong, is not breach of any duty, essentially or accidentally necessary, neither in the thing itself, nor to the person; that is, he is neither bound to the article, nor to any endeavors or antecedent acts of volition and choice; and the man who may safely be ignorant of the proposition is not tied at all to search it out, and if not at all to search it, then certainly not to find it. All the obligation we are capable of is not to be malicious or voluntarily criminal in any kind; and then if by accident we find out a truth, we are obliged to believe it; and so will every wise or good man do; indeed he cannot do otherwise. But if he disbelieves an article without malice, or design, or involuntarily, or unknowingly, it is contradiction to say it is a sin to him who might totally have been ignorant of it; for that he believes it in the wrong sense, it is his ignorance, and it is impossible that where he hath heartily endeavored to find out a truth, that this endeavor should make him guilty of a sin which would never have been laid to his charge if he had taken no pains at all: his ignorance in this case is not a fault at all; possibly it might, if there had been no endeavor to have cured it.

So that there is wholly a mistake in this proposition: for true it is, there are some propositions which if a man never hear of, they will not be required of him; and they who cannot read might safely be ignorant that Melchizedec was king of Salem; but he who reads it in the Scripture may not safely contradict it, although before that knowledge did arrive to him he might safely have been ignorant of it. But this, although it be true, is not pertinent to our question; for *in sensu diviso* this is true, that which at one time a man may be ignorant of, at some other time he may not disbelieve: but *in sensu conjuncto* it is false; for at what time, and in what circumstance soever it is no sin to be ignorant, at that time and in that conjuncture, it is no sin to disbelieve; and such is the nature of all questions disputable, which are therefore not required of us to be believed in any one particular sense, because the nature of the thing is such as not to be necessary to be known at all simply and absolutely; and such is the ambiguity and cloud of its face and represent-ment as not to be necessary so much as by accident, and therefore not to the particular sense of any one person.

And yet such is the iniquity of men that they suck in opinions as wild asses do the wind, without distinguishing the wholesome from the corrupted air, and then live upon it at a venture; and when all their confidence is built upon zeal and mistake, yet therefore because they are zealous and mistaken, they are impatient of contradiction.

But besides that against this I have laid prejudice enough

from the dictates of Holy Scripture, it is observable that
this with its appendant degrees, I mean restraint of prophesying, imposing upon other men's understanding, being masters of their consciences and larding it over their faith, came
in with the retinue and train of Antichrist; that is, they came
in as other abuses and corruptions of the church did, by
reason of the iniquity of times, and the cooling of the first
heats of Christianity, and the increase of interest, and the
abatements of Christian simplicity, when the church's fortune grew better, and her sons grew worse, and some of her
fathers worst of all. For in the first three hundred years
there was no sign of persecuting any man for his opinion,
though at that time there were very horrid opinions commenced, and such which were exemplary and parallel enough
to determine this question; for they then were assaulted by
new sects which destroyed the common principles of nature, of Christianity, of innocence and public society; and
they who used all the means Christian and spiritual for their
disimprovement and conviction, thought not of using corporal force otherwise than by blaming such proceedings: and
therefore I do not only urge their not doing it as an argument of the unlawfulness of such proceeding, but their de-
fying it and speaking against such practices as unreasonable
and destructive of Christianity. For so Tertullian is express, *humani juris et naturalis potestatis est unicuique quod
putaverit colere; . . . sed nec religionis est cogere reli-
gionem, quæ suscipi debet sponte non vi:* The same is the
doctrine of S. Cyprian, Lactantius, S. Hilary, Minutius Felix,
Sulpitius Severus, S. Chrysostom, S. Hierome, S. Austin,
Damascene, Theophylact, Socrates Scholasticus, and S. Bernard, as they are severally referred to and urged upon occasion in the following discourse.

   To which I add, that all wise princes, till they were over-
borne with faction or solicited by peevish persons, gave toleration to differing sects whose opinions did not disturb the
public interest: but at first, there were some heretical per-

sons that were also impatient of an adversary, and they were
the men who at first entreated with the emperors to persecute the Catholics; but till four hundred years after Christ,
no Catholic persons, or very few, did provoke the secular
army, or implore its aid against the heretics, save only that
Arius behaved himself so seditiously and tumultuarily that
the Nicene fathers procured a temporary decree of his rele-
gation; but it was soon taken off and God left to be his judge,
who indeed did it to some purpose, when he was trusted with
it and the matter wholly left to him.

But as the ages grew worse, so men grew more cruel and
unchristian, and in the Greek church Atticus, and Nestorius
of Constantinople, Theodosius of Synada, and some few
others who had forgotten the mercies of their great Master
and their own duty, grew implacable and furious and impatient of contradiction. It was a bold and arrogant speech
which Nestorius made in his sermon before Theodosius the
younger, *Da mihi, O imperator, terram ab hæreticis re-
purgatam, et ego tibi vicissim cœlum dabo: disperde mecum
hæreticos, et ego tecum disperdam Persas*: it was as groundless and unwarrantable as it was bloody and inhuman.

And we see the contrary events prove truer than this
groundless and unlearned promise: for Theodosius and Val-
entinian were prosperous princes, and have to all ages a
precious memory and the reputation of a great piety; but
they were so far from doing what Nestorius had suggested
that they restrained him from his violence and immanity,
and Theodosius did highly commend the good bishop Proclus
for his sweetness of deportment towards erring persons, far
above the cruelty of his predecessor Atticus. And the experience which Christendom hath had in this last age is argument enough that toleration of differing opinions is so far
from disturbing the public peace, or destroying the interest
of princes and commonwealths, that it does advantage to
the public, it secures peace, because there is not so much
as the pretense of religion left to such persons to contend for

it, being already indulged to them. When France fought against the Huguenots, the spilling of her own blood was argument enough of the imprudence of that way of promoting religion; but since she hath given permission to them, the world is witness how prosperous she hath been ever since. But the great instance is in the differing temper, government, and success which Margaret of Parma and the Duke of Alva had: the clemency of the first had almost extinguished the flame; but when she was removed, Alva succeeded and managed the matter of religion with fire and sword; he made the flame so great that his religion and his prince too hath been almost quite turned out of the country. *Pelli è medio sapientiam, quoties vi res agitur,* said Ennius; and therefore the best of men, and the most glorious of princes, were always ready to give toleration, but never to make executions for matters disputable: Eusebius in his second Book of the life of Constantine reports these words of the emperor, *Parem cum fidelibus ii qui errant, pacis et quietis fruitionem gaudentes accipiant; ipsa siquidem communicationis et societatis restitutio ad rectam etiam veritatis viam perducere potest. Nemo cuiquam molestus sit; quisque quod animo destinat, hoc etiam faciat.*

And indeed there is great reason for princes to give toleration to disagreeing persons whose opinions by fair means cannot be altered; for if the persons be confident, they will serve God according to their persuasions; and if they be publicly prohibited, they will privately convene: and then all those inconveniences and mischiefs which are arguments against the permission of conventicles, are arguments for the public permissions of differing religions, because the denying of the public worship will certainly produce private conventicles, against which all wise princes and commonwealths have upon great reasons made edicts and severe sanctions: *Quicquid enim agitur absente rege, in caput ejus plerumque redundat,* say the politics; for the face of a man is as the face of a lion, and scatters all base machinations which breathe not but in the dark. It is a proverbial saying, *quod nimia familiaritas servorum est conspiratio adversus dominum,* and they who for their security run into grots and cellars, and retirements, think that, they being upon the defensive, those princes and those laws that drive them to it are their enemies, and therefore they cannot be secure unless the power of the one and the obligation of the other be lessened and rescinded; and then the being restrained and made miserable, endears the discontented persons mutually and makes more hearty and dangerous confederations. King James of blessed memory, in his letters to the States of the United Provinces, dated 6 March, 1613, thus wrote, *Magis autem è re fore si sopiantur authoritate publica, ita ut prohibeatis ministros vestros ne eas disputationes in suggestum aut plebem ferant; ac districte imperitis ut pacem colant se invicem tolerando in ista opinionum ac sententiarum discrepantia. . . . Eoque justius videmur vobis hoc ipsum suadere debere, quod . . . neutram comperimus adeo deviam ut non possit et cum fidei Christianæ veritate et cum animarum salute consistere,* &c. The like counsel in the divisions of Germany, at the first reformation was thought reasonable by the Emperor Ferdinand, and his excellent son Maximilian; for they had observed that violence did exasperate, was unblessed, unsuccessful and unreasonable, and therefore they made decrees of toleration, and appointed tempers and expedients to be drawn up by discreet persons; and George Cassander was designed to this great work, and did something towards it; and Emanuel Philibert, Duke of Savoy, repenting of his war undertaken for religion against the Pedemontans, promised them toleration, and was as good as his word; as much is done by the nobility of Polonia. So that the best princes and the best bishops gave toleration and impunities; but it is known that the first persecutions of disagreeing persons were by the Arians, by the Circumcellians and Donatists; and from them, they of the church took examples, who in small numbers did sometime persuade it, sometime prac-

tice it. And among the Greeks it became a public and authorized practice, till the question of images grew hot and
high; for then the worshipers of images having taken their
example from the empress Irene, who put her son's eyes out
for making an edict against images, began to be as cruel
as they were deceived, especially being encouraged by the
popes of Rome, who then blew the coals to some purpose.

And that I may upon this occasion give account of this
affair in the Church of Rome, it is remarkable that till the
time of Justinian the emperor, A.D. 525, the Catholics and
Novations had churches indifferently permitted even in Rome
itself, but the bishops of Rome whose interest was much
concerned in it, spoke much against it, and labored the
eradication of the Novations; and at last when they got
power into their hands they served them accordingly; but
it is observed by Socrates that when the first persecution
was made against them at Rome by Pope Innocent I, at
the same instant the Goths invaded Italy, and became lords
of all, it being just in God to bring a persecution upon them
for true belief, who, with an incompetent authority and insufficient grounds, do persecute an error less material, in
persons agreeing with them in the profession of the same
common faith. And I have heard it observed as a blessing
upon S. Austin (who was so merciful to erring persons as
the greatest part of his life in all senses, even when he had
twice changed his mind, yet to tolerate them, and never to
endure they should be given over to the secular power to
be killed) that the very night the vandals set down before
his city of Hippo to besiege it, he died and went to God,
being (as a reward of his merciful doctrine) taken from the
miseries to come; and yet that very thing was also a particular issue of the Divine Providence upon that city, who
not long before had altered their profession into truth by
force, and now were falling into their power, who afterward
by a greater force turned them to be Arians.

But in the Church of Rome, the popes were the first

preachers of force and violence in matters of opinion, and
that so zealously that Pope Vigilius suffered himself to be
imprisoned and handled roughly by the emperor Justinian,
rather than he would consent to the restitution and peace
of certain disagreeing persons; but as yet it came not so
far as death. The first that preached that doctrine was Dominic, the founder of the begging order of friars, the friars
preachers; in memory of which the Inquisition is intrusted
only to the friars of his order; and if there be any force in
dreams, or truth in legends (as there is not much in either),
this very thing might be signified by his mother's dream,
who the night before Dominic was born, dreamed she was
brought to bed of a huge dog with a fire-brand in his mouth.
Sure enough, however his disciples expound the dream, it
was a better sign that he should prove a rabid, furious in-
cendiary than anything else; whatever he might be in the
other parts of his life, in this doctrine he was not much better,
as appears in his deportment toward the Albigenses, against
whom he so preached, *adeo quidem ut centum hæreticorum
millia ab octo millibus catholicorum fusa et interfecta fuisse
perhibeantur,* saith one of him; and of those who were taken,
one hundred eighty were burned to death because they would
not abjure their doctrine: this was the first example of
putting erring persons to death that I find in the Roman
church; for about one hundred and seventy years before,
Berengarius fell into opinion concerning the blessed sacrament which they called heresy, and recanted, and relapsed,
and recanted again, and fell again two or three times, saith
Gerson writing against *Romant of the Rose,* and yet he died
sicca morte, his own natural death, and with the hope of
heaven, and yet Hildebrand was once his judge; which shows
that at that time Rome was not come to do great heights
of bloodshed. In England, although the pope had as great
power here as anywhere, yet there were no executions for
matter of opinion known till the time of Henry the Fourth,
who (because he usurped the crown) was willing by all

means to endear the clergy by destroying their enemies, that so he might be sure of them to all his purposes.[18] And, indeed, it may become them well enough, who are wiser in their generations than the children of light; it may possibly serve the policies of evil persons, but never the pure and chaste designs of Christianity, which admits no blood but Christ's, and the imitating blood of martyrs, but knows nothing how to serve her ends by persecuting any of her erring children.

By this time I hope it will not be thought reasonable to say, he that teaches mercy to erring persons, teaches indifferency in religion, unless so many fathers, and so many churches, and the best of emperors, and all the world (till they were abused by tyranny, popery, and faction) did teach indifferency, for I have shown that Christianity does not punish corporally persons erring spiritually, but indeed popery does; the Donatists, and Circumcellians, and Arians, and the Itaciani, they of old did: in the middle ages, the patrons of images did, and the papists at this day do, and have done ever since they were taught it by their S. Dominic.

Seventhly, and yet after all this, I have something more to exempt myself from the clamor of this objection: for let all errors be as much and as zealously suppressed as may be (the doctrine of the following discourse contradicts not that), but let it be done by such means as are proper instruments of their suppression, by preaching and disputation (so that neither of them breed disturbance), by charity and sweetness, by holiness of life, assiduity of exhortation, by the word of God and prayer.

For these ways are most natural, most prudent, most peaceable, and effectual. Only let not men be hasty in calling every disliked opinion by the name of heresy; and when they have resolved that they will call it so, let them use the erring person like a brother, not beat him like a dog, or con-

[18] Cf. Fuller's *Church History of Britain*, Bk. IV. cent. 15.

vince him with a gibbet, or vex him out of his understanding and persuasions.

And now if men still say, I persuade to indifferency, there is no help for me, for I have given reasons against it; I must bear it as well as I can; I am not yet without remedy as they are, for patience will help me, and reason will not cure them; let them take their course, and I'll take mine.

Only I will take leave to consider this (and they would do well to do so too), that unless faith be kept within its own latitude and not called out to patrocinate every less necessary opinion, and the interest of every sect, or peevish person; and if damnation be pronounced against Christians believing the creed, and living good lives, because they are deceived, or are said to be deceived in some opinions less necessary, there is no way in the world to satisfy unlearned persons in the choice of their religion, or to appease the unquietness of a scrupulous conscience: for suppose an honest citizen whose employment and parts will not enable him to judge the disputes and arguings of great clerks, sees factions commenced and managed with much bitterness by persons who might on either hand be fit enough to guide him; when if he follows either, he is disquieted and pronounced damned by the other (who also if he be the most unreasonable in his opinion, will perhaps be more furious in his sentence), what shall this man do, where shall he rest the sole of his foot? Upon the doctrine of the church where he lives? Well! but that he hears declaimed against perpetually, and other churches claim highly and pretend fairly for truth, and condemn his church. If I tell him that he must live a good life, and believe the creed, and not trouble himself with their disputes, or interesting himself in sects and factions, I speak reason: because no law of God ties him to believe more than what is of essential necessity, and whatsoever he shall come to know to be revealed by God. Now if he believes his creed, he believes all that is necessary to all, or of itself; and if he do his moral endeavor beside, he can do no more toward finding out all the rest, and then he is secured; but then if this will secure him, why do men press further and pretend every opinion as necessary, and that in so high degree that if they all said true, or any two indeed of them, in five hundred sects which are in the world (and for ought I know there may be five thousand) it is five hundred to one but that every man is damned; for every sect damns all but itself, and that is damned of four hundred ninety-nine, and it is excellent fortune then if that escape; and there is the same reason in every one of them, that is, it is extreme unreasonableness in all of them to pronounce damnation against such persons, against whom clearly and dogmatically holy Scripture hath not: *In odiosis quod minimum est sequimur, in favoribus quod est maximum,* saith the law, and therefore we should say anything, or make any excuse that is any degree reasonable, rather than condemn all the world to hell; especially if we consider these two things, that we ourselves are as apt to be deceived as any are, and that they who are deceived when they used their moral industry that they might not be deceived, if they perish for this, they perish for what they could not help.

But, however, if the best security in the world be not in neglecting all sects and subdivisions of men, and fixing ourselves on points necessary and plain, and on honest and pious endeavors according to our several capacities and opportunities for all the rest; if I say, all this be not through the mercies of God the best security to all unlearned persons, and learned too, where shall we fix? where shall we either have peace or security? If you bid me follow your doctrine, you must tell me why; and perhaps when you have, I am not able to judge; or if I be as able as other people are, yet when I have judged, I may be deceived too, and so may you, or any man else you bid me follow, so that I am no whit the nearer truth or peace.

And then if we look abroad, and consider how there is

scarce any church but is highly charged by many adversaries
in many things, possibly we may see a reason to charge every
one of them in some things; and what shall we do then? The
church of Rome hath spots enough, and all the world is inquisitive enough to find out more, and to represent these to
her greatest disadvantage. The Greek church denies the
procession of the Holy Ghost from the Son; if that be false
doctrine, she is highly to blame; if it be not, then all the
western churches are to blame for saying the contrary. And
there is no church that is in prosperity, but alters her doctrine every age, either by bringing in new doctrines, or by
contradicting her old; which shows that none are satisfied
with themselves or with their own confessions: and since
all churches believe themselves fallible, that only excepted
which all other churches say is most of all deceived, it were
strange if in so many articles which make up their several
bodies of confessions, they had not mistaken every one of
them in something or other. The Lutheran churches maintain consubstantiation, the Zuinglians are sacramentaries,
the Calvinists are fierce in the matters of absolute predetermination, and all these reject Episcopacy, which the primitive church would have made no doubt to have called heresy.
The Socinians profess a portentous number of strange opinions: they deny the holy Trinity, and the satisfaction of our
blessed Saviour: the Anabaptists laugh at Pædo-baptism; the
Ethiopian churches are Nestorian: where then shall we fix
our confidence, or join communion? to pitch upon any one
of these is to throw the dice, if salvation be to be had only
in one of them, and that every error that by chance hath
made a sect, and is distinguished by a name, be damnable.

If this consideration does not deceive me, we have no
other help in the midst of these distractions and disunions,
but all of us to be united in that common term, which as it
does constitute the church in its being such, so it is the
medium of the communion of saints; and that is the creed
of the apostles; and in all other things an honest endeavor

to find out what truths we can, and a charitable and mutual permission to others that disagree from us and our opinions. I am sure this may satisfy us, for it will secure us; but I know not anything else that will; and no man can be reasonably persuaded, or satisfied in anything else, unless he throws himself upon chance, or absolute predestination, or his own confidence, in every one of which it is two to one at least but he may miscarry.

Thus far I thought I had reason on my side, and I suppose I have made it good upon its proper grounds in the pages following. But then if the result be that men must be permitted in their opinions, and that Christians must not persecute Christians; I have also as much reason to reprove all those oblique arts which are not direct persecutions of men's persons, but they are indirect proceedings, ungentle and unchristian, servants of faction and interest, provocations to zeal and animosities, and destructive of learning and ingenuity. And these are suppressing all the monuments of their adversaries, forcing them to recant, and burning their books.

For it is a strange industry, and an importune diligence that was used by our forefathers; of all those heresies which gave them battle and employment, we have absolutely no record or monument, but what themselves who were adversaries have transmitted to us; and we know that adversaries, especially such who observed all opportunities to discredit both the persons and doctrines of the enemy, are not always the best records or witnesses of such transactions. We see it now in this very age, in the present distemperatures, that parties are no good registers of the actions of the adverse side: and if we cannot be confident of the truth of a story now, now I say that it is possible for any man, and likely that the interested adversary will discover the imposture, it is far more unlikely that after ages should know any other truth but such as serves the ends of the representers. I am sure such things were never taught us by

Christ and his apostles, and if we were sure that ourselves
spoke truth, or that truth were able to justify herself, it were
better if to preserve a doctrine we did not destroy a commandment, and out of zeal pretending to Christian religion,
lose the glories and rewards of ingenuity and Christian simplicity.

Of the same consideration is mending authors, not to their
own mind but to ours, that is, to mend them so as to spoil
them; forbidding the publication of books in which there
is nothing impious or against the public interest, leaving
out clauses in translations, disgracing men's persons, charging disavowed doctrines upon men, and the persons of the
men with the consequents of their doctrine, which they deny
either to be true or to be consequent, false reporting of
disputations and conferences, burning books by the hand
of the hangman, and all such arts, which show that we either
distrust God for the maintenance of his truth, or that we
distrust the cause, or distrust ourselves and our abilities.
I will say no more of these, but only concerning the last, I
shall transcribe a passage out of Tacitus in the life of Julius
Agricola,[19] who gives this account of it, *Veniam non petis-
sem, nisi incusaturas tam sæva et infesta virtutibus tem-
pora. Legimus quum Aruleno Rustico Pætus Thrasea, Heren-
nio Senecioni Priscus Helvidius laudati essent, capitale
fuisse: neque in ipsos modo authores, sed in libros quoque
eorum sævitum delegato Triumviris ministerio ut monu-
menta clarissimorum ingeniorum in comitio ac foro urerentur.
Scilicet illo igne vocem populi Romani et libertatem senatus
et conscientiam generis humani aboleri arbitrabantur, ex-
pulsis insuper sapientiæ professoribus, atque omni bona arte
in exsilium acta, ne quid usquam honestum occurreret.* It is
but an illiterate policy to think that such indirect and
uningenuous proceedings can amongst wise and free men disgrace the authors and disrepute their discourses; and I have
seen that the price hath been trebled upon a forbidden or a

[19] Book IV, Chap. ii.

condemned book; and some men in policy have got a prohibition, that their impression might be the more certainly
vendible, and author himself thought considerable.

The best way is to leave tricks and devices, and to fall upon
that way which the best ages of the church did use: with
the strength of argument, and allegations of Scripture, and
modesty of deportment, and meekness, and charity to the
persons of men, they converted misbelievers, stopped the
mouths of adversaries, asserted truth, and discountenanced
error; and those other stratagems and arts of support and
maintenance to doctrines, were the issues of heretical brains;
the old Catholics had nothing to secure themselves but the
ἓν μέγα of truth and plain dealing. . . .

Ralph Cudworth 1617-1688

THE SEVENTEENTH century is notable for its great theologians and preachers, first for the Caroline divines and later for the Cambridge Platonists. The latter group, especially, emphasized inner spiritual life and severe moral discipline, believing that one's spiritual vision became clearer as the result of moral obedience. They held that the fruit of both philosophy and religion was conduct and that the supreme motivation of conduct was the love of God and man. Cudworth has been recognized as the most learned of that learned group, which comprised such men as Benjamin Whichcote, Henry More, John Smith, and Nathanael Culverwell.

He was born in Aller, Somerset, not a great distance from the birthplace of Locke. He was privately prepared by his stepfather, Dr. Stoughton, for entrance into Emmanuel College, Cambridge, in 1632. He took his B.A. and M.A. degrees there and was made a fellow in 1639. He was a popular tutor, numbering among his distinguished students Sir William Temple.

He became Master of Clare Hall in 1645 and proceeded to a B.D. in the following year. Here he was also Regius Professor in Hebrew. He became Master of Christ's College in 1654, continued there the remainder of his life, and is buried in the College Chapel. His daughter became Lady Masham and was Locke's benefactress, providing a home for Locke over many years. In *Some Thoughts Concerning Education* there are frequent references to the educational methods employed in teaching Lady Masham's son. After Cudworth's death his widow also joined her daughter's household.

Cudworth's most famous sermon was preached before the House of Commons on March 31, 1647. Though Parliament was full of vigorous Presbyterians, Cudworth fearlessly called for the dismissal of party differences and a pattern of life based upon the life of Christ. His sermon is a great plea for a liberal attitude founded upon inner spiritual security.

He undertook to work out a system of philosophy, but this enormous task was never completed. *The True Intellectual System of the Universe* is a part of this project and is directed against the growing materialism which stemmed from Hobbes. Cudworth was very slow about publication and his *Treatise of Immutable Morality* was not published until 1731, many years after his death. A number of other manuscripts remain unpublished.

From A SERMON PREACHED BEFORE THE HONORABLE HOUSE OF COMMONS, MARCH 31, 1647.[1]

[*The Law of Love*]

I do not urge the law written upon tables of stone without us (though there is still a good use of that too) but the law of holiness written within upon the fleshly tables of our hearts. The first, though it work us into some outward conformity to God's commandments, and so hath a good effect upon the world, yet we are all this while but like dead instruments of music that sound sweetly and harmoniously when they are only struck and played upon from without by the musician's hand, who hath the theory and law of music living within himself. But the second, the living law of the gospel, the law of the spirit of life within us, is as if the soul of music should incorporate itself with the instrument and live in the strings and make them of their own accord, without any touch or impulse from without, dance up and down and warble out their harmonies. They that are acted only by an outward law are but like neurospasts, or those little puppets that skip nimbly up and down and seem to be full of quick and sprightly motion, whereas they are all the while moved artificially by certain wires and strings from without, and not by any principle of motion from themselves within: or else like clocks and watches that go pretty regularly for a while, but are moved by weights and plummets or some other artificial springs that must be ever now and then wound up, or else they cease. But they that are acted by the new law of the gospel, by the law of the spirit, they have an inward principle of life within, that from the center of itself puts forth itself freely and constantly into all obedi-

[1] Text: Facsimile of original edition, 1647, in the library of Union Theological Seminary (New York, 1930).

ence to the will of Christ. This new law of the gospel, it is
a kind of musical soul, informing the dead organ of our
hearts, that makes them of their own accord delight to act
harmoniously according to the rule of God's word. The law
that I speak of, it is the law of love, which is the most powerful law in the world; and yet it freeth us in a manner from
all law without us because it maketh us become a law unto
ourselves. The more it prevaileth in us, the more it eateth
up and devoureth all other laws without us; just as Aaron's
living rod did swallow up those rods of the magicians that
were made only to counterfeit a little life:[2]

> *Sius legem det amantibus?*
> *Major lex amor est sibi.*

Love is at once a freedom from all law, a state of purest
liberty, and yet a law, too, of the most constraining and in-
dispensable necessity. The worst law in the world is the
law of sin, which is in our members, which keeps us in a
condition of most absolute slavery when we are wholly under
the tyrannical commands of our lusts: this is a cruel Pharaoh
indeed that sets his hard taskmasters over us and makes us
wretchedly drudge in mire and clay. The law of the letter
without us sets us in a condition of a little more liberty by
restraining of us from many outward acts of sin, but yet it
doth not disenthrall us from the power of sin in our hearts.
But the law of the spirit of life, the gospel-law of love, it
puts us into a condition of most pure and perfect liberty;
and whosoever really entertains this law, he hath cast out
the bondwoman and her children,[3] from henceforth Sarah,
the free woman, shall live forever with him, and she shall
be to him a mother of many children: her seed shall be as
the sand of the seashore for number and as the stars of
heaven. Here is evangelical liberty, here is gospel freedom,
when the law of the spirit of life in Christ Jesus hath made

[2] Exod. 7:10–12.
[3] Gen. 21:10–20, 22:17.

us free from the law of sin and death: [4] when we have a liberty from sin, and not a liberty to sin; for our dear Lord and Master hath told us that *Whosoever committeth sin, he is the servant of it.*[5] He that lies under the power and vassalage of his base lusts and yet talks of gospel freedom, he is but like a poor condemned prisoner that in his sleep dreams of being set at liberty and of walking up and down wheresoever he pleaseth; whilst his legs are all the while locked fast in fetters and irons. To please ourselves with a notion of gospel liberty whilst we have not a gospel principle of holiness within us to free us from the power of sin, it is nothing else but to gild over our bonds and fetters and to fancy ourselves to be in a golden cage. There is a straitness, slavery, and narrowness in all sin: sin crowds and crumples up our souls, which if they were freely spread abroad, would be as wide and as large as the whole universe. No man is truly free but he that hath his own will enlarged to the extent of God's own will, by loving whatsoever God loves and nothing else. Such a one doth not fondly hug this and that particular created good thing and envassal himself unto it, but he loveth everything that is lovely, beginning at God and descending down to all his creatures, according to the several degrees of perfection in them. He enjoys a boundless liberty and a boundless sweetness, according to his boundless love. He enclaspeth the whole world within his outstretched arms; his soul is as wide as the whole universe, as big as yesterday, today, and forever. Whosoever is once acquainted with this disposition of spirit, he never desires anything else; and he loves the life of God in himself dearer than his own life. To conclude this therefore, if we love Christ and keep his commandments, his commandments will not be grievous to us: His yoke will be easy and his burden light; [6] it will not put us into a state of bondage, but of perfect liberty. For it is most true of evangelical obedience, what the wise man speaketh of wisdom: *her ways are ways*

[4] Rom. 8:2.   [5] John 8:34.   [6] Matt. 11:29.

of pleasantness, and all her paths are peace; she is a tree of life to those that lay hold upon her, and happy are all they that retain her.[7]

I will now shut up all with one or two considerations to persuade you further to the keeping of Christ's commandments.

First, from the desire which we all have of knowledge; if we would indeed know divine truths, the only way to come to this is by keeping of Christ's commandments. The grossness of our apprehensions in spiritual things and our many mistakes that we have about them, proceed from nothing but those dull and foggy steams which rise up from our foul hearts and becloud our understandings. If we did but heartily comply with Christ's commandments and purge our hearts from all gross and sensual affections, we should not then look about for truth wholly without ourselves, and enslave ourselves to the dictates of this and that teacher and hang upon the lips of men; but we should find the great eternal God inwardly teaching our souls and continually instructing us more and more in the mysteries of his will: and out of our bellies should flow rivers of living waters. Nothing puts a stop and hindrance to the passage of truth in the world, but the carnality of our hearts, the corruption of our lives. 'Tis not wrangling disputes and syllogistical reasonings that are the mighty pillars that underprop truth in the world; if we would but underset it with the holiness of our hearts and lives, it should never fail. Truth is a prevailing and conquering thing and would quickly overcome the world, did not the earthiness of our dispositions and the darkness of our false hearts hinder it. Our saviour Christ bids the blind man wash off the clay that was upon his eyes in the Pool of Siloam,[8] and then he should see clearly, intimating this to us, that it is the earthiness of men's affections that darkens the eye of their understandings in spiritual things. Truth is always ready and near at hand if our eyes

---

[7] Prov. 3:17–18.   [8] John 9:7.

were not closed up with mud that we could but open them to look upon it. Truth always waits upon our souls and offers itself freely to us, as the sun offers its beams to every eye that will but open and let them shine in upon it. If we could but purge our hearts from that filth and defilement which hangeth about them, there would be no doubt of all of truth's prevailing in the world. For truth is great, and stronger than all things; all the earth calleth upon truth, and the heaven blesseth it, all works shake and tremble at it. The truth endureth, and is always strong; it liveth and conquereth forevermore. She is the strength, kingdom, power, and majesty of all ages. Blessed be the God of truth.

Last of all, if we desire a true Reformation, as we seem to do, let us begin here in reforming our hearts and lives, in keeping of Christ's commandments. All outward forms and models of reformation, though they be never so good in their kind, yet they are of little worth to us without this inward reformation of the heart. Tin or lead or any other baser metal, if it be cast into never so good a mold and made up into never so elegant a figure, yet it is but tin or lead still; it is the same metal that it was before. And if we be molded into never so good a form of outward government, unless we new mold our hearts within too, we are but little better than we were before. If adulterate silver that hath much alloy or dross in it have never so current a stamp put upon it, yet it will not pass notwithstanding when the touchstone trieth it. We must be reformed within with a spirit of fire, and a spirit of burning to purge us from the dross and corruption of our hearts, and refine us as gold and silver, and then we shall be reformed truly and not before. When this once comes to pass, then shall Christ be set upon his throne indeed; then the glory of the Lord shall overflow the land; then we shall be a people acceptable unto him, and as Mount Sion, which he dearly loved.

COWLEY attended Westminster School, where he showed unusual poetic talent and at fifteen published his first book of poems, *Poetical Blossoms*. When he entered Trinity College, Cambridge, this had reached a second edition, and soon two plays followed. There were other poets at Cambridge at this time, but none so precocious as Cowley. Crashaw became his warm friend, and later in Paris Cowley was able to be of practical service to Crashaw, whom he found in great need.

Cowley had just won a Fellowship to Trinity when the Puritan Commissioners reached Cambridge in April, 1644, making flight necessary. First at Oxford and then in France he was closely associated with the court, was employed in secret correspondence, and was sent on missions of state. In 1654 he was in England and, coming under suspicion, was imprisoned for a time. For safety he enrolled as a student of medicine at Oxford, receiving his degree in 1657. He also saw his collected poems through the press during this time.

After Cromwell's death Cowley returned to France but found a cool reception, for Charles II suspected him of defection in his loyalty. After the Restoration he retired to the quiet country life he had long desired, settling at Barn Elms on land given him by the queen. Later he moved to Chertsey, which had a more healthful climate and was nearer London.

In his own day Cowley was considered a superior poet to Milton. *The Mistress,* his major collection of poems, shows the influence of Donne in certain mannerisms, but does not achieve Donne's intensity. His *Anacreontics* and *Pindaric Odes* are more interesting and important, and point the way toward eighteenth century poetry. The *Davideis,* an incomplete biblical epic in couplets which preceded *Paradise Lost* by a decade, found few readers. In contrast with his contemporary reputation, Cowley's reputation today depends chiefly upon his familiar essays. In this type of personal writing he is following Montaigne; yet the voice is Cowley's own, expressing his thoughts in the phrases of daily speech rather than in the balanced terseness of Bacon or the elaboration of the writers of poetic prose. *A Proposition for the Advancement of Experimental Philosophy* is a distinguished contribution in the development of modern education, and was suggestive in the founding of the Royal Scientific Society. Since its purpose was informative and practical, it was written with a clarity and directness that seem very modern.

A PROPOSITION FOR THE ADVANCEMENT
OF EXPERIMENTAL PHILOSOPHY

The Preface [1]

ALL KNOWLEDGE must either be of God or of his creatures, that is, of nature; the first is called from the object, divinity; the latter, natural philosophy, and is divided into the contemplation of the immediate or mediate creatures of God, that is, the creatures of his creature man. Of this latter kind are all arts for the use of human life, which are thus again divided: some are purely human, or made by man alone, and as it were entirely spun out of himself, without relation to other creatures; such are grammar and logic, to improve his natural qualities of internal and external speech; as likewise rhetoric and politics (or law) to fulfill and exalt his natural inclination to society. Others are mixed, and are man's creatures no otherwise than by the result which he effects by conjunction and application of the creatures of God. Of these parts of philosophy, that which treats of God Almighty (properly called divinity), which is almost only to be sought out of his revealed will and therefore requires only the diligent and pious study of that, and of the best interpreters upon it; and that part which I call purely human, depending solely upon memory and wit, that is, reading and invention, are both excellently well provided for by the constitution of our universities. But the other two parts, the inquisition into the nature of God's creatures, and the application of them to human uses (especially the latter) seem to be very slenderly provided for, or rather almost totally neglected, except only some small assistances to physic and the mathematics. And therefore the founders of our colleges have taken ample care to supply the students with multitude of books, and to appoint tutors and frequent exercises, the one to interpret, and the other to confirm their

[1] Text: 1661, first edition.

582

reading, as also to afford them sufficient plenty and leisure for the opportunities of their private study, that the beams which they receive by lecture may be doubled by reflections of their own wit; but towards the observation and application, as I said, of the creatures themselves, they have allowed no instruments, materials, or conveniences. Partly because the necessary expense thereof is much greater than of the other; and partly from that idle and pernicious opinion which had long possessed the world, that all things to be searched in nature had been already found and discovered by the ancients, and that it were a folly to travel about for that which others had before brought home to us. And the great importer of all truths they took to be Aristotle, as if (as Macrobius [2] speaks foolishly of Hippocrates) he could neither deceive nor be deceived, or as if there had been not only no lies in him, but all verities. O true philosophers in one sense! and contented with very little! Not that I would disparage the admirable wit and worthy labors of the ancients, much less of Aristotle, the most eminent among them; but it were madness to imagine that the cisterns of men should afford us as much, and as wholesome waters, as the fountains of nature. As we understand the manners of men by conversation among them, and not by reading romances, the same is our case in the true apprehension and judgment of things. And no man can hope to make himself as rich by stealing out of others' trunks as he might by opening and digging of new mines. If he conceive that all are already exhausted, let him consider that many lazily thought so a hundred years ago, and yet nevertheless since that time whole regions of art have been discovered, which the ancients as little dreamt of as they did of America. There is yet many a *terra incognita* behind to exercise our diligence, and let us exercise it never so much, we shall leave work enough too for our posterity.

[2] Macrobius flourished about A.D. 400. In his commentary on Cicero's *Dream of Scipio* he refers to Hippocrates.

This therefore being laid down as a certain foundation, that we must not content ourselves with that inheritance of knowledge which is left us by the labor and bounty of our ancestors, but seek to improve those very grounds and add to them with new and greater purchases; it remains to be considered by what means we are most likely to attain the ends of this virtuous covetousness.

And certainly the solitary and inactive contemplation of nature, by the most ingenious persons living, in their own private studies can never effect it. Our reasoning faculty as well as fancy does but dream when it is not guided by sensible objects. We shall compound where nature has divided, and divide where nature has compounded, and create nothing but either deformed monsters, or at best pretty but impossible mermaids. 'Tis like painting by memory and imagination, which can never produce a picture to the life. Many persons of admirable abilities (if they had been wisely managed and profitably employed) have spent their whole time and diligence in commentating upon Aristotle's philosophy, who could never go beyond him, because their design was only to follow, not grasp, or lay hold on, or so much as touch nature, because they caught only at the shadow of her in their own brains. And therefore we see that for above a thousand years together nothing almost of ornament or advantage was added to the uses of human society, except only guns and printing, whereas since the industry of men has ventured to go abroad, out of books and out of themselves, and to work among God's creatures, instead of playing among their own, every age has abounded with excellent inventions, and every year perhaps might do so, if a considerable number of select persons were set apart, and well directed, and plentifully provided for the search of them. But our universities, having been founded in those former times that I complain of, it is no wonder if they be defective in their constitution as to this way of learning, which was not then thought on.

For the supplying of which defect, it is humbly proposed to his sacred Majesty, his most honorable Parliament, and Privy Council, and to all such of his subjects as are willing and able to contribute anything towards the advancement of real and useful learning, that by their authority, encouragement, patronage, and bounty, a Philosophical College may be erected, after this ensuing, or some such model.

SEVERAL DISCOURSES BY WAY OF
ESSAYS, IN VERSE AND PROSE [1]

Of Solitude

Nunquam minus solus, quam cum solus is now become a very vulgar saying. Every man, and almost every boy, for these seventeen hundred years has had it in his mouth. But it was first spoken by the excellent Scipio, who was without question a most eloquent and witty person, as well as the most wise, most worthy, most happy, and the greatest of all mankind. His meaning, no doubt, was this, that he found more satisfaction to his mind, and more improvement of it, by solitude than by company; and to show that he spoke not this loosely, or out of vanity, after he had made Rome mistress of almost the whole world, he retired himself from it by a voluntary exile, and at a private house in the middle of a wood near Linternum, passed the remainder of his glorious life no less gloriously. This house Seneca went to see so long after with great veneration; and, among other things, describes his baths to have been of so mean a structure that now, says he, the basest of the people would despise them, and cry out, "Poor Scipio understood not how to live." What an authority is here for the credit of retreat! and happy had it been for Hannibal, if adversity could have taught him as much wisdom as was learnt by Scipio from the highest prosperities. This would be no wonder if it were as truly as it is colorably and wittily said by Montaigne "that ambition itself might teach us to love solitude; there's nothing does so much hate to have companions." [2] 'Tis true, it loves to have its elbows free, it detests to have company on either side; but it delights above all things in a train behind; aye, and ushers too before it. But the greatest part of men are so far from the opinion of that noble Roman that,

---

[1] Text: 1668, first edition.   [2] Montaigne, *Essays,* lib. 1. 38.

if they chance at any time to be without company, they're like a becalmed ship; they never move but by the wind of other men's breath and have no oars of their own to steer withal. It is very fantastical and contradictory in human nature that men should love themselves above all the rest of the world and yet never endure to be with themselves. When they are in love with a mistress, all other persons are importunate and burdensome to them. *Tecum vivere amem, tecum obeam libens,*[3] they would live and die with her alone.

> *Sic ego secretis possum bene vivere silvis,*
> *Qua nulla humano sit via trita pede.*
> *Tu mihi curarum requies, tu nocte vel atra*
> *Lumen, et in solis tu mihi turba locis.*[4]

> With thee forever I in woods could rest,
> Where never human foot the ground has prest.
> Thou from all shades the darkness canst exclude,
> And from a desert banish solitude.

And yet our dear self is so wearisome to us that we can scarcely support its conversation for an hour together. This is such an odd temper of mind as Catullus expresses towards one of his mistresses, whom we may suppose to have been of a very unsociable humor:

> *Odi, et amo: quonam id faciam ratione requiras*
> *Nescio; sed fieri sentio, et excrucior.*[5]

> I hate, and yet I love thee too;
> How can that be? I know not how;
> Only that it is so I know,
> And feel with torment that 'tis so.

It is a deplorable condition, this, and drives a man sometimes to pitiful shifts in seeking how to avoid himself.

[3] Horace, *Odes,* III. 9. 24.   [4] Tibullus, iv. 13. 9.
[5] Catullus, *De Amore suo,* 83.

The truth of the matter is, that neither he who is a fop in the world is a fit man to be alone; nor he who has set his heart much upon the world, though he have never so much understanding; so that solitude can be well fitted and sit right but upon a very few persons. They must have enough knowledge of the world to see the vanity of it, and enough virtue to despise all vanity; if the mind be possessed with any lust or passions, a man had better be in a fair than in a wood alone. They may, like petty thieves, cheat us perhaps, and pick our pockets in the midst of company; but like robbers they use to strip and bind or murder us when they catch us alone. This is but to retreat from men and fall into the hands of devils. 'Tis like the punishment of parricides among the Romans, to be sewed into a bag with an ape, a dog, and a serpent.

The first work, therefore, that a man must do, to make himself capable of the good of solitude, is the very eradication of all lusts; for how is it possible for a man to enjoy himself while his affections are tied to things without himself? In the second place, he must learn the art and get the habit of thinking; for this, too, no less than well speaking, depends upon much practice; and cogitation is the thing which distinguishes the solitude of a god from a wild beast. Now, because the soul of man is not by its own nature or observation furnished with sufficient materials to work upon, it is necessary for it to have continual recourse to learning and books for fresh supplies, so that the solitary life will grow indigent and be ready to starve without them; but if once we be thoroughly engaged in the love of letters, instead of being wearied with the length of any day, we shall only complain of the shortness of our whole life.

> *O vita, stulto longa, sapienti brevis!* [6]
> O life, long to the fool, short to the wise!

[6] Publius Syrus, *Sententiæ*, 202.

The first minister of state has not so much business in public as a wise man has in private: if the one have little leisure to be alone, the other has less leisure to be in company; the one has but part of the affairs of one nation, the other all the works of God and nature under his consideration. There is no saying shocks me so much as that which I hear very often, that a man does not know how to pass his time. 'Twould have been but ill spoken by Methusalem in the nine hundred sixty-ninth year of his life; so far it is from us, who have not time enough to attain the utmost perfection of any part of science, to have cause to complain that we are forced to be idle for want of work. But this, you'll say, is work only for the learned; others are not capable either of the employments or divertisements that arrive from letters. I know they are not; and therefore cannot much recommend solitude to a man wholly illiterate. But if any man be so unlearned as to want entertainment of the little intervals of accidental solitude, which frequently occur in almost all conditions (except the very meanest of the people, who have business enough in the necessary provisions of life), it is truly a great shame both to his parents and himself; for a very small portion of any ingenious art will stop up all those gaps of our time: either music, or painting, or designing, or chemistry, or history, or gardening, or twenty other things, will do it usefully and pleasantly; and, if he happen to set his affections upon poetry (which I do not advise him to immoderately), that will overdo it; no wood will be thick enough to hide him from the importunities of company or business, which would abstract him from his beloved.

O qui me gelidis in vallibus Hæmi
Sistat, et ingenti ramorum protegat umbra? [7]

[7] From Virgil's *Georgics*, II. 489 (adapted: *O quis me gelidis sub montibus Æmi*). "O that some one would set me down in the cool valleys of Hamus and shield with a mighty shade of boughs."

Of Agriculture

THE FIRST wish of Virgil (as you will find anon by his verses) was to be a good philosopher, the second, a good husbandman: and God (whom he seemed to understand better than most of the most learned heathens) dealt with him just as he did with Solomon; because he prayed for wisdom in the first place, he added all things else which were subordinately to be desired. He made him one of the best philosophers and the best husbandmen; and, to adorn and communicate both those faculties, the best poet. He made him, besides all this, a rich man, and a man who desired to be no richer. *O fortunatus nimium, et bona qui sua novit:* To be a husbandman is but a retreat from the city; to be a philosopher, from the world; or rather, a retreat from the world, as it is man's, into the world, as it is God's.

But, since nature denies to most men the capacity or appetite, and fortune allows but to a very few the opportunities or possibility of applying themselves wholly to philosophy, the best mixture of human affairs that we can make are the employments of a country life. It is, as Columella [1] calls it, *Res sine dubitatione proxima, et quasi consanguinea sapientiæ,* the nearest neighbor, or rather next in kindred, to philosophy. Varro [2] says, the principles of it are the same which Ennius made to be the principles of all nature, earth, water, air, and the sun. It does certainly comprehend more parts of philosophy than any one profession, art, or science in the world besides: and therefore Cicero says, the pleasures of a husbandman, *mihi ad sapientis vitam proxime videntur accedere,* [3] come very nigh to those of a philosopher. There is no other sort of life that affords so many branches of

---

[1] Columella, Roman writer of the first century A.D., author of *De Re Rustica,* I. 1.

[2] Varro, 116–27(?) B.C., Roman writer, author of *Rerum Rusticarum,* I. 4.

[3] *De Senectute,* xv. 51.

praise to a panegyrist: the utility of it to a man's self; the
usefulness, or rather necessity, of it to all the rest of mankind; the innocence, the pleasure, the antiquity, the dignity.

The utility (I mean plainly the lucre of it) is not so great
now in our nation as arises from merchandise and the trading of the city, from whence many of the best estates and
chief honors of the kingdom are derived: we have no men
now fetched from the plow to be made lords, as they were in
Rome to be made consuls and dictators; the reason of which
I conceive to be from an evil custom, now grown as strong
among us as if it were a law, which is, that no men put their
children to be bred up apprentices in agriculture, as in other
trades, but such who are so poor that, when they come to
be men, they have not wherewithal to set up in it, and so
can only farm some small parcel of ground, the rent of which
devours all but the bare subsistence of the tenant: whilst
they who are proprietors of the land are either too proud,
or, for want of that kind of education, too ignorant, to improve their estates, though the means of doing it be as easy
and certain in this as in any other track of commerce. If
there were always two or three thousand youths, for seven
or eight years bound to this profession, that they might learn
the whole art of it, and afterwards be enabled to be masters
in it, by a moderate stock, I cannot doubt but that we should
see as many aldermen's estates made in the country, as now
we do out of all kind of merchandising in the city. There
are as many ways to be rich, and, which is better, there is
no possibility to be poor, without such negligence as can
neither have excuse nor pity; for a little ground will, without question, feed a little family, and the superfluities of
life (which are now in some cases by custom made almost
necessary) must be supplied out of the superabundance of
art and industry, or contemned by as great a degree of philosophy.

As for the necessity of this art, it is evident enough, since
this can live without all others, and no one other without

this. This is like speech, without which the society of man cannot be preserved; the others, like figures and tropes of speech, which serve only to adorn it. Many nations have lived, and some do still, without any art but this: not so elegantly, I confess, but still they live; and almost all the other arts, which are here practiced, are beholding to this for most of their materials.

The innocence of this life is the next thing for which I commend it; and if husbandmen preserve not that, they are much to blame, for no men are so free from the temptations of iniquity. They live by what they can get by industry from the earth; and others, by what they can catch by craft from men. They live upon an estate given them by their mother; and others, upon an estate cheated from their brethren. They live, like sheep and kine, by the allowances of nature; and others, like wolves and foxes, by the acquisitions of rapine. And I hope I may affirm (without any offense to the great) that sheep and kine are very useful, and that wolves and foxes are pernicious creatures. They are, without dispute, of all men the most quiet and least apt to be inflamed to the disturbance of the commonwealth: their manner of life inclines them, and interest binds them, to love peace; in our late mad and miserable civil wars, all other trades, even to the meanest, set forth whole troops and raised up some great commanders, who became famous and mighty for the mischiefs they had done; but I do not remember the name of any one husbandman who had so considerable a share in the twenty years' ruin of his country as to deserve the curses of his countrymen.

And if great delights be joined with so much innocence, I think it is ill done of men not to take them here, where they are so tame and ready at hand, rather than hunt for them in courts and cities, where they are so wild and the chase so troublesome and dangerous.

We are here among the vast and noble scenes of nature; we are there among the pitiful shifts of policy: we walk here in the light and open ways of the divine bounty; we grope there in the dark and confused labyrinths of human malice: our senses are here feasted with the clear and genuine taste of their objects, which are all sophisticated there, and for the most part overwhelmed with their contraries. Here, pleasure looks (methinks) like a beautiful, constant, and modest wife; it is there an impudent, fickle, and painted harlot. Here is harmless and cheap plenty; there, guilty and expenseful luxury.

I shall only instance in one delight more, the most natural and best-natured of all other, a perpetual companion of the husbandman; and that is, the satisfaction of looking round about him, and seeing nothing but the effects and improvements of his own art and diligence: to be always gathering of some fruits of it, and at the same time to behold others ripening, and others budding; to see all his fields and gardens covered with the beauteous creatures of his own industry; and to see, like God, that all his works are good:

—Hinc atque hinc glomerantur Oreades: ipsi
Agricolæ tacitum pertentant gaudia pectus.

On his heart-strings a secret joy does strike.

The antiquity of his art is certainly not to be contested by any other. The three first men in the world were a gardener, a plowman, and a grazier; and if any man object that the second of these was a murderer, I desire he would consider that as soon as he was so, he quitted our profession and turned builder. It is for this reason, I suppose, that Ecclesiasticus forbids us to hate husbandry; because (says he) "the Most High has created it." We were all born to this art and taught by nature to nourish our bodies by the same earth out of which they were made, and to which they must return, and pay at last for their sustenance.

Behold the original and primitive nobility of all those

great persons, who are too proud now, not only to till the ground, but almost to tread upon it. We may talk what we please of lilies, and lions rampant, and spread-eagles, in fields d'or or d'argent; but, if heraldry were guided by reason, a plow in a field arable would be the most noble and ancient arms.

All these considerations make me fall into the wonder and complaint of Columella, how it should come to pass that all arts or sciences (for the dispute, which is an art, and which a science, does not belong to the curiosity of us husbandmen) : metaphysic, physic, morality, mathematics, logic, rhetoric &c., which are all, I grant, good and useful faculties (except only metaphysic, which I do not know whether it be anything or no); but even vaulting, fencing, dancing, attiring, cookery, carving, and such like vanities, should all have public schools and masters, and yet that we should never see or hear of any man, who took upon him the profession of teaching this so pleasant, so virtuous, so profitable, so honorable, so necessary art.

A man would think, when he is in serious humor, that it were but a vain, irrational, and ridiculous thing for a great company of men and women to run up and down in a room together, in a hundred several postures and figures, to no purpose, and with no design; and therefore dancing was invented first, and only practiced anciently, in the ceremonies of the heathen religion, which consisted all in mummery and madness; the latter being the chief glory of the worship, and accounted divine inspiration: this, I say, a severe man would think; though I dare not determine so far against so customary a part, now, of good-breeding. And yet, who is there among our gentry that does not entertain a dancing-master for his children as soon as they are able to walk? But did ever any father provide a tutor for his son to instruct him betimes in the nature and improvements of that land which he intended to leave him? That is at least a superfluity, and this a defect, in our manner of education; and therefore I could wish (but cannot in these times much hope to see it) that one college in each university were erected, and appropriated to this study, as well as there are to medicine and the civil law: there would be no need of making a body of scholars and fellows with certain endowments, as in other colleges; it would suffice if, after this manner of halls in Oxford, there were only four professors constituted (for it would be too much work for only one master, or principal, as they call him there) to teach these four parts of it: first, aration, and all things relating to it; secondly, pasturage; thirdly, gardens, orchards, vineyards, and woods; fourthly, all parts of rural economy, which would contain the government of bees, swine, poultry, decoys, ponds, &c. and all that which Varro calls *villaticas pastiones,* together with the sports of the field (which ought to be looked upon not only as pleasures, but as parts of housekeeping) and the domestical conservation and uses of all that is brought in by industry abroad. The business of these professors should not be, as is commonly practiced in other arts, only to read pompous and superficial lectures out of Virgil's Georgics, Pliny, Varro, or Columella; but to instruct their pupils in the whole method and course of this study, which might be run through perhaps, with diligence, in a year or two: and the continual succession of scholars, upon a moderate taxation for their diet, lodging and learning, would be a sufficient constant revenue for maintenance of the house and the professors, who should be men not chosen for the ostentation of critical literature, but for solid and experimental knowledge of the things they teach; such men, so industrious and public-spirited, as I conceive Mr. Hartlib to be, if the gentleman be yet alive. But it is needless to speak further of my thoughts of this design, unless the present disposition of the age allowed more probability of bringing it into execution. What I have further to say of the country life shall be borrowed from the poets, who were always the most faithful and affectionate friends to it. Poetry was born among the shepherds.

> *Nescio qua natale solum dulcedine Musas*
> *Ducit, et immemores non sinit esse sui.*

The Muses still love their own native place;
'T has secret charms, which nothing can deface.

The truth is, no other place is proper for their work; one might as well undertake to dance in a crowd, as to make good verses in the midst of noise and tumult.

As well might corn, as verse, in cities grow;
In vain the thankless glebe we plow and sow;
Against th' unnatural soil in vain we strive;
'Tis not a ground in which these plants will thrive.

It will bear nothing but the nettles and thorns of satire, which grow most naturally in the worst earth; and therefore almost all poets, except those who were not able to eat bread without the bounty of great men, that is, without what they could get by flattering of them, have not only withdrawn themselves from the vices and vanities of the grand world,

> *pariter vitiisque jocisque*
> *Altius humanis exeruere caput*

into the innocent happiness of a retired life; but have commended and adorned nothing so much by their ever-living poems. Hesiod [4] was the first or second poet in the world that remains yet extant (if Homer, as some think, preceded him, but I rather believe they were contemporaries); and he is the first writer too of the art of husbandry: "and he

---

[4] Hesiod, Greek epic poet who lived in the eighth century B.C.

has contributed (says Columella) not a little to our profession"; I suppose he means not a little honor, for the matter of his instructions is not very imporant: his great antiquity is visible through the gravity and simplicity of his style. The most acute of all his sayings concerns our purpose very much and is couched in the reverend obscurity of an oracle. Πλεόν ἥμισυ παντὸς, the half is more than the whole. The occasion of the speech is this: his brother Perses had, by corrupting some great men (βασιλῆας Δωροφάγους, great bribe-eaters he calls them), gotten from him the half of his estate. It is no matter (says he); they have not done me so much prejudice as they imagine.

Νήπιοι, οὐδὲ ἴσασιν ὅσῳ Πλέον ἥμισυ Παντός
Οὐδ' ὅσον ἐν μαλάχῃ τε καὶ ασφοδέλῳ μέγ' ὄνειαρ,
Κρύψαντες γὰρ ἔχουσι θεοὶ Βίον ἀνθρώποισι.

Unhappy they to whom God has not revealed,
By a strong light which must their sense control,
That half a great estate's more than the whole.
Unhappy, from whom still concealed does lie,
Of roots and herbs, the wholesome luxury.

This I conceive to be honest Hesiod's meaning. From Homer, we must not expect much concerning our affairs. He was blind, and could neither work in the country, nor enjoy the pleasures of it; his helpless poverty was likeliest to be sustained in the richest places; he was to delight the Grecians with fine tales of the wars and adventures of their ancestors; his subject removed him from all commerce with us, and yet, methinks, he made a shift to show his good will a little. For, though he could do us no honor in the person of his hero Ulysses (much less of Achilles), because his whole time was consumed in wars and voyages; yet he makes his father Laertes a gardener all that while, and seeking his consolation for the absence of his son in the pleasure of planting and even dunging his own grounds. Ye see, he did not contemn us peasants; nay, so far was he from that insolence that he always styles Eumæus, who kept the hogs, with wonderful respect, Δῖον ὑφορβόν, the divine swine-herd; he could have done no more for Menelaus or Agamemnon. And Theocritus (a very ancient poet, but he was one of our own tribe, for he wrote nothing but pastorals) gave the same epithet to an husbandman, ʼΑμείβετο Δῖος ἀγρώτης. The divine husbandman replied to Hercules, who was but Δῖος himself. These were civil Greeks, and who understood the dignity of our calling!

Among the Romans we have, in the first place, our truly divine Virgil, who, though, by the favor of Mæcenas and Augustus, he might have been one of the chief men of Rome, yet chose rather to employ much of his time in the exercise, and much of his immortal wit in the praise and instructions, of a rustic life; who, though he had written before whole books of pastorals and georgics, could not abstain, in his great and imperial poem, from describing Evander, one of his best princes, as living just after the homely manner of an ordinary countryman. He seats him in a throne of maple, and lays him but upon a bear's skin; the kine and oxen are lowing in his court-yard; the birds under the eves of his window call him up in the morning; and when he goes abroad, only two dogs go along with him for his guard: at last, when he brings Æneas into his royal cottage, he makes him say this memorable compliment, greater than even yet was spoken at the Escurial, the Louvre, or our Whitehall:

> ———*Hæc (inquit) limina victor*
> *Alcides subiit, hæc illum regia cepit:*
> *Aude, hospes, contemnere opes, et te quoque dignum*
> *Finge Deo, rebusque veni non asper egenis.*

This humble roof, this rustic court (said he),
Receiv'd Alcides, crown'd with victory:

Scorn not, great guest, the steps where he has trod;
But contemn wealth, and imitate a God.

The next man, whom we are much obliged to, both for his
doctrine and example, is the next best poet in the world to
Virgil, his dear friend Horace; who, when Augustus had
desired Mæcenas to persuade him to come and live do-
mestically and at the same table with him, and to be secretary of state of the whole world under him, or rather jointly
with him, for he says, *ut nos in epistolis scribendis adjuvet,*
could not be tempted to forsake his Sabine or Tiburtin
manor, for so rich and so glorious a trouble. There was never,
I think, such an example of this in the world, that he should
have so much moderation and courage as to refuse an offer
of such greatness, and the emperor so much generosity and
good-nature as not to be at all offended with his refusal,
but to retain still the same kindness, and express it often
to him in most friendly and familiar letters, part of which
are still extant. If I should produce all the passages of this
excellent author upon the several subjects which I treat of
in this book, I must be obliged to translate half his works;
of which I may say more truly than, in my opinion, he did
of Homer.

> *Qui, quid sit pulchrum, quid turpe, quid utile,*
> *quid non,*
> *Plenius et melius Chrysippo et Crantore dicit.*

I shall content myself upon this particular theme with
three only, one out of his *Odes,* the other out of his *Satires,*
the third out of his *Epistles;* and shall forbear to collect
the suffrages of all other poets, which may be found scattered
up and down through all their writings, and especially in
Martial's. But I must not omit to make some excuse for the
bold-undertaking of my own unskillful pencil upon the beauties of a face that has been drawn before by so many great
masters; especially, that I should dare to do it in Latin

verses (though of another kind), and have the confidence to translate them. I can only say that I love the matter, and that ought to cover many faults; and that I run not to contend with those before me, but follow to applaud them.

Of Myself

IT IS a hard and nice subject for a man to write of himself; it grates his own heart to say anything of disparagement, and the reader's ears to hear anything of praise from him. There is no danger from me of offending him in this kind; neither my mind, nor my body, nor my fortune, allow me any materials for that vanity. It is sufficient for my own contentment that they have preserved me from being scandalous, or remarkable on the defective side. But besides that, I shall here speak of myself only in relation to the subject of these precedent discourses, and shall be likelier thereby to fall into the contempt than rise up to the estimation of most people. As far as my memory can return back into my past life, before I knew, or was capable of guessing what the world, or glories, or business of it were, the natural affections of my soul gave me a secret bent of aversion from them, as some plants are said to turn away from others, by an antipathy imperceptible to themselves, and inscrutable to man's understanding. Even when I was a very young boy at school, instead of running about on holidays and playing with my fellows, I was wont to steal from them and walk into the fields, either alone with a book, or with some one companion, if I could find any of the same temper. I was then, too, so much an enemy to all constraint, that my masters could never prevail on me, by any persuasions or encouragements, to learn without book the common rules of grammar, in which they dispensed with me alone, because they found I made a shift to do the usual exercise out of my own reading and observation. That I was then of the same mind as I am now (which, I confess, I wonder at myself) may appear by the latter end of an ode, which I made when I was but thirteen years old, and which was then printed with many other verses. The beginning of it is boyish, but of this part which I here set down (if a very little were corrected) I should hardly now be much ashamed.

9.

This only grant me, that my means may lie
Too low for envy, for contempt too high.
    Some honor I would have,
Not from great deeds, but good alone.
The unknown are better than ill known.
    Rumor can ope' the grave.
Acquaintance I would have, but when 't depends
Not on the number, but the choice of friends.

10.

Book should, not business, entertain the light,
And sleep, as undisturb'd as death, the night.
    My house a cottage, more
Than palace, and should fitting be
For all my use, no luxury.
    My garden painted o're
With nature's hand, not art's; and pleasures yield,
Horace might envy in his Sabine field.

11.

Thus would I double my life's fading space,
For he that runs it well, twice runs his race.
    And in this true delight,
These unbought sports, this happy state,
I would not fear nor wish my fate,
    But boldly say each night,
Tomorrow let my sun his beams display,
Or in clouds hide them; I have liv'd today.

You may see by it, I was even then acquainted with the poets (for the conclusion is taken out of Horace),[5] and perhaps it was the immature and immoderate love of them which stamped first, or rather engraved these characters in me: they were like letters cut into the bark of a young tree, which with the tree still grow proportionably. But how this love came to be produced in me so early is a hard question. I believe I can tell the particular little chance that filled my head first with such chimes of verse as have never since left ringing there: for I remember when I began to read, and to take some pleasure in it, there was wont to lie in my mother's parlor (I know not by what accident, for she herself never in her life read any book but of devotion), but there was wont to lie Spenser's Works; this I happened to fall upon, and was infinitely delighted with the stories of the knights, and giants, and monsters, and brave houses, which I found everywhere there (though my understanding had little to do with all this); and by degrees with the tinkling of the rhyme and dance of the numbers, so that I think I had read him all over before I was twelve years old, and was thus made a poet as immediately as a child is made an eunuch. With these affections of mind, and my heart wholly set upon letters, I went to the university; but was soon torn from thence by that violent public storm which would suffer nothing to stand where it did, but rooted up every plant, even from the princely cedars to me, the hyssop. Yet I had as good fortune as could have befallen me in such a tempest; for I was cast by it into the family of one of the best persons,[6] and into the court of one of the best princesses of the world. Now though I was here engaged in ways most contrary to the original design of my life, that is, into much company, and no small business, and into a daily sight of greatness, both militant and triumphant (for that was the

[5] *Odes*, III, 29, 41–45.
[6] The reference is to Lord Jermyn, in whose service he attended Queen Henrietta Maria during her exile in France.

state then of the English and French courts), yet all this
was so far from altering my opinion, that it only added the
confirmation of reason to that which was before but natural
inclination. I saw plainly all the paint of that kind of life,
the nearer I came to it; and that beauty which I did not
fall in love with, when, for ought I knew, it was real, was
not like to bewitch or entice me when I saw that it was
adulterate. I met with several great persons, whom I liked
very well, but could not perceive that any part of their
greatness was to be liked or desired, no more than I would
be glad or content to be in a storm, though I saw many ships
which rode safely and bravely in it: a storm would not agree
with my stomach, if it did with my courage. Though I was
in a crowd of as good company as could be found anywhere,
though I was in business of great and honorable trust,
though I ate at the best table, and enjoyed the best conveniences for present subsistence that ought to be desired
by a man of my condition in banishment and public distress; yet I could not abstain from renewing my old schoolboy's wish in a copy of verses to the same effect.

> Well then; I now do plainly see
> This busy world and I shall ne'er agree, &c.

And I never then proposed to myself any other advantage
from His Majesty's happy Restoration, but the getting into
some moderately convenient retreat in the country, which
I thought in that case I might easily have compassed, as well
as some others, with no greater probabilities or pretenses
have arrived to extraordinary fortunes: but I had before
written a shrewd prophecy against myself, and I think Apollo
inspired me in the truth, though not in the elegance of it.

> Thou, neither great at court nor in the war,
> Nor at th' Exchange shal't be, nor at the wrangling bar;
> Content thyself with the small barren praise
> Which neglected verse does raise, &c.

However, by the failing of the forces which I had expected, I did not quit the design which I had resolved on; I cast myself into it a *corps perdu,* without making capitulations or taking counsel of fortune. But God laughs at a man who says to his soul, "Take thy ease": [7] I met presently not only with many little encumbrances and impediments, but with so much sickness (a new misfortune to me) as would have spoiled the happiness of an emperor as well as mine; yet I do neither repent nor alter my course. *Non ego perfidum dixi sacramentum;* [8] nothing shall separate me from a mistress which I have loved so long and have now at last married, though she neither has brought me a rich portion, nor lived yet so quietly with me as I hoped from her.

> ————*Nec vos, dulcissima mundi*
> *Nomina, vos Musæ, libertas, otia, libri,*
> *Hortique sylvæque anima remanente relinquam.*

> Nor by me e'er shall you,
> You of all names the sweetest, and the best,
> You Muses, books, and liberty and rest;
> You gardens, fields, and woods forsaken be,
>   As long as life itself forsakes not me.

But this is a very petty ejaculation; because I have concluded all the other chapters with a copy of verses, I will maintain the humor to the last.

[7] Luke 12:16–21.   [8] Horace, *Odes,* II. 17.

William Allen, *Pseud.*   d. 1658

i.e., EDWARD SEXBY

Killing No Murder was first published in Holland in 1657 under the name of William Allen. It is a satire in Swift's manner, reminding one in tone and method of *A Modest Proposal*. It is dedicated to Cromwell and presents the idea that since Cromwell desired the good of the people and this good would be best served by his death, he should gladly die. That the book was also known in England in 1657 is evidenced by the title of Michael Hawke's "Killing is Murder and no Murder: or an exercitation concerning a scurrilous pamphlet of one W. Allen . . . entitled Killing No Murder." It was attributed for a time to Silas Titus, who claimed the authorship, but both from internal evidence and from the confession which Edward Sexby made shortly before his death in the Tower, it is clear that Sexby wrote the book. Since Titus was his friend, however, he may have had some share in the composition.

There is apparently no information concerning the time or place of Sexby's birth. From about 1643 he belonged to Cromwell's regiment of horse and for a time served under Fairfax. He seems not to have been formally connected with the army after some time in 1647, but he undertook several important commissions, including a trip to France for the intelligence committee of the council of state. In 1651 he was in charge of a force in Scotland and was given the rank of colonel. He was accused of "detaining" the pay of his soldiers, was tried, and was deprived of his rank.

After Cromwell became Protector, Sexby separated from him and became the leader of several plots against him. Forced to flee from England, he took refuge in Flanders. From here he negotiated with Spain to bring about a revolt in England against the Protector and was involved in a number of other plots. He said, "Either I or Cromwell must perish."

When his book had reached England, he ventured to go over in disguise, hoping to be instrumental in bringing to pass his satirical recommendations. Just as he seemed to be making a safe escape again, he was detected and held in the Tower. Here he died on January 13, 1658.

KILLING NO MURDER [1]

And all the people of the land rejoiced, and the city was quiet, after that they had slain Athaliah with the sword.
—II Chron. 23:21.

Now after that time that Amaziah did turn away from following the Lord, they made a conspiracy against him in Jerusalem, and he fled to Lachish; but they sent to Lachish after him, and slew him there.
—II Chron. 25:27.

To his Highness

OLIVER CROMWELL

May it please your Highness,
How I have spent some hours of the leisure your Highness has been pleased to give me, this following paper will give your Highness an account; how you will please to interpret it I cannot tell; but I can with confidence say my intention in it is to procure your Highness that justice nobody yet does you, and to let the people see the longer they defer it, the greater injury they do both themselves and you. To your Highness justly belongs the honor of dying for the people; and it cannot choose but be an unspeakable consolation to you in the last moments of your life to consider with how much benefit to the world you are like to leave it. 'Tis then only (my Lord) the titles you now usurp will be truly yours; you will then be indeed the deliverer of your country and free it from a bondage little inferior to that from which Moses delivered his. You will then be that true reformer which you would now be thought; religion shall be then restored, lib-

[1] Text: 1689. The notes are reproduced in full so that the reader can see the weight of authority with which the author supported his arguments. The reference number frequently precedes the passage.

erty asserted, and parliaments have those privileges they have fought for; we shall then hope that other laws will have place besides those of the sword, and that justice shall be otherwise defined than the will and pleasure of the strongest; and we shall then hope men will keep oaths again, and not have the necessity of being false and perfidious to preserve themselves and be like their rulers: all this we hope from your Highness's happy expiration, who are the true father of your country; for while you live, we can call nothing ours, and it is from your death that we hope for our inheritances. Let this consideration arm and fortify your Highness's mind against the fears of death and the terrors of your evil conscience, that the good you will do by your death will somewhat balance the evils of your life. And if in the black catalogue of high malefactors, few can be found that have lived more to the affliction and disturbance of mankind than your Highness hath done, yet your greatest enemies will not deny but there are likewise as few that have expired more to the universal benefit of mankind than your Highness is like to do. To hasten this great good is the chief end of my writing this paper, and if it have the effects I hope it will, your Highness will quickly be out of the reach of men's malice, and your enemies will only be able to wound you in your memory, which strokes you will not feel. That your Highness may be speedily in this security, is the universal wishes of your grateful country; this is the desire and the prayer of the good and of the bad; and, it may be, is the only thing wherein all sects and factions do agree in their devotions, and is our only common prayer. But amongst all that put in their requests and supplications for your Highness's speedy deliverance from all earthly troubles, none is more assiduous nor more fervent than he that with the rest of the nation hath the honor to be (may it please your Highness)

Your Highness's present slave and vassal,

W. A.

To all those Officers and Soldiers of the Army that remember their Engagements and dare to be honest.

I heartily wish for England's sake that your number may be far greater than I fear it is, and that his Highness's frequent purgations may have left any amongst you that by these characters are concerned in this dedication. That I, and all men, have reason to make this a doubt, your own actions, as well as your tame sufferings, do but too plainly manifest. For you that were the champions of our liberty, and to that purpose were raised, are not you become the instruments of our slavery? And your hands, that the people employed to take off the yoke from our necks, are not those the very hands that now do put it on? Do you remember that you were raised to defend the privileges of Parliament, and have sworn to do it; and will you be employed to force elections and dissolve Parliaments because they will not establish the tyrant's iniquity and our slavery by a law? I beseech you, think upon what you have promised, and what you do, and give not posterity, as well as your own generation, the occasion to mention you with infamy, and to curse that unfortunate valor and success of yours, that only hath gained victories (as you use them) against the Commonwealth. Could ever England have thought to have seen that army that was never mentioned without the titles of religious, zealous, faithful, courageous, the fence of her liberty at home, the terror of her enemies abroad, become her jailers? Not her guard, but her oppressors? Not her soldiers, but a tyrant's executioners, drawing to blocks and gibbets all that dare be honester than themselves? This you do and this you are; nor can you ever redeem your own honor, the trust and love of your country, the estimation of brave men, or' the prayers of good, if you let not speedily the world see you have been deceived; which they will only then believe when they see your vengeance upon his faithless head that did it. This if you defer too long to do, you will find too late to attempt, and your repentance will neither vindicate you nor help us. To let you see you may do this as a lawful action and to persuade you to it as a glorious one is the principal intent of this following paper, which, whatever effects it hath upon you, I shall not absolutely fail of my ends; for if it excites not your virtue and courage, it will yet exprobrate your cowardice and baseness. This is from one that was once amongst you, and will be so again when you dare be as you were.

KILLING NO MURDER, ETC.

It is not any ambition to be in print, when so few spare paper and the press, nor any instigations of private revenge or malice (though few that dare be honest now want their causes) that have prevailed with me to make myself the author of a pamphlet, and to disturb that quiet which at present I enjoy by his Highness's great favor and injustice. Nor am I ignorant to how little purpose I shall employ that time and pains which I shall bestow upon this paper. For to think that any reasons or persuasions of mine, or convictions of their own, shall draw men from anything wherein they see profit or security, or to anything where they fear loss or see danger is to have a better opinion both of myself and them than either of us both deserve.

Besides, the subject itself is of that nature that I am not only to expect danger from ill men, but censure and disallowance from many that are good; for these opinions only looked upon, not looked into (which all have not eyes for), will appear bloody and cruel; and these appellations I must expect from those that have a zeal, but not according to knowledge. If therefore I had considered myself, I had spared whatever this is of pains, and not distasted so many to please so few as are in mankind (the honest and the wise). But at such a time as this, when God is not only exercising us with a usual and common calamity of letting us fall into slavery, that used our liberty so ill, but is pleased so far to blind our understandings, and to debase our spirits, as to suffer us to court our bondage, and to place it among the requests we put up to him; indignation makes a man break that silence that prudence would persuade him to use, if not to work upon other men's minds, yet to ease his own.

A late pamphlet tells us of a great design discovered against the person of his Highness, and of the Parliament's coming (for so does that Junto profane that name) to congratulate with his Highness, his happy deliverance from that wicked and bloody attempt. Besides this, that they have ordered that God Almighty shall be mocked with a day of thanks, as I think the world is with the plot, and that the people shall give public thanks for the public calamity, and that God is yet pleased to continue his judgments upon them, and to frustrate all means that are used for their deliverance. Certainly none will now deny that the English are a very thankful people. But I think if we had read in Scripture that the Israelites had cried unto the Lord, not for their own deliverance, but the preservation of their taskmasters, and that they had thanked God with solemnity that Pharaoh was yet living, and that there was still great hopes of the daily increase of the number of their bricks: though that people did so many things, not only impiously and profanely, but ridiculously and absurdly; yet certainly they did nothing we should more have wondered at than to have found them ceremoniously thankful to God for plagues, that were commonly so brutishly unthankful for mercies; and we should have thought that Moses had done them a great deal of wrong, if he had not suffered them to enjoy slavery, and left them to their tasks and garlic.

I can with justice say, my principal intention in this paper is not to declaim against my Lord Protector or his accomplices, for were it not more to justify others than to accuse them, I should think their own actions did that work sufficiently, and I should not take pains to tell the world what they knew before; my design is to examine whether if there hath been such a plot as we hear of, and that it was contrived by Mr. Sindercombe against my Lord Protector, and not by my Lord Protector against Mr. Sindercombe (which is doubtful), whether it deserves those epithets Mr. Speaker is pleased to give it, of bloody, wicked, and proceeding from the Prince of Darkness. I know very well how incapable the vulgar are of considering what is extraordinary and singular in every case, and that they judge of things, and name them by their exterior appearances, without penetrating at all into their causes or natures: and without doubt when they hear the Protector was to be killed, they straight conclude a man was to be murdered, not a malefactor punished; for they think the formalities always make them the things themselves, and that 'tis the judge and the crier that makes the justice, and the jail the criminal. And therefore when they read in the pamphlet Mr. Speaker's speech, they certainly think he gives these plotters their right titles, and, as readily as a High Court of Justice, they condemn them, without ever examining whether they would have killed a magistrate, or destroyed a tyrant, over whom every man is naturally a judge and an executioner, and whom the laws of God, of nature, and of nations expose, like beasts of prey, to be destroyed as they are met.

That I may be as plain as I can, I shall first make it a question (which indeed is none) whether my Lord Protector be a tyrant or not? Secondly, if he be, whether it is lawful to do justice upon him without solemnity, that is, to kill him? Thirdly, if it be lawful, whether it is likely to prove profitable or noxious to the Commonwealth?

The civil law makes tyrants of two sorts: *tyrannus sine titulo,* and *tyrannus exercitio:* The one is called a tyrant because he has no right to govern; the other because he governs tyrannically. We will briefly discourse of them both, and see whether the Protector may not with great justice put in his claim to both titles.

We shall sufficiently demonstrate who they are that have not a right to govern, if we show who they are that have; and what it is that makes the power just, which those that rule have over the natural liberty of other men. To fathers within their private families, nature hath given a supreme power. Every man, says Aristotle,[2] of right governs his wife and children; and this power was necessarily exercised [3] everywhere, whilst families lived dispersed, before the con-

[2] *Politics,* lib. 1. c. i.   [3] Gen. 34:24.

stitutions of commonwealths; [4] and in many places it continued after, as appears by the laws of Solon, and the most ancient of those of Rome. And indeed, as by the laws of God [5] and nature, the care, defense and support of the family lies upon every man whose it is; so by the same law, there is due unto every man from his family a subjection and obedience in compensation of that support. But several families uniting themselves together to make up one body of a commonwealth, and being independent one of another without any natural superiority or obligation, nothing can introduce amongst them a disparity of rule and subjection, but some power that is over them, which power none can pretend to have but God and themselves: wherefore all power which is lawfully exercised over such a society of men (which, from the end of its institution, we call a commonwealth) must necessarily be derived either from the appointment of God Almighty, who is Supreme Lord of all and every part, or from the consent of the society itself, who have the next power to his of disposing of their own liberty as they shall think fit for their own good. This power God hath given to societies of men,[6] as well as he gave it to particular [7] persons; and when he interposes not his own authority and appoints not himself who shall be his vicegerents and rule under him, he leaves it to none but the people themselves to make the election, whose benefit is the end of all government. Nay, when he himself hath been pleased to appoint rulers for that people which he was pleased particularly to own, he many times made the choice, but left the confirmation and ratification of that choice to the people themselves. So Saul [8] was chosen by God, and anointed king by his prophet, but made king by all the people at Gilgal.[9] David was anointed king [10] by the same prophet; but was afterwards, after Saul's death, con-

---

[4] Aristotle, *op. cit.*   [5] I Tim. 5:8.
[6] *Vid.* Hooker, *Eccles. Pol.*, lib. 1. c. 10.
[7] Exod. 21:5.   [8] I Sam. 10:1.
[9] I Sam. 12:2.   [10] I Sam. 16:14.

firmed by the people of Juda [11] and seven years after by the elders of [12] Israel, the people's deputies, at Hebron: And it is observable that, though they knew that David was appointed king by God and anointed by his prophet, yet they likewise knew that God allowed to themselves not only his confirmation, but likewise the limitation of his power; for before his inauguration they made a league [13] with him, that is, obliged him by compact to the performance of such conditions as they thought necessary for the securing their liberty. Nor is it less remarkable that when God gives directions to his people concerning their government, he plainly leaves the form to themselves; *statues super te regem;* but, [14] *si dixeris statuam.* And it is plain in that place, that God gives the people the choice of their king, for he there instructs them whom they shall choose, *e medio fratrum tuorum,* one out of the midst of thy brethren; much more might we say, if it were a less manifest truth, that all just power of government is founded upon these two bases of God's immediate command, or the people's consent. And therefore, whosoever arrogates to himself that power, or any part of it, that cannot produce one of these two titles, is not a ruler but an invader, and those that are subject to that power are not governed but oppressed.

This being considered, have not the people of England much reason to ask the Protector this question: *Quis constituit te virum principem et judicem super nos?* Who made thee a prince and a judge over us? If God made thee, make it manifest to us; if the people, where did we meet to do it? Who took our subscriptions? To whom deputed we our authority? And when and where did these deputies make the choice? Sure these interrogations are very natural, and, I believe, would much trouble his Highness's Council and his Junto to answer. In a word, that I may not tire my reader (who will not want proofs for what I say if he wants not

---

[11] II Sam. 2:4.   [12] II Sam. 5:3.
[13] *Ibid.*   [14] Deut. 17:14.

memory), if to change the government without the people's consent; if to dissolve the representatives by force, and disannul their acts; if to give the name of the people's representatives to confederates of his own, that he may establish iniquity by a law; if to take away men's lives out of all course of law, by certain murderers of his own appointment, whom he names a High Court of Justice; if to decimate men's estates, and by his own power to impose upon the people what taxes he pleases, and to maintain this by force of arms: if, I say, all this does make a tyrant, his own impudence cannot deny but he is as complete a one as ever hath been since there have been societies of men. He that hath done, and does all this, is the person for whose preservation the people of England must pray; but certainly if they do, 'tis for the same reason that the old woman of Syracuse prayed for the long life of the tyrant Dionysius, lest the devil should come next.

Now, if instead of God's command or the people's consent, his Highness hath no other title but force and fraud, which is to want all title: and if to violate all laws and propose none to rule by but those of his own will, be to exercise that tyranny he hath usurped and to make his administration conformable to his claim; then the first question we proposed is a question no longer.

But before we come to the second, because things are more easily perceived and found by the description of their exterior accidents and qualities than the defining their essences, it will not be amiss to see whether his Highness hath not as well the outward mark and characters by which tyrants are known, as he hath their nature and essential properties: whether he hath not the skin of the lion and tail of the fox, as well as he hath the violence of the one and deceit of the other. Now in this delineation which I intend to make of a tyrant, all the lineaments, all the colors, will be found so naturally to correspond with the life, that it cannot but be doubted whether his Highness be the original or the copy;

whether I have in drawing the tyrant represented him; or in representing him, expressed a tyrant: and therefore lest I should be suspected to deal insincerely with his Highness, and not to have applied these following characters, but made them, I shall not give you any of my own stamping, but such as I find in Plato, Aristotle, Tacitus, and his Highness's own evangelist, Machiavel.[15]

1. Almost all tyrants have been first captains and generals for the people, under pretenses of vindicating or defending their liberties. *Ut imperium evertant libertatem præferunt; cum preverterunt, ipsam aggrediuntur,* says Tacitus,[16] to subvert the present government, they pretend liberty for the people; when the government is down, they then invade that liberty themselves: this needs no application.

2. Tyrants accomplish their ends much more by fraud than force. Neither virtue nor force (says Machiavel) [17] are so necessary to that purpose as *una astutia fortunata,* a lucky craft; which, says he,[18] without force has been often found sufficient, but never force without that. And in another place [19] he tells us, their way in *aggirare icervelli de gli huomini, con astutia,* etc. With cunning plausible pretenses to impose upon men's understandings, and in the end they master those that had so little wit as to rely upon their faith and integrity.

'Tis but unnecessary to say, that had not his Highness had a faculty to be fluent in his tears, and eloquent in his execrations; had he not had spongy eyes, and a supple conscience; and besides, to do with a people of great faith but little wit: his courage and the rest of his moral virtues, with the help of his janizaries, had never been able so far to

---

[15] The Marks of a Tyrant. Aristotle, *Politics* lib. 5. c. ix. (Loeb). *Vid.* Machiavel, *Discor.,* lib. 1. c. 40.

[16] *Annals,* lib 1. *Idem alibi veterum libertas et speciosa nomina prætexuntur, nec quisquam alienam servitium, et dominationem sibi concupivit, ut non eadem ista vocabula usurparet.*

[17] Machiavel, *Discor.,* lib. 2. c. 13; *Prince,* c. 9.

[18] *Discor.,* lib. 2. c. 13.

[19] *Prince,* c. 18.

advance him out of the reach of justice that we should have
need to call for any other hand to remove him, but that of
the hangman.

3. They abase all excellent persons, and rid out of the way
all that have noble minds. *Et terræ filios extollunt,* and advance sons of the earth.

To put Aristotle into other words,[20] they purge both Parliament and army, till they leave few or none there that have
either honor or conscience, wit, interest, or courage to oppose their designs. And in these purgations (saith Plato)
tyrants do quite contrary to physicians; for they purge us
of our humors, but tyrants of our spirits.

4. They dare suffer no assemblies, not so much as horse
races.

5. In all places they have their spies and delators, that
is, they have their Fleetwoods, their Broughals, their St.
Johns (besides innumerable small spies), to appear discontented and not to side with them; that under that disguise
they may get trust and make discoveries. They likewise have
their emissaries to send with forged letters. If anyone doubt
this, let him send to Major General Brown, and he will
satisfy him.

6. They stir not without a guard, nor his Highness without his life-guard.

7. They impoverish the people that they may want the
power, if they have the will, to attempt anything against
them. His Highness's way is by taxes, excise, decimation, etc.

8. They make war to divert and busy the people, and besides to have a pretense to raise moneys and to make new
levies, if they either distrust their old forces, or think them
not sufficient. The war with Spain serveth his Highness to
this purpose; and upon no other justice was it begun at first,
or is still continued.[21]

9. They will seem to honor and provide for good men: that

---

[20] Aristotle, *Politics,* lib. 5. c. ix.
[21] Aristotle, *ibid.,* and Plato, *De Repub.,* lib. 9.

is, if the ministers will be orthodox and flatter; if they will wrest and torture the Scripture to prove his government lawful, and furnish him with titles; his Highness will likewise be then content to understand Scripture in their favor, and furnish them with titles.[22]

10. Things that are odious and distasteful they make others executioners of; and when the people are discontented, they appease them by sacrificing those ministers they employ.[23] I leave it to his Highness's major generals, to ruminate a little upon this point.

11. In all things they pretend to be wonderful careful of the public; to give general accompts of the money they receive, which they pretend to be levied for the maintenance of the state and the prosecuting of the war. His Highness made an excellent comment upon this place of Aristotle, in his speech to this Parliament.[24]

12. All things set aside for religious uses they set to sale; that while those things last, they may exact the less of the people. The cavaliers would interpret this of the Dean and Chapter's lands.

13. They pretend inspiration from gods, and responses from oracles, to authorize what they do; his Highness hath been ever an enthusiast. And as Hugh Capet, in taking the crown, pretended to be admonished to it in a dream by St. Valery and St. Richard; so I believe his Highness will do the same, at the instigation of S. Henry and S. Richard, his two sons.

14. Lastly, above all things they pretend a love to God and religion. This Aristotle calls *artuæ tyrannicaræ potissimam;* the surest and best of all the arts of tyrants; and we all know his Highness has found it so by experience. He hath found indeed, that in godliness there is great gain, and that

[22] Machiavel, *Prince,* c. 19.
[23] Machiavel adds, "And do grateful things themselves." But that I omit; for I really am unprovided of an instance for his Highness for I have not yet heard of any good he has done himself.
[24] Aristotle, *ibid.,* Plato, *De Repub.,* lib. 8.

preaching and praying, well-managed, will obtain other kingdoms as well as that of heaven.[25] His indeed have been pious
arms, for he hath conquered most of those of the church,
by prayers and [26] tears. But the truth is, were it not for our
honor to be governed by one that can manage both the spiritual and temporal sword, and Roman-like, to have our
emperor our high priest, we might have had preaching at a
much cheaper rate, and it would have cost us but our tithes,
which now cost us all.

Other marks and rules there are mentioned by Aristotle
to know tyrants by; but they being unsuitable to his Highness's actions, and impracticable to his temper, I insist not
on them. As among other things [27] Aristotle would not have
a tyrant insolent in his behavior, nor strike people. But his
Highness is naturally choleric, and must call men rogues,
and go to cuffs. At last he concludes he should so fashion
his manners as neither to be really good, nor absolutely
bad, but half one, half t'other. Now this half good is too
great a proportion for his Highness, and much more than
his temper will bear.

But to speak truths more seriously, and to conclude this
first question: certainly whatever these characters make any
man, it cannot be denied but his Highness is, and then if he
be not a tyrant, we must confess we have no definition nor
description of a tyrant left us, and may well imagine there
is no such thing in nature and that 'tis only a notion and a
name. But if there be such a beast, and we do at all believe
what we see and feel, let us now inquire, according to the
method we proposed, whether this be a beast of game that
we are to give law to, or a beast of prey to destroy which
all means are allowable and fair?

In deciding this question authors very much differ, as far
as it concerns supreme magistrates, who degenerate into

---

[25] Hist. of France, Aristotle, lib. 5. c. ix.
[26] *Preces et lacrymæ sunt arma Ecclesiæ.*
[27] *Politics,* lib. 5. c. ix.

tyrants. Some think they are to be borne with as bad [28] parents and place them in the number of those mischiefs [29] that have no other cure but our patience; others think they may be questioned by the supreme law of the people's safety, and that they are answerable to the people's representatives for the breach of their trust. But none of sober sense make private persons judges of their actions, which were indeed to subvert all government. But on the other side, I find none that have not been frighted or corrupted out of their reason, that have been so great enemies to common justice and the liberty of mankind as to give any kind of indemnity to a usurper, who can pretend no title but that of being stronger, nor challenge the people's obedience upon any other obligation but that of their necessity and fear. Such a person, as one out of all bounds of human protection, all men make the Ishmael [30] against whom is every man's hand, as his is against every man. To him they give no more security than Cain, his fellow-murderer and oppressor, promised to himself, to be destroyed by him that found him first.

The reason why a tyrant's case is particular, and why in that every man hath that vengeance given him which in other cases is reserved to God and the magistrate, cannot be obscure if we rightly consider what a tyrant is, what his crimes are, and in what state he stands with the Commonwealth and with every member of it. And certainly, if we find him an enemy to all human society, and subverter of all laws, and one that by the greatness of his villainies secures himself against all ordinary course of justice; we shall not at all think it strange, if then he have no benefit from human society, no protection from the law, and if, in his case, justice dispenses with her forms. We are therefore to consider that the end for which men enter into society is not barely to live, which they may do dispersed as other animals, but to

---

[28] *Ames parentem si æquus est; si non feras.*
[29] *Sicut sterilitatem, aut nimios imbres,* etc. (Tacitus).
[30] Gen. 16:12.

live happily, and a life answerable to the dignity and excellency of their kind. Out of society this happiness is not to be had, for singly we are impotent and defective, unable to procure those things that are either of necessity or ornament for our lives; and as unable to defend and keep them when they are acquired. To remedy these defects, we associate together, that what we can neither enjoy nor keep singly, by natural benefits and assistances of one another, we may be able to do both. We cannot possibly accomplish these ends if we submit not our passions and appetites to the laws of reason and justice; for the depravity of man's will makes him as unfit to live in society, as his necessity makes him unable to live out of it; and if that perverseness be not regulated by laws, men's appetites to the same things, their avarice, their lust, their ambition, would quickly make society as unsafe, or more, than solitude itself, and we should associate only to be nearer our misery and our ruin. That therefore by which we accomplish the ends of a sociable life is our subjection and submission to laws; these are the nerves and sinews of every society or commonwealth, without which they must necessarily dissolve and fall asunder. And indeed (as Augustine says) [31] those societies where law and justice is not, are not commonwealths or kingdoms, but *magna latrocinia,* great confederacies of thieves and robbers: those therefore that submit to no law are not to be reputed in the society of mankind, which cannot consist without a law: therefore Aristotle [32] saith, tyranny is against the law of nature, that is, the law of human society, in which human nature is preserved. For this reason, they deny a tyrant to be *partem civitatis,* for every part is subject to the whole; and a citizen (says the same author) [33] is he who is as well obliged to the duty of obeying as he is capable of the power of commanding: and indeed he does obey whilst he does command; that is, he obeys the laws, which (says Tully) *magistratibus præsunt, ut magistratus præsunt populo,* are

[31] *De Civit. Dei.*   [32] *Politics,* lib. 3. c. xi.   [33] *Ibid.,* lib. 3. c. vii.

above the magistrates, as the magistrates are above the people. And therefore a tyrant that submits to no law, but his will and lust are the law by which he governs himself and others, is no magistrate, no citizen, or member of any society, but an ulcer and a disease that destroys it; and if it be rightly considered, a commonwealth by falling into a tyranny absolutely loses that name and is actually another thing: *non est civitas quæ unius est viri* (says Sophocles), that which is one man's is no city. For there is no longer king and people, or parliament and people, but those names are changed (at least their natures) into masters and servants, lords and slaves; and *servoræ non civitas erit sed magna familia* (says Grotius) [34] where all are slaves, 'tis not a city but a great family: and the truth is, we are all members of Whitehall, and when our master pleaseth, he may send for us thither, and there bore through our ears at the door-posts. But to conclude, a tyrant, as we have said, being no part of a commonwealth, nor submitting to the laws of it, but making himself above all law, there is no reason he should have the protection that is due to a member of a commonwealth, nor any defense from laws, that does acknowledge none. He is therefore in all reason to be reckoned in the number of those savage beasts that fall not with others into any herd, that have no other defense but their own strength, making a prey of all that is weaker, and by the same justice, being a prey to all that is stronger than themselves.

In the next place, let it be considered, that a tyrant making himself above all law, and defending his injustice by a strength which no power of magistrates is able to oppose, he becomes above all punishment, above all other justice than that he receives from the stroke of some generous hand: and certainly the safety of mankind were but ill provided for, if they [sic] were no kind of justice to reach great villainies, but tyrants should be *immunditie scelerum tuti,* secured by the greatness of their crimes. Our laws would be then but cobwebs

[34] *De Jure Belli,* lib. 3. c. 8.

indeed, made only to catch flies, but not to hold wasps or hornets; and it might be then said of all commonwealths, that was said of Athens, that there only small thieves were hanged, but the great ones were free, and condemned the rest. But he that will secure himself of all hands must know he secures himself from none: he that flies justice in the court must expect to find it in the street; and he that goes armed against every man arms every man against himself. *Bellum est in eos, qui judiciis coerceri non possunt* (says Cicero), we have war with those against whom we can have no law. The same author, *cum duo sint decertandi genera,* etc., there being two ways of deciding differences, the one by judgment and arbitration, the other by force; the one proper to men, the other to beasts. We must have recourse to the latter, when the former cannot be obtained.[35] And certainly by the law of nature, *ubi cessat judicium,* when no justice can be had, every man may be his own magistrate and do justice for himself; for the law (says Grotius) [36] that forbids me to pursue my right but by a course of law, certainly supposes, *ubi copia est judicii,* where law and justice is to be had; otherwise, that law were a defense for injuries, not one against them; and quite contrary to the nature of all laws would become the protection of the guilty against the innocent, not of the innocent against the guilty.[37] Now as it is contrary to the laws of God and nature, that men who are partial to themselves and therefore unjust to others should be their own judges, where others are to be had, so it is as contrary to the law of nature, and the common safety of mankind, that when the law can have no place, men should be forbidden to repel force by force, and so be left without all defense and remedy against injuries. God himself left not the slave without remedy against the cruel master: [38] and what analogy can it hold with reason that the slave, that is but his master's money and but part of his household-stuff, should find re-

---

[35] Grotius, *De Jure Belli,* lib. 1. c. 8.
[36] *Ibid.*   [37] Deut. 17.   [38] Exod. 21.

dress against the injuries and insolences of an imperious master; and a free people, who have no superior but their God,
should have none at all against the injustice and oppression
of a barbarous tyrant? And were not the incongruity full as
great, that the law of God permitting every man to kill a
thief if he took him breaking open his house in the night,
because then it might be supposed he could not bring him to
justice: but a tyrant, that is the common robber of mankind,
and one whom no law can take hold on, his person should be
sacrosanct, *cui nihil sacrum aut sanctum,* to whom nothing
is sacred, nothing inviolable! But the vulgar judge ridiculously, like themselves: the glister of things dazzles their
eyes, and they judge of them by their appearances and the
colors that are put on them. For who can be more absurd in
nature and contrary to all common sense, than to call him
thief and kill him that comes alone, or with a few, to rob me;
and to call him Lord Protector and obey him that robs me
with regiments and troops? [39] As if to rove with two or three
ships were to be a pirate, but with fifty, an admiral. But if
it be the number of adherents only, not the cause, that makes
the difference between a robber and a Protector, I wish that
number were defined, that we might know where the thief
ends and the prince begins; and be able to distinguish between a robbery and a tax. But sure no Englishman can be
ignorant that it is his birthright to be master of his own
estate, and that none can command any part of it but [by] his
own grant and consent, either made expressly by himself, or
virtually by a parliament.[40] All other ways are mere robberies
in other names; *auferre, trucidare, rapere, falsis nominibus
imperium, atque ubi solitudinem faciunt, pacem appellant;*
to rob, to extort, to murder tyrants falsely called to govern,
and to make desolation, they call to settle peace; in every
assessment we are robbed: the excise is robbery; the customs
robbery; and without doubt, whenever 'tis prudent, 'tis lawful to kill the thieves, whom we can bring to no other justice:

[39] Exod. 22:2.   [40] Tacitus, *Vit. Agric.*

and not only lawful and to do ourselves right, but glorious and to deserve of mankind, to free the world of that common robber, that universal pirate, under whom and for whom the lesser beasts prey. This fire-brand I would have any way extinguished; this ulcer I would have any hand to lance: and I cannot doubt but God will suddenly sanctify some hand to do it, and bring down that bloody and deceitful man who lives not only to the misery but the infamy of our nation.

I shall have reason to be much less confident of the justice of this opinion, if it were new, and only grounded upon collections and interpretations of my own. But herein, if I am deceived, I shall, however, have the excuse to have been drawn into that error by the examples that are left us by the greatest and most virtuous, and the opinions of the wisest and gravest men that have left their memoirs to posterity. Out of the great plenty of confirmations I could bring for this opinion from examples and authorities, I shall select a very few; for manifest truths have not need of those supports; and I have as little mind to tire myself as my reader.

First, therefore, a usurper, that by only force possesseth himself of government, and by force only keeps it, is yet in the state of war with every man, says the learned Grotius: and therefore everything is lawful against him that is lawful against an open enemy, whom every private man hath a right to kill. *Hostis hostem occidere volui,* says Scævola to Porsena, when he was taken, after he had failed in his attempt to kill him; I am an enemy, and an enemy I would have killed; which every man hath a right to do.[41]

Contra publicos hostes, et Majestatis reos, omnis homo miles est (says Tertullian), against common enemies and those that are traitors to the commonwealth, every man is a soldier: this opinion the most celebrated nations have approved both by their laws and practices. The Grecians (as Xenophon tells us), who suffered not murderers to come into their temples, in those very temples they erected statues to

---

[41] In *Bel.,* lib. 1. c. 4. *Luc.,* lib. 2.

those that killed tyrants, thinking it fit to place their deliverers amongst their gods.[42] Cicero was an eyewitness of the honors that were done such men, *Græci homines,* etc. The Greeks (saith he) attribute the honors of the gods to those that killed tyrants: what have I seen in Athens and other cities of Greece! What religion paid to such men! What songs! What elegies! by which they are consecrated to immortality, and almost deified! In Athens, by Solon's law, death was not only decreed for the tyrant that oppressed the state, but for all those that took any charge,[43] or did bear any office while the tyranny remained. And Plato tells us the ordinary course they took with tyrants in Greece: [44] if (says he) the tyrant cannot be expulsed by accusing him to the citizens, then by secret practices they dispatch him.

Amongst the Romans the Valerian Law was, *si quis injussu populi,* etc., whosoever took magistracy upon him without the command of the people, it was lawful for any man to kill him. Plutarch makes this law more severe, *ut injudicatum occidere eum liceret, qui dominatum concupisceret.* That it was lawful by that law, before any judgment past, to kill him that but aspired to tyranny. Likewise the consular law, which was made after the suppression of the tyranny of the decemvirate, made it lawful to kill any man that went about to create magistrates, *sine provocatione,* etc., without reference and appeal to the people. By these laws, and innumerable testimonies of authors, it appears that the Romans, with the rest of their philosophy, had learned from the Grecians what was the natural remedy against a tyrant: nor did they honor those less that durst apply it. Who, as Polybius says (speaking of conspiracies against tyrants), were not *deterrimi civium, sed generosissimi quique, et maximi animi;* [45] not the worst and meanest of the citizens, but the most generous, and those of greatest

---

[42] *Pro Milone.*   [43] Plut. in *Solon.*
[44] Let His Highness's Junto mark this. *De Repub.* lib. 8. In Public.
[45] *Hist.* lib. 6.

virtue: so were most of those that conspired against Julius Cæsar; he himself thought Brutus worthy to succeed him in the empire of the world. And Cicero, who had the title of *pater patriæ*, if he were not conscious of the design, yet he at least affected the honor of being thought so: *quæ enim res unquam*, etc.[46] What act, says he, O Jupiter, more glorious! more worthy of eternal memory, hath been done not only in this city, but in the whole world! In this design, as the Trojan horse, I willingly suffer myself to be included with the princes. In the same place he tells us what all virtuous Romans thought of the fact as well as he: *omnes boni, quantum in ipsis fuit, Cæsarem occiderunt: aliis consilium: aliis animus: aliis occasio defuit, voluntas nemini*: All good men (saith he) as much as lay in them, killed Cæsar: some wanted capacity, some courage, others opportunity, but none the will to do it. But yet we have not declared the exent of their severity against a tyrant: they exposed him to fraud, as well as force, and left him no security in oaths and compacts, that neither law nor religion might defend him that violated both. *Cum tyranno Romanis nulla fides, nulla jurisjurandi religio,* saith Brutus in Appian; with a tyrant the Romans think no faith to be kept, observe no religion of an oath: Seneca gives the reason, *quia quicquid erat, quo mihi cohæreret,* etc.[47] For whatever there was of mutual obligation betwixt us, his destroying the laws of human society, hath dissolved; so these that thought that there was *in hostem nefas*, that a villainy might be committed against an enemy: these that professed *non minus juste quam fortiter arma gerere,*[48] to manage their arms with justice as well as courage: these that thought faith was to be kept even with the perfidious; [49] yet they thought a tyrant could receive

[46] *Philip.* 2.

[47] Appian, lib. 7 [*Civil Wars*, II. 19]. Seneca, *De Beneficiis*, lib. 7. c. 19.

[48] Seneca, *idem.*

[49] *Regulus qui longum semper fama,* etc. Seneca in *Exerc.* 4. 7. Michael of Ephesus, *Commentary on Aristotle*, on the fifth book of *Nicomachean Ethics*.

no injustice, but to be let live; and that the most lawful way to destroy him was the readiest, no matter whether by force or fraud; for against beasts of prey men use the toil and the net, as well as the spear and the lance. But so great was their detestation of a tyrant that it made some take their opinions from their passions, and vent things which they could but ill justify to their morality; they thought a tyrant had so absolutely forfeited all title to humanity, and all kind of protection they could give him or his, that they left his wife without any other guard for her chastity but age and deformity; and thought it not adultery what was committed with her. Many more testimonies might I bring, for 'tis harder to make choice than to find plenty. But I shall conclude with authorities that are much more authentic, and examples we may much more safely imitate.

The law of God itself decreed certain [50] death to that man that would do presumptuously, and submit to no decision of justice. Who can read this and think a tyrant ought to live? But certainly, neither that nor any other law were to any effect if there were no way to put it in execution. But in a tyrant's case, process and citation have no place, and if we will only have formal remedies against him, we are sure to have none. There's small hopes of justice where the malefactor hath a power to condemn the judge.

All remedy therefore against a tyrant is Ehud's dagger, without which all our laws were fruitless and we helpless. This is that high court of justice where Moses brought the Egyptian, whither Ehud brought Eglon; Samson, the Philistines; Samuel, Agag; and Jehoiada, the she-tyrant Athaliah.

Let us a little consider in particular these several examples, and see whether they may be proportioned to our purpose.

First, as to the case of Moses and the Egyptian: certainly every Englishman hath as much call as Moses, and more cause than he,[51] to slay this Egyptian that is always laying

[50] *Utique morietur vir ille,* Deut. 17:12.
[51] Exod. 2:11, 12.

on burdens, and always smiting both our brethren and ourselves: for as to his call, he had no other than we read, but the necessity his brother stood in of his help. He looked on his brethren's burdens, and seeing an Egyptian smiting an Hebrew, knowing he was out of the reach of all other kind of justice, he slew him. Certainly this was and is as lawful for any man to do, as it was for Moses, who was then but a private man and had no authority for what he did but what the law of nature gives every man, to oppose force to force, and to make justice where he finds none. As to the cause of that action, we have much more to say than Moses had; he saw one Hebrew smitten, we many Englishmen murdered; he saw his brethren's burdens and their blows; we our brethren's burdens, imprisonments, and deaths. Now sure if it were lawful for Moses to kill that Egyptian that oppressed one man, being there was no way to procure an ordinary course of justice against him; it cannot be but absurd to think it unlawful to kill him [52] that oppresses a whole nation, and one that justice as little reaches as it defends.

The example of Ehud shows us the natural and almost the only remedy against a tyrant, and the way to free an oppressed people from the slavery of an insulting Moabite: 'tis done by prayers and tears, with the help of a dagger, by [53] crying to the Lord, and the left hand of an Ehud. Devotion and action go well together; for believe it, a tyrant is not of that kind of devil that is to be cast out by only fasting and prayer: and here the Scripture shows us what the Lord thought a fit message to send a tyrant from himself, a dagger of a cubit in his belly; and every worthy man that desires to be an Ehud, a deliverer of his country, will strive to be the messenger.[54]

We may here likewise observe in this and many places of

[52] *Vid. Et. Governador Christiano*, c. 8. p. 40.
[53] *Qualquiera cuidadano me de repeter la fuerca,* etc.
[54] Judges 3:11, 19, 20.

Judges, that when the Israelites fell to idolatry,[55] which of all sins certainly is one of the greatest, God Almighty, to proportion the punishment to the offense, still delivered them into the hands of tyrants, which sure is one of the greatest of all plagues.

In the story of Samson 'tis manifest [56] that the denying him his wife and the burning her and her father, which though they were great, yet were but private injuries, he took for sufficient grounds to make war upon the Philistines, being himself but a private man, and not only not assisted, but opposed by his servile country men.[57] He knew what the law of nature allowed him, where other laws have no place, and thought it a sufficient justification for smiting the Philistines hip and thigh, to answer for himself, that as they did unto him so had he done unto them.

Now that which was lawful for Samson to do against many oppressors, why is it unlawful for us to do against one? Are our injuries less? Our friends and relations are daily murdered before our faces: have we other ways for reparation? Let them be named and I am silenced: but if we have none, the firebrands, or the jaw-bone, the first weapons our just fury can lay hold on, may certainly be lawfully employed against that uncircumcised Philistine that oppresses us. We have too the oppositions and discouragements that Samson had, and therefore have the more need of his courage and resolution: as he had the men of Judah, so we have the men of Levi, crying to us out of the pulpit as from the top of the rock Etam, "Know you not that the Philistine is a ruler over you?" [58] The truth is, they would fain make him so and bind us with Samson in new cords, but we hope they will become as flax and that they will either loose from our hands or we shall have the courage to cut them.

Upon the same grounds of retaliation did Samuel do justice with his own hand upon the tyrant Agag: as thy

[55] Judges 20.   [56] Judges 15.   [57] Judges 15:11.
[58] Judges 15:14.

sword (says the prophet) hath made women childless, so shall thy mother be childless among women. Nor is there any law more natural and more just.[59]

How many mothers has our Agag, for his own ambition, made childless? How many children fatherless? How many have this reason to hew this Amalekite in pieces before the Lord? And let his own relations and all theirs that are confederates with him beware, lest men come at last to revenge their own relations in them.[60] They make many a woman husbandless, and many a father childless: their wives may come at last to know what 'tis to want a husband, and themselves to lose their children. Let them remember what their great apostle Machiavel tells them: that in contestations for the preserving their liberty, people many times use moderation; but when they come to vindicate it, their rigor exceeds all mean; like beasts that have been kept up and are afterwards let loose, they always are more fierce and cruel.

To conclude with the example Jehoiada hath left us:[61] six years he hid the right heir of the crown in the house of the Lord, and without all doubt, amongst the rest of God's services there he was all that time contriving the destruction of the tyrant that had aspired to the throne by the destruction of those that had the right to it.[62] Jehoiada had no pretense to authorize this action but the equity and justice of the act itself: he pretended no immediate command from God for what he did, nor any authority from the Sanhedrim; and therefore any man might have done what Jehoiada did as lawfully, that could have done it as effectually as he. Now what citation was given to Athaliah, what appearance was she called to before any court of justice? Her fact was her trial; she was without any expostulation taken forth of the ranges [63] and only let live till she got out of the temple, that that holy place might not be defiled by the blood

[59] I Sam. 15:33.   [60] In *Discor.*   [61] II Kings 11.
[62] II Chron. 23.   [63] II Chron. 23:14.

of a tyrant, which was fitter to be shed on a dunghill; and so they slew her at the horse gate. And by the king's house, the very Whitehall where she had caused the blood royal to be spilt, and which herself had so long unjustly possessed, there by Providence did she receive her punishment, where she had acted so great a part of her crimes. How the people approved of this glorious action of destroying a tyrant, this chapter tells us at the last verse: And all the people of the land rejoiced, and the city was quiet, after that they had slain Athaliah with the sword.[64] And that it may appear they no less honored the authors of such actions than other nations did; as in his lifetime they obeyed Jehoiada as a king, so after his death, for the good he had done in Israel (saith the Scripture), they likewise buried him amongst the kings.[65]

I must not conclude this story without observing that Jehoiada commanded that whosoever followed Athaliah should be put to death; letting us see what they deserve that are confederates with tyrants, and will side with them, and but appear to defend them, or allow them: his Highness's Council, his Junto, and the Agags of his janizaries may, if they please, take notice of this, and repent, lest they likewise perish.[66] And likewise his Highness's chaplains, and triers, who are to admit none into the ministry that will preach liberty with the gospel, may, if they think fit, observe that with the tyrant fell Mattan the priest of Baal. And indeed, none but Baal's priests will preach for tyrants: and certainly those priests which sacrifice to our Baal, our idol of a magistrate, deserve as well to be hanged before their pulpits as ever Mattan did to fall before his altar.[67]

I should think now I had said much more than enough to the second question, and should come to the third and last I proposed in my method; but I meet with two objections lying in my way: the first is, that these examples out of

---

[64] II Chron. 23:21.   [65] II Chron. 24:16.
[66] Mr. Sindercombe's judge and jury may likewise consider of this point.
[67] II Chron. 23:17.

Scripture are of men that were inspired of God, and that therefore they had that call and authority for their actions which we cannot pretend to; so that it would be unsafe for us to draw their actions into examples, except we had likewise their justification to allege.

The other objection is, that there being now no opposition made to the government of his Highness, that the people following their callings and traffic at home and abroad, making use of the laws and appealing to his Highness's courts of justice: that all this argues the people's tacit consent to the government; and that therefore now 'tis to be reputed lawful, and the people's obedience voluntary.

To the first, I answer with learned Milton, that if God commanded these things, 'tis a sign they were lawful and are commendable. But secondly, as I observed in the relations of the examples themselves: neither Samson nor Samuel alleged any other cause or reason for what they did, but retaliation and the apparent justice of the actions themselves. Nor had God appeared to Moses in the bush when he slew the Egyptian; nor did Jehoiada allege any prophetical authority or other call to do what he did, but that common call which all men have, to do all actions of justice that are within their power, when the ordinary course of justice ceases.

To the second, my answer is that if commerce and pleadings were enough to argue the people's consent and give tyranny the name of government, there was never yet any tyranny of many weeks' standing in this world. Certainly, we then extremely wrong Caligula and Nero in calling them tyrants, and they were rebels that conspired against them; except we will believe that all the while they reigned, that in Rome they kept their shops shut, and opened not their temples or their courts. We are likewise with no less absurdity to imagine that the whole eighteen years' time which Israel served Eglon, and six years that Athaliah reigned, that the Israelites quite desisted from traffic, pleadings, and all public acts; otherwise Ehud and Jehoiada were both traitors, the one for killing his king, the other his queen.

Having shown what a tyrant is, his marks and practices, I can scarce persuade myself to say anything to that I made my third question, whether the removing him is like to prove of advantage to the Commonwealth or not? for methinks 'tis to inquire whether 'tis better the man to die or the imposthume be lanced, or the gangrened limb be cut off? But yet there be some whose cowardice and avarice furnish them with some arguments to the contrary; and they would fain make the world believe that to be base and degenerate is to be cautious and prudent, and what is in truth a servile fear, they falsely call a Christian patience. It will not therefore be amiss to make appear that there is indeed that necessity which we think there is, of saving the vineyard of the Commonwealth, if possible, by destroying the wild boar that is broke into it. We have already showed that it is lawful, and now we shall see whether it is expedient. First, I have already told you that to be under a tyrant is not to be a commonwealth, but a great family, consisting of master and slaves. *Vir bonæ servorum nulla est unquam civitas,* says an old poet, a number of slaves make not a city. So that whilst this monster lives, we are not members of a commonwealth, but only his living tools and instruments, which he may employ to what use he pleases. *Servi tua est fortuna, ratio ad te nihil,* says another; thy condition is a slave's, thou art not to inquire a reason: nor must we think we must continue long in the condition of slaves, and not degenerate into the habit and temper that is natural to that condition: our minds will grow low with our fortunes and by being accustomed to live like slaves, we shall become unfit to be anything else. *Etiam fera animalia si clausa teneas virtutis obliviscuntur,* says Tacitus,[68] the fiercest creatures, by long constraint, lose their courage. And says Sir Francis Bacon, the blessing of Issachar and that of Judah falls not upon one people, to be asses crouching under burdens, and

[68] *Hist.* lib. 4.

to have the spirit of lions. And with their courage 'tis no wonder if they lose their fortune, as the effect with the cause, and act as ignominiously abroad as they suffer at home. 'Tis Machiavel's observation, that the Roman armies that were always victorious under consuls, all the while they were under the slavery of the decemviri never prospered. And certainly people have reason to fight but faintly, where they are to gain the victory against themselves; when every success shall be a confirmation of their slavery, and a new link to their chain.[69]

But we shall not only lose our courage, which is a useless and unsafe virtue under a tyrant, but by degrees we shall, after the example of our master, all turn perfidious, deceitful, irreligious, flatterers, and whatever is villainous and infamous in mankind. See but to what degree we are come already: can there any oath be found so fortified by all religious ties, which we easily find not a distinction to break when either profit or danger persuades us to it? Do we remember any engagements, or if we do, have we any shame in breaking them? Can any man think with patience upon what we have professed when he sees what we wildly do and tamely suffer? What have we of nobility among us but the name, the luxury and vices of it? Poor wretches, those that now carry that title are so far from having any of the virtues that should grace and indeed give them their titles, that they have not so much as the generous vices that attend greatness; they have lost all ambition and indignation. As for our ministers,[70] what have they, or indeed desire they, of their calling, but the tithes? etc. How do these horrid prevaricators search for distinctions to piece contrary oaths? How do they rake Scriptures for flatteries, and impudently apply them to his monstrous Highness? What is the city but a great tame beast, that eats and carries, and cares not who rides it? What's the thing called a Parliament,

[69] *Discor.*, lib. 1. c. 24.
[70] Dr. Locker, Dr. Owen, Mr. Jenkins, etc.

but a mock, composed of a people that are only suffered to sit there because they are known to have no virtue, after the exclusion of all others that were but suspected to have any? What are they but pimps of tyranny, who are only employed to draw in the people to prostitute their liberty? What will not the army fight for? what will they not fight against? What are they but janizaries, slaves themselves, and making all others so? What are the people in general but knaves, fools, and cowards, principled for ease, vice, and slavery? This is our temper, this tyrant hath brought us to already; and if it continues, the little virtue that is yet left to stock the nation must totally extinguish; and then his Highness hath completed his work of reformation.[71] And the truth is, till then his Highness cannot be secure. He must not endure virtue for that will not endure him. He that will maintain tyranny must kill Brutus, says Machiavel. A tyrant, says Plato,[72] must dispatch all virtuous persons, or he cannot be safe; so that he is brought to that unhappy necessity, either to live amongst base and wicked persons, or not to live at all.

Nor must we expect any cure from our patience; [73] *inxanno si gli huomini,* says Machiavel, *credendo con la humilita vincere la superbia.* Men deceive themselves, that think to mollify arrogancy with humility; a tyrant is never modest but when he is weak; 'tis in the winter of his fortune when this serpent bites not: we must not therefore suffer ourselves to be cozened with hopes of his amendment; for, *nemo unquam* [74] *imperium flagitio quæsitum bonis artibus exercuit,* never did any man manage the government with justice, that got it by villainy. The longer the tyrant lives, the more the tyrannical humor increases in him, says [75] Plato, like those beasts that grow more curst as they grow old. New occasions daily happen that necessitate them to new mischiefs; and he must defend one villainy with another.

---

[71] *Discor.,* lib. 3. c. 3.   [72] *De Repub.,* lib. 8.   [73] *Discor.,* lib. 2. c. 14.
[74] Tacitus, *Hist.* lib. 1.   [75] *De Repub.,* lib. 9.

But suppose the contrary of all this, that his Highness were *vi dominationis convulsus, et mutatus,* changed to the better by great fortune (of which he gives no symptoms), what, notwithstanding, could be more miserable than to have no other security for our liberty, no other law for our safety, than the will of a man, though the most just living? We have all our beast within us; and whosoever (says [76] Aristotle) is governed by a man without a law, is governed by a man and by a beast. *Etiam si non sit molestus dominus: tamen est miserrimum posse si velit* (says [77] Tully), though a master does not tyrannize, yet 'tis a most miserable thing that 'tis in his power to do so if he will. If he be good, so was Nero for five years; and how shall we secure that he will not change? Besides, the power that is allowed to a good man, we may be sure will be claimed and taken by an ill; and therefore it hath been the custom of good princes [78] to abridge their own power, it may be distrusting themselves, but certainly fearing their successors, to the chance of whose being virtuous, they would not hazard the welfare of their people. An unlimited power therefore is to be trusted to none, which if it does not find a tyrant, commonly makes one; or if one uses it modestly, 'tis no argument that others will; and therefore Augustus Cæsar must have no greater power given him than you would have Tiberius take. And [79] Cicero's moderation is to be trusted with a consideration, that there are others to be consuls as well as he.

But before I press this business farther, if it needs be any farther pressed, that we should endeavor to rescue the honor, the virtue, and liberty of our nation, I shall answer to some few objections that have occurred to me. This I shall do very briefly.

Some I find of a strange opinion, that it were a generous and a noble action to kill his Highness in the field; but to

---

[76] *Politics,* lib. 3. c. xi.   [77] Cicero, *Phil.* 4.
[78] Lycurgus Theopomp. Plut. in *Lycurg.*
[79] *Vid. Orat. Cæsaris* in Sallust. *Consp. Cat.*

do it privately they think it is unlawful, but know not why; as if it were not generous to apprehend a thief till his sword were drawn and he in a posture to defend himself and kill me. But these people do not consider that whosoever is possessed of power any time will be sure to engage so many either in guilt or profit, or both, that to go about to throw him out by open force will very much hazard the total ruin of the Commonwealth.[80] A tyrant is a devil that tears the body in the exorcising; and they are all of Caligula's temper, that if they could, they would have the whole frame of nature fall with them. 'Tis an opinion that deserves no other refutation than the manifest absurdity of itself; that it should be lawful for me to destroy a tyrant with hazard, blood, and confusion, but not without.

Another objection, and more common, is the fear of what may succeed if his Highness were removed. One would think the world were bewitched. I am fallen into a ditch, where I shall certainly perish if I lie; but I refuse to be helped out for fear of falling into another: I suffer a certain misery for fear of a contingent one, and let the disease kill me, because there is a hazard in the cure. Is not this ridiculous policy, *ne moriare mori,* to die for fear of dying. Sure 'tis frenzy not to desire a change when we are sure we cannot be worse. [81] *Et non incurrere in pericula, ubi quies centi paria metuuntur,* and not then to hazard, when the danger and the mischiefs are the same in lying still.

Hitherto I have spoken in general to all Englishmen; now I address my discourse particularly to those that certainly best deserve that name, ourselves, that have fought, however unfortunately, for our liberties under this tyrant; and in the end, cozened by his oaths and tears, have purchased nothing but our slavery with the price of our blood. To us particularly it belongs to bring this monster to justice, whom he hath made the instruments of his villainy, and sharers in the curse and detestation that is due to himself from all

[80] Sueton., *Vit. Calig.*   [81] Seneca.

good men: others only have their liberty to vindicate; we our liberty and our honor. We engaged to the people with him, and to the people for him, and from our hands they may justly expect a satisfaction of punishment, being they cannot have that of performance. What the people at present endure, and posterity shall suffer, will be all laid at our doors; for only we, under God, have the power to pull down this Dagon which we have set up: and if we do it not, all mankind will repute us approvers of all the villainies he hath done, and authors of all to come. Shall we, that would not endure a king attempting tyranny, shall we suffer a professed tyrant? We that resisted the lion assailing us, shall we submit to the wolf tearing us? If there be no remedy to be found, we have great reason to exclaim,[82] *utinam te potius* (Carole) *retinuissemus quam hunc habuissemus, non quod ulla sit optanda servitus, sed quod ex dignitate domini minus turpis est conditio servi*, We wish we had rather endured thee (O Charles) than have been condemned to this mean tyrant; not that we desire any kind of slavery, but that the quality of the master something graces the condition of the slave.

But if we consider it rightly, what our duty, our engagements, and our honor exact from us, both our safety and our interest oblige us to; and 'tis unanswerable in us, to discretion, as 'tis to virtue, to let this viper live: for first, he knows very well 'tis only we that have the power to hurt him, and therefore of us he will take any course to secure himself: he is conscious to himself how falsely and perfidiously he hath dealt with us; and therefore he will always fear that from our revenge which he knows he hath so well deserved.

Lastly, he knows our principles, how directly contrary they are to that arbitrary power he must govern by, and therefore he may reasonably suspect that we that have already ventured our lives against tyranny will always have the

[82] Cicero, *Epist. ad Octav.*

will, when we have the opportunity, to do the same again.

These considerations will easily persuade him to secure himself of us, if we prevent him not and secure ourselves of him. He reads in his practice of piety, *chi diviene patron,* etc.,[83] he that makes himself master of a city that has been accustomed to liberty, if he destroys it not, he must expect to be destroyed by it. And we may read too in the same author, and believe him, that those that are the occasion that one becomes powerful, always ruins them, if they want the wit and courage to secure themselves.[84]

Now as to our interest, we must never expect that he will ever trust those that he has provoked and fears: he will be sure to keep us down, lest we should pluck down him. 'Tis the rule that tyrants observe when they are in power, never to make much use of those that helped them to it; and indeed 'tis their interest and security not to do it: for those that have been the authors of their greatness, being conscious of their own merit, they are bold with the tyrant and less industrious to please him: they think all he can do for them is their due, and still they expect more; and when they fail in their expectations (as 'tis impossible to satisfy them), their disappointments make them discontented, and their discontents dangerous. Therefore all tyrants follow the example of Dionysius, who was said to use his friends as he did his bottles: when he had use for them, he kept them by him; when he had none, that they should not trouble him and lie in his way, he hung them up.

But to conclude this already over-long paper, let every man to whom God hath given the spirit of wisdom and courage be persuaded by his honor, his safety, his own good and his country's, and indeed the duty he owes to his generation, and to mankind, to endeavor by all rational means to free the world of this pest. Let not other nations have the occasion to think so meanly of us, as if we resolved to sit still and have our ears bored, or that any discouragements

[83] Machiavel, *Prince,* c. 5.   [84] *Ibid.,* c. 3.

or disappointments can ever make us desist from attempting
our liberty till we have purchased it, either by this monster's
death or by our own. Our nation is not yet so barren of virtue that we want noble examples to follow amongst ourselves.
The brave Sindercombe hath showed as great a mind as
any old Rome could boast of; and had he lived there, his
name had been registered with Brutus and Cato and he had
had his statues as well as they.

But I will not have so sinister an opinion of ourselves
(as little generosity as slavery hath left us) as to think
so great a virtue can want its monuments even amongst us.
Certainly in every virtuous mind there are statues reared
to Sindercombe. Whenever we read the elegies of those that
have died for their country; when we admire those great
examples of magnanimity that have tired tyrants' cruelties;
when we extol their constancy, whom neither bribe nor
terrors could make betray their friends; 'tis then we erect
Sindercombe statues, and grave him monuments, where all
that can be said of a great and noble mind, we justly make
an epitaph for him: and though the tyrant caused him to
be smothered, lest the people should hinder an open murder,
yet he will never be able either to smother his memory or
his own villainy. His poison was but a poor and common
device to impose only on those that understood not tyrants'
practices and are unacquainted (if any be) with his cruelties
and falsehoods. He may therefore, if he please, take away
the stake from Sindercombe's grave, and if he have a mind
it should be known how he died, let him send thither the
pillows and feather-beds with which Barkstead and his hangman smothered him. But to conclude, let not this monster
think himself the more secure that he has suppressed one
great spirit,[85] he may be confident that *longus post tillum
sequitur ordo idem potentium decus.*
There is a great roll behind, even of those that are in
his own muster-rolls, and are ambitious of the name of the

[85] And what may Cecil and Toop expect for their treachery and perjury?

deliverers of their country; and they know what the action is that will purchase it. His bed, his table, is not secure, and he stands in need of other guards to defend him against his own. Death and destruction pursues him wherever he goes; they follow him everywhere, like his fellow-travelers, and at last they will come upon him like armed men.[86] Darkness is hid in his secret places; a fire not blown shall consume him; it shall go ill with him that is left in his tabernacle.[87] He shall flee from the iron weapon, and a bow of steel shall strike him through. Because he hath oppressed, and forsaken the poor; because he hath violently taken away a house which he builded not; [88] we may be confident, and so may he, ere long all this will be accomplished; for the triumphing of the wicked is but short, and the joy of the hypocrite but for a moment. Though his Excellency [89] mount up to the heavens, and his head reacheth unto the clouds, yet he shall perish forever like his own dung. They that have seen him shall say, "Where is he?"

POSTSCRIPT

Courteous Reader,
Expect another sheet or two of paper on this subject, if I escape the tyrant's hands, although he gets (in the interim) the crown upon his head, which he hath (underhand) put his confederates on to petition his acceptance thereof.

[86] Job 20.
[87] Whitehall, Hampton Court, etc.
[88] Job 20:5.
[89] He hath now left that title for Highness and will shortly leave that for King.

Margaret Cavendish   c. 1625[1]-1673

DUCHESS OF NEWCASTLE

MARGARET was the daughter of Thomas Lucas of St. John's near Colchester. She was one of eight children, and their pleasant early life together is described with great charm in her autobiography. When the court moved to Oxford, Margaret went also to become a lady-in-waiting to Henrietta Maria. Later she accompanied the Queen to Paris, and it was there that Newcastle, who fled from England, first saw her. He had, however, previously heard of her from her brother, Lord Lucas, who had served under Newcastle in the wars. There was opposition to this love affair both by the Queen and by various members of the court, but finally the marriage took place in December, 1645. Margaret shared the Duke's sixteen-year exile on the Continent, and upon their return to England lived in retirement in the country as happy in her writing as he was in raising horses. She was granted the privilege of burial in Westminster Abbey, where before his death, the Duke erected a monument for them both.

When she set down *A True Relation of My Birth, Breeding, and Life,* the Duchess of Newcastle made a notable contribution to the development of autobiographical writing. This work was first published in *Nature's Picture drawn by Fancy's Pencil to the Life,* 1656, and was later appended to her *Life of William Cavendish, Duke of Newcastle,* 1667. Her descriptions of people and places are vivid, and the analysis of her own character is made with pleasing candor.

Her biography of her husband, though violently disliked by Pepys, has been called "one of the lesser classics of

[1] Henry Ten Eyck Perry accepts 1623 as the probable year of birth. See *The First Duchess of Newcastle* (New York, 1918), pp. 46–47.

English biographical literature." It is valuable not only for its historical information and its portrayal of the sacrificial support given by the Cavaliers to their king, but also for the insight it gives into the manners and customs of daily life in the seventeenth century.

The works in philosophy and science, which she considered her serious contribution, have no real value. She boasted of writing "according to my own natural cogitations," but her work suffered because she had no background for the cogitations. Her twenty-six plays were criticized, as she herself comments, for not being "made up so exactly as they should be, having no plots, designs, catastrophes, and such like, I know not what." Though her literary effort reaches thirteen volumes of a variety of types, she is known today for the two lives and a volume of *Sociable Letters*. She is chiefly remembered as one of the first women in England to take up writing as a profession.

A TRUE RELATION OF MY BIRTH, BREEDING, AND LIFE [1]

MY FATHER was a gentleman, which title is grounded and given by merit, not by princes; and 'tis the act of time, not favor: and though my father was not a peer of the realm, yet there were few peers who had much greater estates, or lived more noble therewith. Yet at that time great titles were to be sold, and not at so high rates but that his estate might have easily purchased, and was pressed for to take; but my father did not esteem titles, unless they were gained by heroic actions; and the kingdom being in a happy peace with all other nations, and in itself being governed by a wise king, King James, there were no employments for heroic spirits; and towards the latter end of Queen Elizabeth's reign, as soon as he came to man's estate, he unfortunately killed one Mr. Brooks in a single duel. For my father by the laws of honor could do no less than call him to the field, to question him for an injury he did him, where their swords were to dispute, and one or both of their lives to decide the argument, wherein my father had the better; and though my father by honor challenged him, with valor fought him, and in justice killed him, yet he suffered more than any person of quality usually does in cases of honor; for though the laws be rigorous, yet the present princes most commonly are gracious in those misfortunes, expecially to the injured: but my father found it not, for his exile was from the time of his misfortunes to Queen Elizabeth's death; for the Lord Cobham being then a great man with Queen Elizabeth, and this gentleman, Mr. Brooks, a kind of a favorite, and as I take it brother to the then Lord Cobham, which made Queen Elizabeth so severe, not to pardon him: but King James of blessed memory graciously gave him his

[1] *The Life of William Cavendish, Duke of Newcastle: To Which Is Added the True Relation of My Birth, Breeding, and Life.* Ed. by C. H. Firth (London, 1915).

pardon, and leave to return home to his native country, wherein he lived happily, and died peaceably, leaving a wife and eight children, three sons and five daughters, I being the youngest child he had, and an infant when he died.

As for my breeding, it was according to my birth, and the nature of my sex; for my birth was not lost in my breeding, for as my sisters were or had been bred, so was I in plenty, or rather with superfluity. Likewise we were bred virtuously, modestly, civilly, honorably, and on honest principles: as for plenty, we had not only for necessity, conveniency, and decency, but for delight and pleasure to a superfluity; 'tis true we did not riot, but we lived orderly; for riot, even in kings' courts and princes' palaces, brings ruin without content or pleasure, when order in less fortunes shall live more plentifully and deliciously than princes, that live in a hurly-burly, as I may term it, in which they are seldom well served. For disorder obstructs; besides, it doth disgust life, distract the appetites, and yield no true relish to the senses; for pleasure, delight, peace and felicity live in method and temperance.

As for our garments, my mother did not only delight to see us neat and cleanly, fine and gay, but rich and costly; maintaining us to the height of her estate, but not beyond it; for we were so far from being in debt, before these wars, as we were rather beforehand with the world, buying all with ready money, not on the score. For although after my father's death the estate was divided between my mother and her sons, paying such a sum of money for portions to her daughters, either at the day of their marriage, or when they should come to age; yet by reason she and her children agreed with a mutual consent, all their affairs were managed so well, as she lived not in a much lower condition than when my father lived; 'tis true, my mother might have increased her daughters' portions by a thrifty sparing, yet she chose to bestow it on our breeding, honest pleasure, and harmless delights, out of an opinion that if she bred us with needy necessity, it might chance to create in us sharking [2] qualities, mean thoughts, and base actions, which she knew my father as well as herself did abhor. Likewise, we were bred tenderly, for my mother naturally did strive to please and delight her children, not to cross or torment them, terrifying them with threats, or lashing them with slavish whips; but instead of threats, reason was used to persuade us, and instead of lashes, the deformities of vice were discovered, and the graces and virtues were presented unto us, also we were bred with respectful attendance, everyone being severally waited upon, and all her servants in general used the same respect to her children (even those that were very young) as they did to herself; for she suffered not her servants either to be rude before us, or to domineer over us, which all vulgar servants are apt, and ofttimes which some have leave to do. Likewise she never suffered the vulgar serving-men to be in the nursery among the nursemaids, lest their rude love-making might do unseemly actions, or speak unhandsome words in the presence of her children, knowing that youth is apt to take infection by ill examples, having not the reason of distinguishing good from bad. Neither were we suffered to have any familiarity with the vulgar servants, or conversation: yet caused us to demean ourselves with a humble civility towards them, as they with a dutiful respect to us. Not because they were servants were we so reserved, for many noble persons are forced to serve through necessity; but by reason the vulgar sort of servants are as ill-bred as meanly born, giving children ill examples and worse counsel.

As for tutors, although we had for all sorts of virtues,[3] as singing, dancing, playing on music, reading, writing, working, and the like, yet we were not kept strictly thereto; they were rather for formality than benefit, for my mother

---

[2] "Shark" means "to swindle."
[3] "Virtues" used in the sense of accomplishments. It is said that the Duchess later changed the word to "virtuosos."

cared not so much for our dancing and fiddling, singing and prating of several languages, as that we should be bred virtuously, modestly, civilly, honorably, and on honest principles.

As for my brothers, of which I had three, I know not how they were bred. First, they were bred when I was not capable to observe, or before I was born; likewise the breeding of men was after different manner of ways from those of women: but this I know, that they loved virtue, endeavored merit, practiced justice, and spoke truth; they were constantly loyal, and truly valiant. Two of my three brothers were excellent soldiers, and martial discipliners, being practiced therein, for though they might have lived upon their own estates very honorably, yet they rather chose to serve in the wars under the States of Holland, than to live idly at home in peace: my brother, Sir Thomas Lucas, there having a troop of horse; my brother, the youngest, Sir Charles Lucas, serving therein. But he served the States not long, for after he had been at the siege and taking of some towns, he returned home again; and though he had the less experience, yet he was like to have proved the better soldier, if better could have been, for naturally he had a practical genius to the warlike arts, or arts in war, as natural poets have to poetry: but his life was cut off before he could arrive to the true perfection thereof; yet he wrote "A Treatise of the Arts in War," but by reason it was in characters, and the key thereof lost, we cannot as yet understand anything therein, at least not so as to divulge it. My other brother, the Lord Lucas, who was heir to my father's estate, and as it were the father to take care of us all, is not less valiant than they were, although his skill in the discipline of war was not so much, being not bred therein. Yet he had more skill in the use of the sword, and is more learned in other arts and sciences than they were, he being a great scholar, by reason he is given much to studious contemplation.

Their practice was, when they met together, to exercise

themselves with fencing, wrestling, shooting, and such like exercises, for I observed they did seldom hawk or hunt, and very seldom or never dance, or play on music, saying it was too effeminate for masculine spirits. Neither had they skill, or did use to play, for ought I could hear, at cards or dice, or the like games, nor given to any vice, as I did know, unless to love a mistress were a crime, not that I know any they had, but what report did say, and usually reports are false, at least exceed the truth.

As for the pastimes of my sisters when they were in the country, it was to read, work, walk, and discourse with each other. For though two of my three brothers were married (my brother the Lord Lucas to a virtuous and beautiful lady, daughter to Sir Christopher Nevil, son to the Lord Abergavenny, and my brother Sir Thomas Lucas to a virtuous lady of an ancient family, one Sir John Byron's daughter), likewise, three of my sisters (one married Sir Peter Killegrew, the other Sir William Walter, the third Sir Edmund Pye, the fourth as yet unmarried), yet most of them lived with my mother, especially when she was at her country-house, living most commonly at London half the year, which is the metropolitan city of England. But when they were at London, they were dispersed into several houses of their own, yet for the most part they met every day, feasting with each other like Job's children. But this unnatural war came like a whirlwind, which felled down their houses, where some in the wars were crushed to death, as my youngest brother Sir Charles Lucas, and my brother Sir Thomas Lucas; and though my brother Sir Thomas Lucas died not immediately of his wounds, yet a wound he received on his head in Ireland shortened his life.

But to rehearse their recreations. There customs were in winter to go sometimes to plays, or to ride in their coaches about the streets to see the concourse and recourse of people; and in the spring time to visit the Spring-Garden, Hyde Park, and the like places; and sometimes they would have music, and sup in barges upon the water. These harmless recreations they would pass their time away with; for I observed, they did seldom make visits, nor never went abroad with strangers in their company, but only themselves in a flock together, agreeing so well that there seemed but one mind amongst them. And not only my own brothers and sisters agreed so, but my brothers- and sisters-in-law, and their children, although but young, had the like agreeable natures and affectionable dispositions; for to my best remembrance I do not know that ever they did fall out, or had any angry or unkind disputes. Likewise, I did observe that my sisters were so far from mingling themselves with any other company, that they had no familiar conversation or intimate acquaintance with the families to which each other were linked to by marriage, the family of the one being as great strangers to the rest of my brothers and sisters as the family of the other.

But sometime after this war began, I knew not how they lived; for though most of them were in Oxford, wherein the King was, yet after the Queen went from Oxford, and so out of England, I was parted from them. For when the Queen was in Oxford, I had a great desire to be one of her maids of honor, hearing the Queen had not the same number she was used to have. Whereupon I wooed and won my mother to let me go; for my mother, being fond of all her children, was desirous to please them, which made her consent to my request. But my brothers and sisters seemed not very well pleased, by reason I had never been from home, nor seldom out of their sight; for though they knew I would not behave myself to their, or my own dishonor, yet they thought I might to my disadvantage, being inexperienced in the world. Which indeed I did, for I was so bashful when I was out of my mother's, brothers' and sisters' sight, whose presence used to give me confidence (thinking I could not do amiss whilst any one of them was by, for I knew they would gently reform me if I did; besides, I was ambitious they should approve of my actions and behavior), that when I was gone from them, I was like one that had no foundation to stand, or guide to direct me, which made me afraid, lest I should wander with ignorance out of the ways of honor, so that I knew not how to behave myself. Besides, I had heard that the world was apt to lay aspersions even on the innocent, for which I durst neither look up with my eyes, nor speak, nor be any way sociable, insomuch as I was thought a natural fool. Indeed I had not much wit, yet I was not an idiot, my wit was according to my years; and though I might have learned more wit, and advanced my understanding by living in a court, yet being dull, fearful, and bashful, I neither heeded what was said or practiced, but just what belonged to my loyal duty, and my own honest reputation. And, indeed, I was so afraid to dishonor my friends and family by my indiscreet actions that I rather chose to be accounted a fool than to be thought rude or wanton. In truth, my bashfulness and fears made me repent my going from home to see the world abroad, and much I did desire to return to my mother again, or to my sister Pye, with whom I often lived when she was in London, and loved with a supernatural affection: but my mother advised me there to stay, although I put her to more charges than if she had kept me at home, and the more, by reason she and my brothers were sequestered from their estates, and plundered of all their goods, yet she maintained me so, that I was in condition rather to lend than to borrow, which courtiers usually are not, being always necessitated by reason of great expenses courts put them to. But my mother said it would be a disgrace for me to return out of the court so soon after I was placed; so I continued almost two years, until such time as I was married from thence.[4] For my Lord the Marquis of Newcastle did approve of those bashful fears which many condemned, and would choose such a wife as he might bring to his own humors, and

----

[4] She accompanied Queen Henrietta Maria to Paris and was married in Paris in 1645.

not such an one as was wedded to self-conceit, or one that had been tempered to the humors of another; for which he wooed me for his wife; and though I did dread marriage, and shunned men's companies as much as I could, yet I could not, nor had not the power to refuse him, by reason my affections were fixed on him, and he was the only person I ever was in love with. Neither was I ashamed to own it, but gloried therein, for it was not amorous love: I never was infected therewith; it is a disease, or a passion, or both, I only know by relation, not by experience. Neither could title, wealth, power, or person entice me to love; but my love was honest and honorable, being placed upon merit, which affection joyed at the fame of his worth, pleased with delight in his wit, proud of the respects he used to me, and triumphing in the affections he professed for me, which affections he confirmed to me by a deed of time, sealed by constancy, and assigned by an unalterable decree of his promise; which makes me happy in despite of Fortune's frowns. For though misfortunes may and do oft dissolve base, wild, loose, and ungrounded affections, yet she hath no power of those that are united either by merit, justice, gratitude, duty, fidelity, or the like; and though my Lord hath lost his estate, and banished out of his country for his loyalty to his king and country, yet neither despised poverty nor pinching necessity could make him break the bonds of friendship, or weaken his loyal duty to his king or country.

But not only the family I am linked to is ruined, but the family from which I sprung, by these unhappy wars; which ruin my mother lived to see, and then died, having lived a widow many years, for she never forgot my father so as to marry again. Indeed, he remained so lively in her memory, and her grief was so lasting, as she never mentioned his name, though she spoke often of him, but love and grief caused tears to flow, and tender sighs to rise, mourning in sad complaints. She made her house her cloister, enclosing herself as it were therein, for she seldom went abroad, unless to church; but these unhappy wars forced her out, by reason she and her children were loyal to the king; for which they plundered her and my brothers of all their goods, plate, jewels, money, corn, cattle, and the like, cut down their woods, pulled down their houses, and sequestered them from their lands and livings; but in such misfortunes my mother was of an heroic spirit, in suffering patiently where there is no remedy, or to be industrious where she thought she could help. She was of a grave behavior, and had such a majestic grandeur, as it were continually hung about her, that it would strike a kind of an awe to the beholders, and command respect from the rudest (I mean the rudest of civilized people, I mean not such barbarous people as plundered her and used her cruelly, for they would have pulled God out of heaven, had they had power, as they did royalty out of his throne). Also her beauty was beyond the ruin of time, for she had a well-favored loveliness in her face, a pleasing sweetness in her countenance, and a well-tempered complexion, as neither too red nor too pale, even to her dying hour, although in years; and by her dying, one might think death was enamored with her, for he embraced her in a sleep, and so gently, as if he were afraid to hurt her. Also she was an affectionate mother, breeding her children with a most industrious care and tender love, and having eight children, three sons and five daughters, there was not any one crooked, or any ways deformed, neither were they dwarfish, or of a giant-like stature, but every ways proportionable; likewise well-featured, clear complexions, brown hair (but some lighter than others), sound teeth, sweet breaths, plain speeches, tunable voices (I mean not so much to sing as in speaking, as not stuttering, nor wharling [5] in the throat, or speaking through the nose, or hoarsely, unless they had a cold, or squeakingly, which impediments many have) : neither were their voices of too low a strain, or too high, but their

[5] Firth quotes from Halliwell's *Dictionary of Archaic and Provincial Words*, "an inability in anyone to pronounce the letter R."

notes and words were tunable and timely. I hope this truth
will not offend my readers, and lest they should think I am
a partial register, I dare not commend my sisters, as to say
they were handsome; although many would say they were
very handsome: but this I dare say, their beauty, if any they
had, was not so lasting as my mother's, time making sud-
dener ruin in their faces than in hers. Likewise my mother
was a good mistress to her servants, taking care of her
servants in their sickness, not sparing any cost she was able
to bestow for their recovery; neither did she exact more
from them in their health than what they with ease or rather
like pastime could do: she would freely pardon a fault and
forget an injury, yet sometimes she would be angry; but
never with her children, the sight of them would pacify her;
neither would she be angry with others but when she had
cause, as with negligent or knavish servants that would
lavishly or unnecessarily waste, or subtilely and thievishly
steal. And though she would often complain that her family
was too great for her weak management, and often pressed
my brother to take it upon him, yet I observe she took a
pleasure, and some little pride, in the governing thereof:
she was very skillful in leases, and setting of lands, and court-
keeping, ordering of stewards, and the like affairs. Also I
observed, that my mother, nor brothers, before these wars,
had never any lawsuits but what an attorney dispatched in
a term with small cost, but if they had, it was more than
I knew of. But, as I said, my mother lived to see the ruin of
her children, in which was her ruin, and then died: my
brother Sir Thomas Lucas soon after, my brother Sir
Charles Lucas after him, being shot to death for his
loyal service, for he was most constantly loyal and cou-
rageously active; indeed he had a superfluity of courage.
My eldest sister died sometime before my mother, her death
being, as I believe, hastened through grief of her only daughter, on which she doted, being very pretty, sweet natured,
and had an extraordinary wit for her age. She dying of a

consumption, my sister, her mother, died some half a year after of the same disease; and though time is apt to waste remembrance as a consumptive body, or to wear it out like a garment into rags, or to molder it into dust; yet I find the natural affections I have for my friends are beyond the length, strength, and power of time: for I shall lament the loss so long as I live, also the loss of my Lord's noble brother, which died not long after I returned from England (he being then sick of an ague), whose favors and my thankfulness, ingratitude shall never disjoin; for I will build his monument of truth, though I cannot of marble, and hang my tears and scutcheons on his tomb. He was nobly generous, wisely valiant, naturally civil, honestly kind, truly loving, virtuously temperate; his promise was like a fixed decree, his words were destiny, his life was holy, his disposition mild, his behavior courteous, his discourse pleasing; he had a ready wit, and a spacious knowledge, a settled judgment, a clear understanding, a rational insight; he was learned in all arts and sciences, but especially in the mathematics, in which study he spent most part of his time; and though his tongue preached not moral philosophy, yet his life taught it; indeed he was such a person that he might have been a pattern for all mankind to take. He loved my Lord his brother with a doting affection, as my Lord did him, for whose sake I suppose he was so nobly generous, carefully kind, and respectful to me; for I dare not challenge his favors as to myself, having not merits to deserve them. He was for a time the preserver of my life, for after I was married some two or three years, my Lord traveled out of France, from the city of Paris, in which city he resided the time he was there, so went into Holland, to a town called Rotterdam, in which place he stayed some six months. From thence he returned to Brabant, unto the city of Antwerp, which city we passed through when we went into Holland; and in that city my Lord settled himself and family, choosing it for the most pleasantest, and quietest place to retire himself and ruined fortunes in. But after we had remained some time therein, we grew extremely necessitated, tradesmen being there not so rich as to trust my Lord for so much, or so long, as those of France; yet they were so civil, kind and charitable, as to trust him for as much as they were able; but at last necessity enforced me to return into England to seek for relief. For I hearing my Lord's estate, amongst the rest of many more estates, was to be sold, and that the wives of the owners should have an allowance therefrom, it gave me hopes I should receive a benefit thereby; so being accompanied with my Lord's only brother, Sir Charles Cavendish, who was commanded to return, to live therein or to lose his estate, which estate he was forced to buy with a great composition before he could enjoy any part thereof; so over I went. But when I came there I found their hearts as hard as my fortunes, and their natures as cruel as my miseries, for they sold all my Lord's estate, which was a very great one, and gave me not any part thereof, or any allowance thereof, which few or no other was so hardly dealt withal. Indeed, I did not stand as a beggar at the Parliament door, for I never was at the Parliament House, nor stood I ever at the door, as I do know, or can remember, I am sure not as a petitioner. Neither did I haunt the committees, for I never was at any, as a petitioner, but one in my life, which was called Goldsmiths' Hall [6] but I received neither gold nor silver from them, only an absolute refusal, I should have no share of my Lord's estate; for my brother, the Lord Lucas, did claim in my behalf such a part of my Lord's estate as wives had allowed them, but they told him that, by reason I was married since my Lord was made a delinquent, I could have nothing, nor should have anything, he being the greatest traitor to the state, which was to be the most loyal subject to his king and country. But I whisperingly spoke to my brother to conduct me out of

[6] This committee heard the cases of delinquents and compounded with them according to the degree of guilt.

that ungentlemanly place, so without speaking to them
one word good or bad, I returned to my lodgings, and as
that committee was the first, so was it the last, I ever was
at as a petitioner. 'Tis true I went sometimes to Drury House
to inquire how the land was sold, but no other ways, although some reported I was at the Parliament House, and
at this committee and at that committee, and what I should
say, and how I was answered. But the customs of England
being changed as well as the laws, where women become
pleaders, attorneys, petitioners and the like, running about
with their several causes, complaining of their several grievances, exclaiming against their several enemies, bragging of
their several favors they receive from the powerful; thus
trafficking with idle words bring in false reports and vain
discourse; for the truth is, our sex doth nothing but justle
for the pre-eminence of words (I mean not for speaking
well, but speaking much), as they do for the pre-eminence
of place, words rushing against words, thwarting and crossing
each other, and pulling with reproaches, striving to throw
each other down with disgrace, thinking to advance themselves thereby. But if our sex would but well consider, and
rationally ponder, they will perceive and find that it is
neither words nor place that can advance them, but worth
and merit : nor can words or place disgrace them, but inconstancy and boldness; for an honest heart, a noble soul, a
chaste life, and a true speaking tongue, is the throne, scepter,
crown, and footstool that advances them to an honorable renown, I mean not noble, virtuous, discreet, and worthy persons, whom necessity did enforce to submit, comply, and
follow their own suits, but such as had nothing to lose, but
made it their trade to solicit. But I despairing, being positively denied at Goldsmiths' Hall,—besides I had a firm
faith, or strong opinion, that the pains were more than the
gains—and being unpracticed in public employments, unlearned in their uncouth ways, ignorant of the humors and
dispositions of those persons to whom I was to address my

suit, and not knowing where the power lay, and being not a good flatterer, I did not trouble myself or petition my enemies. Besides I am naturally bashful, not that I am ashamed of my mind or body, my birth or breeding, my actions or fortunes, for my bashfulness is in my nature, not for any crime, and though I have strived and reasoned with myself, yet that which is inbred, I find is difficult to root out; but I do not find that my bashfulness is concerned with the qualities of the persons, but the number, for were I to enter amongst a company of Lazaruses, I should be as much out of countenance, as if they were all Cæsars or Alexanders, Cleopatras or Queen Didos. Neither do I find my bashfulness riseth so often in blushes, as contracts my spirits to a chill paleness. But the best of it is, most commonly it soon vanisheth away, and many times before it can be perceived; and the more foolish, or unworthy, I conceive the company to be, the worse I am, and the best remedy I ever found was, is to persuade myself that all those persons I meet are wise and virtuous. The reason I take to be is that the wise and virtuous censure less, excuse more, praise best, esteem rightly, judge justly, behave themselves civilly, demean themselves respectfully, and speak modestly, when fools or unworthy persons are apt to commit absurdities, as to be bold, rude, uncivil both in words and actions, forgetting or not well understanding themselves or the company they are with. And though I never met such sorts of ill-bred creatures, yet naturally I have such an aversion to such kind of people, as I am afraid to meet them, as children are afraid of spirits, or those that are afraid to see or meet devils; which makes me think this natural defect in me, if it be a defect, is rather a fear than a bashfulness, but whatsoever it is, I find it troublesome, for it hath many times obstructed the passage of my speech, and perturbed my natural actions, forcing a constrainedness or unusual motions. But, however, since it is rather a fear of others than a bashful distrust of myself, I despair of a perfect cure, unless na-

ture as well as human governments could be civilized and
brought into a methodical order, ruling the words and actions with a supreme power of reason, and the authority of
discretion: but a rude nature is worse than a brute nature,
by so much more as man is better than beast, but those that
are of civil natures and gentle dispositions are as much
nearer to celestial creatures as those that are of rude or
cruel are to devils. But in fine, after I had been in England
a year and a half,[7] in which time I gave some half a score
visits, and went with my Lord's brother to hear music in
one Mr. Lawes his house,[8] three or four times, as also some
three or four times to Hyde Park with my sisters, to take
the air, else I never stirred out of my lodgings, unless to see
my brothers and sisters, nor seldom did I dress myself, as
taking no delight to adorn myself, since he I only desired
to please was absent, although report did dress me in a hundred several fashions ('tis true when I did dress myself,
I did endeavor to do it to my best becoming, both in respect
to myself and those I went to visit, or chanced to meet),
but after I had been in England a year and a half, part of
which time I wrote a book of poems, and a little book called
my *Philosophical Fancies,* to which I have written a large
addition since I returned out of England, besides this book
and one other (as for my book entitled *The World's Olio,*
I wrote most part of it before I went into England), but
being not of a merry, although not of a froward or peevish
disposition, became very melancholy, by reason I was from
my Lord, which made my mind so restless, as it did break
my sleeps, and distemper my health, with which growing
impatient of a longer delay, I resolved to return, although
I was grieved to leave Sir Charles, my Lord's brother, he

[7] Mr. Firth divides this sentence at a point which leaves the meaning
suspended. Without its many parenthetical statements the sentence reads,
"But in fine, after I had been in England a year and a half . . . I resolved
to return . . ."

[8] Henry Lawes, musician associated with the Bridgewater family and
composer of the music for *Comus.* See also Milton's sonnet in praise of
Lawes.

being sick of an ague, of which sickness he died. For though his ague was cured, his life was decayed; he being not of a strong constitution could not, as it did prove, recover his health, for the dregs of his ague did put out the lamp of his life; yet heaven knows I did not think his life was so near to an end, for his doctor had great hopes of his perfect recovery, and by reason he was to go into the country for change of air, where I should have been a trouble, rather than any ways serviceable, besides, more charge the longer I stayed, for which I made the more haste to return to my Lord, with whom I had rather be as a poor beggar than to be mistress of the world absented from him; yet heaven hitherto hath kept us, and though fortune hath been cross, yet we do submit, and are both content with what is, and cannot be mended, and are so prepared that the worst of fortunes shall not afflict our minds, so as to make us unhappy, howsoever it doth pinch our lives with poverty. For, if tranquillity lives in an honest mind, the mind lives in peace, although the body suffer: but patience hath armed us, and misery hath tried us, and finds us fortune-proof, for the truth is, my Lord is a person whose humor is neither extravagantly merry nor unnecessarily sad, his mind is above his fortune as his generosity is above his purse, his courage above danger, his justice above bribes, his friendship above self-interest, his truth too firm for falsehood, his temperance beyond temptation. His conversation is pleasing and affable, his wit is quick, and his judgment is strong, distinguishing clearly without clouds of mistakes, dissecting truth, so as it justly admits not of disputes: his discourse is always new upon the occasion, without troubling the hearers with old historical relations, nor stuffed with useless sentences. His behavior is manly without formality, and free without constraint, and his mind hath the same freedom. His nature is noble, and his disposition sweet; his loyalty is proved by his public service for his king and country, by his often hazarding his life, by the loss of his estate, and the banishment of his person, by his necessitated condition, and his constant and patient suffering. But, howsoever our fortunes are, we are both content, spending our time harmlessly, for my Lord pleaseth himself with the management of few horses, and exercises himself with the use of the sword; which two arts he hath brought by his studious thoughts, rational experience, and industrious practice, to an absolute perfection; and though he hath taken as much pains in those arts, both by study and practice, as chemists for the philosopher's stone, yet he hath this advantage of them, that he hath found the right and the truth thereof and therein, which chemists never found in their art, and I believe never will. Also he recreates himself with his pen, writing what his wit dictates to him, but I pass my time rather with scribbling than writing, with words than wit: not that I speak much, because I am addicted to contemplation, unless I am with my Lord, yet then I rather attentively listen to what he says, than impertinently speak. Yet when I am writing any sad feigned stories, or serious humors, or melancholy passions, I am forced many times to express them with the tongue before I can write them with the pen, by reason those thoughts that are sad, serious, and melancholy are apt to contract and to draw too much back, which oppression doth as it were overpower or smother the conception in the brain. But when some of those thoughts are sent out in words, they give the rest more liberty to place themselves in a more methodical order, marching more regularly with my pen, on the ground of white paper; but my letters seem rather as a ragged rout than a well-armed body, for the brain being quicker in creating than the hand in writing or the memory in retaining, many fancies are lost, by reason they ofttimes outrun the pen; where I, to keep speed in the race, write so fast as I stay not so long as to write my letters plain, insomuch as some have taken my handwriting for some strange character, and being accustomed so to do, I cannot now write very plain, when I strive to write my best; indeed, my ordinary hand-writing is so bad as few can read it, so as to write it fair for the press; but however, that little wit I have, it delights me to scribble it out, and disperse it about. For I being addicted from my childhood to contemplation rather than conversation, to solitariness rather than society, to melancholy rather than mirth, to write with the pen than to work with a needle, passing my time with harmless fancies, their company being pleasing, their conversation innocent (in which I take such pleasure, as I neglect my health, for it is as great a grief to leave their society as a joy to be in their company), my only trouble is, lest my brain should grow barren, or that the root of my fancies should become insipid, withering into a dull stupidity for want of maturing subjects to write on. For I being of a lazy nature, and not of an active disposition, as some are that love to journey from town to town, from place to place, from house to house, delighting in variety of company, making still one where the greatest number is; likewise in playing at cards, or any other games, in which I neither have practised, nor have I any skill therein: as for dancing, although it be a graceful art, and becometh unmarried persons well, yet for those that are married, it is too light an action, disagreeing with the gravity thereof; and for reveling I am of too dull a nature to make one in a merry society; as for feasting, it would neither agree with my humor or constitution, for my diet is for the most part sparing, as a little boiled chicken, or the like, my drink most commonly water; for though I have an indifferent good appetite, yet I do often fast, out of an opinion that if I should eat much, and exercise little, which I do, only walking a slow pace in my chamber, whilst my thoughts run apace in my brain, so that the motions of my mind hinders the active exercises of my body; for should I dance or run, or walk apace, I should dance my thoughts out of measure, run my fancies out of breath, and tread out the feet of my numbers. But because I would not bury myself quite from the sight of the world, I go sometimes abroad, seldom to visit, but only in my coach about the town, or about some of the streets, which we call here a tour, where all the chief of the town go to see and to be seen, likewise all strangers of what quality soever, as all great princes or queens that make any short stay. For this town being a passage or thorough-fare to most parts, causeth many times persons of great quality to be here, though not as inhabitants, yet to lodge for some short time; and all such, as I said, take a delight, or at least go to see the customs thereof, which most cities of note in Europe, for all I can hear, hath such like recrea-tions for the effeminate sex, although for my part I had rather sit at home and write, or walk, as I said, in my chamber and contemplate; but I hold necessary sometimes to appear abroad, besides I do find that several objects do bring new materials for my thoughts and fancies to build upon. Yet I must say this in the behalf of my thoughts, that I never found them idle; for if the senses bring no work in, they will work of themselves, like silkworms that spin out of their own bowels; neither can I say I think the time tedious when I am alone, so I be near my Lord and know he is well.

But now I have declared to my readers, my birth, breed-ing, and actions, to this part of my life, I mean the material parts, for should I write every particular, as my childish sports and the like, it would be ridiculous and tedious; but I have been honorably born and nobly matched; I have been bred to elevated thoughts, not to a dejected spirit, my life hath been ruled with honesty, attended by modesty, and directed by truth. But since I have written in general thus far of my life, I think it fit I should speak something of my humor, particular practice, and disposition. As for my humor, I was from my childhood given to contemplation, being more taken or delighted with thoughts than in conversation with a society, insomuch as I would walk two or three hours, and never rest, in a musing, considering, contemplating manner, reasoning with myself of everything my senses did present. But when I was in the company of my natural friends, I was very attentive of what they said or did; but for strangers I regarded not much what they said, but many times I did observe their actions, whereupon my reason as judge, and my thoughts as accusers, or excusers, or approvers and commenders, did plead, or appeal to accuse, or complain thereto. Also I never took delight in closets, or cabinets of toys, but in the variety of fine clothes, and such toys as only were to adorn my person. Likewise I had a natural stupidity towards the learning of any other language than my native tongue, for I could sooner and with more facility understand the sense than remember the words, and for want of such memory makes me so unlearned in foreign languages as I am. As for my practice, I was never very active, by reason I was given much to contemplation; besides my brothers and sisters were for the most part serious, and staid in their actions, not given to sport nor play, nor dance about, whose company I keeping, made me so too: but I observed that although their actions were staid, yet they would be very merry amongst themselves, delighting in each other's company: also they would in their discourse express the general actions of the world, judging, condemning, approving, commending, as they thought good, and with those that were innocently harmless, they would make themselves merry therewith. As for my study of books it was little, yet I chose rather to read than to employ my time in any other work, or practice, and when I read what I understood not, I would ask my brother, the Lord Lucas, he being learned, the sense of meaning thereof. But my serious study could not be much, by reason I took great delight in attiring, fine dressing, and fashions, especially such fashions as I did invent myself, not taking that pleasure in such fashions as were invented by others; also I did dislike any should follow my fashions, for I always took delight in a singularity, even in accouterments of habits. But whatsoever I was addicted to, either in

fashion of clothes, contemplation of thoughts, actions of
life, they were lawful, honest, honorable, and modest, of
which I can avouch to the world with a great confidence, because it is a pure truth. As for my disposition, it is more inclining to be melancholy than merry, but not crabbed or
peevishly melancholy, but soft, melting, solitary, and contemplating melancholy; and I am apt to weep rather than
laugh, not that I do often either of them. Also I am tender
natured, for it troubles my conscience to kill a fly, and the
groans of a dying beast strike my soul. Also where I place
a particular affection, I love extraordinarily and constantly,
yet not fondly, but soberly and observingly, not to hang
about them as a trouble, but to wait upon them as a servant;
but this affection will take no root, but where I think or
find merit, and have leave both from divine and moral laws;
yet I find this passion so troublesome, as it is the only torment
to my life, for fear any evil misfortune or accident, or sickness, or death, should come unto them, insomuch as I am
never freely at rest. Likewise I am grateful, for I never
received a courtesy but I am impatient and troubled until
I can return it. Also I am chaste, both by nature and education, insomuch as I do abhor an unchaste thought. Likewise
I am seldom angry, as my servants may witness for me, for
I rather choose to suffer some inconveniences than disturb
my thoughts, which makes me wink many times at their
faults; but when I am angry, I am very angry, but yet it is
soon over, and I am easily pacified, if it be not such an injury as may create a hate. Neither am I apt to be exceptious
or jealous; but if I have the least symptom of this passion,
I declare it to those it concerns, for I never let it lie smother-
ing in my breast to breed a malignant disease in the mind,
which might break out into extravagant passions, or railing
speeches, or indiscreet actions; but I examine moderately,
reason soberly, and plead gently in my own behalf, through
a desire to keep those affections I had, or at least thought to
have. And truly I am so vain, as to be so self-conceited, or

so naturally partial, to think my friends have as much reason
to love me as another, since none can love more sincerely
than I, and it were an injustice to prefer a fainter affection,
or to esteem the body more than the mind. Likewise I am
neither spiteful, envious, nor malicious; I repine not at the
gifts that nature or fortune bestows upon others, yet I am
a great emulator; for though I wish none worse than they
are, yet it is lawful for me to wish myself the best, and to
do my honest endeavor thereunto; for I think it no crime
to wish myself the exactest of nature's works, my thread of
life the longest, my chain of destiny the strongest, my mind
the peaceablest, my life the pleasantest, my death the easiest,
and the greatest saint in heaven; also to do my endeavor,
so far as honor and honesty doth allow of, to be the highest
on fortune's wheel, and to hold the wheel from turning, if I
can. And if it be commendable to wish another's good, it
were a sin not to wish my own; for as envy is a vice, so
emulation is a virtue, but emulation is in the way to ambition, or indeed it is a noble ambition. But I fear my ambition inclines to vainglory, for I am very ambitious; yet 'tis
neither for beauty, wit, titles, wealth, or power, but as they
are steps to raise me to fame's tower, which is to live by
remembrance in after-ages. Likewise I am, that the vulgar
calls, proud, not out of a self-conceit, or to slight or condemn any, but scorning to do a base or mean act, and dis-
daining rude or unworthy persons; insomuch that if I
should find any that were rude, or too bold, I should be apt
to be so passionate as to affront them, if I can, unless discretion should get betwixt my passion and their boldness,
which sometimes perchance it might, if discretion should
crowd hard for place. For though I am naturally bashful,
yet in such a cause my spirits would be all on fire; otherwise
I am so well-bred as to be civil to all persons, of all degrees
or qualities. Likewise I am so proud, or rather just to my
Lord, as to abate nothing of the quality of his wife, for if
honor be the mark of merit, and his master's royal favor,

who will favor none but those that have merit to deserve, it were a baseness for me to neglect the ceremony thereof. Also in some cases I am naturally a coward, and in other cases very valiant; as for example, if any of my nearest friends were in danger, I should never consider my life in striving to help them, though I were sure to do them no good, and would willingly, nay cheerfully, resign my life for their sakes; likewise I should not spare my life, if honor bids me die. But in a danger where my friends or my honor is not concerned, or engaged, but only my life to be unprofitably lost, I am the veriest coward in nature, as upon the sea, or any dangerous places, or of thieves, or fire, or the like; nay the shooting of a gun, although but a pot-gun, will make me start, and stop my hearing, much less have I courage to discharge one; or if a sword should be held against me, although but in jest, I am afraid. Also as I am not covetous, so I am not prodigal, but of the two I am inclining to be prodigal, yet I cannot say to a vain prodigality, because I imagine it is to a profitable end; for perceiving the world is given, or apt, to honor the outside more than the inside, worshiping show more than substance; and I am so vain, if it be a vanity, as to endeavor to be worshiped, rather than not to be regarded; yet I shall never be so prodigal as to impoverish my friends, or go beyond the limits or facility of our estate. And though I desire to appear to the best advantage, whilst I live in the view of the public world, yet I could most willingly exclude myself, so as never to see the face of any creature but my Lord as long as I live, enclosing myself like an anchorite, wearing a frieze gown tied with a cord about my waist. But I hope my readers will not think me vain for writing my life, since there have been many that have done the like, as Cæsar, Ovid, and many more, both men and women, and I know no reason I may not do it as well as they: but I verily believe some censuring readers will scornfully say, why hath this lady written her own life? since none cares to know whose daughter she was, or whose wife she is, or how she was bred, or what fortunes she had, or how she lived, or what humor or disposition she was of. I answer that it is true, that 'tis to no purpose to the readers, but it is to the authoress, because I write it for my own sake, not theirs. Neither did I intend this piece for to delight, but to divulge; not to please the fancy, but to tell the truth, lest after-ages should mistake, in not knowing I was daughter to one Master Lucas of St. John's, near Colchester, in Essex, second wife to the Lord Marquis of Newcastle; for my Lord having had two wives, I might easily have been mistaken, especially if I should die and my Lord marry again.

John Aubrey

Because Aubrey was frail in his childhood, he began his education at home, where he was fortunate in having as his teacher the Reverend Robert Latimer, who also instructed Hobbes. Later on he entered grammar school for a while and proceeded to Trinity College, Oxford. He had to leave Oxford on account of an epidemic of smallpox; and in the confused state resulting from the civil war, he did not return. After three years in the country, he entered the Middle Temple for the study of law, but never went into practice.

His father had several estates, and Aubrey assisted him with his business affairs. Frequently he had the opportunity to devote himself to antiquarian research, in which he was much interested. Upon his father's death in 1652 he inherited considerable property and was kept busy by a number of lawsuits. He lived extravagantly, with the result that he soon lost his inheritance and became so poor that he had to sell his books. His affairs continued to run "kim-kam," and he turned to his friends and patrons for maintenance. His careless buoyancy was irresistible, and he was welcome wherever he went.

He assisted Anthony à Wood in collecting biographical notes for his *Athenæ Oxonienses,* but his interest was in anecdote and personal details rather than in factual information. His work is extremely unmethodical, and countless gaps which he meant to fill in are marked by the reminder, *quære.* Even so, his unfinished manuscripts convey the human quality which Wood's completed sketches lack.

Much of his research has been incorporated by someone else or left in manuscript. Aubrey was not a finisher and the heterogeneous state of his mass of notes has been a deterrent in making known the extent of his work.

BRIEF LIVES [1]

Francis Bacon

CHANCELLOR BACON :—The learned and great Cardinal Richelieu was a great admirer of the Lord Bacon.

So was Monsieur Balzac: e.g. *Les Œuvres diverses,* dissertation sur un tragédie, à Monsieur Huygens de Zuylichen, p.
158—"Croyons, pour l'amour du chancilier Bacon, que toutes
les folies des anciens sont sages et tous leur songes mysteries."

Quære if I have inserted his irrigation in the spring
showers. [2]

Vide Court of King James by Sir Anthony Weldon, where
is an account of his being viceroy here when the king was in
Scotland, and gave audience to ambassadors in the banqueting house.

Lord Chancellor Bacon:—Memorandum, this Oct. 1681,
it rang over all St. Albans that Sir Harbottle Grimston, Master of the Rolls, had removed the coffin of this most renownèd
Lord Chancellor to make room for his own to lie in, in the
vault there at St. Michael's church.

Sir Francis Bacon, Knight, Baron of Verulam and Viscount
of St. Albans, and Lord High Chancellor of England:—*vide*
his life writ by Dr. William Rawley before *Baconi Resus-
citatio,* in folio.

It appears by this following inscription that Mr. Jeremiah Betenham of Gray's Inn was his Lordship's intimate
and dearly beloved friend. This inscription is on the frieze
of the summer house on the mount in the upper garden of
Gray's Inn, built by the Lord Chancellor Bacon. The north
side of the inscription is now perished. The fane was a Cupid
drawing his bow.

Franciscus Bacon, Regis Solicitator Generalis, executor
testamenti Jeremie Betenham nuper lectoris hujus hospitii,

---

[1] Text edited by Andrew Clark. 2 vols. (Oxford, Clarendon Press, 1898).
[2] "That is, in the life in MS. Aubrey 6." [Clark's note]

viri innocentis et abstinentis et contemplativi, hanc sedem
in memoriam ejusden Jeremie extruxit, anno Domini, 1609.

In his Lordship's prosperity Sir Fulke Greville, Lord
Brooke, was his great friend and acquaintance; but when he
was in disgrace and want, he was so unworthy as to forbid
his butler to let him have any more small beer, which he had
often sent for, his stomach being nice and the small beer of
Gray's Inn not liking his palate. This has done his memory
more dishonor than Sir Philip Sidney's friendship engraven
on his monument hath done him honor. *Vide* . . . History,
and (I think) Sir Anthony Weldon.

. . . Faucet, of Marybone in the county of Middlesex,
esqr., was his friend and acquaintance, as appears by this
letter which I copied from his own handwriting (an elegant
Roman hand). 'Tis in the hands of Walter Charlton, M.D.,
who begged it not long since of Mr. Faucet's grandson.[3]

Richard, earl of Dorset,[4] was a great admirer and friend
of the Lord Chancellor Bacon, and was wont to have Sir
Thomas Billingsley along with him to remember and put
down in writing my Lord's sayings at table.

Edward, lord Herbert of Cherbury.

John Donne, dean of Paul's.

George Herbert.

Mr. Ben Jonson was one of his friends and acquaintance,
as doth appear by his excellent verses on his Lordship's birthday in his second volume, and in his *Underwoods,* where
he gives him a character and concludes that "about his time,
and within his view were born all the wits that could honor
a nation or help study."

Lord Bacon's Birthday

Hail, happy genius of this ancient pile,
How comes it all things so about thee smile?
The fire, the wine, the men! and in the midst

[3] Aubrey left a blank space for the letter but did not insert it.
[4] Richard Sackville, third Earl of Dorset.

Thou stand'st as if some mystery thou didst!
Pardon, I read it in thy face, the day,
For whose returns, and many, all these pray:
And so do I. This is the sixtieth year
Since Bacon, and my lord, was born, and here,
Son to the grave wise Keeper of the Seal,
Fame and foundation of the English weal.
What then his father was, that since is he,
Now with a title more to the degree,
England's High Chancellor, the destin'd heir
In his soft cradle of his father's chair,
Whose even thread the Fates spin round and full
Out of their choicest and their whitest wool.
'Tis a brave cause of joy; let it be known,
For 'twere a narrow gladness, kept thine own.
Give me a deep-crown'd bowl, that I may sing
In raising him the wisdom of my king.

       —Underwoods, p. 222.

Discoveries, p. 101.

 Yet there happened in my time one noble speaker who was full
of gravity in his speaking. His language (where he could spare
or pass by a jest) was nobly censorious. No man ever spake more
neatly, more pres[ent]ly, more weightily, or suffered less emptiness, less idleness, in what he utter'd. No member of his speech
but consisted of the own graces: his hearers could not cough,
or look aside from him, without loss. He commanded where he
spoke, and had his judges angry and pleased at his devotion. No
man had their affections more in his power. The fear of every
man that heard him was lest he should make an end.

 Cicero is said to be the only wit that the people of Rome had,
equaled to their empire, *ingenium par imperio.* We had many,
and in their several ages (to take in but the former *seculum*) Sir
Thomas Moore, the elder Wyatt, Henry Earl of Surrey, Chal-
loner, Smith, Eliot, Bishop Gardiner, were for their times admirable; Sir Nicholas Bacon was singular and almost alone in

the beginning of Queen Elizabeth's time; Sir Philip Sidney and Mr. Hooker (in different matter) grew great masters of wit and language and in whom all vigor of invention and strength of judgment met; the Earl of Essex, noble and high; and Sir Walter Raleigh, not to be contemned either for judgment or style; Sir Henry Saville, grave and truly lettered; Sir Edwin Sandys, excellent in both; Lord Egerton, the Chancellor, a grave and great orator, and best when he was provoked; but his learned and able (though unfortunate) successor is he who hath filled up all numbers, and performed that in our tongue which may be compared or preferred either to insolent Greece or haughty Rome. In short, within his view and about his times were all the wits born that could honor a language or help study. Now things daily fall, wits grow downward and eloquence grows backward, so that he may be named and stand as the mark and ἀκμή of our language.

I have ever observed it to have been the office of a wise patriot among the greatest affairs of the state to take care of the commonwealth of learning; for schools they are the seminaries of state, and nothing is worthier the study of a statesman than that part of the republic which we call the advancement of letters. Witness the care of Julius Cæsar, who in the heat of the civil war wrote his books of analogy and dedicated them to Tully. This made the lord St. Albans entitle his work *Novum Organum,* which though by the most of superficial men who cannot get beyond the title of nominals, it is not penetrated nor understood, it really openeth all defects of learning whatsoever, and is a book

Qui longum noto scriptori porriget œvum.[5]

My conceit of his person was never increased towards him by his place or honor, but I have and do reverence him for the greatness that was only proper to himself, in that he seemed to me ever by his work one of the greatest men and most worthy of admiration that have been in many ages. In his adversity I ever prayed that God would give him strength, for greatness he could not want. Neither could I condole in a word or syllable for him,

[5] Horace, *Ars Poet.,* 346.

as knowing no accident could do harm to virtue, but rather help to make it manifest.

He came often to Sir John Danvers at Chelsey. Sir John told me that when his Lordship had written the *History of Henry VII*, he sent the manuscript copy to him to desire his opinion of it before 'twas printed. Qd. Sir John, "Your Lordship knows that I am no scholar." " 'Tis no matter," said my Lord, "I know what a scholar can say; I would know what you can say." Sir John read it, and gave his opinion what he misliked which Tacitus did not omit (which I am sorry I have forgot) which my Lord acknowledged to be true, and mended it: "Why," said he, "a scholar would never have told me this."

Mr. Thomas Hobbes (Malmesburiensis) was beloved by his Lordship, who was wont to have him walk with him in his delicate groves where he did meditate: and when a notion darted into his mind, Mr. Hobbes was presently to write it down, and his Lordship was wont to say that he did it better than anyone else about him; for that many times when he read their notes, he scarce understood what they wrote because they understood it not clearly themselves.

In short, all that were *great and good* loved and honored him.

Sir Edward Coke, Lord Chief Justice, always envied him, and would be undervaluing his law, as you may find in my Lord's letters, and I knew old lawyers that remembered it.

He was Lord Protector during King James's progress into Scotland, and gave audience in great state to ambassadors in the banqueting house at Whitehall.

His Lordship would many times have music in the next room where he meditated.

The aviary at York house was built by his Lordship; it did cost 300 li.

At every meal, according to the season of the year, he had his table strewed with sweet herbs and flowers, which he said did refresh his spirits and memory.

When his Lordship was at his country house at Gorham-
bury, St. Albans seemed as if the court were there, so nobly
did he live. His servants had liveries with his crest (a
boar . . .) ; his watermen were more employed by gentlemen than any other, even the king's.

King James sent a buck to him, and he gave the keeper
fifty pounds.

He was wont to say to his servant Hunt (who was a notable
thrifty man, and loved this world, and the only servant he
had that he could never get to become bound for him), "The
world was made for man, Hunt ; and not man for the world."
Hunt left an estate of 1000 li. per annum in Somerset.

None of his servants durst appear before him without
Spanish leather boots : for he would smell the neat's-leather,
which offended him.

The East India merchants presented his Lordship with a
cabinet of jewels, which his page, Mr. Cockaine, received,
and deceived his Lord.

Three of his Lordship's servants kept their coaches, and
some kept race-horses—*vide* Sir Anthony Weldon's *Court of
King James.*

He was a παιδεραστής. His Ganymedes and favorites took
bribes ; but his Lordship always gave judgment *secundum
æquum et bonum.* His decrees in Chancery stand firm, i.e.,
there are fewer of his decrees reversed than of any other
Chancellor.

His dowager married her gentleman-usher, Sir (Thomas I
think) Underhill, whom she made deaf and blind with too
much of Venus. She was living since the beheading of the
late king.—*Quære* where and when she died.

He had a delicate, lively hazel eye ; Dr. Harvey told me
it was like the eye of a viper.

I have now forgotten what Mr. Bushell said, whether his
Lordship enjoyed his Muse best at night, or in the morning.

His Lordship was a good poet, but concealed, as appears
by his letters. See excellent verses of his Lordship's which

Mr. Farnaby translated into Greek, and printed both in his Ἀνθολογία, *scil.*

> The world's a bubble, and the life of man
> Less than a span, etc.

Ἀνθολογία: *Florilegium epigrammatum selectorum;* Thomas Farnaby, London, 1629, pag. 8.—"Huc elegantem viri clarissimi domini Verulamii παρῳδίαν adjicere adlubuit"—opposite to it on the other page—"*quam* παρῳδίαν *e nostrati bona nos Græcam qualemcunque sic fecimus, et rhythmice.*" [6]

His Lordship being in York House garden looking on fishers as they were throwing their net, asked them what they would take for their draught; they answered *so much:* his Lordship would offer them no more but *so much.* They drew up their net, and in it were only 2 or 3 little fishes: his Lordship then told them it had been better for them to have taken his offer. They replied, they hoped to have had a better draught; "but," said his Lordship, "hope is a good breakfast, but an ill supper."

When his Lordship was in disfavor, his neighbors, hearing how much he was indebted, came to him with a motion to buy Oakwood of him. His Lordship told them, "He would not sell his feathers."

The Earl of Manchester being removed from his place of Lord Chief Justice of the Common Pleas to be Lord President of the Council, told my Lord (upon his fall) that he was sorry to see him made such an example. Lord Bacon replied, "It did not trouble him since *he* was made *a President.*"

The Bishop of London did cut down a noble cloud of trees at Fulham. The Lord Chancellor told him that he was a good expounder of dark places.

Upon his being in disfavor, his servants suddenly went away; he compared them to the flying of the vermin when the house was falling.

[6] Aubrey quotes the entire poem.

One told his Lordship it was not time to look about him. He replied, "I do not look *about* me, I look *above* me."

Sir Julius Cæsar (Master of the Rolls) sent to his Lordship in his necessity a hundred pounds for a present; [7] *quære de hoc* of Michael Malet. His Lordship would often drink a good draught of strong beer (March beer) to-bedwards, to lay his working fancy asleep: which otherwise would keep him from sleeping great part of the night.

I remember Sir John Danvers told me that his Lordship much delighted in his curious garden at Chelsey, and as he was walking there one time, he fell down in a dead swoon. My Lady Danvers rubbed his face, temples, etc. and gave him cordial water: as soon as he came to himself, said he, "Madam, I am no good footman."

Mr. Hobbes told me that the cause of his Lordship's death was trying an experiment: *viz.*, as he was taking the air in a coach with Dr. Witherborne (a Scotchman, physician to the king) towards Highgate, snow lay on the ground, and it came into my Lord's thoughts why flesh might not be preserved in snow as in salt. They were resolved they would try the experiment presently. They alighted out of the coach and went into a poor woman's house at the bottom of Highgate hill and bought a hen, and made the woman exenterate it, and then stuffed the body with snow, and my Lord did help to do it himself. The snow so chilled him that he immediately fell so extremely ill that he could not return to his lodgings (I suppose then at Gray's Inn), but went to the Earl of Arundel's house at Highgate, where they put him into a good bed warmed with a pan, but it was a damp bed that had not been lain-in, in about a year before, which gave him such a cold that in 2 or 3 days, as I remember he i.e., Hobbes told me, he died of suffocation.

Mr. George Herbert, Orator of the University of Cambridge, has made excellent verses on this great man. So has

---

[7] "Most of these informations I have from Sir John Danvers." [Aubrey's note]

Mr. Abraham Cowley in his Pindarics. Mr. Thomas Randolph of Trinity College in Cambridge has in his poems verses on him.

In the north side of the chancel of St. Michael's church (which, as I remember, is within the walls of Verulam) is the Lord Chancellor Bacon's monument in white marble in a niche as big as the life, sitting in his chair in his gown, and hat cocked, leaning his head on his right hand. Underneath is this inscription which they say was made by his friend Sir Henry Wotton:

Franciscus Bacon, Baro de Verulam
Sti Albani Vicecomes, seu, notioribus titulis,
Scientiarum Lumen, Facundiæ Lex,
sic sedebat.
Qui postquam omnia Naturalis sapientiæ
et Civilis arcana evolvisset,
Naturæ decretum explevit
'Composita solvantur,'
Anno Domini MDCXXVI
ætatis LXVI
Tanti viri
mem.
Thomas Meautys [8]
superstitis cultor,
defuncti admirator,
H. P.

He had a uterine brother [9] Anthony Bacon, who was a very great statesman and much beyond his brother Francis for the politics, a lame man, he was a pensioner too, and lived with . . . Earl of Essex. And to him he dedicates the first edition of his *Essays,* a little book no bigger than a primer, which I have seen in the Bodleian Library.

His sisters were ingenious and well-bred; they well un-

---

[8] "His Lordship's secretary, who married a kinswoman . . ." [Aubrey's note]

[9] "His mother was Anne Cook, sister of ———— Cook of Giddy-hall in Essex. 2nd wife to Sir Nicholas Bacon." [Aubrey's note]

derstood the use of the globes, as you may find in the preface of Mr. Blundevill of the *Sphere:* see if it is not dedicated to them. One of them was married to Sir John Constable of Yorkshire. To this brother-in-law he dedicates his second edition of his *Essays,* in 8vo; his last, in 4to, to the Duke of Bucks.

Blundevill's *Exercises,* preface:—"I began this arithmetic more than seven years since for that virtuous gentlewoman Miss Elizabeth Bacon, the daughter of Sir Nicholas Bacon, knight (a man of most excellent wit and of a most deep judgment and sometimes Lord Keeper of the Great Seal of England), and lately the loving and faithful wife of my worshipful friend Mr. Justice Windham, who for his integrity of life and for his wisdom and justice daily showed in government and also for his good hospitality deserved great commendation; and though at her request I had made this arithmetic so plain and easy as was possible (as to my seeming) yet her continual sickness would not suffer her to exercise herself therein."

Thomas Fuller

THOMAS FULLER, D.D., born at Orwincle [1] in Northamptonshire. His father was minister there, and married . . . one of the sisters of John Davenant, Bishop of Sarum.—From Dr. Edward Davenant.

He was a boy of a pregnant wit, and when the bishop and his father were discoursing, he would be by and hearken, and now and then put in, and sometimes beyond expectation or his years.

He was of a middle stature; strong set; curled hair; a very working head, in so much that, walking and meditating before dinner, he would eat up a penny loaf, not knowing

---

[1] "John Dryden, poet, was born here." [Aubrey's note] Aubrey refers to Aldwincle.

that he did it. His natural memory was very great, to which he had added the *art of memory:* he would repeat to you forwards and backwards all the signs from Ludgate to Charing Cross.

He was fellow of Sidney College in Cambridge, where he wrote his *Divine Poems.* He was first minister of Broad Windsor in Dorset, and prebendary of the church of Sarum. He was sequestered minister of Waltham Abbey, and preacher of the Savoy, where he died and is buried.

He was a pleasant facetious person, and a *bonus socius.*

Scripsit *Holy War; Pisgah Sight; England's Worthies;* several Sermons, among others, a funeral sermon on Henry Danvers, esq., the eldest son of Sir John Danvers (and only [son] by his second wife, Dantesey), brother of Henry Earl of Danby, preached at Lavington in Wilts 1654;*obiit* 19 November.

He was minister of Waltham Cross in Essex, and also of the Savoy in the Strand, where he died (and lies buried) not long after the restoration of His Majesty.

John Milton

Quære Christopher Milton, his brother, of the Inner Temple, bencher.[1]

Mr. John Milton was of an Oxfordshire family. His grandfather, ————— (a Roman Catholic), of Holton, in Oxfordshire, near Shotover.

His father was brought up in the University of Oxon, at Christ Church, and his grandfather disinherited him because he kept not to the Catholic religion.[2] So thereupon he came to London, and became a scrivener (brought up by a friend of his; was not an apprentice) and got a plentiful estate by it, and left it off many years before he died. He was

---

[1] A genealogical table follows.
[2] *"Quære*—he found a Bible in English in his chamber." [Aubrey's note]

an ingenious man; delighted in music; composed many songs now in print, especially that of *Oriana*.[3]

I have been told that the father composed a song of fourscore parts for the Landgrave of Hess, for which his Highness sent a medal of gold, or a noble present. He died about 1647; buried in Cripplegate church, from his house in the Barbican.

His son John was born in Bread Street, in London, at the Spread Eagle, which was his house [he had also in that street another house, the Rose; and other houses in other places].

(John Milton was born the 9th of December 1608, *die Veneris*,[4] half an hour after 6 in the morning.) [5]

Anno Domini 1619, he was ten years old, as by his picture; and was then a poet.

His school-master then was a Puritan, in Essex, who cut his hair short.

He went to school to old Mr. Gill, at Paul's school. Went, at his own charge only, to Christ's College in Cambridge at fifteen, where he stayed eight years at least.[6] Then he traveled into France and Italy (had Sir H. Wotton's commendatory letters). At Geneva he contracted a great friendship with the learned Dr. Diodati of Geneva:—*vide* his poems. He was acquainted with Sir Henry Wotton, ambassador at Venice, who delighted in his company. He was several years beyond sea,[7] and returned to England just upon the breaking out of the civil wars.

From his brother, Christopher Milton:—when he went to school, when he was very young, he studied very hard,

---

[3] *"Quære* Mr. J. Playford *pro* Wilky's set of *Oriana."* [Aubrey's note]
[4] "i.e., Friday."
[5] These facts appear at another place in the MS. At this point Aubrey leaves blanks to be filled in from information to be secured from Christopher Milton: "He was born *anno Domini* . . . the . . . day of . . . about . . . a clock, in the. . . ."
  "Quære Mr. Christopher Milton to see the date of his brother's birth."
[6] After receiving the M.A. degree at Cambridge, 1632, he went to Horton, where his father now lived, and spent about five years in private study.
[7] *"Quære,* how many. *Resp.* two years." [Aubrey's note]

and sat up very late, commonly till 12 or one a clock at night, and his father ordered the maid to sit up for him, and in those years (10) composed many copies of verses which might well become a riper age. And was a very hard student in the University, and performed all his exercises there with very good applause.

His first tutor there was Mr. Chappell; from whom receiving some unkindness,[8] he was afterwards (though it seemed contrary to the rules of the college) transferred to the tuition of one Mr. Tovell [Tovey] who died parson of Lutterworth.

He went to travel about the year 1638 and was abroad about a year's space, chiefly in Italy.

Immediately after his return he took a lodging at Mr. Russell's, a tailor, in St. Bride's churchyard, and took into his tuition his sister's two sons, Edward and John Phillips, the first 10, the other 9 years of age; and in a year's time made them capable of interpreting a Latin author at sight, etc. And within three years they went through the best of Latin and Greek poets—Lucretius and Manilius,[9] of the Latins; Hesiod, Aratus, Dionysius Afer, Oppian, Apollonii *Argonautica,* and Quintus Calaber. Cato, Varro, and Columella *De re rustica* were the very first authors they learned. As he was severe on one hand, so he was most familiar and free in his conversation to those to whom most sour in his way of education. N.B. he made his nephews songsters, and sing, from the time they were with him.

He married his first wife [10] [Mary] Powell, of Fosthill, at Shotover, in Oxonshire, *anno Domini* . . . ; [11] by whom he had 4 children. [He] hath two daughters living: Deborah was his amanuensis (he taught her Latin, and to read Greek

8 "Whipped him." [Aubrey's note]
9 "And with him the use of the globes, and some rudiments of arithmetic and geometry." [Aubrey's note]
10 "She was a zealous royalist and went without her husband's consent to her mother in the king's quarters." [Aubrey's note]
11 Probably 1642.

to him when he had lost his eyesight, which was *anno Domini* . . .).

(She went from him to her mother's at . . . in the king's quarters, near Oxford), *anno Domini* . . . ; and [he] wrote the *Triplechord* about divorce.

Two opinions do not well on the same bolster. She was a . . . royalist, and went to her mother to the king's quarters, near Oxford. I have perhaps so much charity to her that she might not wrong his bed: but what man, especially contemplative, would like to have a young wife environed and stormed by the sons of Mars, and those of the enemy party?

His first wife (Mrs. Powell, a royalist) was brought up and lived where there was a great deal of company and merriment. And when she came to live with her husband, at Mr. Russell's, in St. Bride's churchyard, she found it very solitary; no company came to her; oftentimes heard his nephews beaten and cry. This life was irksome to her, and so she went to her parents at Fosthill. He sent for her, after some time; and I think his servant was evilly entreated: but as for matter of wronging his bed, I never heard the least suspicions; nor had he, of that, any jealousy.

He had a middle wife, whose name (he [12] thinks Katharine) Woodcock. No child living by her.

He married his second wife, Elizabeth Minshull, *anno* . . .[13] (the year before the sickness) : a gent. person, a peaceful and agreeable humor.

He was Latin secretary to the Parliament.

His sight began to fail him at first upon his writing against Salmasius, and before 'twas fully completed one eye absolutely failed. Upon the writing of other books, after that, his other eye decayed.

His eyesight was decaying about 20 years before his death: *quære,* when stark blind? His father read without spectacles

---

[12] "Probably Edward Philips." [Clark's note]
[13] February 24, 1663. He means third wife.

at 84. His mother had very weak eyes, and used spectacles presently after she was thirty years old.

After he was blind he wrote these following books, *viz.* *Paradise Lost, Paradise Regained, Grammar, Dictionary* (imperfect)—*quære+*.

I heard that after he was blind that he was writing a Latin Dictionary (in the hands of Moyses Pitt). *Vidua affirmat* she gave all his papers (among which this dictionary, imperfect) to his nephew, a sister's son, that he brought up . . . Phillips, who lives near the Maypole in the Strand (*quære*). She had a great many letters by her from learned men, his acquaintance, both of England and beyond sea.

He lived in several places, e.g., Holborn near King's gate. He died in Bunhill, opposite to the Artillery-garden wall.

He died of the gout struck in, the 9th or 10th of November, 1674, as appears by his apothecary's book.

He lies buried in St. Giles's Cripplegate, upper end of chancel at the right hand, *vide* his gravestone.—Memorandum his stone is now removed; for, about two years since (now, 1681), the two steps to the communion table were raised. I guess John Speed and he lie together.

His harmonical and ingenious soul did lodge in a beautiful and well-proportioned body:

> *In toto nusquam corpore menda fuit.*
> —Ovid. (1 *Amor.* 5, 18)

He was a spare man. He was scarce so tall as I am—*quære, quot* feet I am high: *resp.*, of middle stature.

He had auburn hair. His complexion exceeding fair—he was so fair that they called him *the lady of Christ's College.* Oval face. His eye a dark gray.

He had a delicate tunable voice, and had good skill. His father instructed him. He had an organ in his house: he played on that most.

Of a very cheerful humor.—He would be cheerful even in his gout-fits, and sing.

He was very healthy and free from all diseases: seldom took any physic (only sometimes he took manna): only towards his latter end he was visited with the gout, spring and fall.

He had a very good memory; but I believe that his excellent method of thinking and disposing did much to help his memory.

He pronounced the letter R (*littera canina*) very hard— a certain sign of a satirical wit—from John Dryden.

Write his name in red letters on his pictures, with his widow, to preserve.[14]

His widow has his picture, drawn very well and like, when a Cambridge scholar.

She has his picture when a Cambridge scholar, which ought to be engraven; for the pictures before his books are not *at all* like him.

His exercise was chiefly walking.

He was an early riser (*scil.* at 4 a clock *manè*); yea, after he lost his sight. He had a man read to him. The first thing he read was the Hebrew Bible, and that was at 4 h. *manè* ½ h+. Then he contemplated. At 7 his man came to him again, and then read to him again, and wrote till dinner: the writing was as much as the reading. His (2) daughter, Deborah, could read to him Latin, Italian and French, and Greek. [She] married in Dublin to one Mr. Clarke (sells silk, etc.); very like her father. The other sister is (1) Mary, more like her mother.

After dinner he used to walk 3 or four hours at a time (he always had a garden where he lived); went to bed about 9. Temperate man, rarely drank between meals. Extreme pleasant in his conversation, and at dinner, supper, etc.; but satirical.

From Mr. E. Phillips:—All the time of writing his *Paradise Lost,* his vein began at the autumnal æquinoctial, and ceased at the vernal (or thereabouts: I believe about May):

---

[14] Obviously Aubrey's note to himself.

and this was 4 or 5 years of his doing it. He began about 2 years before the king came in, and finished about three years after the king's restoration.

In the 4th book of *Paradise Lost* there are about six verses of Satan's exclamation to the sun, which Mr. E. Phillips remembers about 15 or 16 years before ever his poem was thought of. Which verses were intended for the beginning of a tragedy which he had designed, but was diverted from it by other business.

[Whatever he wrote against monarchy was out of no animosity to the king's person, or out of any faction or interest, but out of a pure zeal to the liberty of mankind, which he thought would be greater under a free state than under a monarchal government. His being so conversant in Livy and the Roman authors, and the greatness he saw done by the Roman commonwealth, and the virtue of their great commanders induced him to.] [15]

From Mr. Abraham Hill:—Memorandum: his sharp writing against Alexander More, of Holland, upon a mistake, notwithstanding he had given him by the ambassador [16] all satisfaction to the contrary: *viz.* that the book called "Clamor" was written by Peter du Moulin. Well, that was all one; he having written it, it should go into the world; one of them was as bad as the other.

Memorandum:—Mr. Theodore Haak, Regiæ Societatis Socius, hath translated half his *Paradise Lost* into High Dutch in such blank verse, which is very well liked of by Germanus Fabricius, Professor at Heidelberg, who sent to Mr. Haak a letter upon this translation:—*incredibile est quantum nos omnes affecerit gravitas styli, et copia lectissimorum verborum*, etc.—*vide* the letter.

Mr. John Milton made two admirable panegyrics, as to sublimity of wit, one on Oliver Cromwell, and the other on

---

[15] "This paragraph is not in Aubrey's hand." [Clark's note]

[16] "*Quære* the ambassador's name of Mr. Hill. *Resp.*, Newport, the Dutch Ambassador." [Aubrey's note]

Thomas, Lord Fairfax, both which his nephew Mr. Phillips hath. But he hath hung back these two years, as to imparting copies to me for the collection of mine with you.[17] Wherefore I desire you in your next to intimate your desire of having these two copies of verses aforesaid. Were they made in commendation of the devil, 'twere all one to me: 'tis the ὕψος that I look after. I have been told 'tis beyond Waller's or anything in that kind.

Quære his nephew, Mr. Edward Phillips, for a perfect catalogue of his writings. Memorandum, he wrote a little tract of education.[18]

Quære Mr. (Andrew) Allam, of Edmund-hall, Oxon, of John Milton's life written by himself: *vide* pagg . . .

He was visited much by learned [men]; more than he did desire.

He was mightily importuned to go into France and Italy. Foreigners came much to see him, and much admired him, and offered to him great preferments to come over to them: and the only inducement of several foreigners that came over into England was chiefly to see Oliver Protector and Mr. John Milton; and would see the house and chamber where he was born. He was much more admired abroad than at home.

His familiar learned acquaintance were Mr. Andrew Marvell, Mr. Skinner, Dr. Paget, M.D., Mr. [Cyriack] Skinner, who was his disciple.

John Dryden, esq., Poet Laureate, who very much admires him, and went to him to have leave to put his *Paradise Lost* into a drama in rhyme. Mr. Milton received him civilly, and told him he would give him leave to tag his verses.

His widow assures me that Mr. T. Hobbes was not one of his acquaintance, that her husband did not like him at all, but he would acknowledge him to be a man of great parts, and a learned man. Their interests and tenets did run counter to each other; *vide* in Hobbes' *Behemoth*.

---

[17] That is, with Anthony à Wood.   [18] A list of his works is here given.

John Bunyan 1628-1688

JOHN BUNYAN was born in the village of Elstow, Bedford-shire. His only schooling was that of the grammar school, and he was young when he entered his father's trade as tinker. He acquired a reputation for great wickedness; and later in *Grace Abounding to the Chief of Sinners* he revealed how his own tender conscience magnified his sins and made the devil seem a real person constantly leering and tugging at him.

At sixteen he was levied into the Parliamentary forces, where he served until June, 1647. Upon his return, he took up his trade again, and after a year or two married a young woman whose only dowry consisted of two religious books inherited from her father: *The Plain Man's Pathway to Heaven* and *The Practice of Piety*. These, through their influence on Bunyan and his writing, became a dowry to the whole world.

After his own spiritual conflict was resolved, Bunyan felt that he must preach to others. At first he added a kind of lay ministry to his regular occupation, but in 1655 he moved to Bedford and devoted himself to preaching and controversial writing. About 1656 his wife died, leaving him with four small children, one of whom was blind. He made a second fortunate marriage about 1659, but in a year's time was imprisoned for preaching without a license. He spent twelve years in the Bedford jail but was so trusted by his jailer that he could go and come with great freedom. Once he was allowed to pay a visit to London. He took up lace-making to help support his family, and wrote many tracts and books during this period of confinement.

The Declaration of Indulgence in 1672 gave Bunyan his freedom; but when it was repealed after three years, he was again imprisoned. This time, however, he had only about six months in jail, a time spent in writing *Pilgrim's Progress*.

When the imprisonment was over, Bunyan was asked to take a larger parish, but he would not leave the people of Bedford. He would often go to London to preach, however, and there he drew large crowds, including people of high rank. It was in London, in August, 1688, that Bunyan became ill and died at the home of a friend. He was buried among the Dissenters in Bunhill Fields, where the bombing of London during the Second World War opened some of the graves, but left Bunyan untouched among the plane trees.

Bunyan's vivid homely style and his narrative genius give immortality to his books. Though the reader moves among seventeenth-century scenes and meets allegorical figures, the characters are so universal and so full of life that Bunyan's works become timeless.

The Pilgrim's Progress, Grace Abounding, The Holy War, and *The Life and Death of Mr. Badman* are the most famous of Bunyan's works; yet one must not forget that his prose writings were many and varied and that he was also the author of the *Emblem Book* and some other verse.

From GRACE ABOUNDING TO THE CHIEF OF SINNERS [1]

[*The Questions of Election and Grace*]

53. ABOUT THIS time the state and happiness of these poor people at Bedford was thus, in a kind of vision, presented to me. I saw, as if they were set on the sunny side of some high mountain, there refreshing themselves with the pleasant beams of the sun, while I was shivering and shrinking in the cold, afflicted with frost, snow, and dark clouds. Methought, also, betwixt me and them, I saw a wall that did compass about this mountain; now, through this wall my soul did greatly desire to pass; concluding, that if I could, I would go even into the very midst of them, and there also comfort myself with the heat of their sun.

54. About this wall I thought myself to go again and again, still prying as I went, to see if I could find some way or passage by which I might enter therein; but none could I find for some time. At the last, I saw, as it were, a narrow gap, like a little doorway in the wall, through which I attempted to pass; but the passage being very strait and narrow, I made many efforts to get in, but all in vain, even until I was well-nigh quite beat out, by striving to get in; at last, with great striving, methought I at first did get in my head, and after that, by a sidling striving my shoulders, and my whole body; then was I exceeding glad, and went and sat down in the midst of them, and so was comforted with the light and heat of their sun.

55. Now, this mountain and wall, etc., was made out to me—the mountain signifieth the church of the living God; the sun that shone thereon, the comfortable shining of his merciful face on them that were therein; the wall, I thought, was the Word, that did make separation between the Christians and the world; and the gap which was in this wall,

[1] Text: 1688, sixth edition.

I thought, was Jesus Christ, who is the way to God the Father (John 14:6; Matt. 7:14). But forasmuch as the passage was narrow, even so narrow that I could not, but with great difficulty, enter in thereat, it showed me that none could enter into life but those that were in downright earnest; and unless also they left this wicked world behind them; for here was only room for body and soul, but not for body and soul and sin.

56. This resemblance abode upon my spirit many days; all which time I saw myself in a forlorn and sad condition, but yet was provoked to a vehement hunger and desire to be one of that number that did sit in the sunshine. Now also I should pray wherever I was, whether at home or abroad, in house or field, and should also often, with lifting up of heart, sing that of the 51st Psalm, O Lord, consider my distress; for as yet I knew not where I was.

57. Neither as yet could I attain to any considerable persuasion that I had faith in Christ; but instead of having satisfaction, here I began to find my soul to be assaulted with fresh doubts about my future happiness; especially with such as these, Whether was I elected? But how if the day of grace should now be past and gone?

58. By these two temptations I was very much afflicted and disquieted; sometimes by one, and sometimes by the other of them. And first, to speak of that about my questioning my election, I found at this time, that though I was in a flame to find the way to heaven and glory, and though nothing could beat me off from this, yet this question did so offend and discourage me, that I was especially at some times as if the very strength of my body also had been taken away by the force and power thereof. This scripture did also seem to me to trample upon all my desires, *It is neither in him that willeth, nor in him that runneth, but in God that showeth mercy* (Rom. 9).

59. With this scripture I could not tell what to do; for I evidently saw, unless that the great God, of his infinite

grace and bounty, had voluntarily chosen me to be a vessel
of mercy, though I should desire, and long, and labor until
my heart did break, no good could come of it. Therefore this
would still stick with me. How can you tell you are elected?
And what if you should not? How then?

60. O Lord, thought I, what if I should not, indeed? It
may be you are not, said the tempter; it may be so, indeed,
thought I. Why, then, said Satan, you had as good leave off,
and strive no further; for if, indeed, you should not be
elected and chosen of God, there is no talk of your being
saved; *For it is neither in him that willeth, nor in him that
runneth, but in God that showeth mercy.*

61. By these things I was driven to my wits' end, not knowing what to say, or how to answer these temptations. Indeed, I little thought that Satan had thus assaulted me, but
rather that it was my own prudence, thus to start the question; for that the elect only attained eternal life, that I,
without scruple, did heartily close withal; but that myself
was one of them, there lay the question.

62. Thus, therefore, for several days, I was greatly assaulted
and perplexed, and was often, when I have been walking,
ready to sink where I went, with faintness in my mind;
but one day, after I had been so many weeks oppressed and
cast down therewith as I was now quite giving up the ghost
of all my hopes of ever attaining life, that sentence fell
with weight upon my spirit, *Look at the generations of old
and see; did ever any trust in God and were confounded?*

63. At which I was greatly lightened and encouraged in
my soul; for thus, at that very instant, it was expounded to
me. Begin at the beginning of Genesis, and read to the end
of the Revelation, and see if you can find that there was
ever any that trusted in the Lord and was confounded. So,
coming home, I presently went to my Bible to see if I
could find that saying, not doubting but to find it presently;
for it was so fresh, and with such strength and comfort on
my spirit, that I was as if it talked with me.

64. Well, I looked, but I found it not; only it abode upon me; then I did ask first this good man and then another if they knew where it was, but they knew no such place. At this I wondered, that such a sentence should so suddenly, and with such comfort and strength, seize and abide upon my heart, and yet that none could find it, for I doubted not but it was in holy Scripture.

65. Thus I continued above a year, and could not find the place; but at last, casting my eye into the Apocrypha books, I found it in Ecclesiasticus 2 : 10. This, at the first, did somewhat daunt me; but because, by this time I had got more of the experience of the love and kindness of God, it troubled me the less; especially when I considered, that though it was not in those texts that we call holy and canonical, yet forasmuch as this sentence was the sum and substance of many of the promises, it was my duty to take the comfort of it; and I bless God for that word, for it was of God to me: that word doth still, at times, shine before my face.

66. After this, that other doubt did come with strength upon me, But how if the day of grace should be past and gone? How if you have overstood the time of mercy? Now, I remember that one day, as I was walking into the country, I was much in the thoughts of this, But how if the day of grace be past? And to aggravate my trouble, the tempter presented to my mind those good people of Bedford and suggested thus unto me, that these being converted already, they were all that God would save in those parts; and that I came too late, for these had got the blessing before I came.

67. Now was I in great distress, thinking in very deed that this might well be so; wherefore I went up and down bemoaning my sad condition, counting myself far worse than a thousand fools for standing off thus long, and spending so many years in sin as I have done; still crying out, Oh, that I had turned sooner! Oh, that I had turned seven years ago! It made me also angry with myself, to think that I should

have no more wit but to trifle away my time till my soul and heaven were lost.

68. But when I had been long vexed with this fear, and was scarce able to take one step more, just about the same place where I received my other encouragement, these words broke in upon my mind, *Compel them to come in, that my house may be filled; and yet there is room* (Luke 14: 22, 23). These words, but especially them, *And yet there is room,* were sweet words to me; for, truly, I thought that by them I saw there was place enough in heaven for me; and moreover, that when the Lord Jesus did speak these words, he then did think of me; and that he knowing the time would come that I should be afflicted with fear that there was no place left for me in his bosom, did before speak this word and leave it upon record that I might find help thereby against this vile temptation. This I then verily believed.

69. In the light and encouragement of this word I went a pretty while; and the comfort was the more when I thought that the Lord Jesus should think on me so long ago, and that he should speak them words on purpose for my sake; for I did then think, verily, that he did on purpose speak them to encourage me withal.

70. But I was not without my temptations to go back again; temptations, I say, both from Satan, mine own heart, and carnal acquaintance; but I thank God these were outweighed by that sound sense of death and the day of judgment, which abode, as it were, continually in my view; I should often also think on Nebuchadnezzar, of whom it is said, He had given him all the kingdoms of the earth (Dan. 5: 18, 19). Yet, thought I, if this great man had all his portion in this world, one hour in hell fire would make him forget all. Which consideration was a great help to me.

71. I was almost made, about this time, to see something concerning the beasts that Moses counted clean and unclean. I thought those beasts were types of men: the clean, types

of them that were the people of God; but the unclean, types
of such as were the children of the wicked one. Now, I read
that the clean beasts chewed the cud; that is, thought I, they
show us we must feed upon the word of God. They also
parted the hoof; I thought that signified we must part, if
we would be saved, with the ways of ungodly men. And
also, in further reading about them, I found that though
we did chew the cud as the hare, yet if we walked with claws
like a dog, or if we did part the hoof like the swine, yet if
we did not chew the cud as the sheep, we were still for all
that, but unclean; for I thought the hare to be a type of
those that talk of the Word, yet walk in the ways of sin;
and that the swine was like him that parted with his outward
pollutions, but still wanted the Word of faith, without which
there could be no way of salvation, let a man be never so
devout (Deut. 14). After this I found, by reading the Word,
that those that must be glorified with Christ in another
world must be called by him here; called to the partaking
of a share in his Word and righteousness, and to the comforts and first fruits of his Spirit, and to a peculiar interest
in all those heavenly things which do indeed fore-fit the
soul for that rest and house of glory which is in heaven above.

72. Here, again, I was at a very great stand, not knowing
what to do, fearing I was not called; for, thought I, if I
be not called, what then can do me good? None but those
who are effectually called inherit the kingdom of heaven.
But oh! how I now loved those words that spake of a
Christian's calling! as when the Lord said to one, *Follow
me,* and to another, *Come after me.* And oh! thought I,
that he would say so to me too, how gladly would I run after
him!

73. I cannot now express with what longings and break-
ings in my soul I cried to Christ to call me. Thus I continued for a time, all on a flame to be converted to Jesus
Christ; and did also see at that day, such glory in a converted state, that I could not be contented without a share

therein. Gold! could it have been gotten for gold, what could I have given for it! had I had a whole world, it had all gone ten thousand times over for this, that my soul might have been in a converted state.

74. How lovely now was everyone in my eyes that I thought to be converted men and women! they shone, they walked like a people that carried the broad seal of heaven about them. Oh! I saw the lot was fallen to them in pleasant places, and they had a goodly heritage (Ps. 16). But that which made me sick was that of Christ, in Mark, He went up into a mountain and called to him whom he would, and they came unto him (Mark 3: 13).

75. This scripture made me faint and fear, yet it kindled fire in my soul. That which made me fear was this, lest Christ should have no liking for me, for he called *whom he would*. But oh! the glory that I saw in that condition did still so engage my heart that I could seldom read of any that Christ did call, but I presently wished, Would I had been in their clothes; would I had been born Peter; would I had been born John; or would I had been by and had heard him when he called them, how would I have cried, O Lord, call me also. But oh! I feared he would not call me.

76. And truly the Lord let me go thus many months together and showed me nothing; either that I was already, or should be called hereafter. But at last, after much time spent, and many groans to God, that I might be made a partaker of the holy and heavenly calling, that Word came in upon me: *I will cleanse their blood that I have not cleansed: for the Lord dwelleth in Zion* (Joel 3: 21). These words I thought were sent to encourage me to wait still upon God, and signified unto me that if I were not already, yet time might come I might be in truth converted unto Christ.

From THE PILGRIM'S PROGRESS [1]

[The Palace Beautiful and the Conflict with Apollyon]

THUS HE went on his way, but while he was thus bewailing his unhappy miscarriage, he lifted up his eyes, and behold there was a very stately palace before him, the name whereof was Beautiful, and it stood just by the highway side.

So I saw in my dream that he made haste and went forward, that if possible he might get lodging there; now, before he had gone far, he entered into a very narrow passage, which was about a furlong off of the Porter's Lodge; and looking very narrowly before him as he went, he espied two lions in the way. Now, thought he, I see the dangers that Mistrust and Timorous were driven back by. (The lions were chained, but he saw not the chains.) Then he was afraid, and thought also himself to go back after them, for he thought nothing but death was before him. But the porter at the lodge, whose name is Watchful, perceiving that Christian made a halt as if he would go back, cried unto him, saying, "Is thy strength so small? [2] Fear not the lions, for they are chained, and are placed there for trial of faith where it is, and for discovery of those that have none. Keep in the midst of the path, and no hurt shall come unto thee." [3]

Then I saw that he went on, trembling for fear of the lions, but taking good heed to the directions of the porter; he heard them roar, but they did him no harm. Then he clapped his hands, and went on, till he came and stood before the gate where the porter was. Then said Christian to the porter, "Sir, what house is this? And may I lodge here tonight?"

The porter answered, "This house was built by the Lord of the Hill, and he built it for the relief and security of pil-

[1] Text: 1678, first edition, pp. 49–74.
[2] Mark. 13:34.   [3] Isa. 41:10.

grims." The porter also asked whence he was and whither he was going.

CHR. I am come from the City of Destruction, and am going to Mount Zion; but because the sun is now set, I desire, if I may, to lodge here tonight.

PORT. What is your name?

CHR. My name is now Christian, but my name at the first was Graceless; I came of the race of Japhet, whom God will persuade to dwell in the tents of Shem.[4]

PORT. But how doth it happen that you come so late? The sun is set.

CHR. I had been here sooner, but that, wretched man that I am, I slept in the arbor that stands on the hillside; nay, I had, notwithstanding that, been here much sooner, but that in my sleep I lost my evidence, and came without it to the brow of the hill; and then feeling for it, and finding it not, I was forced with sorrow of heart to go back to the place where I slept my sleep, where I found it; and now I am come.

PORT. Well, I will call out one of the virgins of this place, who will, if she likes your talk, bring you in to the rest of the family, according to the rules of the house. So Watchful, the porter, rang a bell, at the sound of which came out at the door of the house a grave and beautiful damsel named Discretion, and asked why she was called.

The porter answered, "This man is in a journey from the City of Destruction to Mount Zion, but being weary and benighted, he asked me if he might lodge here tonight; so I told him I would call for thee, who, after discourse had with him, mayest do as seemeth thee good, even according to the law of the house."

Then she asked him whence he was and whither he was going, and he told her. She asked him also how he got into the way, and he told her. Then she asked him what he had seen and met with in the way, and he told her. At last, she

---

[4] Gen. 9:27.

asked his name; so he said, "It is Christian, and I have so much the more a desire to lodge here tonight, because, by what I perceive, this place was built by the Lord of the Hill, for the relief and security of pilgrims."

So she smiled, but the water stood in her eyes; and after a little pause, she said, "I will call forth two or three more of the family." So she ran to the door and called out Prudence, Piety and Charity, who, after a little more discourse with him, had him in to the family; and many of them, meeting him at the threshold of the house, said, "Come in thou blessed of the Lord; this house was built by the Lord of the Hill, on purpose to entertain such pilgrims in." Then he bowed his head and followed them into the house. So when he was come in and sat down, they gave him something to drink, and consented together, that until supper was ready, some one or two of them should have some particular discourse with Christian, for the best improvement of time; and they appointed Piety, and Prudence [and Charity] to discourse with him; and thus they began.

PIETY. Come, good Christian, since we have been so loving to you, to receive you into our house this night, let us, if perhaps we may better ourselves thereby, talk with you of all things that have happened to you in your pilgrimage.

CHR. With a very good will, and I am glad that you are so well disposed.

PIETY. What moved you at first to betake yourself to a pilgrim's life?

CHR. I was driven out of my native country by a dreadful sound that was in mine ears, to wit, that unavoidable destruction did attend me, if I abode in that place where I was.

PIETY. But how did it happen that you came out of your country this way?

CHR. It was as God would have it; for when I was under the fears of destruction, I did not know whither to go; but by chance there came a man, even to me (as I was trembling and weeping), whose name is Evangelist, and he directed me to the Wicket-gate, which else I should never have found, and so set me into the way that hath led me directly to this house.

PIETY. But did you not come by the House of the Interpreter?

CHR. Yes, and did see such things there, the remembrance of which will stick by me as long as I live; [e]specially three things: to wit, how Christ, in despite of Satan, maintains his work of grace in the heart; how the man had sinned himself quite out of hopes of God's mercy; and also the dream of him that thought in his sleep the day of judgment was come.

PIETY. Why, did you hear him tell his dream?

CHR. Yes, and a dreadful one it was, I thought. It made my heart ache as he was telling of it; but yet I am glad I heard it.

PIETY. Was that all you saw at the House of the Interpreter?

CHR. No, he took me and had me where he showed me a stately palace, and how the people were clad in gold that were in it, and how there came a venturous man and cut his way through the armed men that stood in the door to keep him out, and how he was bid to come in and win eternal glory. Methought those things did ravish my heart. I would have stayed at that good man's house a twelvemonth, but that I knew I had further to go.

PIETY. And what saw you else in the way?

CHR. Saw! why, I went but a little further, and saw one, as I thought in my mind, hang bleeding upon a tree; and the very sight of him made my burden fall off my back; for I groaned under a very heavy burden, but then it fell down from off me. It was a strange thing to me, for I never saw such a thing before; yea, and while I stood looking up, for then I could not forbear looking, three shining ones came to me: one of them testified that my sins were forgiven me; another stripped me of my rags, and gave me this broidered coat which you see; and the third set the mark which you see in my forehead, and gave me this sealed roll. (And with that he plucked it out of his bosom.)

PIETY. But you saw more than this, did you not?

CHR. The things that I have told you were the best; yet some other matters I saw, as namely: I saw three men, Simple, Sloth and Presumption, lie asleep a little out of the way, as I came, with irons upon their heels; but do you think I could awake them? I also saw Formality and Hypocrisy come tumbling over the wall, to go, as they pretended, to Zion; but they were quickly lost, even as I myself did tell them, but they would not believe. But above all, I found it hard work to get up this hill, and as hard to come by the lions' mouths; and truly if it had not been for the good man, the porter that stands at the gate, I do not know but that after all I might have gone back again: but now, I thank God I am here, and I thank you for receiving of me.

Then Prudence thought good to ask him a few questions and desired his answer to them.

PRUD. Do you not think sometimes of the country from which you came?

CHR. Yes, but with much shame and detestation; truly, if I had been mindful of that country from whence I came out, I might have had opportunity to have returned; but now I desire a better country, that is, an heavenly.[5]

PRUD. Do you not yet bear away with you some of the things that then you were conversant withal?

CHR. Yes, but greatly against my will; especially my inward and carnal cogitations, with which all my countrymen, as well as myself, were delighted; but now all those things are my grief; and might I but choose mine own things, I would choose never to think of those things more; but when I would be doing of that which is best, that which is worst is with me.[6]

---

[5] Heb. 11:15, 16.   [6] Rom. 7:15–20.

PRUD. Do you not find sometimes, as if those things are vanquished, which at other times are your perplexity?

CHR. Yes, but that is but seldom; but they are to me golden hours in which such things happen to me.

PRUD. Can you remember by what means you find your annoyances, at time, as if they were vanquished?

CHR. Yes, when I think what I saw at the cross, that will do it; and when I look upon my broidered coat, that will do it; also when I look into the roll that I carry in my bosom, that will do it; and when my thoughts wax warm about whither I am going, that will do it.

PRUD. And what is it that makes you so desirous to go to Mount Zion?

CHR. Why, there I hope to see Him alive that did hang dead on the cross; and there I hope to be rid of all those things that to this day are in me an annoyance to me; there, they say, there is no death; and there I shall dwell with such company as I like best.[7] For, to tell you truth, I love Him, because I was by Him eased of my burden; and I am weary of my inward sickness. I would fain be where I shall die no more, and with the company that shall continually cry, "Holy, Holy, Holy!"

[Then said Charity to Christian,[8] Have you a family? Are you a married man?

CHR. I have a wife and four small children.

CHAR. And why did you not bring them along with you?

CHR. Then Christian wept, and said, Oh, how willingly would I have done it! but they were all of them utterly averse to my going on pilgrimage.

CHAR. But you should have talked to them, and have endeavored to have shown them the danger of being behind.

CHR. So I did; and told them also what God had shown

---

[7] Isa. 25:8; Rev. 21:4.

[8] The dialogue between Charity and Christian is not in the first edition, but I have inserted it here because of the additions to the story which it provides.

to me of the destruction of our city; "but I seemed to them as one that mocked," and they believed me not.[9]

CHAR. And did you pray to God that he would bless your counsel to them?

CHR. And that with much affection: for you must think that my wife and poor children were very dear unto me.

CHAR. But did you tell them of your own sorrow and fear of destruction? for I suppose that destruction was visible enough to you.

CHR. Yes, over, and over, and over. They might also see my fears in my countenance, in my tears, and also in my trembling under the apprehension of the judgment that did hang over our heads; but all was not sufficient to prevail with them to come with me.

CHAR. But what could they say for themselves, why they came not?

CHR. Why, my wife was afraid of losing this world, and my children were given to the foolish delights of youth; so what by one thing, and what by another, they left me to wander in this manner alone.

CHAR. But did you not, with your vain life, damp all that you by words used by way of persuasion to bring them away with you?

CHR. Indeed, I cannot commend my life; for I am conscious to myself of many failings therein: I know also, that a man by his conversation may soon overthrow what by argument or persuasion he doth labor to fasten upon others for their good. Yet this I can say, I was very wary of giving them occasion, by any unseemly action, to make them averse to going on pilgrimage. Yea, for this very thing they would tell me I was too precise, and that I denied myself of things for their sakes in which they saw no evil. Nay, I think I may say that if what they saw in me did hinder them, it was my great tenderness in sinning against God, or of doing any wrong to my neighbor.

[9] Gen. 19:14.

CHAR. Indeed Cain hated his brother, "because his own works were evil, and his brother's righteous"; [10] and if thy wife and children have been offended with thee for this, they hereby show themselves to be implacable to good, and "thou hast delivered thy soul from their blood." [11]]

Now I saw in my dream, that thus they sat talking together until supper was ready. So when they had made ready, they sat down to meat. Now the table was furnished "with fat things, and with wine that was well refined"; [12] and all their talk at the table was about the Lord of the Hill: as, namely, about what he had done, and wherefore he did what he did, and why he had builded that house. And by what they said, I perceived that he had been a great warrior, and had fought with and slain "him that had the power of death," [13] but not without great danger to himself, which made me love him the more.

For, as they said, and as I believe (said Christian) he did it with the loss of much blood; but that which put glory of grace into all he did, was, that he did it out of pure love to his country. And besides, there were some of them of the household that said they had seen and spoke with him since he did die on the cross; and they have attested that they had it from his own lips that he is such a lover of poor pilgrims that the like is not to be found from the east to the west. They, moreover, gave an instance of what they affirmed, and that was, he had stripped himself of his glory, that he might do this for the poor; and that they heard him say and affirm that he would not dwell in the mountain of Zion alone. They said, moreover, that he had made many pilgrims princes, though by nature they were beggars born, and their original had been the dunghill. [14]

Thus they discoursed together till late at night; and after they had committed themselves to their Lord for protection, they betook themselves to rest. The pilgrim they laid in a

[10] I John 3:12. [11] Ezek. 3:19. [12] Isa. 25:6.
[13] Heb. 2:14, 15. [14] I Sam. 2:8; Psalm, 113:7.

large upper chamber, whose window opened toward the sunrising; the name of the chamber was Peace, where he slept till break of day, and then he awoke and sang—

> Where am I now? Is this the love and care
> Of Jesus for the men that pilgrims are?
> Thus to provide that I should be forgiven.
> And dwell already the next door to heaven.

So in the morning they all got up; and, after some more discourse, they told him that he should not depart till they had shown him the rarities of that place. And first they had him into the study, where they showed him records of the greatest antiquity; in which, as I remember in my dream, they showed him first the pedigree of the Lord of the Hill, that he was the son of the Ancient of Days, and came by that eternal generation. Here also was more fully recorded the acts that he had done, and the names of many hundreds that he had taken into his service; and how he had placed them in such habitations that could neither by length of days nor decays of nature be dissolved.

Then they read to him some of the worthy acts that some of his servants had done: as, how they had subdued kingdoms, wrought righteousness, obtained promises, stopped the mouths of lions, quenched the violence of fire, escaped the edge of the sword, out of weakness were made strong, waxed valiant in fight, and turned to flight the armies of the aliens.[15]

They then read again, in another part of the records of the house, where it was showed how willing their Lord was to receive into his favor any, even any, though they in time past had offered great affronts to his person and proceedings. Here also were several other histories of many other famous things, of all which Christian had a view: as of things both ancient and modern, together with prophecies and predictions of things that have their certain accomplishment, both to the

[15] Heb. 11:33, 34.

dread and amazement of enemies, and the comfort and solace of pilgrims.

The next day they took him and had him into the armory, where they showed him all manner of furniture, which their Lord had provided for pilgrims, as sword, shield, helmet, breastplate, all-prayer, and shoes that would not wear out.[16] And there was here enough of this to harness out as many men for the service of their Lord as there be stars in the heaven for multitude.

They also showed him some of the engines with which some of his servants had done wonderful things. They showed him Moses' rod; the hammer and nail with which Jael slew Sisera; the pitchers, trumpets and lamps too, with which Gideon put to flight the armies of Midian. They showed him the ox's goad wherewith Shamgar slew six hundred men. They showed him also the jaw bone with which Samson did such mighty feats; they showed him, moreover, the sling and stone with which David slew Goliath of Gath; and the sword, also, with which their Lord will kill the Man of Sin in the day that he shall rise up to the prey. They showed him, besides, many excellent things, with which Christian was much delighted. This done, they went to their rest again.

Then I saw in my dream that on the morrow he got up to go forward, but they desired him to stay till the next day also; "and then," said they, "we will, if the day be clear, show you the Delectable Mountains," which, they said, would yet further add to his comfort because they were nearer the desired haven than the place where at present he was; so he consented and stayed. When the morning was up, they had him to the top of the house, and bid him look south; so he did, and, behold, at a great distance, he saw a most pleasant mountainous country, beautified with woods, vineyards, fruits of all sorts, flowers also; with springs and fountains, very delectable to behold.[17] Then he asked the name of the country.

[16] Ephes. 6:13–19.   [17] Isa. 33:16, 17.

They said it was Emmanuel's Land; "and it is as common," said they, "as this hill is, to and for all the pilgrims. And when thou comest there, from thence," said they, "thou mayest see to the gate of the Celestial City, as the shepherds that live there will make appear."

Now he bethought himself of setting forward, and they were willing he should. "But first," said they, "let us go again into the armory." So they did; and when they came there, they harnessed him from head to foot with what was of proof, lest, perhaps, he should meet with assaults in the way. He being, therefore, thus accoutered, walketh out with his friends to the gate, and there he asked the porter if he saw any pilgrims pass by. Then the porter answered, Yes.

CHR. Pray, did you know him? said he.

PORT. I asked him his name, and he told me it was Faithful.

CHR. Oh! said Christian, I know him; he is my townsman, my near neighbor; he comes from the place where I was born. How far do you think he may be before?

PORT. He has got by this time below the hill.

CHR. Well, said Christian, good porter, the Lord be with thee, and add to all thy blessings much increase for the kindness that thou hast showed to me.

Then he began to go forward; but Discretion, Piety, [Charity], and Prudence would accompany him down to the foot of the hill. So they went on together, reiterating their former discourses, till they came to go down the hill. Then said Christian, "As it was difficult coming up, so (so far as I can see) it is dangerous going down."

"Yes," said Prudence, "so it is; for it is a harder matter for a man to go down into the Valley of Humiliation, as thou art now, and to catch no slip by the way."

"Therefore," said they, "are we come out to accompany thee down the hill." So he began to go down, but very warily; yet he caught a slip or two.

Then I saw in my dream that these good companions, when Christian was gone to the bottom of the hill, gave him a loaf of bread, a bottle of wine, and a cluster of raisins; and then he went on his way.

But now, in this Valley of Humiliation, poor Christian was hard put to it; for he had gone but a little way, before he espied a foul fiend coming over the field to meet him; his name is Apollyon. Then did Christian begin to be afraid, and to cast in his mind whether to go back or to stand his ground. But he considered again that he had no armor for his back; and therefore thought that to turn the back to him might give him the greater advantage with ease to pierce him with his darts. Therefore he resolved to venture and stand his ground; for, thought he, had I no more in mine eye than the saving of my life, 'twould be the best way to stand.

So he went on and Apollyon met him. Now the monster was hideous to behold: he was clothed with scales like a fish (and they are his pride); he had wings like a dragon, and out of his belly came fire and smoke, and his mouth was as the mouth of a lion. When he was come up to Christian, he beheld him with a disdainful countenance, and thus began to question with him.

APOL. Whence came you and whither are you bound?

CHR. I am come from the City of Destruction, which is the place of all evil, and am going to the City of Zion.

APOL. By this I perceive thou art one of my subjects, for all that country is mine, and I am the prince and god of it. How is it, then, that thou hast run away from thy king? Were it not that I hope thou mayest do me more service, I would strike thee now at one blow to the ground.

CHR. I was born, indeed, in your dominions, but your service was hard, and your wages such as a man could not live on, "for the wages of sin is death"; [18] therefore, when I was come to years, I did as other considerate persons do, look out, if perhaps I might mend myself.

APOL. There is no prince that will thus lightly lose his subjects; neither will I as yet lose thee; but since thou com-

[18] Rom. 6:23.

plainest of thy service and wages, be content to go back : what our country will afford, I do here promise to give thee.

CHR. But I have let myself to another, even to the King of princes; and how can I with fairness go back with thee?

APOL. Thou hast done in this according to the proverb, changed a bad for a worse; but it is ordinary for those that have professed themselves his servants, after a while to give him the slip and return again to me: do thou so too, and all shall be well.

CHR. I have given him my faith, and sworn my allegiance to him; how, then, can I go back from this, and not be hanged as a traitor?

APOL. Thou didst the same to me, and yet I am willing to pass by all, if now thou wilt yet turn again and go back.

CHR. What I promised thee was in my nonage; and besides, I count that the Prince under whose banner now I stand is able to absolve me, yea, and to pardon also what I did as to my compliance with thee; and, besides (O thou destroying Apollyon), to speak truth, I like his service, his wages, his servants, his government, his company, and country better than thine; and therefore leave off to persuade me further; I am his servant, and I will follow him.

APOL. Consider, again, when thou art in cold blood, what thou art like to meet with in the way that thou goest. Thou knowest that, for the most part, his servants come to an ill end, because they are transgressors against me and my ways. How many of them have been put to shameful deaths, and, besides, thou countest his service better than mine, whereas he never came yet from the place where he is to deliver any that served him out of our hands; but as for me, how many times, as all the world very well knows, have I delivered, either by power or fraud, those that have faithfully served me, from him and his, though taken by them; and so I will deliver thee.

CHR. His forbearing at present to deliver them is on purpose to try their love, whether they will cleave to him to the end; and as for the ill end thou sayest they come to, that is most glorious in their account: for, for present deliverance, they do not much expect it; for they stay for their glory, and then they shall have it when their Prince comes in his, and the glory of the angels.

APOL. Thou hast already been unfaithful in thy service to him; and how dost thou think to receive wages of him?

CHR. Wherein, O Apollyon, have I been unfaithful to him?

APOL. Thou didst faint at first setting out, when thou wast almost choked in the Gulf of Despond. Thou didst attempt wrong ways to be rid of thy burden, whereas thou shouldest have stayed till thy Prince had taken it off; thou didst sinfully sleep and lose thy choice thing; thou wast, also, almost persuaded to go back, at the sight of the lions; and when thou talkest of thy journey, and of what thou hast heard and seen, thou art inwardly desirous of vainglory in all that thou sayest or doest.

CHR. All this is true, and much more which thou hast left out; but the Prince whom I serve and honor is merciful, and ready to forgive. But besides, these infirmities possessed me in thy country, for there I sucked them in; and I have groaned under them, been sorry for them, and have obtained pardon of my Prince.

APOL. Then Apollyon broke out into a grievous rage, saying, I am an enemy to this Prince; I hate his person, his laws, and people; I am come out on purpose to withstand thee.

CHR. Apollyon, beware what you do, for I am in the King's highway, the way of holiness; therefore take heed to yourself.

APOL. Then Apollyon straddled quite over the whole breadth of the way, and said, I am void of fear in this matter; prepare thyself to die for I swear thou shalt go no further; here will I spill thy soul.

And with that he threw a flaming dart at his breast; but Christian had a shield in his hand, with which he caught it, and so prevented the danger of that.

Then did Christian draw, for he saw 't was time to bestir him; and Apollyon as fast made at him, throwing darts as thick as hail; by the which, notwithstanding all that Christian could do to avoid it, Apollyon wounded him in his head, his hand, and his foot. This made Christian give a little back; Apollyon therefore followed his work amain, and Christian again took courage, and resisted as manfully as he could. This sore combat lasted for above half a day, even till Christian was almost quite spent; for you must know that Christian, by reason of his wounds, must grow weaker and weaker.

Then Apollyon, espying his opportunity, began to gather up close to Christian, and wrestling with him, gave him a dreadful fall; and with that Christian's sword flew out of his hand. Then, said Apollyon, "I am sure of thee now." And with that he had almost pressed him to death, so that Christian began to despair of life. But as God would have it, while Apollyon was fetching of his last blow, thereby to make a full end of this good man, Christian nimbly reached out his hand for his sword, and caught it, saying, "Rejoice not against me, O mine enemy; when I fall I shall arise," [19] and with that gave him a deadly thrust, which made him give back, as one that had received his mortal wound. Christian perceiving that, made at him again, saying, "Nay, in all these things we are more than conquerors through him that loved us." [20] And with that Apollyon spread forth his dragon's wings, and sped him away, that Christian for a season saw him no more.[21]

In this combat no man can imagine, unless he had seen and heard as I did, what yelling and hideous roaring Apollyon made all the time of the fight—he spake like a dragon: and,

[19] Micah 7:8; II Cor. 12:9.   [20] Rom. 8:37.
[21] James 4:7.

on the other side, what sighs and groans burst from Christian's heart. I never saw him all the while give so much as one pleasant look, till he perceived he had wounded Apollyon with his two-edged sword; then, indeed, he did smile, and look upward; but it was the dreadfulest fight that ever I saw.

So when the battle was over, Christian said, "I will here give thanks to him that delivered me out of the mouth of the lion, to him that did help me against Apollyon." And so he did, saying—

> Great Beelzebub, the captain of this fiend,
> Designed my ruin; therefore to this end
> He sent him harnessed out: and he, with rage
> That hellish was, did fiercely me engage.
> But blessed Michael helped me, and I
> By dint of sword, did quickly make him fly,
> Therefore to him let me give lasting praise,
> And thank and bless his holy name always.

Then there came to him a hand, with some of the leaves of the tree of life,[22] the which Christian took, and applied to the wounds that he had received in the battle, and was healed immediately. He also sat down in that place to eat bread, and to drink of the bottle that was given to him a little before; so, being refreshed, he addressed himself to his journey, with his sword drawn in his hand; for he said, I know not but some other enemy may be at hand. But he met with no other affront from Apollyon quite through this valley.

[*Vanity Fair*] [23]

[CHRISTIAN, FAITHFUL, TALKATIVE]

Thus they went on talking of what they had seen by the way; and so made that way easy, which would otherwise,

---

[22] Rev. 22:2.   [23] 1678, pp. 120–37.

no doubt, have been tedious to them: for now they went through a wilderness.

Then I saw in my dream that when they were got out of the wilderness, they presently saw a town before them, and the name of that town is Vanity; and at the town there is a Fair kept, called Vanity Fair. It is kept all the year long; it beareth the name of Vanity Fair because the town where 'tis kept is lighter than Vanity, and also because all that is there sold, or that cometh thither, is Vanity. As is the saying of the wise, "All that cometh is vanity." [24]

This fair is no new-erected business, but a thing of ancient standing; I will show you the original of it.

Almost five thousand years agone, there were pilgrims walking to the Celestial City, as these two honest persons are; and Beelzebub, Apollyon, and Legion, with their companions, perceiving by the path that the pilgrims made, that their way to the City lay through this town of Vanity, they contrived here to set up a fair: a fair wherein should be sold of all sorts of vanity and that it should last all the year long. Therefore at this fair are all such merchandise sold, as houses, lands, trades, places, honors, preferments, titles, countries, kingdoms, lusts, pleasures, and delights of all sorts, as whores, bawds, wives, husbands, children, masters, servants, lives, blood, bodies, souls, silver, gold, pearls, precious stones, and what not. And moreover, at this fair there is at all times to be seen jugglings, cheats, games, plays, fools, apes, knaves, and rogues, and that of all sorts. Here are to be seen, and that for nothing, thefts, murders, adulteries, false-swearers, and that of a blood-red color. And as in other fairs of less moment, there are several rows and streets under their proper names, where such and such wares are vended; so here likewise, you have the proper places, rows, streets (viz. countries and kingdoms) where the wares of this fair are soonest to be found: here is the Britain Row, the French Row, the Italian Row, the Spanish Row, the German Row,

[24] Isa. 40:17; Eccl. 1:11; 2:17.

where several sorts of vanities are to be sold. But as in other fairs, some one commodity is as the chief of all the fair, so the ware of Rome and her merchandise is greatly promoted in this fair; only our English nation, with some others, have taken a dislike thereat.

Now, as I said, the way to the Celestial City lies just through this town where this lusty fair is kept; and he that will go to the city, and yet not go through this town, must needs go out of the world.[25] The Prince of princes himself, when here, went through this town to his own country, and that upon a fair-day, too: yea, and as I think, it was Beelzebub, the chief lord of this fair, that invited him to buy of his vanities; [26] yea, would have made him lord of the fair, would he but have done him reverence as he went through the town. Yea, because he was such a person of honor, Beelzebub had him from street to street and showed him all the kingdoms of the world in a little time, that he might, if possible, allure that Blessed One to cheapen and buy some of his vanities. But he had no mind to the merchandise, and therefore left the town without laying out so much as one farthing upon these vanities. This fair therefore is an ancient thing of long standing, and a very great fair.

Now these pilgrims, as I said, must needs go through this fair: well, so they did; but behold, even as they entered into the fair, all the people in the fair were moved, and the town itself as it were in a hubbub about them; and that for several reasons, for,

First, the pilgrims were clothed with such kind of raiment as was diverse from the raiment of any that traded in that fair. The people therefore of the fair made a great gazing upon them: some said they were fools, some they were bedlams, and some they were outlandish men.

Secondly, and as they wondered at their apparel, so they did likewise at their speech,[27] for few could understand what

25 I Cor. 5:10.   26 Matt. 4:8; Luke 4:5, 6, 7.
27 I Cor. 2:7, 8.

they said: they naturally spoke the language of Canaan, but they that kept the fair, were the men of this world; so that from one end of the fair to the other, they seemed barbarians each to the other.

Thirdly, but that which did not a little amuse the merchandisers, was that these pilgrims set very light by all their wares; they cared not so much as to look upon them, and if they called upon them to buy, they would put their fingers in their ears, and cry, "Turn away mine eyes from beholding vanity," [28] and look upwards, signifying that their trade and traffic was in heaven.

One chanced mockingly, beholding the carriages of the men, to say unto them, "What will ye buy?" but they, looking gravely upon him said, "We buy the truth." [29] At that, there was an occasion taken to despite the men the more, some mocking, some taunting, some speaking reproachfully, and some calling upon others to smite them. At last things came to an hubbub and great stir in the fair, insomuch that all order was confounded. Now was word presently brought to the Great One of the fair, who quickly came down and deputed some of his most trusty friends to take these men into examination, about whom the fair was almost overturned. So the men were brought to examination; and they that sat upon them asked them whence they came, whither they went, and what they did there in such an unusual garb. The men told them that they were pilgrims and strangers in the world, and that they were going to their own country, which was the heavenly Jerusalem, and that they had given none occasion to the men of the town, nor yet to the merchandisers thus to abuse them, and to let them in their journey, except it was for that, when one asked them what they would buy, they said they would buy the truth. But they that were appointed to examine them did not believe them to be any other than bedlams and mad, or else such as came to put all things into confusion in the fair. Therefore

[28] Psalm 119:37; Phil. 3:19, 20.   [29] Prov. 23:23.

they took them and beat them, and besmeared them with dirt, and then put them into the cage, that they might be made a spectacle to all the men of the fair. There therefore they lay for some time and were made the objects of any man's sport, or malice, or revenge, the Great One of the fair laughing still at all that befell them.

But the men being patient, and not rendering railing for railing, but contrariwise blessing, and giving good words for bad, and kindness for injuries done, some men in the fair that were more observing and less prejudiced than the rest began to check and blame the baser sort for their continual abuses done by them to the men. They, therefore, in angry manner let fly at them again, counting them as bad as the men in the cage, and telling them that they seemed confederates and should be made partakers of their misfortunes. The others replied that for ought they could see, the men were quiet and sober, and intended nobody any harm; and that there were many that traded in their fair that were more worthy to be put into the cage, yea, and pillory, too, than were the men that they had abused. Thus, after divers words had passed on both sides (the men themselves behaving themselves all the while very wisely and soberly before them), they fell to some blows and did harm to one another.

Then were these two poor men brought before their examiners again, and there charged as being guilty of the late hubbub that had been in the fair. So they beat them pitifully, and hanged irons upon them, and led them in chains up and down the fair, for an example and a terror to the others, lest any should further speak in their behalf, or join themselves unto them. But Christian and Faithful behaved themselves yet more wisely, and received the ignominy and shame that was cast upon them with so much meekness and patience that it won to their side (though but few in comparison of the rest) several of the men in the fair. This put the other party yet into a greater rage, insomuch that they concluded

the death of these two men. Wherefore they threatened that
the cage nor irons should serve their turn, but that they
should die for the abuse they had done, and for deluding the
men of the fair.

Then were they remanded to the cage again until further
order should be taken with them. So they put them in, and
made their feet fast in the stocks. Then a convenient time
being appointed, they brought them forth to their trial, in
order to their condemnation. When the time was come, they
were brought before their enemies and arraigned; the judge's
name was Lord Hategood. Their indictment was one and
the same in substance, though somewhat varying in form;
the contents whereof were this: that they were enemies and
disturbers of their trade; that they had made commotions
and divisions in the town, and had won a party to their own
most dangerous opinions, in contempt of the law of their
Prince.

Then Faithful began to answer, that he had only set himself against that which had set itself against him that is
higher than the highest. And said he, "As for disturbance,
I make none, being myself a man of peace; the party that
were won to us were won by beholding our truth and innocence, and they are only turned from the worse to the better.
And as to the king you talk of, since he is Beelzebub, the
enemy of our Lord, I defy him and all his angels."

Then proclamation was made that they that had ought to
say for their lord the king against the prisoners at the bar
should forthwith appear, and give in their evidence. So there
came in three witnesses, to wit, Envy, Superstition, and
Pickthank. They were then asked if they knew the prisoner
at the bar, and what they had to say for their lord the king
against him.

Then stood forth Envy and said to this effect: "My Lord,
I have known this man a long time, and will attest upon
my oath before this honorable bench that he is—"

JUDGE. Hold, give him his oath.

So they sware him. Then he said, "My Lord, this man, notwithstanding his plausible name, is one of the vilest men in our country; he neither regardeth prince nor people, law nor custom, but doth all that he can to possess all men with certain of his disloyal notions, which he in the general calls principles of faith and holiness. And in particular, I heard him once affirm that Christianity, and the customs of our town of Vanity, were diametrically opposite and could not be reconciled. By which saying, my Lord, he doth at once not only condemn all our laudable doings, but us in the doing of them."

JUDGE. Then did the judge say to him, "Hast thou any more to say?"

ENV. My Lord, I could say much more, only I would not be tedious to the court. Yet if need be, when the other gentlemen have given their evidence, rather than anything shall be wanting that will dispatch him, I will enlarge my testimony against him. So he was bid stand by.

Then they called Superstition and bid him look upon the prisoner; they also asked, what he could say for their lord the king against him. Then they sware him; so he began.

SUPER. My Lord, I have no great acquaintance with this man, nor do I desire to have further knowledge of him; however, this I know, that he is a very pestilent fellow, from some discourse that the other day I had with him in this town; for then talking with him, I heard him say that our religion was naught, and such by which a man could by no means please God: which sayings of his, my Lord, your Lordship very well knows what necessarily thence will follow, to wit, that we still do worship in vain, are yet in our sins, and finally shall be damned; and this is that which I have to say.

Then was Pickthank sworn, and bid him say what he knew in behalf of their lord the king against the prisoner at the bar.

PICK. My Lord, and you gentlemen all, this fellow I have known of a long time and have heard him speak things that ought not to be spoke. For he hath railed on our noble Prince Beelzebub and hath spoke contemptibly of his honorable friends, whose names are Lord Old Man, the Lord Carnal Delight, the Lord Luxurious, the Lord Desire of Vainglory, my old Lord Lechery, Sir Having Greedy, with all the rest of our nobility; and he hath said, moreover, that if all men were of his mind, if possible, there is not one of these noble men should have any longer a being in this town. Besides, he hath not been afraid to rail on you, my Lord, who are now appointed to be his judge, calling you an ungodly villain, with many other such vilifying terms, by which he hath bespattered most of the gentry of our town.

When this Pickthank had told his tale, the judge directed his speech to the prisoner at the bar, saying, "Thou renegate, heretic, and traitor, hast thou heard what these honest gentlemen have witnessed against thee?"

FAITH. May I speak a few words in my own defense?

JUDGE. Sirrah, sirrah, thou deservest to live no longer, but to be slain immediately upon the place; yet that all men may see our gentleness towards thee, let us see what thou hast to say.

FAITH. 1. I say then in answer to what Mr. Envy hath spoken, I never said ought but this, That what rule, or laws, or custom, or people were flat against the word of God are diametrically opposite to Christianity. If I have said amiss in this, convince me of my error, and I am ready here before you to make my recantation.

2. As to the second, to wit, Mr. Superstition, and his charge against me, I said only this, That in the worship of God there is required a divine faith; but there can be no divine faith without a divine revelation of the will of God: therefore whatever is thrust into the worship of God that is not agreeable to divine revelation cannot be done but by an human faith, which faith will not profit to eternal life.

3. As to what Mr. Pickthank hath said, I say (avoiding terms, as that I am said to rail, and the like), that the prince

of this town, with all the rabblement of his attendants, by this gentleman named, are more fit for being in hell than in this town and country; and so the Lord have mercy upon me.

Then the judge called to the jury (who all this while stood by to hear and observe) : "Gentlemen of the jury, you see this man about whom so great an uproar hath been made in this town; you have also heard what these worthy gentlemen have witnessed against him; also you have heard his reply and confession. It lieth now in your breasts to hang him, or save his life. But yet I think meet to instruct you into our law. There was an act made in the days of Pharaoh the Great, servant to our prince, that lest those of ordinary religion should multiply and grow too strong for him, their males should be thrown into the river. There was also an act made in the days of Nebuchadnezzar the Great, another of his servants, that whoever would not fall down and worship his golden image should be thrown into a fiery furnace. There was also an act made in the days of Darius, that whoso for some time called upon any god but his should be cast into the lions' den. Now the substance of these laws this rebel has broken, not only in thought (which is not to be borne) but also in word and deed; which must therefore needs be intolerable. For that of Pharaoh, his law was made upon a supposition to prevent mischief, no crime being yet apparent; but here is a crime apparent. For the second and third, you see he disputeth against our religion; and for the treason he hath confessed, he deserveth to die the death."

Then went the jury out, whose names were Mr. Blindman, Mr. No-good, Mr. Malice, Mr. Love-lust, Mr. Live-loose, Mr. Heady, Mr. High-mind, Mr. Enmity, Mr. Liar, Mr. Cruelty, Mr. Hate-light, and Mr. Implacable, who everyone gave in his private verdict against him among themselves, and afterwards unanimously concluded to bring him in guilty before the judge. And first Mr. Blindman, the foreman, said, "I see clearly that this man is an heretic."

Then said Mr. No-good, "Away with such a fellow from the earth."

"Ay," said Mr. Malice, "for I hate the very looks of him."

Then said Mr. Love-lust, "I could never endure him."

"Nor I," said Mr. Live-loose, "for he would always be condemning my way."

"Hang him, hang him," said Mr. Heady.

"A sorry scrub," said Mr. High-mind.

"My heart riseth against him," said Mr. Enmity.

"He is a rogue," said Mr. Liar.

"Hanging is too good for him," said Mr. Cruelty.

"Let's dispatch him out of the way," said Mr. Hate-light.

Then said Mr. Implacable, "Might I have all the world given me, I could not be reconciled to him; therefore let us forthwith bring him in guilty of death."

And so they did; therefore he was presently condemned to be had from the place where he was, to the place from whence he came, and there to be put to the most cruel death that could be invented.

They therefore brought him out to do with him according to their law; and first they scourged him, then they buffeted him, then they lanced his flesh with knives; after that they stoned him with stones, then pricked him with their swords, and last of all they burned him to ashes at the stake. Thus came Faithful to his end. Now I saw that there stood behind the multitude a chariot and a couple of horses waiting for Faithful, who (so soon as his adversaries had dispatched him) was taken up into it, and straightway was carried up through the clouds with sound of trumpet, the nearest way to the celestial gate. But as for Christian, he had some respite, and was remanded back to prison; so there he remained for a space: but he that over-rules all things, having the power of their rage in his own hand, so wrought it about that Christian for that time escaped them and went his way.

And as he went, he sang, saying:

Well, Faithful, thou hast faithfully professed
Unto thy Lord: with him thou shalt be blessed;
When faithless ones, with all their vain delights,
Are crying out under their hellish plights,
Sing, Faithful, sing; and let thy name survive;
For though they killed thee, thou art yet alive.

Now I saw in my dream that Christian went not forth
alone, for there was one whose name was Hopeful (being
made so by the beholding of Christian and Faithful in their
words and behavior, in their sufferings at the fair) who
joined himself unto him, and entering into a brotherly covenant, told him that he would be his companion. Thus one
died to make testimony to the truth, and another rises out
of his ashes to be a companion with Christian. This Hopeful also told Christian that there were many more of the
men in the fair that would take their time and follow after.

John Dryden 1631-1700

John Dryden was born in Aldwincle, Northamptonshire, but was educated at Westminster School, London, and Trinity College, Cambridge. His first position was with his cousin, who was in Cromwell's service; but after Cromwell's death Dryden became a Royalist, later giving full support to the king by his brilliant satires against the Shaftesbury Plot.

Literature was his calling, and with the opening of the theaters, he naturally turned to the writing of plays as the only income-producing type of writing. It was especially necessary for him to continue in this field after his marriage to Lady Elizabeth Howard in 1663. Between this time and 1678 he averaged more than one new play a year. His audience was made up chiefly of the nobility, and therefore he took as his model the popular French heroic romance. His extravagant heroic dramas are built around the conflict between love and honor, and his characters all belong to the aristocracy.

Dryden's early poems had been stimulated by special occasions, first, the death of Cromwell and then the restoration of Charles II. In 1666 the Dutch war and the London fire afforded themes for his first really distinguished poem, the *Annus Mirabilis*. In 1668 his superiority as a writer of prose was established by the publication of *An Essay of Dramatic Poesy*. In recognition of his abilities he was appointed to the laureateship upon Davenant's death and made Historiographer Royal.

His versatility was further demonstrated by his great political satires, *Absalom and Achitophel* and *MacFlecknoe*. The former depicted the plot to put Monmouth on the throne, in terms of Absalom's plot against David; and the latter attacked the minor poet, Shadwell, who had been engaged by the Whigs to reply to Dryden. Dryden's use of the couplet is brilliant, but it is his superb depiction of characters which gives permanent fame to these satires.

Theological argument is transmuted into poetry in *Religio Laici* and *The Hind and the Panther*. In the former Dryden supported the Established Church, but after his conversion to Catholicism he wrote the equally powerful defense of the Catholic Church.

With the coming of William and Mary, Dryden lost his various positions, including that of Poet Laureate, and to support himself turned to writing more plays and to translating some of the Latin poets. In 1693 he completed his Juvenal and Persius, prefaced by the excellent *A Discourse Concerning the Original and Progress of Satire*. His Virgil appeared four years later, and the year before his death he published *Fables Ancient and Modern*, containing translations not only of some of the Roman poets but also of Boccaccio and Chaucer.

Dryden's prefaces to his plays and translations reveal the principles of literary taste current in the Restoration period. Independent and incisive, his mind gets to the center of each critical tenet. In the famous *Essay of Dramatic Poesy*, for example, he is able to make an impartial presentation of the several opposing points of view debated by the critics. In all of his prose there is clarity and ease ; the supple naturalness of speech has supplanted the highly adorned poetic prose of the earlier part of the century. The leader in almost every type of writing, Dryden became the great literary dictator presiding at Will's Coffee House and determining the fate of younger writers.

From AN ESSAY OF DRAMATIC POESY [1]

[*French and English Plays*]

"IF THE question had been stated," replied Lisideius, "who had writ best, the French or English, forty years ago, I should have been of your opinion, and adjudged the honor to our own nation; but since that time" (said he, turning towards Neander), "we have been so long together bad Englishmen that we had not leisure to be good poets. Beaumont, Fletcher, and Jonson (who were only capable of bringing us to that degree of perfection which we have) were just then leaving the world; as if in an age of so much horror, wit and those milder studies of humanity had no further business among us. But the Muses, who ever follow peace, went to plant in another country: it was then that the great Cardinal of Richelieu began to take them into his protection; and that, by his encouragement, Corneille, and some other Frenchmen, reformed their theater, which before was as much below ours, as it now surpasses it and the rest of Europe. But because Crites in his discourse for the ancients has prevented me, by observing many rules of the stage which the moderns have borrowed from them, I shall only, in short, demand of you, whether you are not convinced that of all nations the French have best observed them? In the unity of time you find them so scrupulous that it yet remains a dispute among their poets, whether the artificial day of twelve hours, more or less, be not meant by Aristotle, rather than the natural one of twenty-four; and consequently, whether all plays ought not to be reduced into that compass. This I can testify, that in all their

[1] Text: 1693, third edition. This essay is a critical discussion in dialogue concerning ancient drama, French and English plays and the merits of "regular" drama, and the use of rhyme in tragedy. There are four speakers: Eugenius, Charles Sackville, later sixth Earl of Dorset; Crites, Sir Robert Howard, Dryden's brother-in-law; Lisideius, Sir Charles Sedley; and Neander, Dryden.

dramas writ within these last twenty years and upwards, I have not observed any that have extended the time to thirty hours: in the unity of place they are full as scrupulous; for many of their critics limit it to that very spot of ground where the play is supposed to begin; none of them exceed the compass of the same town or city. The unity of action in all their plays is yet more conspicuous; for they do not burden them with under-plots, as the English do: which is the reason why many scenes of our tragi-comedies carry on a design that is nothing of kin to the main plot; and that we see two distinct webs in a play, like those in ill-wrought stuffs; and two actions, that is, two plays, carried on together, to the confounding of the audience; who, before they are warm in their concernments for one part, are diverted to another; and by that means espouse the interest of neither. From hence likewise it arises that the one half of our actors are not known to the other. They keep their distances, as if they were Montagues and Capulets, and seldom begin an acquaintance till the last scene of the fifth act, when they are all to meet upon the stage. There is no theater in the world has anything so absurd as the English tragi-comedy; 'tis a drama of our own invention, and the fashion of it is enough to proclaim it so; here a course of mirth, there another of sadness and passion, and a third of honor and a duel: thus, in two hours and a half, we run through all the fits of Bedlam. The French affords you as much variety on the same day, but they do it not so unseasonably, or *mal à propos,* as we: our poets present you the play and the farce together; and our stages still retain somewhat of the original civility of the Red Bull: [2]

Atque ursum et pugiles media inter carmina poscunt.[3]

The end of tragedies or serious plays, says Aristotle, is to beget admiration, compassion, or concernment; but are not

[2] The Red Bull, a theater in St. John's Street, Clerkenwell, where an attempt was made to revive old plays.

[3] In the midst of the verses they demand either the bear or the pugilists.

mirth and compassion things incompatible? and is it not evident that the poet must of necessity destroy the former by intermingling of the latter? that is, he must ruin the sole end and object of his tragedy, to introduce somewhat that is forced into it, and is not of the body of it. Would you not think that physician mad, who, having prescribed a purge, should immediately order you to take restringents?

"But to leave our plays, and return to theirs. I have noted one great advantage they have had in the plotting of their tragedies; that is, they are always grounded upon some known history: according to that of Horace, *Ex noto fictum carmen sequar;* [4] and in that they have surpassed them. For the ancients, as was observed before, took for the foundation of their plays some poetical fiction, such as under that consideration could move but little concernment in the audience, because they already knew the event of it. But the French goes farther:

> *Atque ita mentitur, sic veris falsa remiscet*
> *Primo ne medium, medio ne discrepet imum.* [5]

He so interweaves truth with probable fiction that he puts a pleasing fallacy upon us; mends the intrigues of fate, and dispenses with the severity of history, to reward that virtue which has been rendered to us there unfortunate. Sometimes the story has left the success so doubtful that the writer is free, by the privilege of a poet, to take that which of two or more relations will best suit with his design: as for example, in the death of Cyrus, whom Justin and some others report to have perished in the Scythian war, but Xenophon affirms to have died in his bed of extreme old age. Nay, more, when the event is past dispute, even then

---

[4] Horace, *Ars Poet.*, 240.
[5]   "And so adroitly mingles false with true,
          So with his fair illusions cheats the view,
          That all the parts—beginning, middle, end—
          In one harmonious compound sweetly blend."
                    (*De Arte Poetica*, 151, 152 ; Howes.)

we are willing to be deceived, and the poet, if he contrives
it with appearance of truth, has all the audience of his party,
at least during the time his play is acting: so naturally we
are kind to virtue, when our own interest is not in question,
that we take it up as the general concernment of mankind.
On the other side, if you consider the historical plays of
Shakespeare, they are rather so many chronicles of kings,
or the business many times of thirty or forty years, cramped
into a representation of two hours and a half; which is not
to imitate or paint nature, but rather to draw her in minia-
ture, to take her in little; to look upon her through the wrong
end of a perspective, and receive her images not only much
less, but infinitely more imperfect than the life: this, instead of making a play delightful, renders it ridiculous:

> *Quodcunque ostendis mihi sic, incredulus odi.*[6]

For the spirit of man cannot be satisfied but with truth, or
at least verisimility; and a poem is to contain, if not τα ἔυμα,
yet ἐτύμοισιν ὁμοῖα,[7] as one of the Greek poets has expressed it.

"Another thing in which the French differ from us and
from the Spaniards, is that they do not embarrass, or cumber
themselves with too much plot; they only represent so much
of a story as will constitute one whole and great action sufficient for a play; we, who undertake more, do but multiply
adventures which, not being produced from one another, as
effects from causes, but rarely following, constitute many
actions in the drama, and consequently make it many plays.

"But by pursuing closely one argument, which is not
cloyed with many turns, the French have gained more liberty
for verse, in which they write; they have leisure to dwell
on a subject which deserves it; and to represent the passions (which we have acknowledged to be the poet's work)
without being hurried from one thing to another, as we are
in the plays of Calderon, which we have seen lately upon
our theaters under the name of Spanish plots. I have taken

---

[6] *Ars Poet.*, 188.   [7] Homer, *Odyssey*, xix, 203.

notice but of one tragedy of ours whose plot has that uni-
formity and unity of design in it which I have commended
in the French; and that is *Rollo,* or rather, under the name
of Rollo, the Story of Bassianus and Geta in Herodian: there
indeed the plot is neither large nor intricate, but just enough
to fill the minds of the audience, not to cloy them. Besides,
you see it founded upon the truth of history, only the time
of the action is not reducible to the strictness of the rules;
and you see in some places a little farce mingled, which is
below the dignity of the other parts, and in this all our poets
are extremely peccant: even Ben Jonson himself, in *Sejanus*
and *Catiline,* has given us this olio of a play, this unnatural
mixture of comedy and tragedy; which to me sounds just
as ridiculously as the history of David with the merry humors
of Golia's. In *Sejanus* you may take notice of the scene betwixt Livia and the physician which is a pleasant satire
upon the artificial helps of beauty: in *Catiline* you may see
the parliament of women; the little envies of them to one
another; and all that passes betwixt Curio and Fulvia: scenes
admirable in their kind, but of an ill mingle with the
rest.

"But I return again to the French writers, who, as I have
said, do not burden themselves too much with plot, which
has been reproached to them by an ingenious person of our
nation as a fault; for, he says, they commonly make but
one person considerable in a play; they dwell on him, and
his concernments, while the rest of the persons are only
subservient to set him off. If he intends this by it, that there
is one person in the play who is of greater dignity than the
rest, he must tax, not only theirs, but those of the ancients,
and which he would be loath to do, the best of ours; for it
is impossible but that one person must be more conspicuous
in it than any other, and consequently the greatest share in
the action must devolve on him. We see it so in the management of all affairs; even in the most equal aristocracy, the
balance cannot be so justly poised but some one will be
superior to the rest, either in parts, fortune, interest, or the

consideration of some glorious exploit; which will reduce the greatest part of business into his hands.

"But, if he would have us to imagine that in exalting one character the rest of them are neglected, and that all of them have not some share or other in the action of the play, I desire him to produce any of Corneille's tragedies, wherein every person, like so many servants in a well-governed family, has not some employment, and who is not necessary to the carrying on of the plot, or at least to your understanding it.

"There are indeed some protatic [8] persons in the ancients, whom they make use of in their plays, either to hear or give the relation: but the French avoid this with great address, making their narrations only to or by such who are some way interested in the main design. And now I am speaking of relations, I cannot take a fitter opportunity to add this in favor of the French, that they often use them with better judgment and more *à propos* than the English do. Not that I commend narrations in general, but there are two sorts of them. One, of those things which are antecedent to the play and are related to make the conduct of it more clear to us. But 'tis a fault to choose such subjects for the stage as will force us on that rock, because we see they are seldom listened to by the audience, and that is many times the ruin of the play; for, being once let pass without attention, the audience can never recover themselves to understand the plot; and indeed it is somewhat unreasonable that they should be put to so much trouble, as that, to comprehend what passes in their sight, they must have recourse to what was done, perhaps, ten or twenty years ago.

"But there is another sort of relations, that is, of things happening in the action of the play, and supposed to be done behind the scenes; and this is many times both convenient and beautiful; for by it the French avoid the tumult to which we are subject in England, by representing duels, battles, and the like; which renders our stage too like the theaters where they fight for prizes. For what is more ri-

---

[8] Characters who appear only in the first of the play.

diculous than to represent an army with a drum and five men behind it; all which the hero of the other side is to drive in before him; or to see a duel fought, and one slain with two or three thrusts of the foils, which we know are so blunted that we might give a man an hour to kill another in good earnest with them.

"I have observed that in all our tragedies, the audience cannot forbear laughing when the actors are to die; it is the most comic part of the whole play. All *passions* may be lively represented on the stage, if to the well-writing of them the actor supplies a good commanded voice, and limbs that move easily, and without stiffness; but there are many *actions* which can never be imitated to a just height: dying especially is a thing which none but a Roman gladiator could naturally perform on the stage, when he did not imitate or represent, but do it; and therefore it is better to omit the representation of it.

"The words of a good writer, which describe it lively, will make a deeper impression of belief in us than all the actor can insinuate into us, when he seems to fall dead before us; as a poet in the description of a beautiful garden, or a meadow, will please our imagination more than the place itself can please our sight. When we see death represented, we are convinced it is but fiction; but when we hear it related, our eyes, the strongest witnesses, are wanting, which might have undeceived us; and we are all willing to favor the sleight, when the poet does not too grossly impose on us. They therefore who imagine these relations would make no concernment in the audience, are deceived, by confounding them with the other, which are of things antecedent to the play: those are made often in cold blood, as I may say, to the audience; but these are warmed with our concernments, which were before awakened in the play. What the philosophers say of motion, that, when it is once begun, it continues of itself, and will do so to eternity, without some stop put to it, is clearly true on this occasion: the soul, being already moved with the characters and fortunes of those imaginary persons, continues going of its own accord; and we are no more weary to hear what becomes of them when they are not on the stage, than we are to listen to the news of an absent mistress. But it is objected that, if one part of the play may be related, then why not all? I answer, some parts of the action are more fit to be represented, some to be related. Corneille says judiciously that the poet is not obliged to expose to view all particular actions which conduce to the principal: he ought to select such of them to be seen, which will appear with the greatest beauty, either by the magnificence of the show or the vehemence of passions they produce, or some other charm which they have in them; and let the rest arrive to the audience by narration. 'Tis a great mistake in us to believe the French present no part of the action on the stage; every alteration or crossing of a design, every new-sprung passion, and turn of it, is a part of the action, and much the noblest, except we conceive nothing to be action till the players come to blows; as if the painting of the hero's mind were not more properly the poet's work than the strength of his body. Nor does this anything contradict the opinion of Horace, where he tells us,

> *Segnius irritant animos demissa per aurem,*
> *Quam quæ sunt oculis subjecta fidelibus.*[9]

For he says immediately after,

> *Non tamen intus*
> *Digna geri promes in scenam ; multaque ;*
> *tolles*
> *Ex oculis, quæ mox narret facundia præsens.*[10]

[9] "Those which a tale shall through the ear impart,
With fainter characters impress the heart
Than those which, subject to the eye's broad gaze
[The pleased spectator to himself conveys]."
(*Ars Poet.*, 180–182)

[10] "Yet drag not on the stage each horrid scene,
Nor shock the sight with what should pass within.
This let description's milder medium show,
And leave to eloquence her tale of woe."
(*Ibid.*, 182–184)

Among which many he recounts some:

Nec pueros coram populo Medea trucidet,
Aut in avem Progne mutetur, Cadmus in anguem, etc.[11]

That is, those actions which by reason of their cruelty will
cause aversion in us, or by reason of their impossibility, unbelief, ought either wholly to be avoided by a poet, or only
delivered by narration. To which we may have leave to add
such as to avoid tumult (as was before hinted), or to reduce
the plot into a more reasonable compass of time, or for defect of beauty in them, are rather to be related than presented to the eye. Examples of all these kinds are frequent,
not only among all the ancients, but in the best received of
our English poets. We find Ben Jonson using them in his
Magnetic Lady,[12] where one comes out from dinner, and relates the quarrels and disorders of it, to save the undecent
appearance of them on the stage, and to abbreviate the
story; and this in express imitation of Terence, who had
done the same before him in his *Eunuch,* where Pythias
makes the like relation of what happened within at the
soldiers' entertainment. The relations likewise of Sejanus's
death, and the prodigies before it, are remarkable; the one
of which was hid from sight, to avoid the horror and tumult
of the representation; the other, to shun the introducing of
things impossible to be believed. In that excellent play, *The
King and no King,* Fletcher goes yet farther, for the whole
unravelling of the plot is done by narration in the fifth act,
after the manner of the ancients; and it moves great concernment in the audience, though it be only a relation of
what was done many years before the play. I could multiply
other instances, but these are sufficient to prove that there

---

[11]   "Let not the cruel Colchian mother slay
        Her smiling infants in the face of day; . . .
        Nor Procne's form the rising plumage take,
        Nor Cadmus sink into a slimy snake."
                                        (*Ibid.,* 185–187)
[12] Act ii, sc. 2.

is no error in choosing a subject which requires this sort of narrations; in the ill management of them, there may.

"But I find I have been too long in this discourse, since the French have many other excellencies not common to us; as that you never see any of their plays end with a conversion, or simple change of will, which is the ordinary way which our poets use to end theirs. It shows little art in the conclusion of a dramatic poem, when they who have hindered the felicity during the four acts, desist from it in the fifth, without some powerful cause to take them off their design; and though I deny not but such reasons may be found, yet it is a path that is cautiously to be trod, and the poet is to be sure he convinces the audience that the motive is strong enough. As for example, the conversion of the Usurer in *The Scornful Lady* seems to me a little forced; for, being an Usurer, which implies a lover of money to the highest degree of covetousness (and such the poet has represented him), the account he gives for the sudden change is, that he has been duped by the wild young fellow; which in reason might render him more wary another time, and make him punish himself with harder fare and coarser clothes, to get up again what he had lost: but that he should look on it as a judgment, and so repent, we may expect to hear in a sermon, but I should never endure it in a play.

"I pass by this; neither will I insist on the care they take that no person after his first entrance shall ever appear, but the business which brings him upon the stage shall be evident; which rule, if observed, must needs render all the events in the play more natural; for there you see the probability of every accident, in the cause that produced it; and that which appears chance in the play will seem so reasonable to you, that you will find it almost necessary: so that in the exit of the actor you have a clear account of his purpose and design in the next entrance (though, if the scene be well wrought, the event will commonly deceive you); for there is nothing so absurd, says Corneille, as for an actor to leave the stage only because he has no more to say.

"I should now speak of the beauty of their rhyme, and the just reason I have to prefer that way of writing in tragedies before ours in blank verse; but because it is partly received by us, and therefore not altogether peculiar to them, I will say no more of it in relation to their plays. For our own, I doubt not but it will exceedingly beautify them; and I can see but one reason why it should not generally obtain, that is, because our poets write so ill in it. This indeed may prove a more prevailing argument than all others which are used to destroy it, and therefore I am only troubled when great and judicious poets, and those who are acknowledged such, have writ or spoke against it: as for others, they are to be answered by that one sentence of an ancient author:—*Sed ut primo ad consequendos eos quos priores ducimus, accendimur, ita ubi aut præteriri, aut æquari eos posse desperavimus, studium cum spe senescit: quod, scilicet, assequi non potest, sequi desinit; . . . præteritoque eo in quo eminere non possumus, aliquid in quo nitamur, conquirimus.*"

Lisideius concluded in this manner; and Neander, after a little pause, thus answered him:

"I shall grant Lisideius, without much dispute, a great part of what he has urged against us; for I acknowledge that the French contrive their plots more regularly, and observe the laws of comedy and decorum of the stage (to speak generally) with more exactness than the English. Farther, I deny not but he has taxed us justly in some irregularities of ours, which he has mentioned; yet, after all, I am of opinion that neither our faults nor their virtues are considerable enough to place them above us.

"For the lively imitation of nature being in the definition of a play, those which best fulfill that law ought to be esteemed superior to the others. 'Tis true, those beauties of the French poesy are such as will raise perfection higher where it is, but are not sufficient to give it where it is not: they are indeed the beauties of a statue, but not of a man, because not animated with the soul of poesy, which is imitation of humor and passions: and this Lisideius himself, or any other, however biased to their party, cannot but acknowledge, if he will either compare the humors of our comedies, or the characters of our serious plays, with theirs. He who will look upon theirs which have been written till these last ten years, or thereabouts, will find it a hard matter to pick out two or three passable humors amongst them. Corneille himself, their arch-poet, what has he produced except *The Liar,* and you know how it was cried up in France; but when it came upon the English stage, though well translated, and that part of Durant acted to so much advantage as I am confident never received in its own country, the most favorable to it would not put it in competition with many of Fletcher's or Ben Jonson's. In the rest of Corneille's comedies you have little humor; he tells you himself his way is first to show two lovers in good intelligence with each other; in the working up of the play to embroil them by some mistake, and in the latter end to clear it and reconcile them.

"But of late years Molière, the younger Corneille, Quinault,[13] and some others, have been imitating afar off the quick turns and graces of the English stage. They have mixed their serious plays with mirth, like our tragi-comedies, since the death of Cardinal Richelieu; which Lisideius and many others not observing, have commended that in them for a virtue which they themselves no longer practice. Most of their new plays are, like some of ours, derived from the Spanish novels.[14] There is scarce one of them without a veil, and a trusty Diego,[15] who drolls much after the rate of *The Adventures.* But their humors, if I may grace them with that name, are so thin-sown that never above one of them

---

[13] Philippe Quinault (1635–1688) whose *Les Rivals* seems to imitate the *Rival Ladies,* etc.

[14] Middleton's *Spanish Gypsy,* for example, is from Cervantes.

[15] Diego is a servant in the play, *The Adventures of Five Hours.* He was also often called Philipin; see below.

comes up in any play. I dare take upon me to find more variety of them in some one play of Ben Jonson's than in all theirs together; as he who has seen *The Alchemist, The Silent Woman,* or *Bartholomew Fair* cannot but acknowledge with me.

"I grant the French have performed what was possible on the ground-work of the Spanish plays; what was pleasant before, they have made regular: but there is not above one good play to be writ on all these plots; they are too much alike to please often; which we need not the experience of our own stage to justify. As for their new way of mingling mirth with serious plot, I do not, with Lisideius, condemn the thing, though I cannot approve of their manner of doing it. He tells us, we cannot so speedily recollect ourselves after a scene of great passion and concernment, as to pass to another of mirth and humor, and to enjoy it with any relish: but why should he imagine the soul of man more heavy than his senses? Does not the eye pass from an unpleasant object to a pleasant in a much shorter time than is required to this? and does not the unpleasantness of the first commend the beauty of the latter? The old rule of logic might have convinced him, that contraries, when placed near, set off each other. A continued gravity keeps the spirit too much bent; we must refresh it sometimes, as we bait in a journey that we may go on with greater ease. A scene of mirth, mixed with tragedy, has the same effect upon us which our music has betwixt the acts; which we find a relief to us from the best plots and language of the stage, if the discourses have been long. I must therefore have stronger arguments, ere I am convinced that compassion and mirth in the same subject destroy each other; and in the meantime cannot but conclude, to the honor of our nation, that we have invented, increased, and perfected a more pleasant way of writing for the stage, than was ever known to the ancients or moderns of any nation, which is tragi-comedy.

"And this leads me to wonder why Lisideius and many

others should cry up the barrenness of the French plots above the variety and copiousness of the English. Their plots are single; they carry on one design, which is pushed forward by all the actors, every scene in the play contributing and moving towards it. Our plays, besides the main design, have under-plots or by-concernments, of less considerable persons and intrigues, which are carried on with the motion of the main plot; as they say the orb of the fixed stars, and those of the planets, though they have motions of their own, are whirled about by the motion of the *primum mobile,* in which they are contained. That similitude expresses much of the English stage; for if contrary motions may be found in nature to agree; if a planet can go east and west at the same time, one way by virtue of his own motion, the other by the force of the first mover, it will not be difficult to imagine how the under-plot, which is only different, not contrary to the great design, may naturally be conducted along with it.

"Eugenius has already shown us, from the confessions of the French poets, that the unity of action is sufficiently preserved, if all the imperfect actions of the play are conducing to the main design; but when those petty intrigues of a play are so ill ordered that they have no coherence with the other, I must grant that Lisideius has reason to tax that want of due connection; for co-ordination in a play is as dangerous and unnatural as in a state. In the meantime he must acknowledge, our variety, if well ordered, will afford a greater pleasure to the audience.

"As for his other argument, that by pursuing one single theme they gain an advantage to express and work up the passions, I wish any example he could bring from them would make it good; for I confess their verses are to me the coldest I have ever read. Neither, indeed, is it possible for them, in the way they take, so to express passion as that the effects of it should appear in the concernment of an audience, their speeches being so many declamations, which tire us with their length; so that instead of persuading us to grieve for their imaginary heroes, we are concerned for our own trouble, as we are in tedious visits of bad company; we are in pain till they are gone. When the French stage came to be reformed by Cardinal Richelieu, those long harangues were introduced to comply with the gravity of a churchman. Look upon the *Cinna* and the *Pompey;* they are not so properly to be called plays, as long discourses of reason of state; and *Polieucte* [16] in matters of religion is as solemn as the long stops upon our organs. Since that time it is grown into a custom, and their actors speak by the hour-glass, like our parsons; nay, they account it the grace of their parts, and think themselves disparaged by the poet if they may not twice or thrice in a play entertain the audience with a speech of an hundred lines. I deny not but this may suit well enough with the French; for as we, who are a more sullen people, come to be diverted at our plays, so they, who are of an airy and gay temper, come thither to make themselves more serious: and this I conceive to be one reason why comedies are more pleasing to us, and tragedies to them. But to speak generally: it cannot be denied that short speeches and replies are more apt to move the passions and beget concernment in us, than the other; for it is unnatural for anyone in a gust of passion to speak long together, or for another in the same condition to suffer him, without interruption. Grief and passion are like floods raised in little brooks by a sudden rain; they are quickly up; and if the concernment be poured unexpectedly in upon us, it overflows us: but a long sober shower gives them leisure to run out as they came in, without troubling the ordinary current. As for comedy, repartee is one of its chiefest graces; the greatest pleasure of the audience is a chase of wit, kept up on both sides, and swiftly managed. And this our forefathers, if not we, have had in Fletcher's plays, to a much higher degree of perfection than the French poets can reasonably hope to reach.

"There is another part of Lisideius his discourse, in which

[16] Pierre Corneille was the author of *Cinna, Pompey,* and *Polieucte.*

he rather excused our neighbors than commended them; that is, for aiming only to make one person considerable in their plays. 'Tis very true what he has urged, that one character in all plays, even without the poet's care, will have advantage of all the others; and that the design of the whole drama will chiefly depend on it. But this hinders not that there may be more shining characters in the play: many persons of a second magnitude, nay, some so very near, so almost equal to the first, that greatness may be opposed to greatness, and all the persons be made considerable, not only by their quality, but their action. 'Tis evident that the more the persons are, the greater will be the variety of the plot. If then the parts are managed so regularly that the beauty of the whole be kept entire, and that the variety become not a perplexed and confused mass of accidents, you will find it infinitely pleasing to be led in a labyrinth of design, where you see some of your way before you, yet discern not the end till you arrive at it. And that all this is practicable, I can produce for examples many of our English plays: as *The Maid's Tragedy, The Alchemist, The Silent Woman.* I was going to have named *The Fox*, but that the unity of design seems not exactly observed in it; for there appear two actions in the play; the first naturally ending with the fourth act; the second forced from it in the fifth: which yet is the less to be condemned in him, because the disguise of Volpone, though it suited not with his character as a crafty or covetous person, agreed well enough with that of a voluptuary; and by it the poet gained the end at which he aimed, the punishment of vice, and the reward of virtue, both which that disguise produced. So that to judge equally of it, it was an excellent fifth act, but not so naturally proceeding from the former.

"But to leave this, and pass to the latter part of Lisideius his discourse, which concerns relations: I must acknowledge with him, that the French have reason to hide that part of the action which would occasion too much tumult on the stage, and to choose rather to have it made known by narration to the audience. Farther, I think it very convenient, for the reasons he has given, that all incredible actions were removed; but whether custom has so insinuated itself into our countrymen, or nature has so formed them to fierceness, I know not; but they will scarcely suffer combats and other objects of horror to be taken from them. And indeed, the indecency of tumults is all which can be objected against fighting: for why may not our imagination as well suffer itself to be deluded with the probability of it, as with any other thing in the play? For my part, I can with as great ease persuade myself that the blows are given in good earnest, as I can that they who strike them are kings or princes, or those persons which they represent. For objects of incredibility, I would be satisfied from Lisideius, whether we have any so removed from all appearance of truth as are those of Corneille's *Andromède*; a play which has been frequented the most of any he has writ. If the Perseus, or the son of a heathen god, the Pegasus, and the Monster, were not capable to choke a strong belief, let him blame any representation of ours hereafter. Those indeed were objects of delight; yet the reason is the same as to the probability: for he makes it not a ballet or masque, but a play, which is to resemble truth. But for death, that it ought not to be represented, I have, besides the arguments alleged by Lisideius, the authority of Ben Jonson, who has forborne it in his tragedies; for both the death of Sejanus and Catiline are related: though in the latter I cannot but observe one irregularity of that great poet; he has removed the scene in the same act from Rome to Catiline's army, and from thence again to Rome; and besides, has allowed a very inconsiderable time, after Catiline's speech, for the striking of the battle, and the return of Petreius, who is to relate the event of it to the senate: which I should not animadvert on him, who was otherwise a painful observer of τὸ πρέπον, or the *decorum* of the stage, if he had not used extreme severity in his judgment on the incomparable Shakespeare for the same fault.—To conclude on this subject of relations; if we are to be blamed for showing too much of the action, the French are as faulty for discovering too little of it: a mean betwixt both should be observed by every judicious writer, so as the audience may neither be left unsatisfied by not seeing what is beautiful, or shocked by beholding what is either incredible or undecent.

"I hope I have already proved in this discourse that, though we are not altogether so punctual as the French in observing the laws of comedy, yet our errors are so few, and little, and those things wherein we excel them so considerable, that we ought of right to be preferred before them. But what will Lisideius say, if they themselves acknowledge they are too strictly bounded by those laws, for breaking which he has blamed the English? I will allege Corneille's words, as I find them in the end of his Discourse of the Three Unities: *Il est facile aux spéculatifs d'estre sévères,* etc. ' 'Tis easy for speculative persons to judge severely; but if they would produce to public view ten or twelve pieces of this nature, they would perhaps give more latitude to the rules than I have done, when by experience they had known how much we are limited and constrained by them, and how many beauties of the stage they banished from it.' To illustrate a little what he has said: By their servile observations of the unities of time and place, and integrity of scenes, they have brought on themselves that dearth of plot, and narrowness of imagination, which may be observed in all their plays. How many beautiful accidents might naturally happen in two or three days, which cannot arrive with any probability in the compass of twenty-four hours? There is time to be allowed also for maturity of design, which, amongst great and prudent persons, such as are often represented in tragedy, cannot, with any likelihood of truth, be brought to pass at so short a warning. Farther; by tying themselves strictly to the unity of place, and unbroken scenes, they are

forced many times to omit some beauties which cannot be
shown where the act began; but might, if the scene were
interrupted, and the stage cleared for the persons to enter in
another place; and therefore the French poets are often
forced upon absurdities; for if the act begins in a chamber,
all the persons in the play must have some business or other
to come thither, or else they are not to be shown that act;
and sometimes their characters are very unfitting to appear
there: as, suppose it were the king's bed-chamber; yet the
meanest man in the tragedy must come and dispatch his
business there, rather than in the lobby or courtyard (which
is fitter for him), for fear the stage should be cleared, and
the scenes broken. Many times they fall by it in a greater
inconvenience; for they keep their scenes unbroken, and yet
change the place; as in one of their newest plays,[17] where
the act begins in the street. There a gentleman is to meet
his friend; he sees him with his man, coming out from his
father's house; they talk together, and the first goes out:
the second, who is a lover, has made an appointment with
his mistress; she appears at the window, and then we are
to imagine the street lies under it. This gentleman is called
away, and leaves his servant with his mistress; presently her
father is heard from within; the young lady is afraid the
serving-man should be discovered, and thrusts him into a
place of safety, which is supposed to be her closet. After
this, the father enters to the daughter, and now the scene
is in a house; for he is seeking from one room to another
for this poor Philipin, or French Diego, who is heard from
within, drolling and breaking many a miserable conceit on
the subject of his sad condition. In this ridiculous manner
the play goes forward, the stage being never empty all the
while: so that the street, the window, the houses, and the
closet, are made to walk about, and the persons to stand

[17] Thomas Corneille's *L'Amour à la Mode*, Act III, with some inac-
curacies.

still. Now what, I beseech you, is more easy than to write a regular French play, or more difficult than to write an irregular English one, like those of Fletcher, or of Shakespeare?

"If they content themselves, as Corneille did, with some flat design, which, like an ill riddle, is found out ere it be half proposed, such plots we can make every way regular, as easily as they; but whenever they endeavor to rise to any quick turns and counterturns of plot, as some of them have attempted, since Corneille's plays have been less in vogue, you see they write as irregularly as we, though they cover it more speciously. Hence the reason is perspicuous why no French plays, when translated, have, or ever can succeed on the English stage. For if you consider the plots, our own are fuller of variety; if the writing, ours are more quick and fuller of spirit; and therefore 'tis a strange mistake in those who decry the way of writing plays in verse, as if the English therein imitated the French. We have borrowed nothing from them; our plots are weaved in English looms: we endeavor therein to follow the variety and greatness of characters which are derived to us from Shakespeare and Fletcher; the copiousness and well-knitting of the intrigues we have from Jonson; and for the verse itself we have the English precedents of elder date than any of Corneille's plays. Not to name our old comedies before Shakespeare, which were all writ in verse of six feet, or Alexandrines, such as the French now use, I can show in Shakespeare many scenes of rhyme together, and the like in Ben Jonson's tragedies: in *Catiline* and *Sejanus* sometimes thirty or forty lines, I mean besides the Chorus, or the monologues; which, by the way, showed Ben no enemy to this way of writing, especially if you read his *Sad Shepherd*, which goes sometimes on rhyme, sometimes on blank verse, like an horse who eases himself on trot and amble. You find him likewise commending Fletcher's pastoral of *The Faithful Shepherdess*, which is for the most part rhyme, though not refined to that purity to which it hath since been brought. And these examples are enough to clear us from a servile imitation of the French.

"But to return whence I have digressed: I dare boldly affirm these two things of the English drama: First, that we have many plays of ours as regular as any of theirs, and which, besides, have more variety of plot and characters; and secondly, that in most of the irregular plays of Shakespeare or Fletcher (for Ben Jonson's are for the most part regular), there is a more masculine fancy and greater spirit in the writing than there is in any of the French. I could produce, even in Shakespeare's and Fletcher's works, some plays which are almost exactly formed; as *The Merry Wives of Windsor*, and *The Scornful Lady:* but because (generally speaking) Shakespeare, who writ first, did not perfectly observe the laws of comedy, and Fletcher, who came nearer to perfection, yet through carelessness made many faults; I will take the pattern of a perfect play from Ben Jonson, who was a careful and learned observer of the dramatic laws, and from all his comedies I shall select *The Silent Woman;* of which I will make a short examen, according to those rules which the French observe."

As Neander was beginning to examine *The Silent Woman*, Eugenius, earnestly regarding him; "I beseech you, Neander," said he, "gratify the company, and me in particular, so far, as before you speak of the play, to give us a character of the author; and tell us frankly your opinion, whether you do not think all writers, both French and English, ought to give place to him."

"I fear," replied Neander, "that in obeying your commands I shall draw some envy on myself. Besides, in performing them, it will be first necessary to speak somewhat of Shakespeare and Fletcher, his rivals in poesy; and one of them, in my opinion, at least his equal, perhaps his superior.

"To begin, then, with Shakespeare. He was the man who

of all modern, and perhaps ancient poets, had the largest and most comprehensive soul. All the images of nature were still present to him, and he drew them, not laboriously, but luckily; when he describes anything, you more than see it, you feel it too. Those who accuse him to have wanted learning give him the greater commendation: he was naturally learned; he needed not the spectacles of books to read nature; he looked inwards, and found her there. I cannot say he is everywhere alike; were he so, I should do him injury to compare him with the greatest of mankind. He is many times flat, insipid; his comic wit degenerating into clenches, his serious swelling into bombast. But he is always great when some great occasion is presented to him; no man can say he ever had a fit subject for his wit and did not then raise himself as high above the rest of poets,

Quantum lenta solent inter viburna cupressi.[18]

The consideration of this made Mr. Hales [19] of Eton say that there is no subject of which any poet ever writ, but he would produce it much better done in Shakespeare; and however others are now generally preferred before him, yet the age wherein he lived, which had contemporaries with him Fletcher and Jonson, never equalled them to him in their esteem: and in the last king's court, when Ben's reputation was at highest, Sir John Suckling, and with him the greater part of the courtiers, set our Shakespeare far above him.

"Beaumont and Fletcher, of whom I am next to speak, had, with the advantage of Shakespeare's wit, which was their precedent, great natural gifts, improved by study: Beaumont especially being so accurate a judge of plays that Ben Jonson, while he lived, submitted all his writings to his censure, and, 'tis thought, used his judgment in correcting,

---

[18] As the cypresses tower among the humbler trees of the wayside.— Virgil, *Ec.*, I. 25.
[19] John Hales, Fellow of Eton, author of *The Golden Remains,* 1659.

if not contriving, all his plots. What value he had for him, appears by the verses he writ to him; and therefore I need speak no farther of it. The first play that brought Fletcher and him in esteem was their *Philaster:* for before that, they had written two or three very unsuccessfully, as the like is reported of Ben Jonson, before he writ *Every Man in His Humor.* Their plots were generally more regular than Shakespeare's, especially those which were made before Beaumont's death; and they understood and imitated the conversation of gentlemen much better; whose wild debaucheries, and quickness of wit in repartees, no poet before them could paint as they have done. Humor, which Ben Jonson derived from particular persons, they made it not their business to describe: they represented all the passions very lively, but above all, love. I am apt to believe the English language in them arrived to its highest perfection: what words have since been taken in, are rather superfluous than ornamental. Their plays are now the most pleasant and frequent entertainments of the stage; two of theirs being acted through the year for one of Shakespeare's or Jonson's: the reason is, because there is a certain gaiety in their comedies, and pathos in their more serious plays, which suit generally with all men's humors. Shakespeare's language is likewise a little obsolete, and Ben Jonson's wit comes short of theirs.

"As for Jonson, to whose character I am now arrived, if we look upon him while he was himself (for his last plays were but his dotages),[20] I think him the most learned and judicious writer which any theater ever had. He was a most severe judge of himself, as well as others. One cannot say he wanted wit, but rather that he was frugal of it. In his works you find little to retrench or alter. Wit, and language, and humor also in some measure we had before him; but something of art was wanting to the drama till he came. He managed his strength to more advantage than any who preceded him. You seldom find him making love in any of his scenes, or endeavoring to move the passions; his genius was too sullen

[20] *New Inn* and *Tale of a Tub.*

and saturnine to do it gracefully, especially when he knew he came after those who had performed both to such an height. Humor was his proper sphere; and in that he delighted most to represent mechanic people. He was deeply conversant in the ancients, both Greek and Latin, and he borrowed boldly from them: there is scarce a poet or historian among the Roman authors of those times whom he has not translated in *Sejanus* and *Catiline*. But he has done his robberies so openly, that one may see he fears not to be taxed by any law. He invades authors like a monarch; and what would be theft in other poets is only victory in him. With the spoils of these writers he so represents old Rome to us, in its rites, ceremonies, and customs, that if one of their poets had written either of his tragedies, we had seen less of it than in him. If there was any fault in his language, 'twas that he weaved it too closely and laboriously, in his comedies especially: perhaps, too, he did a little too much Romanize our tongue, leaving the words which he translated almost as much Latin as he found them: wherein, though he learnedly followed their language, he did not enough comply with the idiom of ours. If I would compare him with Shakespeare, I must acknowledge him the more correct poet, but Shakespeare the greater wit. Shakespeare was the Homer, or father of our dramatic poets; Jonson was the Virgil, the pattern of elaborate writing; I admire him, but I love Shakespeare. To conclude of him: as he has given us the most correct plays, so in the precepts which he has laid down in his *Discoveries*, we have as many and profitable rules for perfecting the stage as any wherewith the French can furnish us.

"Having thus spoken of the author, I proceed to the examination of his comedy, *The Silent Woman.*

Examen of the Silent Woman

"To begin first with the length of the action; it is so far from exceeding the compass of a natural day that it takes not up an artificial one. 'Tis all included in the limits of three

hours and a half, which is no more than is required for the
presentment on the stage: a beauty perhaps not much observed; if it had, we should not have looked on the Spanish
translation of *Five Hours* with so much wonder. The scene of
it is laid in London; the latitude of place is almost as little
as you can imagine; for it lies all within the compass of two
houses, and after the first act, in one. The continuity of scenes
is observed more than in any of our plays, except his own *Fox*
and *Alchemist*. They are not broken above twice or thrice
at most in the whole comedy; and in the two best of Corneille's
plays, the *Cid* and *Cinna,* they are interrupted once. The action of the play is entirely one; the end or aim of which is the
settling Morose's estate on Dauphine. The intrigue of it is
the greatest and most noble of any pure unmixed comedy in
any language; you see in it many persons of various characters and humors, and all delightful. At first, Morose, or an
old man, to whom all noise but his own talking is offensive.
Some who would be thought critics, say this humor of his is
forced: but to remove that objection, we may consider him
first to be naturally of a delicate hearing, as many are, to
whom all sharp sounds are unpleasant; and secondly, we
may attribute much of it to the peevishness of his age, or
the wayward authority of an old man in his own house, where
he may make himself obeyed; and to this the poet seems
to allude in his name Morose. Besides this, I am assured
from divers persons that Ben Jonson was actually acquainted
with such a man, one altogether as ridiculous as he is here
represented. Others say, it is not enough to find one man
of such an humor; it must be common to more, and the more
common the more natural. To prove this, they instance in
the best of comical characters, Falstaff: there are many men
resembling him: old, fat, merry, cowardly, drunken, amorous,
vain, and lying. But to convince these people, I need but
tell them that humor is the ridiculous extravagance of conversation, wherein one man differs from all others. If then
it be common, or communicated to many, how differs it

from other men's? or what indeed causes it to be ridiculous
so much as the singularity of it? As for Falstaff, he is not
properly one humor, but a miscellany of humors or images,
drawn from so many several men: that wherein he is singular
is his wit, or those things he says *præter expectatum,* unexpected by the audience; his quick evasions, when you imagine
him surprised, which, as they are extremely diverting of
themselves, so receive a great addition from his person; for
the very sight of such an unwieldy old debauched fellow is
a comedy alone. And here, having a place so proper for it,
I cannot but enlarge somewhat upon this subject of humor
into which I am fallen. The ancients had little of it in their
comedies; for the τὸ γελοῖον of the old comedy, of which
Aristophanes was chief, was not so much to imitate a man,
as to make the people laugh at some odd conceit, which had
commonly somewhat of unnatural or obscene in it. Thus,
when you see Socrates brought upon the stage, you are not
to imagine him made ridiculous by the imitation of his actions, but rather by making him perform something very
unlike himself; something so childish and absurd, as by comparing it with the gravity of the true Socrates, makes a
ridiculous object for the spectators. In their new comedy
which succeeded, the poets sought indeed to express the ἦθος,
as in their tragedies the πάθος of mankind. But this ἦθος contained only the general characters of man and manners; as
old men, lovers, serving-men, courtesans, parasites, and such
other persons as we see in their comedies; all which they
made alike: that is, one old man or father, one lover, one
courtesan, so like another as if the first of them had begot
the rest of every sort: *Ex homine hunc natum dicas.*[21] The
same custom they observed likewise in their tragedies. As
for the French, though they have the word *humeur* among
them, yet they have small use of it in their comedies or
farces; they being but ill imitations of the *ridiculum,* or
that which stirred up laughter in the old comedy. But among

---

[21] Terent. *Eun.* iii. 2. 7. "The one is the born image of the other."

the English 'tis otherwise: where by humor is meant some extravagant habit, passion, or affection, particular (as I have said before) to some one person, by the oddness of which he is immediately distinguished from the rest of men; which being lively and naturally represented, most frequently begets that malicious pleasure in the audience which is testified by laughter; as all things which are deviations from customs are ever the aptest to produce it: though by the way this laughter is only accidental, as the person represented is fantastic or bizarre, but pleasure is essential to it, as the imitation of what is natural. The description of these humors, drawn from the knowledge and observation of particular persons, was the particular genius and talent of Ben Jonson; to whose play I now return.

"Besides Morose, there are at least nine or ten different characters and humors in *The Silent Woman;* all which persons have several concernments of their own, yet are all used by the poet to the conducting of the main design to perfection. I shall not waste time in commending the writing of this play; but I will give you my opinion, that there is more wit and acuteness of fancy in it than in any of Ben Jonson's. Besides that he has here described the conversation of gentlemen in the persons of True-Wit and his friends with more gaiety, air, and freedom, than in the rest of his comedies. For the contrivance of the plot, 'tis extreme, elaborate, and yet withal easy; for the λύσις, or untying of it, 'tis so admirable, that when it is done, no one of the audience would think the poet could have missed it; and yet it was concealed so much before the last scene, that any other way would sooner have entered into your thoughts. But I dare not take upon me to commend the fabric of it, because it is altogether so full of art, that I must unravel every scene in it to commend it as I ought. And this excellent contrivance is still the more to be admired, because 'tis comedy where the persons are only of common rank, and their business private, not elevated by passions or high concernments, as in serious plays. Here everyone is a proper judge of all he sees, nothing is represented but that with which he daily converses: so that by consequence all faults lie open to discovery, and few are pardonable. 'Tis this which Horace has judiciously observed:

> *Creditur, ex medio quia res arcessit, habere*
> *Sudoris minimum; sed habet Comedia tanto*
> *Plus oneris, quanto veniæ minus.*[22]

"But our poet who was not ignorant of those difficulties has made use of all advantages; as he who designs a large leap takes his rise from the highest ground. One of these advantages is that which Corneille has laid down as the greatest which can arrive to any poem, and which he himself could never compass above thrice in all his plays; *viz.,* the making choice of some signal and long-expected day, whereon the action of the play is to depend. This day was that designed by Dauphine for the settling of his uncle's estate upon him; which to compass, he contrives to marry him. That the marriage had been plotted by him long beforehand is made evident by what he tells True-Wit in the second act, that in one moment he had destroyed what he had been raising many months.

"There is another artifice of the poet, which I cannot here omit, because by the frequent practice of it in his comedies he has left it to us almost as a rule; that is, when he has any character or humor wherein he would show a *coup de maistre,* or his highest skill, he recommends it to your observation by a pleasant description of it before the person first appears. Thus, in *Bartholomew Fair* he gives you the pictures of Numps and Cokes, and in this those of Daw, Lafoole, Morose, and the Collegiate Ladies; all which you hear described before you see them. So that before they come upon the stage, you have a longing expectation of them, which prepares you to receive them favorably; and

[22] Horace, *Epistles,* ii. 1. 168.

when they are there, even from their first appearance you are so far acquainted with them that nothing of their humor is lost to you.

"I will observe yet one thing further of this admirable plot: the business of it rises in every act. The second is greater than the first; the third than the second; and so forward to the fifth. There too you see, till the very last scene, new difficulties arising to obstruct the action of the play; and when the audience is brought into despair that the business can naturally be effected, then, and not before, the discovery is made. But that the poet might entertain you with more variety all this while, he reserves some new characters to show you, which he opens not till the second and third act; in the second Morose, Daw, the Barber, and Otter; in the third the Collegiate Ladies: all which he moves afterwards in by-walks, or under-plots, as diversions to the main design, lest it should grow tedious, though they are still naturally joined with it, and somewhere or other subservient to it. Thus, like a skillful chess-player, by little and little he draws out his men, and makes his pawns of use to his greater persons.

"If this comedy and some others of his were translated into French prose (which would now be no wonder to them, since Molière has lately given them plays out of verse, which have not displeased them), I believe the controversy would soon be decided betwixt the two nations, even making them the judges. But we need not call our heroes to our aid. Be it spoken to the honor of the English, our nation can never want in any age such who are able to dispute the empire of wit with any people in the universe. And though the fury of a civil war, and power for twenty years together abandoned to a barbarous race of men, enemies of all good learning, had buried the Muses under the ruins of monarchy; yet, with the restoration of our happiness, we see revived poesy lifting up its head, and already shaking off the rubbish which lay so heavy on it. We have seen since His Majesty's return, many dramatic poems which yield not to those of any foreign nation, and which deserve all laurels but the English. I will set aside flattery and envy: it cannot be denied but we have had some little blemish either in the plot or writing of all those plays which have been made within these seven years; (and perhaps there is no nation in the world so quick to discern them, or so difficult to pardon them, as ours): yet if we can persuade ourselves to use the candor of that poet, who, though the most severe of critics, has left us this caution by which to moderate our censures—

> *ubi plura nitent in carmine, non ego paucis*
> *Offendar maculis;—* [23]

if, in consideration of their many and great beauties, we can wink at some and little imperfections, if we, I say, can be thus equal to ourselves, I ask no favor from the French. And if I do not venture upon any particular judgment of our late plays, 'tis out of the consideration which an ancient writer gives me: *vivorum ut magna admiratio, ita censura difficilis:* betwixt the extremes of admiration and malice, 'tis hard to judge uprightly of the living. Only I think it may be permitted me to say that as it is no lessening to us to yield to some plays, and those not many, of our own nation in the last age, so can it be no addition to pronounce of our present poets, that they have far surpassed all the ancients, and the modern writers of other countries."

[23]   "If then a poem charm me in the main,
        Slight faults I'll not too rigidly arraign."
                    (Horace, *Ars Poet.,* 351, 352)

From the PREFACE TO THE TRANSLATION OF OVID'S EPISTLES [1]

ALL TRANSLATION, I suppose, may be reduced to these three heads.

First, that of metaphrase, or turning an author word by word and line by line from one language into another. Thus, or near this manner, was Horace his *Art of Poetry* translated by Ben Jonson. The second way is that of paraphrase, or translation with latitude, where the author is kept in view by the translator so as never to be lost, but his words are not so strictly followed as his sense; and that too is admitted to be amplified, but not altered. Such is Mr. Waller's translation of Virgil's Fourth *Æneid*. The third way is that of imitation, where the translator (if now he has not lost that name) assumes the liberty, not only to vary from the words and sense, but to forsake them both as he sees occasion; and taking only some general hints from the original, to run division on the groundwork, as he pleases. Such is Mr. Cowley's practice in turning two Odes of Pindar and one of Horace into English.

Concerning the first of these methods, our master Horace has given us this caution:

> *Nec verbum verbo curabis reddere, fidus*
> *Interpres . . .*

> Nor word for word too faithfully translate;

as the Earl of Roscommon has excellently rendered it. Too faithfully is, indeed, pedantically: 'Tis a faith like that which proceeds from superstition, blind and zealous. Take it in the expression of Sir John Denham to Sir Richard Fanshaw, on his version of the *Pastor Fido*:

[1] Text: 1683, third edition.

756

That servile path thou nobly dost decline,
Of tracing word by word, and line by line:
A new and nobler way thou dost pursue,
To make translations and translators too:
They but preserve the ashes, thou the flame,
True to his sense, but truer to his fame.

'Tis almost impossible to translate verbally, and well,
at the same time; for the Latin (a most severe and compendious language) often expresses that in one word, which
either the barbarity or the narrowness of modern tongues
cannot supply in more. 'Tis frequent, also, that the conceit
is couched in some expression which will be lost in English:

Atque iidem venti vela fidemque ferent.

What poet of our nation is so happy as to express this thought
literally in English, and to strike wit, or almost sense, out of
it?

In short, the verbal copier is encumbered with so many
difficulties at once that he can never disentangle himself
from all. He is to consider at the same time the thought of
his author and his words, and to find out the counterpart to
each in another language; and, besides this, he is to confine himself to the compass of numbers and the slavery of
rhyme. 'Tis much like dancing on ropes with fettered legs:
a man may shun a fall by using caution; but the gracefulness of motion is not to be expected: and when we have said
the best of it, 'tis but a foolish task; for no sober man would
put himself into a danger for the applause of escaping without breaking his neck. We see Ben Jonson could not avoid
obscurity in his literal translation of Horace, attempted in
the same compass of lines; nay, Horace himself could scarce
have done it to a Greek poet:

Brevis esse laboro, obscurus fio:

either perspicuity or gracefulness will frequently be wanting. Horace has indeed avoided both these rocks in his translation of the three first lines of Homer's *Odysseis,* which
he has contracted into two:

> *Dic mihi musa virum captæ post tempora Trojæ,*
> *Qui mores hominum multorum vidit, et urbes.*

Muse, speak the man, who, since the siege of Troy,
So many towns, such change of manners saw.
                                    —Earl of Roscommon

But then the sufferings of Ulysses, which are a considerable part of the sentence, are omitted:

> Ὃς μάλα πολλὰ πλάγχθη.

The consideration of these difficulties, in a servile, literal
translation, not long since made two of our famous wits, Sir
John Denham and Mr. Cowley, to contrive another way of
turning authors into our tongue, called, by the latter of
them, imitation. As they were friends, I suppose they communicated their thoughts on this subject to each other;
and therefore their reasons for it are little different, though
the practice of one is much more moderate. I take imitation
of an author, in their sense, to be an endeavor of a later poet
to write like one who has written before him on the same
subject; that is, not to translate his words or to be confined
to his sense, but only to set him as a pattern and to write
as he supposes that author would have done, had he lived
in our age and in our country. Yet I dare not say that either
of them have [sic] carried this libertine way of rendering
authors (as Mr. Cowley calls it) so far as my definition
reaches; for in the *Pindaric Odes,* the customs and ceremonies of ancient Greece are still preserved. But I know not
what mischief may arise hereafter from the example of such
an innovation when writers of unequal parts to him shall
imitate so bold an undertaking. To add and to diminish what

we please, which is the way avowed by him, ought only to
be granted to Mr. Cowley, and that too only in his translation of Pindar; because he alone was able to make him
amends by giving him better of his own, whenever he refused his author's thoughts. Pindar is generally known to
be a dark writer, to want connection (I mean as to our understanding), to soar out of sight, and leave his reader at a
gaze. So wild and ungovernable a poet cannot be translated
literally; his genius is too strong to bear a chain, and Samson-
like he shakes it off. A genius so elevated and unconfined as
Mr. Cowley's, was but necessary to make Pindar speak English, and that was to be performed by no other way than
imitation. But if Virgil, or Ovid, or any regular intelligible
authors, be thus used, 'tis no longer to be called their work,
when neither the thoughts nor words are drawn from the
original; but instead of them there is something new produced, which is almost the creation of another hand. By this
way, 'tis true, somewhat that is excellent may be invented,
perhaps more excellent than the first design; though Virgil
must still be excepted, when that *perhaps* takes place. Yet
he who is inquisitive to know an author's thoughts will be
disappointed in his expectation; and 'tis not always that a
man will be contented to have a present made him, when he
expects the payment of a debt. To state it fairly, imitation
of an author is the most advantageous way for a translator
to show himself, but the greatest wrong which can be done
to the memory and reputation of the dead. Sir John Denham
(who advised more liberty than he took himself) gives his
reason for his innovation, in his admirable Preface before
the translation of the Second Æneid: *Poetry is of so subtile
a spirit, that, in pouring out of one language into another, it
will all evaporate; and, if a new spirit be not added in the
transfusion, there will remain nothing but a caput mortuum.*
I confess this argument holds good against a literal translation; but who defends it? Imitation and verbal version are,
in my opinion, the two extremes which ought to be avoided;

and therefore, when I have proposed the mean betwixt them, it will be seen how far this argument will reach.

No man is capable of translating poetry, who, besides a genius to that art, is not a master both of his author's language and of his own; nor must we understand the language only of the poet, but his particular turn of thoughts and expression, which are the characters that distinguish, and as it were individuate him from all other writers. When we are come thus far, 'tis time to look into ourselves, to conform our genius to his, to give his thought either the same turn, if our tongue will bear it, or, if not, to vary but the dress, not to alter or destroy the substance. The like care must be taken of the more outward ornaments, the words. When they appear (which is but seldom) literally graceful, it were an injury to the author that they should be changed. But since every language is so full of its own proprieties, that which is beautiful in one is often barbarous, nay sometimes nonsense, in another, it would be unreasonable to limit a translator to the narrow compass of his author's words: 'tis enough if he choose out some expression which does not vitiate the sense. I suppose he may stretch his chain to such a latitude; but by the innovation of thoughts, methinks he breaks it. By this means the spirit of an author may be transfused and yet not lost: and thus 'tis plain, that the reason alleged by Sir John Denham has no further force than to expression; for thought, if it be translated truly, cannot be lost in another language; but the words that convey it to our apprehension (which are the image and ornament of that thought) may be so ill chosen, as to make it appear in an unhandsome dress, and rob it of its native luster. There is, therefore, a liberty to be allowed for the expression; neither is it necessary that words and lines should be confined to the measure of their original. The sense of an author, generally speaking, is to be sacred and inviolable. If the fancy of Ovid be luxuriant, 'tis his character to be so; and if I retrench it, he is no longer Ovid. It will be replied, that he receives the advantage by this lopping of his superfluous branches; but I rejoin, that a translator has no such right. When a painter copies from the life, I suppose he has no privilege to alter features and lineaments under pretense that his picture will look better: perhaps the face which he has drawn would be more exact if the eye or nose were altered; but 'tis his business to make it resemble the original. In two cases only there may a seeming difficulty arise; that is, if the thought be notoriously trivial or dishonest; but the same answer will serve for both, that then they ought not to be translated:

> *Et quæ*
> *Desperes tractata nitescere posse, relinquas.*

Thus I have ventured to give my opinion on this subject against the authority of two great men, but I hope without offense to either of their memories; for I both loved them living and reverence them now they are dead. But if, after what I have urged, it be thought by better judges that the praise of a translation consists in adding new beauties to the piece, thereby to recompense the loss which it sustains by change of language, I shall be willing to be taught better and to recant. In the meantime it seems to me that the true reason why we have so few versions which are tolerable is not from the too close pursuing of the author's sense, but because there are so few who have all the talents which are requisite for translation, and that there is so little praise and so small encouragement for so considerable a part of learning . . .

PREFACE TO THE "FABLES" [1]

'TIS WITH a poet, as with a man who designs to build and is very exact, as he supposes, in casting up the cost beforehand; but, generally speaking, he is mistaken in his account and reckons short of the expense he first intended. He alters his mind as the work proceeds and will have this or that convenience more, of which he had not thought when he began. So has it happened to me; I have built a house, where I intended but a lodge; yet with better success than a certain nobleman, who, beginning with a dog-kennel, never lived to finish the palace he had contrived.[2]

From translating the first of Homer's *Iliads* (which I intended as an essay to the whole work), I proceeded to the translation of the twelfth book of Ovid's *Metamorphoses,* because it contains, among other things, the causes, the beginning, and ending of the Trojan war. Here I ought in reason to have stopped; but the speeches of Ajax and Ulysses lying next in my way, I could not balk 'em. When I had compassed them, I was so taken with the former part of the fifteenth book (which is the masterpiece of the whole *Metamorphoses*), that I enjoined myself the pleasing task of rendering it into English. And now I found by the number of my verses that they began to swell into a little volume, which gave me an occasion of looking backward on some beauties of my author in his former books; there occurred to me the *Hunting of the Boar, Cinyras and Myrrha,* the good-natured story of *Baucis and Philemon,* with the rest, which I hope I have translated closely enough, and given them the same turn of verse which they had in the original; and this, I may say without vanity, is not the talent of every poet. He who has arrived the nearest to it, is the ingenious

---

[1] Text: first edition, 1700.

[2] Scott notes this as a probable allusion to the Duke of Buckingham's mansion at Cliveden.

and learned Sandys,[3] the best versifier of the former age; if I may properly call it by that name, which was the former part of this concluding century. For Spenser and Fairfax [4] both flourished in the reign of Queen Elizabeth; great masters in our language, and who saw much further into the beauties of our numbers than those who immediately followed them. Milton was the poetical son of Spenser, and Mr. Waller of Fairfax; for we have our lineal descents and clans as well as other families. Spenser more than once insinuates that the soul of Chaucer was transfused into his body, and that he was begotten by him two hundred years after his decease. Milton has acknowledged to me that Spenser was his original, and many besides myself have heard our famous Waller own that he derived the harmony of his numbers from *Godfrey of Bulloigne,* which was turned into English by Mr. Fairfax.

But to return: having done with Ovid for this time, it came into my mind that our old English poet, Chaucer, in many things resembled him, and that with no disadvantage on the side of the modern author, as I shall endeavor to prove when I compare them; and as I am, and always have been, studious to promote the honor of my native country, so I soon resolved to put their merits to the trial by turning some of the *Canterbury Tales* into our language, as it is now refined; for by this means, both the poets being set in the same light, and dressed in the same English habit, story to be compared with story, a certain judgment may be made betwixt them by the reader, without obtruding my opinion on him. Or, if I seem partial to my countryman and predecessor in the laurel, the friends of antiquity are not few; and, besides many of the learned, Ovid has almost all the beaux and the whole fair sex, his declared patrons. Perhaps I have assumed somewhat more to myself than they allow me, be-

[3] George Sandys (1578–1644). Sandys' translation of the Psalms was published 1636. His *Ovid's Metamorphoses, Englished By G.S.,* 1626.

[4] Edward Fairfax (d. 1635). *Godfrey of Bulloigne* is an excellent translation of Tasso's *Jerusalem Delivered,* 1600.

cause I have adventured to sum up the evidence; but the
readers are the jury, and their privilege remains entire, to
decide according to the merits of the cause; or, if they please,
to bring it to another hearing before some other court. In the
meantime, to follow the thread of my discourse (as thoughts,
according to Mr. Hobbes, have always some connection),
so from Chaucer I was led to think on Boccace, who was
not only his contemporary, but also pursued the same studies:
wrote novels in prose, and many works in verse; particularly
is said to have invented the octave rhyme, or stanza of eight
lines, which ever since has been maintained by the practice
of all Italian writers who are, or at least assume the title
of, heroic poets. He and Chaucer, among other things, had
this in common, that they refined their mother-tongues;
but with this difference, that Dante had begun to file their
language, at least in verse, before the time of Boccace, who
likewise received no little help from his master Petrarch;
but the reformation of their prose was wholly owing to Boccace himself, who is yet the standard of purity in the Italian
tongue, though many of his phrases are become obsolete,
as in process of time it must needs happen. Chaucer (as you
have formerly been told by our learned Mr. Rymer) first
adorned and amplified our barren tongue from the Provençal,[5] which was then the most polished of all the modern
languages; but this subject has been copiously treated by
that great critic, who deserves no little commendation from
us his countrymen. For these reasons of time, and resemblance of genius in Chaucer and Boccace, I resolved to join
them in my present work; to which I have added some
original papers of my own, which whether they are equal
or inferior to my other poems, an author is the most improper judge; and therefore I leave them wholly to the mercy
of the reader. I will hope the best, that they will not be
condemned; but if they should, I have the excuse of an

[5] Rymer was in error on this point; see "Provencial Poetry" in the *Short
View of Tragedy.*

old gentleman, who, mounting on horseback before some ladies, when I was present, got up somewhat heavily, but desired of the fair spectators that they would count four-score-and-eight before they judged him. By the mercy of God, I am already come within twenty years of his number; a cripple in my limbs, but what decays are in my mind the reader must determine. I think myself as vigorous as ever in the faculties of my soul, excepting only my memory, which is not impaired to any great degree: and if I lose not more of it, I have no great reason to complain. What judgment I had, increases rather than diminishes; and thoughts, such as they are, come crowding in so fast upon me, that my only difficulty is to choose or to reject, to run them into verse, or to give them the other harmony of prose; I have so long studied and practiced both, that they are grown into a habit, and become familiar to me. In short, though I may lawfully plead some part of the old gentleman's excuse, yet I will reserve it till I think I have greater need and ask no grains of allowance for the faults of this my present work, but those which are given of course to human frailty. I will not trouble my reader with the shortness of time in which I writ it, or the several intervals of sickness. They who think too well of their own performances are apt to boast in their prefaces how little time their works have cost them, and what other business of more importance interfered; but the reader will be as apt to ask the question, why they allowed not a longer time to make their work more perfect? and why they had so despicable an opinion of their judges as to thrust their in-digested stuff upon them, as if they deserved no better?

With this account of my present undertaking, I conclude the first part of this discourse; in the second part, as at a second sitting, though I alter not the draft, I must touch the same features over again, and change the dead-coloring of the whole. In general I will only say that I have written nothing which savors of immorality or profaneness; at least, I am not conscious to myself of any such intention.

If there happen to be found an irreverent expression, or a thought too wanton, they are crept into my verses through my inadvertency; if the searchers find any in the cargo, let them be staved or forfeited, like counter-banned goods; at least, let their authors be answerable for them, as being but imported merchandise, and not of my own manufacture. On the other side, I have endeavored to choose such fables, both ancient and modern, as contain in each of them some instructive moral; which I could prove by induction, but the way is tedious, and they leap foremost into sight without the reader's trouble of looking after them. I wish I could affirm, with a safe conscience, that I had taken the same care in all my former writings; for it must be owned, that supposing verses are never so beautiful or pleasing, yet, if they contain anything which shocks religion or good manners, they are at best what Horace says of good numbers without good sense, *Versus inopes rerum, nugæque conoræ.* Thus far, I hope, I am right in court, without renouncing to my other right of self-defense, where I have been wrongfully accused, and my sense wire-drawn into blasphemy or bawdry, as it has often been by a religious lawyer, in a late pleading against the stage;[6] in which he mixes truth with falsehood, and has not forgotten the old rule of calumniating strongly that something may remain.

I resume the thread of my discourse with the first of my translations, which was the first *Iliad* of Homer. If it shall please God to give me longer life and moderate health, my intentions are to translate the whole *Ilias;* provided still that I meet with those encouragements from the public which may enable me to proceed in my undertaking with some cheerfulness. And this I dare assure the world beforehand, that I have found, by trial, Homer a more pleasing task than Virgil (though I say not the translation will be less laborious); for the Grecian is more according to my

---

[6] Jeremy Collier (1650–1726), whose *Short View of the Immorality and Profaneness of the Stage* was published in 1698.

genius than the Latin poet. In the works of the two authors we may read their manners and natural inclinations, which are wholly different. Virgil was of a quiet, sedate temper; Homer was violent, impetuous, and full of fire. The chief talent of Virgil was propriety of thoughts and ornament of words; Homer was rapid in his thoughts and took all the liberties, both of numbers and of expressions, which his language and the age in which he lived, allowed him. Homer's invention was more copious, Virgil's more confined; so that if Homer had not led the way, it was not in Virgil to have begun heroic poetry; for nothing can be more evident than that the Roman poem is but the second part of the *Ilias:* a continuation of the same story, and the persons already formed. The manners of Æneas are those of Hector, super-added to those which Homer gave him. The adventures of Ulysses in the *Odysseis* are imitated in the first six books of Virgil's *Æneis;* and though the accidents are not the same (which would have argued him of a servile copying, and total barrenness of invention), yet the seas were the same in which both heroes wandered; and Dido cannot be denied to be the poetical daughter of Calypso. The six latter books of Virgil's poem are the four-and-twenty *Iliads* contracted: a quarrel occasioned by a lady, a single combat, battles fought, and a town besieged. I say not this in derogation to Virgil, neither do I contradict anything which I have formerly said in his just praise; for his episodes are almost wholly of his own invention, and the form which he has given to the telling makes the tale his own, even though the original story had been the same. But this proves, however, that Homer taught Virgil to design; and if invention be the first virtue of an epic poet, then the Latin poem can only be allowed a second place. Mr. Hobbes, in the preface to his own bald translation of the *Ilias* (studying poetry as he did mathe-matics, when it was too late), Mr. Hobbes, I say, begins the praise of Homer where he should have ended it. He tells us that the first beauty of an epic poem consists in diction; that is, in the choice of words, and harmony of numbers. Now the words are the coloring of the work, which, in the order of nature, is last to be considered. The design, the disposition, the manners, and the thoughts, are all before it: where any of those are wanting or imperfect, so much wants or is imperfect in the imitation of human life, which is in the very definition of a poem. Words, indeed, like glaring colors, are the first beauties that arise and strike the sight; but, if the draft be false or lame, the figures ill disposed, the manners obscure or inconsistent, or the thoughts unnatural, then the finest colors are but daubing, and the piece is a beautiful monster at the best. Neither Virgil nor Homer were [sic] deficient in any of the former beauties; but in this last, which is expression, the Roman poet is at least equal to the Grecian, as I have said elsewhere; supplying the poverty of his language by his musical ear, and by his diligence.

But to return: our two great poets being so different in their tempers, one choleric and sanguine, the other phlegmatic and melancholic; that which makes them excel in their several ways is that each of them has followed his own natural inclination, as well in forming the design, as in the execution of it. The very heroes show their authors: Achilles is hot, impatient, revengeful—

Impiger, iracundus, inexorabilis, acer, etc.

Æneas patient, considerate, careful of his people, and merciful to his enemies; ever submissive to the will of heaven—

. . . quo fata trahunt retrahuntque, sequamur.

I could please myself with enlarging on this subject, but am forced to defer it to a fitter time. From all I have said, I will only draw this inference, that the action of Homer, being more full of vigor than that of Virgil, according to the temper of the writer, is of consequence more pleasing to the reader. One warms you by degrees; the other sets you on fire all at once and never intermits his heat. 'Tis the same

difference which Longinus makes betwixt the effects of eloquence in Demosthenes and Tully.[7] One persuades, the other
commands. You never cool while you read Homer, even not
in the second book (a graceful flattery to his countrymen);
but he hastens from the ships, and concludes not that book
till he has made you an amends by the violent playing of a
new machine.[8] From thence he hurries on his action with
variety of events, and ends it in less compass than two months.
This vehemence of his, I confess, is more suitable to my
temper; and, therefore, I have translated his first book with
greater pleasure than any part of Virgil; but it was not a
pleasure without pains. The continual agitations of the spirits
must needs be a weakening of any constitution, especially
in age; and many pauses are required for refreshment betwixt the heats; the *Iliad* of itself being a third part longer
than all Virgil's works together.

This is what I thought needful in this place to say of
Homer. I proceed to Ovid and Chaucer, considering the
former only in relation to the latter. With Ovid ended the
Golden Age of the Roman tongue; from Chaucer the purity
of the English tongue began. The manners of the poets were
not unlike. Both of them were well-bred, well-natured, amorous, and libertine, at least in their writings: it may be also
in their lives. Their studies were the same, philosophy and
philology. Both of them were knowing in astronomy; of
which Ovid's books of the Roman Feasts, and Chaucer's
Treatise of the Astrolabe, are sufficient witnesses. But Chaucer was likewise an astrologer, as were Virgil, Horace, Persius,
and Manilius. Both writ with wonderful facility and clearness; neither were great inventors: for Ovid only copied the
Grecian fables, and most of Chaucer's stories were taken
from his Italian contemporaries, or their predecessors. Boccace his *Decameron* was first published, and from thence
our Englishman has borrowed many of his *Canterbury Tales;*

---

[7] Longinus, *On the Sublime*, c. 12.
[8] Dryden has reversed the chronology here.

yet that of *Palamon and Arcite* was written, in all probability, by some Italian wit, in a former age, as I shall prove hereafter. The tale of Griselda was the invention of Petrarch; by him sent to Boccace, from whom it came to Chaucer. *Troilus and Criseyde* was also written by a Lombard author, but much amplified by our English translator, as well beautified; the genius of our countrymen, in general, being rather to improve an invention than to invent themselves, as is evident not only in our poetry, but in many of our manufactures. I find I have anticipated already, and taken up from Boccace before I come to him; but there is so much less behind; and I am of the temper of most kings, who love to be in debt, are all for present money, no matter how they pay it afterwards; besides, the nature of a preface is rambling, never wholly out of the way, nor in it. This I have learned from the practice of honest Montaigne, and return at my pleasure to Ovid and Chaucer, of whom I have little more to say.

Both of them built on the inventions of other men; yet since Chaucer had something of his own, as *The Wife of Bath's Tale, The Cock and the Fox,* which I have translated, and some others, I may justly give our countryman the precedence in that part; since I can remember nothing of Ovid which was wholly his. Both of them understood the manners, under which name I comprehend the passions, and, in a larger sense, the descriptions of persons, and their very habits. For an example, I see Baucis and Philemon as perfectly before me, as if some ancient painter had drawn them; and all the pilgrims in the *Canterbury Tales,* their humors, their features, and the very dress, as distinctly as if I had supped with them at the Tabard in Southwark. Yet even there, too, the figures of Chaucer are much more lively, and set in a better light; which though I have not time to prove, yet I appeal to the reader, and am sure he will clear me from partiality. The thoughts and words remain to be considered in the comparison of the two poets, and I have saved myself one-half of that labor, by owning that Ovid lived when the Roman tongue was in its meridian; Chaucer, in the dawning of our language; therefore that part of the comparison stands not on an equal foot, any more than the diction of Ennius and Ovid, or of Chaucer and our present English. The words are given up, as a post not to be defended in our poet, because he wanted the modern art of fortifying. The thoughts remain to be considered; and they are to be measured only by their propriety; that is, as they flow more or less naturally from the persons described, on such and such occasions. The vulgar judges, which are nine parts in ten of all nations, who call conceits and jingles wit, who see Ovid full of them and Chaucer altogether without them, will think me little less than mad for preferring the Englishman to the Roman. Yet, with their leave, I must presume to say that the things they admire are only glittering trifles, and so far from being witty, that in a serious poem they are nauseous, because they are unnatural. Would any man who is ready to die for love describe his passion like Narcissus? Would he think of *inopem me copia fecit,* and a dozen more of such expressions, poured on the neck of one another, and signifying all the same thing? If this were wit, was this a time to be witty, when the poor wretch was in the agony of death? This is just John Littlewit, in *Bartholomew Fair,* who had a conceit (as he tells you) left him in his misery; a miserable conceit. On these occasions the poet should endeavor to raise pity; but, instead of this, Ovid is tickling you to laugh. Virgil never made use of such machines when he was moving you to commiserate the death of Dido: he would not destroy what he was building. Chaucer makes Arcite violent in his love, and unjust in the pursuit of it; yet when he came to die, he made him think more reasonably: he repents not of his love, for that had altered his character; but acknowledges the injustice of his proceedings, and resigns Emilia to Palamon. What would Ovid have done on this occasion? He would certainly have made Arcite witty on his death-bed; he had complained he was further off from possession, by being so near, and a thousand such boyisms, which Chaucer rejected as below the dignity of the subject. They who think otherwise, would, by the same reason, prefer Lucan and Ovid to Homer and Virgil, and Martial to all four of them. As for the turn of words, in which Ovid particularly excells all poets, they are sometimes a fault and sometimes a beauty, as they are used properly or improperly; but in strong passions always to be shunned, because passions are serious, and will admit no playing. The French have a high value for them; and, I confess, they are often what they call delicate, when they are introduced with judgment; but Chaucer writ with more simplicity, and followed nature more closely than to use them. I have thus far, to the best of my knowledge, been an upright judge betwixt the parties in competition, not meddling with the design nor the disposition of it; because the design was not their own; and in the disposing of it they were equal. It remains that I say somewhat of Chaucer in particular.

In the first place, as he is the father of English poetry, as I hold him in the same degree of veneration as the Grecians held Homer, or the Romans Virgil. He is a perpetual fountain of good sense; learned in all sciences; and, therefore, speaks properly on all subjects. As he knew what to say, so he knows also when to leave off; a continence which is practiced by few writers, and scarcely by any of the ancients, excepting Virgil and Horace. One of our late great poets [9] is sunk in his reputation, because he could never forgive any conceit which came in his way; but swept like a drag-net, great and small. There was plenty enough, but the dishes were ill sorted; whole pyramids of sweet-meats for boys and women, but little of solid meat for men. All this proceeded not from any want of knowledge, but of judgment. Neither did he want that in discerning the beauties and faults of other poets, but only indulged himself in the luxury of writing;

[9] Cowley.

and perhaps knew it was a fault, but hoped the reader would not find it. For this reason, though he must always be thought a great poet, he is no longer esteemed a good writer; and for ten impressions which his works have had in so many successive years, yet at present a hundred books are scarcely purchased once a twelve-month; for, as my last lord Rochester said, though somewhat profanely, "Not being of God, he could not stand."

Chaucer followed nature everywhere, but was never so bold to go beyond her; and there is a great difference of being *poeta* and *nimis poeta*, if we may believe Catullus,[10] as much as betwixt a modest behavior and affectation. The verse of Chaucer, I confess, is not harmonious to us; but 'tis like the eloquence of one whom Tacitus commends, it was *auribus istius temporis accommodata:* they who lived with him, and some time after him, thought it musical; and it continues so, even in our judgment, if compared with the numbers of Lydgate and Gower, his contemporaries; there is the rude sweetness of a Scotch tune in it, which is natural and pleasing, though not perfect. 'Tis true, I cannot go so far as he who published the last edition of him; [11] for he would make us believe the fault is in our ears, and that there were really ten syllables in a verse where we find but nine; but this opinion is not worth confuting; 'tis so gross and obvious an error that common sense (which is a rule in everything but matters of faith and revelation) must convince the reader that equality of numbers in every verse which we call heroic was either not known, or not always practiced in Chaucer's age. It were an easy matter to produce some thousands of his verses which are lame for want of half a foot, and sometimes a whole one, and which no pronunciation can make otherwise. We can only say that he lived in the infancy of our poetry, and that nothing is brought to perfection at the first. We must be children be-

---

[10] Dryden means Martial. See *Epigrams*, iii. 44.
[11] Thomas Speght. See the Preface for the passage.

fore we grow men. There was an Ennius, and in process of
time a Lucilius, and a Lucretius before Virgil and Horace;
even after Chaucer there was a Spenser, a Harington,[12] a
Fairfax, before Waller and Denham were in being; and our
numbers were in their nonage till these last appeared. I need
say little of his parentage, life, and fortunes; they are to
be found at large in all the editions of his works. He was
employed abroad, and favored by Edward the Third, Richard
the Second, and Henry the Fourth, and was poet, as I suppose, to all three of them. In Richard's time, I doubt, he
was a little dipped in the rebellion of the Commons; and
being brother-in-law to John of Gaunt, it was no wonder if
he followed the fortunes of that family; and was well with
Henry the Fourth when he had deposed his predecessor.
Neither is it to be admired that Henry, who was a wise as
well as a valiant prince, who claimed by succession, and
was sensible that his title was not sound, but was rightfully
in Mortimer, who had married the heir of York; it was not
to be admired, I say, if that great politician should be
pleased to have the greatest wit of those times in his interests, and to be the trumpet of his praises. Augustus had
given him the example, by the advice of Mæcenas, who
recommended Virgil and Horace to him; whose praises
helped to make him popular while he was alive, and after
his death have made him precious to posterity. As for the
religion of our poet, he seems to have some little bias towards
the opinions of Wycliffe after John of Gaunt his patron;
somewhat of which appears in the tale of *Piers Plowman;*
yet I cannot blame him for inveighing so sharply against
the vices of the clergy in his age: their pride, their ambition, their pomp, their avarice, their worldly interest, deserved the lashes which he gave them, both in that and in
most of his *Canterbury Tales.* Neither has his contemporary
Boccace spared them; yet both those poets lived in much
esteem with good and holy men in orders, for the scandal

---

[12] Sir John Harington, translator of Ariosto's *Orlando Furioso,* 1591.

which is given by particular priests reflects not on the sacred
function. Chaucer's Monk, his Canon, and his Friar took
not from the character of his Good Parson. A satirical poet
is the check of the laymen on bad priests. We are only to
take care that we involve not the innocent with the guilty in
the same condemnation. The good cannot be too much honored, nor the bad too coarsely used; for the corruption of
the best becomes the worst. When a clergyman is whipped,
his gown is first taken off, by which the dignity of his order
is secured. If he be wrongfully accused, he has his action
of slander; and 'tis at the poet's peril if he transgress the
law. But they will tell us that all kind of satire, though never
so well deserved by particular priests, yet brings the whole
order into contempt. Is then the peerage of England anything dishonored when a peer suffers for his treason? If he
be libeled or any way defamed, he has his *scandalum mag-
natum* to punish the offender. They who use this kind of
argument seem to be conscious to themselves of somewhat
which has deserved the poet's lash, and are less concerned
for their public capacity than for their private; at least there
is pride at the bottom of their reasoning. If the faults of
men in orders are only to be judged among themselves, they
are all in the same sort parties; for, since they say the honor
of their order is concerned in every member of it, how can
we be sure that they will be impartial judges? How far I
may be allowed to speak my opinion in this case, I know not;
but I am sure a dispute of this nature caused mischief in
abundance betwixt a King of England and an Archbishop
of Canterbury; [13] one standing up for the laws of his land,
and the other for the honor (as he called it) of God's church;
which ended in the murder of the prelate, and in the whipping
of his Majesty from post to pillar for his penance. The
learned and ingenious Dr. Drake [14] has saved me the labor

[13] Henry II and Thomas à Becket.
[14] James Drake's answer to Collier, *The Ancient and Modern Stages Re-
viewed,* was published in 1699.

of inquiring into the esteem and reverence which the priests
have had of old; and I would rather extend than diminish
any part of it; yet I must needs say that when a priest pro-
vokes me without any occasion given him, I have no reason,
unless it be the charity of a Christian, to forgive him: *prior
læsit* is justification sufficient in the civil law. If I answer
him in his own language, self-defense I am sure must be
allowed me; and if I carry it further, even to a sharp re-
crimination, somewhat may be indulged to human frailty.
Yet my resentment has not wrought so far but that I have
followed Chaucer in his character of a holy man, and have
enlarged on that subject with some pleasure; reserving to
myself the right, if I shall think fit hereafter, to describe
another sort of priests, such as are more easily to be found
than the Good Parson; such as have given the last blow to
Christianity in this age by a practice so contrary to their
doctrine. But this will keep cold till another time. In the
meanwhile, I take up Chaucer where I left him.

He must have been a man of a most wonderful comprehensive nature, because, as it has been truly observed of
him, he has taken into the compass of his *Canterbury Tales*
the various manners and humors (as we now call them) of
the whole English nation, in his age. Not a single character
has escaped him. All his pilgrims are severally distinguished
from each other; and not only in their inclinations but in
their very physiognomies and persons. Baptista Porta [15]
could not have described their natures better than by the
marks which the poet gives them. The matter and manner
of their tales, and of their telling, are so suited to their different educations, humors, and callings that each of them
would be improper in any other mouth. Even the grave and
serious characters are distinguished by their several sorts
of gravity: their discourses are such as belong to their age,
their calling, and their breeding; such as are becoming of

---

[15] A physician of Naples who wrote on physiognomy.

them, and of them only. Some of his persons are vicious, and some virtuous; some are unlearned, or (as Chaucer calls them) lewd, and some are learned. Even the ribaldry of the low characters is different: the Reeve, the Miller, and the Cook are several men, and distinguished from each other as much as the mincing Lady-Prioress and the broad-speaking, gap-toothed Wife of Bath. But enough of this; there is such a variety of game springing up before me that I am distracted in my choice, and know not which to follow. 'Tis sufficient to say, according to the proverb, that here is God's plenty. We have our forefathers and great-grand-dames all before us as they were in Chaucer's days: their general characters are still remaining in mankind, and even in England, though they are called by other names than those of monks, and friars, and canons, and lady-abbesses, and nuns; for mankind is ever the same, and nothing lost out of nature, though everything is altered. May I have leave to do myself the justice (since my enemies will do me none, and are so far from granting me to be a good poet that they will not allow me so much as to be a Christian, or a moral man), may I have leave, I say, to inform my reader that I have confined my choice to such tales of Chaucer as savor nothing of immodesty. If I had desired more to please than to instruct, the Reeve, the Miller, the Shipman, the Merchant, the Sumner, and, above all, the Wife of Bath, in the prologue to her tale, would have procured me as many friends and readers as there are beaux and ladies of pleasure in the town. But I will no more offend against good manners: I am sensible as I ought to be of the scandal I have given by my loose writings; and make what reparation I am able, by this public acknowledgment. If anything of this nature, or of profaneness, be crept into these poems, I am so far from defending it that I disown it. *Totum hoc indictum volo.* Chaucer makes another manner of apology for his broad speaking, and Boccace makes the like, but I will follow neither of

them. Our countryman, in the end of his Characters, before
the *Canterbury Tales,* thus excuses the ribaldry, which is
very gross in many of his novels—

> But firste, I pray you, of your courtesy,
> That ye ne arrete it not my villany,
> Though that I plainly speak in this mattere,
> To tellen you her words, and eke her chere;
> Ne though I speak her words properly,
> For this ye knowen as well as I,
> Who shall tellen a tale after a man,
> He mote rehearse as nye as ever he can:
> Everich word of it ben in his charge,
> All speke he, never so rudely, ne large:
> Or else he mote tellen his tale untrue,
> Or feine things, or find words new:
> He may not spare, altho he were his brother,
> He mote as wel say o word as another.
> Crist spake himself full broad in holy Writ
> And well I wote no villany is it,
> Eke Plato saith, who so can him rede,
> The words mote been cousin to the dede.

Yet if a man should have inquired of Boccace or of Chaucer, what need they had of introducing such characters,
where obscene words were proper in their mouths, but very
indecent to be heard, I know not what answer they could
have made; for that reason, such tales shall be left untold
by me. You have here a specimen of Chaucer's language,
which is so obsolete that his sense is scarce to be understood;
and you have likewise more than one example of his unequal numbers, which were mentioned before. Yet many
of his verses consist of ten syllables, and the words not much
behind our present English; as for example, these two lines,
in the description of the Carpenter's young wife—

Wincing she was, as is a jolly colt,
Long as a mast, and upright as a bolt.

I have almost done with Chaucer, when I have answered
some objections relating to my present work. I find some
people are offended that I have turned these tales into modern English; because they think them unworthy of my pains,
and look on Chaucer as a dry, old-fashioned wit, not worth
reviving. I have often heard the late Earl of Leicester say
that Mr. Cowley himself was of that opinion; who, having
read him over at my Lord's request, declared he had no taste
of him. I dare not advance my opinion against the judgment
of so great an author; but I think it fair, however, to leave
the decision to the public. Mr. Cowley was too modest to
set up for a dictator, and, being shocked perhaps with his
old style, never examined into the depth of his good sense.
Chaucer, I confess, is a rough diamond and must first be
polished ere he shines. I deny not likewise, that, living in
our early days of poetry, he writes not always of a piece;
but sometimes mingles trivial things with those of greater
moment. Sometimes also, though not often, he runs riot, like
Ovid, and knows not when he has said enough. But there
are more great wits besides Chaucer whose fault is their
excess of conceits, and those ill-sorted. An author is not to
write all he can, but only all he ought. Having observed this
redundancy in Chaucer (as it is an easy matter for a man
of ordinary parts to find a fault in one of greater), I have
not tied myself to a literal translation; but have often
omitted what I judged unnecessary, or not of dignity enough
to appear in the company of better thoughts. I have presumed
further in some places and added somewhat of my own where
I thought my author was deficient, and had not given his
thoughts their true luster, for want of words in the beginning
of our language. And to this I was the more emboldened,
because (if I may be permitted to say it myself) I found I

had a soul congenial to his, and that I had been conversant in the same studies. Another poet, in another age, may take the same liberty with my writings; if at least they live long enough to deserve correction. It was also necessary sometimes to restore the sense of Chaucer which was lost or mangled in the errors of the press. Let this example suffice at present; in the story of *Palamon and Arcite,* where the temple of Diana is described, you find these verses, in all the editions of our author:

> There saw I Danè turned unto a tree,
> I mean not the goddess Diane,
> But Venus daughter, which that hight Danè.

Which, after a little consideration, I knew was to be reformed into this sense, that Daphne, the daughter of Peneus, was turned into a tree. I durst not make thus bold with Ovid, lest some future Milbourne should arise and say I varied from my author because I understood him not.

But there are other judges, who think I ought not to have translated Chaucer into English, out of a quite contrary notion; they suppose there is a certain veneration due to his old language; and that it is little less than profanation and sacrilege to alter it. They are farther of opinion, that somewhat of his good sense will suffer in this transfusion and much of the beauty of his thoughts will infallibly be lost, which appear with more grace in their old habit. Of this opinion was that excellent person whom I mentioned, the late Earl of Leicester, who valued Chaucer as much as Mr. Cowley despised him. My Lord dissuaded me from this attempt (for I was thinking of it for some years before his death), and his authority prevailed so far with me as to defer my undertaking while he lived, in deference to him; yet my reason was not convinced with what he urged against it. If the first end of a writer be to be understood, then, as his language grows obsolete, his thoughts must grow obscure:

Multa renascentur, quæ nunc cecidere; cadentque
Quæ nunc sunt in honore vocabula, si volet usus,
Quem penes arbitrium est et jus et norma loquendi.[16]

When an ancient word for its sound and significancy deserves to be revived, I have that reasonable veneration for antiquity to restore it. All beyond this is superstition. Words are not like landmarks, so sacred as never to be removed; customs are changed, and even statutes are silently repealed when the reason ceases for which they were enacted. As for the other part of the argument, that his thoughts will lose of their original beauty by the innovation of words; in the first place, not only their beauty, but their being is lost, where they are no longer understood, which is the present case. I grant that something must be lost in all transfusion, that is, in all translations; but the sense will remain, which would otherwise be lost, or at least be maimed, when it is scarce intelligible, and that but to a few. How few are there who can read Chaucer so as to understand him perfectly! And if imperfectly, then with less profit, and no pleasure. 'Tis not for the use of some old Saxon friends, that I have taken these pains with him: let them neglect my version, because they have no need of it. I made it for their sakes who understand sense and poetry as well as they, when that poetry and sense is put into words which they understand. I will go farther, and dare to add, that what beauties I lose in some places, I give to others which had them not originally: but in this I may be partial to myself; let the reader judge, and I submit to his decision. Yet I think I have just occasion to complain of them who, because they understand Chaucer, would deprive the greater part of their countrymen of the same advantage, and hoard him up, as misers do their grandam gold, only to look on it themselves and hinder others from making use of it. In sum, I seriously protest that no man ever had, or can have, a greater veneration for Chaucer than

[16] Horace, *Ars Poetica*, 70–72.

myself. I have translated some part of his works, only that
I might perpetuate his memory, or at least refresh it, amongst
my countrymen. If I have altered him anywhere for the
better, I must at the same time acknowledge that I could
have done nothing without him. *Facile est inventis addere*
is no great commendation; and I am not so vain to think I
have deserved a greater. I will conclude what I have to say
of him singly, with this one remark: a lady of my acquaintance who keeps a kind of correspondence with some authors
of the fair sex in France, has been informed by them that
Mademoiselle de Scudéry, who is as old as Sibyl, and inspired like her by the same God of Poetry, is at this time
translating Chaucer into modern French. From which I
gather that he has been formerly translated into the old
Provençal (for how she should come to understand Old English, I know not). But the matter of fact being true, it makes
me think that there is something in it like fatality; that,
after certain periods of time, the fame and memory of great
wits should be renewed, as Chaucer is both in France and
England. If this be wholly chance, 'tis extraordinary; and I
dare not call it more, for fear of being taxed with superstition.

Boccace comes last to be considered, who, living in the
same age with Chaucer, had the same genius, and followed
the same studies. Both writ novels, and each of them cultivated his mother-tongue. But the greatest resemblance of
our two modern authors being in their familiar style and
pleasing way of relating comical adventures, I may pass it
over, because I have translated nothing from Boccace of
that nature. In the serious part of poetry, the advantage is
wholly on Chaucer's side; for though the Englishman has
borrowed many tales from the Italian, yet it appears that
those of Boccace were not generally of his own making, but
taken from authors of former ages, and by him only modeled;
so that what there was of invention in either of them, may
be judged equal. But Chaucer has refined on Boccace, and

has mended the stories which he had borrowed, in his way of telling; though prose allows more liberty of thought, and the expression is more easy when unconfined by numbers. Our countryman carries weight, and yet wins the race at disadvantage. I desire not the reader should take my word; and, therefore, I will set two of their discourses, on the same subject, in the same light, for every man to judge betwixt them. I translated Chaucer first, and amongst the rest, pitched on *The Wife of Bath's Tale;* not daring, as I have said, to adventure on her Prologue, because 'tis too licentious. There Chaucer introduces an old woman of mean parentage, whom a youthful knight of noble blood was forced to marry, and consequently loathed her. The crone being in bed with him on the wedding-night and finding his aversion, endeavors to win his affection by reason, and speaks a good word for herself (as who could blame her?) in hope to mollify the sullen bridegroom. She takes her topics from the benefits of poverty, the advantages of old age and ugliness, the vanity of youth, and the silly pride of ancestry and titles without inherent virtue, which is the true nobility. When I had closed Chaucer, I returned to Ovid, and translated some more of his fables; and, by this time, had so far forgotten *The Wife of Bath's Tale* that, when I took up Boccace, unawares I fell on the same argument, of preferring virtue to nobility of blood and titles, in the story of Sigismonda; which I had certainly avoided, for the resemblance of the two discourses, if my memory had not failed me. Let the reader weigh them both; and, if he thinks me partial to Chaucer, 'tis in him to right Boccace.

I prefer, in our countryman, far above all his other stories, the noble poem of *Palamon and Arcite,* which is of the epic kind, and perhaps not much inferior to the *Ilias* or the *Æneis.* The story is more pleasing than either of them, the manners as perfect, the diction as poetical, the learning as deep and various, and the disposition full as artful; only it includes a greater length of time, as taking up seven years at least; but Aristotle has left undecided the duration of the action; which yet is easily reduced into the compass of a year by a narration of what preceded the return of Palamon to Athens. I had thought, for the honor of our narration, and more particularly for his, whose laurel, though unworthy, I have worn after him, that this story was of English growth, and Chaucer's own; but I was undeceived by Boccace; for, casually looking on the end of his seventh *Giornata,* I found Dioneo (under which name he shadows himself), and Fiametta (who represents his mistress, the natural daughter of Robert, King of Naples), of whom these words are spoken: *Dioneo e Fiametta gran pezza cantarono insieme d'Arcita, e di Palemone;* by which it appears that this story was written before the time of Boccace; but the name of its author being wholly lost, Chaucer is now become an original; and I question not but the poem has received many beauties by passing through his noble hands. Besides this tale there is another of his own invention, after the manner of the Provençals, called *The Flower and the Leaf,* with which I was so particularly pleased, both for the invention and the moral, that I cannot hinder myself from recommending it to the reader.

As a corollary to this preface, in which I have done justice to others, I owe somewhat to myself; not that I think it worth my time to enter the lists with one M———,[17] or one B———,[18] but barely to take notice, that such men there are, who have written scurrilously against me, without any provocation. M———, who is in orders, pretends, amongst the rest, this quarrel to me, that I have fallen foul on priesthood: if I have, I am only to ask pardon of good priests, and am afraid his part of the reparation will come to little. Let him be satisfied that he shall not be able to force himself upon me for an adversary. I contemn him too

---

[17] M——— is the Rev. Luke Milbourne, who attacked Dryden's translation of the *Æneid.*

[18] B——— is Sir Richard Blackmore, London physician and author of a number of epics, including *Prince Arthur* and *King Arthur.*

much to enter into competition with him. His own translations of Virgil have answered his criticisms on mine. If (as
they say he has declared in print) he prefers the version of
Ogilby to mine, the world has made him the same compliment; for 'tis agreed, on all hands, that he writes even below
Ogilby. That, you will say, is not easily to be done; but
what cannot M——— bring about? I am satisfied, however, that, while he and I live together, I shall not be thought
the worst poet of the age.[19] It looks as if I had desired him
underhand to write so ill against me; but upon my honest
word I have not bribed him to do me this service, and am
wholly guiltless of his pamphlet. 'Tis true, I should be glad
if I could persuade him to continue his good offices and write
such another critique on anything of mine; for I find, by
experience, he has a great stroke with the reader when he
condemns any of my poems, to make the world have a better
opinion of them. He has taken some pains with my poetry;
but nobody will be persuaded to take the same with his.
If I had taken to the church (as he affirms, but which was
never in my thoughts), I should have had more sense, if not
more grace, than to have turned myself out of my benefice
by writing libels on my parishioners. But his account of
my manners and my principles are of a piece with his cavils
and his poetry; and so I have done with him forever.

As for the city bard, or knight physician, I hear his quarrel
to me is, that I was the author of *Absalom and Achitophel,*
which, he thinks, is a little hard on his fanatic patrons in
London.

But I will deal the more civilly with his two poems, because nothing ill is to be spoken of the dead; and therefore
peace be to the *manes* of his Arthurs. I will only say, that it
was not for this noble knight that I drew the plan of an epic
poem on King Arthur, in my preface to the translation of

[19] A similar remark was made by Sir John Denham, who saved Wither's
life because "whilst [Wither] lived, he should not be the worst poet in
England."

Juvenal. The guardian angels of kingdoms were machines too ponderous for him to manage; and therefore he rejected them, as Dares did the whirl-bats of Eryx when they were thrown before him by Entellus: [20] yet from that preface, he plainly took his hint; for he began immediately upon the story, though he had the baseness not to acknowledge his benefactor, but instead of it, to traduce me in a libel.

I shall say the less of Mr. Collier, because in many things he has taxed me justly; and I have pleaded guilty to all thoughts and expressions of mine which can be truly argued of obscenity, profaneness, or immorality, and retract them. If he be my enemy, let him triumph; if he be my friend, as I have given him no personal occasion to be otherwise, he will be glad of my repentance. It becomes me not to draw my pen in the defense of a bad cause, when I have so often drawn it for a good one. Yet it were not difficult to prove that in many places he has perverted my meaning by his glosses, and interpreted my words into blasphemy and bawdry of which they were not guilty. Besides that, he is too much given to horse-play in his raillery, and comes to battle like a dictator from the plow. I will not say, "The zeal of God's house has eaten him up"; but I am sure it has devoured some part of his good manners and civility. It might also be doubted, whether it were altogether zeal which prompted him to this rough manner of proceeding; perhaps it became not one of his functions to rake into the rubbish of ancient and modern plays: a divine might have employed his pains to better purpose than in the nastiness of Plautus and Aristophanes, whose examples, as they excuse not me, so it might be possibly supposed that he read them not without some pleasure. They who have written commentaries on those poets, or on Horace, Juvenal, and Martial, have explained some vices which, without their interpretation, had been unknown to modern times. Neither has he judged impartially betwixt the former age and us. There is more bawdry

[20] The reference is to the *Æneid*, v. 400.

in one play of Fletcher's called *The Custom of the Country*, than in all ours together. Yet this has been often acted on the stage in my remembrance. Are the times so much more reformed now than they were five-and-twenty years ago? If they are, I congratulate the amendment of our morals. But I am not to prejudice the cause of my fellow poets, though I abandon my own defense: they have some of them answered for themselves; and neither they nor I can think Mr. Collier so formidable an enemy that we should shun him. He has lost ground, at the latter end of the day, by pursuing his point too far, like the Prince of Condé, at the battle of Senneph: [21] from immoral plays to no plays, *ab abusu ad usum, non valet consequentia*. But, being a party, I am not to erect myself into a judge. As for the rest of those who have written against me, they are such scoundrels that they deserve not the least notice to be taken of them. B——— and M——— are only distinguished from the crowd by being remembered to their infamy:

> . . . *Demetri, teque, Tigelli,*
> *Discipulorum inter jubeo plorare cathedras.*[22]

---

[21] The Prince of Condé at the battle of Senef, August 11, 1674, attacked the rear guard of the Prince of Orange, who was already in retreat.

[22] Horace, *Satires*, I. x. 90–91.

Anthony à Wood 1632-1695

For Wood as for Burton, Oxford encompassed life. He entered Merton College in 1647 and was seldom out of it thereafter. He took his B.A. in 1652, his excuse for the additional year being that he suffered from "slowness of apprehension" because Mutton the university carrier's horse stepped on his head when he was a boy. He continued his study to an M.A. in 1655.

Though only slenderly provided for by his father's will, he had enough to maintain himself in some garret rooms of the old family home across the street from Merton, where he lived until he was buried in the college. Books and documents were near, and his life was absorbed by constant study, as his enormous antiquarian works indicate. Inspired by Sir William Dugdale's *The Antiquities of Warwickshire* he set to work to write the *History and Antiquities of Oxford,* a book which brought him much honor. His next work was the *Athenæ Oxonienses,* which contains biographical sketches of all the alumni of Oxford who had distinguished themselves in any way. There were a number of assistants who gathered material for this work, among them John Aubrey. The work is a monument to enormous industry, and has continued to be the invaluable source for factual information concerning the lives of Oxford men. He was sometimes a severe critic, and it was said that he "had set all Oxford in a flame." His caustic remarks about the Lord Chancellor Clarendon resulted in his being expelled from Oxford and this section of his book publicly burned.

Wood had a disagreeable nature, and his austere life as a recluse provided no counteracting influences. He lacks the warmth and human interest which would bring his subjects to life, but he is appreciated for the generally reliable and orderly material which his massive volumes contain.

ATHENÆ OXONIENSES [1]

James Howell

JAMES HOWELL was born in Caermarthenshire, particularly, as I conceive, at Abernant, of which place his father was minister. In what year he was born I cannot precisely tell you, yet he himself saith that his ascendant was that hot constellation of Cancer about the midst of the dog-days.

After he had been educated in grammar learning in the free school at Hereford, he was sent to Jesus College in the beginning of 1610, aged 16 years, took a degree in arts, and then, being a pure cadet, a true cosmopolite, not born to land, lease, house, or office, was in a manner put to it to see his fortune; but by the endeavors of friends and some money that his father assisted him with, he traveled for three years into various countries, whereby he advantaged himself much in the understanding of several languages.

Some years after his return, he was sent into Spain, 1622, to recover of the king of that place a rich English ship seized on by his viceroy of Sardinia for his master's use, upon some pretense of prohibited goods therein.

Three years after his return (in which interval he was elected fellow of Jesus College, 1623), he was entertained by Emanuel Lord Scroop, Earl of Sunderland and Lord President of the North, and by him was made his secretary. So that residing in York for that purpose, he was by the mayor and aldermen of Richmond chosen a burgess for their corporation for that parliament that began at Westminster in the year 1627.

Four years after he went secretary to Robert, Earl of Leicester, ambassador extraordinary from our king to the king of Denmark; before whom and his children he showed himself a quaint orator by divers Latin speeches spoken before them, showing the occasion of their embassy, to con-

---

[1] Text ed. by Philip Bliss (London, 1813, 1815, 1817, 1820), 4 vols.

dole the death of Sophia, queen dowager of Denmark, grand-mother to Charles I of England.

Afterwards going through several beneficial employments, particularly the assisting the clerks of the Council, he was at length, in the beginning of the civil war, made one of those clerks; but being prodigally inclined, and therefore running much into debt, he was seized by order of a certain com-mittee (after the king was forced from his parliament) and committed prisoner to the Fleet.[2] So that having nothing to trust to but his wits, and to the purchase of a small spot of ground upon Parnassus (which he held in fee of the Muses), he solely dedicated himself to write and translate books; which though several of them are mere scribbles, yet they brought him in a comfortable subsistence during his long stay there.

After the king's return in 1660, we never heard of his restoration to his place of clerk of the council (having before flattered Oliver and sided with the Commonwealth's men), only that he was made the king's historiographer, being the first in England that have that title; and having no beneficial employment, he wrote books to his last.

He had a singular command of his pen, whether in verse or prose, and was well read in modern histories, especially in those of the countries wherein he had traveled, had a para-bolical and allusive fancy, according to his motto *Senesco non Segnesco*. But the reader is to know that his writings having been only to gain a livelihood, and by their dedica-tions to flatter great and noble persons, are very trite and empty, stolen from other authors without acknowledgment, and fitted only to please the humors of novices. . . .[3]

At length after he had taken many rambles in this world in his younger years, and had suffered confinement in his last, gave way to fate in the beginning of November in 1666, and was buried on the north side of Temple Church in London,

[2] His imprisonment appears to have been for political reasons.
[3] An extensive list of his works follows this paragraph.

near the round walk. Soon after was a monument set up in the wall over his grave, with this inscription thereon.

Jacobus Howell Cambro-Britannus, Regius Historio-graphus (in Anglia primus) qui post varias perigrinationes, tandem naturæ cursum peregit, satur annorum et famæ, domi forisque huc usque erraticus, hic fixus 1666. This monument was pulled down in 1683, when the said Temple Church was beautified and repaired.

Robert Burton

ROBERT BURTON, known otherwise to scholars as Democritus Junior, younger brother to Will Burton, whom I shall mention under the year 1645, was born of an ancient and genteel family at Lindley, in Leicestershire, 8 Feb. 1576, and therefore in the titles of several of his choice books which he gave to the public library, he added to his surname *Lindliacus Leicestrensis.* He was educated in grammar learning in the free-school of Sutton-Coldfield in Warwickshire, whence he was sent to Brasenose College in the long vacation, *an.* 1593, where he made a considerable progress in logic and philosophy in the condition of a commoner. In 1599 he was elected student of Christ Church and for form sake, though he wanted not a tutor, he was put under the tuition of Dr. John Bancroft, afterwards bishop of Oxon. In 1614 he was admitted to the reading of the sentences, and on 29 Nov. 1616, he had the vicarage of St. Thomas's parish in the west suburb of Oxon conferred on him by the dean and canons of Christ Church (to the parishioners whereof he always gave the sacrament in wafers), which, with the rectory of Segrave in Leicestershire, given to him some years after by George, Lord Berkeley, he kept with much ado to his dying day. He was an exact mathematician, a curious calculator of nativities, a general read scholar, a thorough paced philologist, and one that understood the surveying of lands well. As he was by many accounted a severe student, a devourer of authors,[1] a melancholy and humorous person, so by others who knew him well, a person of great honesty, plain dealing, and charity. I have heard some of the ancients of Christ Church often say that his company was very merry, facete, and juvenile, and no man in his time did surpass him for his ready and dexterous interlarding his common discourses among them with verses from the poets or sentences from classical authors. Which being then all the fashion in the university made his company more acceptable. He hath written:

The Anatomy of Melancholy. First printed in quarto [1621] and afterwards several times in folio *an.* 1624, 1632, '38, and 1652, etc.,[2] to the great profit of the bookseller, who got an estate by it. 'Tis a book so full of variety of reading that gentlemen who have lost their time and are put to a push for invention, may furnish themselves with matter for common scholastical discourse and writing. Several authors have unmercifully stolen matter from the said book without any acknowledgment, particularly one Will. Greenwood, in his book entitled *A Description of the Passion of Love,* etc., London, 1657, octavo. Who, as others of the like humor do sometimes take his quotations without the least mention of Democritus Junior.[3]

He, the said R. Burton, paid his last debt to nature in his chamber in Christ's Church, at, or very near that time which he had some years before foretold from the calculation of his own nativity. Which being exact, several of the students did

---

[1] In "Democritus Junior to the Reader" Burton says of his own writing: "I have only this of Macrobius to say of myself, *Omne meum, nihil meum,* 'tis all mine and none mine. As a good housewife out of divers fleeces weaves one piece of cloth, a bee gathers wax and honey out of many flowers and makes a new bundle of all,

Floriferis ut apes in saltibus omnia bibant,

I have laboriously collected this *cento* out of divers writers and that *sine iniuria;* I have wronged no authors but given every man his own . . . I cite and quote mine authors."

[2] Bliss, the editor of Wood, adds in brackets the editions of 1628, 1660, and 1676.

[3] In the eighteenth century Sterne happily pillaged the *Anatomy.*

not forbear to whisper among themselves that rather than there should be a mistake in the calculation, he sent up his soul to heaven through a slip about his neck. His body was afterwards with due solemnity buried near that of Dr. Robert Weston, in the north aisle, which joins next to the choir of the Cathedral of Christ Church, on the 27 of January in sixteen hundred thirty-and-nine. Over his grave was soon after erected a comely monument on the upper pillar of the said aisle, with his bust painted to the life: on the right hand of which is the calculation of his nativity, and under the bust this inscription made by himself; all put up by the care of William Burton his brother. "Paucis notus paucioribus ignotus, hic jacet Democritus junior, cui vitam dedit, et mortam melancholia. Obiit viii. Id. Jan. A.D. MDCXXXIX." He left behind him a very choice library of books,[4] many of which he bequeathed to that of Bodley, and a hundred pounds to buy five pounds yearly for the supplying of Christ Church library with books. [Burton's monument and bust has been engraved for Nichol's *History of Leicestershire* to which I refer for everything relative to the author, although Wood has diligently collected all that is material. His *Melancholy* is in the hands of every reader of taste and information. It was the only work, Dr. Johnson said, that could force him from his bed two hours earlier than he wished to rise.

There is a small head of Burton engraved by C. Le Blon, in the frontispiece to his *Anatomy of Melancholy*.] [5]

[4] "The bequest to the Bodleian library is, without exception, one of the most curious, and, according to the taste of the present day, valuable additions that repository possesses. Burton's books consist of all the historical, political, and poetical tracts of his own time, with a large collection of miscellaneous accounts of murders, monsters, and accidents. In short, he seems to have purchased indiscriminately everything that was published, which accounts for the uncommon treasures of St. Paul's Churchyard, which are now to be found only in the Oxford Vatican."
[5] The material in brackets was added by Bliss.

Jeremy Taylor

JEREMY TAYLOR tumbled out of his mother's womb into the laps of the Muses at Cambridge, was educated in Gonvill and Caius College, there till he was M. of A. Afterwards entering into holy orders, he supplied for a time the divinity lecturer's place in the Cathedral of St. Paul in London, where behaving himself with great credit and applause far above his years, came to the cognizance of that great encourager of learning, ingenuity, and virtue, Dr. Laud, Archbishop of Canterbury, who thinking it for the advantage of the world that such mighty parts should be afforded better opportunities of study and improvement than a course of constant preaching would allow of, he caused him to be elected fellow of All Souls College, 1636: where being settled, love and admiration still waited upon him; while he improved himself much in books. But this the reader is to know that though he came in merely by the paramount interest of the said archbishop, yet it was done against the statutes of the college in these two respects. First, because he had exceeded the age within which the said statutes made candidates capable of being elected, and secondly, that he had not been of three years' standing in the university of Oxon, only a week or two before he was put in. However, he being a person of most wonderful parts and like to be an ornament thereunto, he was dispensed with, and thereby obtained in that house much of that learning wherewith he was enabled to write casuistically. About the same time he was in a ready way to be confirmed a member of the Church of Rome, as many of that persuasion have said, but upon a sermon delivered in St. Mary's church in Oxon on the fifth of November (Gun-powder-treason day) in the year 1638, wherein several things were put in against the papists by the then vice chancellor, he was afterwards rejected with scorn by those of that party, particularly by Fr. à St. Clara, his intimate acquaintance; to whom afterwards he expressed some sorrow for those things he had said against them, as the said St. Clara hath several times told me.

About that time he became one of the chaplains to the said Archbishop of Canterbury, who bestowed upon him the rectory of Uppingham in Rutlandshire, and other matters he would have done for him in order to his advance in the church, had not the rebellion unluckily broke out. In the year 1642 he was with others, by virtue of His Majesty's letters sent to this university, actually created Doctor of Divinity in that noted convocation held on the first day of November the same year, he being then chaplain in ordinary to His said Majesty, and a frequent preacher before him and the court at Oxon. Afterwards he attended in His Majesty's army in the condition of chaplain; where though he had not a command of his time and books, yet he laid the foundation of several treatises in defense of episcopacy, the liturgy, ministry, and Church of England.

Upon the declining of the king's cause, he retired into Wales, where he was suffered under the loyal Earl of Carbury of the Golden Grove in Caermarthenshire to officiate, and keep school, to maintain him and his children. For which, though it continued but a few years, were several youths most loyally educated, and afterwards sent to the universities. In this solitude he began to write his excellent discourses, which are enough of themselves to furnish a library, and will be famous to all succeeding generations for the exactness of wit, profoundness of judgment, richness of fancy, clearness of expression, copiousness of invention, and general usefulness to all the purposes of a Christian. By which he soon after got a great reputation among all persons of judgment and indifference and his name grew greater still, as the world grew better and wiser. When he had spent some years in this retirement, in a private corner, as it were, of the world, his family was visited with sickness, and thereby lost the dear pledges of God's favor, three sons of great hopes, within the space of two or three months. And though he had learned a quiet submission to the divine will, yet this affliction touched him so sensibly that it made him desirous to leave the country: and going to London, he there for a time officiated in a private congregation of loyalists to his great hazard and danger. At length meeting with Edward, Lord Conway, a person of great honor and generosity, that lord, after he had understood his condition, made him a kind proffer, which our author Taylor embracing, it carried him over into Ireland and settled him at Portmore, a place made for study and contemplation, which he therefore dearly loved. And there he wrote his *Cases of Conscience,* a book that is able alone to give its author immortality.

By this time the wheel of Providence brought about the king's happy restoration, and out of a confused chaos, beauty and order began to appear: whereupon our loyal author went over to congratulate the prince and people's happiness and bear a part in the universal triumph. It was not long after, his sacred Majesty began the settlement of the church, and Dr. Taylor being resolved upon for the bishopric of Down and Connor, was consecrated thereunto at Dublin on the 27th of January, 1660, and on the 21st of June, 1661, he had the administration of the see of Dromore granted to him by His Majesty in consideration that he had been the church's champion and that he had suffered much in defense of its cause. With what care and faithfulness he discharged his office, all upon the place knew well, and what good rules and directions he gave to his clergy, and how he taught them the practice of them by his own example.

Upon his being made bishop, he was constituted a privy councilor, and the University of Dublin gave him their testimony by recommending him for their vice-chancellor, which honorable office he kept to his dying day. He was esteemed by the generality of persons a complete artist, accurate logician, exquisite, quick and accurate in his reasonings, a person of great fluency in his language and of prodigious readiness in learning. A noted Presbyterian [1] also (his antagonist) doth ingenuously confess that Dr. Taylor "is a man of admirable wit, great parts, hath a quick and elegant pen, is of abilities in critical learning, and of profound skill in antiquity," etc., and another [2] who knew him well tells us that "he was a rare humanist, and hugely versed in all the polite parts of learning, and had thoroughly concocted all the ancient moralists, Greek and Roman poets and orators; and was not unacquainted with the refined wits of the latter ages, whether French or Italian," etc.

But he had not only the accomplishments of a gentleman, but so universal were his parts that they were proportioned to everything. And though his spirit and humor were made up of smoothness and gentleness, yet he could bear with the harshness and roughness of the schools, and was not unseen in their subtilities and spinosities. His skill was great both in the civil and canon law and casuistical divinity: and he was a rare conductor of souls, and knew how to counsel and to advise; to solve difficulties, and determine cases, and quiet consciences. To these may be added his great acquaintance with the fathers and ecclesiastical writers, and the doctors of the first and purest ages both of the Greek and Latin church; which he hath made use of against the Roman Catholics, to vindicate the Church of England from the challenge of innovation, and to prove her ancient, catholic, and apostolical. Add to all these, he was a person of great humility, had nothing in him of pride and humor, but was courteous and affable and of easy access. He was withal a person of great charity and hospitality: and whosoever compares his plentiful incomes with the inconsiderable estate he left at his death will be easily convinced that charity was steward for a great proportion of his revenue. To sum up all in a few words of another author, "This great prelate had the good humor of

---

[1] Henry Jeanes, "Epistle to the Reader," *Certain Letters Between Him and Jeremy Taylor*, London, 1660.
[2] George Rust, *Sermon at Bishop Taylor's Funeral*.

a gentleman, the eloquence of an orator, the fancy of a poet, the acuteness of a schoolman, the profoundness of a philosopher, the wisdom of a chancellor, the sagacity of a prophet, the reason of an angel, and the piety of a saint. He had devotion enough for a cloister, learning enough for an university, and wit enough for a college of virtuosi. And had his parts and endowments been parceled out among his poor clergy that he left behind him, it would perhaps have made one of the best dioceses in the world. . . ." [3]

These are all the books and sermons, as I conceive, that this most worthy and eminent author hath written, and therefore I shall only add, that he being overtaken with a violent fever, surrendered up his pious soul to the Omnipotent at Lisburne alias Lisnegarvy on the thirteenth day of August in sixteen hundred sixty-and-seven, and was buried in a chapel of his own erection on the ruins of the old cathedral of Dromore. In that see succeeded his most dear and excellent friend (who preached his funeral sermon, and afterwards made it public) named George Rust, D.D. sometime fellow of Christ's College in Cambridge, a learned divine, and an eloquent preacher; who dying in December (about St. Thomas's day) in 1670, was buried in the same vault wherein the said Bishop Taylor had been deposited. After him succeeded in the same see (Dromore) Dr. Essex Digby, and him, Capel Wiseman, dean of Raphoe, sometime fellow of All Souls College, 1683.

[3] George Rust, *op. cit.* A list of Taylor's works follows.

John Locke   1632-1704

LOCKE's father, who lived near the vigorous city of Bristol, was a county attorney sympathetic toward the parliamentary cause and after the beginning of the Civil War, a captain in the parliamentary forces. When Locke entered Christ Church College, Oxford, he continued to be under liberal influences, for Cromwell was then Chancellor; John Owen, an Independent with liberal views, was dean; and his tutor was a Puritan. At first he seems to have intended going into the ministry, but he became interested in medicine and abandoned this idea. He received his A.B. in 1656 and his M.A. a little more than two years later. In 1660 he was appointed Greek lecturer in his own college, and later held other lectureships.

His first trip to the Continent was as secretary to Walter Vane, who had been sent on a mission to the Elector of Brandenburg. It is significant that the thing which most impressed Locke was the religious toleration which he observed.

Upon his return to England he continued his medical studies at Oxford, though he did not take his degree in medicine until 1674. In July 1666 he met Lord Ashley, later Earl of Shaftesbury, and out of their friendship grew an arrangement whereby Locke served as physician for the family and tutor to Ashley's son. When the Earl of Shaftesbury was made Lord High Chancellor, 1672, Locke acted as his secretary.

The fall of Shaftesbury three years later resulted in Locke's going for a prolonged stay on the Continent; but upon Shaftesbury's reinstatement, he resumed his secretaryship. Further plotting, however, led to Shaftesbury's flight to Holland, and Locke then returned to Oxford for study and writing. But he was under suspicion, and in 1683 also went to Holland, where he remained in hiding for a time. He was not in England again until after William of Orange came to the throne.

William III offered Locke an important diplomatic post,

but he was not well enough to undertake it. Finding that London was injurious to his health, he went to the home of his friends, Sir Francis and Lady Masham, in Essex, where he was made welcome the remainder of his life.

Though Locke's practice as a physician was limited to Shaftesbury's family, his interest in science showed itself in various ways. When he was at Oxford, the group which was later to become the Royal Scientific Society sometimes met in his rooms. He was a friend of Sydenham and Boyle, and kept up a correspondence with some of the French scientists. He was elected Fellow of the Royal Scientific Society, but seems never to have been an active participant.

Locke's greatest work, the *Essay on the Human Understanding*, though first planned in 1671, was not published until 1690, and even then underwent revision through the fourth edition. This essay makes an important contribution through the application of the scientific method to philosophy in the attempt to define the nature of ideas. It presents the conclusion that all knowledge is based on the evidence presented by the five senses. Two other influential works should be mentioned here: the *Letters on Toleration,* the first of which appeared in 1689, helped to prepare the way for the Act of Toleration; and *Thoughts on Education* advanced the idea, which was already receiving attention, that the road to learning should be shortened. Though the importance of his work should not be underestimated, Locke's enormous popularity in the seventeenth and eighteenth centuries was in part the result of a number of fortunate circumstances which combined to give him a favorable reception. On the other hand, the clarity and dignity of his prose style and his exact use of language constitute a permanent contribution to the development of prose.

From OF HUMAN UNDERSTANDING [1]

Book II, Chapter I, s. 1–9

Of Ideas in General, and Their Original

1. EVERY MAN being conscious to himself that he thinks, and that which his mind is employed about whilst thinking being the ideas that are there, it is past doubt that men have in their minds several ideas, such as are those expressed by the words, whiteness, hardness, sweetness, thinking, motion, man, elephant, army, drunkenness, and others: it is in the first place then to be inquired, how he comes by them. I know it is a received doctrine that men have native ideas and original characters stamped upon their minds in their very first being. This opinion I have at large examined already; and, I suppose, what I have said in the foregoing book will be much more easily admitted when I have showed whence the understanding may get all the ideas it has, and by what ways and degrees they may come into the mind; for which I shall appeal to everyone's own observation and experience.

2. Let us then suppose the mind to be, as we say, white paper, void of all characters, without any ideas; how comes it to be furnished? Whence comes it by that vast store which the busy and boundless fancy of man has painted on it with an almost endless variety? Whence has it all the materials of reason and knowledge? To this I answer, in one word, from experience: in that, all our knowledge is founded; and from that it ultimately derives itself. Our observation, employed either about external, sensible objects, or about the internal operations of our minds, perceived and reflected on by ourselves, is that which supplies our understandings with all the materials of thinking. These two are the fountains of knowledge, from whence all the ideas we have, or can naturally have, do spring.

[1] Text: 1690, first edition.

3. First, our senses, conversant about particular sensible objects, do convey into the mind several distinct perceptions of things, according to those various ways wherein those objects do affect them: and thus we come by those ideas we have of yellow, white, heat, cold, soft, hard, bitter, sweet, and all those which we call sensible qualities. This great source of most of the ideas we have, depending wholly upon our senses, and derived by them to our understanding, I call sensation.

4. Secondly, the other fountain, from which experience furnisheth the understanding with ideas, is the perception of the operations of our own minds within us, as it is employed about the ideas it has got; which operations, when the soul comes to reflect on and consider, do furnish the understanding with another set of ideas, which could not be had from things without; and such are, perception, thinking, doubting, believing, reasoning, knowing, willing, and all the different actings of our own minds; which we being conscious of, and observing in ourselves, do from these receive into our understanding as distinct ideas as we do from bodies affecting our senses. This source of ideas, every man has wholly in himself: and though it be not sense, as having nothing to do with external objects, yet it is very like it and might properly enough be called internal sense. But as I call the other sensation, so I call this reflection, the ideas it affords being such only as the mind gets by reflecting on its own operations within itself. By reflection then, in the following part of this discourse, I would be understood to mean, that notice which the mind takes of its own operations and the manner of them, by reason whereof there come to be ideas of these operations in the understanding. These two, I say, *viz.* eternal, material things as the objects of sensation and the operations of our own minds within as the objects of reflection, are, to me, the only originals from whence all our ideas take their beginnings. The term *operations* here, I use in a large sense, as comprehending not barely the actions of the mind about its ideas, but some sort of passions arising sometimes

from them, such as is the satisfaction or uneasiness arising from any thought.

5. The understanding seems to me not to have the least glimmering of any ideas which it doth not receive from one of these two: external objects furnish the mind with the ideas of sensible qualities, which are all those different perceptions they produced in us; and the mind furnishes the understanding with ideas of its own operations. These, when we have taken a full survey of them, we shall find to contain all our whole stock of ideas; and that we have nothing in our minds which did not come in, one of these two ways. Let anyone examine his own thoughts, and thoroughly search into his understanding, and then let him tell me, whether all the original ideas he has there are any other than of the objects of his senses, or of the operations of his mind considered as objects of his reflection: and how great a mass of knowledge soever he imagines to be lodged there, he will, upon taking a strict view, see that he has not any idea in his mind but what one of those two have imprinted, though perhaps with infinite variety compounded and enlarged by the understanding, as we shall see hereafter.

6. He that attentively considers the state of a child at his first coming into the world will have little reason to think him stored with plenty of ideas that are to be the matter of his future knowledge. 'Tis by degrees he comes to be furnished with them: and though the ideas of obvious and familiar qualities imprint themselves before the memory begins to keep a register of time and order, yet it is often so late before some unusual qualities come in the way that there are few men that cannot recollect the beginning of their acquaintance with them; and if it were worth while, no doubt a child might be so ordered as to have but a very few even of the ordinary ideas till he were grown up to a man. But being surrounded with bodies that perpetually and diversely affect us, variety of ideas, whether care be taken about it or no, are imprinted on the minds of children. Light

and colors are busy and at hand everywhere when the eye is but open; sounds and some tangible qualities fail not to solicit their proper senses and force an entrance to the mind; but yet I think it will be granted easily that if a child were kept in a place where he never saw any other but black and white till he were a man, he would have no more ideas of scarlet or green than he that from his childhood never tasted an oyster or a pineapple has of those particular relishes.

7. Men then come to be furnished with fewer or more simple ideas from without, according as the objects they converse with afford greater or lesser variety; and from the operation of their minds within, according as they more or less reflect on them. For, though he that contemplates the operations of his mind cannot but have plain and clear ideas of them, yet unless he turn his thoughts that way, and considers them attentively, he will no more have clear and distinct ideas of all the operations of his mind and all that may be observed therein, than he will have all the particular ideas of any landscape, or of the parts and motions of a clock, who will not turn his eyes to it and with attention heed all the parts of it. The picture or clock may be so placed that they may come in his way every day; but yet he will have but a confused idea of all the parts they are made up of till he applies himself with attention to consider them each in particular.

8. And hence we see the reason why it is pretty late before most children get ideas of the operations of their own minds; and some have not any very clear or perfect ideas of the greatest part of them all their lives. Because, though they pass there continually, yet, like floating visions, they make not deep impressions enough to leave in the mind clear and distinct, lasting ideas till the understanding turn inwards upon itself, and reflect on its own operations, and make them the object of its own contemplation. Whereas children at their first coming into the world seek particularly after nothing but what may ease their hunger or other pain, but

take all other objects as they come, are generally pleased with all new ones that are not painful; and so growing up in a constant attention to outward sensations, seldom make any considerable reflection on what passes within them till they come to be of riper years; and some scarce ever at all.

9. To ask at what time a man has first any ideas is to ask when he begins to perceive; having ideas, and perception, being the same thing. I know it is an opinion that the soul always thinks, and that it has the actual perception of ideas in itself constantly as long as it exists; and that actual thinking is as inseparable from the soul as actual extension is from the body: which if true, to inquire after the beginning of a man's ideas is the same as to inquire after the beginning of his soul. For by this account, soul and ideas, as body and extension, will begin to exist both at the same time.

From SOME THOUGHTS CONCERNING EDUCATION [1]

154. As soon as he can speak English, 'tis time for him to learn some other language: this nobody doubts of when French is proposed. And the reason is, because people are accustomed to the right way of teaching that language, which is by talking it into children in constant conversation, and not by grammatical rules. The Latin tongue would easily be taught the same way if his tutor, being constantly with him, would talk nothing else to him, and make him answer still in the same language. But because French is a living language and to be used more in speaking, that should be first learned, that the yet pliant organs of speech might be accustomed to a due formation of those sounds and he get the habit of pronouncing French well, which is the harder to be done the longer it is delayed.

155. When he can speak and read French well, which in this method is usually in a year or two, he should proceed to Latin, which 'tis a wonder parents, when they have had the experiment in French, should not think ought to be learned the same way, by talking and reading. Only care is to be taken whilst he is learning these foreign languages by speaking and reading nothing else with his tutor, that he do not forget to read English, which may be preserved by his mother, or somebody else, hearing him read some chosen parts of the Scripture or other English book every day.

156. Latin, I look upon as absolutely necessary to a gentleman; and indeed, custom, which prevails over everything, has made it so much a part of education that even those children are whipped to it, and made spend many hours of their precious time uneasily in Latin, who, after they are

[1] Text: 1693, first edition, beginning section 154, p. 192. The 1693 edition is used because the expanded editions are very repetitious.

once gone from school, are never to have more to do with it as long as they live. Can there be anything more ridiculous than that a father should waste his own money and his son's time in setting him to learn the Roman language, when at the same time he designs him for a trade, wherein he, having no use for Latin, fails not to forget that little which he brought from school, and which 'tis ten to one he abhors for the ill usage it procured him? Could it be believed, unless we had everywhere amongst us examples of it, that a child should be forced to learn the rudiments of a language which he is never to use in the course of life [that] he is designed to, and neglect all the while the writing a good hand and casting account, which are of great advantage in all conditions of life, and to most trades indispensably necessary? But though these qualifications, requisite to trade and commerce and the business of the world, are seldom or never to be had at grammar schools, yet thither, not only gentlemen send their younger sons, intended for trades, but even tradesmen and farmers fail not to send their children, though they have neither intention nor ability to make them scholars. If you ask them why they do this, they think it is a strange question as if you should ask them why they go to church. Custom serves for reason, and has, to those who take it for reason, so consecrated this method that it is almost religiously observed by them, and they stick to it as if their children had scarce an orthodox education unless they learned Lily's grammar.

157. But how necessary soever Latin be to some, and is thought to be to others to whom it is of no manner of use or service, yet the ordinary way of learning it in a grammar school is that which having had thoughts about, I cannot be forward to encourage. The reasons against it are so evident and cogent, that they have prevailed with some intelligent persons to quit the ordinary road, not without success, though the method made use of was not exactly that which I imagine the easiest, and in short, is this: to trouble the child with no

grammar at all, but to have Latin, as English had been, without the perplexity of rules, talked into him; for if you will consider it, Latin is no more unknown to a child when he comes into the world than English; and yet he learns English without master, rule, or grammar; and so might he Latin too as Tully did, if he had somebody always to talk to him in this language. And when we often see a French woman teach an English girl to speak and read French perfectly in a year or two without any rule of grammar, or anything else but prattling to her, I cannot but wonder how gentlemen have over-seen this way for their sons and thought them more dull or incapable than their daughters. If therefore a man could be got, who himself speaks good Latin, who would always be about your son, and talk constantly to him, and make him read Latin, that would be the true, genuine way and easy way of teaching him Latin, and that I could wish, since besides teaching him a language without pains or chiding (which children are wont to be whipped for at school six or seven years together), he might at the same time not only form his mind and manners but instruct him also in several sciences, such as are a good part of geography, astronomy, chronology, anatomy, besides some parts of history, and all other parts of knowledge of things that fall under the senses and require little more than memory. For there, if we would take the true way, our knowledge should begin, and in those things be laid the foundation; and not in the abstract notions of logic and metaphysics, which are fitter to amuse than inform the understanding in its first setting out towards knowledge: in which abstract speculations, when young men have had their heads employed a while without finding the success and improvement, or that use of them which they expected, they are apt to have mean thoughts, either of learning or themselves, to quit their studies and throw away their books, as containing nothing but hard words and empty sounds; or else concluding that if there be any real knowledge in them, they themselves have not the understandings capable of it; and that this is so, perhaps I could assure you upon my own experience. Amongst other things to be learned by a young man in this method, whilst others of his age are wholly taken up with Latin and languages, I may also set down geometry for one, having known a young gentleman, bred something after this way, able to demonstrate several propositions in Euclid before he was thirteen.

158. But if such a man cannot be got, who speaks good Latin, and being able to instruct your son in all these parts of knowledge, will undertake it by this method, the next best is to have him taught as near this way as may be, which is by taking some easy and pleasant book, such as *Æsop's Fables,* and writing the English translation (made as literal as it can be) in one line, and the Latin words which answer each of them just over it in another. These let him read every day, over and over again, till he perfectly understands the Latin (but have a care still, whatever you are teaching him, of clogging him with too much at once, or making anything his business but down-right virtue; or reproving him for anything but vice); and then go on to another fable, till he be also perfect in that, not omitting what he is already perfect in, but sometimes reviewing that to keep it in his memory. And when he comes to write, let these be set him for copies, which with the exercise of the hand will also advance him in Latin. This being a more imperfect way than by talking Latin into him; the formation of the verbs first, and afterwards the declensions of the nouns and pronouns perfectly learned by heart, may facilitate his acquaintance with the genius and manner of the Latin tongue, which varies the signification of verbs and nouns, not as the modern languages do by participles prefixed, but by changing the last syllables. More than this of grammar I think he need not have till he can read himself Sanctii Minerva,[2] with Scoppius's notes.

[2] Francis Sanctius, author of *Minerva, seu de causis linguæ Latinæ Commentarius.*

159. When by this way of interlining Latin and English one with another, he has got a moderate knowledge of the Latin tongue, he may then be advanced a little farther to the reading of some other easy Latin book, such as Justin or Eutropius; and to make the reading and understanding of it the less tedious and difficult to him, let him help himself if he please with the English translation. Nor let the objection that he will then know it only by rote (which is not when well-considered of any moment against, but plainly for this way of learning a language) fright anyone. For languages are only to be learned by rote; and a man who does not speak English or Latin perfectly by rote so that having thought of the thing he would speak of, his tongue of course, without thought of rule or grammar, falls into the proper expression and idiom of that language, does not speak it well, nor is master of it. And I would fain have anyone name to me that tongue that anyone can learn, or speak as he should do, by the rules of grammar. Languages were made not by rules of art but by accident, and the common use of the people; and he that will speak them well has no other rule than that, nor anything to trust to but his memory and the habit of speaking after the fashion learned from those that are allowed to speak properly, which in other words is only to speak by rote.

160. For the exercise of his writing, let him sometimes translate Latin into English. But the learning of Latin being nothing but the learning of words, a very unpleasant business both to young and old, join as much other real knowledge with it as you can, beginning still with that which lies most obvious to the senses, such as is the knowledge of minerals, plants, and animals; and particularly timber and fruit trees, their parts and ways of propagation: wherein a great deal may be taught a child, which will not be useless to the man. But more especially geography, astronomy, and anatomy.

161. But if, after all, his fate be to go to school to get the Latin tongue, 'twill be in vain to talk to you concerning the

method I think best to be observed in schools; you must submit to that you find there; nor expect to have it changed for your son: but yet by all means obtain, if you can, that he be not employed in making Latin themes and declamations, and least of all, verses of any kind. You may insist on it, if it will do any good, that you have no design to make him either a Latin orator, or a poet, but barely would have him understand perfectly a Latin author; and that you observe [that] those who teach any of the modern languages, and that with success, never amuse their scholars to make speeches or verses, either in French or Italian, their business being language barely, and not invention.

162. But to tell you a little more fully why I would not have him exercised in making of themes and verses. 1. As to themes, they have, I confess, the pretense of something useful, which is to teach people to speak handsomely and well on any subject; which if it could be attained this way, I own would be a great advantage, there being nothing more becoming a gentleman, nor more useful in all the occurrences of life than to be able on any occasion to speak well and to the purpose. But this I say, that the making of themes, as is usual in schools, helps not one jot toward it. For do but consider what 'tis in making a theme, that a young lad is employed about: 'tis in making a speech on some Latin saying as, *omnia vincit amor;* or *non licet in bello bis peccare,* etc. And here the poor lad, who wants knowledge of those things he is to speak of, which is to be had only from time and observation, must set his invention on the rack to say something, where he knows nothing, which is a sort of Egyptian tyranny to bid them make bricks who have not any of the materials. And therefore it is usual in such cases for the poor children to go to those of higher forms with this petition, "Pray give me a little sense"; which whether it be more reasonable or more ridiculous is not easy to determine. Before a man can be in any capacity to speak on any subject, 'tis necessary he be acquainted with it; or else it is as

foolish to set him to discourse of it as to set a blind man to talk of colors or a deaf man of music. And would you not think him a little cracked who would require another to make an argument on a moot point, who understands nothing of our laws? And what, I pray, do school boys understand concerning those matters which are used to be proposed to them in their themes as subjects to discourse on to whet and exercise their fancies?

163. In the next place consider the language that their themes are made in: 'tis Latin, a language foreign to their country and long since dead everywhere: a language which your son, 'tis a thousand to one, shall never have an occasion once to make a speech in as long as he lives, after he comes to be a man; and a language wherein the manner of expressing oneself is so far different from ours, that to be perfect in that would very little improve the purity and facility of his English style. Besides that, there is now so little room or use for set speeches in our own language in any part of our English business that I can see no pretense for this sort of exercise in our schools, unless it can be supposed that the making of set Latin speeches should be the way to teach men to speak well in English extempore. The way to that I should think rather to be this: that there should be proposed to young gentlemen rational and material questions [suited to their age and capacities and on subjects not wholly unknown to them nor out of their way: such as these] when they are of fit age for such exercise which they should extempore, or after a little meditation in the place, speak to without penning of anything. For, I ask, if we will examine the effects of this way of learning to speak well, who speak best in any business when occasion calls them to it upon any debate, either those who have accustomed themselves to compose and write down beforehand what they would say, or those, who thinking only of the matter, to understand that as well as they can, use themselves only to speak extempore? And he that shall judge by this will be little apt to think that

the accustoming him to studied speeches and set composi-
tions is the way to fit a young gentleman for business.

164. But, perhaps, we shall be told, 'tis to improve and perfect them in the Latin tongue. 'Tis true that this is their
proper business at school; but the making of themes is not
the way to it: that perplexes their brains about invention of
things to be said, not about the signification of words to be
learned; and when they are making a theme, 'tis thoughts
they search and sweat for, and not language. But the learning and mastery of a tongue, being uneasy and unpleasant
enough in itself, should not be cumbered with any other
difficulties, as is done in this way of proceeding. In fine, if
boys' invention be to be quickened by such exercise, let them
make themes in English, where they have facility and a command of words, and will better see what kind of thoughts
they have when put into their own language: and if the
Latin tongue be to be learned, let it be done the easiest way,
without toiling and disgusting the mind by so uneasy an employment as that of making speeches joined to it.

165. If these be any reasons against children's making
Latin themes at school, I have much more to say, and of
more weight, against making verses: verses of any sort. For
if he have no genius to poetry, 'tis the most unreasonable
thing in the world to torment a child and waste his time about
that which can never succeed: and if he have a poetic vein,
'tis to me the strangest thing in the world that the father
should desire or suffer it to be cherished or improved. Methinks the parents should labor to have it stifled and suppressed as much as may be; and I know not what reason a
father can have to wish his son a poet, who does not desire
to have him bid defiance to all other callings and business,
which is not yet the worst of the case; for if he prove a suc-
cessful rhymer and get once the reputation of a wit, I desire
it may be considered what company and places he is like
to spend his time in, nay, and estate too: for it is very seldom seen that anyone discovers mines of gold or silver in

Parnassus. 'Tis a pleasant air, but a barren soil; and there are very few instances of those who have added to their patrimony by anything they have reaped from thence. Poetry and gaming, which usually go together, are alike in this too, that they seldom bring any advantage but to those who have nothing else to live on. Men of estates almost constantly go away losers; and 'tis well if they escape at a cheaper rate than their whole estates, or the greatest part of them. If therefore you would not have your son the fiddle to every jovial company, without whom the sparks could not relish their wine nor know how to pass an afternoon idly; if you would not have him waste his time and estate to divert others and condemn the dirty acres left him by his ancestors, I do not think you will much care he should be a poet, or that his school-master should enter him in versifying. But yet, if anyone will think poetry a desirable quality in his son, and that the study of it would raise his fancy and parts, he must needs yet confess that to that end reading the excellent Greek and Roman poets is of more use than making bad verses of his own in a language that is not his own. And he, whose design it is to excel in English poetry, would not, I guess, think the ways to it were to make his first essays in Latin verses.

166. Another thing very ordinary in the vulgar method of grammar schools there is, of which I see no use at all, unless it be to balk young lads in the way to learning languages, which, in my opinion, should be made as easy and pleasant as may be; and that which was painful in it, as much as possible, quite removed. That which I mean, and here complain of, is their being forced to learn by heart great parcels of the authors which are taught them, wherein I can discover no advantage at all, especially to the business they are upon. Languages are to be learned only by reading and talking, and not by scraps of authors got by heart; which when a man's head is stuffed with, he has got the just furniture of a pedant, and 'tis the ready way to make him one, than which there

is nothing less becoming a gentleman. For what can be more ridiculous than to mix the rich and handsome thoughts and sayings of others with a deal of poor stuff of his own, which is thereby the more exposed, and has no other grace in it, nor will otherwise recommend the speaker than a threadbare russet coat would, that was set off with large patches of scarlet and glittering brocade. Indeed, where a passage comes in the way, whose matter is worth remembrance and the expression of it very close and excellent (as there are many such in the ancient authors), it may not be amiss to lodge it in the mind of young scholars, and with such admirable strokes of those great masters, sometimes exercise the memory of schoolboys. But their learning of their lessons by heart, as they happen to fall out in their books, without choice or distinction, I know not what it serves for, but to misspend their time and pains and give them disgust and aversion to their books, wherein they find nothing but useless trouble.

167. But under whose care soever the child is put to be taught during the tender and flexible years of his life, this is certain, it should be one who thinks Latin and language the least part of education; one who, knowing how much virtue and a well-tempered soul is to be preferred to any sort of learning or language, makes it his chief business to form the mind of his scholars and give them a right disposition, which if once got, though all the rest should be neglected, would in due time produce all the rest: and which if it be not got and settled, so as to keep out ill and vicious habits, languages and sciences and all the other accomplishments of education will be to no purpose but to make the worse or more dangerous man. And indeed, whatever stir there is made about getting of Latin, as the great and difficult business, his mother may teach it him herself, if she will but spend two or three hours in a day with him and make him read the Evangelists in Latin to her: for she need but buy a Latin Testament, and, having got somebody to mark the last syllable but one where it is long in words above two syllables (which is enough to

regulate her pronunciation and accenting the words), read daily the Gospels, and then let her avoid understanding them in Latin if she can. And when she understands the Evangelists in Latin, let her in the same manner read *Æsop's Fables,* and so proceed on to Eutropius, Justin, and such other books, I do not mention this as an imagination of what I fancy may do, but as of a thing I have known done, and the Latin tongue with ease got this way.

But to return to what I was saying: he that takes on him the charge of bringing up young men, especially young gentlemen, should have something more in him than Latin, more than even a knowledge in the liberal sciences: he should be a person of eminent virtue and prudence, and with good sense, have good humor and the skill to carry himself with gravity, ease, and kindness, in a constant conversation with his pupils.

168. At the same time that he is learning French and Latin, a child, as has been said, may also be entered in arithmetic, geography, chronology, history and geometry too. For if these be taught him in French or Latin, when he begins once to understand either of these tongues, he will get a knowledge in these sciences, and the language to boot.

Geography I think should be begun with: for the learning of the figure of the globe, the situation and boundaries of the four parts of the world, and that of particular kingdoms and countries, being only an exercise of the eyes and memory, a child with pleasure will learn and retain them. And this is so certain, that I now live in the house with a child whom his mother has so well instructed this way in geography that he knew the limits of the four parts of the world, could readily point, being asked, to any country upon the globe, or any county in the map of England; knew all the great rivers, promontories, straits and bays in the world; and could find the longitude and latitude of any place, before he was six years old.[3] These things, that he will thus learn by sight, and have

[3] The reference is to Frank Masham, son of Lady Masham in whose home Locke spent his later years.

by rote in his memory, are not all, I confess, that he is to learn upon the globes. But yet it is a good step and preparation to it, and will make the remainder much easier, when his judgment is grown ripe enough for it: besides that, it gets so much time now; and by the pleasure of knowing things, leads him on insensibly to the gaining of languages.

169. When he has the natural parts of the globe well fixed in his memory, it may then be time to begin arithmetic. By the natural parts of the globe, I mean the several positions of the parts of the earth and sea, under different names and distinctions of countries, not coming yet to those artificial and imaginary lines which have been invented, and are only supposed for the better improvement of that science.

170. Arithmetic is the easiest, and consequently the first sort of abstract reasoning, which the mind commonly bears or accustoms itself to: and is of so general use in all parts of life and business that scarce anything is to be done without it. This is certain, a man cannot have too much of it, nor too perfectly: he should therefore begin to be exercised in counting as soon, and as far as he is capable of it; and do something in it every day till he is master of the art of numbers. When he understands addition and subtraction, he then may be advanced farther in geography, after he is acquainted with the poles, zones, parallel circles, and meridians, be taught longitude and latitude, and the use of maps; and by that time he is perfected in these circles of the globes, with the horizon and ecliptic, he may be taught the same thing also on the celestial globe, with the figure and position of the several constellations which may be showed him first upon the globe and then in the heavens.

When that is done, and he knows pretty well the constellations of this our hemisphere, it may be time to give him some notions of this our planetary world; and to that purpose, it may not be amiss to make him a draught of the Copernican system, and therein explain to him the situation of the planets, their respective distances from the sun, the center of their revolutions. This will prepare him to understand the motion and theory of the planets the most easy and natural way. For since astronomers no longer doubt of the motion of the planets about the sun, it is fit he should proceed upon that hypothesis, which is not only the simplest and least perplexed for a learner, but also the likeliest to be true in itself. But in this, as in all other parts of instruction, great care must be taken with children, to begin with that which is plain and simple, and to teach them as little as can be at once, and settle that well in their heads before you proceed to the next, or anything new in that science. Give them first one simple idea, and see that they take it right, and perfectly comprehend it before you go any farther, and then add some other simple idea which lies next in your way to what you aim at; and so proceeding by gentle and insensible steps, children without confusion and amazement will have their understandings opened and their thoughts extended farther than could have been expected. And when anyone has learned anything himself, there is no such way to fix it in his memory and to encourage him to go on as to set him to teach it to others.

171. When he has once got such an acquaintance with the globes as is above mentioned, he may be fit to be tried in a little geometry; wherein I think the first six books of Euclid enough for him to be taught. For I am in some doubt whether more to a man of business be necessary or useful. At least, if he have a genius and inclination to it, being entered so far by his tutor, he will be able to go on of himself without a teacher.

The globes therefore must be studied, and that diligently; and I think may be begun betimes, if the tutor will be but careful to distinguish what the child is capable of knowing, and what not; for which this may be a rule that perhaps will go a pretty way, *viz.* that children may be taught anything that falls under their senses, especially their sight, as far as their memories only are exercised: and thus a child very young may learn which is the equator, which the meridian, etc., which Europe, and which England, upon the globes, as soon almost as he knows the rooms of the house he lives in, if care be taken not to teach him too much at once, nor to set him upon a new part till that which he is upon be perfectly learned and fixed in his memory.

172. With geography, chronology ought to go hand in hand. I mean the general part of it, so that he may have in his mind a view of the whole current of time, and the several considerable epochs that are made use of in history. Without these two, history, which is the great mistress of prudence and civil knowledge, and ought to be the proper study of a gentleman, or man of business in the world; without geography and chronology, I say, history will be very ill retained, and very little useful; but be only a jumble of matters of fact, confusedly heaped together without order or instruction. 'Tis by these two that the actions of mankind are ranked into their proper places of time and countries, under which circumstances they are not only much easier kept in the memory, but in that natural order are only capable to afford those observations which make a man the better and the abler for reading them.

When I speak of chronology as a science he should be perfect in, I do not mean the little controversies that are in it. These are endless, and most of them of so little importance to a gentleman as not to deserve to be inquired into, were they capable of an easy decision. And therefore all that learned noise and dust of the chronologist is wholly to be avoided. The most useful book I have seen in that part of learning is a small treatise of Strauchius,[4] which is printed in twelves, under the title of *Breviarium Chronologicum*, out of which may be selected all that is necessary to be taught a young gentleman concerning chronology; for all that is in that treatise a learner need not be cumbered with. He has in him the most remarkable or useful epochs reduced all to that of the Julian Period, which is the easiest and plainest

[4] Giles Strauchius of Wittenberg, 1632–1682.

and surest method that can be made use of in chronology. To this treatise of Strauchius, Helvicus's [5] tables may be added, as a book to be turned to on all occasions.

173. As nothing teaches, so nothing delights more than history. The first of these recommends it to the study of grown men; the latter makes me think it the fittest for a young lad, who as soon as he is instructed in chronology, and acquainted with the several epochs in use in this part of the world, and can reduce them to the Julian Period, should then have some Latin history put into his hand. The choice should be directed by the easiness of the style; for wherever he begins, chronology will keep it from confusion; and the pleasantness of the subject inviting him to read, the language will insensibly be got without that terrible vexation and uneasiness which children suffer where they are put into books beyond their capacity; such as are the Roman orators and poets, only to learn the Roman language. When he has by reading mastered the easier, such perhaps as Justin, Eutropius, Quintus Curtius,[6] etc., the next degree to these will give him no great trouble: and thus by a gradual progress from the plainest and easiest historians, he may at last come to read the most difficult and sublime of the Latin authors, such as are Tully, Virgil, and Horace.

174. The knowledge of virtue, all along from the beginning, in all the instances he is capable of, being taught him more by practice than rules; and the love of reputation, instead of satisfying his appetite, being made habitual in him, I know not whether he should read any other discourses of morality but what he finds in the Bible; or have any system of ethics put into his hand till he can read Tully's *Offices* not as a schoolboy to learn Latin, but as one that would be informed in the principles and precepts of virtue for the conduct of his life.

[5] Christopher Helvicus, 1581–1617.
[6] Three early Roman historians: Justin (Junianus Justinus) author of *Historiarum Philippicarum;* Eutropius, author of *Breviarium Historiæ Romanæ;* Quintus Curtius, author of *De rebus gestis Alexandri magni.*

175. When he has pretty well digested Tully's *Offices,* it may be seasonable to set him upon Grotius' *De Jure Belli et Pacis,* or, which perhaps is the better of the two, Pufendorf's *De Jure Naturali et Gentium;* [7] wherein he will be instructed in the natural rights of men, and the original and foundations of society, and the duties resulting from thence. This general part of civil law and history are studies which a gentleman should not barely touch at, but constantly dwell upon, and never have done with. A virtuous and well-behaved young man, that is well-versed in the general part of the civil law (which concerns not the chicane of private cases, but the affairs and intercourse of civilized nations in general, grounded upon principles of reason), understands Latin well, and can write a good hand, one may turn loose into the world with great assurance that he will find employment and esteem everywhere.

176. It would be strange to suppose an English gentleman should be ignorant of the law of his country. This, whatever station he is in, is so requisite, that from a Justice of the Peace to a Minister of State I know no place he can well fill without it. I do not mean the chicane or wrangling and captious part of the law: a gentleman, whose business is to seek the true measures of right and wrong, and not the arts how to avoid doing the one and secure himself in doing the other, ought to be as far from such a study of the law, as he is concerned diligently to apply himself to that wherein he may be serviceable to his country. And to that purpose, I think the right way for a gentleman to study our law, which he does not design for his calling, is to take a view of our English constitution and government in the ancient books of the common law, and some more modern writers, who out of them have given an account of this government. And having got a true idea of that, then to read our history, and

---

[7] Samuel Pufendorf (1632–1694) carried forward the theories of Grotius, applying some of the doctrines of Hobbes, but assuming as basic the conception that a state of peace rather than a state of war is the state of nature.

with it join in every king's reign the laws then made. This will give an insight into the reason of our statutes, and show the true ground upon which they came to be made, and what weight they ought to have.

177. Rhetoric and logic being the arts that in the ordinary method usually follow immediately after grammar,[8] it may perhaps be wondered that I have said so little of them. The reason is, because of the little advantage young people receive by them; for I have seldom or never observed anyone to get the skill of reasoning well, or speaking handsomely, by studying those rules which pretend to teach it: and therefore I would have a young gentleman take a view of them in the shortest systems could be found, without dwelling long on the contemplation and study of those formalities. Right reasoning is founded on something else than the *predicaments* and *predicables,* and does not consist in talking in *mode* and *figure* itself. But 'tis beside my present business to enlarge upon this speculation. To come therefore to what we have in hand; if you would have your son reason well, let him read Chillingworth;[9] and if you would have him speak well, let him be conversant in Tully, to give him the true idea of eloquence; and let him read those things that are well-written in English, to perfect his style in the purity of our language. If the use and end of right reasoning be to have right notions and a right judgment of things, to distinguish betwixt truth and falsehood, right and wrong, and to act accordingly; be sure not to let your son be bred up in the art and formality of disputing, either practicing it himself or admiring it in others; unless instead of an able man, you desire to have him an insignificant wrangler, opiniator in discourse, and priding himself in contradicting others; or, which is worse, questioning everything, and thinking there is no such thing as truth to be sought, but only victory, in

[8] The trivium consisted of these three subjects.
[9] William Chillingworth, 1602–1644, a distinguished English divine whose *The Religion of Protestants* is one of the great works of the century.

disputing. Truth is to be found and maintained by a mature and due consideration of things themselves, and not by artificial terms and ways of arguing; which lead not men so much into the discovery of truth, as into a captious and fallacious use of doubtful words, which is the most useless and disingenuous way of talking and most unbecoming a gentleman or a lover of truth of anything in the world.

[178.] Natural philosophy, as a speculative science, I think we have none, and perhaps I may think I have reason to say we never shall. The works of nature are contrived by a wisdom, and operate by ways too far surpassing our faculties to discover or capacities to conceive, for us ever to be able to reduce them into a science. Natural philosophy being the knowledge of the principles, properties and operations of things as they are in themselves, I imagine there are two parts of it, one comprehending spirits, with their nature and qualities, and the other bodies. The first of these is usually referred to metaphysics: but under what title soever the consideration of spirits comes, I think it ought to go before the study of matter and body, not as a science that can be methodized into a system and treated of upon principles of knowledge; but as an enlargement of our minds towards a truer and fuller comprehension of the intellectual world to which we are led both by reason and revelation. And since the clearest and largest discoveries we have of other spirits, besides God and our own souls, is imparted to us from heaven by revelation, I think the information that at least young people should have of them should be taken from that revelation. To this purpose, I think, it would be well if there were made a good history of the Bible for young people to read; wherein everything that is fit to be put into it, being laid down in its due order of time, and several things omitted which were suited only to riper age, that confusion which is usually produced by promiscuous reading of the Scripture, as it lies now bound up in our Bibles, would be avoided. And also this other good obtained, that by reading of it constantly, there would be instilled into the minds of children a notion and belief of spirits, they having so much to do in all the transactions of that history, which will be a good preparation to the study of bodies. For without the notion and allowance of spirits, our philosophy will be lame and defective in one main part of it when it leaves out the contemplation of the most excellent and powerful part of the creation.

179. Of this *History of the Bible,* I think too it would be well if there were a short and plain epitome made, containing the chief and most material heads, for children to be conversant in as soon as they can read. This, though it will lead them early into some notion of spirits, yet it is not contrary to what I said above, that I would not have children troubled, whilst young, with notions of spirits; whereby my meaning was, that I think it inconvenient that their yet tender minds should receive early impressions of goblins, specters, and apparitions, wherewith their maids and those about them are apt to fright them into a compliance with their orders, which often proves a great inconvenience to them all their lives after, by subjecting their minds to frights, fearful apprehensions, weakness and superstition; which when coming abroad into the world and conversation they grow weary and ashamed of, it not seldom happens that, to make, as they think, a thorough cure, and ease themselves of a load which has sat so heavy on them, they throw away the thoughts of all spirits together, and so run into the other, but worse, extreme.

180. The reason why I would have this premised to the study of bodies, and the doctrine of the Scriptures well imbibed before young men be entered in natural philosophy, is, because matter, being a thing that all our senses are constantly conversant with, it is so apt to possess the mind, and exclude all other beings but matter, that prejudice, grounded on such principles, often leaves no room for the admittance of spirits, or the allowing any such things as immaterial beings *in rerum natura ;* when yet it is evident that

by mere matter and motion none of the great phænomena of nature can be resolved, to instance but in that common one of gravity, which I think impossible to be explained by any natural operation of matter, or any other law of motion, but the positive will of a superior being so ordering it. And therefore since the deluge cannot be well explained without admitting something out of the ordinary course of nature, I propose it to be considered whether God's altering the center of gravity in the earth for a time (a thing as intelligible as gravity itself, which perhaps a little variation of causes unknown to us would produce) will not more easily account for Noah's flood than any hypothesis yet made use of to solve it. But this I mention by the bye, to show the necessity of having recourse to something beyond bare matter and its motion in the explication of nature; to which the notions of spirits and their power, to whose operation so much is attributed in the Bible, may be a fit preparative, reserving to a fitter opportunity a fuller explication of this hypothesis, and the application of it to all the parts of the deluge, and any difficulties can be supposed in the history of the flood as recorded in the Bible.

181. But to return to the study of natural philosophy. Though the world be full of systems of it, yet I cannot say I know any one which can be taught a young man as a science wherein he may be sure to find truth and certainty, which is what all sciences give an expectation of. I do not hence conclude that none of them are to be read. It is necessary for a gentleman in this learned age to look into some of them to fit himself for conversation: but whether that of Descartes be put into his hands, as that which is most in fashion, or it be thought fit to give him a short view of that and several others also, I think the systems of natural philosophy that have obtained in this part of the world are to be read more to know the hypotheses, and to understand the terms and ways of talking of the several sects, than with hopes to gain thereby a comprehensive, scientifical, and satis-

factory knowledge of the works of nature. Only this may be said, that the modern Corpuscularians talk in most things more intelligently than the Peripatetics, who possessed the schools immediately before them. He that would look further back and acquaint himself with the several opinions of the ancients, may consult Dr. Cudworth's *Intellectual System,* wherein that very learned author hath with such accurateness and judgment collected and explained the opinions of the Greek philosophers, that what principles they built on and what were the chief hypotheses that divided them is better to be seen in him than anywhere else that I know. But I would not deter anyone from the study of nature because all the knowledge we have or possibly can have of it cannot be brought into a science. There are very many things in it that are convenient and necessary to be known to a gentleman; and a great many other that will abundantly reward the pains of the curious with delight and advantage. But these, I think, are rather to be found amongst such writers as have employed themselves in making rational experiments and observations than in starting barely speculative systems. Such writings therefore, as many of Mr. Boyle's [10] are, with others that have writ of husbandry, planting, gardening, and the like, may be fit for a gentleman, when he has a little acquainted himself with some of the systems of the natural philosophy in fashion.

182. Though the systems of physic that I have met with afford little encouragement to look for certainty or science in any treatise which shall pretend to give us a body of natural philosophy from the first principles of bodies in general, yet the incomparable Mr. Newton has shown how far mathematics applied to some parts of nature may, upon principles that matter of fact justify, carry us in the knowledge of some, as I may so call them, particular provinces of the incomprehensible universe. And if others could give us so good and clear an account of other parts of nature, as he

[10] Robert Boyle, 1627–1691.

has of this our planetary world, and the most considerable phænomena observable in it, in his admirable book, *Philosophiæ naturalis Principia Mathematica,* we might in time hope to be furnished with more true and certain knowledge in several parts of this stupendous machine than hitherto we could have expected. And though there are very few that have mathematics enough to understand his demonstrations, yet the most accurate mathematicians who have examined them allowing them to be such, his book will deserve to be read, and give no small light and pleasure to those, who, willing to understand the motions, properties, and operations of the great masses of matter in this our solar system, will but carefully mind his conclusions, which may be depended on as propositions well proved.

183. This is, in short, what I have thought concerning a young gentleman's studies; wherein it will possibly be wondered that I should omit Greek, since amongst the Grecians is to be found the original as it were, and foundation of all that learning which we have in this part of the world. I grant it so; and will add that no man can pass for a scholar that is ignorant of the Greek tongue. But I am not here considering the education of a professed scholar, but of a gentleman, to whom Latin and French, as the world now goes, is by everyone acknowledged to be necessary. When he comes to be a man, if he has a mind to carry his studies farther, and look into the Greek learning, he will then easily get that tongue himself: and if he has not that inclination, his learning of it under a tutor will be but lost labor, and much of his time and pains spent in that which will be neglected and thrown away as soon as he is at liberty. For how many are there of an hundred, even amongst scholars themselves, who retain the Greek they carried from school; or ever improve it to a familiar reading and perfect understanding of Greek authors?

184. Besides what is to be had from study and books, there are other accomplishments necessary to a gentleman, to be

got by exercise, and to which time is to be allowed, and for which masters must be had.

Dancing being that which gives graceful motions all the life, and above all things manliness and a becoming confidence to young children, I think it cannot be learned too early, after they are once of an age and strength capable of it. But you must be sure to have a good master, that knows, and can teach what is graceful and becoming, and what gives a freedom and easiness to all the motions of the body. One that teaches not this is worse than none at all: natural unfashionableness being much better than apish affected postures; and I think it much more passable to put off the hat and make a leg like an honest country gentleman than like an ill-fashioned dancing master. For as for the jigging part, and the figures of dances, I count that little or nothing, farther than as it tends to perfect graceful carriage.

185. Music is thought to have some affinity with dancing, and a good hand upon some instruments is by many people mightily valued. But it wastes so much of a young man's time to gain but a moderate skill in it, and engages often in such odd company, that many think it much better spared: and I have amongst men of parts and business so seldom heard anyone commended or esteemed for having an excellency in music, that amongst all those things that ever came into the list of accomplishments, I think I may give it the last place. Our short lives will not serve us for the attainment of all things; nor can our minds be always intent on something to be learned. The weakness of our constitutions both of mind and body requires that we should be often unbent: and he that will make a good use of any part of his life must allow a large portion of it to recreation. At least, this must not be denied to young people; unless whilst you with too much haste make them old, you have the displeasure to set them in their graves or a second childhood sooner than you could wish. And therefore, I think that the time and pains allotted to serious improvements

should be employed about things of most use and consequence, and that too in the methods the most easy and short
that could be at any rate obtained: and perhaps, as I have
above said, it would be none of the least secrets of education to make the exercises of the body and the mind the
recreation one to another. I doubt not but that something
might be done in it by a prudent man that would well consider the temper and inclination of his pupil. For he that
is wearied either with study or dancing does not desire
presently to go to sleep, but to do something else which may
divert and delight him. But this must be always remembered,
that nothing can come into the account of recreation that
is not done with delight.

186. Fencing and riding the great horse are looked upon
so necessary parts of breeding that it would be thought a
great omission to neglect them; the latter of the two, being
for the most part to be learned only in great towns, is one
of the best exercises for health which is to be had in those
places of ease and luxury: and upon that account makes a
fit part of a young gentleman's employment during his abode
there. And as far as it conduces to give a man a firm and
graceful seat on horseback, and to make him able to teach
his horse to stop and turn quick, and to rest on his haunches,
is of use to a gentleman both in peace and war. But whether
it be of moment enough to be made a business of, and deserve to take up more of his time than should barely for
his health be employed at due intervals in some such vigorous
exercise, I shall leave to the discretion of parents and tutors;
who will do well to remember, in all the parts of education,
that most time and application is to be bestowed on that
which is like to be of greatest consequence and frequentest
use in the ordinary course and occurrences of that life the
young man is designed for.

187. As for fencing, it seems to me a good exercise for
health, but dangerous to the life; the confidence of their
skill being apt to engage in quarrels those that think they

have some skill and to make them often more touchy than needs on point of honor and slight occasions. Young men, in their warm blood, are forward to think they have in vain learned to fence, if they never show their skill and courage in a duel; and they seem to have reason. But how many sad tragedies that reason has been the occasion of, the tears of many a mother can witness. A man that cannot fence will be more careful to keep out of bullies' and gamesters' company, and will not be half so apt to stand upon punctilios, nor to give affronts, or fiercely justify them when given, which is that which usually makes the quarrel. And when a man is in the field, a moderate skill in fencing rather exposes him to the sword of his enemy than secures him from it. And certainly a man of courage who cannot fence at all and therefore will put all upon one thrust and not stand parrying, has the odds against a moderate fencer, especially if he has skill in wrestling. And therefore, if any provision be to be made against such accidents, and a man be to prepare his son for duels, I had much rather mine should be a good wrestler than an ordinary fencer, which is the most a gentleman can attain to in it, unless he will be constantly in the fencing-school and every day exercising. But since fencing and riding the great horse are so generally looked upon as necessary qualifications in the breeding of a gentleman, it will be hard wholly to deny anyone of that rank these marks of distinction. I shall leave it therefore to the father to consider how far the temper of his son and the station he is like to be in will allow or encourage him to comply with fashions which, having very little to do with civil life, were yet formerly unknown to the most warlike nations, and seem to have added little of force or courage to those who have received them; unless we will think martial skill or prowess have been improved by dueling, with which fencing came into, and with which I presume it will go out of the world.

188. These are my present thoughts concerning learning

and accomplishments. The great business of all is virtue and wisdom:

Nullum numen abest si sit Prudentia.[11]

Teach him to get a mastery over his inclinations, and submit his appetite to reason. This being obtained, and by constant practice settled into habit, the hardest part of the task is over. To bring a young man to this, I know nothing which so much contributes as the love of praise and commendation, which should therefore be instilled into him by all arts imaginable. Make his mind as sensible of credit and shame as may be; and when you have done that, you have put a principle into him which will influence his actions when you are not by, to which the fear of a little smart of a rod is not comparable, and which will be the proper stock whereon afterwards to graff the true principles of morality and religion.

189. I have one thing more to add, which as soon as I mention I shall run the danger of being suspected to have forgot what I am about, and what I have above written concerning education all tending towards a gentleman's calling, with which a trade seems wholly inconsistent. And yet I cannot forbear to say, I would have him learn a trade, a manual trade: nay two or three, but one more particularly.

190. The busy inclination of children being always to be directed to something that may be useful to them, the advantage may be considered of two kinds: 1. Where the skill itself that is got by exercise is worth the having. Thus skill not only in languages and learned sciences, but in painting, turning, gardening, tempering and working in iron, and all other useful arts is worth the having. 2. Where the exercise itself, without any consideration, is necessary or useful for health. Knowledge in some things is so necessary to be got by children whilst they are young, that some part of their

[11] From Juvenal: "No deity is absent where there is Prudence."

time is to be allotted to their improvement in them, though those employments contribute nothing at all to their health. Such are reading and writing and all other sedentary studies for the improvement of the mind, which are the unavoidable business of gentlemen quite from their cradles. Other manual arts, which are both got and exercised by labor, do many of them by their exercise contribute to our health too, especially such as employ us in the open air. In these, then, health and improvement may be joined together; and of these should some fit ones be chosen, to be made the recreations of one whose chief business is with books and study. In this choice the age and inclination of the person is to be considered, and constraint always to be avoided in bringing him to it. For command and force may often create, but can never cure, an aversion: and whatever anyone is brought to by compulsion, he will leave as soon as he can, and be little profited and less recreated by, whilst he is at it.

191. That which of all others would please me best, would be a painter, were there not an argument or two against it not easy to be answered. First, ill painting is one of the worst things in the world; and to attain a tolerable degree of skill in it requires too much of a man's time. If he have a natural inclination to it, it will endanger the neglect of all other more useful studies to give way to that; and if he have no inclination to it, all the time, pains, and money shall be employed in it, will be thrown away to no purpose. Another reason why I am not for painting in a gentleman is because it is a sedentary recreation, which more employs the mind than the body. A gentleman's more serious employment I look on to be study; and when that demands relaxation and refreshment, it should be in some exercise of the body, which unbends the thought, and confirms the health and strength. For these two reasons I am not for painting.

192. In the next place, for a country gentleman I should propose one, or rather both these, *viz.* gardening and working in wood, as a carpenter, joiner, or turner, as being fit and

healthy recreations for a man of study or business. For since
the mind endures not to be constantly employed in the same
thing or way, and sedentary or studious men should have
some exercise that at the same time might divert their minds
and employ their bodies, I know none that could do it better
for a country gentleman than these two; the one of them
affording him exercise when the weather or season keeps him
from the other. Besides that by being skilled in the one of
them, he will be able to govern and teach his gardener; by
the other, contrive and make a great many things both of
delight and use: though these I propose not as the chief end
of his labor, but as temptations to it; diversion from his other
more serious thoughts and employments by useful and healthy
manual exercise being what I chiefly aim at in it.

193. Nor let it be thought that I mistake, when I call these
or the like trades diversions or recreations: for recreation
is not being idle (as everyone may observe) but easing the
wearied part by change of business: and he that thinks diversion may not lie in hard and painful labor, forgets the early
rising, hard riding, heat, cold, and hunger of huntsmen, which
is yet known to be the constant recreation of men of the
greatest condition. Delving, planting, inoculating, or any the
like profitable employments, would be no less a diversion
than any of the idle sports in fashion, if men could but be
brought to delight in them, which custom and skill in a
trade will quickly bring anyone to do. And I doubt not but
there are to be found those who, being frequently called to
cards or any other play by those they could not refuse, have
been more tired with these recreations than with any the
most serious employment of life, though the play has been
such as they have naturally had no aversion to, and with
which they could willingly sometimes divert themselves.

194. Though when one reflects on these and other like
pastimes (as they are called) one finds they leave little satisfaction behind them, when they are over; and most commonly give more vexation than delight to people whilst they

are actually engaged in them, and neither profit the mind nor the body. They are a plain instance to me that men cannot be perfectly idle; they must be doing something. The skill should be, so to order their time of recreation, that it may relax and refresh the part that has been exercised and is tired, and yet do something which besides the present delight and ease, may produce what will afterwards be profitable. It has been nothing but the vanity and pride of greatness and riches that has brought unprofitable and dangerous pastimes into fashion, and persuaded people into a belief that the learning or putting their hands to anything that was useful could not be a diversion fit for a gentleman. This has been that which has given cards, dice and drinking so much credit in the world: and a great many throw away their spare hours in them, through the prevalency of custom and want of some better employment to pass their time, more than from any real delight is to be found in them, only because it being very irksome and uneasy to do nothing at all, they had never learned any laudable manual art wherewith to divert themselves, and so they betake themselves to those foolish or ill ways in use, to help off their time, which a rational man, till corrupted by custom, could find very little pleasure in.

195. I say not this, that I would never have a young gentleman accommodate himself to the innocent diversions in fashion amongst those of his age and condition. I am so far from having him austere and morose to that degree that I would persuade him to more than ordinary complaisance for all the gaieties and diversions of those he converses with, and be averse or testy in nothing they should desire of him, that might become a gentleman and an honest man. But allowance being made for idle and jovial conversation and all fashionable becoming recreations; I say, a young man will have time enough from his serious and main business, to learn almost any trade. 'Tis want of application, and not of time, that men are not skillful in more arts than one; and

an hour in a day, constantly employed in such a way of diversion, will carry a man in a short time a great deal farther than he can imagine: which, if it were of no other use but to drive the common, vicious, useless, and dangerous pastimes out of fashion, and to show there was no need of them, would deserve to be encouraged. If men from their youth were weaned from that sauntering humor wherein some out of custom let a good part of their lives run uselessly away, without either business or recreation, they would find time enough to acquire dexterity and skill in hundreds of things, which, though remote from their proper callings, would not at all interfere with them. And therefore, I think, for this, as well as other reasons before-mentioned, a lazy, listless humor that idly dreams away the time, is of all others the least to be indulged or permitted in young people. It is the proper state of one sick and out of order in his health, and is tolerable in nobody else of what age or condition soever.

196. To the arts above-mentioned may be added perfuming, varnishing, graving, and several sorts of working in iron, brass, and silver; and if, as it happens to most young gentlemen, that a considerable part of his time be spent in a great town, he may learn to cut, polish, and set precious stones, or employ himself in grinding and polishing optical glasses. Amongst the great variety there is of ingenious manual arts, 'twill be impossible that no one should be found to please and delight him, unless he be either idle or debauched, which is not to be supposed in a right way of education. And since he cannot be always employed in study, reading, and conversation, there will be many an hour, besides what his exercises will take up, which, if not spent this way, will be spent worse. For I conclude, a young man will seldom desire to sit perfectly still and idle; or, if he does, 'tis a fault that ought to be mended.

197. But if his mistaken parents, frighted with the disgraceful names of mechanic and trade, shall have an aversion to anything of this kind in their children; yet there is one

thing relating to trade, which, when they consider, they will think absolutely necessary for their sons to learn.

Merchants' accompts, though a science not likely to help a gentleman to get an estate, yet possibly there is not anything of more use and efficacy, to make him preserve the estate he has. 'Tis seldom observed that he who keeps an accompt of his income and expenses, and thereby has constantly under view the course of his domestic affairs lets them run to ruin: and I doubt not but many a man gets behindhand before he is aware, or runs farther on when he is once in, for want of this care, or the skill to do it. I would therefore advise all gentlemen to learn perfectly merchants' accompts, and not to think it is a skill that belongs not to them, because it has received its name from, and has been chiefly practiced by men of traffic.

198. When my young master has once got the skill of keeping accounts (which is a business of reason more than arithmetic) perhaps it will not be amiss that his father from thenceforth require him to do it in all his concernments. Not that I would have him set down every pint of wine or play that costs him money; the general name of expenses will serve for such things well enough: nor would I have his father look so narrowly into these accompts, as to take occasion from thence to criticise on his expenses; he must remember that he himself was once a young man, and not forget the thoughts he had then, nor the right his son has to have the same and to have allowance made for them. If therefore I would have the young gentleman obliged to keep an account, it is not at all to have that way a check upon his expenses (for what the father allows him, he ought to let him be fully master of) but only that he might be brought early into the custom of doing it and that it might be made familiar and habitual to him betimes, which will be so useful and necessary to be constantly practiced the whole course of his life. A noble Venetian, whose son wallowed in the plenty of his father's riches, finding his son's expenses grow very high and

extravagant, ordered his cashier to let him have for the future no more money than what he should count when he received it. This one would think no great restraint to a young gentleman's expenses; who could freely have as much money as he would tell. But yet this, to one that was used to nothing but the pursuit of his pleasures, proved a very great trouble, which at last ended in this sober and advantageous reflection: if it be so much pains to me barely to count the money I would spend, what labor and pains did it cost my ancestors, not only to count, but get it? This rational thought, suggested by this little pains imposed upon him, wrought so effectually upon his mind that it made him take up, and from that time forwards prove a good husband. This, at least, everybody must allow, that nothing is likelier to keep a man within compass, than the having constantly before his eyes the state of his affairs in a regular course of accompt.

199. The last part usually in education is travel, which is commonly thought to finish the work, and complete the gentleman. I confess travel into foreign countries has great advantages, but the time usually chosen to send young men abroad, is, I think, of all other, that which renders them least capable of reaping those advantages. Those which are proposed, as to the main of them, may be reduced to these two: first, language, secondly, an improvement in wisdom and prudence, by seeing men and conversing with people of tempers, customs and ways of living, different from one another, and especially from those of his parish and neighborhood. But from sixteen to one-and-twenty, which is the ordinary time of travel, men are, of all their lives, the least suited to these improvements. The first season to get foreign languages and form the tongue to their true accents, I should think, should be from seven to fourteen or sixteen, and then too a tutor with them is useful and necessary, who may with those languages teach them other things. But to put them out of their parents' view at a great distance under a gov-

ernor, when they think themselves to be too much men to be governed by others, and yet have not prudence and experience enough to govern themselves, what is it but to expose them to all the greatest dangers of their whole life, when they have the least fence and guard against them? Till that boiling boisterous part of life comes in, it may be hoped the tutor may have some authority: neither the stubbornness of age, nor the temptation or examples of others, can take him from his tutor's conduct till fifteen or sixteen: but then, when he begins to comfort himself with men, and thinks himself one; when he comes to relish and pride himself in manly vices, and thinks it a shame to be any longer under the control and conduct of another, what can be hoped from even the most careful and discreet governor, when neither he has power to compel, nor his pupil a disposition to be persuaded; but on the contrary, has the advice of warm blood and prevailing fashion, to hearken to the temptations of his companions, just as wise as himself, rather than to the persuasions of his tutor, who is now looked on as an enemy to his freedom? And when is a man so like to miscarry, as when at the same time he is both raw and unruly? This is the season of all his life that most requires the eye and authority of his parents and friends to govern it. The flexibleness of the former part of a man's age, not yet grown up to be headstrong, makes it more governable and safe; and in the afterpart, reason and foresight begin a little to take place, and mind a man of his safety and improvement. The time therefore I should think the fittest for a young gentleman to be sent abroad, would be, either when he is younger, under a tutor, whom he might be the better for; or when he is some years older, without a governor; when he is of age to govern himself, and make observations of what he finds in other countries worthy his notice, and that might be of use to him after his return; and when too, being thoroughly acquainted with the laws and fashions, the natural and moral advantages and defects of his own country, he has something to exchange with those abroad, from whose conversation he hoped to reap any knowledge.

200. The ordering of travel otherwise, is that, I imagine, which makes so many young gentlemen come back so little improved by it. And if they do bring home with them any knowledge of the places and people they have seen, it is often an admiration of the worst and vainest fashions they met with abroad; retaining a relish and memory of those things wherein their liberty took its first swing, rather than of what should make them better and wiser after their return. And indeed how can it be otherwise, going abroad at the age they do under a governor who is to provide their necessaries, and make their observations for them? Thus under the shelter and pretense of a governor, thinking themselves excused from standing upon their own legs or being accountable for their own conduct, they very seldom trouble themselves with inquiries or making useful observations of their own. Their thoughts run after play and pleasure, wherein they take it as a lessoning to be controlled; but seldom trouble themselves to examine the designs, observe the address, and consider the arts, tempers, and inclinations of men they meet with; that so they may know how to comport themselves towards them. Here he that travels with them is to screen them; get them out when they have run themselves into the briars; and in all their miscarriages be answerable for them. I confess, the knowledge of men is so great a skill that it is not to be expected a young man should presently be perfect in it. But yet his going abroad is to little purpose if travel does not sometimes open his eyes, make him cautious and wary, and accustom him to look beyond the outside, and, under the inoffensive guard of a civil and obliging carriage, keep himself free and safe in his conversation with strangers and all sorts of people without forfeiting their good opinion. He that is sent out to travel at the age, and with the thoughts of a man designing to improve himself, may get into the conversation and acquaint-

ance of persons of condition where he comes; which, though a thing of most advantage to a gentleman that travels, yet I ask, amongst our young men that go abroad under tutors, what one is there of an hundred, that ever visits any person of quality? Much less makes an acquaintance with such, from whose conversation he may learn what is good breeding in that country, and what is worth observation in it; though from such persons it is, one may learn more in one day, than in a year's rambling from one inn to another. Nor indeed, is it to be wondered; for men of worth and parts will not easily admit the familiarity of boys who yet need the care of a tutor; though a young gentleman and stranger, appearing like a man, and showing a desire to inform himself in the customs, manners, laws, and government of the country he is in, will find welcome assistance and entertainment amongst the best and most knowing persons everywhere, who will be ready to receive, encourage, and countenance an ingenuous and inquisitive foreigner.

201. This, how true soever it be, will not I fear alter the custom, which has cast the time of travel upon the worst part of a man's life; but for reasons not taken from their improvement. The young lad must not be ventured abroad at eight or ten, for fear of what may happen to the tender child, though he then runs ten times less risk than at sixteen or eighteen. Nor must he stay at home till that dangerous, heady age be over, because he must be back again by one-and-twenty, to marry and propagate. The father cannot stay any longer for the portion, nor the mother for a new set of babies to play with; and so my young master, whatever comes on it, must have a wife looked out for him by that time he is of age; though it would be no prejudice to his strength, his parts, or his issue, if it were respited for some time, and he had leave to get, in years and knowledge, the start a little of his children, who are often found to tread too near upon the heels of their fathers, to the no great satisfaction either of son or father. But the young gentleman being got

within view of matrimony, 'tis time to leave him to his mistress.

202. Though I am now come to a conclusion of what obvious remarks have suggested to me concerning education, I would not have it thought that I look on it as a just treatise on this subject. There are a thousand other things that may need consideration; especially if one should take in the various tempers, different inclinations, and particular defaults, that are to be found in children, and prescribe proper remedies. The variety is so great that it would require a volume; nor would that reach it. Each man's mind has some peculiarity, as well as his face, that distinguishes him from all others; and there are possibly scarce two children who can be conducted by exactly the same method. Besides that, I think a prince, a nobleman, and an ordinary gentleman's son, should have different ways of breeding. But having had here only some general views in reference to the main end and aims in education, and those designed for a gentleman's son, whom, being then very little, I considered only as white paper, or wax to be molded and fashioned as one pleases; I have touched little more than those heads which I judged necessary for the breeding of a young gentleman of his condition in general; and have now published these my occasional thoughts with this hope, that though this be far from being a complete treatise on this subject, or such as that everyone may find what will just fit his child in it, yet it may give some small light to those whose concern for their dear little ones makes them so irregularly bold that they dare venture to consult their own reason in the education of their children, rather than wholly to rely upon old custom.

Samuel Pepys 1633-1702

FLEET STREET, London, in which Pepys' early home was located, provided a fitting scene for the development of one who was to become the recorder of a cross section of Restoration life. We do not know many of the details of his life before 1660 when he began the *Diary*. He was a St. Paul's boy and then went to Cambridge, where the Pepysian library at Magdalene College is a constant reminder that this was his college. In 1655 he married a girl of fifteen, who until her early death at twenty-nine stirred him alternately to jealousy and to admiration. He had a very humble start as secretary to a relative, Sir Edward Montagu, but about a year after his marriage was made Clerk of the Exchequer. He accompanied Sir Edward on the expedition to bring Charles II back to England, serving as Secretary to the Admirals of the Fleet. After his return he was made Clerk of the Acts of the Navy. His conscientious and tireless work, his ability and his vision were recognized: in 1673 he was made Secretary to the Admiralty and in 1685 he was elected to Parliament.

A man of Pepys' temperament could not have made such progress without some mishaps. In 1679 he was accused of giving Naval information to the French government and sent to the Tower. Although he was soon released on bail, he was not discharged for about a year. During this time and for a period of retirement following, he lived at the home of a loyal friend, William Hewer. In 1683 he was again in public service as Secretary to Lord Dartmouth on an expedition to Tangier. His account of this expedition and of his travels is given in his *Second Diary*. Again in England, he was reappointed Secretary to the Admiralty and served until after the exile of James II. His *Memoirs of the Royal Navy*, which he wrote after his official career ended, is an important contribution to the understanding of the development of the

English navy. Other honors also came to him, among which one of the most important was the election as President of the Royal Scientific Society.

Pepys' *Diary*, which covers nine years following the Restoration, is remarkable for both human and historical interest. Written in shorthand as a personal record, it shows the man himself in a peculiarly intimate way; but because of his breadth of interest, it becomes also a record of literature, art, music, science, social and political life, and the great events of the time. We see Pepys enjoying the music and the pageantry of the coronation of Charles II; we watch with him the growing Bill of the dead during the plague of 1665; we walk with him the hot streets of London in the confusion of the fire of 1666; and we wait tensely with him for reports of the fleet during the Dutch wars. This is a book which contains that "potency of life" about which Milton spoke, and it gives to its author "a life beyond life."

From THE DIARY OF SAMUEL PEPYS [1]

3rd [February,1663/4]. . . . In Covent Garden tonight going to fetch home my wife, I stopped at the great Coffee
House there,[2] where I never was before; where Dryden, the
poet (I knew at Cambridge), and all the wits of the town,
and Harris the player, and Mr. Hoole of our college. And
had I had time then, or could at other times, it will be good
coming thither, for there, I perceive, is very witty and pleasant discourse. But I could not tarry, and as it was late, they
were all ready to go away.

4th [February, 1664]. Up and to the office, where after
a while sitting, I left the board upon pretense of serious business, and by coach to Paul's School, where I heard some good
speeches of the boys that were to be elected this year. Thence
by and by with Mr. Pullen and Barnes (a great Nonconformist) with several others of my old acquaintance to the
Nag's Head Tavern, and there did give them a bottle of
sack, and away again and I to the School and up to hear
the upper form examined; and there was kept by very many
of the Mercers, Clutterbuck, Barker, Harrington, and others;
and with great respect used by them all, and had a notable
dinner. Here they tell me that in Dr. Colet's [3] will he says
that he would have a Master found for the School that hath
good skill in Latin, and (if it could be) one that had some
knowledge of the Greek; so little was Greek known here at
the time. Dr. Wilkins [4] and one Mr. Smallwood, Posers.
After great pleasure there, and specially to Mr. Crumlum, so
often to tell of my being a benefactor to the School, I to my
bookseller's and there spent an hour looking over *Theatrum*

---

[1] Text: *The Diary of Samuel Pepys,* Transcribed from the Pepysian
Library, Magdalene College, Cambridge, by the Rev. Mynors Bright. With
Lord Braybrooke's notes. Ed. with additions by Henry B. Wheatley.
10 vols. (London, 1923).

[2] Will's Coffee House, where Dryden presided as literary dictator.

[3] John Colet, 1464–1519, dean of St. Paul's and founder of the school.

[4] John Wilkins, 1614–1672, one of the founders of the Royal Society.

Urbium and *Flandria illustrata,* with excellent cuts, with great content. So homeward, and called at my little milliner's, where I chatted with her, her husband out of the way, and a mad merry slut she is. So home to the office, and by and by comes my wife home from the burial of Captain Grove's wife at Wapping (she telling me a story how her maid Jane going into the boat did fall down and show her arse in the boat), and along comes my uncle Wight and Mr. Maes with the state of their case, which he told me very discreetly, and I believe is a very hard one, and so after drinking a bottle of ale or two they had gone, and I a little more to the office, and so home to prayers and to bed. This evening I made an end of my letter to Creed about his pieces of eight, and sent it away to him. I pray God give good end to it to bring me some money, and that duly as from him.

13th [June, 1664]. So up at 5 o'clock, and with Captain Taylor on board her [5] at Deptford, and found all out of order, only the soldiers civil and Sir Arthur Bassett a civil person. I rated at Captain Taylor, whom, contrary to my expectation, I found a lying and a very stupid blundering fellow, good for nothing, and yet we talk of him in the navy as if he had been an excellent officer; but I find him a lying knave and of no judgment or dispatch at all. After finding the condition of the ship, no master, not above four men, and many ship's provisions, sails, and other things wanting, I went back and called upon Fudge, whom I found like a lying rogue unready to go on board, but I did so jeer him that I made him get everything ready, and left Taylor and H. Russell to quicken him, and so away and I by water to Whitehall, where I met His Royal Highness at a Tangier Committee about this very thing, and did there satisfy him how things are, at which all was pacified without any trouble, and I hope may end well, but I confess I am at a real trouble for fear the rogue should not do his work, and I come to shame and loss of the money I did justly hope to have got by it. Thence

[5] A ship for Tangier.

walked with Mr. Coventry to St. James's and there spent by his desire the whole morning reading of some old navy books given him of old Sir John Coke's [6] by the Archbishop of Canterbury that now is: wherein the order that was observed in the navy then, above what it is now, is very observable, and fine things we did observe in our reading. Anon to dinner to discourse of the business of the Dutch war, wherein he tells me the Dutch do in every particular, which are but few and small things that we can demand of them, whatever cry we unjustly make, do seem to offer at an accommodation, for they do own that it is not for their profit to have war with England. We did also talk of a history of the navy of England, how fit it were to be writ; and he did say that it hath been in his mind to propose to me the writing of the history of the late Dutch war, which I am glad to hear, it being a thing I much desire, and sorts mightily with my genius; and if well done, may recommend me much. So he says he will get me an order for making of searches to all records, etc., in order thereto, and I shall take great delight in doing of it. Thence by water down to the Tower, and thither sent for Mr. Creed to my house, where he promised to be; and he and I down to the ship and find all things in pretty good order, and I hope will end to my mind. Thence having a galley down to Greenwich, and there saw the king's works, which are great, a-doing there, and so to the Cherry Garden, [7] and so carried some cherries home, and after supper to bed, my wife lying with me, which from my not being thoroughly well, nor she, we have not done above these two or three weeks.

2nd [August 1664]. . . . To the King's playhouse, and there saw "Bartholomew Fair," which do still please me; and is, as it is acted, the best comedy in the world, I believe.

[6] Sir John Coke (1563–1644) in 1618 was one of a special commission appointed for the examination of the state of the navy.
[7] The Cherry Garden was a place of public entertainment at Rotherhithe.

I chanced to sit by Tom Killegrew, who tells me that he is setting up a nursery; that is, is going to build a house in Moorefields, wherein he will have common plays acted. But four operas it shall have in the year, to act six weeks at a time; where we shall have the best scenes and machines, the best music, and everything as magnificent as in Christendom; and to that end hath sent for voices and painters and other persons from Italy. Thence homeward called upon my Lord Marlborough.

10th [September, 1664]. Up and to the office, where we sat all the morning, and I much troubled to think what the end of our great sluggishness will be, for we do nothing in this office like people able to carry on a war. We must be put out, or other people put in. Dined at home, and then my wife and I and Mercer to the Duke's House, and there saw "The Rivals," [8] which is no excellent play, but good acting in it; especially Gosnell comes and sings and dances finely, but, for all that, fell out of the key, so that the music could not play to her afterwards, and so did Harris also go out of the tune to agree with her. Thence home and late writing letters, and this night I received, by Will, £105, the first-fruits of my endeavors in the late contract for victualing of Tangier, for which God be praised! for I can with a safe conscience say that I have therein saved the king £5,000 per annum, and yet got myself a hope of £300 per annum without the least wrong to the king. So to supper and to bed.

9th [January 1664/65]. Up and walked to Whitehall, it being still a brave frost, and I in perfect health, blessed be God! In my way saw a woman that broke her thigh, in her heels slipping up upon the frosty streets. To the Duke, and there did our usual work. Here I saw the Royal Society bring their new book,[9] wherein is nobly writ their charter and laws,

[8] A comedy by Sir William Davenant, first published in 1668. It is an alteration of *The Two Noble Kinsmen.*
[9] The Charter Book contains the signatures of the Fellows of the Society from the foundation. See Birch, *History,* II, 4.

and comes to be signed by the Duke as a Fellow; and all the Fellows' hands are to be entered there and lie as a monument; and the King hath put his with the word Founder. . . .

March 1st [1664/65]. Up and this day being the day that by a promise a great while ago made to my wife, I was to give her £20 to lay out in clothes against Easter, she did, notwithstanding last night's falling out, come to peace with me and I with her, but did boggle mightily at the parting with my money, but at last did give it her, and then she abroad to buy her things, and I to my office, where busy all the morning. At noon I to dinner at Trinity House, and thence to Gresham College, where Mr. Hooke read a second very curious lecture about the late comet; among other things proving very probably that this is the very same comet that appeared before in the year 1618, and that in such a time probably it will appear again, which is a very new opinion; but all will be in print. Then to the meeting, where Sir G. Carteret's two sons, his own, and Sir N. Slaning [10] were admitted to the Society: and this day I did pay my admission money, 40s. to the Society. Here was very fine discourses and experiments, but I do lack philosophy enough to understand them, and so cannot remember them. Among others, a very particular account of the making of the several sorts of bread in France, which is accounted the best place for bread in the world. So home, where very busy getting an answer to some question of Sir Philip Warwick touching the expense of the navy, and that being done, I by coach at 8 at night with my wife and Mercer to Sir Philip's and discoursed with him (leaving them in the coach), and then back with them home and to supper and to bed.

31st [August, 1665]. Up; and after putting several things in order to my removal, to Woolwich; the plague having a great increase this week, beyond all expectation of almost 2,000, making the general Bill 7,000, odd 100; and the plague

---

[10] Sir Nicholas Slaning, K.B., who married a daughter of Sir George Carteret.

above 6,000. I down by appointment to Greenwich, to our office, where I did some business, and there dined with our company and Sir W. Boreman, and Sir The. Biddulph, at Mr. Boreman's, where a good venison pasty; and after a good merry dinner, I to my office, and there late writing letters, and then to Woolwich by water, where pleasant with my wife and people, and after supper to bed. Thus the month ends with great sadness upon the public, through the greatness of the plague everywhere through the kingdom almost. Every day sadder and sadder news of its increase. In the city died this week 7,496, and of them 6,102 of the plague. But it is feared that the true number of the dead this week is near 10,000; partly from the poor that cannot be taken notice of through the greatness of the number, and partly from the Quakers and others that will not have any bell ring for them. Our fleet gone out to find the Dutch, we having about 100 sail in our fleet, and in them the "Sovereign" one; so that it is a better fleet than the former with the "Duke" was. All our fear is that the Dutch should be got in before them; which would be a very great sorrow to the public, and to me particularly, for my Lord Sandwich's sake. A great deal of money being spent, and the kingdom not in a condition to spare, nor a parliament without much difficulty to meet to give more. And to that to have it said, "What hath been done by our late fleets?" As to myself I am very well, only in fear of the plague, and as much of an ague by being forced to go early and late to Woolwich, and my family to lie there continually. My late gettings have been very great to my content, and am likely to have yet a few more profitable jobs in a little while; for which Tangier and Sir W. Warren I am wholly obliged to.

5th [October, 1665]. Lay long in bed, talking among other things of my sister Pall, and my wife of herself is very willing that I should give her £400 to her portion and would have her married soon as we could; but this great sickness time do make it unfit to send for her up. I abroad to the office and thence to the Duke of Albemarle, all my way reading a book of Mr. Evelyn's translating and sending me as a present, about directions for gathering a library; [11] but the book is above my reach, but the epistle to my Lord Chancellor is a very fine piece. . . . So away to Mr. Evelyn's, to discourse of our confounded business of prisoners and sick and wounded seamen, wherein he and we are so much put out of order. And here he showed me his gardens, which are, for variety of evergreens and hedge of holly, the finest things I ever saw in my life. Thence in his coach to Greenwich, and there to my office, all the way having fine discourse of trees and the nature of vegetables. And so to write letters, I very late to Sir W. Coventry of great concernment, and so to my last night's lodging, but my wife is gone home to Woolwich. The Bill, blessed be God! is less this week by 740 of what it was last week. Being come to my lodging, I got something to eat, having eat little all the day, and so to bed, having this night renewed my promises of observing my vows as I used to do: for I find that, since I left them off, my mind is run a' wool-gathering and my business neglected.

5th (Lord's day) [November, 1665]. . . . By water to Deptford, and there made a visit to Mr. Evelyn, who, among other things, showed me most excellent painting in little, in distemper, Indian ink, water colors, graving, and, above all, the whole secret of mezzo-tinto and the manner of it, which is very pretty, and good things done with it. He read to me very much also of his discourse, he hath been many years and now is about, about gardenage; which will be a most noble and pleasant piece. He read me part of a play or two of his making, very good, but not as he conceits them, I think, to be. He showed me his *Hortus Hiemalis;* leaves laid up in a book of several plants kept dry, which preserve color, however, and look very finely, better than any Herbal. In fine, a

---

[11] "Instructions concerning erecting of a Library, presented to my Lord the President De Mesme by Gilbert Naudeus and now interpreted by Jo. Evelyn, Esquire, London, 1621." This little book was dedicated to Lord Clarendon by the translator.

most excellent person he is, and must be allowed a little for a little conceitedness; but he may well be so, being a man so much above others. He read me, though with too much gusto, some little poems of his own, that were not transcendent, yet one or two very pretty epigrams; among others, of a lady looking in at a grate and being pecked at by an eagle that was there. . . .

6th [December, 1665]. Up betimes, it being fast-day; and by water to the Duke of Albemarle, who came to town from Oxford last night. He is mighty brisk, and very kind to me, and asks my advice principally in everything. He surprises me with the news that my Lord Sandwich goes ambassador to Spain speedily; though I know not whence this arises; yet I am heartily glad of it. He did give me several directions what to do, and so I home by water again and to church a little, thinking to have met Mrs. Pierce in order to our meeting at night; but she not there, I home and dined, and comes presently by appointment my wife. I spent the afternoon upon a song of Solyman's words to Roxalana [12] that I have set, and so with my wife walked and Mercer to Mrs. Pierce's, where Captain Rolt and Mrs. Knipp, Mr. Colman and his wife, and Lanier, Mrs. Worshipp and her singing daughter met; and by and by unexpectedly comes Mr. Pierce from Oxford. Here the best company for music that I ever was in, in my life, and wish I could live and die in it, both for music and the face of Mrs. Pierce and my wife and Knipp,[13] who is pretty enough, but the most excellent, mad-humored thing, and sings the noblest that ever I heard in my life, and Rolt with her, some things together most excellently. I spent the night in an ecstasy almost; and, having invited them to my house a day or two hence, we broke up. . . .

25th (Christmas Day) [December, 1665]. To church in the morning, and there saw a wedding in the church, which

---

[12] From *The Siege of Rhodes*, Part II, Act iv, sc. 2. "Beauty retire."
[13] Mrs. Knipp, the actress at the King's House, 1664–1678.

I have not seen many a day; and the young people so merry one with another; and strange to see what delight we married people have to see these poor fools decoyed into our condition, every man and woman gazing and smiling at them. Here I saw again my beauty Lethulier. Thence to my Lord Bruncker's by invitation and dined there, and so home to look over and settle my papers, both of my accounts private, and those of Tangier, which I have let go so long that it were impossible for any soul, had I died, to understand them, or ever come to any good in them. I hope God will never suffer me to come to that disorder again.

3rd [January, 1665/66]. Up, and all the morning till three in the afternoon examining and fitting up my Pursers' paper and sent it away by an express. Then comes my wife, and I set her to get supper ready against I go to the Duke of Albemarle and back again; and at the Duke's with great joy I received the good news of the decrease of the plague this week to 70, and but 253 in all; which is the least Bill hath been known these twenty years in the city. Through the want of people in London is it, that must make it so low below the ordinary number for Bills. So home, and find all my good company I had bespoke, as Colman and his wife, and Lanier, Knipp and her surly husband; and good music we had, and among other things, Mrs. Colman sang my words I set, of "Beauty, retire," and I think it is a good song, and they praise it mightily. Then to dancing and supper, and mighty merry till Mr. Rolt came in, whose pain of the tooth-ache made him no company, and spoilt ours; so he away, and then my wife's teeth fell of aching, and she to bed. So forced to break off with a good song, and so to bed.

28th [January, 1665/66]. . . . After dinner took coach, and to [Hampton] Court, where we find the King, and Duke, and Lords, all in Council; so we walked up and down, there being none of the ladies come, and so much the more business I hope will be done. The council being up, out comes the King, and I kissed his hand, and he mighty kind, and Sir W. Coventry. I found my Lord Sandwich there, poor man! I see with a melancholy face, and suffers his beard to grow on his upper lip more than usual. I took him a little aside to know when I should wait on him, and where; he told me, and that it would be best to meet at his lodgings, without being seen to walk together. Which I liked very well; and lord! to see in what difficulty I stand, that I dare not walk with Sir W. Coventry for fear my Lord or Sir G. Carteret should see me; nor with either of them, for fear Sir W. Coventry should. After changing a few words with Sir W. Coventry, who assures me of his respect and love of me, and his concernment for my health in all this sickness, I went down into one of the courts and there met the King and Duke; and the Duke called me to him. And the King come to me of himself and told me, "Mr. Pepys," says he, "I do give you thanks for your good service all this year, and I assure you I am very sensible of it." And the Duke of York did tell me with pleasure that he had read over my discourse about pursers and would have it ordered in my way, and so fell from one discourse to another. . . .

19th (Lord's day) [August, 1666]. Up, and to my chamber, and there began to draw out fair and methodically my accounts of Tangier, in order to show them to the lords. But by and by comes by agreement Mr. Reeves, and after him Mr. Spong, and all day with them, both before and after dinner, till ten o'clock at night, upon optic inquiries, he bringing me a frame he closes on, to see how the rays of light do cut one another, and in a dark room with smoke, which is very pretty. He did also bring a lanthorn, with pictures in glass, to make strange things appear on a wall, very pretty. We did also at night see Jupiter and his girdle and satellites, very fine, with my twelve-foot glass, but could not Saturn, he being very dark. Spong and I had also several fine discourses upon the globes this afternoon, particularly why the fixed stars do not rise and set at the same hour all the year long, which he could not demonstrate, nor I neither, the reason of. But it vexed me to understand no more from Reeves and his glasses touching the nature and reason of the several refractions of the several figured glasses, he understanding the acting part, but not one bit the theory, nor can make anybody understand it, which is a strange dullness, methinks. I did not hear anything yesterday or at all to confirm either Sir Thos. Allen's news of the 10 or 12 ships taken, nor of the disorder at Amsterdam upon the news of the burning of the ships, that he [De Witt] should be fled to the Prince of Orange, it being generally believed that he was gone to France before.

2nd (Lord's day) [September, 1666]. Some of the maids sitting up late last night to get things ready against our feast today, Jane called us up about three in the morning to tell us of a great fire they saw in the city. So I rose and slipped on my nightgown and went to her window; and thought it to be on the back-side of Mark Lane at the farthest; but, being unused to such fires as followed, I thought it far enough off; and so went to bed again and to sleep. About seven rose again to dress myself, and there looked out at the window and saw the fire not so much as it was and further off. So to my closet to set things to rights after yesterday's cleaning. By and by Jane comes and tells me that she hears that above 300 houses have been burned down tonight by the fire we saw and that it is now burning down all Fish Street by London Bridge. So I made myself ready presently, and walked to the Tower; and there got up upon one of the high places, Sir J. Robinson's little son going up with me; and there I did see the houses at that end of the bridge all on fire and an infinite great fire on this and the other side the end of the bridge; which, among other people, did trouble me for poor little Michell and our Sarah on the bridge. So down, with my heart full of trouble, to the lieutenant of the Tower, who tells me that it begun this morning in the king's baker's house in Pudding Lane [14] and that it had burned down St. Magnus's Church and most part of Fish Street already. So I down to the waterside, and there got a boat,

---

[14] Pudding Lane led from Eastcheap to Lower Thames Street.

and through bridge, and there saw a lamentable fire. Poor Michell's house, as far as the Old Swan, already burned that way, and the fire running further, that in a very little time it got as far as the Steel-yard, while I was there. Everybody endeavoring to remove their goods, and flinging into the river or bringing them into lighters that lay off; poor people staying in their houses as long as till the very fire touched them, and then running into boats or clambering from one pair of stairs by the waterside to another. And among other things, the poor pigeons, I perceive, were loath to leave their houses, but hovered about the windows and balconies till they were, some of them burned, their wings, and fell down. Having stayed and in an hour's time seen the fire rage every way, and nobody, to my sight, endeavoring to quench it, but to remove their goods and leave all to the fire, and having seen it get as far as the Steel-yard, and the wind mighty high and driving it into the city; and everything, after so long a drought, proving conbustible, even the very stones of churches; and among other things, the poor steeple [15] by which pretty Mrs. ——— lives, and whereof my old school-fellow Elborough is parson, taken fire in the very top, and there burned till it fell down: I to Whitehall (with a gentleman with me, who desired to go off from the Tower, to see the fire, in my boat); and there up to the King's closet in the chapel, where people came about me, and I did give them an account dismayed them all, and word was carried in to the King. So I was called for, and did tell the King and Duke of York what I saw; and that, unless His Majesty did command houses to be pulled down, nothing could stop the fire. They seemed much troubled, and the King commanded me to go to my Lord Mayor from him and command him to spare no houses, but to pull down before the fire every way. The Duke of York bid me tell him that if he would have any more soldiers, he shall; and so did my Lord Arlington afterwards, as a great secret. Here meeting with Captain Cocke,

[15] St. Lawrence Poultney of which Thomas Elborough was curate.

I in his coach, which he lent me, and Creed with me to Paul's; and there walked along Watling Street, as well as I could, every creature coming away laden with goods to save, and, here and there, sick people carried away in beds. Extraordinary good goods carried in carts and on backs. At last met my Lord Mayor in Canning Street, like a man spent, with handkercher about his neck. To the King's message he cried, like a fainting woman, "Lord! what can I do? I am spent: people will not obey me. I have been pulling down houses; but the fire overtakes us faster than we can do it." That he needed no more soldiers; and that, for himself, he must go and refresh himself, having been up all night. So he left me, and I him, and walked home; seeing people all almost distracted, and no manner of means used to quench the fire. The houses, too, so very thick thereabouts, and full of matter for burning, as pitch and tar, in Thames Street; and warehouses of oil and wines and brandy and other things. Here I saw Mr. Isaac Houblon, the handsome man, prettily dressed and dirty at his door in Dowgate, receiving some of his brother's things, whose houses were on fire; and, as he says, have been removed twice already; and he doubts (as it soon proved) that they must be in a little time removed from his house also, which was a sad consideration. And to see the churches all filling with goods by people, who themselves should have been quietly there at this time. By this time it was about twelve o'clock; and so home, and there find my guests, who were Mr. Wood and his wife Barbary Shelden, and also Mr. Moone: she mighty fine, and her husband, for all I see, a likely man. But Mr. Moone's design and mine, which was to look over my closet, and please him with the sight thereof, which he hath long desired, was wholly disappointed; for we were in great trouble and disturbance at this fire, not knowing what to think of it. However, we had an extraordinary good dinner, and as merry as at this time we could be. While at dinner Mrs. Batelier came to inquire after Mr. Woolfe and Stanes (who it seems is related to them), whose houses in Fish Street are all burned, and they in sad condition. She would not stay in the fright. Soon as dined, I and Moone away, and walked through the city, the streets full of nothing but people, and horses and carts loaden with goods, ready to run over one another, and removing goods from one burned house to another. They now removing out of Canning Street (which received goods in the morning) into Lombard Street, and further; amongst others I now saw my little goldsmith, Stokes, receiving some friend's goods, whose house itself was burned the day after. We parted at Paul's; he home, and I to Paul's Wharf, where I had appointed a boat to attend me, and took in Mr. Carcasse and his brother, whom I met in the street, and carried them below the bridge and above bridge too, and again to see the fire, which was now got further, both below and above, and no likelihood of stopping it. Met with the king and Duke of York in their barge, and with them to Queenhithe, and there called Sir Richard Browne to them. Their order was only to pull down houses apace, and so below bridge at the waterside; but this little was or could be done, the fire coming upon them so fast. Good hopes there was of stopping it at the Three Cranes above, and at Buttulph's Wharf below bridge, if care be used; but the wind carries it into the city so as we know not, by the waterside, what it do there. River full of lighters and boats taking in goods, and good goods swimming in the water; and only I observed that hardly one lighter or boat in three that had the goods of a house in but there was a pair of virginals in it. Having seen as much as I could now, I away to Whitehall by appointment, and there walked to St. James's Park; and there met my wife and Creed and Wood and his wife, and walked to my boat; and there upon the water again, and to the fire up and down, it still increasing and the wind great. So near the fire as we could for smoke; and all over the Thames, with one's face in the wind you were almost burned with a shower of fire-drops. This is very true: so as houses were burned

by these drops and flakes of fire, three or four, nay, five or
six houses one from another. When we could endure no more
upon the water, we to a little ale house on the Bankside over
against the Three Cranes, and there stayed till it was dark
almost, and saw the fire grow; and, as it grew darker, appeared more and more; and in corners and upon steeples and
between churches and houses, as far as we could see up the
hill of the city, in a most horrid, malicious, bloody flame,
not like the fine flame of an ordinary fire. Barbary and her
husband away before us. We stayed till, it being darkish, we
saw the fire as only one entire arch of fire from this to the
other side of the bridge and in a bow up the hill for an arch
of above a mile long. It made me weep to see it. The churches,
houses, and all on fire and flaming at once; and a horrid
noise the flames made, and the cracking of houses at their
ruin. So home with a sad heart, and there find everybody
discoursing and lamenting the fire; and poor Tom Hater
come with some few of his goods saved out of his house, which
was burned upon Fish Street Hill. I invited him to lie at
my house, and did receive his goods; but was deceived in
his lying there, the news coming every moment of the growth
of the fire; so as we were forced to begin to pack up our own
goods and prepare for their removal; and did by moonshine
(it being brave, dry, and moonshine, and warm weather)
carry much of my goods into the garden; and Mr. Hater and
I did remove my money and iron chests into my cellar, as
thinking that the safest place. And got my bags of gold into
my office, ready to carry away, and my chief papers of accounts also there, and my tallies into a box by themselves.
So great was our fear, as Sir W. Batten hath carts come out
of the country to fetch away his goods this night. We did
put Mr. Hater, poor man, to bed a little; but he got but
very little rest, so much noise being in my house, taking
down of goods.

3rd. About four o'clock in the morning, my Lady Batten

sent me a cart to carry away all my money, and plate, and best things, to Sir W. Rider's at Bethnal Green, which I did, riding myself in my nightgown in the cart; and Lord! to see how the streets and the highways are crowded with people running and riding, and getting of carts at any rate to fetch away things. I find Sir W. Rider tired with being called up all night and receiving things from several friends. His house full of goods, and much of Sir W. Batten's and Sir W. Penn's. I am eased at my heart to have my treasure so well secured. Then home, and with much ado to find a way, nor any sleep all this night to me nor my poor wife. But then all this day she and I, and all my people, laboring to get away the rest of our things, and did get Mr. Tooker to get me a lighter to take them in, and we did carry them (myself some) over Tower Hill, which was by this time full of people's goods, bringing their goods thither; and down to the lighter, which lay at the next quay, above the Tower Dock. And here was my neighbor's wife, Mrs. ———, with her pretty child, and some few of her things, which I did willingly give way to be saved with mine; but there was no passing with anything through the postern, the crowd was so great. The Duke of York came this day by the office and spoke to us, and did ride with his guard up and down the city to keep all quiet (he being now general and having the care of all). This day Mercer being not at home, but against her mistress's order gone to her mother's, and my wife going thither to speak with W. Hewer, met her there and was angry; and her mother saying that she was not a 'prentice girl, to ask leave every time she goes abroad, my wife with good reason was angry, and when she came home, bid her be gone again. And so she went away, which troubled me, but yet less than it would, because of the condition we are in, in fear of coming in a little time to being less able to keep one in her quality. At night lay down a little upon a quilt of W. Hewer's in the office, all my own things being packed up or gone; and after

me my poor wife did the like, we having fed upon the remains of yesterday's dinner, having no fire nor dishes, nor
opportunity of dressing anything.

4th. Up by break of day to get away the remainder of my
things; which I did by a lighter at the Iron gate:[16] and my
hands so few, that it was afternoon before we could get them
all away. Sir W. Penn and I to Tower Street, and there met
the fire burning three or four doors beyond Mr. Howell's,
whose goods, poor man, his trays, and dishes, shovels, etc.,
were flung all along Tower Street in the kennels, and people
working therewith from one end to the other; the fire coming on in that narrow street on both sides with infinite fury.

Sir W. Batten, not knowing how to remove his wine, did
dig a pit in the garden, and laid it in there; and I took
the opportunity of laying all the papers of my office that
I could not otherwise dispose of. And in the evening Sir W.
Penn and I did dig another and put our wine in it; and I
my parmesan cheese as well as my wine and some other things.
The Duke of York was at the office this day, at Sir W. Penn's;
but I happened not to be within. This afternoon, sitting melancholy with Sir W. Penn in our garden, and thinking of
the certain burning of this office, without extraordinary means,
I did propose for the sending up of all our workmen from
the Woolwich and Deptford yards (none whereof yet appeared), and to write to Sir W. Coventry to have the Duke
of York's permission to pull down houses, rather than lose
this office, which would much hinder the king's business. So
Sir W. Penn went down this night in order to the sending
them up tomorrow morning; and I wrote to Sir W. Coventry
about the business, but received no answer. This night, Mrs.
Turner (who, poor woman, was removing her goods all this
day, good goods into the garden, and knows not how to dispose of them) and her husband supped with my wife and
me at night in the office upon a shoulder of mutton from the
cook's without any napkin or anything, in a sad manner, but

[16] Irongate Stairs, at the bottom of Little Tower Hill.

were merry. Only now and then, walking into the garden, saw how horridly the sky looks, all on a fire in the night, was enough to put us out of our wits; and, indeed, it was extremely dreadful, for it looks just as if it was at us, and the whole heaven on fire. I after supper walked in the dark down to Tower Street, and there saw it all on fire, at the Trinity House on that side and the Dolphin Tavern on this side, which was very near us; and the fire with extraordinary vehemence. Now begins the practice of blowing up of houses in Tower Street, those next the Tower, which at first did frighten people more than anything; but it stopped the fire where it was done, it bringing down the houses to the ground in the same places they stood, and then it was easy to quench what little fire was in it, though it kindled nothing almost. W. Hewer this day went to see how his mother did, and comes late home, telling us how he hath been forced to remove her to Islington, her house in Pye Corner being burned; so that the fire is got so far that way and to the Old Bailey, and was running down to Fleet Street; and Paul's is burned and all Cheapside. I wrote to my father this night, but the post-house being burned, the letter could not go.

5th. I lay down in the office again upon W. Hewer's quilt, being mighty weary and sore in my feet with going till I was hardly able to stand. About two in the morning my wife calls me up and tells me of new cries of fire, it being come to Barking Church, which is the bottom of our lane.[17] I up; and finding it so, resolved presently to take her away, and did, and took my gold, which was about £2,350, W. Hewer and Jane, down by Proundy's boat to Woolwich. But Lord! what a sad sight it was by moonlight to see the whole city almost on fire that you might see it as plain at Woolwich as if you were by it. There, when I come, I find the gates shut, but no guard kept at all; which troubled me, because of discourses now begun that there is a plot in it and that the

---

[17] Barking Church was Allhallows Barking in Great Tower Street, almost opposite the end of Seething Lane.

French had done it. I got the gates open, and to Mr. Shelden's, where I locked up my gold and charged my wife and W. Hewer never to leave the room without one of them in it night and day. So back again, by the way seeing my goods well in the lighters at Deptford and watched well by people. Home, and whereas I expected to have seen our house on fire, it being now about seven o'clock, it was not. But to the fire, and there find greater hopes than I expected; for my confidence of finding our office on fire was such that I durst not ask anybody how it was with us till I come and saw it was not burned. But going to the fire, I find by the blowing up of houses and the great help given by the workmen out of the king's yards, sent up by Sir W. Penn, there is a good stop given to it, as well at Mark Lane end as ours; it having only burned the dial of Barking Church and part of the porch and was there quenched. I up to the top of Barking steeple and there saw the saddest sight of desolation that I ever saw; everywhere great fires, oil-cellars and brimstone and other things burning. I became afraid to stay there long, and therefore down again as fast as I could, the fire being spread as far as I could see it; and to Sir W. Penn's, and there eat a piece of cold meat, having eaten nothing since Sunday but the remains of Sunday's dinner. Here I met with Mr. Young and Whistler; and, having removed all my things and received good hopes that the fire at our end is stopped, they and I walked into the town, and find Fenchurch Street, Gracious Street, and Lombard Street all in dust. The Exchange a sad sight, nothing standing there of all the statues or pillars but Sir Thomas Gresham's picture in the corner. Into Moorfields (our feet ready to burn walking through the town among the hot coals) and find that full of people and poor wretches carrying their goods there, and everybody keeping his goods together by themselves (and a great blessing it is to them that it is fair weather for them to keep abroad night and day); drank there, and paid two-pence for a plain penny loaf. Thence homeward, having passed through Cheapside and Newgate market, all burned; and seen Anthony Joyce's house on fire; and took up (which I keep by me) a piece of glass of the Mercer's Chapel in the street, where much more was, so melted and buckled with the heat of the fire like parchment. I also did see a poor cat taken out of a hole in a chimney, joining to the wall of the Exchange, with the hair burnt off the body, and yet alive. So home at night, and find there good hopes of saving our office; but great endeavors of watching all night and having men ready; and so we lodged them in the office, and had drink and bread and cheese for them. And I lay down and slept a good night about midnight, though, when I rose, I heard that there had been a great alarm of French and Dutch being risen, which proved nothing. But it is a strange thing to see how long this time did look since Sunday, having been always full of variety and actions, and little sleep, that it looked like a week or more, and I had forgot almost the day of the week.

31st [December, 1666]. . . . To my accounts, wherein at last I find them clear and right; but to my great discontent do find that my gettings this year have been £573 less than my last: it being this year in all but £2,986, whereas the last, I got £3,560. And then again my spendings this year have exceeded my spendings the last by £644: my whole spendings last year being but £509; whereas this year it appears I have spent £1,154, which is a sum not fit to be said that ever I should spend in one year, before I am master of a better estate than I am. Yet, blessed be God! and I pray God make me thankful for it, I do find myself worth in money, all good, above £6,200; which is above £1,800 more than I was the last year. This, I trust in God, will make me thankful for what I have and careful to make up by care next year what by my negligence and prodigality I have lost and spent this year. The doing of this, and entering of it fair with the sorting of all my expenses, to see how and in what points I have exceeded, did make it late work, till my eyes became very sore and ill, and then did give over, and supper, and to bed. Thus ends this year of public wonder and mischief to this nation, and therefore generally wished by all people to have an end. Myself and family well, having four maids and one clerk, Tom, in my house and my brother now with me to spend time in order to his preferment. Our healths all well (only my eyes with overworking them are sore as candlelight comes to them, and not else). Public matters in a most sad condition; seamen discouraged for want of pay and are become not to be governed: nor, as matters are now, can any fleet go out next year. Our enemies, French and Dutch, great, and grow more by our poverty. The Parliament backward in raising, because jealous of the spending of the money; the city less and less likely to be built again, everybody settling elsewhere and nobody encouraged to trade. A sad, vicious, negligent court, and all sober men there fearful of the ruin of the whole kingdom this next year; from which, good God deliver us! One thing I reckon remarkable in my own condition is that I am come to abound in good plate so as at all entertainments to be served wholly with silver plates, having two dozen and a half.

7th [January, 1666/7]. . . . To the Duke's House, and saw *Macbeth*, which, though I saw it lately, yet appears a most excellent play in all respects, but especially in a divertisement, though it be a deep tragedy; which is a strange perfection in a tragedy, it being most proper here and suitable.

12th [June, 1667]. . . . So home, where all our hearts do now ache; for the news is true that the Dutch have broke the chain and burned our ships and particularly "The Royal Charles"; other particulars I know not, but most sad to be sure. And, the truth is, I do fear so much that the whole kingdom is undone that I do this night resolve to study with my father and wife what to do with the little that I have in money by me, for I give [up] all the rest that I have in the King's hands, for Tangier, for lost. So God help us! and God knows what disorders we may fall into and whether any violence on this office or perhaps some severity on our persons, as being reckoned by the silly people, or perhaps may by policy of state be thought fit to be condemned by the King and Duke of York and so put to trouble, though, God knows! I have, in my own person, done my full duty, I am sure. . . .

13th [March, 1668/69]. . . . That which put me in a good humor both at noon and night is the fancy that I am this day made a captain of one of the king's ships, Mr. Wren having this day sent me the Duke of York's commission to be captain of "The Jersey" in order to my being of a court-martial for examining the loss of "The Defiance," and other things; which do give me occasion of much mirth, and may be of some use to me, at least I shall get a little money for the time I have it; it being designed that I must really be a captain to be able to sit in this court. . . .

15th [March 1668/69]. Up, and by water with W. Hewer to the Temple; and thence to the Rolls, where I made inquiry for several rolls and was soon informed in the manner of it: and so spent the whole morning with W. Hewer, he taking little notes in shorthand, while I hired a clerk there to read me about twelve or more several rolls which I did call for. And it was great pleasure to me to see the method wherein their rolls are kept, that when the master of the office, one Mr. Case, do call for them (who is a man that I have heretofore known by coming to my Lord Sandwich's) he did most readily turn to them. At noon they shut up; and W. Hewer and I did walk to the Cock, at the end of Suffolk Street, where I never was, a great ordinary mightily cried up, and there bespoke a pullet which while dressing, he and I walked into St. James's Park, and thence back and dined very handsome with good soup and a pullet for 4s. 6d. the whole. Thence back to the Rolls, and did a little more business; and so by water to Whitehall, whither I went to speak with Mr. Williamson (that if he hath any papers relating to the navy I might see them, which he promises me). And so by water home with great content for what I have this day found, having got almost as much as I desire of the history of the navy from 1618 to 1642, when the King and Parliament fell out.

31st [May, 1669, last entry]. Up very betimes, and continued all the morning with W. Hewer, upon examining and stating my accounts, in order to the fitting myself to go abroad beyond sea, which the ill condition of my eyes and my neglect for a year or two hath kept me behindhand in and so as to render it very difficult now and troublesome to my mind to do it; but I this day made a satisfactory entrance therein. . . . Had another meeting with the Duke of York at Whitehall on yesterday's work, and made a good advance: and so being called by my wife, we to the Park, Mary Batelier, and a Dutch gentleman, a friend of hers, being with us. Thence to "The World's End," a drinking house by the Park; and there merry, and so home late. And thus ends all that I doubt I shall ever be able to do with my own eyes in the keeping of my Journal, I being not able to do it any longer, having done now so long as to undo my eyes almost every time that I take a pen in my hand; and therefore, whatever comes of it, I must forbear: and therefore resolve from this time forward to have it kept by my people in longhand, and must be contented to set down no more than is fit for them and all the world to know; or if there be anything, I must endeavor to keep a margin in my book open, to add here and there a note in shorthand with my own hand. And so I betake myself to that course, which is almost as much as to see myself go into my grave: for which and all the discomforts that will accompany my being blind, the good God prepare me!

Thomas Traherne   1634(?)¹-1674

THERE is little information concerning Traherne's life. He was the son of a shoemaker who lived in Hereford, but we have no record of Traherne's birth either at Hereford or at the village of Ledbury nearby, which also seems to have had some connection with the family. He was probably of Welsh descent, and his sensitivity to nature made his childhood happy in spite of the limited resources of his family. In both his poetry and his prose there are many recollections of the simple joys of his early days.

By some means he was able to attend Oxford University, receiving his A.B. in 1657, his M.A. in 1661, and his B.D. in 1669. Through the patronage of Anabella, Countess Dowager of Kent, he was made country rector at Credenhill, where he remained about ten years. He next enjoyed the patronage of Sir Orlando Bridgman, Lord Keeper of the Seal, and was his private chaplain until Sir Orlando's death. When Sir Orlando was deprived of his office in 1672, Traherne shared his retirement at Teddington. He survived his patron only a few months and was also buried at Teddington.

Traherne has much in common with George Herbert and Henry Vaughan, and anticipates Blake and Wordsworth. He saw God in nature and in childhood, and he felt that in a childlike attitude one could continue the happiness of his early years. In his own childhood he had suddenly perceived that all created things were his to enjoy, and life therefore was overflowing with riches and wonderment. Traherne believes that such a sense of God's presence in the world and man's direct contact with him through his created works is the way in which God wishes man to praise him.

The manuscripts of Traherne's poems and *Centuries of Meditations* were not discovered until 1897. They were un-

¹ For a discussion of this date see Helen C. White, *The Metaphysical Poets* (New York, 1936), p. 316.

signed, but were identified as Traherne's and published by Mr. Bertram Dobell, the poetry in 1903 and the *Centuries* in 1908. A further manuscript of poems, signed by the author, was unearthed among the manuscripts in the British Museum and published by H. I. Bell in 1910. In his lifetime Traherne published only two works, the learned *Roman Forgeries*, 1673, and *Christian Ethics*, which did not come off the press until after his death.

From CHRISTIAN ETHICS [1]

[*Of Magnanimity*]

MAGNANIMITY and contentment are very near allied; like
brothers and sisters they spring from the same parents, but
are of several features. Fortitude and patience are kindred
to this incomparable virtue. Moralists distinguish magnanimity and modesty by making the one the desire of greater,
the other of less and inferior honors. But in my apprehension there is more in magnanimity. It includes all that belongs to a great soul: a high and mighty courage, an invincible
patience, an immovable grandeur which is above the reach
of injuries, a contempt of all little and feeble enjoyments,
and a certain kind of majesty that is conversant with great
things; a high and lofty frame of spirit, allied with the
sweetness of courtesy and respect; a deep and stable resolution founded on humility without any baseness; an infinite
hope and a vast desire; a divine, profound, uncontrollable
sense of one's own capacity; a generous confidence, and a
great inclination to heroical deeds; all these conspire to complete it, with a severe and mighty expectation of bliss incomprehensible. It soars up to heaven, and looks down upon all
dominion of fortune with pity and disdain. Its aims and designs are transcendent to all concerns of this little world. Its
objects and its ends are worthy of a soul that is like God in
nature; and nothing less than the Kingdom of God, his life
and image; nothing beneath the friendship and communion
with him can be its satisfaction. The terrors, allurements,
and censures of men are the dust of its feet: their avarice and
ambition are but feebleness before it. Their riches and contentions, and interests and honors, but insignificant and
empty trifles. All the world is but a little bubble; infinity
and eternity the only great and sovereign things wherewith
it converseth. A magnanimous soul is always awake. The

[1] Text: 1675, first edition.

whole globe of the earth is but a nutshell in comparison of its enjoyments. The sun is its lamp, the sea its fishpond, the stars its jewels, men, angels, its attendants, and God alone its sovereign delight and supreme complacency. The earth is its garden, all palaces its summer houses, cities are its cottages, empires its more spacious courts, all ages and kingdoms its demesnes, monarchs its ministers and public agents, the whole Catholic Church its family, the eternal Son of God its pattern and example. Nothing is great if compared to a magnanimous soul but the sovereign Lord of all Worlds.

———

From CENTURIES OF MEDITATIONS [1]

The First Century

1

AN EMPTY book is like an infant's soul, in which anything may be written. It is capable of all things, but containeth nothing. I have a mind to fill this with profitable wonders. And since love made you put it into my hands, I will fill it with those truths you love without knowing them: and with those things which, if it be possible, shall shew my love: to you, in communicating most enriching truths; to truth, in exalting her beauties in such a soul.

10

To think well is to serve God in the interior court: to have a mind composed of divine thoughts and set in frame, to be like him within. To conceive aright and to enjoy the world is to conceive the Holy Ghost, and to see his love: which is the mind of the Father. And this more pleaseth him than many worlds, could we create as fair and great as this. For when you are once acquainted with the world, you will find the goodness and wisdom of God so manifest therein that it was impossible another, or better, should be made. Which being made to be enjoyed, nothing can please or serve him more than the soul that enjoys it. For that soul doth accomplish the end of his desire in creating it.

29

You never enjoy the world aright, till the sea itself floweth in your veins, till you are clothed with the heavens, and crowned with the stars: and perceive yourself to be the sole heir of the whole world, and more than so, because men are

[1] Text: reprint of first edition, 1927, with some additions and corrections by Bertram Dobell.

in it who are every one sole heirs as well as you. Till you can sing and rejoice and delight in God, as misers do in gold, and kings in scepters, you never enjoy the world.

30

Till your spirit filleth the whole world, and the stars are your jewels; till you are as familiar with the ways of God in all ages as with your walk and table; till you are intimately acquainted with that shady nothing out of which the world was made: till you love men so as to desire their happiness, with a thirst equal to the zeal of your own; till you delight in God for being good to all: you never enjoy the world. Till you more feel it than your private estate, and are more present in the hemisphere, considering the glories and the beauties there, than in your own house: till you remember how lately you were made, and how wonderful it was when you came into it: and more rejoice in the palace of your glory than if it had been made but today morning.

31

Yet further, you never enjoy the world aright till you so love the beauty of enjoying it that you are covetous and earnest to persuade others to enjoy it. And so perfectly hate the abominable corruption of men in despising it that you had rather suffer the flames of hell than willingly be guilty of their error. There is so much blindness and ingratitude and damned folly in it. The world is a mirror of infinite beauty, yet no man sees it. It is a temple of majesty, yet no man regards it. It is a region of light and peace, did not men disquiet it. It is the Paradise of God. It is more to man since he is fallen than it was before. It is the place of angels and the gate of heaven. When Jacob waked out of his dream, he said "God is here, and I visit it not. How dreadful is this place! This is none other than the House of God, and the Gate of Heaven." [2]

[2] Gen. 28:16.

The Second Century

67

Suppose a river, or a drop of water, an apple or a sand, an ear of corn, or an herb: God knoweth infinite excellencies in it more than we:[3] he seeth how it relateth to angels and men; how it proceedeth from the most perfect Lover to the most perfectly beloved; how it representeth all his attributes; how it conduceth in its place, by the best of means to the best of ends: and for this cause it cannot be beloved too much. God the Author and God the End is to be beloved in it; angels and men are to be beloved in it; and it is highly to be esteemed for all their sakes. O what a treasure is every sand when truly understood! Who can love anything that God made too much? His infinite goodness and wisdom and power and glory are in it. What a world would this be, were everything beloved as it ought to be!

The Third Century

2

All appeared new, and strange at first, inexpressibly rare and delightful and beautiful. I was a little stranger, which at my entrance into the world was saluted and surrounded with innumerable joys. My knowledge was divine. I knew by intuition those things which since my apostasy I collected again by the highest reason. My very ignorance was advantageous. I seemed as one brought into the Estate of Innocence. All things were spotless and pure and glorious: yea, and infinitely mine, and joyful and precious. I knew not that there were any sins, or complaints, or laws. I dreamed not of poverties, contentions, or vices. All tears and quarrels were hidden from mine eyes. Everything was at rest, free and immortal. I knew

---

[3] Cf. William Blake, especially "Auguries of Innocence."

nothing of sickness or death or rents or exaction, either for tribute or bread. In the absence of these I was entertained like an angel with the works of God in their splendor and glory, I saw all in the peace of Eden; heaven and earth did sing my Creator's praises, and could not make more melody to Adam than to me. All time was eternity, and a perpetual Sabbath. Is it not strange that an infant should be heir of the whole world, and see those mysteries which the books of the learned never unfold?

3

The corn was orient and immortal wheat, which never should be reaped, nor was ever sown. I thought it had stood from everlasting to everlasting. The dust and stones of the street were as precious as gold; the gates were at first the end of the world. The green trees when I saw them first through one of the gates transported and ravished me; their sweetness and unusual beauty made my heart to leap, and almost mad with ecstasy, they were such strange and wonderful things. The men! O what venerable and reverend creatures did the aged seem! Immortal cherubims! And young men glittering and sparkling angels, and maids strange seraphic pieces of life and beauty! Boys and girls tumbling in the street, and playing, were moving jewels. I knew not that they were born or should die; but all things abided eternally as they were in their proper places. Eternity was manifest in the light of the day, and something infinite behind everything appeared: which talked with my expectation and moved my desire. The city seemed to stand in Eden, or to be built in heaven. The streets were mine, the temple was mine, the people were mine, their clothes and gold and silver were mine, as much as their sparkling eyes, fair skins, and ruddy faces. The skies were mine, and so were the sun and moon and stars, and all the world was mine; and I the only spectator and enjoyer of it. I knew no churlish proprieties, nor bounds, nor divisions; but all proprieties and divisions were mine: all treasures and the possessors of them. So that with much ado I was corrupted, and made to learn the dirty devices of this world. Which now I unlearn, and become, as it were, a little child again that I may enter into the Kingdom of God.

24

When I heard of any new kingdom beyond the seas, the light and glory of it pleased me immediately; it rose up within me, and I was enlarged wonderfully. I entered into it; I saw its commodities, rarities, springs, meadows, riches, inhabitants; and became possessor of that new room as if it had been prepared for me, so much was I magnified and delighted in it. When the Bible was read, my spirit was present in other ages. I saw the light and splendor of them: the land of Canaan, the Israelites entering into it, the ancient glory of the Amorites, their peace and riches, their cities, houses, vines and fig-trees, the long prosperity of their kings, their milk and honey, their slaughter and destruction, with the joys and triumphs of God's people; all which entered into me, and God among them. I saw all and felt all in such a lively manner, as if there had been no other way to those places, but in spirit only. This showed me the liveliness of interior presence, and that all ages were for most glorious ends, accessible to my understanding, yea with it, yea within it. For without changing place in myself I could behold and enjoy all those: anything when it was proposed, though it was ten thousand ages ago, being always before me.

36

Having been at the University, and received there the taste and tincture of another education, I saw that there were things in this world of which I never dreamed: glorious secrets, and glorious persons past imagination. There I saw that logic, ethics, physics, metaphysics, geometry, astronomy, poesy, medicine, grammar, music, rhetoric, all kinds of arts, trades, and mechanisms that adorned the world pertained to felicity; at least there I saw those things, which afterwards I knew to pertain unto it: and was delighted in it. There I saw into the nature of the sea, the heavens, the sun, the moon and stars, the elements, minerals, and vegetables. All which appeared like the king's daughter, all glorious within; and those things which my nurses, and parents should have talked of, there were taught unto me.

46

When I came into the country, and being seated among silent trees, and meads and hills, had all my time in mine own hands, I resolved to spend it all, whatever it cost me, in search of happiness, and to satiate that burning thirst which nature had enkindled in me from my youth. In which I was so resolute that I chose rather to live upon ten pounds a year, and to go in leather clothes, and feed upon bread and water, so that I might have all my time clearly to myself, than to keep many thousands per annum in an estate of life where my time would be devoured in care and labor. And God was so pleased to accept of that desire that from that time to this, I have had all things plentifully provided for me, without any care at all, my very study of felicity making me more to prosper than all the care in the whole world. So that through his blessing I live a free and a kingly life as if the world were turned again into Eden, or much more, as it is at this day.

The Fifth Century

9

His omnipresence is an ample territory or field of joys, a transparent temple of infinite luster, a strong tower of defense, a castle of repose, a bulwark of security, a palace of delights, an immediate help, and a present refuge in the needful time of trouble, a broad and a vast extent of fame and glory, a theater of infinite excellency, an infinite ocean by means whereof every action, word, and thought is immediately diffused like a drop of wine in a pail of water, and everywhere present, everywhere seen and known, infinitely delighted in, as well as filling infinite spaces. It is the Spirit that pervades all his works, the life and soul of the universe, that in every point of space from the center to the heavens, in every kingdom in the world, in every city, in every wilderness, in every house, every soul, every creature, in all the parts of his infinity and eternity sees our persons, loves our virtues, inspires us with itself, and crowns our actions with praise and glory. It makes our honor infinite in extent, our glory immense, and our happiness eternal. The rays of our light are by this means darted from everlasting to everlasting. This spiritual region makes us infinitely present with God, angels, and men in all places from the utmost bounds of the everlasting hills, throughout all the unwearied durations of his endless infinity, and gives us the sense and feeling of all the delights and praises we occasion, as well as of all the beauties and powers, and pleasures and glories which God enjoyeth or createth.

Thomas Sprat   1635-1713

THOMAS SPRAT was the son of a minister of the same name. He attended Wadham College, Oxford, and took a number of degrees there: A.B., M.A., B.D., and D.D. From the time he took his M.A. in 1657 until his resignation in 1670, he held a Fellowship at Wadham.

Dr. John Wilkins, Principal of Wadham, was deeply interested in science, and Wadham, therefore, became the gathering place for the Oxford branch of the "Invisible College," as the informal organization of scientists in London was called. The Invisible College was later the foundation of the Royal Scientific Society, and Sprat's knowledge of the early meetings was valuable background when he came to write the history of the Society.

After the Restoration, Sprat was appointed chaplain to the Duke of Buckingham and later to Charles II. He held various appointments in the church and finally became Dean of Westminster and then Bishop of Rochester.

He was Cowley's friend and wrote the life of Cowley prefixed to the collected edition of his English works published in 1668. In his own poems he took Cowley as a model, and like him was popular in the seventeenth century as a poet. Also like Cowley his reputation now rests primarily upon his prose. In the *History of the Royal Society* Sprat points out the necessity for a "naked, natural way of speaking" and advocates an English Literary Academy modeled after the French Academy. His own prose illustrates the fine qualities of simple, direct expression in contrast with the ornate prose which had been popular before the Restoration.

From THE HISTORY OF THE ROYAL SOCIETY [1]

The First Part, SECTION XVI

Modern Experimenters

THE THIRD sort of new philosophers have been those who
have not only disagreed from the ancients but have also
proposed to themselves the right course of slow and sure
experimenting; and have prosecuted it as far as the shortness of their own lives or the multiplicity of their other affairs
or the narrowness of their fortunes have given them leave.
Such as these we are to expect to be but few, for they must
divest themselves of many vain conceptions and overcome
a thousand false images, which lie like monsters in their way,
before they can get as far as this. And of these I shall only
mention one great man, who had the true imagination of the
whole extent of this great enterprise as it is now set on foot,
and that is the Lord Bacon. In whose books there are everywhere scattered the best arguments that can be produced for
the defense of experimental philosophy, and the best directions that are needful to promote it. All which he has already adorned with so much art that if my desires could have
prevailed with some excellent friends of mine who engaged
me to this work, there should have been no other preface
to the *History of the Royal Society* but some of his writings.
But methinks in this one man, I do at once find enough occasion to admire the strength of human wit and to bewail
the weakness of mortal condition. For is it not wonderful
that he, who had run through all the degrees of that progression which usually takes up men's whole time; who had
studied and practiced, and governed the common law; who

---

[1] Text: 1667, first edition, pp. 35–36. The Royal Scientific Society had
its beginnings in London at Gresham College and in Oxford at Wadham. It
received its charter in 1662 and was granted a second charter in 1663.

had always lived in the crowd and borne the greatest burden
of civil business, should yet find leisure enough for these
retired studies to excel all those men who separate themselves for this very purpose? He was a man of strong, clear,
and powerful imaginations: his genius was searching and
inimitable; and of this I need give no other proof than his
style itself, which as, for the most part, it describes men's
minds as well as pictures do their bodies, so it did his above
all men living. The course of it vigorous and majestical; the
wit bold and familiar; the comparisons fetched out of the
way, and yet the most easy; in all expressing a soul equally
skilled in men and nature. All this and much more is true of
him; but yet his philosophical works do show that a single
and busy hand can never grasp all this whole design of which
we treat. His rules were admirable, yet his history not so
faithful as might have been wished in many places; he seems
rather to take all that comes than to choose, and to heap
rather than to register. But I hope this accusation of mine
can be no great injury to his memory, seeing at the same time
that I say he had not the strength of a thousand men, I do also
allow him to have had so much as twenty . . .

The First Part, SECTION XX

A Proposal for Erecting an English Academy [2]

I hope now it will not be thought a vain digression if I step
a little aside to recommend the forming of such an Assembly [3]
to the gentlemen of our nation. I know indeed that the English genius is not so airy and discursive as that of some of our
neighbors, but that we generally love to have reason set out
in plain, undeceiving expressions, as much as they to have
it delivered with color and beauty. And besides this, I under-

---

[2] *Ibid.,* pp. 40–43.
[3] Sprat has been speaking of "Modern Academies for Language," such
as the French Academy at Paris.

stand well enough that they have one great assistance to the growth of oratory which to us is wanting: that is, that their nobility live commonly close together in their cities, and ours for the most part scattered in their country houses. For the same reason why our streets are not so well built as theirs will hold also for their exceeding us in the arts of speech: they prefer the pleasures of the town; we, those of the field: whereas it is from the frequent conversations in cities that the humor and wit and variety and elegance of language are chiefly to be fetched. But yet, notwithstanding these discouragements, I shall not stick to say that such a project is now seasonable to set on foot and may make a great reformation in the manner of our speaking and writing. First, the thing itself is no way contemptible. For the purity of speech and greatness of empire have in all countries still met together. The Greeks spoke best when they were in their glory of conquest. The Romans made those times the standard of their wit, when they subdued and gave laws to the world; and from thence by degrees they declined to corruption, as their valor, their prudence, and the honor of their arms did decay; and at last, did even meet the northern nations half way in barbarism, a little before they were over-run by their armies.

But besides, if we observe well the English language, we shall find that it seems at this time more than others to require some such aid to bring it to its last perfection. The truth is, it has been hitherto a little too carelessly handled; and, I think, has had less labor spent about its polishing than it deserves. Till the time of King Henry the Eighth, there was scarce any man regarded it but Chaucer; and nothing was written in it, which one would be willing to read twice but some of his poetry. But then it began to raise itself a little and to sound tolerably well. From that age down to the beginning of our late civil wars, it was still fashioning and beautifying itself. In the wars themselves (which is a time wherein all languages use, if ever, to increase by extraordinary degrees, for in such busy and active times there arise more new thoughts of men, which must be signified and varied by new expressions), then, I say, it received many fantastical terms, which were introduced by our religious sects; and many outlandish phrases, which several writers and translators in that great hurry brought in and made free as they pleased; and with all it was enlarged by many sound and necessary forms and idioms which it before wanted. And now, when men's minds are somewhat settled, their passions allayed, and the peace of our country gives us the opportunity of such diversions; if some sober and judicious men would take the whole mass of our language into their hands as they find it, and would set a mark on the ill words, correct those which are to be retained, admit and establish the good, and make some emendations in the accent and grammar: I dare pronounce that our speech would quickly arrive at as much plenty as it is capable to receive, and at the greatest smoothness which its derivation from the rough German will allow it.

Nor would I have this new English Academy confined only to the weighing words and letters; but there may be also greater works found out for it. By many signs we may guess that the wits of our nation are not inferior to any other, and that they have an excellent mixture of the spirit of the French and the Spaniard; and I am confident that we only want a few more standing examples and a little familiarity with the ancients to excel all the moderns. Now the best means that can be devised to bring that about is to settle a fixed and impartial Court of Eloquence, according to whose censure all books or authors should either stand or fall. And above all, there might be recommended to them one principal work in which we are yet defective, and that is the compiling of a history of our late civil wars. Of all the labors of men's wit and industry I scarce know any that can be more useful to the world than civil history, if it were written with that sincerity and majesty as it ought to be, as a faithful idea of human actions. And it is observable that almost in all civilized countries it has been the last thing that has come to perfection. I may now say that the English can already show many industrious and worthy pieces in this kind; but yet I have some prophetical imagination in my thoughts that there is still behind, something greater than any we have yet seen, reserved for the glory of this age . . .

The Second Part, SECTION XX

Their Manner of Discourse [4]

Thus they have directed, judged, conjectured upon, and improved experiments. But lastly, in these and all other businesses that have come under their care, there is one thing more about which the Society has been most solicitous, and that is the manner of their discourse: which unless they had been very watchful to keep in due temper, the whole spirit and vigor of their design had been soon eaten out by the luxury and redundance of speech. The ill effects of this superfluity of talking have already overwhelmed most other arts and professions; insomuch that when I consider the means of happy living and the causes of their corruption, I can hardly forbear recanting what I said before and concluding that eloquence ought to be banished out of all civil societies as a thing fatal to peace and good manners. To this opinion I should wholly incline if I did not find that it is a weapon which may be as easily procured by bad men as good; and that if these should only cast it away, and those retain it, the naked innocence of virtue would be upon all occasions exposed to the armed malice of the wicked. This is the chief reason that should now keep up the ornaments of speaking in any request, since they are so much degenerated from their original usefulness. They were at first, no doubt, an admirable instrument in the hands of wise men: when they

[4] *Ibid.*, pp. 111–115.

were only employed to describe goodness, honesty, obedience in larger, fairer, and more moving images; to represent truth clothed with bodies; and to bring knowledge back again to our very senses from whence it was at first derived to our understandings. But now they are generally changed to worse uses: they make the fancy disgust the best things if they come sound and unadorned; they are in open defiance against reason, professing not to hold much correspondence with that but with its slaves, the passions; they give the mind a motion too changeable and bewitching to consist with right practice. Who can behold without indignation how many mists and uncertainties these specious tropes and figures have brought on our knowledge? How many rewards, which are due to more profitable and difficult arts, have been still snatched away by the easy vanity of fine speaking? For now I am warmed with this just anger, I cannot withhold myself from betraying the shallowness of all these seeming mysteries, upon which we writers and speakers look so big. And in few words I dare say that of all the studies of men, nothing can be sooner obtained than this vicious abundance of phrase, this trick of metaphors, this volubility of tongue, which makes so great a noise in the world. But I spend words in vain, for the evil is now so inveterate that it is hard to know whom to blame or where to begin to reform. We all value one another so much upon this beautiful deceit, and labor so long after it in the years of our education, that we cannot but ever after think kinder of it than it deserves. And, indeed, in most other parts of learning, I look on it to be a thing almost utterly desperate in its cure; and I think it may be placed among those general mischiefs, such as the dissension of Christian princes, the want of practice in religion, and the like, which have been so long spoken against that men are become insensible about them, everyone shifting off the fault from himself to others; and so they are only made bare commonplaces of complaint. It will suffice my present purpose to point out what has been done by the Royal Society towards the correcting of its excesses in Natural Philosophy, to which it is, of all others, a most professed enemy.

They have therefore been most rigorous in putting in execution the only remedy that can be found for this extravagance: and that has been a constant resolution to reject all the amplifications, digressions, and swellings of style; to return back to the primitive purity and shortness, when men delivered so many things almost in an equal number of words. They have exacted from all their members a close, naked, natural way of speaking, positive expressions, clear senses, a native easiness, bringing all things as near the mathematical plainness as they can, and preferring the language of artisans, countrymen, and merchants before that of wits or scholars.

And here there is one thing not to be passed by, which will render this established custom of the Society well nigh everlasting, and that is the general constitution of the minds of the English. I have already often insisted on some of the prerogatives of England, whereby it may justly lay claim to be the head of a philosophical league, above all other countries in Europe: I have urged its situation, its present genius, and the disposition of its merchants; and many more such arguments to encourage us still remain to be used; but of all others, this which I am now alleging is of the most weighty and important consideration. If there can be a true character given of the universal temper of any nation under heaven, then certainly this must be ascribed to our countrymen: that they have commonly an unaffected sincerity; that they love to deliver their minds with a sound simplicity; that they have the middle qualities between the reserved subtle southern and the rough unhewn northern people; that they are not extremely prone to speak; that they are more concerned what others will think of the strength than of the fineness of what they say; and that an universal modesty possesses them. These qualities are so conspicuous and proper to our soil that we often hear them objected to us by some of our neighbor satirists in more disgraceful expressions. For they are wont to revile the English with a want of familiarity; with a melancholy dumpishness; with slowness, silence, and with the unrefined sullenness of their behavior. But these are only the reproaches of partiality or ignorance: for they ought rather to be commended for an honorable integrity; for a neglect of circumstances and flourishes; for regarding things of greater moment more than less; for a scorn to deceive as well as to be deceived: which are the best endowments that can enter into a philosophical mind. So that even the position of our climate, the air, the influence of the heaven, the composition of the English blood, as well as the embraces of the ocean, seem to join with the labors of the Royal Society to render our country a land of experimental knowledge. And it is a good sign that nature will reveal more of its secrets to the English than to others, because it has already furnished them with a genius so well proportioned for the receiving and retaining its mysteries.

The Third Part, SECTION XL

The Conclusion, being a general recommendation of this design [5]

. . . And now as I have spoken of a Society that prefers works before words, so it becomes their history to endeavor after real fruits and effects. I will therefore conclude by recommending again this undertaking to the English nation: to the bravest people, the most generous design; to the most zealous lovers of liberty, the surest way to ransom the minds of mankind from slavery.

The privileges that our king's dominions enjoy for this end appear to be equaled by no other country. The men we

[5] *Ibid.,* pp. 434–438.

have now living to employ are excellently furnished with all manner of abilities: their method is already settled and placed out of the reach of calumny or contradiction.

The work itself indeed is vast and almost incomprehensible when it is considered in gross; but they have made it feasible and easy by distributing the burden. They have shown to the world this great secret, that philosophy ought not only to be attended by a select company of refined spirits. As they desire that its productions should be vulgar, so they also declare that they may be promoted by vulgar hands. They exact no extraordinary preparations of learning: to have found senses and truth is with them a sufficient qualification. Here is enough business for minds of all sizes: and so boundless is the variety of these studies that here is also enough delight to recompense the labors of them all, from the most ordinary capacities to the highest and most searching wits.

Here first they may take a plain view of all particular things, their kinds, their order, their figure, their place, their motion: and even this naked prospect cannot but fill their thoughts with much satisfaction, seeing it was the first pleasure which the Scripture relates God himself to have taken at the creation: and that not only once, but at the end of every day's work when he saw all that he had made and approved it to be good. From this they may proceed to survey the difference of their composition, their effects, the instruments of their beings and lives, the subtility and structure, the decay and supply of their parts; wherein how large is the space of their delight, seeing the very shape of a mite and the sting of a bee appears so prodigious. From hence they may go to apply things together, to make them work one upon another, to imitate their productions, to help their defects, and with the noblest duty to assist nature, our common mother, in her operations: from hence to all the works of men's hands, the divers artifices of several ages, the various materials, the improvement of trades, the advancement of manufactures: in which last alone there is to be found so great content that many mighty princes of the former and present times, amidst the pleasures of government, which are no doubt the highest in the world, have striven to excel in some manual art.

In this spacious field their observations may wander, and in this whatever they shall meet with, they may call their own. Here they will not only enjoy the cold contentment of learning, but that which is far greater, of discovering. Many things that have been hitherto hidden will arise and expose themselves to their view: many methods of advancing what we have already will come in their way: nay, even many of the lost rarities of antiquity will be hereby restored. Of these a great quantity has been overwhelmed in the ruins of time: and they will sooner be retrieved by our laboring anew in the material subjects whence they first arose, than by our plodding everlastingly on the ancient writings. Their inventions may be soonest regained the same way by which their medals and coins have been found, of which the greatest part has been recovered, not by those who sought for them on purpose in old rubbish, but by digging up foundations to raise new buildings and by plowing the ground to sow new seed.

This is the work we propose to be encouraged, which at once regards the discovering of new secrets and the repairing all the profitable things of antiquity. The supply that is needful to finish it will neither impoverish families nor exhaust a mighty income. So near is mankind to its happiness that so great an attempt may be plentifully endowed by a small part of what is spent on any one single lust or extravagant vanity of the time. So moderate is the society in their desires of assistance that as much charity as is bestowed in England in one year for the relief of particular poverty and diseases were enough forever to sustain a design which endeavors to give aid against all the infirmities and wants of human nature.

If now this enterprise shall chance to fail for want of patronage and revenue, the world will not only be frustrated of their present expectations but will have just ground to despair of any future labors towards the increase of the practical philosophy. If our posterity shall find that an institution so vigorously begun, and so strengthened by many signal advantages could not support itself, they will have reason in all times to conclude that the long barrenness of knowledge was not caused by the corrupt method which was taken, but by the nature of the thing itself. This will be the last great endeavor that will be made in this way if this shall prove ineffectual, and so we shall not only be guilty of our own ignorance, but of the errors of all those that come after us.

But if (as I rather believe and presage) our nation shall lay hold of this opportunity to deserve the applause of mankind, the force of this example will be irresistibly prevalent in all countries round about us; the state of Christendom will soon obtain a new face; while this halcyon knowledge is breeding, all tempests will cease: the oppositions and contentious wranglings of science, falsely so called, will soon vanish away: the peaceable calmness of men's judgments will have an admirable influence on their manners; the sincerity of their understandings will appear in their actions; their opinions will be less violent and dogmatical, but more certain; they will only be gods one to another, and not wolves; the value of their arts will be esteemed by the great things they perform, and not by those they speak: while the old philosophy could only at the best pretend to the portion of Nepthali, to give goodly words, the new will have the blessings of Joseph, the younger and the beloved son: *It shall be like a fruitful bough, even a fruitful bough by a well, whose branches run over the wall: it shall have the blessings of heaven above, the blessings of the deep that lies under, the blessings of the breast and of the womb.*[6] While

[6] Gen. 49:21, 22.

the old could only bestow on us some barren terms and notions, the new shall impart to us the uses of all the creatures, and shall enrich us with all the benefits of fruitfulness and plenty.

Thomas Ellwood 1639-1713

THOMAS ELLWOOD was born at the family home in Crowell, Oxfordshire, but his early childhood was spent in London, where the family lived from 1642 to 1646. In 1659 Ellwood and his father visited Isaac Penington, who had become a Quaker a short time before. Ellwood became greatly interested in the sect and soon after joined them in spite of his father's extreme displeasure. He became the close friend of George Fox and William Penn, and later he was one of the editors of the *Journal* of Fox.

After he recovered from an attack of smallpox in 1662, he was introduced by Isaac Penington to Milton to serve as his amanuensis. Illness interrupted this association, and after his recovery he suffered various imprisonments because of continuing to meet with the Quakers. These "Sufferings and Services" he considered in the cause of truth and therefore bore them with patience. In an interval of about six years between imprisonments he served as tutor to the Penington children.

He wrote many controversial works, which have no literary value; but his autobiography has a pleasing simplicity and vivid directness which give it a place in literature. It records associations with a number of important people, including Milton, and gives insight into the Quaker movement. The accounts of the persecutions endured by the Friends and the descriptions of prison life in the century form an important contribution toward understanding the period.

From THE HISTORY OF THOMAS ELLWOOD WRITTEN BY HIMSELF [1]

[Ellwood and Milton]

AFTER I was well enough to go abroad, with respect to my own health and the safety of others, I went up (in the beginning of the twelfth month, 1661) to my friend Isaac Penington's at Chalfont, and abode there some time for the airing myself more fully that I might be more fit for conversation.

I mentioned before that when I was a boy I had made some good progress in learning and lost it all again before I came to be a man; nor was I rightly sensible of my loss therein until I came amongst the Quakers. But then I both saw my loss and lamented it, and applied myself with utmost diligence at all leisure times to recover it; so false I found that charge to be which in those times was cast as a reproach upon the Quakers that they despised and decried all human learning because they denied it to be essentially necessary to a gospel ministry, which was one of the controversies of those times.

But though I toiled hard and spared no pains to regain what once I had been master of, yet I found it a matter of so great difficulty that I was ready to say as the noble eunuch to Philip in another case, "How can I, unless I had some man to guide me?" [2]

This I had formerly complained of to my especial friend, Isaac Penington, but now more earnestly, which put him upon considering and contriving a means for my assistance.

He had an intimate acquaintance with Dr. Paget, a physician of note in London, and he, with John Milton, a gentleman of great note for learning throughout the learned world,

[1] Text: 1714, pp. 130–37, 233–34. The autobiography was discontinued in 1683, but was supplemented by Joseph Wyeth to fill in the years from 1683 to Ellwood's death in 1714 and published that year.
[2] Acts 8:31.

for the accurate pieces he had written on various subjects and occasions.

This person, having filled a public station in the former times, lived now a private and retired life in London, and having wholly lost his sight, kept always a man to read to him, which usually was the son of some gentleman of his acquaintance, whom in kindness he took to improve in his learning.

Thus by the mediation of my friend Isaac Penington with Dr. Paget and of Dr. Paget with John Milton was I admitted to come to him, not as a servant to him (which at that time he needed not), nor to be in the house with him, but only to have the liberty of coming to his house at certain hours when I would, and to read to him what books he should appoint me, which was all the favor I desired.

But this being a matter which would require some time to bring it about, I in the meanwhile returned to my father's house in Oxfordshire.

I had before received direction by letters from my eldest sister (written by my father's command) to put off what cattle he had left about his house and to discharge his servants; which I had done at the time called Michaelmas before. So that all that winter, when I was at home, I lived like an hermit, all alone, having a pretty large house and nobody in it but myself a' nights especially; but an elderly woman (whose father had been an old servant to the family) came every morning and made my bed, and did what else I had occasion for her to do, till I fell ill of the smallpox, and then I had her with me and the nurse. But now, understanding by letter from my sister that my father did not intend to return to settle there, I made off those provisions which were in the house that they might not be spoiled when I was gone; and because they were what I should have spent if I had tarried there, I took the money made of them to myself for my support at London, if the project succeeded for my going thither.

This done, I committed the care of the house to a tenant of my father's who lived in the town, and taking my leave of Crowell, went up to my sure friend Isaac Penington again; where understanding that the mediation used for my admittance to John Milton had succeeded so well that I might come when I would, I hastened to London and in the first place went to wait upon him.

He received me courteously, as well for the sake of Dr. Paget, who introduced me, as of Isaac Penington, who recommended me; to both whom he bore a good respect. And having inquired divers things of me with respect to my former progression in learning, he dismissed me to provide myself of such accommodations as might be most suitable to my future studies.

I went therefore and took myself a lodging as near to his house (which was then in Jewin Street) as conveniently I could, and from thenceforward went every day in the afternoon, except on the first days of the week, and sitting by him in his dining-room, read to him in such books in the Latin tongue as he pleased to hear me read.

At my first sitting to read to him, observing that I used the English pronunciation, he told me, if I would have the benefit of the Latin tongue, not only to read and understand Latin authors but to converse with foreigners either abroad or at home, I must learn the foreign pronunciation. To this I consenting, he instructed me how to sound the vowels; so different from the common pronunciation used by the English, who speak Anglicè their Latin, that (with some few other variations in sounding some consonants in particular cases, as *c* before *e* or *i* like *ch, sc* before *i* like *sh,* etc.) the Latin thus spoken seemed as different from that which was delivered as the English generally speak it, as if it was another language.

I had before, during my retired life at my father's, by unwearied diligence and industry, so far recovered the rules of grammar (in which I had once been very ready) that I could both read a Latin author and after a sort hammer out his meaning. But this change of pronunciation proved a new difficulty to me. It was now harder to me to read than it was before to understand when read. But

Labor omnia vincit
Improbus:

Incessant pains
The end obtains.

And so did I. Which made my reading the more acceptable to my master. He, on the other hand, perceiving with what earnest desire I pursued learning, gave me not only all the encouragement but all the help he could; for, having a curious ear, he understood by my tone when I understood what I read and when I did not, and accordingly would stop me, examine me, and open the most difficult passages to me.

Thus went I on for about six weeks' time, reading to him in the afternoons; and exercising myself with my own books in my chamber in the forenoons. I was sensible of an improvement.

But, alas! I had fixed my studies in a wrong place. London and I could never agree for health; my lungs (as I suppose) were too tender to bear the sulphurous air of that city, so that I soon began to droop; and in less than two months' time I was fain to leave both my studies and the city and return into the country to preserve life; and much ado I had to get thither.

I chose to go down to Wycombe, and to John Rance's house there: both as he was a physician, and his wife an honest, hearty, discreet, and grave matron, whom I had a very good esteem of, and who (I knew) had a very good regard for me.

There I lay ill a considerable time and to that degree of weakness that scarce any who saw me expected my life. But the Lord was both gracious to me in my illness and was pleased to raise me up again that I might serve him in my generation.

As soon as I had recovered so much strength as to be fit to travel, I obtained of my father (who was then at his house in Crowell to dispose of some things he had there, and who in my illness had come to see me) so much money as would clear all charges in the house, for both physic, food, and attendance: and having fully discharged all, I took leave of my friends in that family and in the town and returned to my studies at London.

I was very kindly received by my master, who had conceived so good an opinion of me that my conversation (I found) was acceptable to him; and he seemed heartily glad of my recovery and return; and into our old method of study we fell again, I reading to him, and he explaining to me as occasion required.

But, as if learning had been a forbidden fruit to me, scarce was I well settled in my work before I met with another diversion, which turned me quite out of my work.

For a sudden storm arising, from I know what surmise of a plot and thereby danger to the government, the meetings of dissenters (such I mean as could be found, which, perhaps, were not many besides the Quakers) were broken up throughout the city, and the prisons mostly filled with our Friends. . . .

Some little time before I went to Aylesbury prison,[3] I was desired by my quondam master, Milton, to take an house for him in the neighborhood where I dwelt, that he might get out of the city for the safety of himself and his family, the pestilence then growing hot in London.[4] I took a pretty box for him in Giles Chalfont, a mile from me, of which I gave him notice, and intended to have waited on

[3] He had been arrested on July 1, 1665 while attending a Quaker funeral and was imprisoned at Aylesbury for a month. He suffered imprisonment several times for his Quaker activities both before and after this experience.
[4] In June, 1665, he took "a pretty box" for Milton at Chalfont St. Giles.

him and seen him well settled in it but was prevented by that imprisonment.

But now being released and returned home, I soon made a visit to him, to welcome him into the country.

After some common discourses had passed betwixt us, he called for a manuscript of his; which, being brought, he delivered to me, bidding me take it home with me and read it at my leisure, and when I had so done, return it to him with my judgment thereupon.

When I came home and had set myself to read it, I found it was that excellent poem which he entitled "Paradise Lost." After I had, with the best attention, read it through, I made him another visit and returned him his book, with due acknowledgment of the favor he had done me in communicating it to me. He asked me how I liked it and what I thought of it, which I modestly but freely told him, and after some further discourse about it, I pleasantly said to him, "Thou hast said much here of 'Paradise Lost,' but what hast thou to say of 'Paradise found'?" He made me no answer, but sat some time in a muse; then brake off that discourse and fell upon another subject.

After the sickness was over and the City well cleansed and become safely habitable again, he returned thither. And when afterwards I went to wait on him there, which I seldom failed of doing whenever my occasions drew me to London, he showed me his second poem, called "Paradise Regained," and in a pleasant tone said to me, "This is owing to you, for you put it into my head by the question you put to me at Chalfont, which before I had not thought of." But from this digression I return to the family I then lived in.

I

Clark, G. N. *The Later Stuarts, 1660–1714.* Oxford History of England. Oxford, Clarendon Press, 1934.

Davies, Godfrey. *The Early Stuarts, 1603–1660.* Oxford History of England. Oxford, Clarendon Press, 1937.

———. *Bibliography of British History: Stuart Period, 1603–1714.* Oxford, Clarendon Press, 1914.

II

Bury, J. B. *A History of Freedom of Thought.* New York, Henry Holt & Co., 1913.

———. *The Idea of Progress: An Inquiry into Its Origin and Growth.* New York, Macmillan Co., 1932.

Gooch, G. P. *English Democratic Ideas in the Seventeenth Century,* 2nd edition. Cambridge (England) University Press, 1927.

Haller, William. *The Rise of Puritanism.* New York, Columbia University Press, 1938.

James, Margaret. *Social Problems and Policy During the Puritan Revolution 1640–1660.* London, George Routledge and Sons, 1930.

Plum, Harry Grant. *Restoration Puritanism: A Study of the Growth of English Liberty.* Chapel Hill, University of North Carolina Press, 1943.

Powell, Chilton L. *English Domestic Relations, 1487–1653.* New York, Columbia University Press, 1917.

Smith, Preserved. *A History of Modern Culture.* 2 vols. New York, Henry Holt & Co., 1930, 1934.

Social and Political Ideas of Some Great Thinkers of the Sixteenth and Seventeenth Centuries. Ed. by F. J. C. Hearnshaw. London, G. G. Harrap, 1926.

Whiting, C. E. *Studies in English Puritanism from the Restoration to the Revolution, 1660–1688.* London and Toronto, Macmillan Co., 1931.

III

Allen, Beverly Sprague. *Tides in English Taste (1619–1800): A Background for the Study of Literature.* 2 vols. Cambridge, Mass., Harvard University Press, 1937.

Dowden, Edward. *Puritan and Anglican*. 3rd edition. New York, Henry Holt & Co., 1910.

Grierson, H. J. C. *Cross Currents in English Literature of the Seventeenth Century*. London, Chatto & Windus, 1929.

Mathew, David. *The Jacobean Age*. London and New York, Longmans, Green & Co., 1938.

Seventeenth Century Studies Presented to Sir Herbert Grierson. Oxford, Clarendon Press, 1938.

Wendell, Barrett. *The Temper of the Seventeenth Century in English Literature*. New York, Charles Scribner's Sons, 1904.

Willey, Basil. *The Seventeenth Century Background: Studies in the Thought of the Age in Relation to Poetry and Religion*. London, Chatto & Windus, 1934.

Wilson, F. P. *Elizabethan and Jacobean*. Oxford, Clarendon Press, 1945.

IV

Charlanne, Louis. *L'Influence française en Angleterre au XVIIᵉ siècle. La Vie sociale—la Vie littéraire*. Paris, Société française d'imprimere et de libraire, 1906.

Upham, A. H. *French Influence in English Literature*. Columbia University Studies in Comparative Literature. New York, Columbia University Press, 1908.

V

James, D. G. *Life of Reason: Hobbes, Locke, Bolingbroke*. London and New York, Longmans, Green & Co., 1949.

Seth, James. *English Philosophers and Schools of Philosophy*. London, J. M. Dent & Sons; New York, E. P. Dutton & Co., 1925.

Sorley, W. R. *History of English Philosophy*. London and New York, G. P. Putnam's Sons, 1921.

VI

Carter, C. S. *The English Church in the Seventeenth Century*. Longmans, Green & Co., 1909.

George, Edward Augustus. *Seventeenth Century Men of Latitude*. New York, Charles Scribner's Sons, 1908.

George, Robert E. G. *Outflying Philosophy*. London, Simpkin and Marshall, 1925.

Henson, H. H. *Studies in English Religion in the Seventeenth Century*. London, J. Murray, 1903.

Inge, W. R. *The Platonic Tradition in English Religious Thought*. New York, Longmans, Green & Co., 1926.

Jordan, W. K. *The Development of Religious Toleration in England, 1640–1660*. 4 vols. London, Allen & Unwin, 1932–40. Vols. II and III.

Powicke, F. J. *The Cambridge Platonists*. London and Toronto, J. M. Dent & Sons, 1926.

Richardson, Caroline F. *English Preachers and Preaching, 1640–1670*. New York, Macmillan Co., 1928.

Spurgeon, Caroline. *Mysticism in English Literature*. Cambridge (England) University Press; New York, G. P. Putnam's Sons, 1913.

Tulloch, John. *Rational Theology and Christian Philosophy in England in the Seventeenth Century*. 2 vols. Edinburgh and London, Blackwood and Sons, 1872–74.

White, Helen C. *English Devotional Literature (Prose), 1600–1640*. University of Wisconsin Studies, Language and Literature, No. 29. Madison, University of Wisconsin Press, 1931.

——. *The Metaphysical Poets: A Study in Religious Experience*. New York, Macmillan Co., 1936.

VII

Burtt, Edwin A. *Metaphysical Foundations of Modern Physical Science*. London, K. Paul, Trench, Trubner & Co., 1925; New York, Harcourt, Brace and Co., rev., 1932.

Clark, G. N. *Science and Social Welfare in the Age of Newton*. Oxford, Clarendon Press, 1937; 2nd edition, 1950.

Jones, R. F. *Ancients and Moderns*. Washington University Studies, New Series, Language and Literature, No. 6. St. Louis, Washington University Press, 1936.

Ornstein, Martha. *The Role of the Scientific Societies in the Seventeenth Century*. 3rd edition. Chicago, University of Chicago Press, 1938.

Sedgwick, W. T., and Tyler, H. W. *A Short History of Science*. New York, Macmillan Co., 1929.

Stimson, Dorothy. *The Gradual Acceptance of the Copernican Theory of the Universe*. New York, Baker & Taylor Co., 1917.

——. *Scientists and Amateurs: A History of the Royal Society*. New York, Henry Schuman, 1948.

Whitehead, A. N. *Science and the Modern World*. New York, Macmillan Co., 1926.

Merton, Robert K. "Science, Technology, and Society in Seventeenth-Century England," *Osiris,* IV (1938), 360–632.

Stimson, Dorothy. "Puritanism and the New Philosophy in Seventeenth Century England," *Bulletin of the Institute of the History of Medicine,* III (1935), 321–34.

VIII

Krapp, George Phillip. *The Rise of English Literary Prose.* London and New York, Oxford University Press, 1915.

Saintsbury, George E. *A History of English Prose Rhythm.* London, Macmillan Co., 1912; reprinted, 1922.

Wilson, F. P. *Elizabethan and Jacobean.* Oxford, Clarendon Press, 1945.

Bennett, Joan. "An Aspect of the Evolution of Seventeenth Century Prose," *Review of English Studies,* XVII (1941), 281–97.

Jones, R. F. "Science and English Prose Style in the Third Quarter of the Seventeenth Century," *Publications of the Modern Language Association,* XLV (1930), 977–1009.

Macdonald, Hugh. "Another Aspect of Seventeenth Century Prose," *Review of English Studies,* XIX (1943), 33–43.

IX

BIOGRAPHY

Dunn, Waldo Hilary. *English Biography.* London, J. M. Dent & Sons; New York, E. P. Dutton & Co., 1916.

Nicolson, Harold. *The Development of English Biography.* New York, Harcourt, Brace and Co., 1928.

Stauffer, Donald A. *English Biography before 1700.* Cambridge, Mass., Harvard University Press, 1930.

CRITICISM

Saintsbury, G. E. *History of English Criticism.* New York, Dodd, Mead and Co., 1911; reprinted, Peter Smith, 1949.

Spingarn, J. E. *Critical Essays of the Seventeenth Century.* 3 vols. Oxford, Clarendon Press, 1908–9.

CHARACTER-BOOKS

Greenough, Chester Noyes. *A Bibliography of the Theophrastian Character in English with Several Portrait Characters.*

Prepared for Publication by J. Milton French. Cambridge, Mass., Harvard University Press, 1927.

Murphy, Gwendolen. *A Bibliography of the English Character-Books, 1608–1700*. Oxford, The Bibliographical Society, 1925.

Character Writings of the Seventeenth Century. Ed. by Henry Morley. London, George Routledge and Sons, 1891.

Smith, David Nichol. *Characters from the Histories and Memoirs of the Seventeenth Century, with an Essay on the Character*. Oxford, Clarendon Press, 1918.

Boyce, Benjamin. *The Theophrastan Character in England to 1642*. With the Assistance of Notes by Chester Noyes Greenough. Cambridge, Mass., Harvard University Press, 1947.

Gordon, G. S. "Theophrastus and His Imitators," *English Literature and the Classics*. Oxford, Clarendon Press, 1912.

ESSAY

Thompson, E. N. S. *The Seventeenth Century English Essay*. University of Iowa Humanistic Studies, III. iii. Iowa City, University of Iowa Press, 1926.

Walker, Hugh. *The English Essay and Essayists*. London and Toronto, J. M. Dent and Sons; New York, E. P. Dutton & Co., 1928.

SERMONS

Mitchell, W. F. *English Pulpit Oratory from Andrewes to Tillotson: A Study of Its Literary Aspects*. London, Society for Promoting Christian Knowledge, 1932.

Jones, R. F. "An Attack on Pulpit Eloquence in the Restoration," *Journal of English and Germanic Philology*, XXX (1931), 188–277.

Cambridge Bibliography of English Literature, Ed. by F. W. Bateson. 4 vols. New York, Macmillan Co., 1941. Vol. I, 600–1600; Vol. II, 1600–1800.

THE HOLY BIBLE

The King James Version of The Holy Bible, 1611.

The Bible and Its Literary Associations. Ed. by M. B. Crook. New York, Abingdon Press, 1937.

Butterworth, C. C. *The Literary Lineage of the King James Bible, 1340–1611.* Philadelphia, University of Pennsylvania Press, 1941.

Daiches, David. *The King James Version of the English Bible.* Chicago, University of Chicago Press, 1941.

FRANCIS BACON

Works. Collected and edited by James Spedding, R. L. Ellis, and D. D. Heath. 15 vols. Boston, Brown and Taggard, 1860–65.

The Advancement of Learning. Ed. by W. A. Wright. 2nd edition. Oxford, Clarendon Press, 1874.

The Advancement of Learning and *Novum Organum.* With a Special Introduction by James Edward Creighton. World's Great Classics. Rev. ed. New York, Willey Book Co., 1944.

Essays. Ed. by Alfred S. West. Pitt Press Series. Cambridge (England) University Press, 1926.

The New Atlantis. Ed. by A. B. Gough. Oxford, Clarendon Press, 1915.

Farrington, Benjamin. *Francis Bacon, Philosopher of Industrial Science.* New York, Henry Schuman, 1949.

Sturt, Mary. *Francis Bacon.* London, K. Paul, Trench, Trubner & Co., 1932.

Bullough, G. "Bacon and the Defence of Learning," *Seventeenth Century Studies Presented to Sir Herbert Grierson.* Oxford, Clarendon Press, 1938, pp. 1–20.

Crane, R. S. "The Relation of Bacon's Essays to His Program for the Advancement of Learning," *Schelling Anniversary Papers.* New York, Century Co., 1928, pp. 87–105.

Crane, William G. "The Essay and the Character," *Wit and Rhetoric in the Renaissance.* New York, Columbia University Press, 1937, pp. 132–61.

Metz, R. "Bacon's Part in the Intellectual Movement of His Time," *Seventeenth Century Studies Presented to Sir Herbert Grierson*. Oxford, Clarendon Press, 1938, pp. 21–32.

Thompson, E. N. S. *The Seventeenth Century English Essay*. Iowa City, University of Iowa Press, 1926, Chap. III.

Zeitlin, J. "The Development of Bacon's Essays, with Special Reference to the Question of Montaigne's Influence upon Them," *Journal of English and Germanic Philology*, XXVII (1928), 496–519.

JOHN DONNE

Keynes, Geoffrey L. *A Bibliography of Dr. John Donne*. 2nd edition. Cambridge (England) University Press, 1932.

White, William. *John Donne since 1900: A Bibliography of Periodical Articles*. Boston, F. W. Faxon Co., 1942.

The Works of John Donne. Ed. by Henry Alford. 6 vols. London, J. W. Parker, 1839.

Devotions upon Emergent Occasions. Ed. by John Sparrow. Cambridge (England) University Press, 1923.

X Sermons . . . chosen from the whole body of Donne's Sermons by Geoffrey Keynes. London, Nonesuch Press, 1923.

Donne's Sermons. Selected passages, with an essay by Logan Pearsall Smith. Oxford, Clarendon Press, 1920.

Donne's Shorter Prose Works. Ed. by Evelyn Simpson, with the assistance of Roger E. Bennett. New York, Farrar, Straus and Co., 1948.

A Garland for John Donne. Ed. by Theodore Spencer. Cambridge, Mass., Harvard University Press, 1931.

Fausset, H. I'A. *John Donne: A Study in Discord*. London, J. Cape, Ltd., 1924.

Gosse, Edmund. *The Life and Letters of John Donne*. 2 vols. London, W. Heinemann, 1899.

Grierson, H. J. C. "Introductions and Commentary," *The Poems of John Donne*. Ed. with introductions and commentary. 2 vols. Oxford, Clarendon Press, 1912. Vol. II.

Coffin, Charles M. *John Donne and the New Philosophy*. Columbia University Studies in English and Comparative Literature, No. 126. New York, Columbia University Press, 1937.

Praz, Mario. *Secentismo e marinismo in Inghilterra: John Donne—Richard Crashaw*. Florence, Società an. Editrice "La Voce," 1925.

Simpson, Evelyn. *A Study of the Prose Works of John Donne*. Oxford, Clarendon Press, 1924; revised and enlarged, 1948.

Battenhouse, R. W. "The Grounds of Religious Toleration in the Thought of John Donne," *Church History*, XI (1942), 217–48.

Bredvold, Louis I. "The Religious Thought of Donne in Relation to Medieval and Later Tradition," *Studies in Shakespeare, Milton, and Donne*. University of Michigan Publications in Language and Literature, Vol. 1. Ann Arbor, University of Michigan Press, 1905.

Roberts, Donald R. "The Death Wish of John Donne," *Publications of the Modern Language Association*, LXII (1947), 958–76.

Sparrow, John. "Donne and Contemporary Preachers," *Essays and Studies by Members of the English Association*, collected by H. J. C. Grierson. Oxford, Clarendon Press, 1931, Vol. XVI, pp. 144–78.

Umbach, Herbert H. "The Merit of Metaphysical Style in Donne's Easter Sermons," *English Literary History*, XII (1945), 108–25.

———. "The Rhetoric of Donne's Sermons," *Publications of the Modern Language Association*, LII (1937), 354–58.

Williamson, George. "Mutability, Decay, and Seventeenth Century Melancholy," *English Literary History*, II (1935), 121–50.

Woolf, Virginia. "Donne after Three Centuries," *The Second Common Reader*. London, Hogarth Press, 1932, pp. 20–37.

BEN JONSON

Tannenbaum, Samuel A. *Ben Jonson (A Concise Bibliography)*. Elizabethan Bibliographies, No. 2. New York, Scholars Facsimiles and Reprints, 1938.

Ben Jonson. Ed. by C. H. Herford, Percy and Evelyn Simpson. 8 vols. Oxford, Clarendon Press, 1925–41.

Timber, or Discoveries and *Conversations with William Drummond.* Ed. by G. B. Harrison. Bodley Head Quartos. New York, E. P. Dutton & Co., 1923.

Timber, or Discoveries. Ed. with an introduction and notes by Felix E. Schelling. Boston, Ginn and Co., 1892.

Castelain, M. *Ben Jonson; l'homme et l'œuvre.* Paris, Libraire Hachette, 1907.

Palmer, Leslie. *Ben Jonson.* London, George Routledge and Sons, 1934.

ROBERT BURTON

Jordan-Smith, Paul. *Bibliographia Burtonia: A Study of Robert Burton's "The Anatomy of Melancholy."* With a bibliography of Burton's Writings. Stanford (Cal.) University Press, 1931.

The Anatomy of Melancholy. Ed. by F. Dell and P. Jordan-Smith. 2 vols. New York, Farrar and Rinehart, 1927. Condensed reissue in one vol., 1929.

The Anatomy of Melancholy. Ed. by A. R. Shiletto. 3 vols. London, G. Bell and Sons, 1912.

Evans, Bergen. *The Psychiatry of Robert Burton.* New York, Columbia University Press, 1944.

Mueller, William R. "Robert Burton's Economic and Political Views," *Huntington Library Quarterly,* XI (1947–48), 341–59.

Murry, John Middleton. "Burton's Anatomy," *Countries of the Mind.* First Series. New edition, revised and enlarged. London, Oxford University Press, 1931.

Patrick, Max. "Robert Burton's Utopianism," *Philological Quarterly,* XXVIII (1949), 345–58.

Whibley, Charles. "Robert Burton," *Literary Portraits.* London and New York, Macmillan Co., 1920, pp. 267–308.

SIR THOMAS OVERBURY

Paylor, W. J. *The Overburian Characters.* Percy Reprints. Oxford, Basil Blackwell, 1936.

Parry, Sir Edward Abbott. *The Overbury Mystery.* London, T. F. Unwin, Ltd., 1925.

Thompson, E. N. S. "Character Books," *Literary Bypaths of the Renaissance.* New Haven, Yale University Press, 1924, pp. 1–27.

Whibley, Charles. "Sir Thomas Overbury," *Essays in Biography.* London, A. Constable and Co., 1913, Chaps. I–II.

THOMAS HOBBES

Leviathan. With an introduction by A. D. Lindsay. Everyman's Library. New York, E. P. Dutton & Co., 1950.

Laird, John. *Hobbes.* Leaders of Philosophy. London, E. Benn, 1934.

Social and Political Ideas of Some Great Thinkers of the Sixteenth and Seventeenth Centuries. Ed. by F. J. C. Hearnshaw. London, G. G. Harrap, 1926, Chap. VII.

Stephen, Sir Leslie. *Hobbes*. Ed. by J. Morley. English Men of Letters Series. London, Macmillan Co., 1904.

Thorpe, C. D. *Aesthetic Theory of Thomas Hobbes*. Ann Arbor, University of Michigan Press, 1940.

Stewart, H. L. "Personality of Thomas Hobbes," *Hibbert Journal*, XLVII (1949), 123–31.

Taylor, A. E. "An Apology for Mr. Hobbes," *Seventeenth Century Studies Presented to Sir Herbert Grierson*. Oxford, Clarendon Press, 1938, pp. 129–37.

IZAAK WALTON

Wood, Arnold. *A Bibliography of the Complete Angler*. New York, Charles Scribner's Sons, 1900.

Butt, J. E. *A Bibliography of Izaak Walton's Lives*. Proceedings, Oxford Bibliographical Society, II, 1930.

The Compleat Angler: The Lives of Donne, Wotton, Hooker, Herbert, and Sanderson. With Love and Truth and Miscellaneous Writings. Ed. by Geoffrey Keynes. London, Nonesuch Press, 1929.

The Compleat Angler. Ed. with an introduction by John Buchan. World's Classics. London, Oxford University Press, 1935.

The Lives of John Donne, Sir Henry Wotton, Richard Hooker, and Robert Sanderson. With an introduction by George Saintsbury. World's Classics. London and New York, Oxford University Press, 1927.

Oliver, H. J. "The Composition and Revisions of 'The Compleat Angler,'" *Modern Language Notes*, XLII (1947), 296–313.

————. "Izaak Walton's Prose Style," *Review of English Studies*, XXI (1945), 280–88.

JAMES HOWELL

Vann, W. H. *Notes on the Writings of James Howell*. Full bibliography. Waco, Texas, Baylor University Press, 1924.

The Familiar Letters of James Howell. With an introduction by Agnes Repplier. 2 vols. Boston and New York, Houghton Mifflin Co., 1908.

Instructions for Foreign Travel. Ed. by E. Arber. English Reprints, No. 16. London, A. Constable and Co., 1903.

JOHN EARLE

Microcosmography. Ed. by Harold Osborne. London, University Tutorial Press, 1933.

OWEN FELLTHAM

Resolves, Divine, Morall, and Politicall. Ed. by Oliphant Smeaton. Temple Classics. London, J. M. Dent & Co., 1904.

Tupper, F. S. "New Facts Regarding Owen Feltham," *Modern Language Notes,* LIV (1939), 199–201.

SIR THOMAS BROWNE

Keynes, Geoffrey. *A Bibliography of Sir Thomas Browne.* Cambridge (England) University Press, 1924.

The Works of Sir Thomas Browne. Ed. by Geoffrey Keynes. 6 vols. London, Faber and Gwyer, Ltd.; New York, W. E. Rudge, 1928–31.

The Works of Sir Thomas Browne. Ed. by A. R. Shiletto, with an introduction by A. H. Bullen. Bohn Library. 3 vols. London, G. Bell and Sons, 1896.

Religio Medici and Hydriotaphia (Urn Burial). With an introduction by Charles Whibley. London, Blackie, 1926.

Gosse, Sir Edmund. *Sir Thomas Browne.* English Men of Letters Series. London and New York, Macmillan Co., 1905.

Leroy, O. *Le Chevalier Thomas Browne, sa vie, sa pensée et son art.* Paris, Libraire J. Gamber, 1931.

Merton, E. S. *Science and the Imagination in Sir Thomas Browne.* New York, King's Crown Press, 1949.

Cline, J. M. "Hydriotaphia," *Five Studies in Literature.* University of California Publications in English, Vol. 8, No. 1. Berkeley, University of California Press, 1940.

Howell, A. C. "Sir Thomas Browne as Wit and Humorist," *Studies in Philology,* XLII (1945), 564–77.

More, P. E. *Shelburne Essays.* Sixth Series. Boston and New York, Houghton-Mifflin Co., 1909, pp. 154–86.

Whibley, Charles. "Sir Thomas Browne," *Essays in Biography.* London, A. Constable and Co., 1913.

THOMAS FULLER

Gibson, S. *Bibliography of Thomas Fuller.* Proceedings, Oxford Bibliographical Society, IV. Oxford, 1936.

The Holy State and the Profane State. Ed. by Maximilian Graff Walten. 2 vols. A facsimile of the first edition, 1642. New York, Columbia University Press, 1938.

Selections from Thomas Fuller, with Essays by Charles Lamb, Leslie Stephen, &c. Ed. by E. H. Broadus. Oxford, Clarendon Press, 1929.

Houghton, Walter Edwards, Jr. *The Formation of Thomas Fuller's Holy and Profane States.* Harvard Studies in English, Vol. XIX. Cambridge, Mass., Harvard University Press, 1938.

Lyman, Dean Belden. *The Great Tom Fuller.* Berkeley, University of California Press, 1935.

Thompson, E. N. S. "A Representative Man of Letters," *Literary Bypaths of the Renaissance.* New Haven, Yale University Press, 1924, pp. 173–83.

JOHN MILTON

Fletcher, H. F. *Contributions to a Milton Bibliography, 1800–1930.* University of Illinois Studies. Urbana, University of Illinois Press, 1931.

Stevens, D. H. *Reference Guide to Milton from 1800 to the Present Day.* Chicago, University of Chicago Press, 1930.

Thompson, E. N. S. *John Milton, Topical Bibliography.* New Haven, Yale University Press, 1916.

The Works of John Milton. Columbia University Edition. 18 vols.; with three supplements and Index, 2 vols. New York, Columbia University Press, 1931–38; 1940.

The Prose Works of John Milton. Ed. by J. A. St. John. Bohn Library. 5 vols. London, G. Bell and Sons, 1848–53; reprinted, 1910.

The Student's Milton. Ed. by F. A. Patterson. Revised edition. New York, Columbia University Press, 1933.

Adamson, J. W. *Pioneers of Modern Education 1600–1700.* Contributions to the History of Education, III. Cambridge, (England) University Press, 1905.

Barker, Arthur. *Milton and the Puritan Dilemma.* Toronto, University of Toronto Press, 1942.

Buck, Philo M., Jr. *Milton on Liberty* (Nebraska) University Studies, Vol. XXV, No. 1. Lincoln, University of Nebraska Press, 1925.

Bush, Douglas. *The Renaissance and English Humanism.* Toronto, University of Toronto Press, 1939.

Diekhoff, John S. *Milton on Himself.* London and New York, Oxford University Press, 1939.

Grierson, H. J. C. *Milton and Wordsworth, Poets and Prophets; a study of their reactions to political events.* Cambridge (England) University Press, 1937.

Hanford, James Holly. *John Milton, Englishman.* New York, Crown Publishers, 1949.

Hutchinson, F. E. *Milton and the English Mind*. London, Hodder and Stoughton, for the English Universities Press, 1946.

Masson, David. *The Life of John Milton Narrated in Connection with the Political, Ecclesiastical, and Literary History of His Time*. 7 vols. London, Macmillan Co., 1859–94.

Tillyard, E. M. W. *Milton*. London, Chatto and Windus, 1934.

Wolfe, D. M. *Milton in the Puritan Revolution*. New York, Thomas Nelson & Sons, 1941.

Ainsworth, Oliver M. "Milton as a Writer on Education," *Transactions of the Wisconsin Academy of Science, Arts, and Letters*, XXI (1924), 41–50.

Brooks, Phillips. "Milton as an Educator," *Journal of Education*, LXVIII (1908), 533–35.

Ekfelt, F. E. "Latinate Diction in Milton's English Prose" (Studies in Milton: Essays in Memory of Elbert N. S. Thompson), *Philological Quarterly*, XXVIII (1949), 53–71.

Firth, C. H. "Milton as an Historian," *Proceedings of the British Academy*, III, 227–57.

Haller, William. "Before Areopagitica," *Publications of the Modern Language Association*, XLII (1927), 875–900.

Thompson, E. N. S. "Milton's *Of Education*," *Studies in Philology*, XV (1918), 159–75.

———. "Milton's Prose Style," *Philological Quarterly*, XIV (1935), 1–15.

———. "The True Bearing of Milton's Prose," *Essays on Milton*. New Haven, Yale University Press, 1914, Chap. III.

Wolfe, Don M. "Milton and Hobbes: A Contrast in Social Temper," *Studies in Philology*, XLI (1944), 410–26.

JEREMY TAYLOR

The Whole Works of Jeremy Taylor. Ed. by R. Heber, revised and corrected by Rev. C. P. Eden. 10 vols. London, Longman, Brown and Co., 1847–54.

The Golden Grove: Selected Passages from the Sermons and Writings of Jeremy Taylor. Ed. by Logan Pearsall Smith. Oxford, Clarendon Press, 1930.

Holy Living and Dying; with Prayers. Bohn Library. London, G. Bell and Sons, 1883.

Brown, W. J. *Jeremy Taylor*. London, Society for Promoting Christian Knowledge; New York, Macmillan Co., 1925.

Gosse, Edmund. *Jeremy Taylor*. English Men of Letters Series. London and New York, Macmillan Co., 1903.

Worley, George. *Jeremy Taylor: a Sketch of His Life and Times.* New York, Longmans, Green & Co., 1904.

Nicolson, Marjorie. "New Material on Jeremy Taylor," *Philological Quarterly,* VII (1929), 321–34.

RALPH CUDWORTH

Sermon Preached before the Honourable House of Commons, at Westminster, March 31, 1647. New York, Facsimile Text Society, 1930.

The True Intellectual System of the Universe. Ed. by John Harrison. 3 vols. London, printed for Thomas Tegg, 1845.

Lowrey, C. E. *Philosophy of Ralph Cudworth.* New York, Phillips and Hunt, 1884.

Muirhead, John Henry. *The Platonic Tradition in Anglo-Saxon Philosophy.* Library of Philosophy. London, Allen & Unwin; New York, Macmillan Co., 1931, Chaps. II–III, pp. 33–71.

Grierson, H. J. C. "Humanism and the Churches," *Cross Currents in English Literature of the Seventeenth Century.* London, Chatto & Windus, 1929.

Nicolson, Marjorie. "Christ's College and the Latitude Men," *Modern Philology,* XXVII (1929), 35–53.

ABRAHAM COWLEY

English Writings of Abraham Cowley. Ed. by A. R. Waller. Cambridge English Classics. 2 vols. Cambridge (England) University Press, 1905–06.

Abraham Cowley: The Essays and Other Prose Writings. Ed. by A. B. Gough. Oxford, Clarendon Press, 1915.

Loiseau, Jean. *Abraham Cowley: sa vie, son œuvre.* Paris, Henri Didier, 1931.

Nethercot, A. H. *Abraham Cowley: the Muse's Hannibal.* London, Oxford University Press, 1931.

———. "Abraham Cowley's Discourse Concerning Style," *Review of English Studies,* II (1926), 385–404.

———. "The Essays of Abraham Cowley," *Journal of English and Germanic Philology,* XXIX (1930), 114–30.

WILLIAM ALLEN (PSEUD.)

Killing No Murder. A Miscellany of Tracts and Pamphlets. Ed. by A. C. Ward. The World's Classics. London, Oxford University Press, 1927.

Firth, C. H. "Killing No Murder," *English Historical Review,*
XVII (1902), 308–11.

MARGARET CAVENDISH, DUCHESS OF NEWCASTLE

*The Life of William Cavendish, Duke of Newcastle, to which is
added the true relation of my birth, breeding, and life.*
Ed. by C. H. Firth. 2nd edition, revised. London, George
Routledge and Sons; New York, E. P. Dutton & Co., 1915.
Perry, Henry Ten Eyck. *The First Duchess of Newcastle and
Her Husband as Figures in Literary History.* Boston, Ginn
and Co., 1918.
Whibley, Charles. "A Princely Woman," *Essays in Biography.*
London, A. Constable and Co., 1913.
Woolf, Virginia. "The Duchess of Newcastle," *The Common
Reader.* London, Hogarth Press, 1925, pp. 101–12.

JOHN AUBREY

Brief Lives. Ed. by Andrew Clark. 2 vols. Oxford, Clarendon
Press, 1898.
Brief Lives. With an Introduction by Oliver Lawson Dick. Lon-
don, Secker and Warburg, 1949.
Powell, Anthony. *John Aubrey and His Friends.* New York,
Charles Scribner's Sons, 1948.

JOHN BUNYAN

Harrison, Frank M. *A Bibliography of the Works of John Bun-
yan.* Oxford, Bibliographical Society, 1932.
Grace Abounding for the Chief of Sinners and *The Pilgrim's
Progress.* Ed. by John Brown. Cambridge (England) Uni-
versity Press, 1907.
The Life and Death of Mr. Badman and *The Holy War.* Ed. by
John Brown. Cambridge (England) University Press, 1905.
The Pilgrim's Progress. Ed. by James B. Wharey. Oxford,
Clarendon Press, 1928.
Brown, John. *John Bunyan: His Life, Times, and Work.* Re-
vised by Frank M. Harrison. London, Hulbert, 1928.
Harrison, G. B. *John Bunyan: A Study in Personality.* London,
J. M. Dent and Sons; New York, E. P. Dutton & Co., 1928.
Knox, Edward A. *John Bunyan in Relation to His Times.* New
York, Longmans, Green & Co., 1928.
Speight, Harold E. B. *The Life and Writings of John Bunyan.*
New York, Harper and Bros., 1928.

Tindall, William Y. *John Bunyan, Mechanick Preacher.* Columbia University Studies in English and Comparative Literature. New York, Columbia University Press, 1934.

Lowes, John L. "The Pilgrim's Progress," *Of Reading Books.* Boston, Houghton Mifflin Co., 1930.

Sharrock, Roger. "Bunyan and the English Emblem Writers," *Review of English Studies,* X (1945), 105–16.

JOHN DRYDEN

Macdonald, Hugh. *John Dryden: a Bibliography of Early Editions and of Drydeniana.* Oxford, Clarendon Press, 1939.

The Dramatic Essays. Ed. by Ernest Rhys. Everyman's Library. New York, E. P. Dutton & Co., 1931.

Essays of John Dryden. Ed. by W. P. Ker. 2 vols. Oxford, Clarendon Press, 1900 and 1926.

Bredvold, Louis I. *The Intellectual Milieu of John Dryden.* University of Michigan Publications in Language and Literature, XII. Ann Arbor, University of Michigan Press, 1934.

Eliot, T. S. *John Dryden, the Poet, the Dramatist, the Critic: Three Essays.* New York, Holliday Press, 1932.

Hollis, Christopher. *Dryden.* London, Duckworth, 1933.

Lubbock, Alan. *The Character of John Dryden.* Hogarth Essays. London, Hogarth Press, 1925.

Osborn, James M. *John Dryden: Some Biographical Facts and Problems.* New York, Columbia University Press, 1940.

Frye, P. H. "Dryden and the Critical Canons of the Eighteenth Century," *Nebraska University Studies,* VII. Lincoln, University of Nebraska Press, 1907.

Legouis, Pierre. "Corneille and Dryden as Dramatic Critics," *Seventeenth Century Studies Presented to Sir Herbert Grierson.* Oxford, Clarendon Press, 1938, pp. 269–91.

Smith, John H. "Dryden's Critical Temper," *Washington University Studies, Humanistic Series,* XII (1925), 201–20.

Trowbridge, Hoyt. "Dryden's Essay on the Dramatic Poetry of the Last Age," *Philological Quarterly,* XXII (1943), 240–50.

ANTHONY À WOOD

Athenæ Oxonienses. . . . Ed. by Phillip Bliss. 4 vols. London, printed for F. C. and J. Rivington, etc., 1813–20.

The Life and Times of Anthony Wood . . . Described by Him-

self. Collected from His Diaries and Other Papers. Ed. by Andrew Clark. Oxford Historical Society. 5 vols. Oxford, Clarendon Press, 1891–1900.

JOHN LOCKE

Christophersen, Hans Oscar. *A Bibliographical Introduction to the Study of John Locke.* Skrifter ut gitt av det Norske Videnskaps-Akademe, Hist.-fil. Klasse, no. 8. Oslo, 1930.

An Essay Concerning Human Understanding. Ed. by A. C. Fraser. 2 vols. Oxford, Clarendon Press, 1894.

The Educational Writings of John Locke. Ed. by William Adamson. London, E. Arnold Co., 1922.

Aaron, Richard I. *John Locke.* Leaders of Philosophy. London and New York, Oxford University Press, 1937.

Gibson, James. *Locke's Theory of Knowledge and Its Historical Relations.* Cambridge (England) University Press, 1931.

Hefelbower, S. G. *Relation of John Locke to English Deism.* Chicago, University of Chicago Press, 1918.

MacLean, Kenneth. *John Locke and English Literature of the Eighteenth Century.* New Haven, Yale University Press, 1936.

SAMUEL PEPYS

Diary. Ed. by Henry B. Wheatley. 10 vols. London, G. Bell and Sons; New York, Harcourt, Brace and Co., 1893–99.

Bradford, Gamaliel. *The Soul of Samuel Pepys.* Boston and New York, Houghton Mifflin Co., 1924.

Bryant, Arthur. *Samuel Pepys.* 3 vols. Cambridge (England) University Press, 1933–36.

Drinkwater, John. *Pepys: His Life and Character.* London, W. Heinemann, 1920.

Marburg, Clara. *Mr. Pepys and Mr. Evelyn.* Philadelphia, University of Pennsylvania Press, 1935.

Ponsonby, Arthur. *Samuel Pepys.* English Men of Letters Series. London, Macmillan Co., 1928.

Tanner, Joseph. *Mr. Pepys: An Introduction to the Diary.* London, G. Bell and Sons, 1925.

Wheatley, Henry B. *Samuel Pepys and the World He Lived In.* 2nd edition. New York, Scribner and Welford, 1880.

THOMAS TRAHERNE

Centuries of Meditations. Ed. by Bertram Dobell. London, P. J. & A. E. Dobell, 1908.

Iredale, Queenie. *Thomas Traherne*. Oxford, Basil Blackwell, 1935.

Wade, Gladys I. *Thomas Traherne*. Princeton, N.J., Princeton University Press; London, Oxford University Press, 1944.

Willett, Gladys E. *Traherne (an Essay)*. Cambridge, W. Heffer, 1919.

Beachcroft, T. O. "Traherne and the Doctrine of Felicity," *Criterion*, IX (1929–30), 291–307.

Gilbert, Alan H. "Thomas Traherne as Artist," *Modern Language Quarterly*, VIII (1947): Sept., pp. 319–41; Dec., pp. 435–47.

Jones, R. M. "Thomas Traherne," *Spiritual Reformers in the Sixteenth and Seventeenth Centuries*. London, Macmillan Co., 1928, pp. 323–35.

Thompson, E. N. S. "The Philosophy of Thomas Traherne," *Philological Quarterly*, VIII (1929), 97–112.

THOMAS SPRAT

History of the Royal Scientific Society. 2nd edition. London, printed by T. R., for J. Martyn and J. Allestry, 1702.

Stimson, Dorothy. *Scientists and Amateurs*. New York, Henry Schuman, 1949, pp. 70–76.

Sonnichsen, C. L. "The Life and Works of Thomas Sprat." Unpublished dissertation, Harvard University.

THOMAS ELLWOOD

History of the Life and Times of Thomas Ellwood. Ed. by C. G. Crump. New York, G. P. Putnam's Sons, 1900.

Brown, Alfred K. "Thomas Ellwood, the Friend of Milton." *Friends Ancient and Modern*, No. 15. London, Headley Bros., 1910.

Index

四十五年之舊曆除夕瞬于翠葉村。

劉以鬯

Fayetteville 95b.